W9-ACO-483

THE ANALECTS

THE ILLUSTRATED LIBRARY OF CHINESE CLASSICS

The Illustrated Library of Chinese Classics brings together a series of immensely appealing and popular graphic narratives about traditional Asian philosophy and literature, all written and illustrated by C. C. Tsai, one of East Asia's most beloved cartoonists. Playful, humorous, and genuinely illuminating, these unique adaptations offer ideal introductions to the most influential writers, works, and schools of ancient Chinese thought.

Confucius
THE ANALECTS

Adapted and illustrated by

C. C. Tsai

Translated by Brian Bruya

Foreword by Michael Puett

Copyright © 2018 by Princeton University Press
Published by Princeton University Press
41 William Street, Princeton, New Jersey 08540
In the United Kingdom: Princeton University Press,
6 Oxford Street, Woodstock, Oxfordshire OX20 1TR
press.princeton.edu
Cover art provided by C. C. Tsai
All Rights Reserved

Library of Congress Cataloging-in-Publication Data

Names: Cai, Zhizhong, 1948– adapter, illustrator. | Bruya, Brian,
    1966– translator. | Confucius. Lun yu. English.
Title: The analects / adapted and illustrated by C.C. Tsai ; translated
    by Brian Bruya ; foreword by Michael Puett.
Other titles: Lun yu. English
Description: Princeton : Princeton University Press, [2018] | Series:
    The illustrated library of Chinese classics | In English with classical
    Chinese original. | Includes bibliographical references and index.
Identifiers: LCCN 2017039858 | ISBN 9780691179759 (pbk. : acid-
    free paper)
Subjects: LCSH: Confucius. Lun yu—Comic books, strips, etc. |
    Confucius—Adaptations. | Graphic novels.
Classification: LCC PL2471.Z7 C3413 2018 | DDC 181/.112—dc23
    LC record available at https://lccn.loc.gov/2017039858

British Library Cataloging-in-Publication Data is available
This book has been composed in News Gothic and Adobe Fangsong
Printed on acid-free paper. ∞
Printed in the United States of America
10 9 8 7 6 5 4 3 2 1

Contents

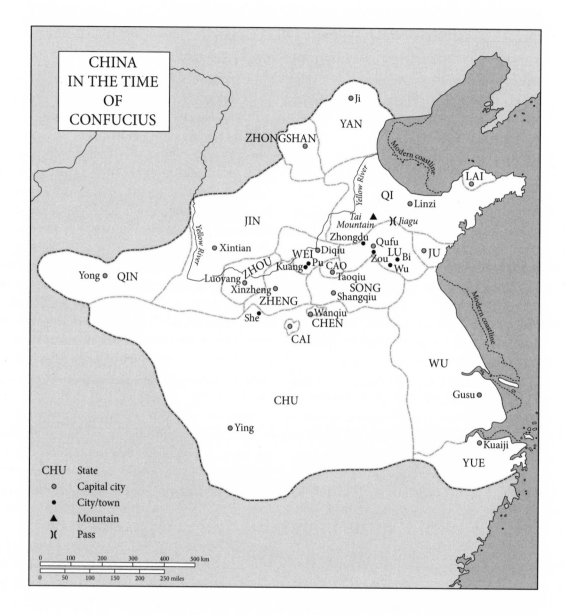

CHINA
IN THE TIME
OF
CONFUCIUS

Ji

YAN

ZHONGSHAN

Modern coastline

LAI

QI

Linzi

JIN

Yellow River

Tai Mountain ▲)(*Jiagu*

Zhongdu

Qufu

Xintian

Diqiu

WEI

Pu

CAO

Zou

LU

Bi

JU

Yellow River

Kuang

Wu

ZHOU

Taoqiu

Luoyang

SONG

Yong ● QIN

Xinzheng

Shangqiu

ZHENG

Wanqiu

She

CHEN

Modern coastline

CAI

WU

Gusu

CHU

Ying

Kuaiji

YUE

CHU State
● Capital city
● City/town
▲ Mountain
)(Pass

0   100   200   300   400   500 km

0   50   100   150   200   250 miles

Foreword

MICHAEL PUETT

It may seem odd at first to think of illustrating a truly great work of philosophy. Would this not reduce the brilliant philosophy found therein to a caricature? Would we ever think of illustrating, for example, Kant's second critique? Well, no, we wouldn't. But the answer to the previous question is no as well. The *Analects* is indeed a truly great philosophical work. But it is not a philosophical text in the way that we often use that term. The philosophy is provided through a series of dialogues between Confucius and his disciples. It portrays Confucius as a figure striving to be good, trying to educate his disciples, and hoping to create a better world. It is a philosophy focused on the art of living. The degree to which the *Analects* works as a philosophical text is tied directly to the degree to which we can picture this art of living in everyday practice—the situations in which Confucius will speak in certain ways to a particular disciple, the way Confucius will hold his body as he offers advice, the expressions Confucius will have when he utters a statement—the ways in which, in short, Confucius can sense those around him and sense what he can say or do that will inspire them to alter their lives for the better.

And what better way to help us envision this philosophy than by allowing us to see it in practice? Chih-chung "C. C." Tsai captures this perfectly; his illustrations bring the dialogues and conversations of the *Analects* to life. When we read Chih-chung Tsai's text, we avoid the danger that so many modern readers of the text fall into—the danger of simply looking for a statement here or there that sounds philosophically profound, pulling it out of the context in which it appears, and ignoring the way the situation is portrayed. For the way to read the text and gain a full understanding of it is to focus precisely on the whole of it—the situations, the moods, the expressions of the utterances. The Confucius as portrayed in this text wants us to change for the better, but the change begins in the seemingly mundane ways we lead our everyday lives. Such a key lesson is lost when we fail to pay attention to the fact that the text itself is fully rooted in the everyday, in how Confucius will alter a situation for the better through, say, an expression or tone of voice. Chih-chung Tsai's rendering makes this wonderfully alive and accessible.

His illustrations also replicate, in a delightful manner, a way of reading the *Analects* that would have been common in earlier times. No one in pre-twentieth century China would have simply read the passages of the *Analects* one after the other without any contextualizing explication. The passages would have always been read through a web of commentaries providing key details concerning the situation and key pieces of background information, thus making it possible for the reader to understand the reasons Confucius speaks as he does to a certain disciple in a certain situation and to grasp the emotions and moods elicited by Confucius' utterances. Chih-chung Tsai's illustrations are based on these commentaries and do much the same work that the commentaries did—but in a very whimsical way.

And, precisely thanks to this whimsy, Chih-chung Tsai captures another aspect of the text that is so often lost on contemporary readers: the *Analects* is a wonderfully humorous text. Confucius is often described as a joyous figure, and among the traits his disciples are learning in the art of living is how to experience the joy that Confucius radiates. Unlike so many recent portraits of Confucius as a boring reciter of platitudes, Chih-chung Tsai captures the playful character of Confucius as portrayed in the text, the humor of Confucius' statements, the self-mocking annoyance that Confucius will express towards a lazy disciple before quoting some lines of poetry with a captivating smile. Far from reducing the brilliant philosophy of the *Analects* to a caricature, Chih-chung Tsai's rendering helps bring it to life.

The text is also superbly translated by Brian Bruya. Not only do Bruya's translations capture the nuanced language of the text beautifully, he also provides key pieces of background information on particular characters mentioned in the text so that Confucius' allusions make sense—thus giving us one bit of the information the commentaries would have provided to a reader that the illustrations alone cannot convey.

In short, Chih-chung Tsai has provided an illustrated version of the *Analects* that both replicates the contextualizing work of the commentarial apparatus and conveys the whimsy, humor, and joyousness of the text. This is a philosophy to be lived, a philosophical text to learn from and laugh with, and a version that captures such a sensibility delightfully.

Introduction

BRIAN BRUYA

I. THE BATTLE OF THE HUNDRED SCHOOLS

The Imperial Period in China began in 221 BCE, when the First Emperor, hailing from the far western state of Qin, completed his conquest of China. From that time until 1911, there were six subsequent major dynasties: the Han, Tang, Song, Yuan, Ming, and Qing. But what about before the Qin? For 789 years, from 1045 to 256 BCE (much longer than any subsequent dynasty), a single lineage held the throne as Son of Heaven, ruler of China. This dynasty's name is Zhou (pronounced *joe*—see the Pronunciation Index in the back of the book for how to pronounce other Chinese names and terms). The period of the Zhou that concerns us is the second half, when traditional order had broken down.

The traditional order was unique among world civilizations. The Zhou Dynasty begins with the victors over the preceding Shang Dynasty fanning out across the country, taking control of key cities and towns—over 150 in total. We can think of each of these newly formed states as a fief, loyal to the Zhou king. Each enfeoffed ruler had local control but served at the pleasure of the king: visiting the king regularly to renew bonds of fealty, sending tribute to the king, and doing the king's bidding when necessary. Each fief was handed down to the ruler's eldest son. In the beginning, these fiefs were close, either in terms of familial relationships or in terms of military loyalty, and the relationship between king and vassal was viewed as like that between father and son. Over time, however, disputes arose, loyalties frayed, and battles occurred. 250 years in, and ties were stretched to the breaking point.

A traditional story (perhaps apocryphal) is often used to illustrate a key turning point in the dynasty. In 773 BCE, the king had just divorced his primary wife and replaced her with his favorite, who was difficult to please. In order to entertain her, the king arranged for a large feast on the outskirts of the capital, and at nightfall he had the warning beacons on the city wall lit. The beacons went up in flame one after another in a spectacular display that reached to the horizon, and after several hours, troops from neighboring states arrived breathless at the capital to bring aid to the king, whom they thought was in grave danger from invasion. The spectacle delighted the queen, but of course the generals and soldiers who had rushed to help were not amused. This happened more than once.

Not long after, the state of Shen, which nursed a grudge against the king, allied with the Quan Rong tribe and attacked the Zhou capital. When the Zhou warning beacons were lit, the neighboring states ignored them. The capital was laid waste, and the king was killed. The Zhou lineage was allowed to continue, but it was forced to move its capital east, its area of direct control was reduced, and it lost the fealty of the major vassals. From that point on, the various states quickly realized it was every state for itself. For the next five and a half centuries the states gradually swallowed each other up until only seven major states remained at the end of the Spring & Autumn Period (770–481 BCE). As armies increased in size during the Warring States Period (481–221 BCE), the disruption of warfare increased as well. The battle for ultimate supremacy continued until Qin was the last state standing.

In this battle for ultimate supremacy it would no longer do for a ruler to simply rely on his circle of close nobility to act as generals and ministers. Every ruler needed the most capable people around. And so an intellectual ferment began. Not only did rulers look beyond the nobility for brains and talent but people of brains and talent began to promote their own views about how best to govern—theories that blossomed to include all kinds of associated philosophical concerns. Over time, similar lines of thinking coalesced into a variety of schools of thought, such as Confucianism, Mohism, Legalism, Daoism, and so on. The Chinese refer to it as the period of the contending voices of a hundred schools of thought.

The first major Confucian text was the *Analects* of Confucius, a handbook for creating a flourishing society through cultural education and strong moral leadership. Mencius, a student of Confucius' grandson, Zisi, was the second major Confucian thinker. His influential book, *The Mencius*, uses memorable analogies and thought experiments (such as the child on the edge of a well) to drive home subtle points about the goodness of human nature and effective governing. Two short pieces that were important to the revival of Confucianism in the Song Dynasty were also products of this time. They are *Advanced Education* (*Da Xue*) and *The Middle Path* (*Zhong Yong*), traditionally attributed to Confucius' student Zengzi and to Zisi, respectively. *Advanced Education* offers a pithy formula for the self-development of caring, world-class leaders, while *The Middle Path* discusses how to achieve balance both internally and externally.

While the Confucians concentrated on creating moral leaders, others, known to us now as Daoists, preferred to concentrate on becoming as close as possible to the natural way of things. The major Daoist texts from this period are the *Zhuangzi* and Laozi's *Daodejing*. The *Zhuangzi* is one of the great works of world literature, simultaneously a profound philosophical study of metaphysics, language, epistemology, and ethics. It's also seriously fun to read for its colorful characters and paradoxical stories. Laozi's *Daodejing* echoes many themes of the *Zhuangzi*, with an emphasis on the sage as leader, non-action, and emptying the mind. Its poetic language and spare style stand it in stark contrast to the *Zhuangzi* but also allow for a richness of interpretation that has made it an all-time favorite of contemplative thinkers across traditions. A third Daoist from this time period, Liezi, had his name placed on a book a few centuries later. The *Liezi* adopts the style and themes of the *Zhuangzi* and continues the whimsical yet profound tradition.

Other thinkers concentrated on ruthless efficiency in government and came to be known as Legalists. One major Legalist thinker was Han Feizi. His book, the *Han Feizi*, condemns ideas from other schools of thought that had devolved into practices that were considered wasteful, corrupt, and inefficient. In response, he speaks directly to the highest levels of leadership, using Daoist terminology and fable-like stories to make his points, advising rulers on how to motivate people, how to organize the government and the military, and how to protect their own positions of power.

Still other thinkers concentrated their theories on military strategy and tactics. The major representative of this genre is, of course, Sunzi, and his classic *Art of War*, a text that so profoundly and succinctly examines how to get the greatest competitive advantage with the least harm done that it is still read today by military leaders and captains of industry.

The political, military, and intellectual battles continued throughout the Warring States Period in a complex interplay until Han Feizi's version of Legalism seemed to tip the balance for the Qin. But the victory was short-lived, and soon a version of Confucianism would rise to the top as the preferred philosophy of political elites. But Daoism, and later Buddhism, had their own periods of dominance and influenced many aspects of Chinese culture over the centuries.

II. CONFUCIUS AND HIS IDEAS

As social roles were changing during the Spring & Autumn Period and rulers were turning to talent outside the nobility, there arose a need for teachers to instruct aspiring leaders. Confucius was, himself, an aspiring leader, but he made his mark as an educator and as a philosopher of education. C. C. Tsai opens this book with the story of Confucius' life, where we see Confucius commonly interacting with his students.

As for his ideas, there are two foundational ideas in Confucius that are prerequisites for understanding and contextualizing all other ideas in the book—one is perfectly familiar to a citizen of a modern liberal democracy like ours and one is quite the opposite. They are culture and hierarchy.

First, culture. In general terms, culture is whatever gets passed down to the next generation. We often narrow the meaning, however, either to something like high art or to touristic caricatures associated with ethnic minorities, like performance of hula dance or Native American drumming. Both of these conceptions of culture are distant from everyday life. For Confucius, culture is a set of practices and traditions that enrich everyday life and engender stability and harmony in society.

Does culture really provide stability and engender harmony? Think about shared holidays, family dinners, birthdays, weddings, funerals, and norms of behavior. What does more in our society to provide stability and engender harmony than the patterns of shared activities that structure our lives? Confucius had a word for this aspect of culture. He called it *li* 禮, which is translated in the book variously as ceremony, propriety, ritual, proper behavior, or sacrifice, depending on the context. It also includes basic etiquette, such as bowing, handshakes, saying "please" and "thank you," and so on. *Li* enriches our lives by providing meaning (think weddings, baptisms, birthday parties), and other aspects of culture (in which *li* is embedded) provide subtle ways of understanding current events and our place in the world (think novels, TV dramas, satirical comedy, songs, etc.). These customs and forms of art and entertainment are avenues of emotional involvement in our world, without which we would be at a loss to both understand our world and express ourselves in it. Our established forms of etiquette are also like this. Imagine if you went to a job interview in a foreign country, and didn't know how to express the good will that is expressed in our society through a common handshake. It would be awkward, and trying to figure out what to do or say would sap your energy and distract you from more important things. *Li* gives us these forms for expression and understanding.

Just like we require our children to read novels or poetry to expand their minds and foster a moral sensibility, so Confucius thought that a primary goal of education was creating a moral person. You can see the emphasis he places on *li*, culture, and education by the number of times they appear in this book. In 7:5, Confucius shows a fervent nostalgia for the Duke of Zhou, whom he understood to be the founder of the cultural forms he espouses. 5:15 gives a definition of "culture" based on inquiry and a love of learning. In 6:20, Confucius shows the necessity of an emotional connection to learning—mere interest is not enough; the best kind of learning is a joyful process. And through learning, one can accomplish great things (14:35), such as creating a moral society. In our society today, we may look to the law for order in society, but Confucius was leery of extrinsic motivation and preferred that each of us do the right thing because we want to, not because we have to. His preference for *li* over law is clear in 2:3. *Li* limits what we're willing to do (6:27, 12:1) and also provides opportunities and avenues for appropriate behavior (3:15, 12:5). More than anything, *li* engenders the kind of humble and deferential behavior that keeps a hierarchical society functioning smoothly.

In our society, we favor equality across the board, so we might expect that a philosophy that favors hierarchy will be about getting power and preserving it. In fact, we see just that in the work of Han Feizi (coming later in this series). For Confucius, though, humility and deference are paramount, no matter where one is in the hierarchy (13:1, 13:19). On top of this, Confucius views hierarchies as dynamic, not static. Just as an infant daughter eventually moves her way up through the hierarchy of a family from dependent child to wife, mother, and aunt, and eventually matriarch, so a commoner can eventually make his way up through the hierarchy of society to become a government official who looks after others. We would think of it today as social mobility.

Social mobility depends on a more fundamental political idea: meritocracy—rule by the able. The idea is simple: The best person for the job is the person best able to do the job. As familiar as this idea is to us today, it has taken a frightfully long time for it to take root in our society. In fact, it really is only since the Civil Rights movement that we have stopped explicitly excluding people based on characteristics unrelated to ability.

The Greeks favored wealth as a criterion of inclusion. Later Europeans favored blood lineage. Other exclusionary criteria have been race, religion, and gender. Although the Chinese long excluded one whole gender from political power, beginning well before the time of Confucius they started the process of elevating men of ability over men of good birth.

Confucius was fully on board with the idea of meritocracy among men. He promoted it through educating all who came to him (7:7), giving them a shot at improving themselves to take on a large role of responsibility in society—one that would have been closed to them in other major cultures around the world, including the early democracies of Greece and Rome. Later, the idea of educating the next generation of leaders was institutionalized in China, and after European contact it contributed to our own institutions of entry into civil service via a process of institutional learning and uniform examination.

So we shouldn't be put off by Confucius' emphasis on hierarchy. Hierarchy is all around us, whether we like it or not. In the sense that you may be a better piano player than me or know more about politics or science, you are higher up the ladder of ability in that respect than I am, and so are in a position to teach me. I am in a position to learn from you. That's a hierarchical relationship in Confucius' eyes, and each of us, if we wish to exploit that differential, should act in certain ways. You should treat me with the care of a mentor and generously guide me. I should treat you with respect while humbly and assiduously learning from you. When these roles are fulfilled, great strides are made. In 6:30, Confucius says, "A benevolent person wishes to establish himself by establishing others and to achieve through helping others achieve." Teachers are mentors. On the other side, students mustn't slack off. In 7:8, Confucius says, "If a student doesn't feel troubled in his studies, I don't enlighten him. If a student doesn't feel frustrated in his studies, I don't explain to him. If I point out one corner, and he can't point out the other three, I don't repeat myself."

According to Confucius, the main virtue guiding the behavior of the mentor/leader is *ren* 仁, translated here as benevolence. The first step in benevolence is developing yourself (12:1, 12:17, 15:10). There are many episodes in this book where Confucius refers to the *junzi* 君子 (translated here as "gentleman"), by which he means the person who is so fully developed in character and virtue that he can act as a model and guide for others: "a gentleman supports the good in people" (12:16). "Gentleman" isn't a perfect translation because in our day it refers to a pretty minimal set of virtues, like holding the door open for others, and it is also gender specific. *Junzi*, on the other hand, is gender neutral and involves well-developed virtues and leadership abilities. A gentleman in Confucius' sense is the kind of person worth looking up to, who has cultivated a genuine concern for others and has the ability to make good on it. Think of someone in your own life who, through kind and patient guidance along with steadfast integrity, has had a strong positive influence on your life, like a coach, a teacher, a grandparent, or a supervisor at work. This is what Confucius meant by a *junzi*. In 6:30, a benevolent leader is someone who spreads kindness to the people, and in 18:1, he goes so far as to sacrifice himself speaking truth to power.

Before one can get to such a high level of moral and social achievement, one must begin at the bottom of the hierarchy and learn the virtues of the follower. The ideal of behavior at the bottom rung is *xiao* 孝, translated here as filial virtue or thoughtfulness toward one's parents. This ideal begins in the home, the most natural hierarchy in Confucius' eyes and the hierarchy that, in its ideal form, should act as a model for the rest of society. In the home, the child is *xiao* to the parents, obeying them and treating them with respect and thoughtfulness when young (1:2) and taking care of them through feelings of respect and gratitude when older (2:7, 4:19). By exercising *xiao* at home, one learns to serve others, which can be naturally extended when one steps onto the bottom rung of the ladder out in society. While working one's way up the ladder, one concentrates on being *zhong* 忠, conscientious (3:19).

Out in society, there will always be temptations to act immorally, to choose one's own short-term interests over the right thing to do more broadly. The term in Chinese for doing the right thing is *yi* 義. We see the idea clearly in 4.16, 9.1, and 14.12. Confucius also reminds us that the right thing to do is often dependent on circumstances and cannot be decided ahead of time according to unbending principles (4.10). There is no final arbiter in the Confucian system, no St. Peter waiting at the Pearly Gates, no god to offer a final judgment, no holy book of commandments to tell us what is right and wrong. This is why self-cultivation is so vitally important for Confucius and why reflection and study must go hand in hand (1.4, 2.15, 19.6).

The philosophy of Confucius is often considered a philosophy of ethics or of politics. It certainly is those—Confucius favors a certain specific set of intertwined virtues, and he favors a government based on the structure of the family. But his philosophy is also a philosophy of education. He advocates a way to create competent, intelligent, sympathetic, moral leaders—the kind of people who instill confidence and cause others to naturally gravitate toward them. In 2:1, he says, "If you govern with virtue, the people will happily follow you—like the North Star, which rests quietly in its place while the other stars revolve around it." Today in China, Confucius is still known as the First Teacher, and is celebrated in the national Teacher's Day holiday, which has precedents going back 2,000 years.

In the *Analects,* nearly every episode has something to do with education, culture, governing, or getting along with others, which to Confucius are various angles on the same thing—how to develop a harmonious society in which inevitable differences work to the benefit of all. This is the kind of wisdom that we can all use more of.

III. THE ARTIST AND HIS WORK

When I was a kid and the daily newspaper was dropped at our doorstep, I loved reading the comic strips and the political cartoons. They could be cute, amusing, and insightful all at once. When I came across C. C. Tsai's illustrated versions of the Chinese classics, I recognized the same brilliant combination of wit and wisdom and fell in love with his books.

I would be remiss if I finished this introduction without introducing the inimitable Chih-chung Tsai (蔡志忠), who goes by "C. C." in English, and whose own story is as amazing as anything he depicts in his books. The way he tells it, he knew at the age of five that he would draw for a living, and at the age of fifteen, his father gave him permission to drop out of school and move from their small town to the metropolis of Taipei, where a comic publisher had welcomed him after receiving an unsolicited manuscript, not realizing how young he was. The young C. C. developed his own humorous comic book characters, all the while honing his skills and learning from other illustrators. During a required three-year stint in the military, he devoted his free time to educating himself in art history and graphic design. On leaving the military he tested into a major movie and television production company, beating out other applicants with their formal educations. There, he had the good fortune of coming across a cache of Disney films, and taught himself animation. Soon he was making his own short films, and then decided to open his own animation studio, winning Taiwan's equivalent of the Oscar just two years later.

Always looking for a new challenge, C. C. began a syndicated comic strip, which quickly expanded to five different strips in magazines and newspapers across Southeast Asia. At the height of his popularity as a syndicated cartoonist, he turned in yet another direction—the illustration of the Chinese classics in comic book format. They were an instant success and propelled him to the top of the bestseller list. That's what you have in your hand.

According to C. C., the secret to his success is not ambition, or even hard work. It's just about having fun and following his interests. One of his interests has been studying the classics. Remember, he dropped out of middle school. By ordinary standards, he should be unable to grasp the language of ancient China. The early Chinese wrote in a language that is to contemporary Chinese as Latin is to contemporary Spanish or Italian. But he is a tireless autodidact, with a nearly photographic memory. He knows as much about the Chinese classics as many Ph.D.'s in the field. The main difference between him and a tenured professor is that he isn't interested in the refined disputes and distinctions on which scholars spend their careers. He merely wants to understand the ideas and share them with others. This book, and others in the series, is the result of playtime in his modest studio—serious and lighthearted, whimsical and profound all at once.

In working with the classics, C. C. stays close to tradition, and in his illustrations he more or less follows the prominent commentaries. This means that the texts that underpin his books are pretty much the same as the texts that underpin other translations you will find on bookstore shelves, with incidental differences here and there that are insignificant to the overall meaning.

C. C. translated the Classical language into contemporary Chinese so that the average reader could understand it. While respecting his interpretive choices where there is ambiguity, I've also chosen to translate with an eye to the Classical language, rather than just from his contemporary Chinese. This helps avoid the attenuation of meaning that happens when communication goes through too many steps—like in the "telephone" game that children play.

In this book, there are just a few places where some explanatory content has been added. For example, in 6:23, C. C. explains why wise people might enjoy water or benevolent people the mountains. That explanation is not in the original, although it can be found in traditional commentaries. This can also be said for the explanation of 9:1. I also added a bit of context for historical figures who would likely be unfamiliar to modern readers. For example, I point out that people mentioned only by name in the original are students, noblemen, etc.

The reader should have full confidence that each classic illustrated by C. C. is the real deal. The advantage that these versions of the classics have over regular, text-only editions is the visual dimension that brings the reader directly into the world of the ancients.

I hope that you enjoy this English version of C. C.'s illustrated *Analects* of Confucius as much as so many others have enjoyed the original Chinese version.

The Life of Confucius

孔子生魯昌平鄉陬邑。其先宋人也，曰孔防叔。防叔生伯夏，伯夏生叔梁紇。紇與顏氏女野合而生孔子，禱於尼丘得孔子。魯襄公二十二年而孔子生。生而首上圩頂，故因名曰丘云。字仲尼，姓孔氏。

丘生而叔梁紇死，葬於防山。防山在魯東，由是孔子疑其父墓處，母諱之也。孔子為兒嬉戲，常陳俎豆，設禮容。

孔子母死，乃殯五父之衢，蓋其慎也。郰人輓父之母誨孔子父墓，然後往合葬於防焉。

孔子要絰，季氏饗士，孔子與往。陽虎絀曰：「季氏饗士，非敢饗子也。」孔子由是退。

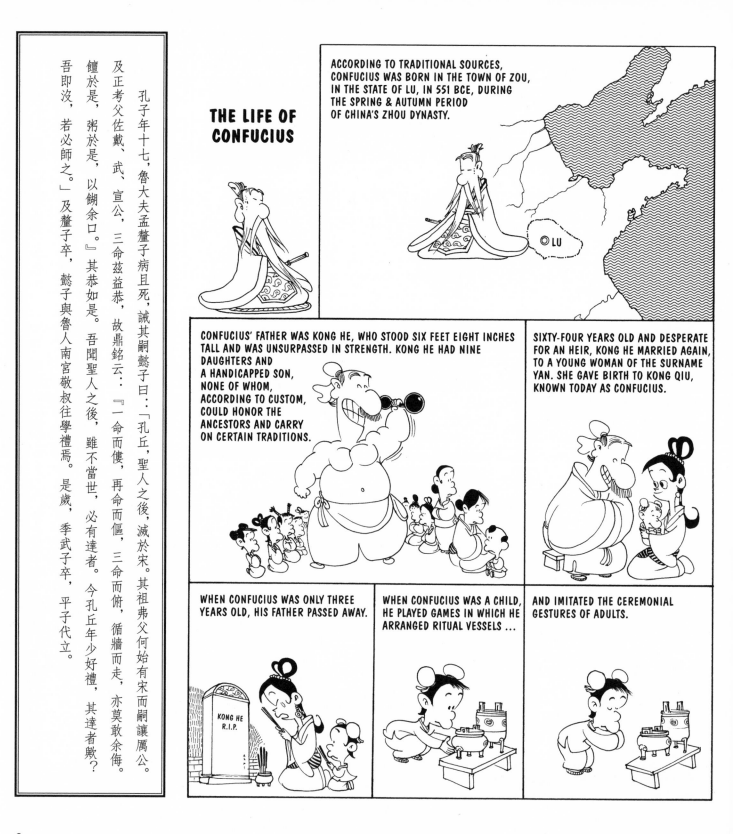

THE LIFE OF CONFUCIUS

ACCORDING TO TRADITIONAL SOURCES, CONFUCIUS WAS BORN IN THE TOWN OF ZOU, IN THE STATE OF LU, IN 551 BCE, DURING THE SPRING & AUTUMN PERIOD OF CHINA'S ZHOU DYNASTY.

LU

CONFUCIUS' FATHER WAS KONG HE, WHO STOOD SIX FEET EIGHT INCHES TALL AND WAS UNSURPASSED IN STRENGTH. KONG HE HAD NINE DAUGHTERS AND A HANDICAPPED SON, NONE OF WHOM, ACCORDING TO CUSTOM, COULD HONOR THE ANCESTORS AND CARRY ON CERTAIN TRADITIONS.

SIXTY-FOUR YEARS OLD AND DESPERATE FOR AN HEIR, KONG HE MARRIED AGAIN, TO A YOUNG WOMAN OF THE SURNAME YAN. SHE GAVE BIRTH TO KONG QIU, KNOWN TODAY AS CONFUCIUS.

WHEN CONFUCIUS WAS ONLY THREE YEARS OLD, HIS FATHER PASSED AWAY.

KONG HE R.I.P.

WHEN CONFUCIUS WAS A CHILD, HE PLAYED GAMES IN WHICH HE ARRANGED RITUAL VESSELS ...

AND IMITATED THE CEREMONIAL GESTURES OF ADULTS.

孔子年十七，魯大夫孟釐子病且死，誡其嗣懿子曰：「孔丘，聖人之後，滅於宋。其祖弗父何始有宋而嗣讓厲公。及正考父佐戴、武、宣公，三命茲益恭，故鼎銘云：『一命而僂，再命而傴，三命而俯，循牆而走，亦莫敢余侮。饘於是，粥於是，以餬余口。』其恭如是。吾聞聖人之後，雖不當世，必有達者。今孔丘年少好禮，其達者歟？吾即沒，若必師之。」及釐子卒，懿子與魯人南宮敬叔往學禮焉。是歲，季武子卒，平子代立。

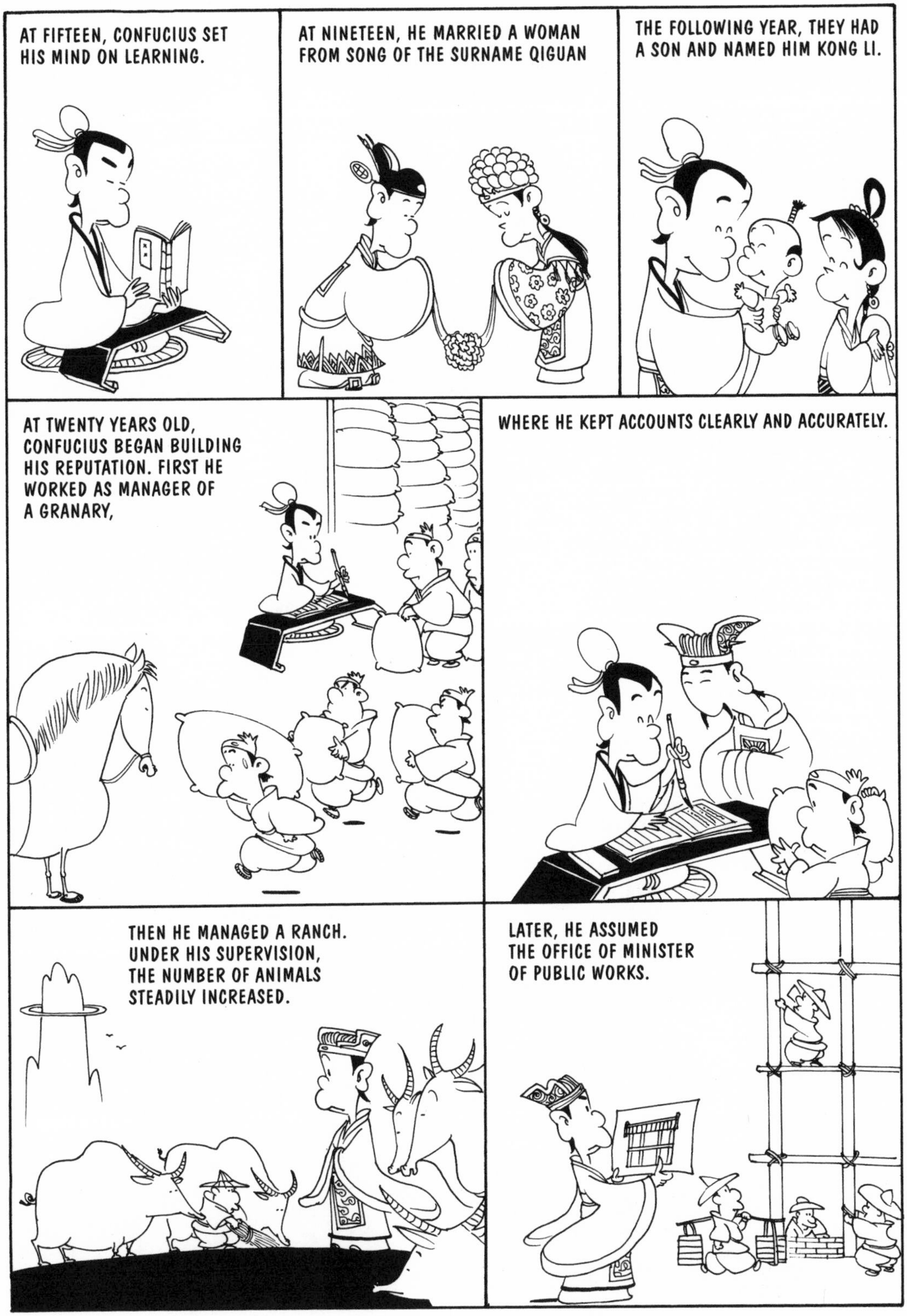
AT FIFTEEN, CONFUCIUS SET HIS MIND ON LEARNING.
AT NINETEEN, HE MARRIED A WOMAN FROM SONG OF THE SURNAME QIGUAN
THE FOLLOWING YEAR, THEY HAD A SON AND NAMED HIM KONG LI.
AT TWENTY YEARS OLD, CONFUCIUS BEGAN BUILDING HIS REPUTATION. FIRST HE WORKED AS MANAGER OF A GRANARY,
WHERE HE KEPT ACCOUNTS CLEARLY AND ACCURATELY.
THEN HE MANAGED A RANCH. UNDER HIS SUPERVISION, THE NUMBER OF ANIMALS STEADILY INCREASED.
LATER, HE ASSUMED THE OFFICE OF MINISTER OF PUBLIC WORKS.

孔子貧且賤。及長，嘗為季氏史，料量平，嘗為司職吏而畜蕃息。由是為司空。已而去魯，斥乎齊，逐乎宋、衛，困於陳蔡之閒，於是反魯。孔子長九尺有六寸，人皆謂之「長人」而異之。魯復善待，由是反魯。魯南宮敬叔言魯君曰：「請與孔子適周。」魯君與之一乘車，兩馬，一豎子俱，適周問禮，蓋見老子云。辭去，而老子送之曰：「吾聞富貴者送人以財，仁人者送人以言。吾不能富貴，竊仁人之號，送子以言，曰：『聰明

深察而近於死者，好議人者也。博辯廣大危其身者，發人之惡者也。為人子者毋以有己，為人臣者毋以有己。』」

孔子自周反于魯，弟子稍益進焉。

是時也，晉平公淫，六卿擅權，東伐諸侯；楚靈王兵彊，陵轢中國；齊大而近於魯。魯小弱，附於楚則晉怒；附於晉則楚來伐；不備於齊，齊師侵魯。

魯昭公之二十年，而孔子蓋年三十矣。齊景公與晏嬰來適魯，景公問孔子曰：「昔秦穆公國小處辟，其霸

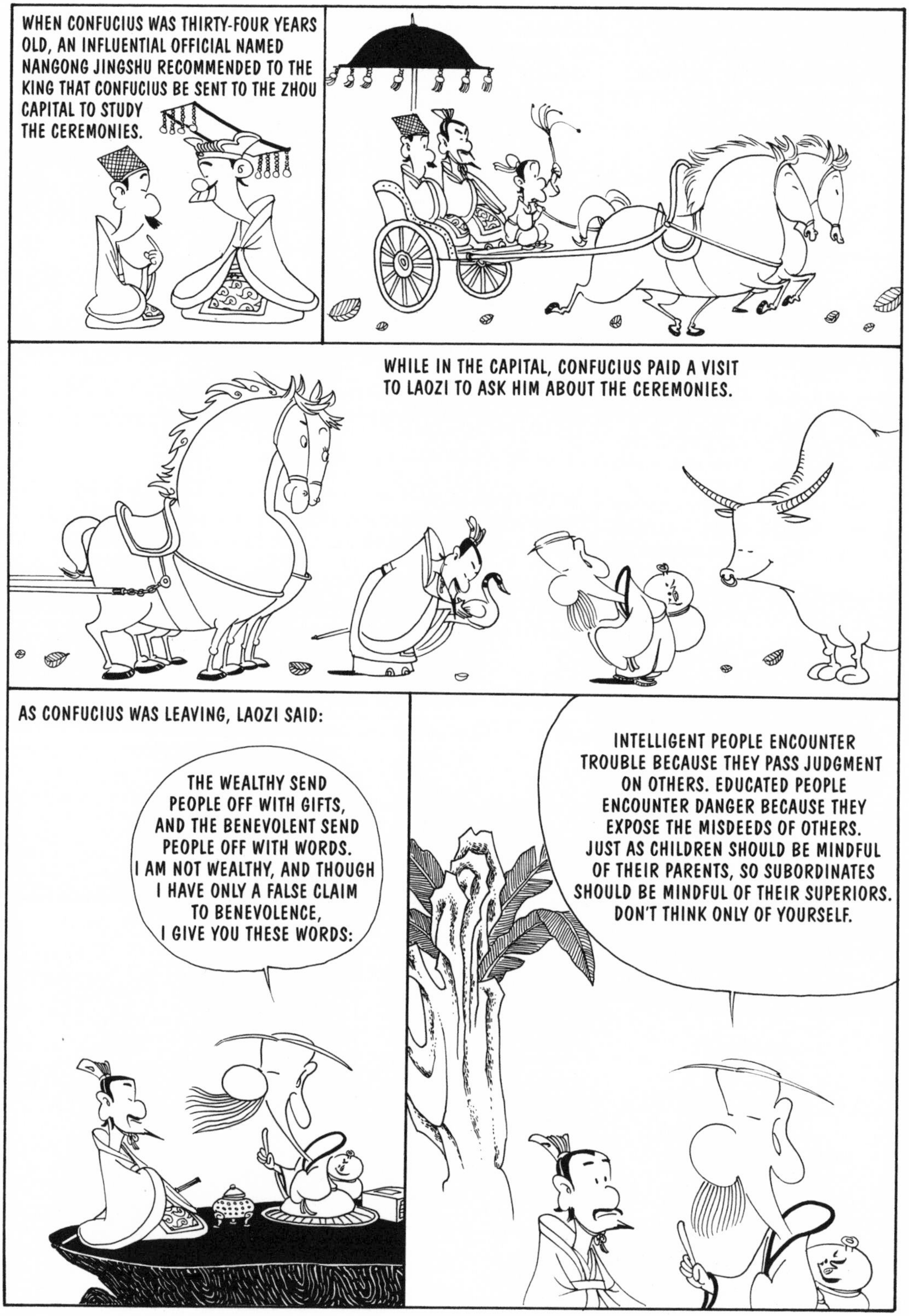
WHEN CONFUCIUS WAS THIRTY-FOUR YEARS OLD, AN INFLUENTIAL OFFICIAL NAMED NANGONG JINGSHU RECOMMENDED TO THE KING THAT CONFUCIUS BE SENT TO THE ZHOU CAPITAL TO STUDY THE CEREMONIES.
WHILE IN THE CAPITAL, CONFUCIUS PAID A VISIT TO LAOZI TO ASK HIM ABOUT THE CEREMONIES.
AS CONFUCIUS WAS LEAVING, LAOZI SAID:
THE WEALTHY SEND PEOPLE OFF WITH GIFTS, AND THE BENEVOLENT SEND PEOPLE OFF WITH WORDS. I AM NOT WEALTHY, AND THOUGH I HAVE ONLY A FALSE CLAIM TO BENEVOLENCE, I GIVE YOU THESE WORDS:
INTELLIGENT PEOPLE ENCOUNTER TROUBLE BECAUSE THEY PASS JUDGMENT ON OTHERS. EDUCATED PEOPLE ENCOUNTER DANGER BECAUSE THEY EXPOSE THE MISDEEDS OF OTHERS. JUST AS CHILDREN SHOULD BE MINDFUL OF THEIR PARENTS, SO SUBORDINATES SHOULD BE MINDFUL OF THEIR SUPERIORS. DON'T THINK ONLY OF YOURSELF.

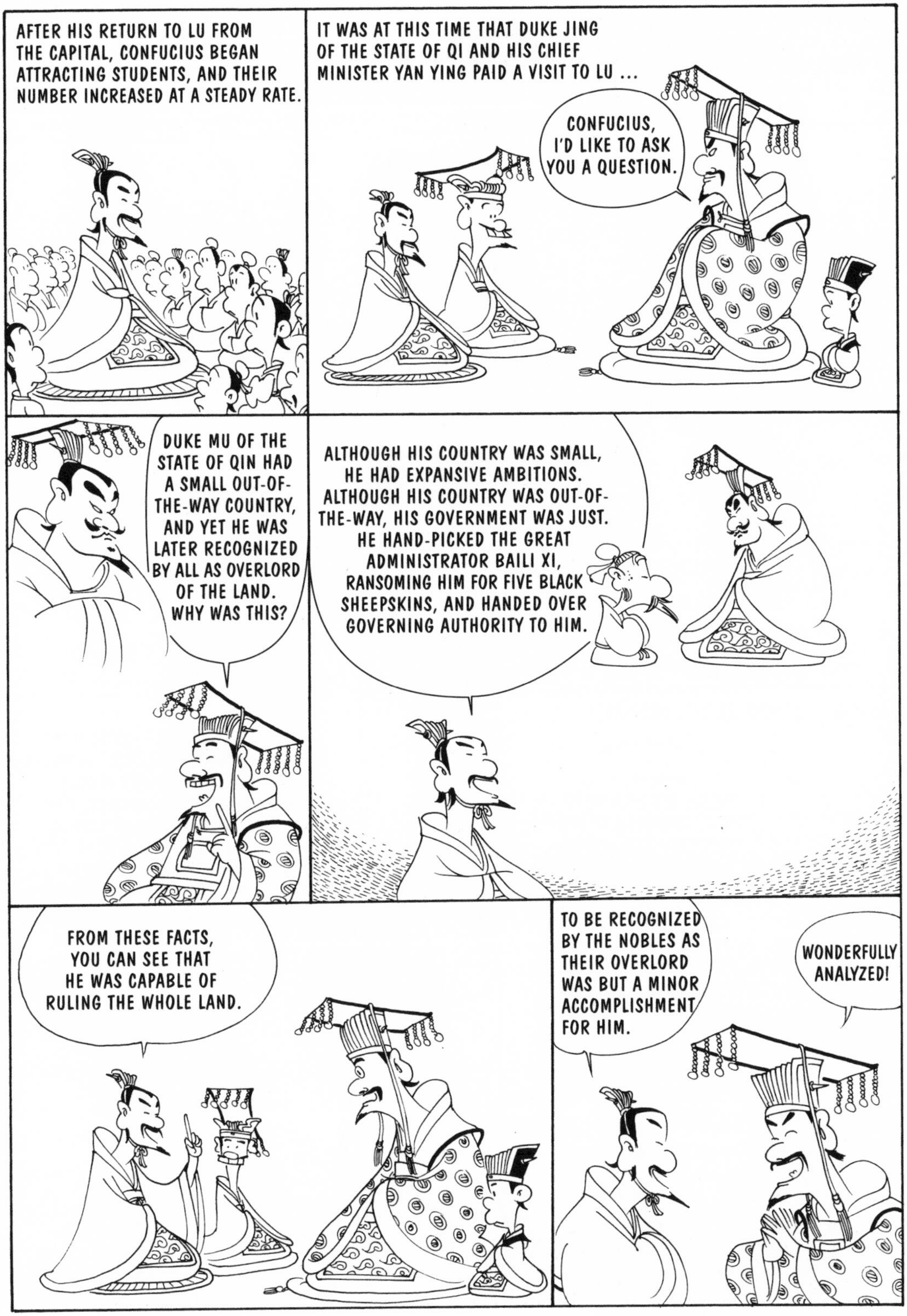
AFTER HIS RETURN TO LU FROM THE CAPITAL, CONFUCIUS BEGAN ATTRACTING STUDENTS, AND THEIR NUMBER INCREASED AT A STEADY RATE.
IT WAS AT THIS TIME THAT DUKE JING OF THE STATE OF QI AND HIS CHIEF MINISTER YAN YING PAID A VISIT TO LU ...
CONFUCIUS, I'D LIKE TO ASK YOU A QUESTION.
DUKE MU OF THE STATE OF QIN HAD A SMALL OUT-OF-THE-WAY COUNTRY, AND YET HE WAS LATER RECOGNIZED BY ALL AS OVERLORD OF THE LAND. WHY WAS THIS?
ALTHOUGH HIS COUNTRY WAS SMALL, HE HAD EXPANSIVE AMBITIONS. ALTHOUGH HIS COUNTRY WAS OUT-OF-THE-WAY, HIS GOVERNMENT WAS JUST. HE HAND-PICKED THE GREAT ADMINISTRATOR BAILI XI, RANSOMING HIM FOR FIVE BLACK SHEEPSKINS, AND HANDED OVER GOVERNING AUTHORITY TO HIM.
FROM THESE FACTS, YOU CAN SEE THAT HE WAS CAPABLE OF RULING THE WHOLE LAND.
TO BE RECOGNIZED BY THE NOBLES AS THEIR OVERLORD WAS BUT A MINOR ACCOMPLISHMENT FOR HIM.
WONDERFULLY ANALYZED!

何也？」對曰：「秦，國雖小，其志大；處雖辟，行中正。身舉五羖，爵之大夫，起纍紲之中，與語三日，授之以政。以此取之，雖王可也，其霸小矣。」景公說。

孔子年三十五，而季平子與郈昭伯以鬬雞故得罪魯昭公，昭公率師擊平子，平子與孟氏、叔孫氏三家共攻昭公，昭公師敗，奔於齊，齊處昭公乾侯。其後頃之，魯亂。孔子適齊，為高昭子家臣，欲以通乎景公。與齊太師語樂，聞《韶》音，學之，三月不知肉味，齊人稱之。

景公問政孔子，孔子曰：「君君，臣臣，父父，子子。」景公曰：「善哉！信如君不君，臣不臣，父不父，子不子，雖有粟，吾豈得而食諸！」他日又復問政於孔子，孔子曰：「政在節財。」景公說，將欲以尼谿田封孔子。晏嬰進曰：「夫儒者滑稽而不可軌法；倨傲自順，不可以為下；崇喪遂哀，破產厚葬，不可以為俗；游說乞貸，不可以為國。自大賢之息，周室既衰，禮樂缺有閒。今孔子盛容飾，繁登降之禮，趨詳之節，累世不能殫其學，當年不能究其禮。

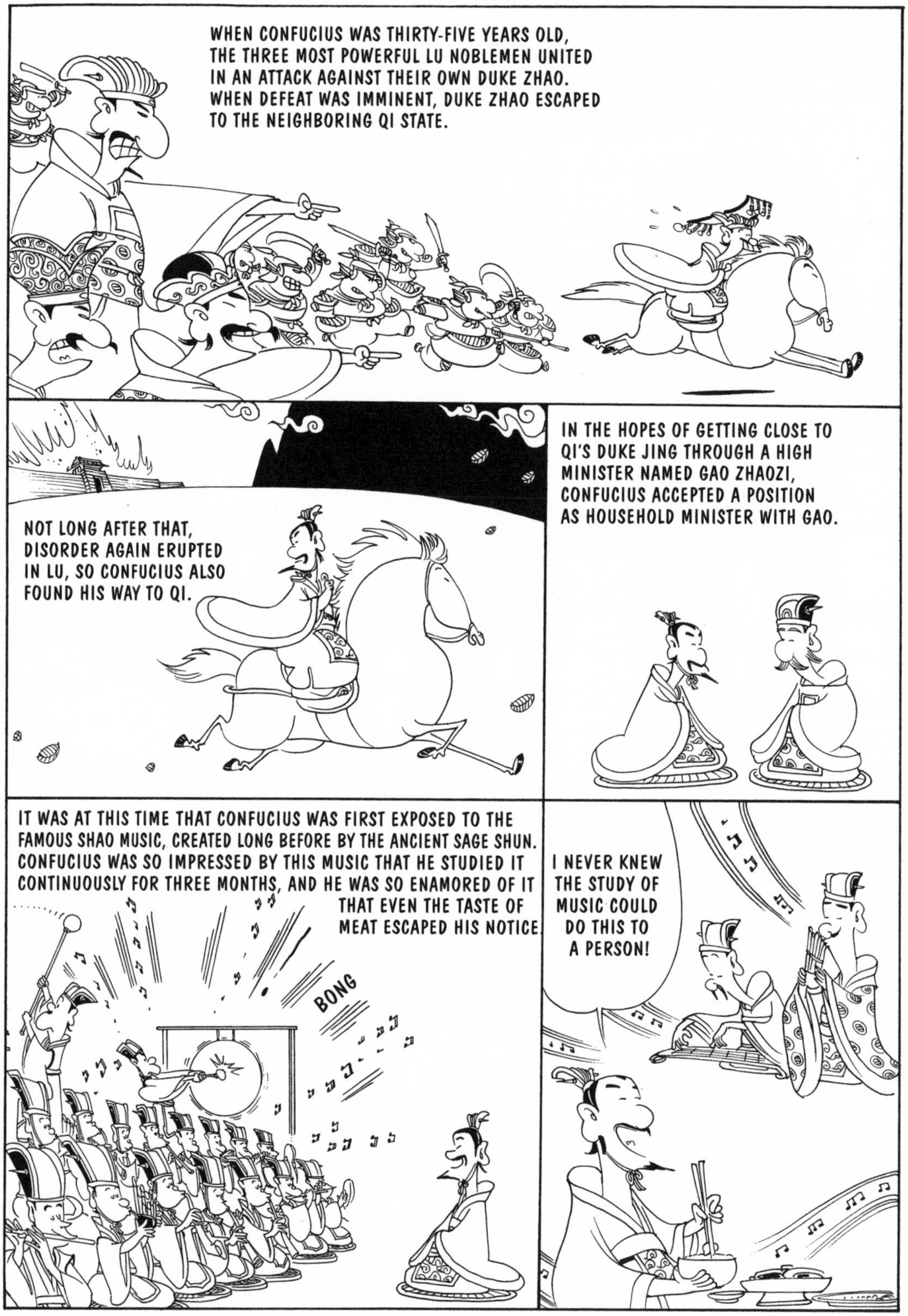
WHEN CONFUCIUS WAS THIRTY-FIVE YEARS OLD, THE THREE MOST POWERFUL LU NOBLEMEN UNITED IN AN ATTACK AGAINST THEIR OWN DUKE ZHAO. WHEN DEFEAT WAS IMMINENT, DUKE ZHAO ESCAPED TO THE NEIGHBORING QI STATE.
NOT LONG AFTER THAT, DISORDER AGAIN ERUPTED IN LU, SO CONFUCIUS ALSO FOUND HIS WAY TO QI.
IN THE HOPES OF GETTING CLOSE TO QI'S DUKE JING THROUGH A HIGH MINISTER NAMED GAO ZHAOZI, CONFUCIUS ACCEPTED A POSITION AS HOUSEHOLD MINISTER WITH GAO.
IT WAS AT THIS TIME THAT CONFUCIUS WAS FIRST EXPOSED TO THE FAMOUS SHAO MUSIC, CREATED LONG BEFORE BY THE ANCIENT SAGE SHUN. CONFUCIUS WAS SO IMPRESSED BY THIS MUSIC THAT HE STUDIED IT CONTINUOUSLY FOR THREE MONTHS, AND HE WAS SO ENAMORED OF IT THAT EVEN THE TASTE OF MEAT ESCAPED HIS NOTICE.
BONG
I NEVER KNEW THE STUDY OF MUSIC COULD DO THIS TO A PERSON!

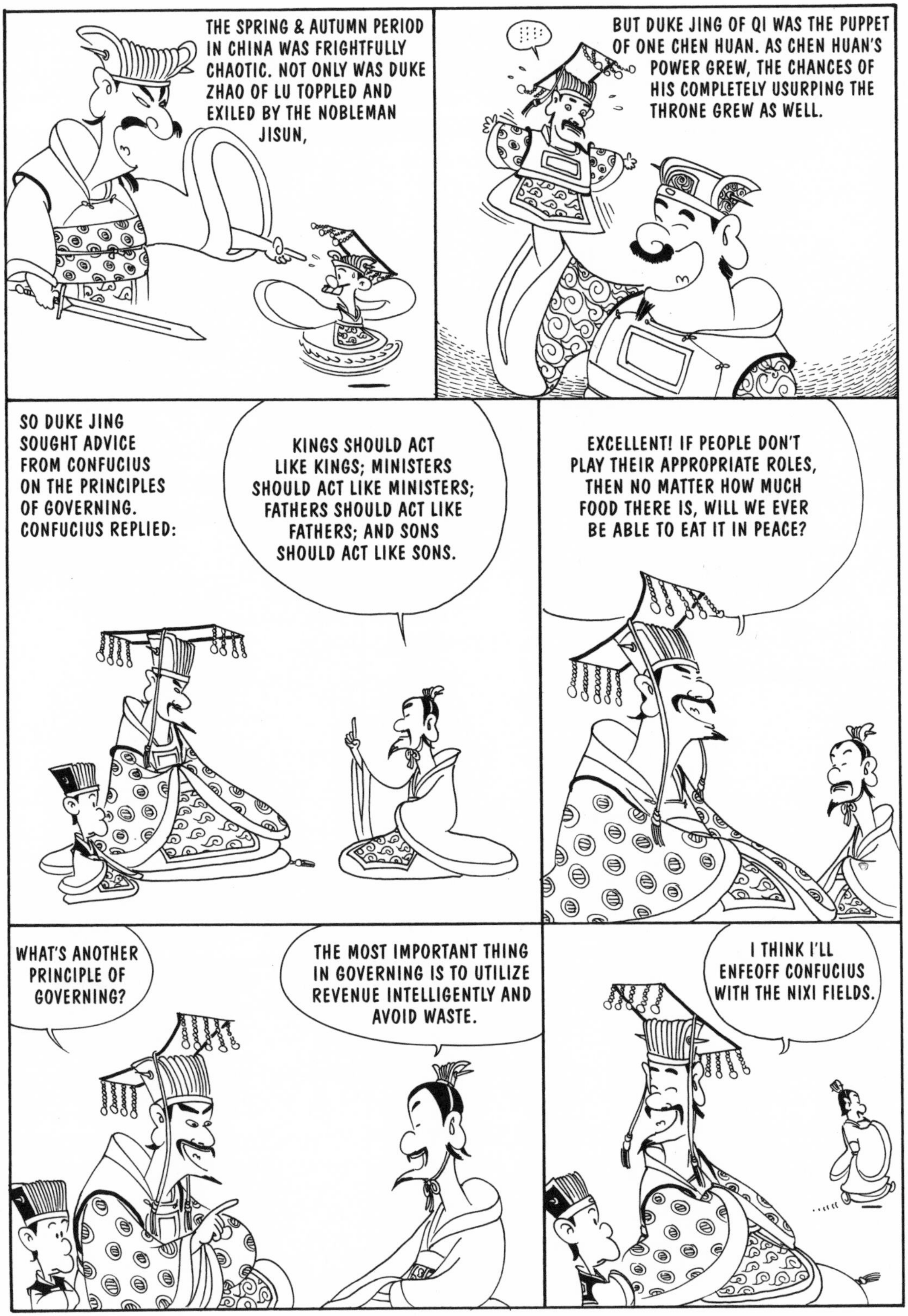
THE SPRING & AUTUMN PERIOD IN CHINA WAS FRIGHTFULLY CHAOTIC. NOT ONLY WAS DUKE ZHAO OF LU TOPPLED AND EXILED BY THE NOBLEMAN JISUN,
BUT DUKE JING OF QI WAS THE PUPPET OF ONE CHEN HUAN. AS CHEN HUAN'S POWER GREW, THE CHANCES OF HIS COMPLETELY USURPING THE THRONE GREW AS WELL.
SO DUKE JING SOUGHT ADVICE FROM CONFUCIUS ON THE PRINCIPLES OF GOVERNING. CONFUCIUS REPLIED:
KINGS SHOULD ACT LIKE KINGS; MINISTERS SHOULD ACT LIKE MINISTERS; FATHERS SHOULD ACT LIKE FATHERS; AND SONS SHOULD ACT LIKE SONS.
EXCELLENT! IF PEOPLE DON'T PLAY THEIR APPROPRIATE ROLES, THEN NO MATTER HOW MUCH FOOD THERE IS, WILL WE EVER BE ABLE TO EAT IT IN PEACE?
WHAT'S ANOTHER PRINCIPLE OF GOVERNING?
THE MOST IMPORTANT THING IN GOVERNING IS TO UTILIZE REVENUE INTELLIGENTLY AND AVOID WASTE.
I THINK I'LL ENFEOFF CONFUCIUS WITH THE NIXI FIELDS.

君欲用之以移齊俗，非所以先細民也。」後景公敬見孔子，不問其禮。異日，景公止孔子曰：「奉子以季氏，吾不能。」以季孟之閒待之。」齊大夫欲害孔子，孔子聞之。景公曰：「吾老矣，弗能用也。」孔子遂行，反乎魯。

孔子年四十二，魯昭公卒於乾侯，定公立。定公立五年，夏，季平子卒，桓子嗣立。季桓子穿井得土缶，中若羊，問仲尼云「得狗」。仲尼曰：「以丘所聞，羊也。丘聞之，木石之怪夔、罔閬，水之怪龍、罔象，土之怪墳羊。」

吳伐越，墮會稽，得骨節專車。吳使使問仲尼：「骨何者最大？」仲尼曰：「禹致群神於會稽山，防風氏後至，禹殺而戮之，其節專車，此為大矣。」吳客曰：「誰為神？」仲尼曰：「山川之神足以綱紀天下，其守為神，社稷為公侯，皆屬於王者。」客曰：「防風何守？」仲尼曰：「汪罔氏之君守封、禺之山，為釐姓。在虞、夏、商為汪罔，於周為長翟，今謂之大人。」客曰：「人長幾何？」仲尼曰：「僬僥氏三尺，短之至也。長者不過十之，數之極也。」於是吳客曰：「善哉聖人！」

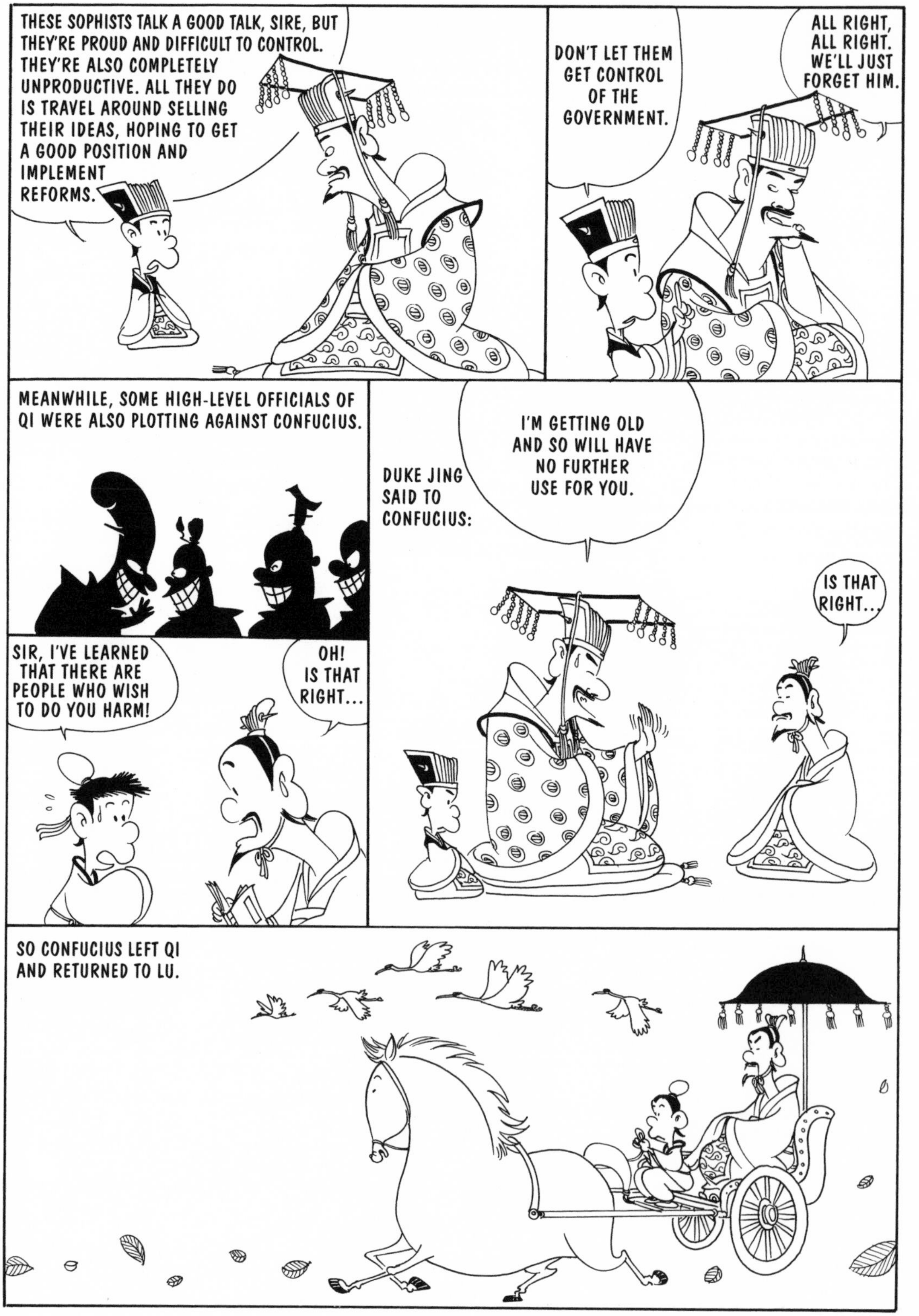
THESE SOPHISTS TALK A GOOD TALK, SIRE, BUT THEY'RE PROUD AND DIFFICULT TO CONTROL. THEY'RE ALSO COMPLETELY UNPRODUCTIVE. ALL THEY DO IS TRAVEL AROUND SELLING THEIR IDEAS, HOPING TO GET A GOOD POSITION AND IMPLEMENT REFORMS.
DON'T LET THEM GET CONTROL OF THE GOVERNMENT.
ALL RIGHT, ALL RIGHT. WE'LL JUST FORGET HIM.
MEANWHILE, SOME HIGH-LEVEL OFFICIALS OF QI WERE ALSO PLOTTING AGAINST CONFUCIUS.
SIR, I'VE LEARNED THAT THERE ARE PEOPLE WHO WISH TO DO YOU HARM!
OH! IS THAT RIGHT...
DUKE JING SAID TO CONFUCIUS:
I'M GETTING OLD AND SO WILL HAVE NO FURTHER USE FOR YOU.
IS THAT RIGHT...
SO CONFUCIUS LEFT QI AND RETURNED TO LU.

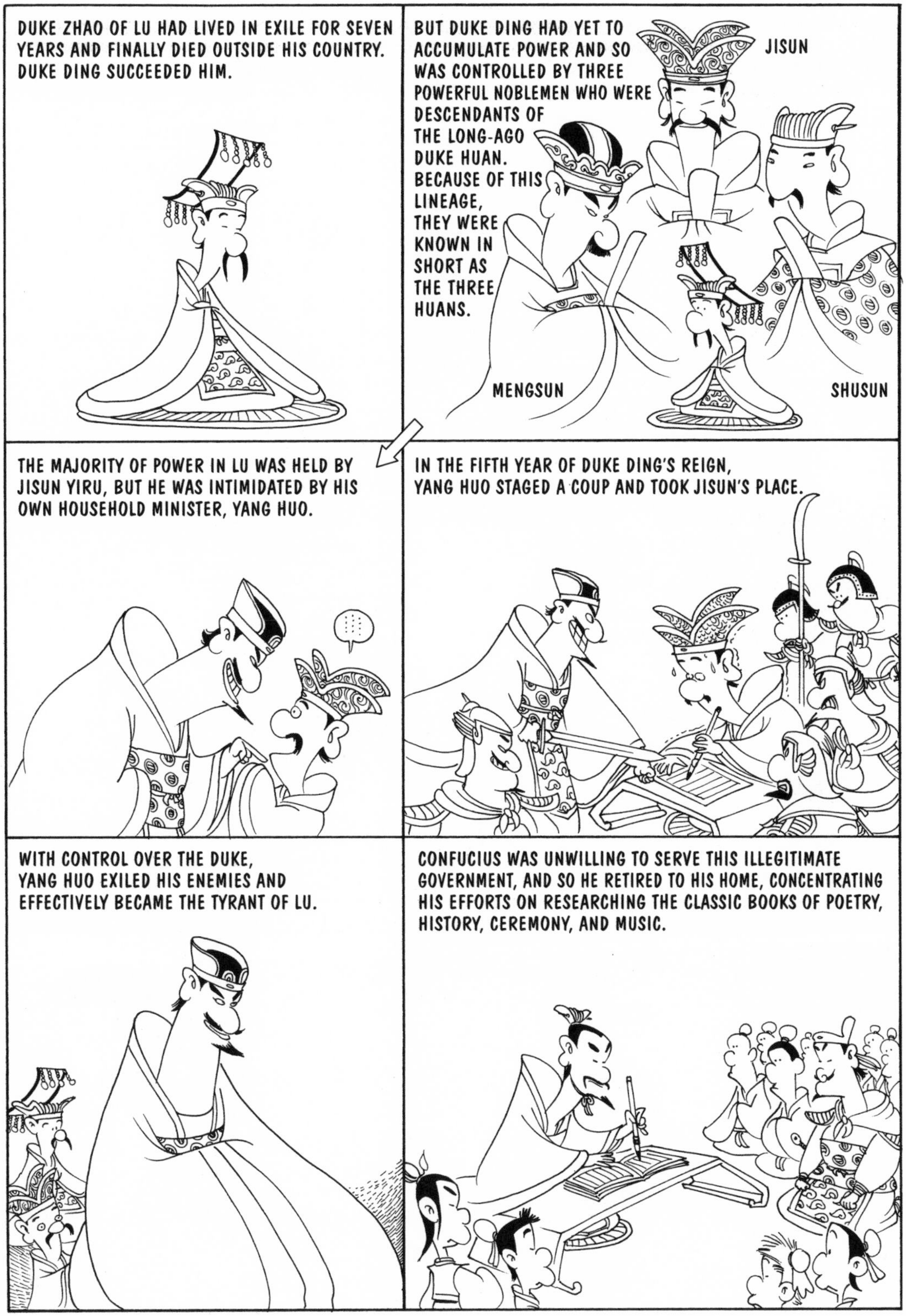
DUKE ZHAO OF LU HAD LIVED IN EXILE FOR SEVEN YEARS AND FINALLY DIED OUTSIDE HIS COUNTRY. DUKE DING SUCCEEDED HIM.
BUT DUKE DING HAD YET TO ACCUMULATE POWER AND SO WAS CONTROLLED BY THREE POWERFUL NOBLEMEN WHO WERE DESCENDANTS OF THE LONG-AGO DUKE HUAN. BECAUSE OF THIS LINEAGE, THEY WERE KNOWN IN SHORT AS THE THREE HUANS.
JISUN
MENGSUN
SHUSUN
THE MAJORITY OF POWER IN LU WAS HELD BY JISUN YIRU, BUT HE WAS INTIMIDATED BY HIS OWN HOUSEHOLD MINISTER, YANG HUO.
IN THE FIFTH YEAR OF DUKE DING'S REIGN, YANG HUO STAGED A COUP AND TOOK JISUN'S PLACE.
WITH CONTROL OVER THE DUKE, YANG HUO EXILED HIS ENEMIES AND EFFECTIVELY BECAME THE TYRANT OF LU.
CONFUCIUS WAS UNWILLING TO SERVE THIS ILLEGITIMATE GOVERNMENT, AND SO HE RETIRED TO HIS HOME, CONCENTRATING HIS EFFORTS ON RESEARCHING THE CLASSIC BOOKS OF POETRY, HISTORY, CEREMONY, AND MUSIC.

桓子嬖臣曰仲梁懷，與陽虎有隙。陽虎欲逐懷，公山不狃止之。其秋，懷益驕，陽虎執懷。桓子怒，陽虎因囚桓子，與盟而醳之。陽虎由此益輕季氏。季氏亦僭於公室，陪臣執國政，是以魯自大夫以下皆僭離於正道。故孔子不仕，退而脩《詩》、《書》、《禮》、《樂》，弟子彌眾，至自遠方，莫不受業焉。

定公八年，公山不狃不得意於季氏，因陽虎為亂，欲廢三桓之適，更立其庶孽陽虎素所善者，遂執季桓子。桓子詐之，得脫。定公九年，陽虎不勝，奔于齊。是時孔子年五十。

公山不狃以費畔季氏，使人召孔子。孔子循道彌久，溫溫無所試，莫能己用，曰：「蓋周文武起豐鎬而王，今費雖小，儻庶幾乎！」欲往。子路不說，止孔子。孔子曰：「夫召我者豈徒哉？如用我，其為東周乎！」然亦卒不行。

其後定公以孔子為中都宰，一年，四方皆則之。由中都宰為司空，由司空為大司寇。

定公十年春，及齊平。夏，齊大夫黎鉏言於景公曰：「魯用孔丘，其勢危齊。」乃使使告魯為好會，

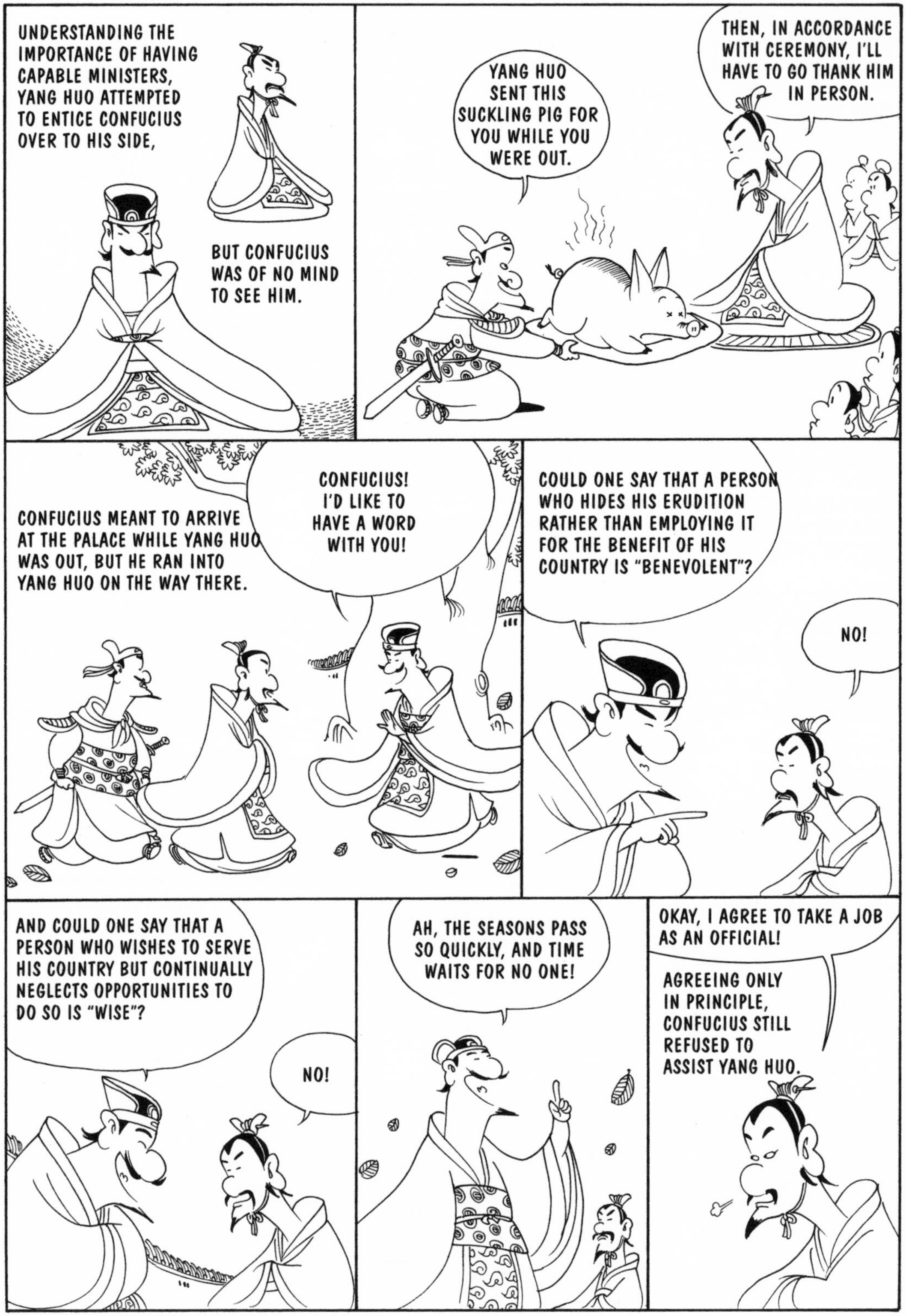

UNDERSTANDING THE IMPORTANCE OF HAVING CAPABLE MINISTERS, YANG HUO ATTEMPTED TO ENTICE CONFUCIUS OVER TO HIS SIDE,
BUT CONFUCIUS WAS OF NO MIND TO SEE HIM.
YANG HUO SENT THIS SUCKLING PIG FOR YOU WHILE YOU WERE OUT.
THEN, IN ACCORDANCE WITH CEREMONY, I'LL HAVE TO GO THANK HIM IN PERSON.
CONFUCIUS MEANT TO ARRIVE AT THE PALACE WHILE YANG HUO WAS OUT, BUT HE RAN INTO YANG HUO ON THE WAY THERE.
CONFUCIUS! I'D LIKE TO HAVE A WORD WITH YOU!
COULD ONE SAY THAT A PERSON WHO HIDES HIS ERUDITION RATHER THAN EMPLOYING IT FOR THE BENEFIT OF HIS COUNTRY IS "BENEVOLENT"?
NO!
AND COULD ONE SAY THAT A PERSON WHO WISHES TO SERVE HIS COUNTRY BUT CONTINUALLY NEGLECTS OPPORTUNITIES TO DO SO IS "WISE"?
NO!
AH, THE SEASONS PASS SO QUICKLY, AND TIME WAITS FOR NO ONE!
OKAY, I AGREE TO TAKE A JOB AS AN OFFICIAL!
AGREEING ONLY IN PRINCIPLE, CONFUCIUS STILL REFUSED TO ASSIST YANG HUO.

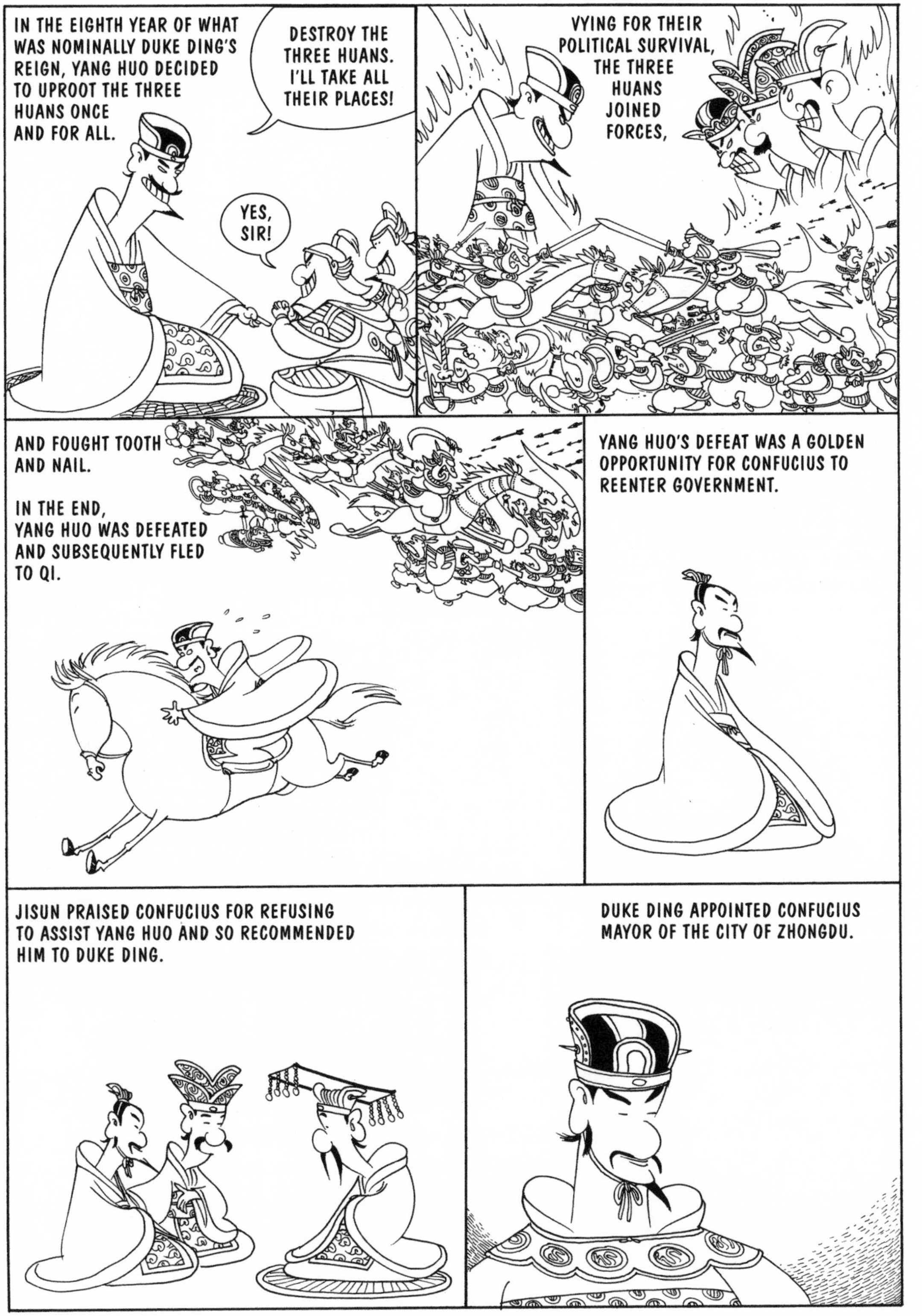
IN THE EIGHTH YEAR OF WHAT WAS NOMINALLY DUKE DING'S REIGN, YANG HUO DECIDED TO UPROOT THE THREE HUANS ONCE AND FOR ALL.
DESTROY THE THREE HUANS. I'LL TAKE ALL THEIR PLACES!
YES, SIR!
VYING FOR THEIR POLITICAL SURVIVAL, THE THREE HUANS JOINED FORCES,
AND FOUGHT TOOTH AND NAIL.
IN THE END, YANG HUO WAS DEFEATED AND SUBSEQUENTLY FLED TO QI.
YANG HUO'S DEFEAT WAS A GOLDEN OPPORTUNITY FOR CONFUCIUS TO REENTER GOVERNMENT.
JISUN PRAISED CONFUCIUS FOR REFUSING TO ASSIST YANG HUO AND SO RECOMMENDED HIM TO DUKE DING.
DUKE DING APPOINTED CONFUCIUS MAYOR OF THE CITY OF ZHONGDU.

會於夾谷。魯定公且以乘車好往。孔子攝相事，曰：「臣聞有文事者必有武備，有武事者必有文備。古者諸侯出疆，必具官以從。請具左右司馬。」定公曰：「諾。」具左右司馬。會齊侯夾谷，為壇位，土階三等，以會遇之禮相見，揖讓而登。獻酬之禮畢，齊有司趨而進曰：「請奏四方之樂。」景公曰：「諾。」於是旍旄羽袚矛戟劍撥鼓噪而至。孔子趨而進，歷階而登，不盡一等，舉袂而言曰：「吾兩君為好會，夷狄之樂何為於此！請命有司！」有司卻之，不去，則左右視晏子與景公。景公心怍，麾而去之。有頃，齊有司趨而進曰：「請奏宮中之樂。」景公曰：「諾。」

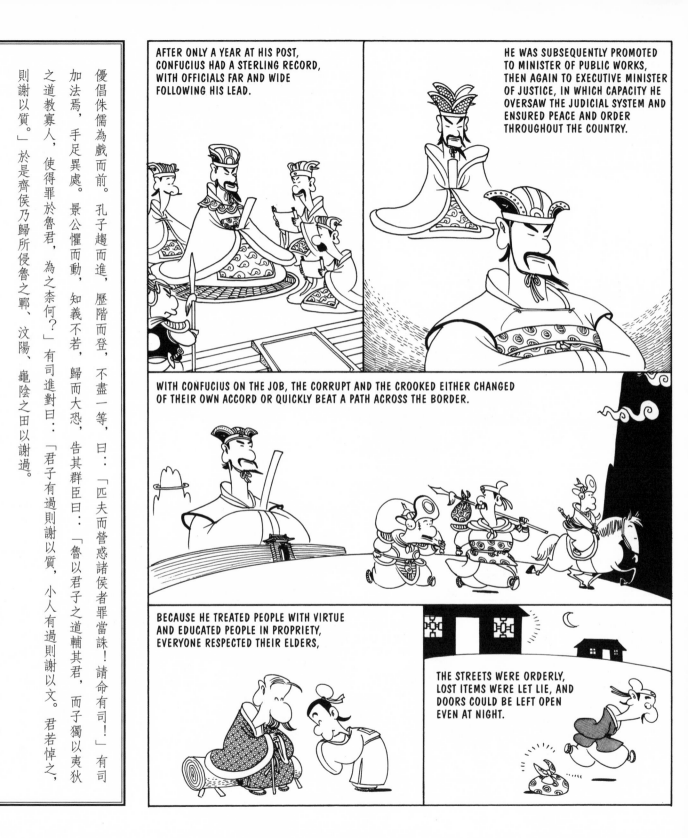

優倡侏儒為戲而前。孔子趨而進，歷階而登，不盡一等，曰：「匹夫而營惑諸侯者罪當誅！請命有司！」有司加法焉，手足異處。景公懼而動，知義不若，歸而大恐，告其群臣曰：「魯以君子之道輔其君，而子獨以夷狄之道教寡人，使得罪於魯君，為之柰何？」有司進對曰：「君子有過則謝以質，小人有過則謝以文。君若悼之，則謝以質。」於是齊侯乃歸所侵魯之鄆、汶陽、龜陰之田以謝過。

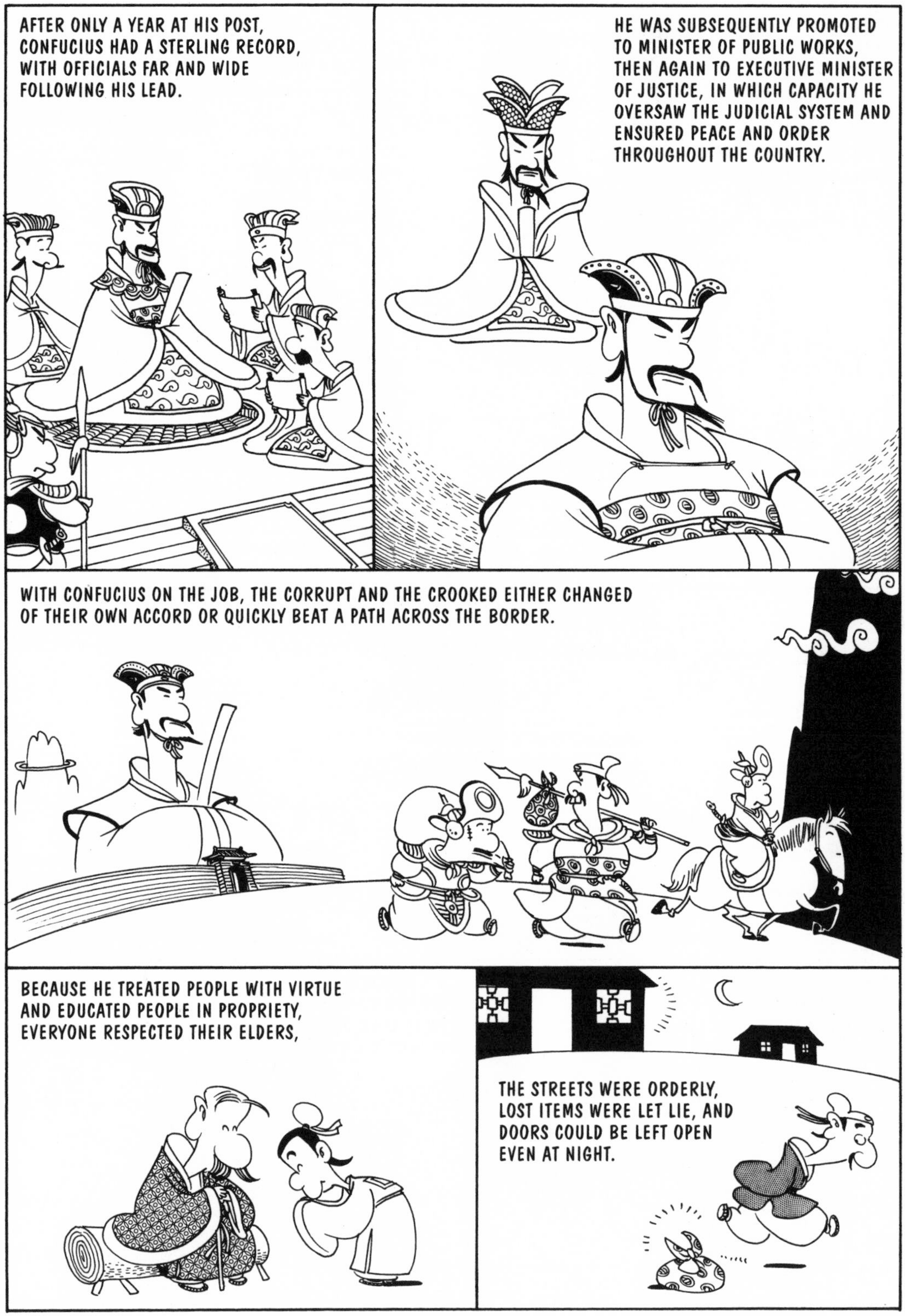

AFTER ONLY A YEAR AT HIS POST, CONFUCIUS HAD A STERLING RECORD, WITH OFFICIALS FAR AND WIDE FOLLOWING HIS LEAD.
HE WAS SUBSEQUENTLY PROMOTED TO MINISTER OF PUBLIC WORKS, THEN AGAIN TO EXECUTIVE MINISTER OF JUSTICE, IN WHICH CAPACITY HE OVERSAW THE JUDICIAL SYSTEM AND ENSURED PEACE AND ORDER THROUGHOUT THE COUNTRY.
WITH CONFUCIUS ON THE JOB, THE CORRUPT AND THE CROOKED EITHER CHANGED OF THEIR OWN ACCORD OR QUICKLY BEAT A PATH ACROSS THE BORDER.
BECAUSE HE TREATED PEOPLE WITH VIRTUE AND EDUCATED PEOPLE IN PROPRIETY, EVERYONE RESPECTED THEIR ELDERS,
THE STREETS WERE ORDERLY, LOST ITEMS WERE LET LIE, AND DOORS COULD BE LEFT OPEN EVEN AT NIGHT.

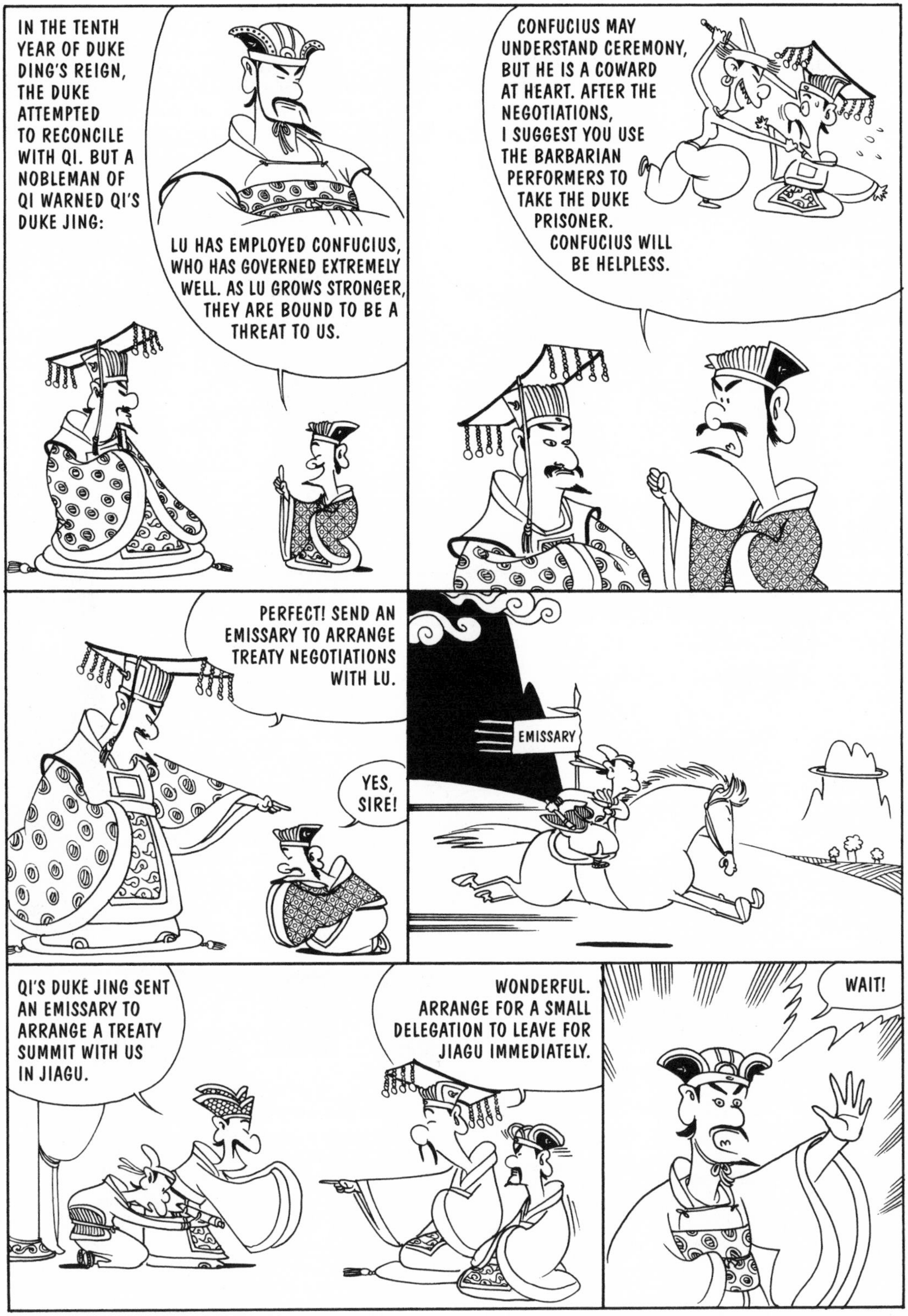
IN THE TENTH YEAR OF DUKE DING'S REIGN, THE DUKE ATTEMPTED TO RECONCILE WITH QI. BUT A NOBLEMAN OF QI WARNED QI'S DUKE JING:
LU HAS EMPLOYED CONFUCIUS, WHO HAS GOVERNED EXTREMELY WELL. AS LU GROWS STRONGER, THEY ARE BOUND TO BE A THREAT TO US.
CONFUCIUS MAY UNDERSTAND CEREMONY, BUT HE IS A COWARD AT HEART. AFTER THE NEGOTIATIONS, I SUGGEST YOU USE THE BARBARIAN PERFORMERS TO TAKE THE DUKE PRISONER. CONFUCIUS WILL BE HELPLESS.
PERFECT! SEND AN EMISSARY TO ARRANGE TREATY NEGOTIATIONS WITH LU.
YES, SIRE!
EMISSARY
QI'S DUKE JING SENT AN EMISSARY TO ARRANGE A TREATY SUMMIT WITH US IN JIAGU.
WONDERFUL. ARRANGE FOR A SMALL DELEGATION TO LEAVE FOR JIAGU IMMEDIATELY.
WAIT!

定公十三年夏，孔子言於定公曰：「臣無藏甲，大夫毋百雉之城。」使仲由為季氏宰，將墮三都。於是叔孫氏先墮郈。季氏將墮費，公山不狃、叔孫輒率費人襲魯。公與三子入于季氏之宮，登武子之臺。費人攻之，弗克，入及公側。孔子命申句須、樂頎下伐之，費人北。國人追之，敗諸姑蔑。二子奔齊，遂墮費。將墮成，公斂處父謂孟孫曰：「墮成，齊人必至于北門。且成，孟氏之保鄣，無成是無孟氏也。我將弗墮。」十二月，公圍成，弗克。

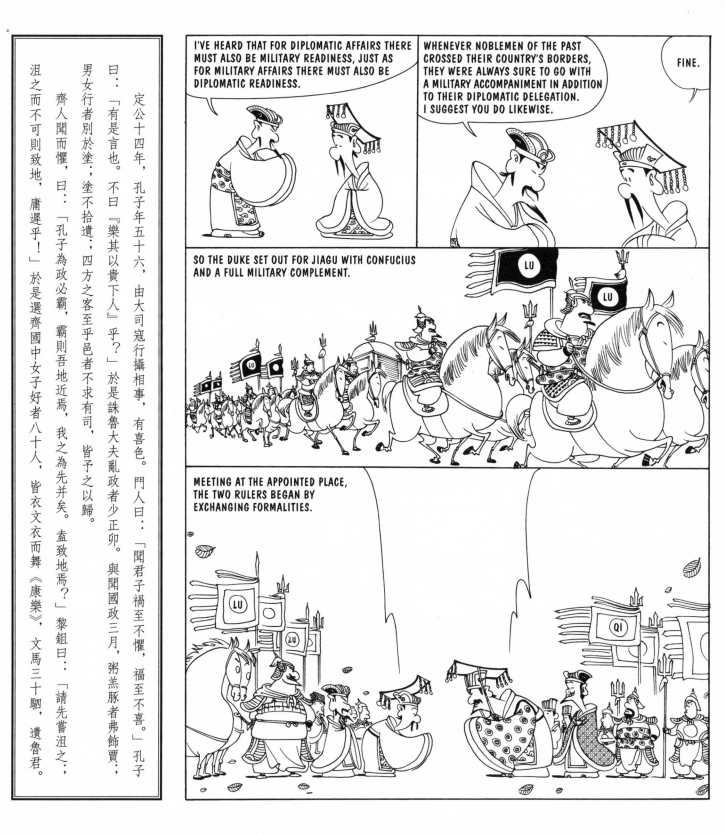

定公十四年，孔子年五十六，由大司寇行攝相事，有喜色。門人曰：「聞君子禍至不懼，福至不喜。」孔子曰：「有是言也。不曰『樂其以貴下人』乎？」於是誅魯大夫亂政者少正卯。與聞國政三月，粥羔豚者弗飾賈；男女行者別於塗；塗不拾遺；四方之客至乎邑者不求有司，皆予之以歸。

齊人聞而懼，曰：「孔子為政必霸，霸則吾地近焉，我之為先并矣。盍致地焉？」黎鉏曰：「請先嘗沮之；沮之而不可則致地，庸遲乎！」於是選齊國中女子好者八十人，皆衣文衣而舞《康樂》，文馬三十駟，遺魯君。

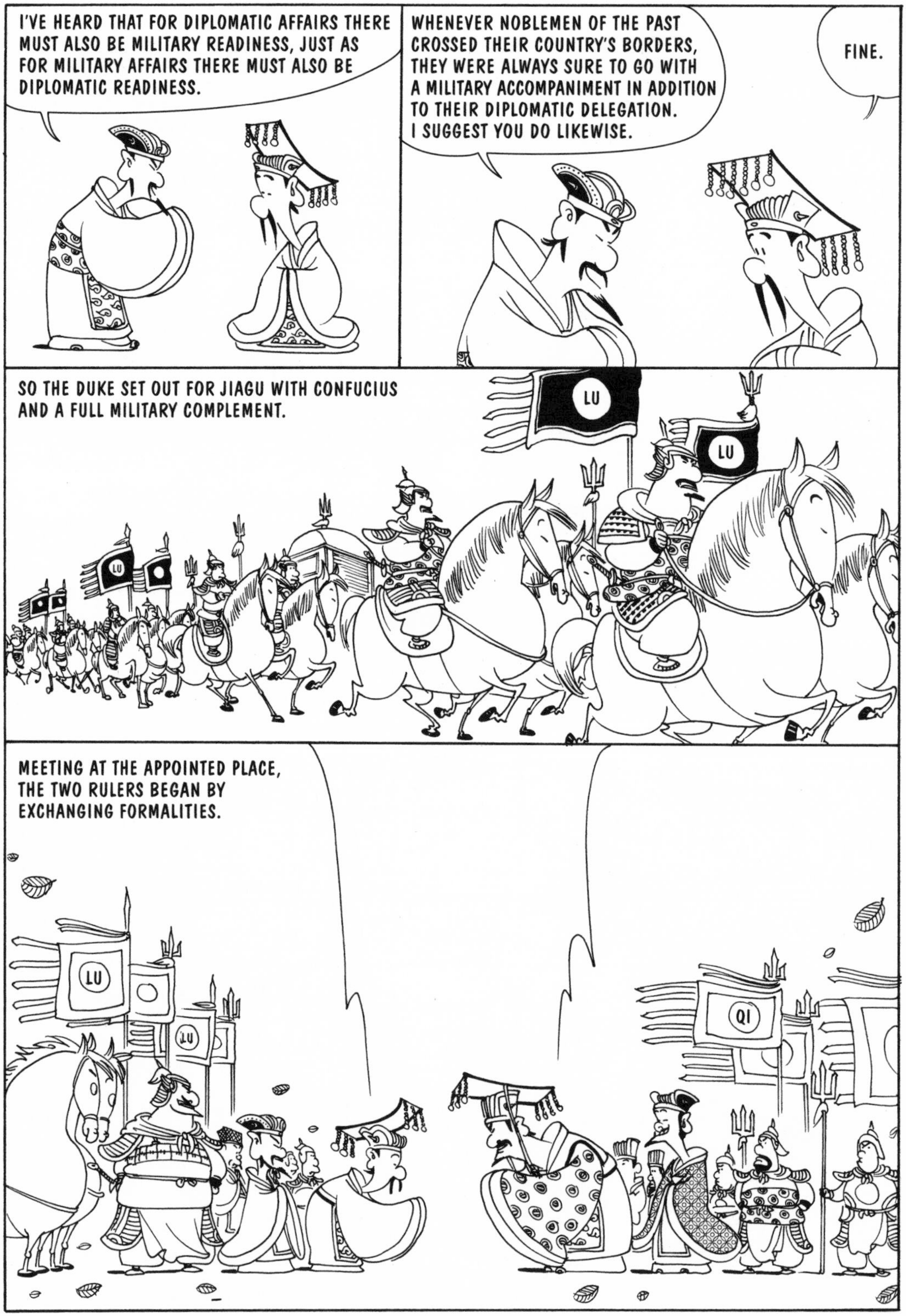
I'VE HEARD THAT FOR DIPLOMATIC AFFAIRS THERE MUST ALSO BE MILITARY READINESS, JUST AS FOR MILITARY AFFAIRS THERE MUST ALSO BE DIPLOMATIC READINESS.
WHENEVER NOBLEMEN OF THE PAST CROSSED THEIR COUNTRY'S BORDERS, THEY WERE ALWAYS SURE TO GO WITH A MILITARY ACCOMPANIMENT IN ADDITION TO THEIR DIPLOMATIC DELEGATION. I SUGGEST YOU DO LIKEWISE.
FINE.
SO THE DUKE SET OUT FOR JIAGU WITH CONFUCIUS AND A FULL MILITARY COMPLEMENT.
LU
LU
LU
MEETING AT THE APPOINTED PLACE, THE TWO RULERS BEGAN BY EXCHANGING FORMALITIES.
LU
LU
QI

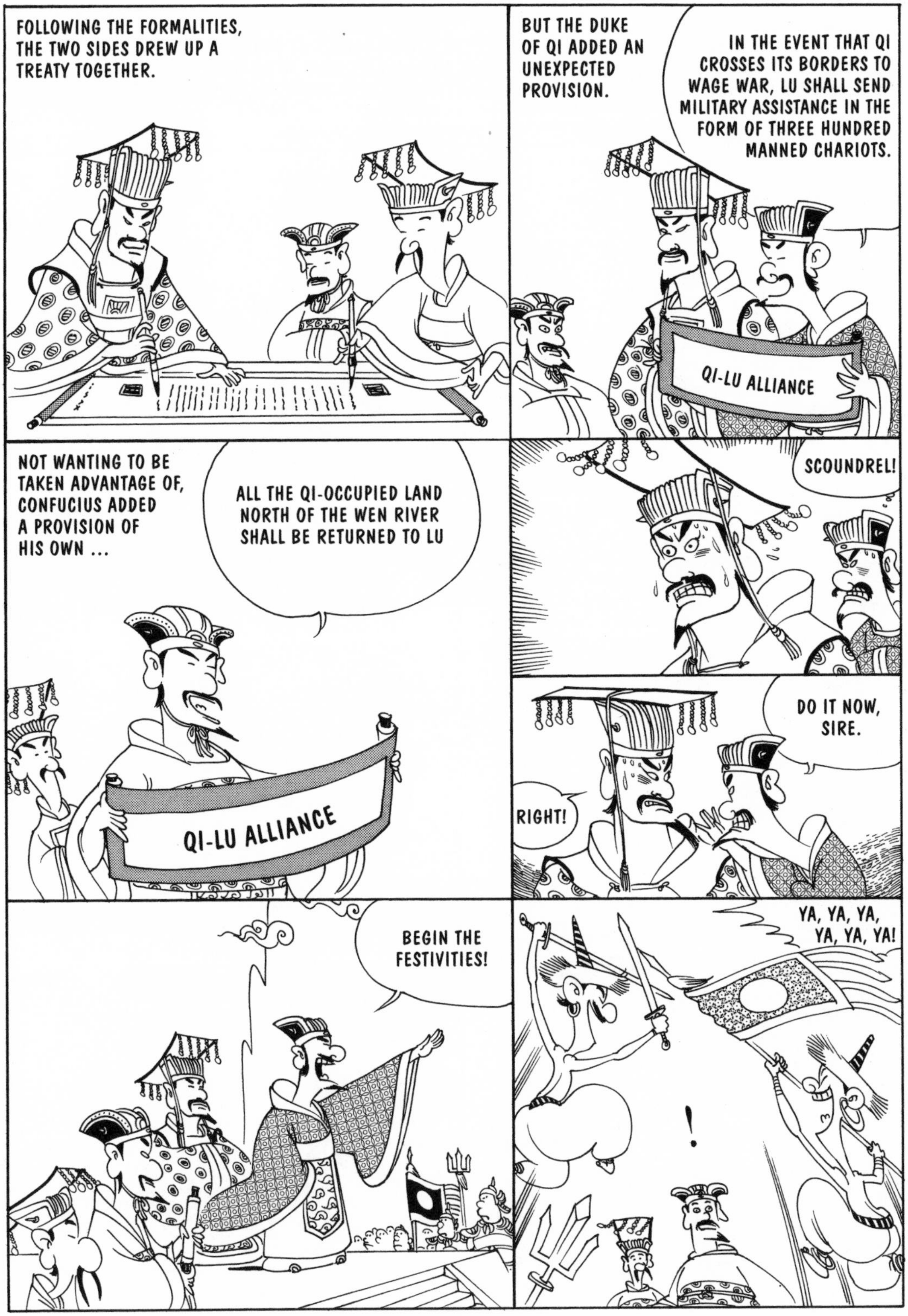
FOLLOWING THE FORMALITIES, THE TWO SIDES DREW UP A TREATY TOGETHER.
BUT THE DUKE OF QI ADDED AN UNEXPECTED PROVISION.
IN THE EVENT THAT QI CROSSES ITS BORDERS TO WAGE WAR, LU SHALL SEND MILITARY ASSISTANCE IN THE FORM OF THREE HUNDRED MANNED CHARIOTS.
QI-LU ALLIANCE
NOT WANTING TO BE TAKEN ADVANTAGE OF, CONFUCIUS ADDED A PROVISION OF HIS OWN ...
ALL THE QI-OCCUPIED LAND NORTH OF THE WEN RIVER SHALL BE RETURNED TO LU
QI-LU ALLIANCE
SCOUNDREL!
DO IT NOW, SIRE.
RIGHT!
BEGIN THE FESTIVITIES!
YA, YA, YA, YA, YA, YA!
!

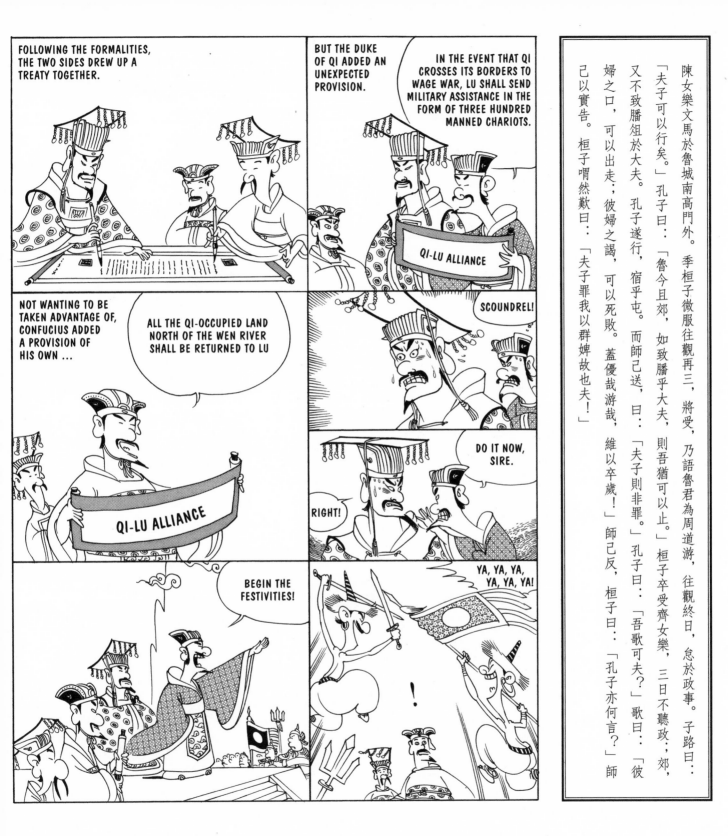

陳女樂文馬於魯城南高門外。季桓子微服往觀再三，將受，乃語魯君為周道游，往觀終日，怠於政事。子路曰：「夫子可以行矣。」孔子曰：「魯今且郊，如致膰乎大夫，則吾猶可以止。」桓子卒受齊女樂，三日不聽政；郊，又不致膰俎於大夫。孔子遂行，宿乎屯。而師己送，曰：「夫子則非罪。」孔子曰：「吾歌可夫？」歌曰：「彼婦之口，可以出走；彼婦之謁，可以死敗。蓋優哉游哉，維以卒歲！」師己反，桓子曰：「孔子亦何言？」師己以實告。桓子喟然歎曰：「夫子罪我以群婢故也夫！」

孔子遂適衛，主於子路妻兄顏濁鄒家。衛靈公問孔子：「居魯得祿幾何？」對曰：「奉粟六萬。」衛人亦致粟六萬。居頃之，或譖孔子於衛靈公。靈公使公孫余假一出一入。孔子恐獲罪焉，居十月，去衛。將適陳，過匡，顏刻為僕，以其策指之曰：「昔吾入此，由彼缺也。」匡人聞之，以為魯之陽虎。陽虎嘗暴匡人，匡人於是遂止孔子。孔子狀類陽虎，拘焉五日。顏淵後，子曰：「吾以汝為死矣。」顏淵曰：「子在，回何敢死！」匡人拘孔子益急，弟子懼。孔子曰：「文王既沒，文不在茲乎？天之將喪斯文也，後死者不得與于斯文也。天

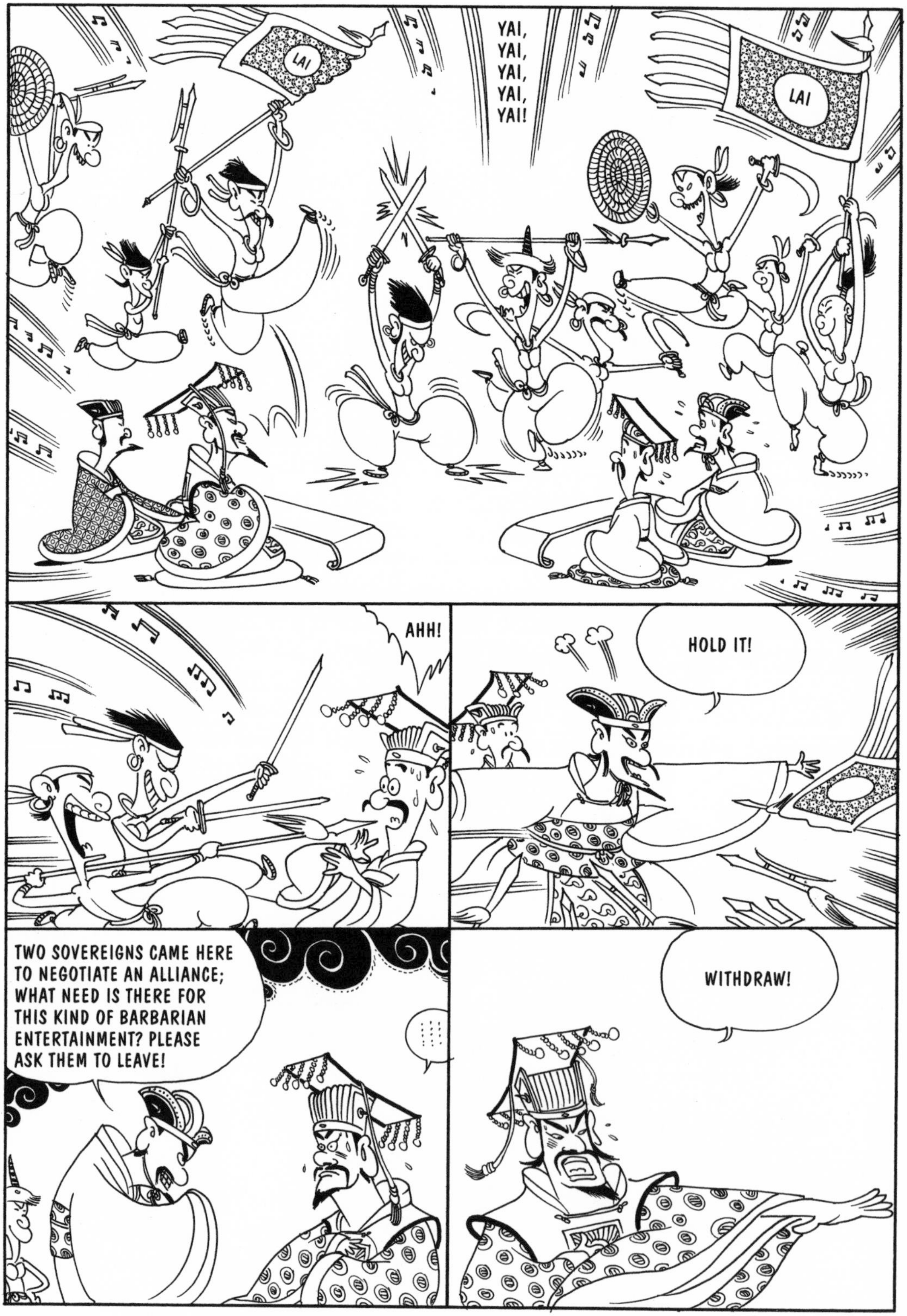
LAI
YAI, YAI, YAI, YAI, YAI!
LAI
AHH!
HOLD IT!
TWO SOVEREIGNS CAME HERE TO NEGOTIATE AN ALLIANCE; WHAT NEED IS THERE FOR THIS KIND OF BARBARIAN ENTERTAINMENT? PLEASE ASK THEM TO LEAVE!
WITHDRAW!

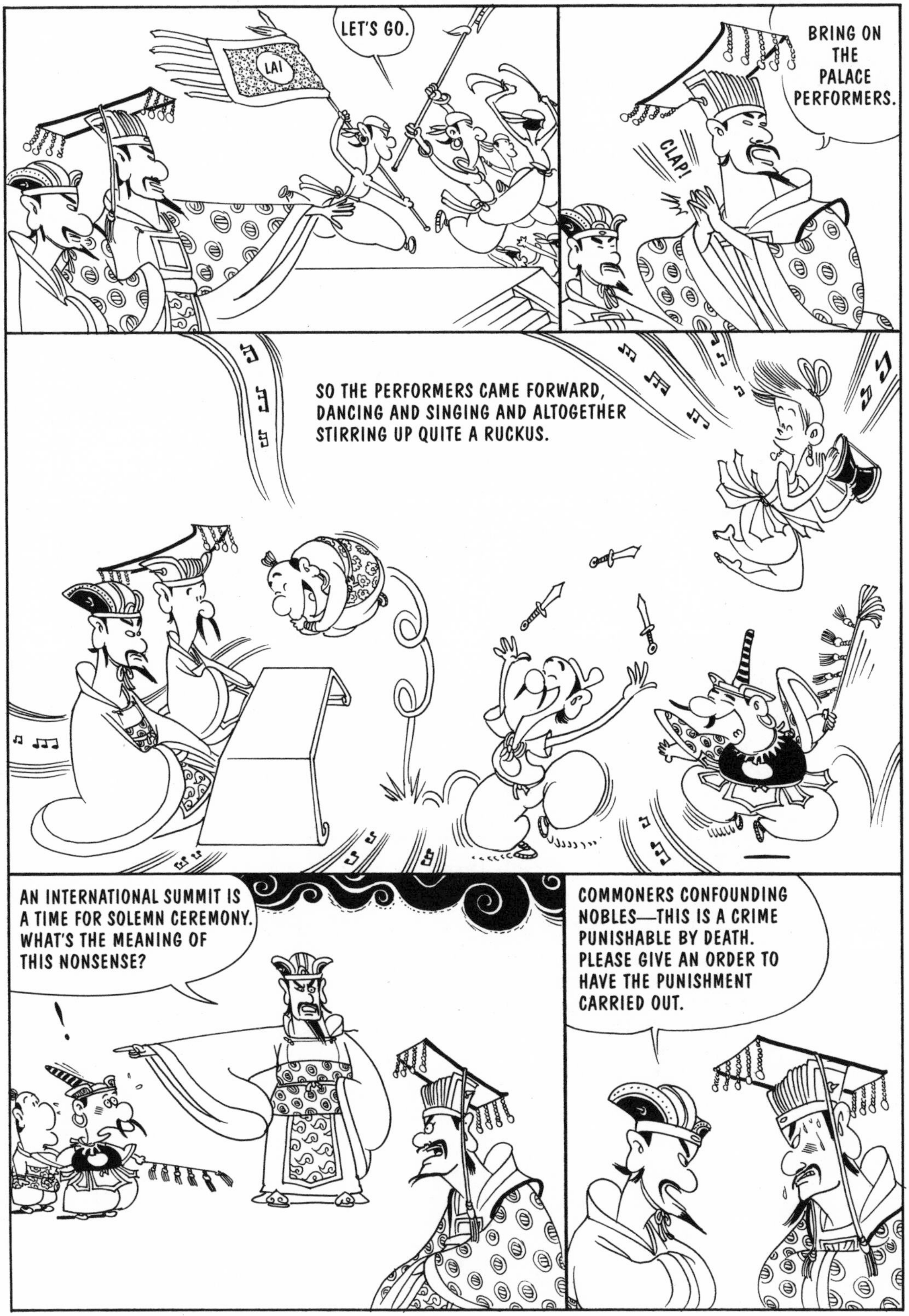
LET'S GO.
LAI
BRING ON THE PALACE PERFORMERS.
CLAP!
SO THE PERFORMERS CAME FORWARD, DANCING AND SINGING AND ALTOGETHER STIRRING UP QUITE A RUCKUS.
AN INTERNATIONAL SUMMIT IS A TIME FOR SOLEMN CEREMONY. WHAT'S THE MEANING OF THIS NONSENSE?
!
COMMONERS CONFOUNDING NOBLES—THIS IS A CRIME PUNISHABLE BY DEATH. PLEASE GIVE AN ORDER TO HAVE THE PUNISHMENT CARRIED OUT.

之未喪斯文也，匡人其如予何！」孔子使從者為甯武子臣於衛，然後得去。

去即過蒲。月餘，反乎衛，主蘧伯玉家。靈公夫人有南子者，使人謂孔子曰：「四方之君子不辱欲與寡君為兄弟者，必見寡小君。寡小君願見。」孔子辭謝，不得已而見之。夫人在絺帷中。孔子入門，北面稽首。夫人自帷中再拜，環珮玉聲璆然。孔子曰：「吾鄉為弗見，見之禮答焉。」子路不說。孔子矢之曰：「予所不者，天厭之！天厭之！」居衛月餘，靈公與夫人同車，宦者雍渠參乘，出，使孔子為次乘，招搖市過之。孔子曰：「吾

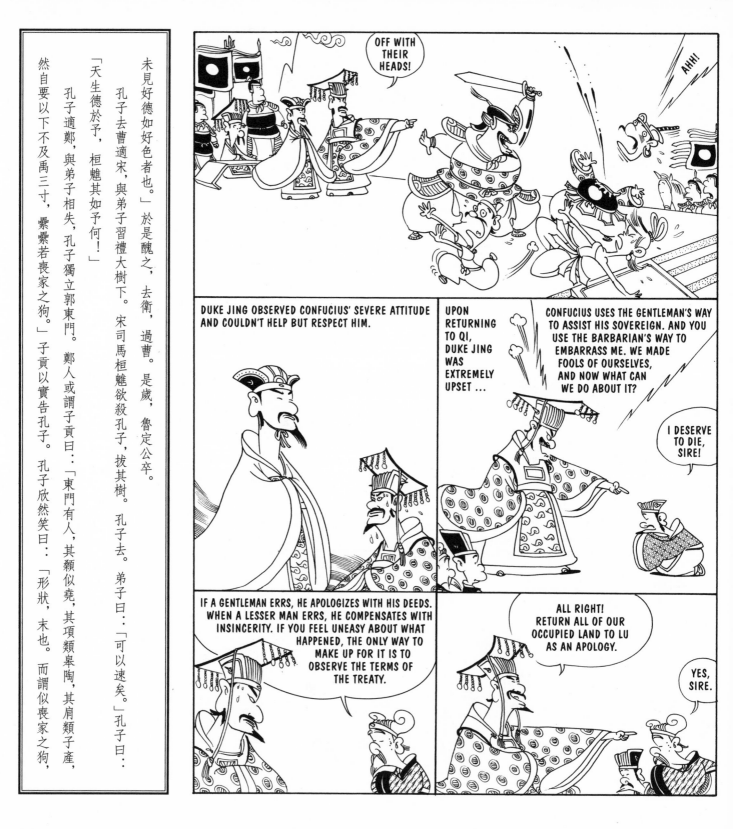

未見好德如好色者也。」於是醜之，去衛，過曹。是歲，魯定公卒。

孔子去曹適宋，與弟子習禮大樹下。宋司馬桓魋欲殺孔子，拔其樹。孔子去。弟子曰：「可以速矣。」孔子曰：「天生德於予，桓魋其如予何！」

孔子適鄭，與弟子相失，孔子獨立郭東門。鄭人或謂子貢曰：「東門有人，其顙似堯，其項類皋陶，其肩類子產，然自要以下不及禹三寸，纍纍若喪家之狗。」子貢以實告孔子。孔子欣然笑曰：「形狀，末也。而謂似喪家之狗，

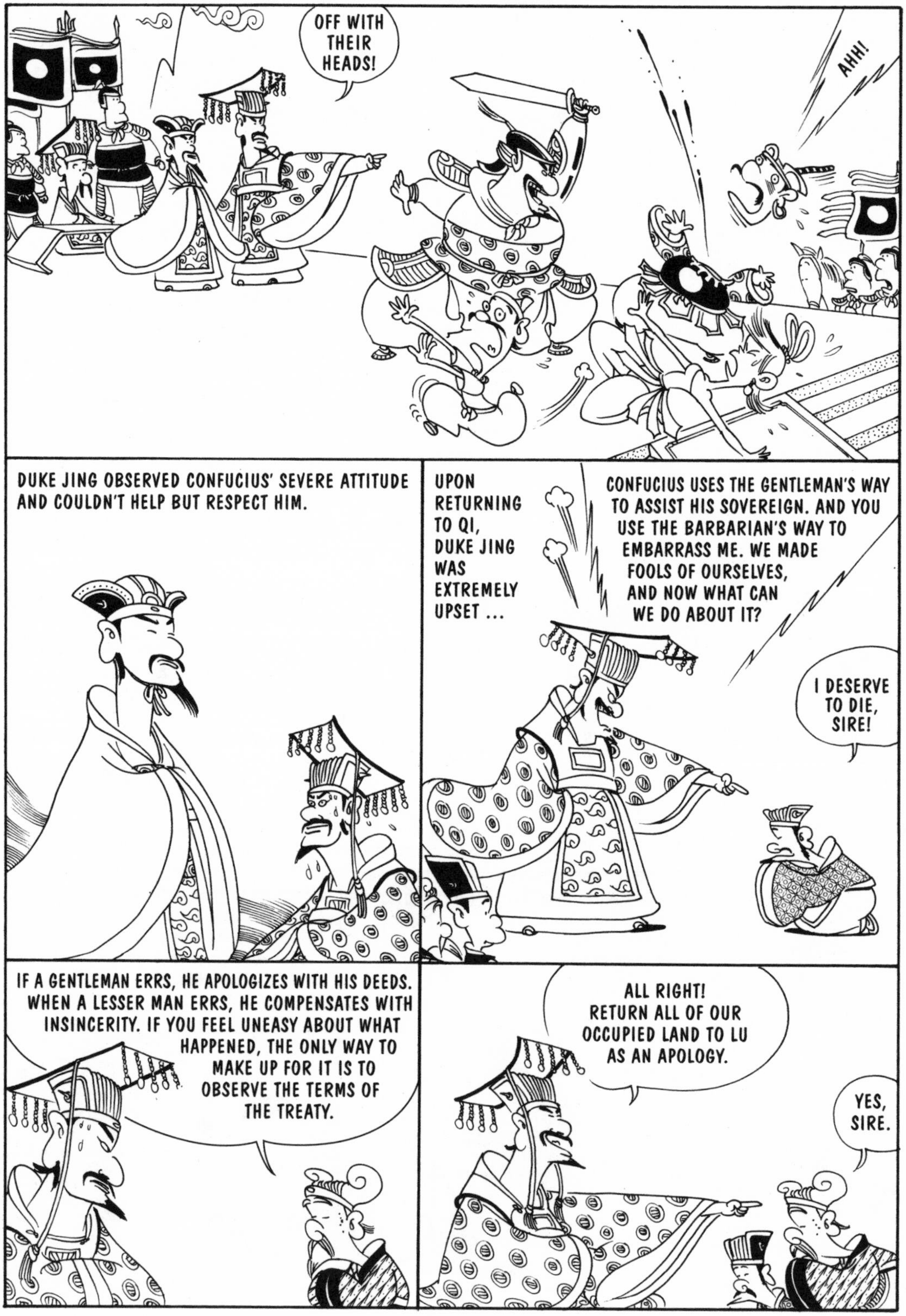

OFF WITH THEIR HEADS!
AHH!
DUKE JING OBSERVED CONFUCIUS' SEVERE ATTITUDE AND COULDN'T HELP BUT RESPECT HIM.
UPON RETURNING TO QI, DUKE JING WAS EXTREMELY UPSET ...
CONFUCIUS USES THE GENTLEMAN'S WAY TO ASSIST HIS SOVEREIGN. AND YOU USE THE BARBARIAN'S WAY TO EMBARRASS ME. WE MADE FOOLS OF OURSELVES, AND NOW WHAT CAN WE DO ABOUT IT?
I DESERVE TO DIE, SIRE!
IF A GENTLEMAN ERRS, HE APOLOGIZES WITH HIS DEEDS. WHEN A LESSER MAN ERRS, HE COMPENSATES WITH INSINCERITY. IF YOU FEEL UNEASY ABOUT WHAT HAPPENED, THE ONLY WAY TO MAKE UP FOR IT IS TO OBSERVE THE TERMS OF THE TREATY.
ALL RIGHT! RETURN ALL OF OUR OCCUPIED LAND TO LU AS AN APOLOGY.
YES, SIRE.

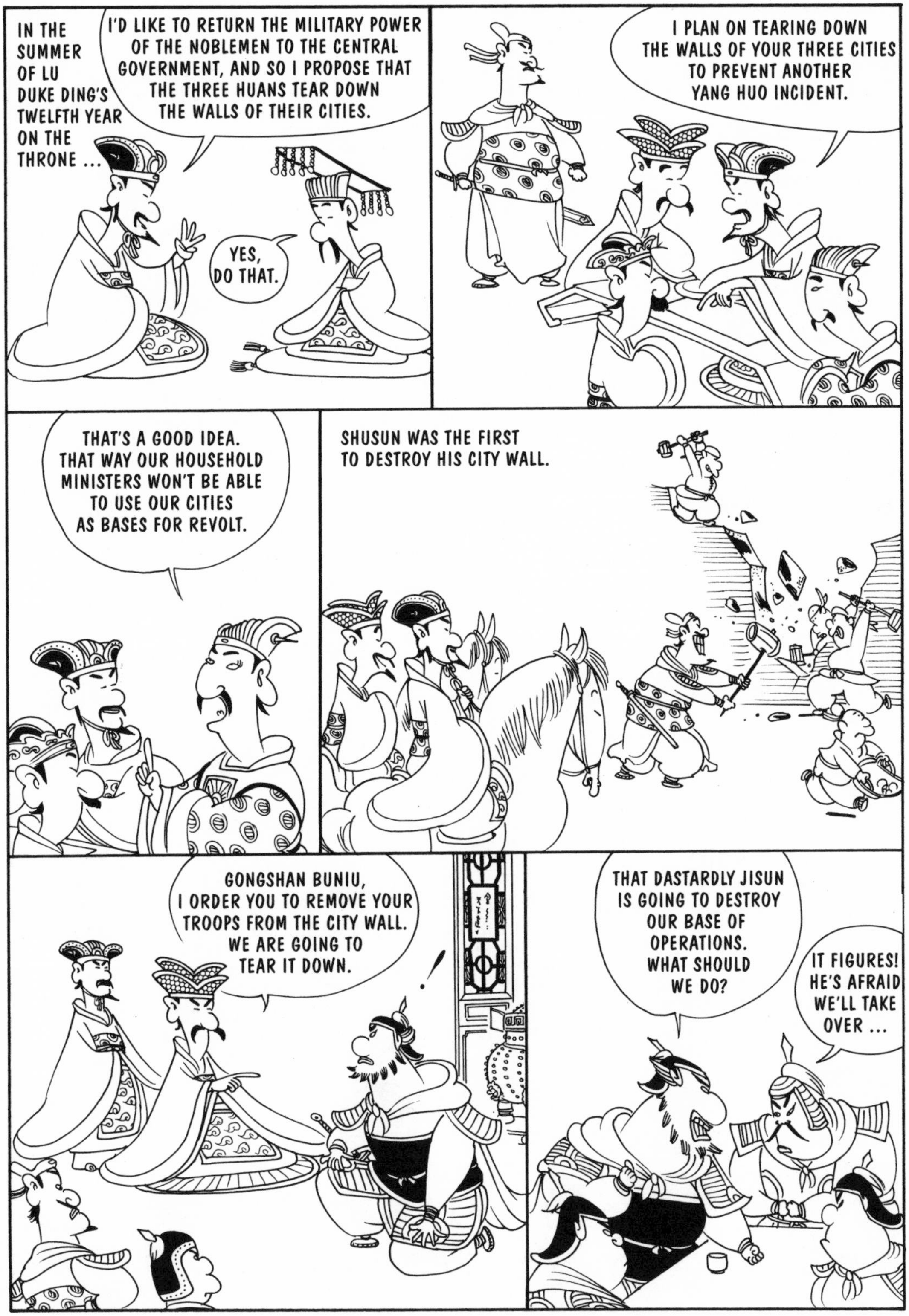
IN THE SUMMER OF LU DUKE DING'S TWELFTH YEAR ON THE THRONE ...
I'D LIKE TO RETURN THE MILITARY POWER OF THE NOBLEMEN TO THE CENTRAL GOVERNMENT, AND SO I PROPOSE THAT THE THREE HUANS TEAR DOWN THE WALLS OF THEIR CITIES.
YES, DO THAT.
I PLAN ON TEARING DOWN THE WALLS OF YOUR THREE CITIES TO PREVENT ANOTHER YANG HUO INCIDENT.
THAT'S A GOOD IDEA. THAT WAY OUR HOUSEHOLD MINISTERS WON'T BE ABLE TO USE OUR CITIES AS BASES FOR REVOLT.
SHUSUN WAS THE FIRST TO DESTROY HIS CITY WALL.
GONGSHAN BUNIU, I ORDER YOU TO REMOVE YOUR TROOPS FROM THE CITY WALL. WE ARE GOING TO TEAR IT DOWN.
!
THAT DASTARDLY JISUN IS GOING TO DESTROY OUR BASE OF OPERATIONS. WHAT SHOULD WE DO?
IT FIGURES! HE'S AFRAID WE'LL TAKE OVER ...

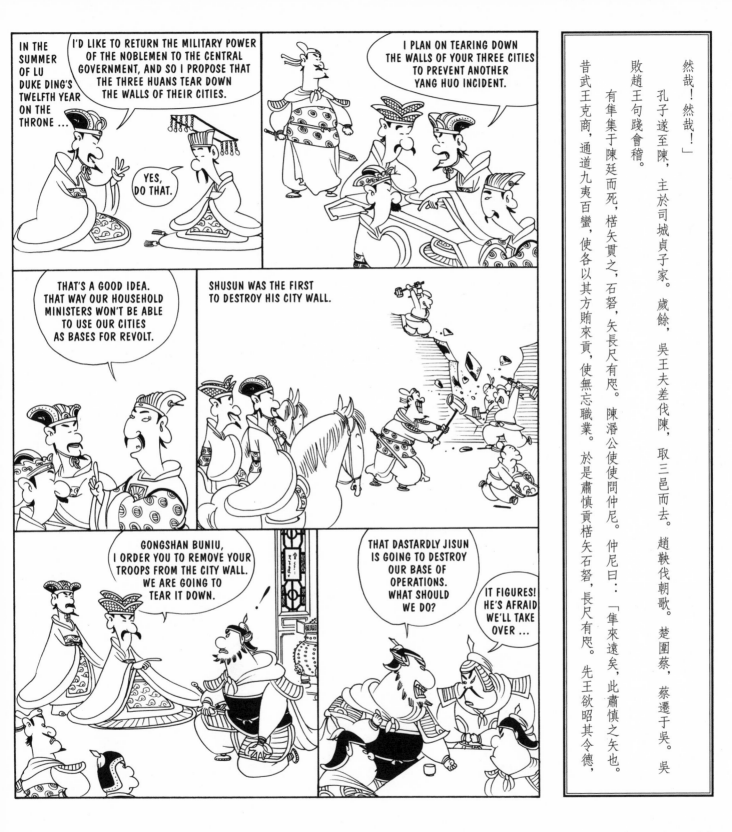

然哉！然哉！」

孔子遂至陳，主於司城貞子家。歲餘，吳王夫差伐陳，取三邑而去。趙鞅伐朝歌。楚圍蔡，蔡遷于吳。吳敗越王句踐會稽。

有隼集于陳廷而死，楛矢貫之，石砮，矢長尺有咫。陳湣公使使問仲尼。仲尼曰：「隼來遠矣，此肅慎之矢也。昔武王克商，通道九夷百蠻，使各以其方賄來貢，使無忘職業。於是肅慎貢楛矢石砮，長尺有咫。先王欲昭其令德，

以肅慎矢分大姬，配虞胡公而封諸陳。分同姓以珍玉，展親；分異姓以遠方職，使無忘服。故分陳以肅慎矢。」

試求之故府，果得之。

孔子居陳三歲，會晉楚爭彊，更伐陳，及吳侵陳，陳常被寇。孔子曰：「歸與歸與！吾黨之小子狂簡，進取不忘其初。」於是孔子去陳。

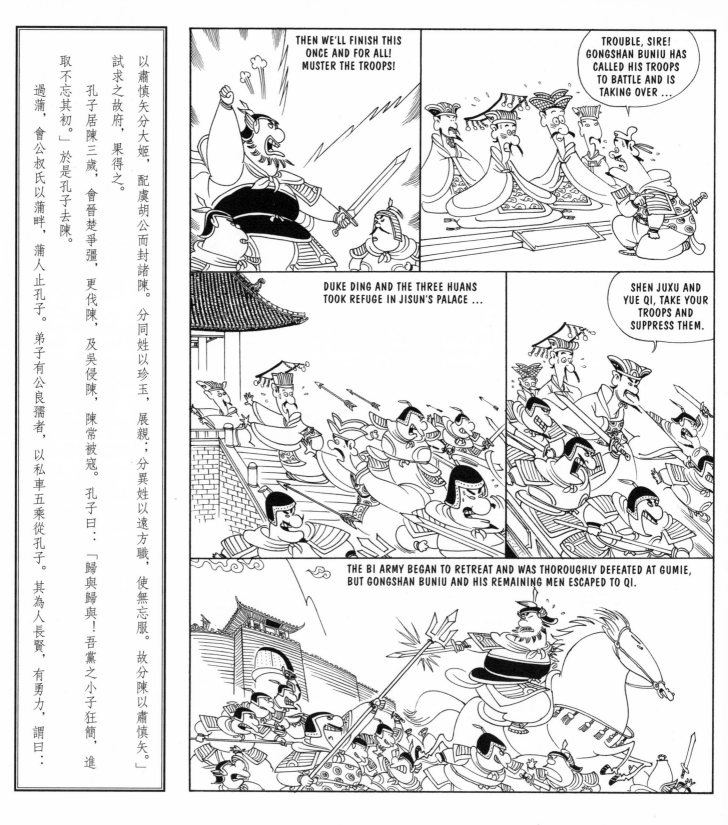

過蒲，會公叔氏以蒲畔，蒲人止孔子。弟子有公良孺者，以私車五乘從孔子。其為人長賢，有勇力，謂曰：

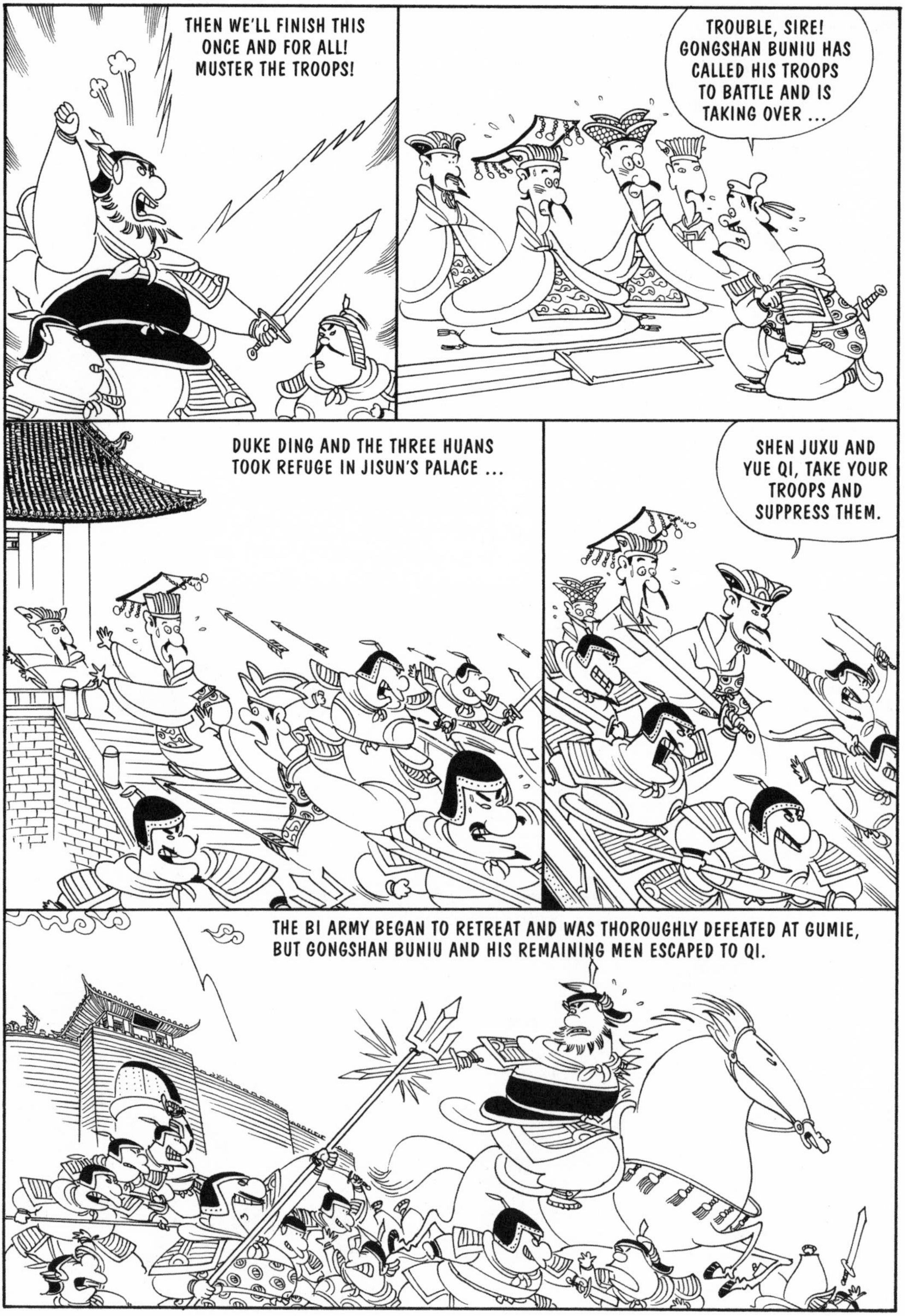
THEN WE'LL FINISH THIS ONCE AND FOR ALL! MUSTER THE TROOPS!
TROUBLE, SIRE! GONGSHAN BUNIU HAS CALLED HIS TROOPS TO BATTLE AND IS TAKING OVER ...
DUKE DING AND THE THREE HUANS TOOK REFUGE IN JISUN'S PALACE ...
SHEN JUXU AND YUE QI, TAKE YOUR TROOPS AND SUPPRESS THEM.
THE BI ARMY BEGAN TO RETREAT AND WAS THOROUGHLY DEFEATED AT GUMIE, BUT GONGSHAN BUNIU AND HIS REMAINING MEN ESCAPED TO QI.

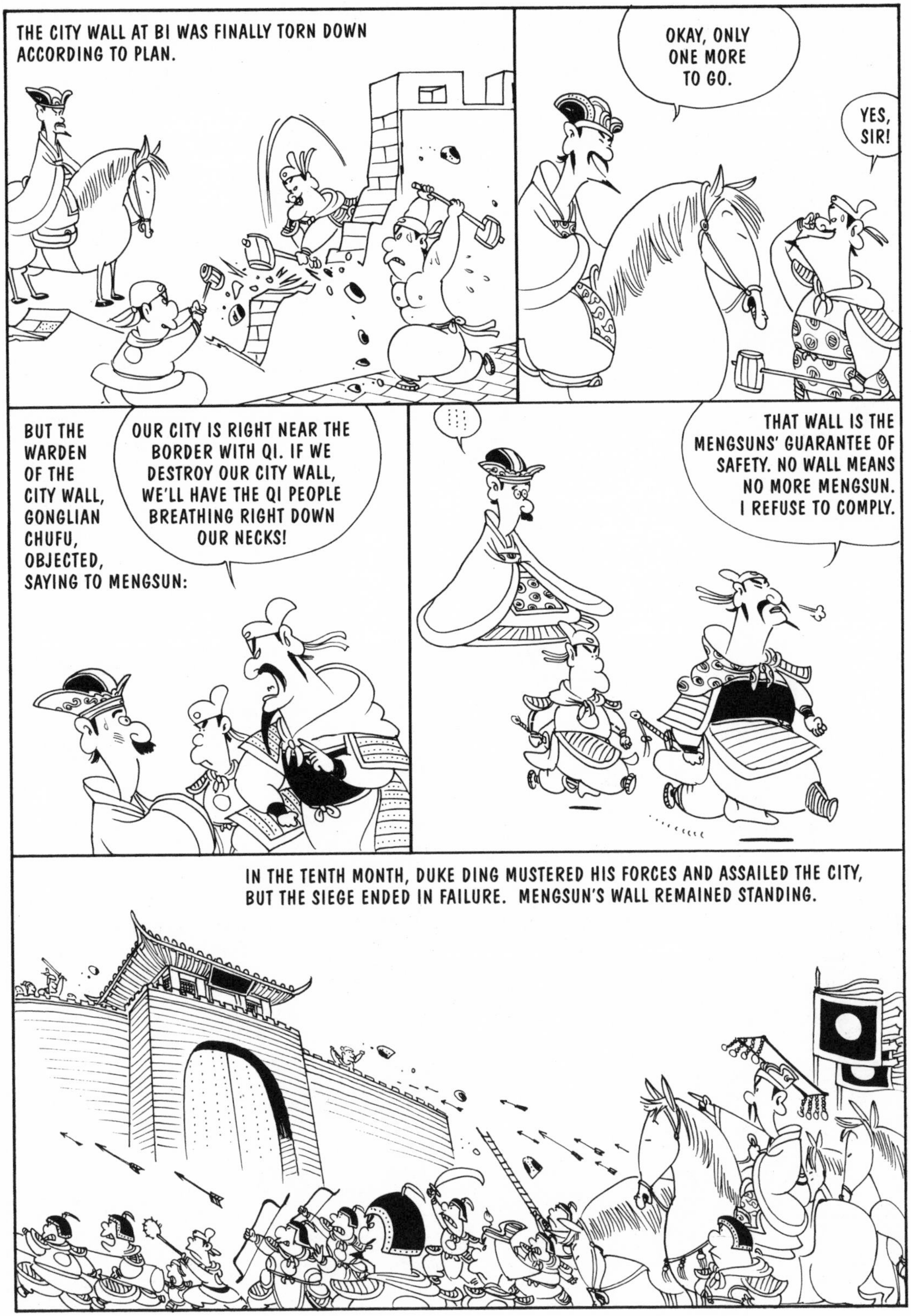
THE CITY WALL AT BI WAS FINALLY TORN DOWN ACCORDING TO PLAN.
OKAY, ONLY ONE MORE TO GO.
YES, SIR!
BUT THE WARDEN OF THE CITY WALL, GONGLIAN CHUFU, OBJECTED, SAYING TO MENGSUN:
OUR CITY IS RIGHT NEAR THE BORDER WITH QI. IF WE DESTROY OUR CITY WALL, WE'LL HAVE THE QI PEOPLE BREATHING RIGHT DOWN OUR NECKS!
THAT WALL IS THE MENGSUNS' GUARANTEE OF SAFETY. NO WALL MEANS NO MORE MENGSUN. I REFUSE TO COMPLY.
IN THE TENTH MONTH, DUKE DING MUSTERED HIS FORCES AND ASSAILED THE CITY, BUT THE SIEGE ENDED IN FAILURE. MENGSUN'S WALL REMAINED STANDING.

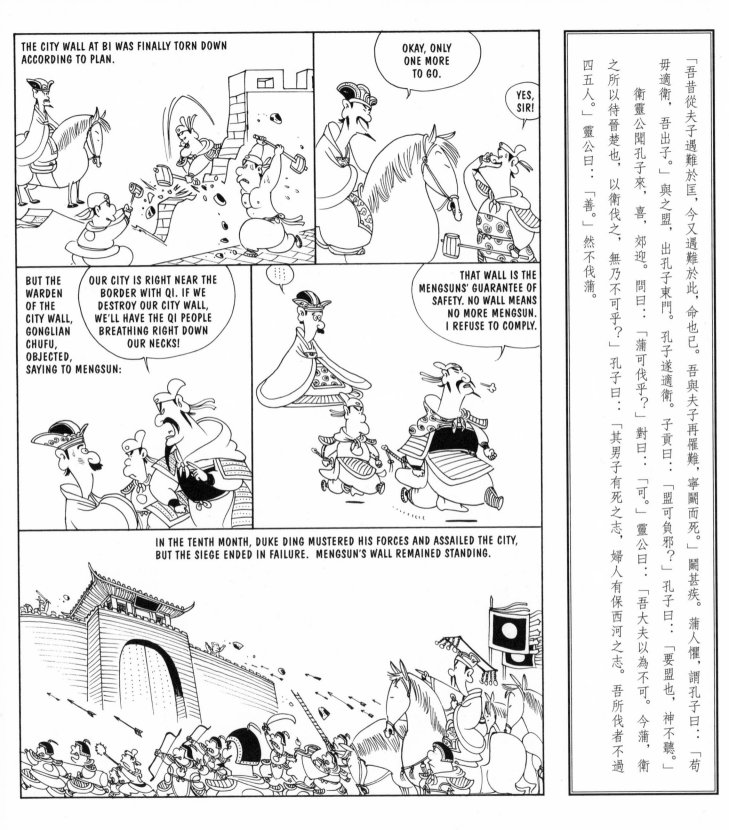

「吾昔從夫子遇難於匡，今又遇難於此，命也已。吾與夫子再罹難，寧鬬而死。」鬬甚疾。蒲人懼，謂孔子曰：「苟毋適衛，吾出子。」與之盟，出孔子東門。孔子遂適衛。子貢曰：「盟可負邪？」孔子曰：「要盟也，神不聽。」

衛靈公聞孔子來，喜，郊迎。問曰：「蒲可伐乎？」對曰：「可。」靈公曰：「吾大夫以為不可。今蒲，衛之所以待晉楚也，以衛伐之，無乃不可乎？」孔子曰：「其男子有死之志，婦人有保西河之志。吾所伐者不過四五人。」靈公曰：「善。」然不伐蒲。

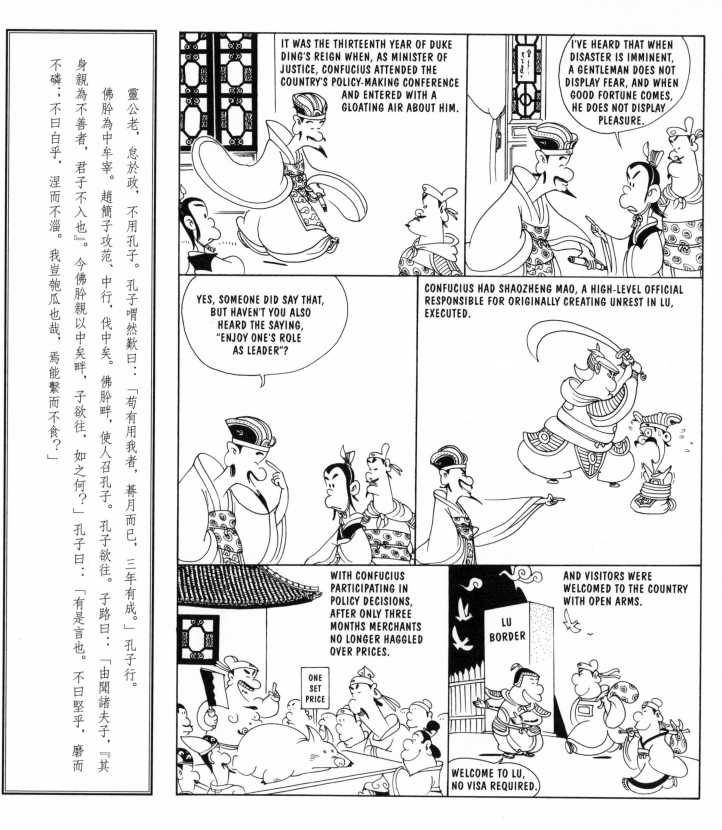

靈公老，怠於政，不用孔子。孔子喟然歎曰：「苟有用我者，朞月而已，三年有成。」孔子行。佛肸為中牟宰。趙簡子攻范、中行，伐中牟。佛肸畔，使人召孔子。孔子欲往。子路曰：「由聞諸夫子，『其身親為不善者，君子不入也』。今佛肸親以中牟畔，子欲往，如之何？」孔子曰：「有是言也。不曰堅乎，磨而不磷；不曰白乎，涅而不淄。我豈匏瓜也哉，焉能繫而不食？」

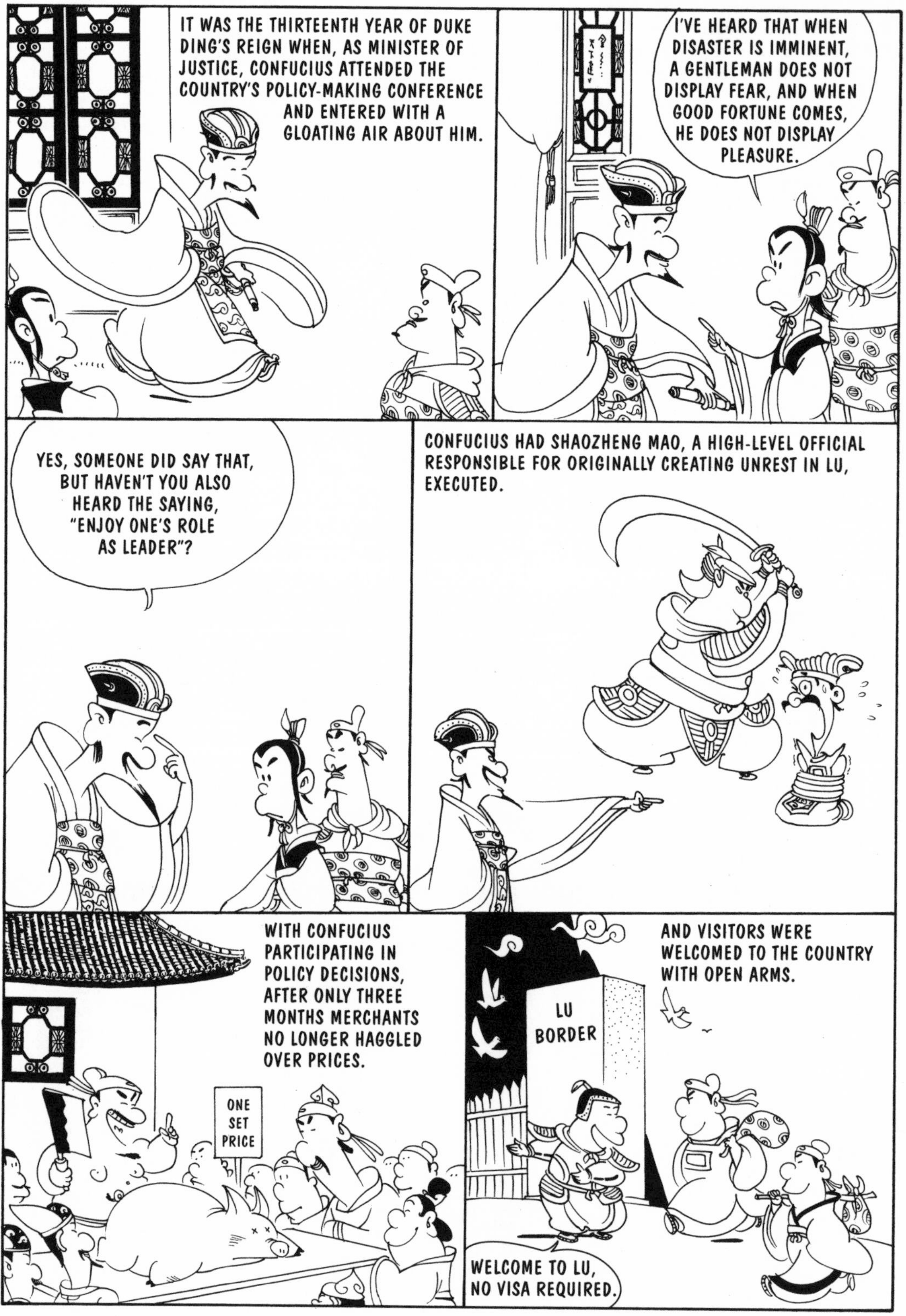
IT WAS THE THIRTEENTH YEAR OF DUKE DING'S REIGN WHEN, AS MINISTER OF JUSTICE, CONFUCIUS ATTENDED THE COUNTRY'S POLICY-MAKING CONFERENCE AND ENTERED WITH A GLOATING AIR ABOUT HIM.
I'VE HEARD THAT WHEN DISASTER IS IMMINENT, A GENTLEMAN DOES NOT DISPLAY FEAR, AND WHEN GOOD FORTUNE COMES, HE DOES NOT DISPLAY PLEASURE.
YES, SOMEONE DID SAY THAT, BUT HAVEN'T YOU ALSO HEARD THE SAYING, "ENJOY ONE'S ROLE AS LEADER"?
CONFUCIUS HAD SHAOZHENG MAO, A HIGH-LEVEL OFFICIAL RESPONSIBLE FOR ORIGINALLY CREATING UNREST IN LU, EXECUTED.
WITH CONFUCIUS PARTICIPATING IN POLICY DECISIONS, AFTER ONLY THREE MONTHS MERCHANTS NO LONGER HAGGLED OVER PRICES.
ONE SET PRICE
AND VISITORS WERE WELCOMED TO THE COUNTRY WITH OPEN ARMS.
LU BORDER
WELCOME TO LU, NO VISA REQUIRED.

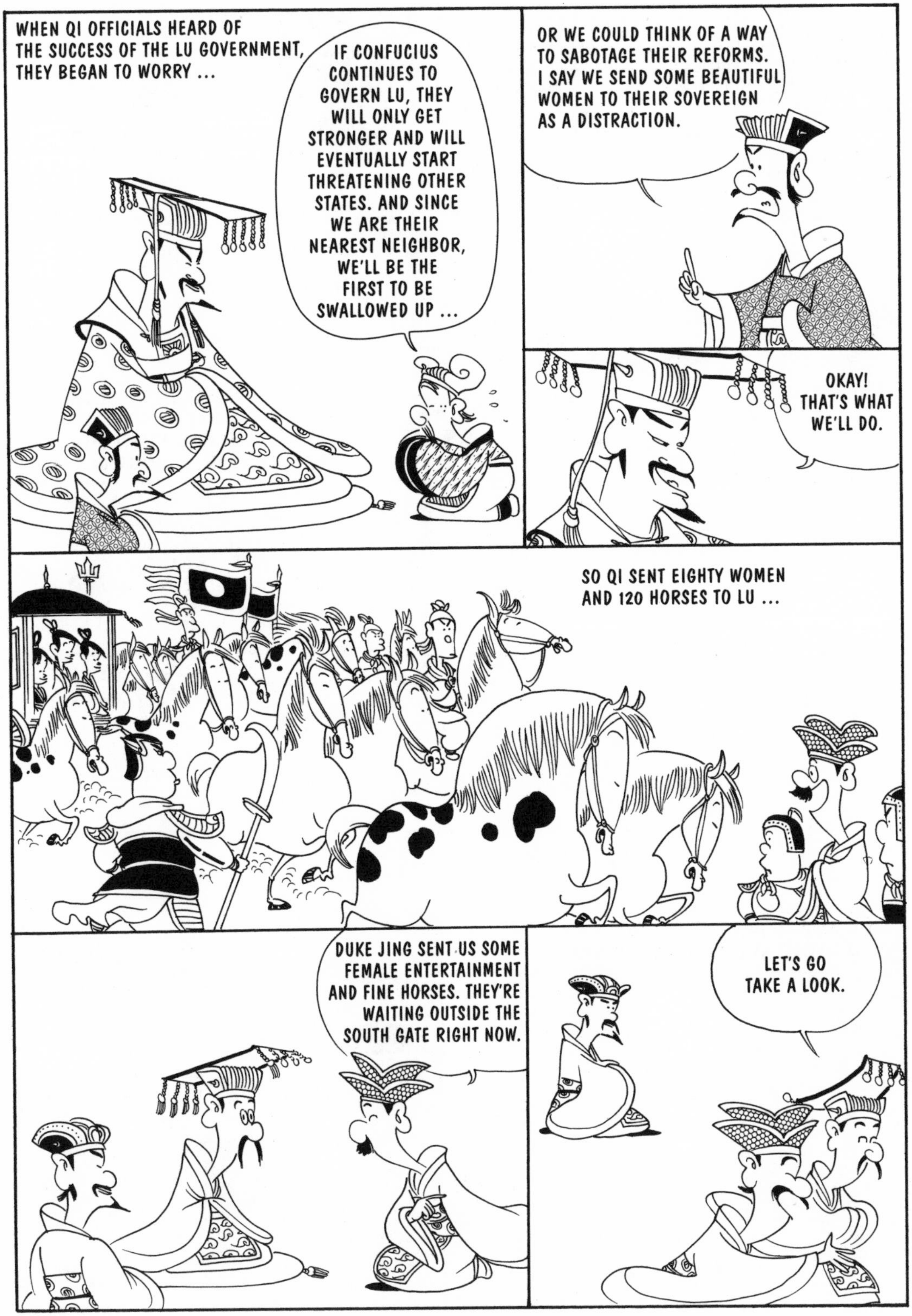
WHEN QI OFFICIALS HEARD OF THE SUCCESS OF THE LU GOVERNMENT, THEY BEGAN TO WORRY ...
IF CONFUCIUS CONTINUES TO GOVERN LU, THEY WILL ONLY GET STRONGER AND WILL EVENTUALLY START THREATENING OTHER STATES. AND SINCE WE ARE THEIR NEAREST NEIGHBOR, WE'LL BE THE FIRST TO BE SWALLOWED UP ...
OR WE COULD THINK OF A WAY TO SABOTAGE THEIR REFORMS. I SAY WE SEND SOME BEAUTIFUL WOMEN TO THEIR SOVEREIGN AS A DISTRACTION.
OKAY! THAT'S WHAT WE'LL DO.
SO QI SENT EIGHTY WOMEN AND 120 HORSES TO LU ...
DUKE JING SENT US SOME FEMALE ENTERTAINMENT AND FINE HORSES. THEY'RE WAITING OUTSIDE THE SOUTH GATE RIGHT NOW.
LET'S GO TAKE A LOOK.

孔子擊磬。有荷蕢而過門者，曰：「有心哉，擊磬乎！硜硜乎，莫己知也夫而已矣！」

孔子學鼓琴師襄子，十日不進。師襄子曰：「可以益矣。」孔子曰：「丘已習其曲矣，未得其數也。」有閒，曰：「已習其數，可以益矣。」孔子曰：「丘未得其志也。」有閒，曰：「已習其志，可以益矣。」孔子曰：「丘未得其為人也。」有閒，曰有所穆然深思焉，有所怡然高望而遠志焉。曰：「丘得其為人，黯然而黑，幾然而長，眼如望羊，如王四國，非文王其誰能為此也！」師襄子辟席再拜，曰：「師蓋云《文王操》也。」

孔子既不得用於衛，將西見趙簡子。至於河而聞竇鳴犢、舜華之死也，臨河而歎曰：「美哉水，洋洋乎！丘之不濟此，命也夫！」子貢趨而進曰：「敢問何謂也？」孔子曰：「竇鳴犢、舜華，晉國之賢大夫也。趙簡子未得志之時，須此兩人而后從政；及其已得志，殺之乃從政。丘聞之也，刳胎殺夭則麒麟不至郊，竭澤涸漁則蛟龍不合陰陽，覆巢毀卵則鳳皇不翔。何則？君子諱傷其類也。夫鳥獸之於不義也尚知辟之，而況乎丘哉！」乃還息乎陬鄉，作為《陬操》以哀之。而反乎衛，入主蘧伯玉家。

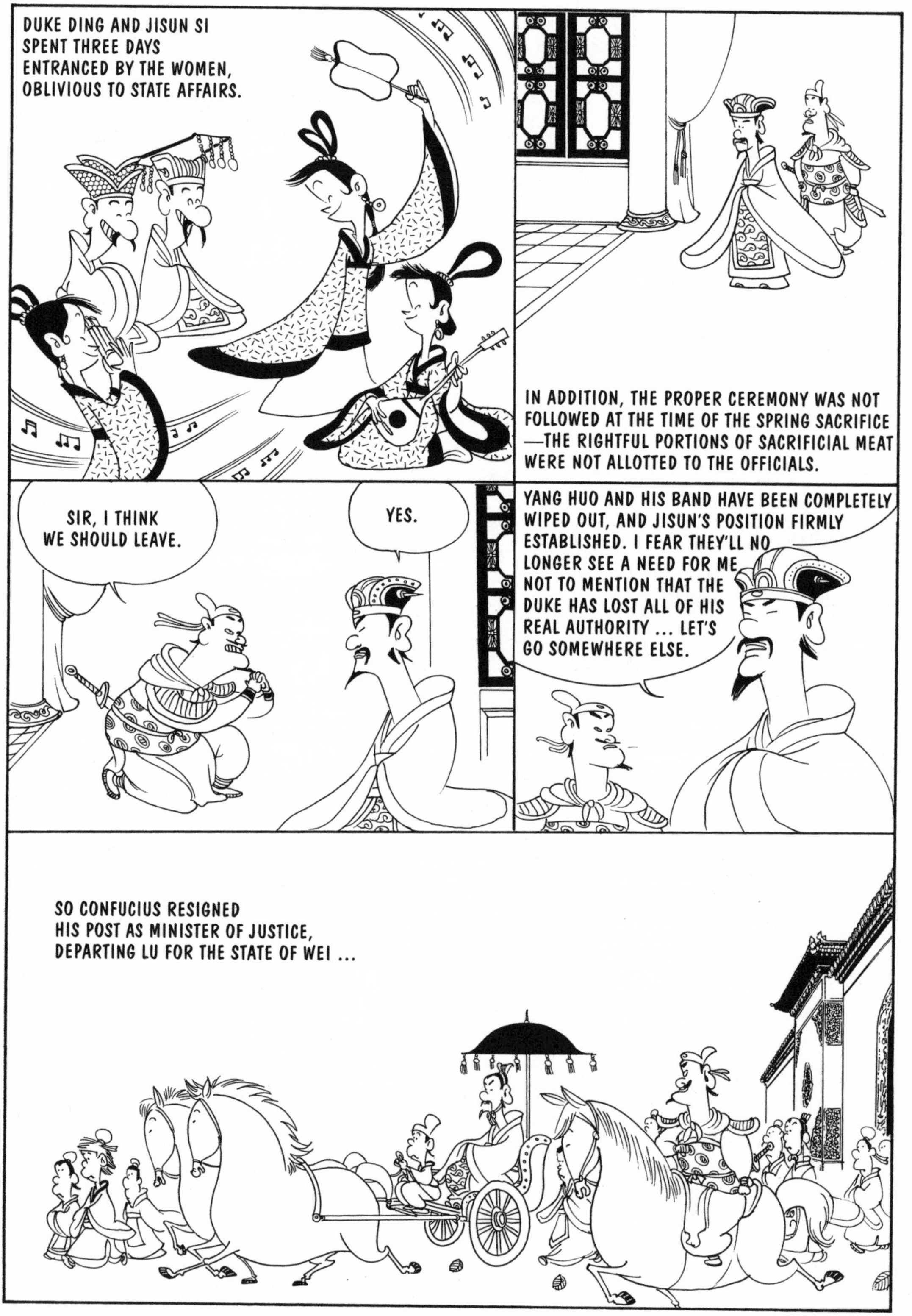
DUKE DING AND JISUN SI SPENT THREE DAYS ENTRANCED BY THE WOMEN, OBLIVIOUS TO STATE AFFAIRS.
IN ADDITION, THE PROPER CEREMONY WAS NOT FOLLOWED AT THE TIME OF THE SPRING SACRIFICE —THE RIGHTFUL PORTIONS OF SACRIFICIAL MEAT WERE NOT ALLOTTED TO THE OFFICIALS.
SIR, I THINK WE SHOULD LEAVE.
YES.
YANG HUO AND HIS BAND HAVE BEEN COMPLETELY WIPED OUT, AND JISUN'S POSITION FIRMLY ESTABLISHED. I FEAR THEY'LL NO LONGER SEE A NEED FOR ME NOT TO MENTION THAT THE DUKE HAS LOST ALL OF HIS REAL AUTHORITY ... LET'S GO SOMEWHERE ELSE.
SO CONFUCIUS RESIGNED HIS POST AS MINISTER OF JUSTICE, DEPARTING LU FOR THE STATE OF WEI ...

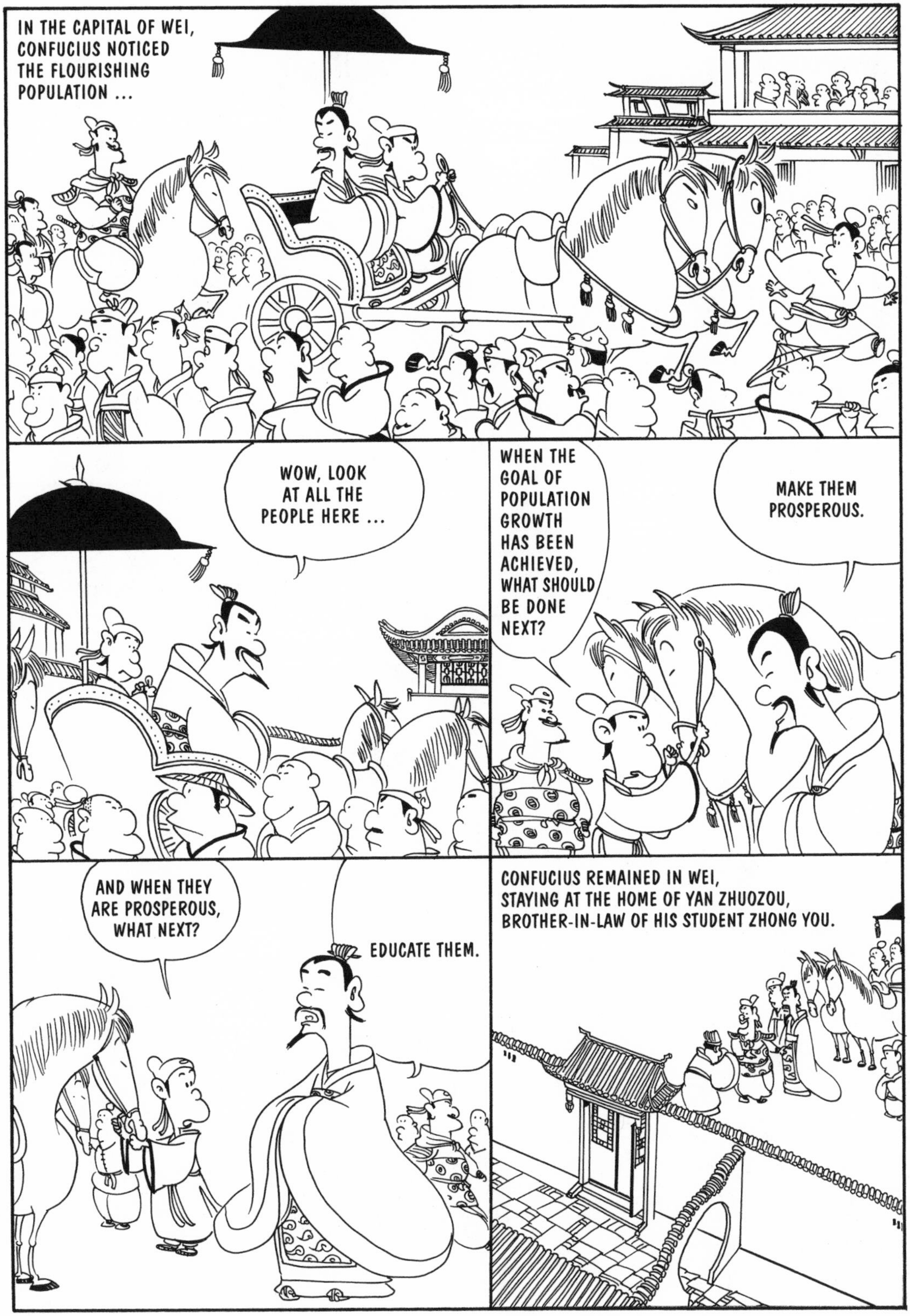
IN THE CAPITAL OF WEI, CONFUCIUS NOTICED THE FLOURISHING POPULATION ...
WOW, LOOK AT ALL THE PEOPLE HERE ...
WHEN THE GOAL OF POPULATION GROWTH HAS BEEN ACHIEVED, WHAT SHOULD BE DONE NEXT?
MAKE THEM PROSPEROUS.
AND WHEN THEY ARE PROSPEROUS, WHAT NEXT?
EDUCATE THEM.
CONFUCIUS REMAINED IN WEI, STAYING AT THE HOME OF YAN ZHUOZOU, BROTHER-IN-LAW OF HIS STUDENT ZHONG YOU.

他日，靈公問兵陳。孔子曰：「俎豆之事則嘗聞之，軍旅之事未之學也。」明日，與孔子語，見蜚鴈，仰視之，色不在孔子。孔子遂行，復如陳。

夏，衛靈公卒，立孫輒，是為衛出公。六月，趙鞅內太子蒯聵于戚。陽虎使太子絻，八人衰絰，偽自衛迎者，哭而入，遂居焉。冬，蔡遷于州來。是歲魯哀公三年，而孔子年六十矣。齊助衛圍戚，以衛太子蒯聵在故也。

夏，魯桓釐廟燔，南宮敬叔救火。孔子在陳，聞之，曰：「災必於桓釐廟乎？」已而果然。

秋，季桓子病，輦而見魯城，喟然歎曰：「昔此國幾興矣，以吾獲罪於孔子，故不興也。」顧謂其嗣康子曰：「我即死，若必相魯；相魯，必召仲尼。」後數日，桓子卒，康子代立。已葬，欲召仲尼。公之魚曰：「昔吾先君用之不終，終為諸侯笑。今又用之，不能終，是再為諸侯笑。」康子曰：「則誰召而可？」曰：「必召冉求。」

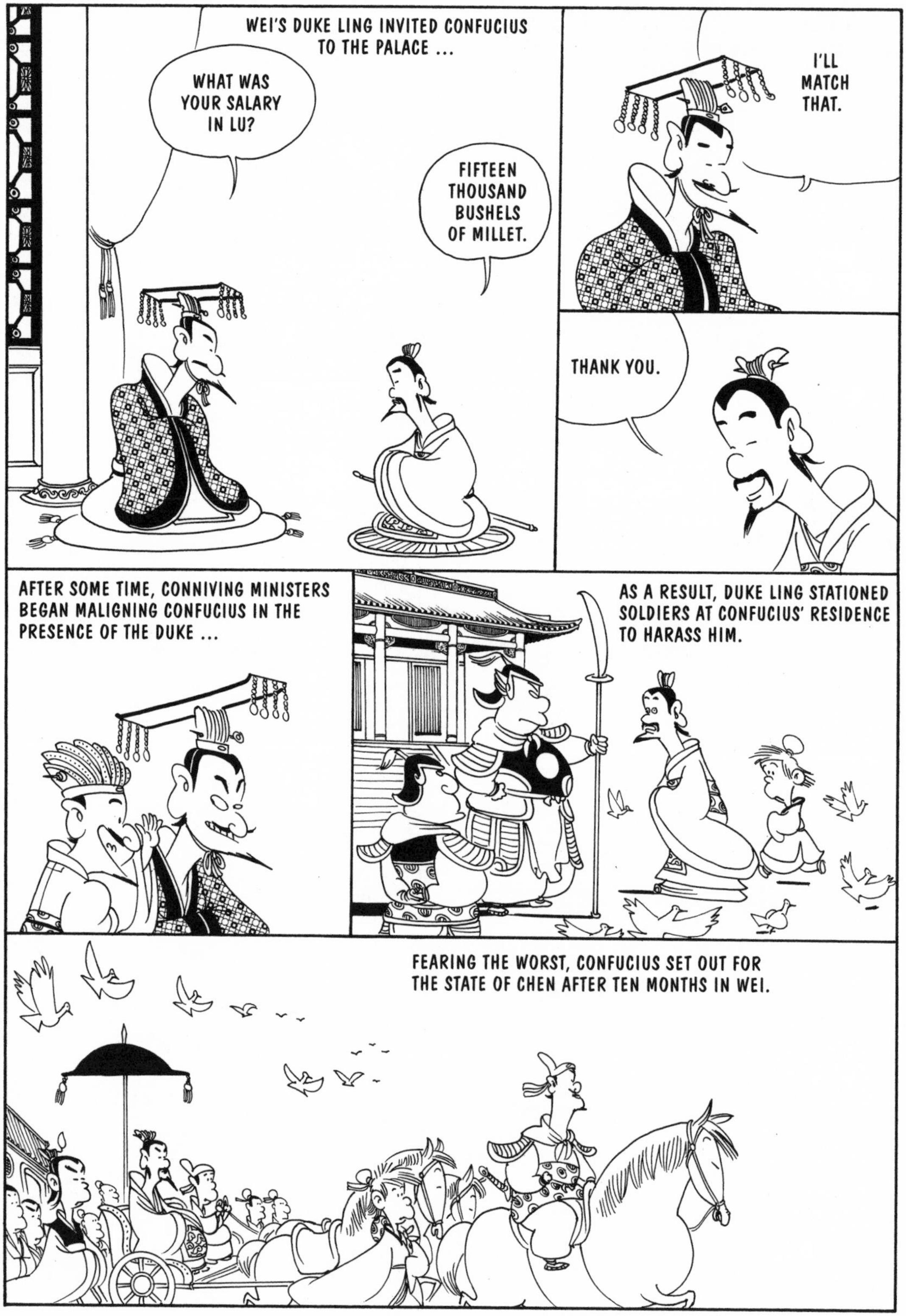
WEI'S DUKE LING INVITED CONFUCIUS TO THE PALACE ...
WHAT WAS YOUR SALARY IN LU?
FIFTEEN THOUSAND BUSHELS OF MILLET.
I'LL MATCH THAT.
THANK YOU.
AFTER SOME TIME, CONNIVING MINISTERS BEGAN MALIGNING CONFUCIUS IN THE PRESENCE OF THE DUKE ...
AS A RESULT, DUKE LING STATIONED SOLDIERS AT CONFUCIUS' RESIDENCE TO HARASS HIM.
FEARING THE WORST, CONFUCIUS SET OUT FOR THE STATE OF CHEN AFTER TEN MONTHS IN WEI.

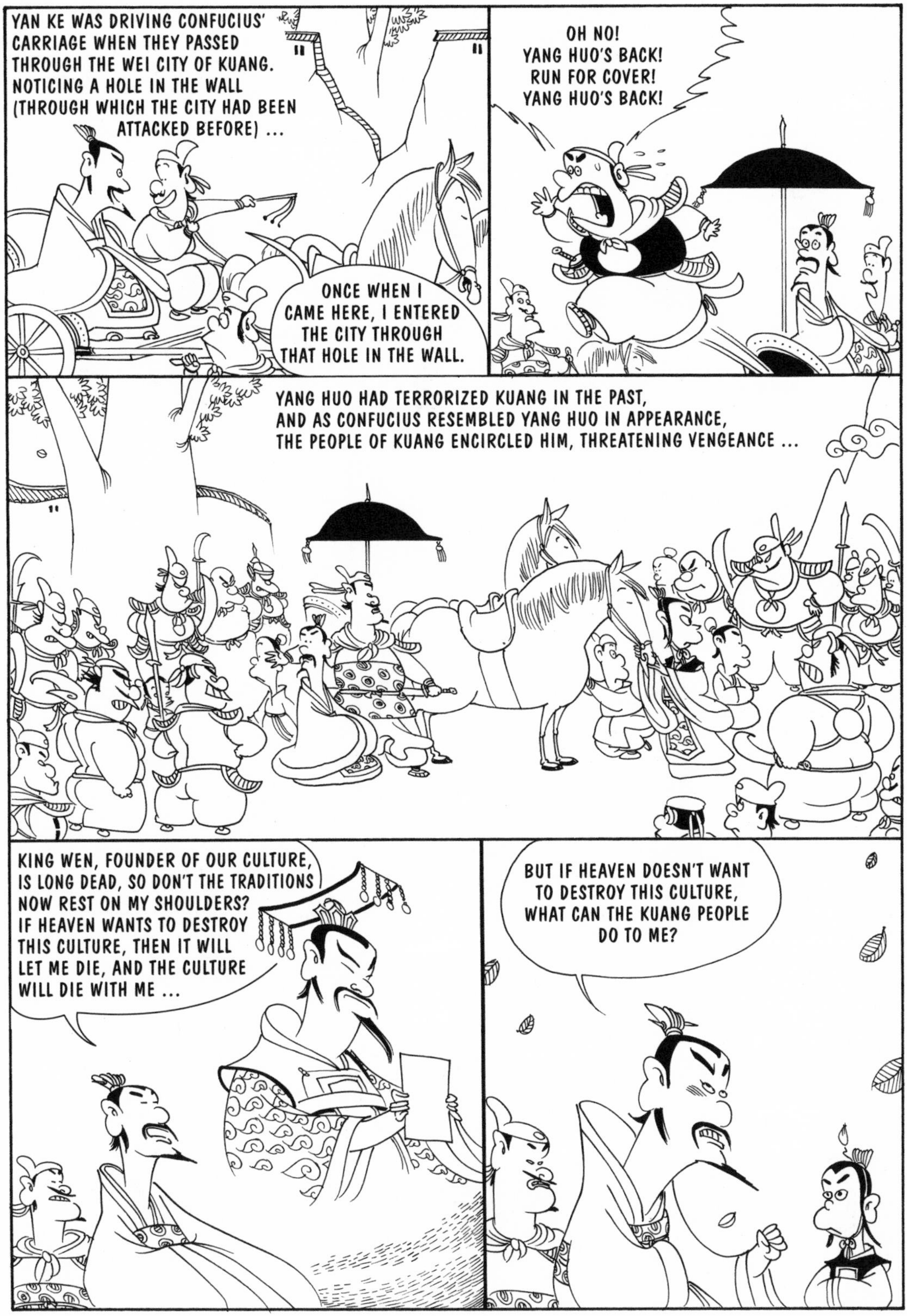
YAN KE WAS DRIVING CONFUCIUS' CARRIAGE WHEN THEY PASSED THROUGH THE WEI CITY OF KUANG. NOTICING A HOLE IN THE WALL (THROUGH WHICH THE CITY HAD BEEN ATTACKED BEFORE) ...
ONCE WHEN I CAME HERE, I ENTERED THE CITY THROUGH THAT HOLE IN THE WALL.
OH NO! YANG HUO'S BACK! RUN FOR COVER! YANG HUO'S BACK!
YANG HUO HAD TERRORIZED KUANG IN THE PAST, AND AS CONFUCIUS RESEMBLED YANG HUO IN APPEARANCE, THE PEOPLE OF KUANG ENCIRCLED HIM, THREATENING VENGEANCE ...
KING WEN, FOUNDER OF OUR CULTURE, IS LONG DEAD, SO DON'T THE TRADITIONS NOW REST ON MY SHOULDERS? IF HEAVEN WANTS TO DESTROY THIS CULTURE, THEN IT WILL LET ME DIE, AND THE CULTURE WILL DIE WITH ME ...
BUT IF HEAVEN DOESN'T WANT TO DESTROY THIS CULTURE, WHAT CAN THE KUANG PEOPLE DO TO ME?

於是使使召冉求。冉求將行，孔子曰：「魯人召求，非小用之，將大用之也。」是日，孔子曰：「歸乎歸乎！吾黨之小子狂簡，斐然成章，吾不知所以裁之。」子贛知孔子思歸，送冉求，因誡曰「即用，以孔子為招」云。

冉求既去，明年，孔子自陳遷于蔡。蔡昭公將如吳，吳召之也。前昭公欺其臣遷州來，後將往，大夫懼復遷，公孫翩射殺昭公。楚侵蔡。秋，齊景公卒。

明年，孔子自蔡如葉。葉公問政，孔子曰：「政在來遠附邇。」他日，葉公問孔子於子路，子路不對。孔子聞之，曰：「由，爾何不對曰『其為人也，學道不倦，誨人不厭，發憤忘食，樂以忘憂，不知老之將至』云爾。」去葉，反于蔡。長沮、桀溺耦而耕，孔子以為隱者，使子路問津焉。長沮曰：「彼執輿者為誰？」子路曰：「為孔丘。」曰：「是魯孔丘與？」曰：「然。」曰：「是知津矣。」桀溺謂子路曰：「子為誰？」曰：「為仲由。」

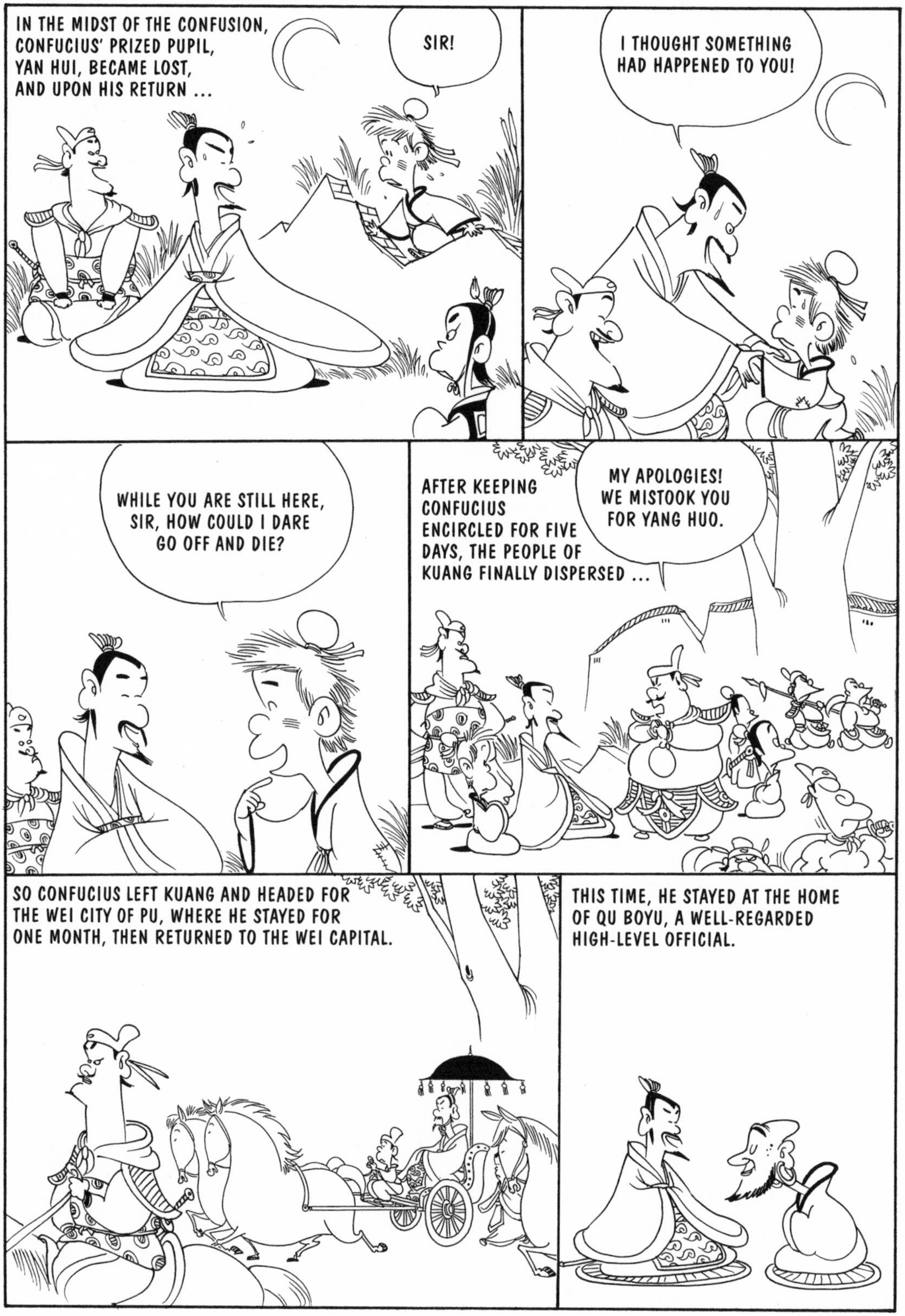

IN THE MIDST OF THE CONFUSION, CONFUCIUS' PRIZED PUPIL, YAN HUI, BECAME LOST, AND UPON HIS RETURN ...
SIR!
I THOUGHT SOMETHING HAD HAPPENED TO YOU!
WHILE YOU ARE STILL HERE, SIR, HOW COULD I DARE GO OFF AND DIE?
AFTER KEEPING CONFUCIUS ENCIRCLED FOR FIVE DAYS, THE PEOPLE OF KUANG FINALLY DISPERSED ...
MY APOLOGIES! WE MISTOOK YOU FOR YANG HUO.
SO CONFUCIUS LEFT KUANG AND HEADED FOR THE WEI CITY OF PU, WHERE HE STAYED FOR ONE MONTH, THEN RETURNED TO THE WEI CAPITAL.
THIS TIME, HE STAYED AT THE HOME OF QU BOYU, A WELL-REGARDED HIGH-LEVEL OFFICIAL.

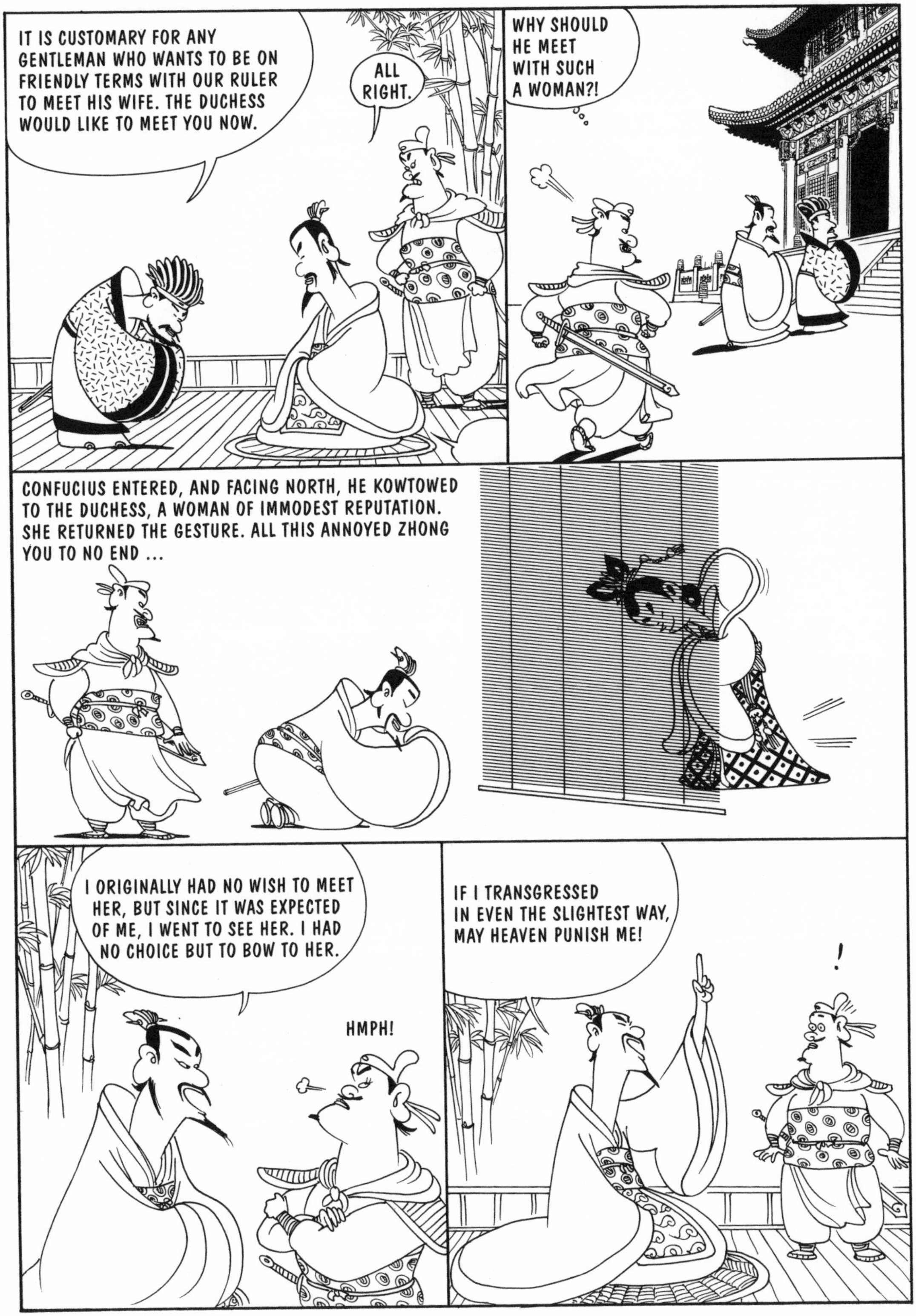
IT IS CUSTOMARY FOR ANY GENTLEMAN WHO WANTS TO BE ON FRIENDLY TERMS WITH OUR RULER TO MEET HIS WIFE. THE DUCHESS WOULD LIKE TO MEET YOU NOW.
ALL RIGHT.
WHY SHOULD HE MEET WITH SUCH A WOMAN?!
CONFUCIUS ENTERED, AND FACING NORTH, HE KOWTOWED TO THE DUCHESS, A WOMAN OF IMMODEST REPUTATION. SHE RETURNED THE GESTURE. ALL THIS ANNOYED ZHONG YOU TO NO END ...
I ORIGINALLY HAD NO WISH TO MEET HER, BUT SINCE IT WAS EXPECTED OF ME, I WENT TO SEE HER. I HAD NO CHOICE BUT TO BOW TO HER.
HMPH!
IF I TRANSGRESSED IN EVEN THE SLIGHTEST WAY, MAY HEAVEN PUNISH ME!
!

曰：「子，孔丘之徒與？」曰：「然。」桀溺曰：「悠悠者天下皆是也，而誰以易之？且與其從辟人之士，豈若從辟世之士哉！」耰而不輟。子路以告孔子，孔子憮然曰：「鳥獸不可與同群。天下有道，丘不與易也。」

他日，子路行，遇荷蓧丈人，曰：「子見夫子乎？」丈人曰：「四體不勤，五穀不分，孰為夫子！」植其杖而芸。子路以告，孔子曰：「隱者也。」復往，則亡。

孔子遷于蔡三歲，吳伐陳。楚救陳，軍于城父。聞孔子在陳蔡之閒，楚使人聘孔子。孔子將往拜禮，陳蔡大夫謀曰：「孔子賢者，所刺譏皆中諸侯之疾。今者久留陳蔡之閒，諸大夫所設行皆非仲尼之意。今楚，大國也，來聘孔子。孔子用於楚，則陳蔡用事大夫危矣。」於是乃相與發徒役圍孔子於野。不得行，絕糧。從者病，莫能興。孔子講誦弦歌不衰。子路慍見曰：「君子亦有窮乎？」孔子曰：「君子固窮，小人窮斯濫矣。」

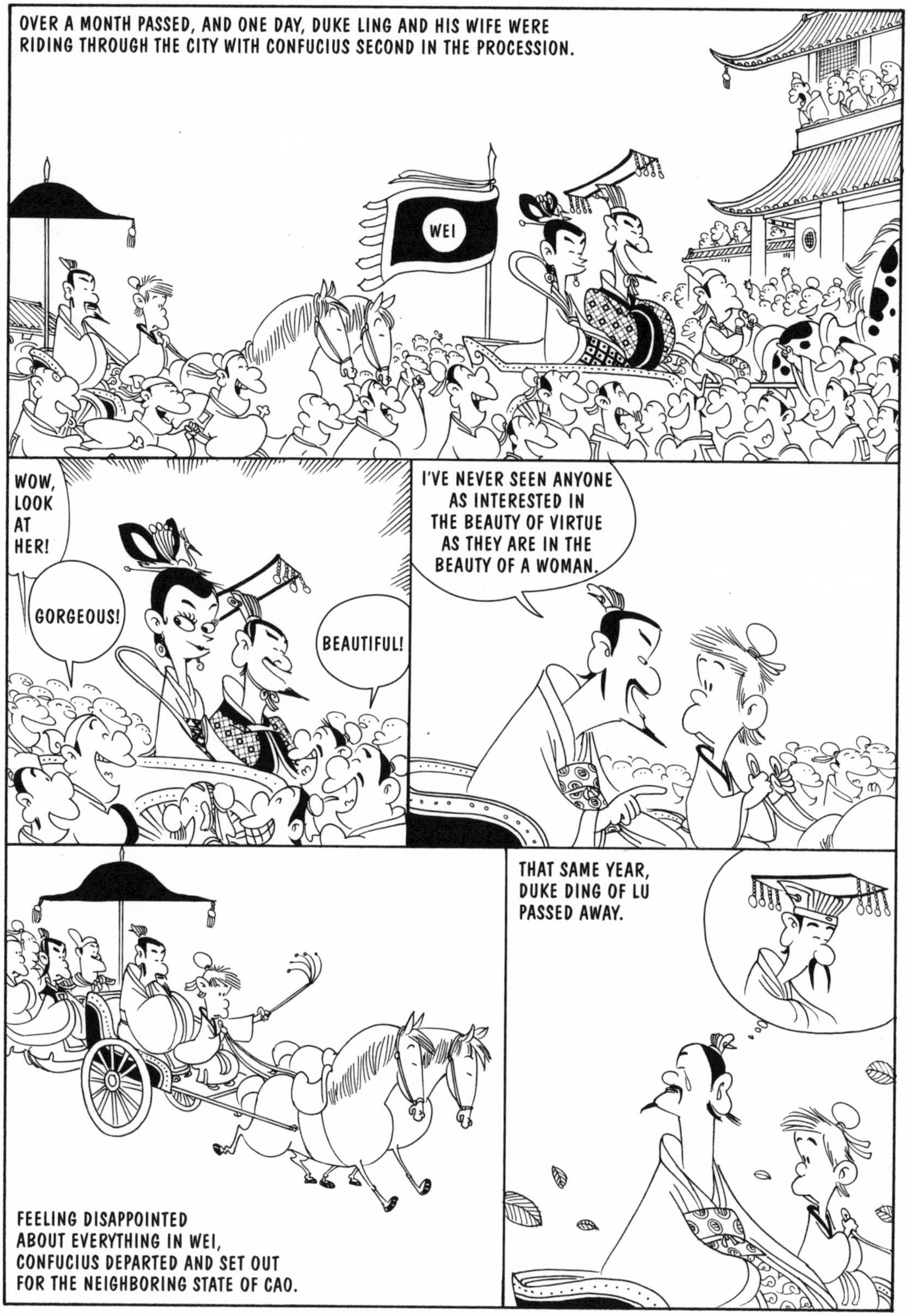

OVER A MONTH PASSED, AND ONE DAY, DUKE LING AND HIS WIFE WERE RIDING THROUGH THE CITY WITH CONFUCIUS SECOND IN THE PROCESSION.
WEI
WOW, LOOK AT HER!
GORGEOUS!
BEAUTIFUL!
I'VE NEVER SEEN ANYONE AS INTERESTED IN THE BEAUTY OF VIRTUE AS THEY ARE IN THE BEAUTY OF A WOMAN.
FEELING DISAPPOINTED ABOUT EVERYTHING IN WEI, CONFUCIUS DEPARTED AND SET OUT FOR THE NEIGHBORING STATE OF CAO.
THAT SAME YEAR, DUKE DING OF LU PASSED AWAY.

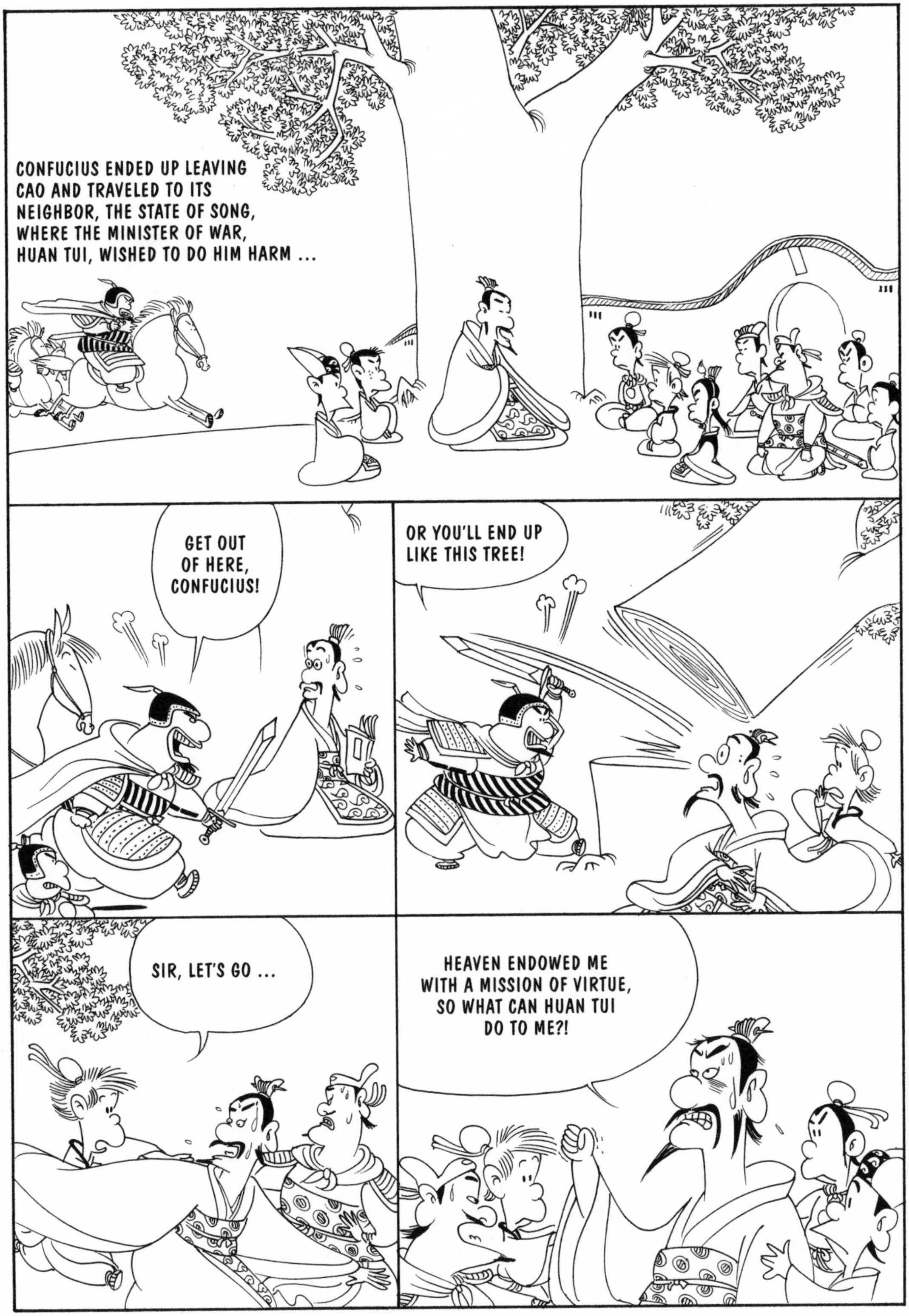
CONFUCIUS ENDED UP LEAVING CAO AND TRAVELED TO ITS NEIGHBOR, THE STATE OF SONG, WHERE THE MINISTER OF WAR, HUAN TUI, WISHED TO DO HIM HARM ...
GET OUT OF HERE, CONFUCIUS!
OR YOU'LL END UP LIKE THIS TREE!
SIR, LET'S GO ...
HEAVEN ENDOWED ME WITH A MISSION OF VIRTUE, SO WHAT CAN HUAN TUI DO TO ME?!

子貢色作。孔子曰：「賜，爾以予為多學而識之者與？」曰：「然。非與？」孔子曰：「非也。予一以貫之。」

孔子知弟子有慍心，乃召子路而問曰：「《詩》云『匪兕匪虎，率彼曠野』。吾道非邪？吾何為於此？」子路曰：「意者吾未仁邪？人之不我信也。意者吾未知邪？人之不我行也。」孔子曰：「有是乎！由，譬使仁者而必信，安有伯夷、叔齊？使知者而必行，安有王子比干？」

子路出，子貢入見。孔子曰：「賜，《詩》云『匪兕匪虎，率彼曠野』。吾道非邪？吾何為於此？」子貢曰：「夫子之道至大也，故天下莫能容夫子。夫子蓋少貶焉？」孔子曰：「賜，良農能稼而不能為穡，良工能巧而不能為順。君子能脩其道，綱而紀之，統而理之，而不能為容。今爾不脩爾道而求為容。賜，而志不遠矣！」

子貢出，顏回入見。孔子曰：「回，《詩》云『匪兕匪虎，率彼曠野』。吾道非邪？吾何為於此？」顏回曰：「夫子之道至大，故天下莫能容。雖然，夫子推而行之，不容何病，不容然後見君子！夫道之不脩也，是吾醜也。

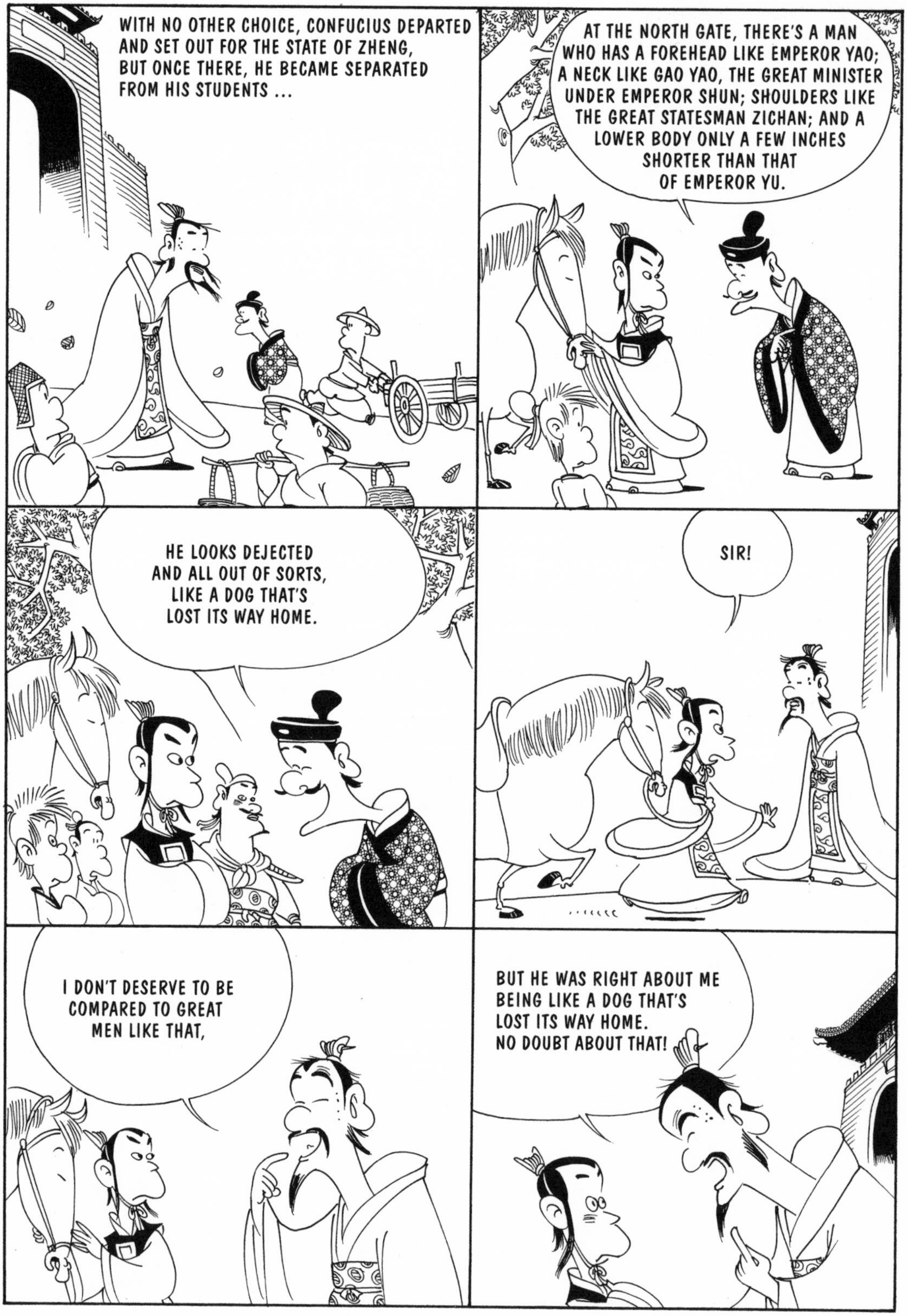
WITH NO OTHER CHOICE, CONFUCIUS DEPARTED AND SET OUT FOR THE STATE OF ZHENG, BUT ONCE THERE, HE BECAME SEPARATED FROM HIS STUDENTS ...
AT THE NORTH GATE, THERE'S A MAN WHO HAS A FOREHEAD LIKE EMPEROR YAO; A NECK LIKE GAO YAO, THE GREAT MINISTER UNDER EMPEROR SHUN; SHOULDERS LIKE THE GREAT STATESMAN ZICHAN; AND A LOWER BODY ONLY A FEW INCHES SHORTER THAN THAT OF EMPEROR YU.
HE LOOKS DEJECTED AND ALL OUT OF SORTS, LIKE A DOG THAT'S LOST ITS WAY HOME.
SIR!
I DON'T DESERVE TO BE COMPARED TO GREAT MEN LIKE THAT,
BUT HE WAS RIGHT ABOUT ME BEING LIKE A DOG THAT'S LOST ITS WAY HOME. NO DOUBT ABOUT THAT!

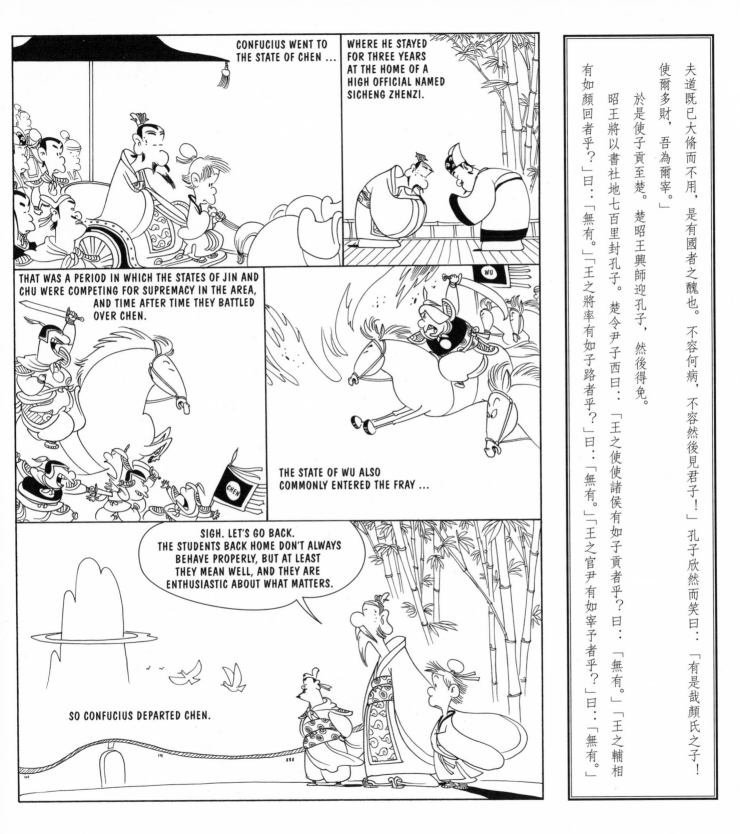

CONFUCIUS WENT TO THE STATE OF CHEN ...

WHERE HE STAYED FOR THREE YEARS AT THE HOME OF A HIGH OFFICIAL NAMED SICHENG ZHENZI.

THAT WAS A PERIOD IN WHICH THE STATES OF JIN AND CHU WERE COMPETING FOR SUPREMACY IN THE AREA, AND TIME AFTER TIME THEY BATTLED OVER CHEN.

THE STATE OF WU ALSO COMMONLY ENTERED THE FRAY ...

SIGH. LET'S GO BACK. THE STUDENTS BACK HOME DON'T ALWAYS BEHAVE PROPERLY, BUT AT LEAST THEY MEAN WELL, AND THEY ARE ENTHUSIASTIC ABOUT WHAT MATTERS.

SO CONFUCIUS DEPARTED CHEN.

夫道既已大脩而不用，是有國者之醜也。不容何病，不容然後見君子！」孔子欣然而笑曰：「有是哉顏氏之子！使爾多財，吾為爾宰。」

於是使子貢至楚。楚昭王興師迎孔子，然後得免。

昭王將以書社地七百里封孔子。楚令尹子西曰：「王之使使諸侯有如子貢者乎？」曰：「無有。」「王之輔相有如顏回者乎？」曰：「無有。」「王之將率有如子路者乎？」曰：「無有。」「王之官尹有如宰予者乎？」曰：「無有。」

33

「且楚之祖封於周，號為子男五十里。今孔丘述三五之法，明周召之業，王若用之，則楚安得世世堂堂方數千里乎？夫文王在豐，武王在鎬，百里之君卒王天下。今孔丘得據土壤，賢弟子為佐，非楚之福也。」昭王乃止。其秋，楚昭王卒于城父。

楚狂接輿歌而過孔子，曰：「鳳兮鳳兮，何德之衰！往者不可諫兮，來者猶可追也！已而已而，今之從政者殆而！」孔子下，欲與之言。趨而去，弗得與之言。

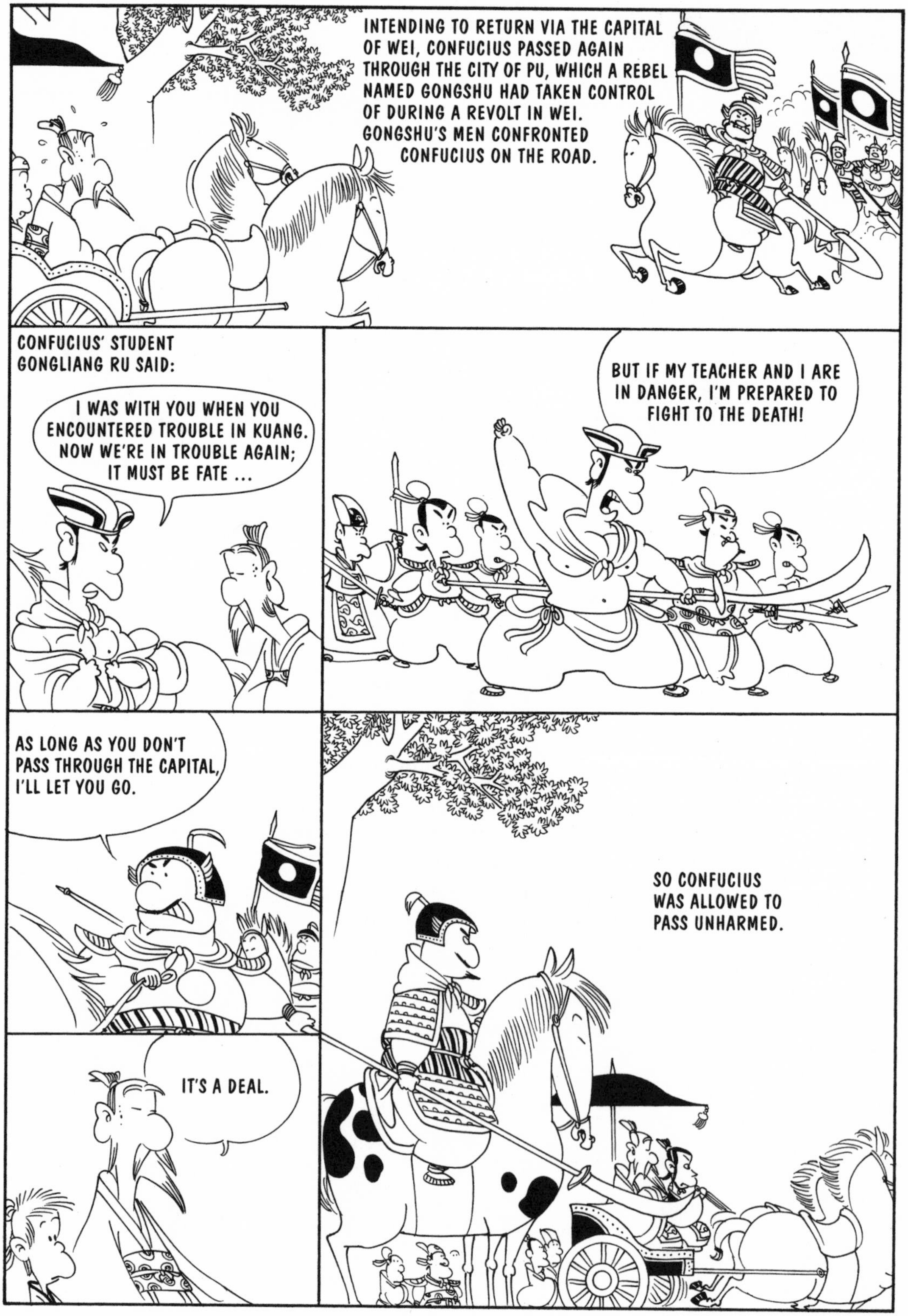
INTENDING TO RETURN VIA THE CAPITAL OF WEI, CONFUCIUS PASSED AGAIN THROUGH THE CITY OF PU, WHICH A REBEL NAMED GONGSHU HAD TAKEN CONTROL OF DURING A REVOLT IN WEI. GONGSHU'S MEN CONFRONTED CONFUCIUS ON THE ROAD.
CONFUCIUS' STUDENT GONGLIANG RU SAID:
I WAS WITH YOU WHEN YOU ENCOUNTERED TROUBLE IN KUANG. NOW WE'RE IN TROUBLE AGAIN; IT MUST BE FATE ...
BUT IF MY TEACHER AND I ARE IN DANGER, I'M PREPARED TO FIGHT TO THE DEATH!
AS LONG AS YOU DON'T PASS THROUGH THE CAPITAL, I'LL LET YOU GO.
IT'S A DEAL.
SO CONFUCIUS WAS ALLOWED TO PASS UNHARMED.

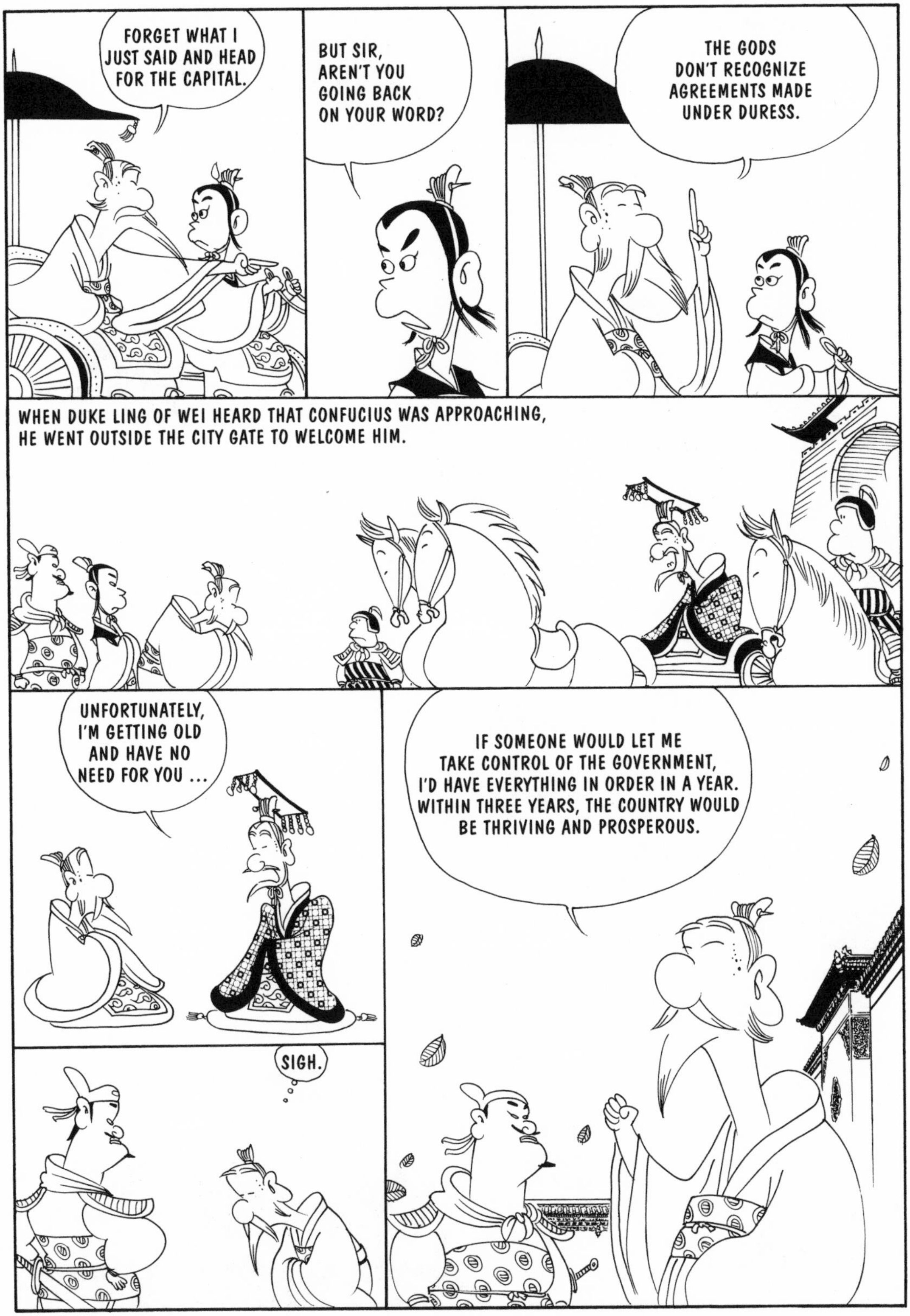
FORGET WHAT I JUST SAID AND HEAD FOR THE CAPITAL.
BUT SIR, AREN'T YOU GOING BACK ON YOUR WORD?
THE GODS DON'T RECOGNIZE AGREEMENTS MADE UNDER DURESS.
WHEN DUKE LING OF WEI HEARD THAT CONFUCIUS WAS APPROACHING, HE WENT OUTSIDE THE CITY GATE TO WELCOME HIM.
UNFORTUNATELY, I'M GETTING OLD AND HAVE NO NEED FOR YOU ...
IF SOMEONE WOULD LET ME TAKE CONTROL OF THE GOVERNMENT, I'D HAVE EVERYTHING IN ORDER IN A YEAR. WITHIN THREE YEARS, THE COUNTRY WOULD BE THRIVING AND PROSPEROUS.
SIGH.

於是孔子自楚反乎衛。是歲也，孔子年六十三，而魯哀公六年也。

其明年，吳與魯會繒，徵百牢。太宰嚭召季康子。康子使子貢往，然後得已。

孔子曰：「魯衛之政，兄弟也。」是時，衛君輒父不得立，在外，諸侯數以為讓。而孔子弟子多仕於衛，衛君欲得孔子為政。子路曰：「衛君待子而為政，子將奚先？」孔子曰：「必也正名乎！」子路曰：「有是哉，子之迂也！何其正也？」孔子曰：「野哉由也！夫名不正則言不順，言不順則事不成，事不成則禮樂不興，禮

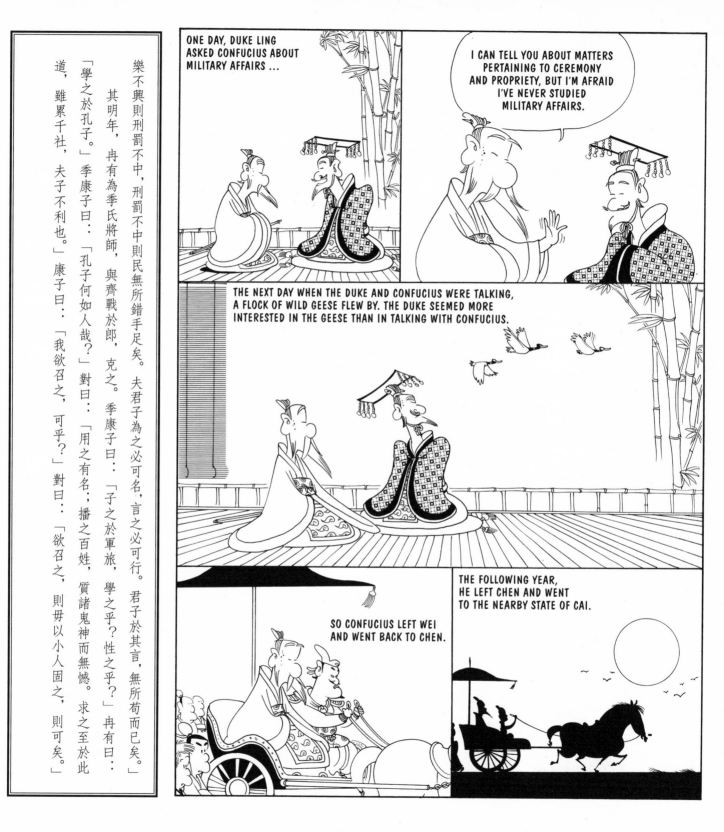

樂不興則刑罰不中，刑罰不中則民無所錯手足矣。夫君子為之必可名，言之必可行。君子於其言，無所苟而已矣。」
其明年，冉有為季氏將師，與齊戰於郎，克之。季康子曰：「子之於軍旅，學之乎？性之乎？」冉有曰：
「學之於孔子。」季康子曰：「孔子何如人哉？」對曰：「用之有名，播之百姓，質諸鬼神而無憾。求之至於此道，雖累千社，夫子不利也。」康子曰：「我欲召之，可乎？」對曰：「欲召之，則毋以小人固之，則可矣。」

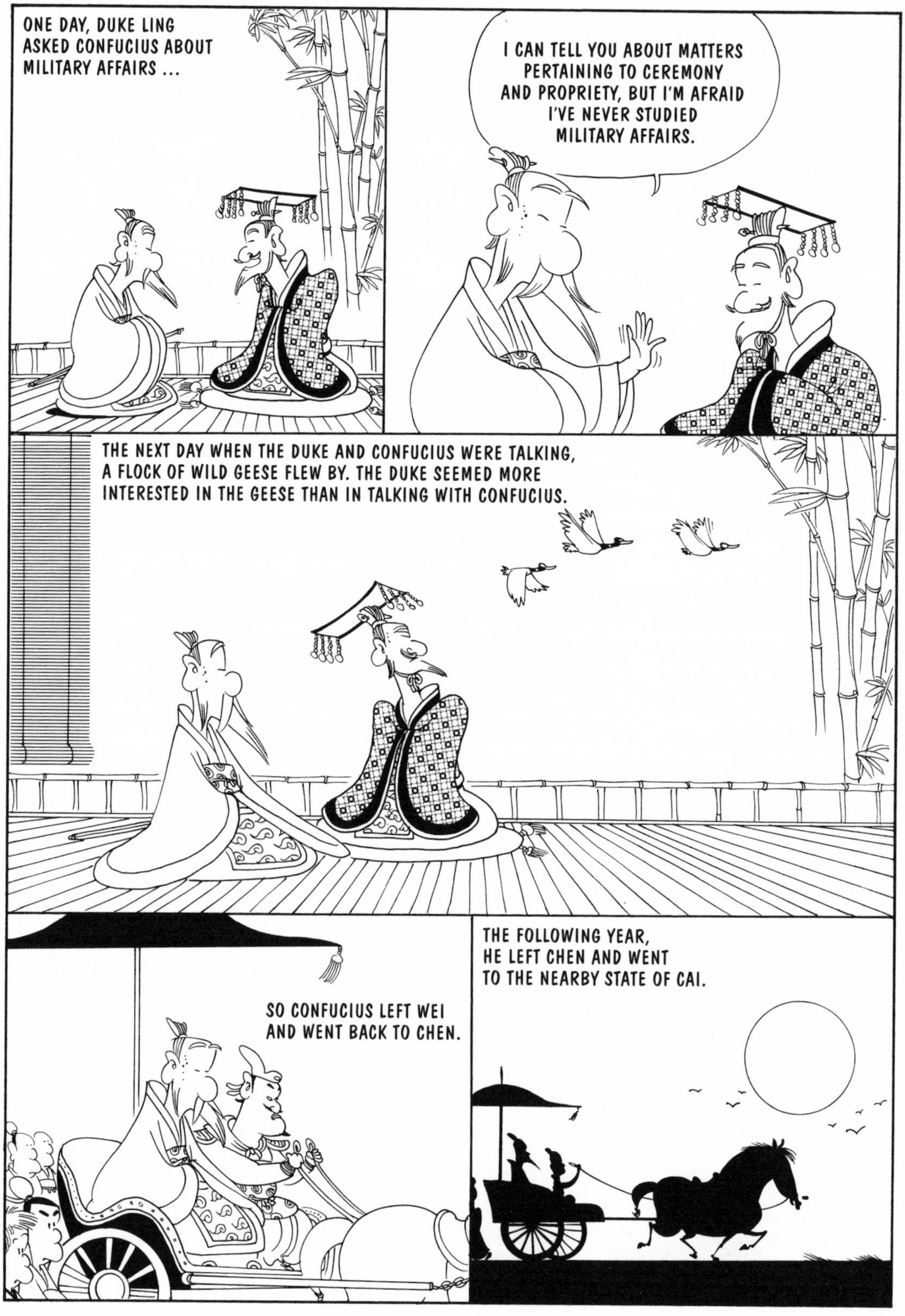
ONE DAY, DUKE LING ASKED CONFUCIUS ABOUT MILITARY AFFAIRS ...
I CAN TELL YOU ABOUT MATTERS PERTAINING TO CEREMONY AND PROPRIETY, BUT I'M AFRAID I'VE NEVER STUDIED MILITARY AFFAIRS.
THE NEXT DAY WHEN THE DUKE AND CONFUCIUS WERE TALKING, A FLOCK OF WILD GEESE FLEW BY. THE DUKE SEEMED MORE INTERESTED IN THE GEESE THAN IN TALKING WITH CONFUCIUS.
SO CONFUCIUS LEFT WEI AND WENT BACK TO CHEN.
THE FOLLOWING YEAR, HE LEFT CHEN AND WENT TO THE NEARBY STATE OF CAI.

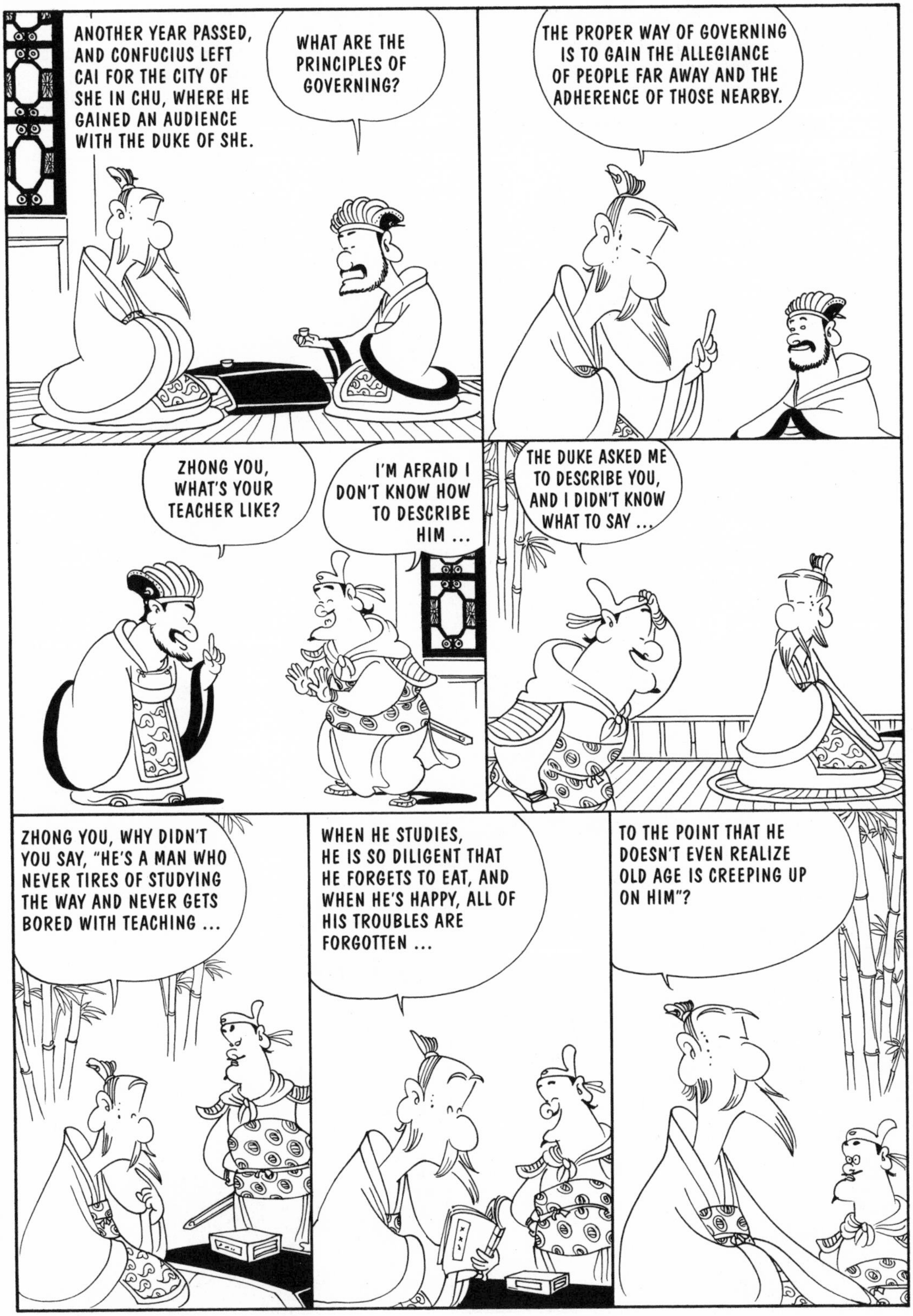
ANOTHER YEAR PASSED, AND CONFUCIUS LEFT CAI FOR THE CITY OF SHE IN CHU, WHERE HE GAINED AN AUDIENCE WITH THE DUKE OF SHE.
WHAT ARE THE PRINCIPLES OF GOVERNING?
THE PROPER WAY OF GOVERNING IS TO GAIN THE ALLEGIANCE OF PEOPLE FAR AWAY AND THE ADHERENCE OF THOSE NEARBY.
ZHONG YOU, WHAT'S YOUR TEACHER LIKE?
I'M AFRAID I DON'T KNOW HOW TO DESCRIBE HIM ...
THE DUKE ASKED ME TO DESCRIBE YOU, AND I DIDN'T KNOW WHAT TO SAY ...
ZHONG YOU, WHY DIDN'T YOU SAY, "HE'S A MAN WHO NEVER TIRES OF STUDYING THE WAY AND NEVER GETS BORED WITH TEACHING ...
WHEN HE STUDIES, HE IS SO DILIGENT THAT HE FORGETS TO EAT, AND WHEN HE'S HAPPY, ALL OF HIS TROUBLES ARE FORGOTTEN ...
TO THE POINT THAT HE DOESN'T EVEN REALIZE OLD AGE IS CREEPING UP ON HIM"?

而衛孔文子將攻太叔，問策於仲尼。仲尼辭不知，退而命載而行，曰：「鳥能擇木，木豈能擇鳥乎！」文子固止。會季康子逐公華、公賓、公林，以幣迎孔子，孔子歸魯。

孔子之去魯凡十四歲而反乎魯。

魯哀公問政，對曰：「政在選臣。」季康子問政，曰：「舉直錯諸枉，則枉者直。」康子患盜，孔子曰：「苟子之不欲，雖賞之不竊。」然魯終不能用孔子，孔子亦不求仕。

孔子之時，周室微而禮樂廢，《詩》、《書》缺。追迹三代之禮，序《書傳》，上紀唐虞之際，下至秦繆，編次其事。曰：「夏禮吾能言之，杞不足徵也。殷禮吾能言之，宋不足徵也。足，則吾能徵之矣。」觀殷夏所損益，曰：「後雖百世可知也，以一文一質。周監二代，郁郁乎文哉。吾從周。」故《書傳》、《禮記》自孔氏。

孔子語魯大師：「樂其可知也。始作翕如，縱之純如，皦如，繹如也，以成。」「吾自衛反魯，然後樂正，《雅》《頌》各得其所。」

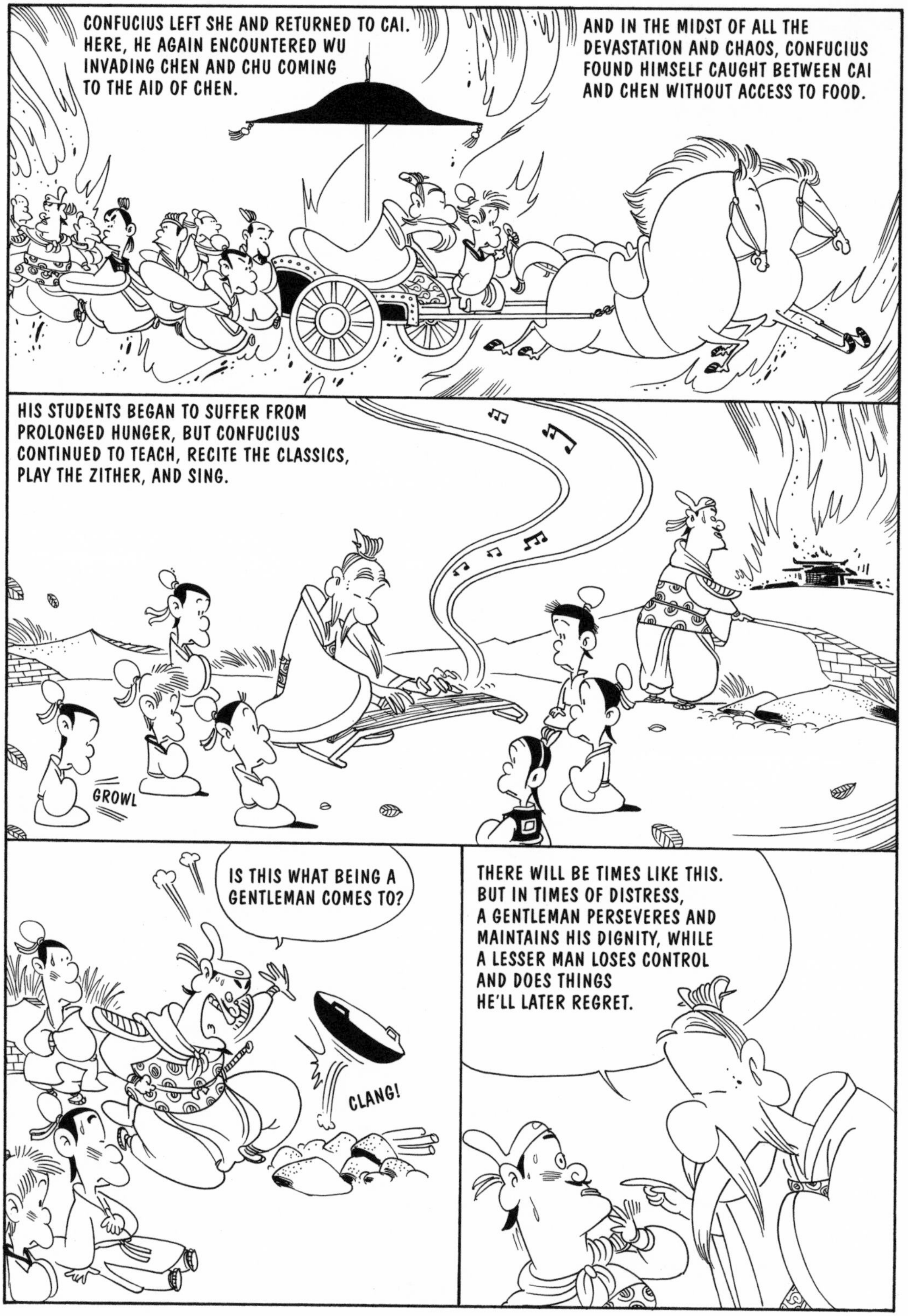

CONFUCIUS LEFT SHE AND RETURNED TO CAI. HERE, HE AGAIN ENCOUNTERED WU INVADING CHEN AND CHU COMING TO THE AID OF CHEN.
AND IN THE MIDST OF ALL THE DEVASTATION AND CHAOS, CONFUCIUS FOUND HIMSELF CAUGHT BETWEEN CAI AND CHEN WITHOUT ACCESS TO FOOD.
HIS STUDENTS BEGAN TO SUFFER FROM PROLONGED HUNGER, BUT CONFUCIUS CONTINUED TO TEACH, RECITE THE CLASSICS, PLAY THE ZITHER, AND SING.
GROWL
IS THIS WHAT BEING A GENTLEMAN COMES TO?
CLANG!
THERE WILL BE TIMES LIKE THIS. BUT IN TIMES OF DISTRESS, A GENTLEMAN PERSEVERES AND MAINTAINS HIS DIGNITY, WHILE A LESSER MAN LOSES CONTROL AND DOES THINGS HE'LL LATER REGRET.

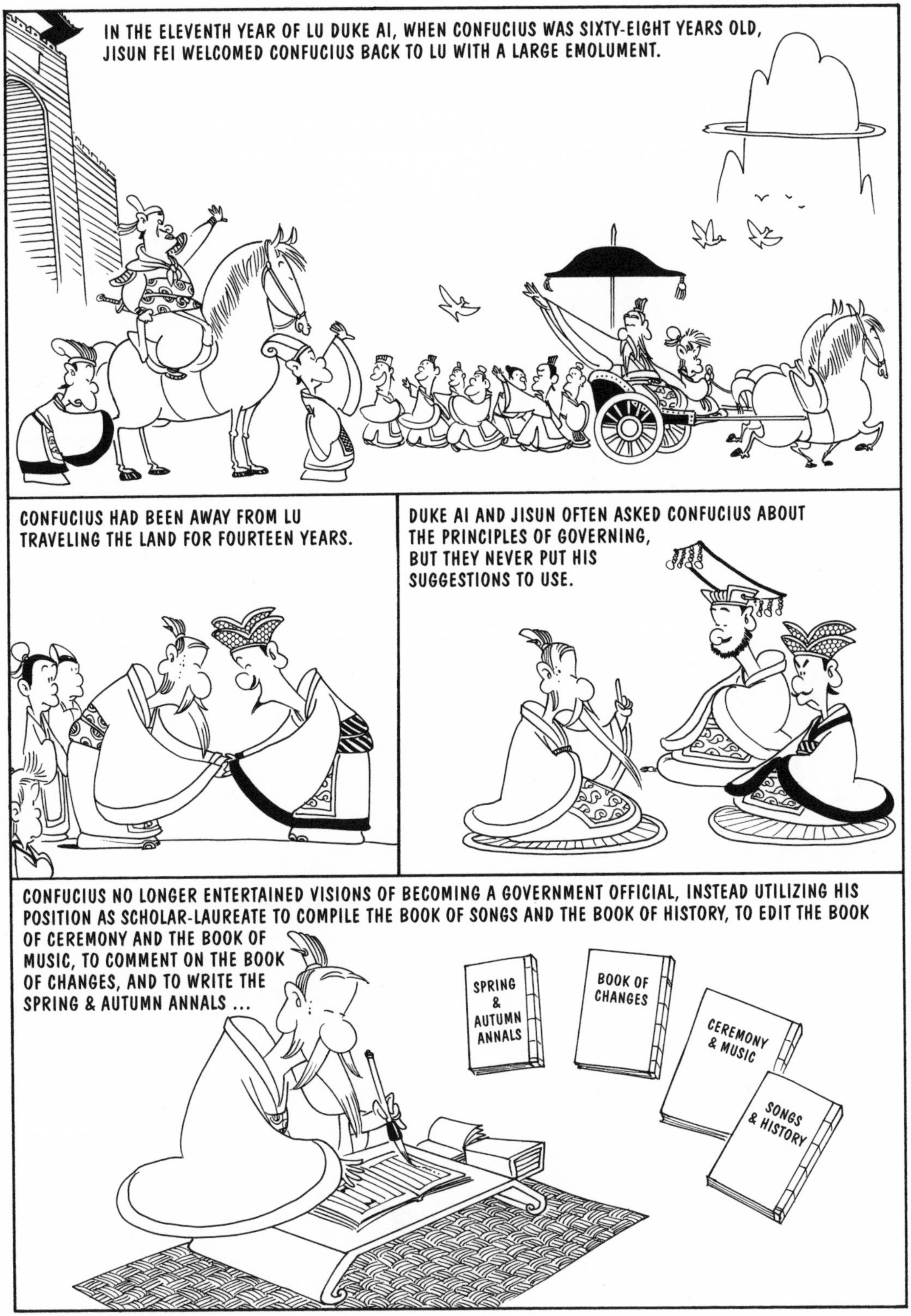
IN THE ELEVENTH YEAR OF LU DUKE AI, WHEN CONFUCIUS WAS SIXTY-EIGHT YEARS OLD, JISUN FEI WELCOMED CONFUCIUS BACK TO LU WITH A LARGE EMOLUMENT.
CONFUCIUS HAD BEEN AWAY FROM LU TRAVELING THE LAND FOR FOURTEEN YEARS.
DUKE AI AND JISUN OFTEN ASKED CONFUCIUS ABOUT THE PRINCIPLES OF GOVERNING, BUT THEY NEVER PUT HIS SUGGESTIONS TO USE.
CONFUCIUS NO LONGER ENTERTAINED VISIONS OF BECOMING A GOVERNMENT OFFICIAL, INSTEAD UTILIZING HIS POSITION AS SCHOLAR-LAUREATE TO COMPILE THE BOOK OF SONGS AND THE BOOK OF HISTORY, TO EDIT THE BOOK OF CEREMONY AND THE BOOK OF MUSIC, TO COMMENT ON THE BOOK OF CHANGES, AND TO WRITE THE SPRING & AUTUMN ANNALS ...
SPRING & AUTUMN ANNALS
BOOK OF CHANGES
CEREMONY & MUSIC
SONGS & HISTORY

古者《詩》三千餘篇，及至孔子，去其重，取可施於禮義，上采契后稷，中述殷周之盛，至幽厲之缺，始於衽席，故曰：「《關雎》之亂以為《風》始，《鹿鳴》為《小雅》始，《文王》為《大雅》始，《清廟》為《頌》始」。三百五篇孔子皆弦歌之，以求合《韶》《武》《雅》《頌》之音。禮樂自此可得而述，以備王道，成六藝。

孔子晚而喜《易》，序《彖》、《繫》、《象》、《說卦》、《文言》。讀《易》，韋編三絕。曰：「假我數年，若是，我於《易》則彬彬矣。」

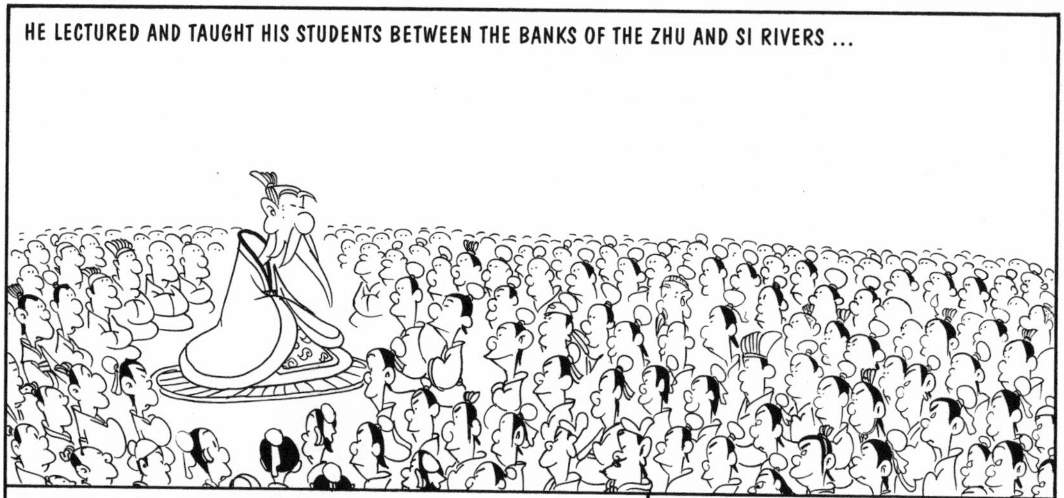
HE LECTURED AND TAUGHT HIS STUDENTS BETWEEN THE BANKS OF THE ZHU AND SI RIVERS ...

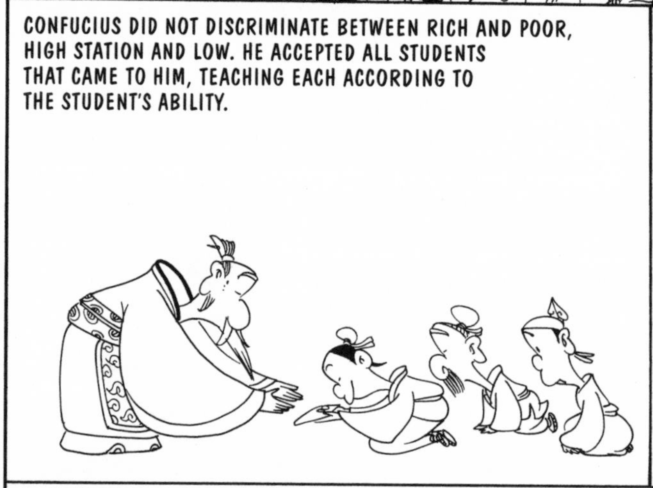
CONFUCIUS DID NOT DISCRIMINATE BETWEEN RICH AND POOR, HIGH STATION AND LOW. HE ACCEPTED ALL STUDENTS THAT CAME TO HIM, TEACHING EACH ACCORDING TO THE STUDENT'S ABILITY.

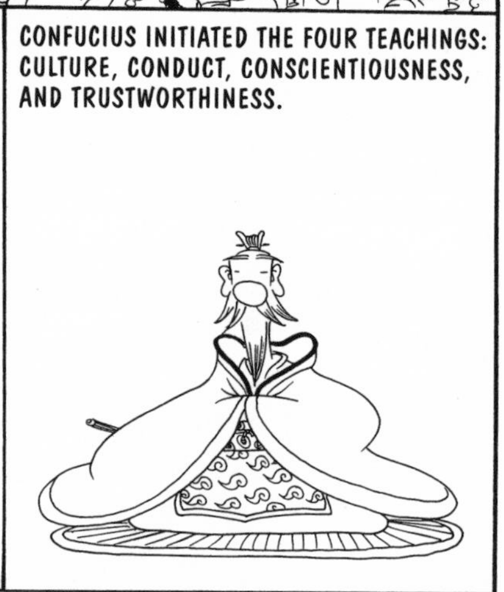
CONFUCIUS INITIATED THE FOUR TEACHINGS: CULTURE, CONDUCT, CONSCIENTIOUSNESS, AND TRUSTWORTHINESS.

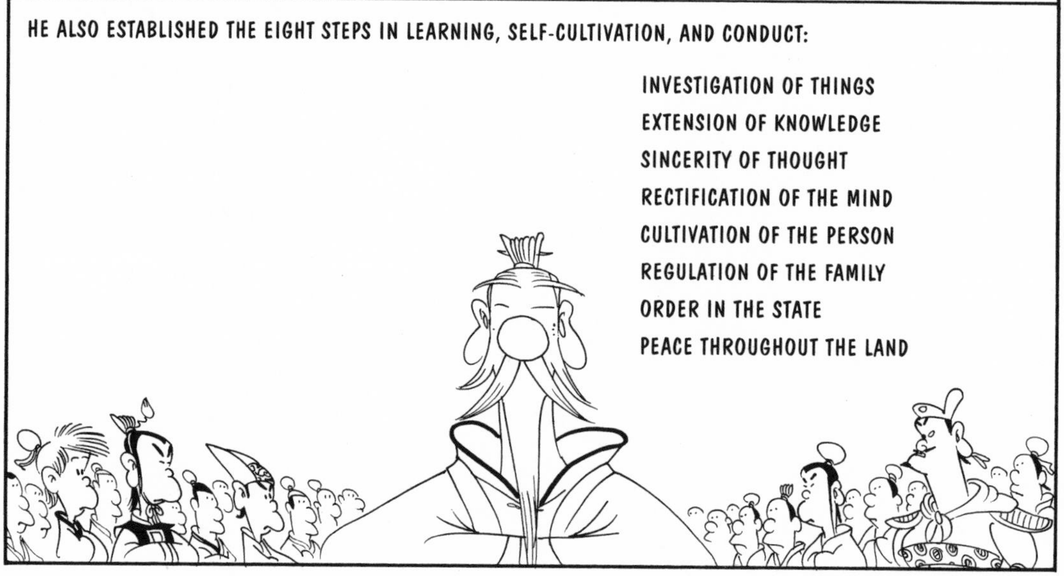
HE ALSO ESTABLISHED THE EIGHT STEPS IN LEARNING, SELF-CULTIVATION, AND CONDUCT:
INVESTIGATION OF THINGS
EXTENSION OF KNOWLEDGE
SINCERITY OF THOUGHT
RECTIFICATION OF THE MIND
CULTIVATION OF THE PERSON
REGULATION OF THE FAMILY
ORDER IN THE STATE
PEACE THROUGHOUT THE LAND

孔子以詩書禮樂教，弟子蓋三千焉，身通六藝者七十有二人。如顏濁鄒之徒，頗受業者甚眾。

孔子以四教：文，行，忠，信。絕四：毋意，毋必，毋固，毋我。所慎：齊，戰，疾。子罕言利與命與仁。

不憤不啟，舉一隅不以三隅反，則弗復也。

其於鄉黨，恂恂似不能言者。其於宗廟朝廷，辯辯言，唯謹爾。朝，與上大夫言，誾誾如也；與下大夫言，侃侃如也。

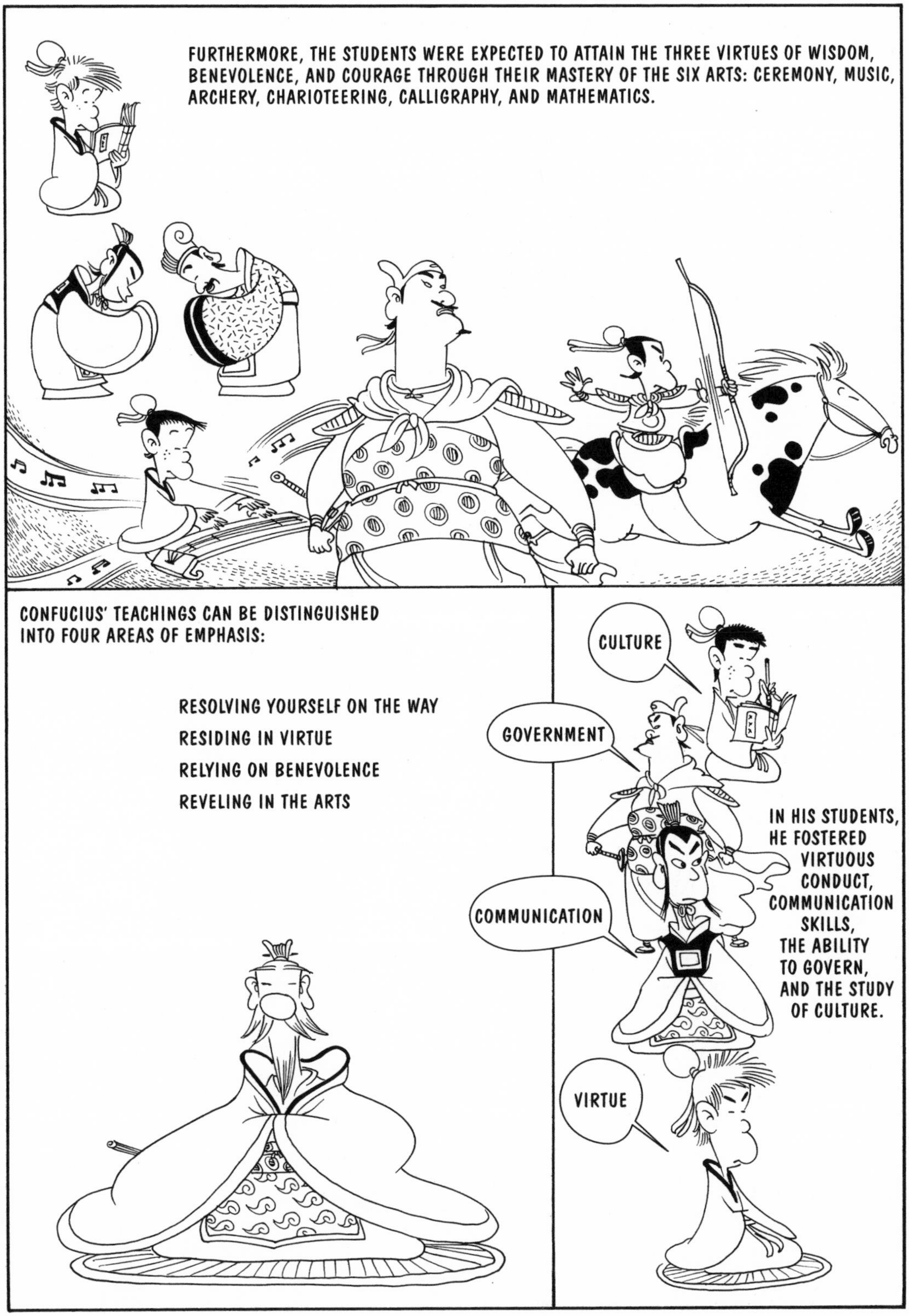
FURTHERMORE, THE STUDENTS WERE EXPECTED TO ATTAIN THE THREE VIRTUES OF WISDOM, BENEVOLENCE, AND COURAGE THROUGH THEIR MASTERY OF THE SIX ARTS: CEREMONY, MUSIC, ARCHERY, CHARIOTEERING, CALLIGRAPHY, AND MATHEMATICS.
CONFUCIUS' TEACHINGS CAN BE DISTINGUISHED INTO FOUR AREAS OF EMPHASIS:
RESOLVING YOURSELF ON THE WAY
RESIDING IN VIRTUE
RELYING ON BENEVOLENCE
REVELING IN THE ARTS
CULTURE
GOVERNMENT
COMMUNICATION
VIRTUE
IN HIS STUDENTS, HE FOSTERED VIRTUOUS CONDUCT, COMMUNICATION SKILLS, THE ABILITY TO GOVERN, AND THE STUDY OF CULTURE.

子貢曰：「夫子之文章，可得聞也。夫子言天道與性命，弗可得聞也已。」顏淵喟然歎曰：「仰之彌高，鑽之彌堅。瞻之在前，忽焉在後。夫子循循然善誘人，博我以文，約我以禮，欲罷不能。既竭我才，如有所立，卓爾。雖欲從之，蔑由也已。」……

明歲，子路死於衛。孔子病，子貢請見。孔子方負杖逍遙於門，曰：「賜，汝來何其晚也？」孔子因歎，歌曰：「太山壞乎！梁柱摧乎！哲人萎乎！」因以涕下。謂子貢曰：「天下無道久矣，莫能宗予。夏人殯於東階，周人於西階，殷人兩柱閒。昨暮予夢坐奠兩柱之閒，予始殷人也。」後七日卒。

孔子年七十三，以魯哀公十六年四月己丑卒。

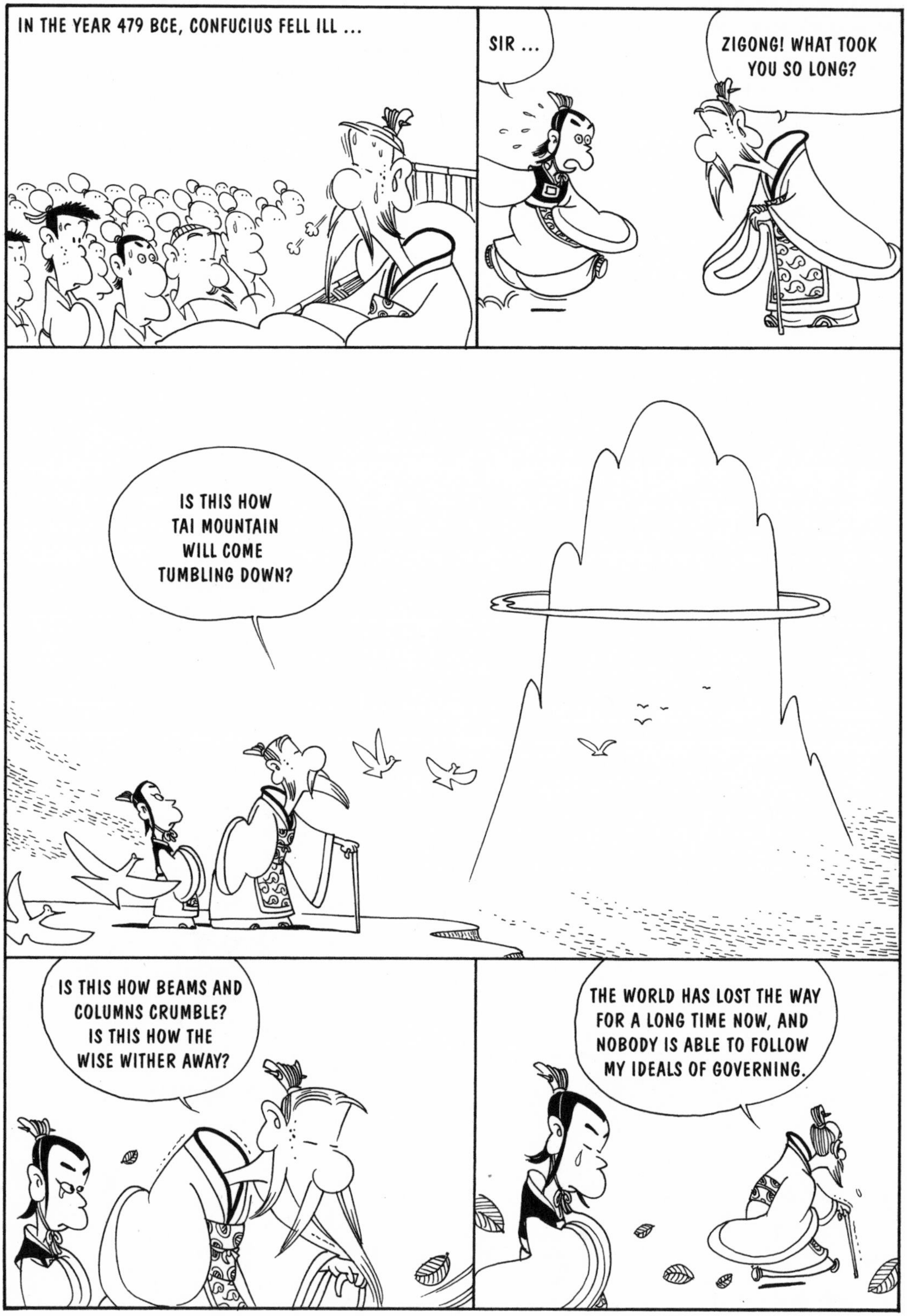
IN THE YEAR 479 BCE, CONFUCIUS FELL ILL ...
SIR ...
ZIGONG! WHAT TOOK YOU SO LONG?
IS THIS HOW TAI MOUNTAIN WILL COME TUMBLING DOWN?
IS THIS HOW BEAMS AND COLUMNS CRUMBLE? IS THIS HOW THE WISE WITHER AWAY?
THE WORLD HAS LOST THE WAY FOR A LONG TIME NOW, AND NOBODY IS ABLE TO FOLLOW MY IDEALS OF GOVERNING.

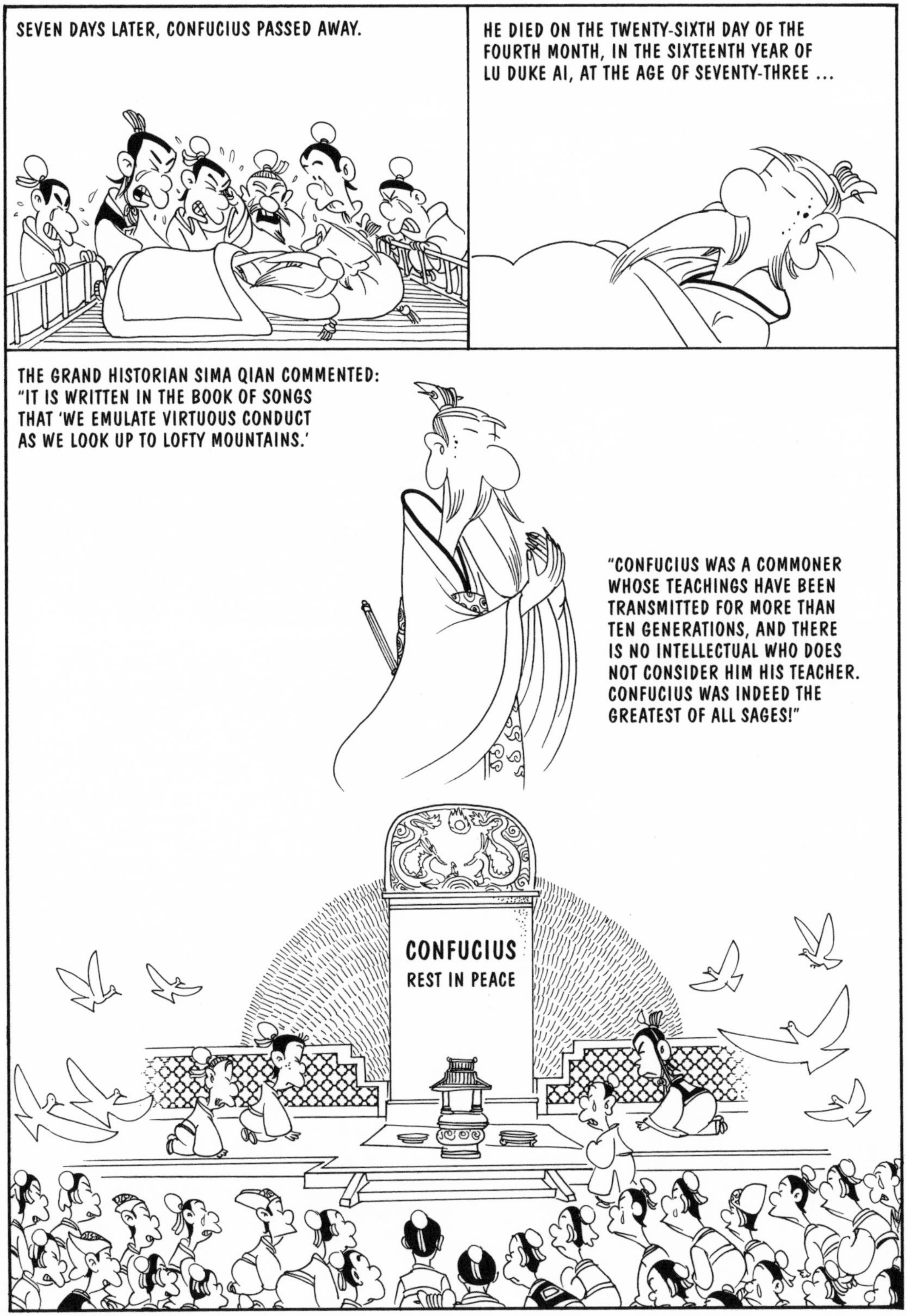
SEVEN DAYS LATER, CONFUCIUS PASSED AWAY.
HE DIED ON THE TWENTY-SIXTH DAY OF THE FOURTH MONTH, IN THE SIXTEENTH YEAR OF LU DUKE AI, AT THE AGE OF SEVENTY-THREE ...
THE GRAND HISTORIAN SIMA QIAN COMMENTED: "IT IS WRITTEN IN THE BOOK OF SONGS THAT 'WE EMULATE VIRTUOUS CONDUCT AS WE LOOK UP TO LOFTY MOUNTAINS.'
"CONFUCIUS WAS A COMMONER WHOSE TEACHINGS HAVE BEEN TRANSMITTED FOR MORE THAN TEN GENERATIONS, AND THERE IS NO INTELLECTUAL WHO DOES NOT CONSIDER HIM HIS TEACHER. CONFUCIUS WAS INDEED THE GREATEST OF ALL SAGES!"
CONFUCIUS
REST IN PEACE

太史公曰：《詩》有之：「高山仰止，景行行止。」雖不能至，然心鄉往之。余讀孔氏書，想見其為人。適魯，觀仲尼廟堂車服禮器，諸生以時習禮其家，余祗迴留之不能去云。天下君王至于賢人眾矣，當時則榮，沒則已焉。孔子布衣，傳十餘世，學者宗之。自天子王侯，中國言《六藝》者折中於夫子，可謂至聖矣！

【史記・孔子世家】

The Analects

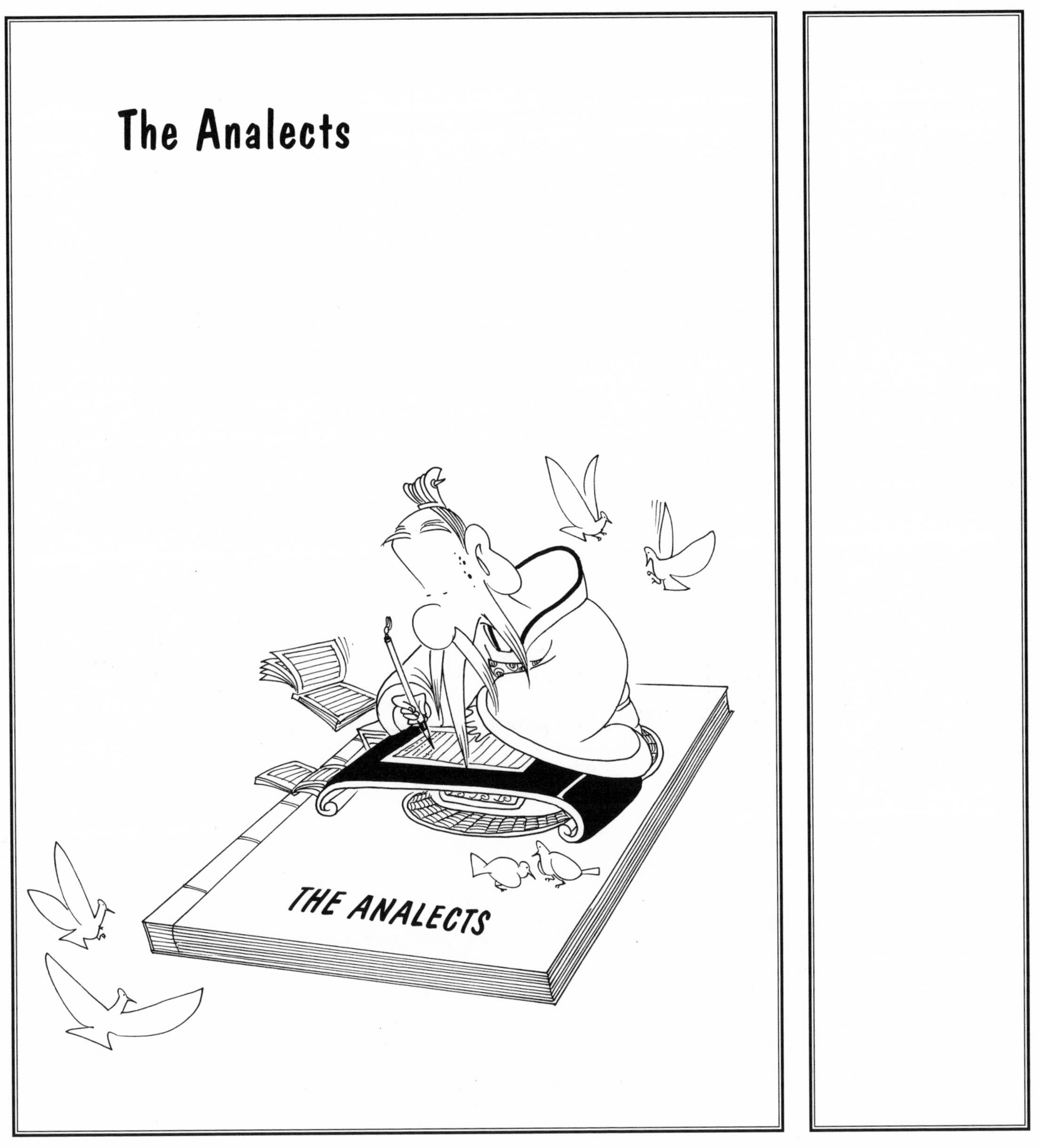
THE ANALECTS

子曰：「學而時習之，不亦說乎？有朋自遠方來，不亦樂乎？人不知而不慍，不亦君子乎？」

1:1

PLEASURE AND DIGNITY

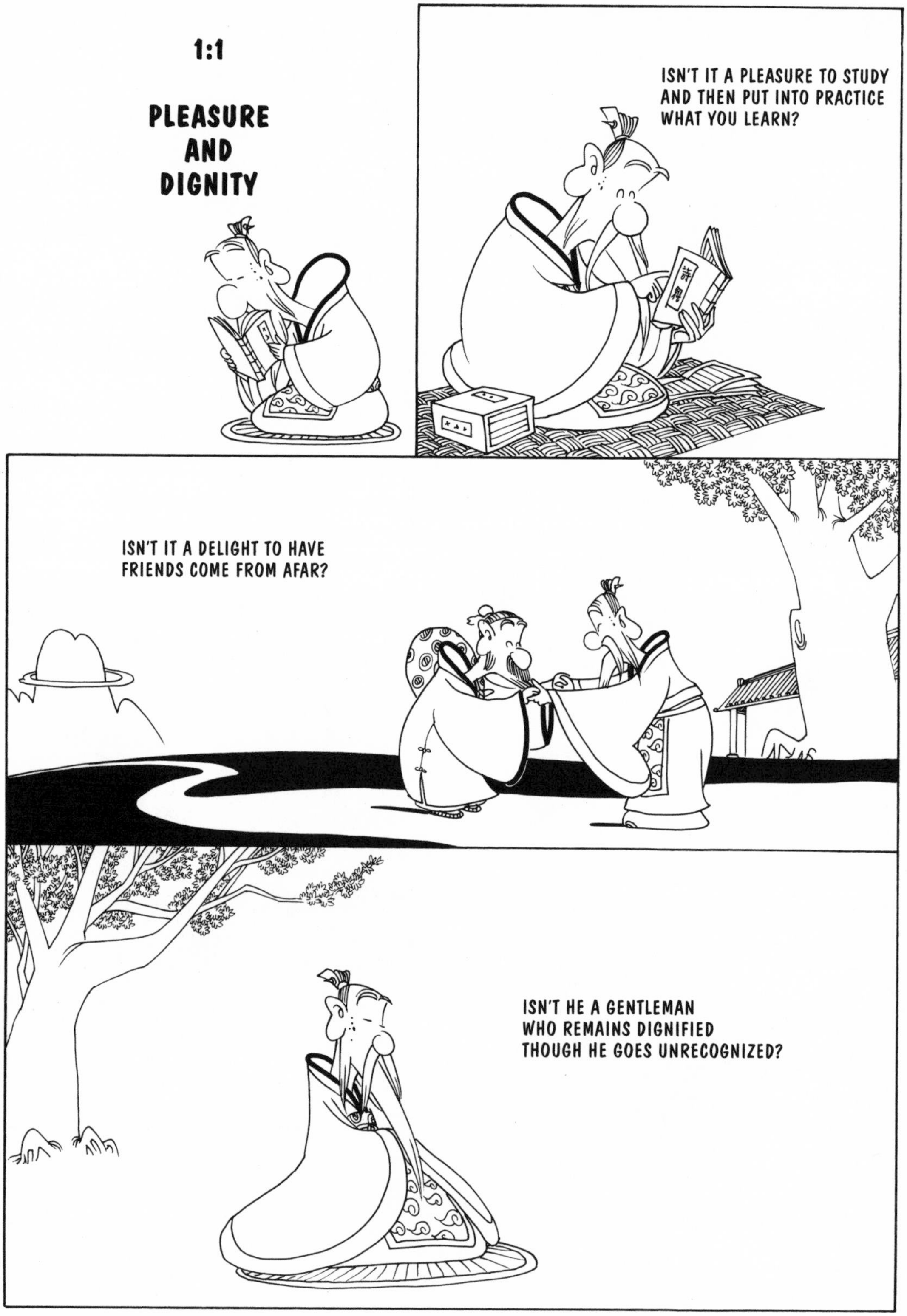
ISN'T IT A PLEASURE TO STUDY AND THEN PUT INTO PRACTICE WHAT YOU LEARN?
ISN'T IT A DELIGHT TO HAVE FRIENDS COME FROM AFAR?
ISN'T HE A GENTLEMAN WHO REMAINS DIGNIFIED THOUGH HE GOES UNRECOGNIZED?

1:2

THE ROOT OF BENEVOLENCE

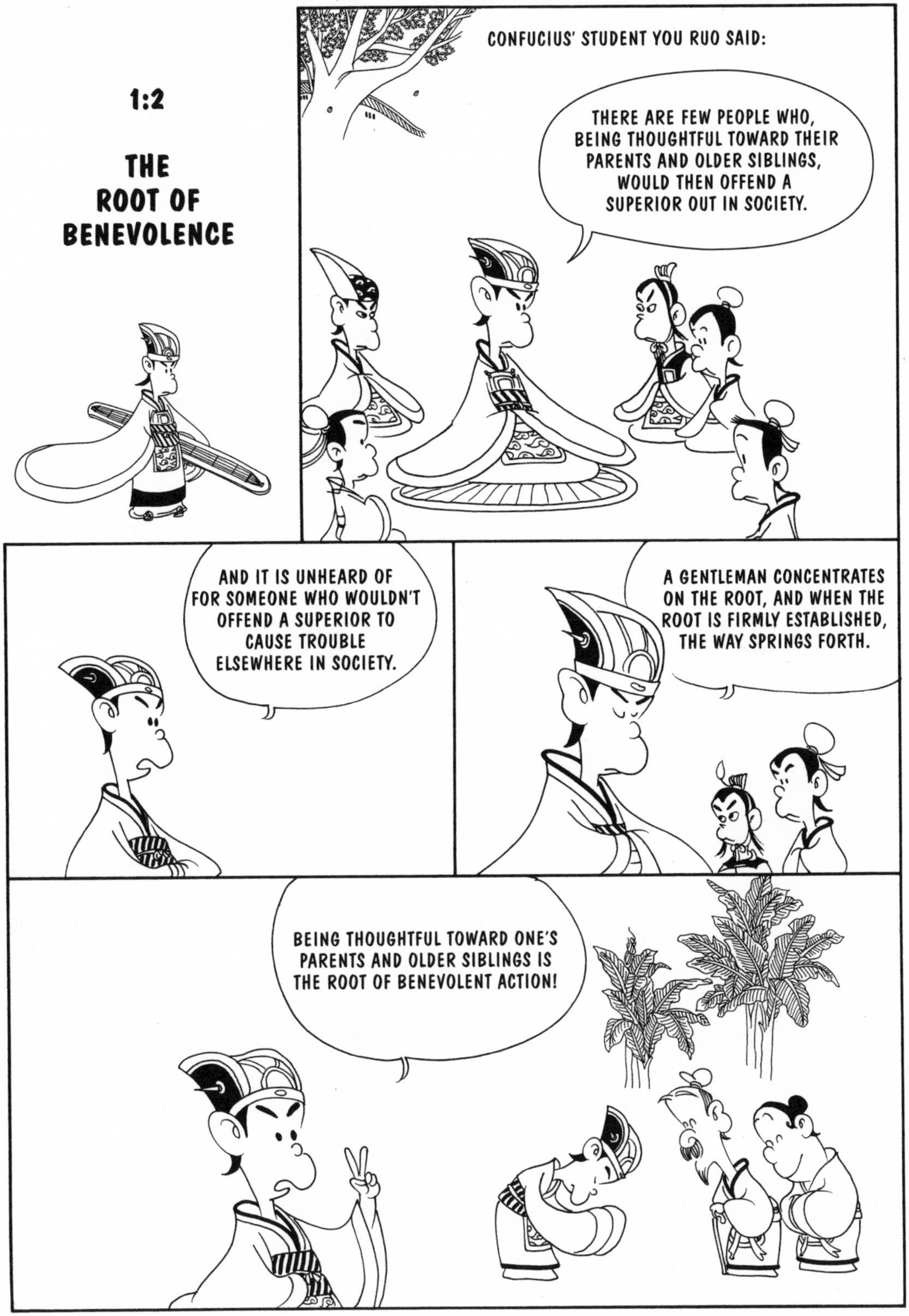
CONFUCIUS' STUDENT YOU RUO SAID:
THERE ARE FEW PEOPLE WHO, BEING THOUGHTFUL TOWARD THEIR PARENTS AND OLDER SIBLINGS, WOULD THEN OFFEND A SUPERIOR OUT IN SOCIETY.
AND IT IS UNHEARD OF FOR SOMEONE WHO WOULDN'T OFFEND A SUPERIOR TO CAUSE TROUBLE ELSEWHERE IN SOCIETY.
A GENTLEMAN CONCENTRATES ON THE ROOT, AND WHEN THE ROOT IS FIRMLY ESTABLISHED, THE WAY SPRINGS FORTH.
BEING THOUGHTFUL TOWARD ONE'S PARENTS AND OLDER SIBLINGS IS THE ROOT OF BENEVOLENT ACTION!

有子曰：「其為人也孝弟，而好犯上者，鮮矣；不好犯上，而好作亂者，未之有也。君子務本，本立而道生。孝弟也者，其為仁之本與！」

曾子曰：「吾日三省吾身：為人謀而不忠乎？與朋友交而不信乎？傳不習乎？」

1:4

SELF-CRITIQUE

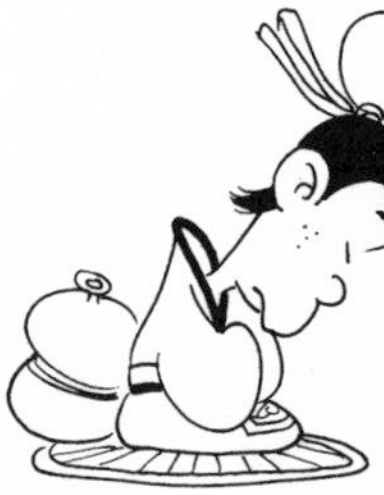

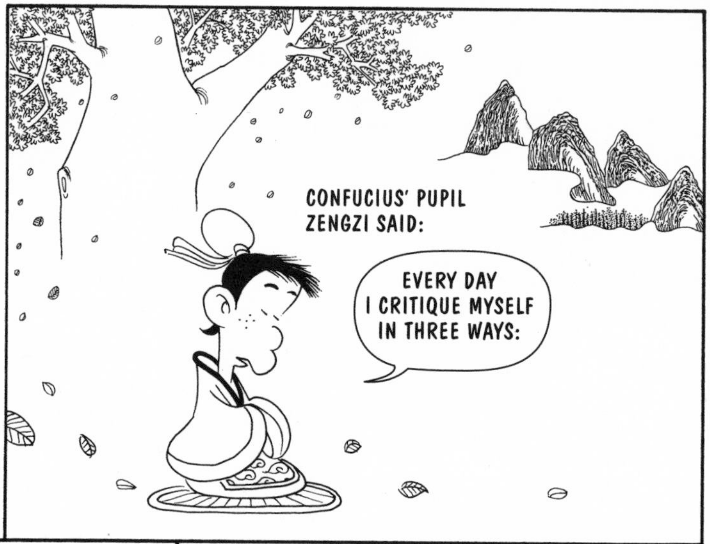
CONFUCIUS' PUPIL ZENGZI SAID:
EVERY DAY I CRITIQUE MYSELF IN THREE WAYS:

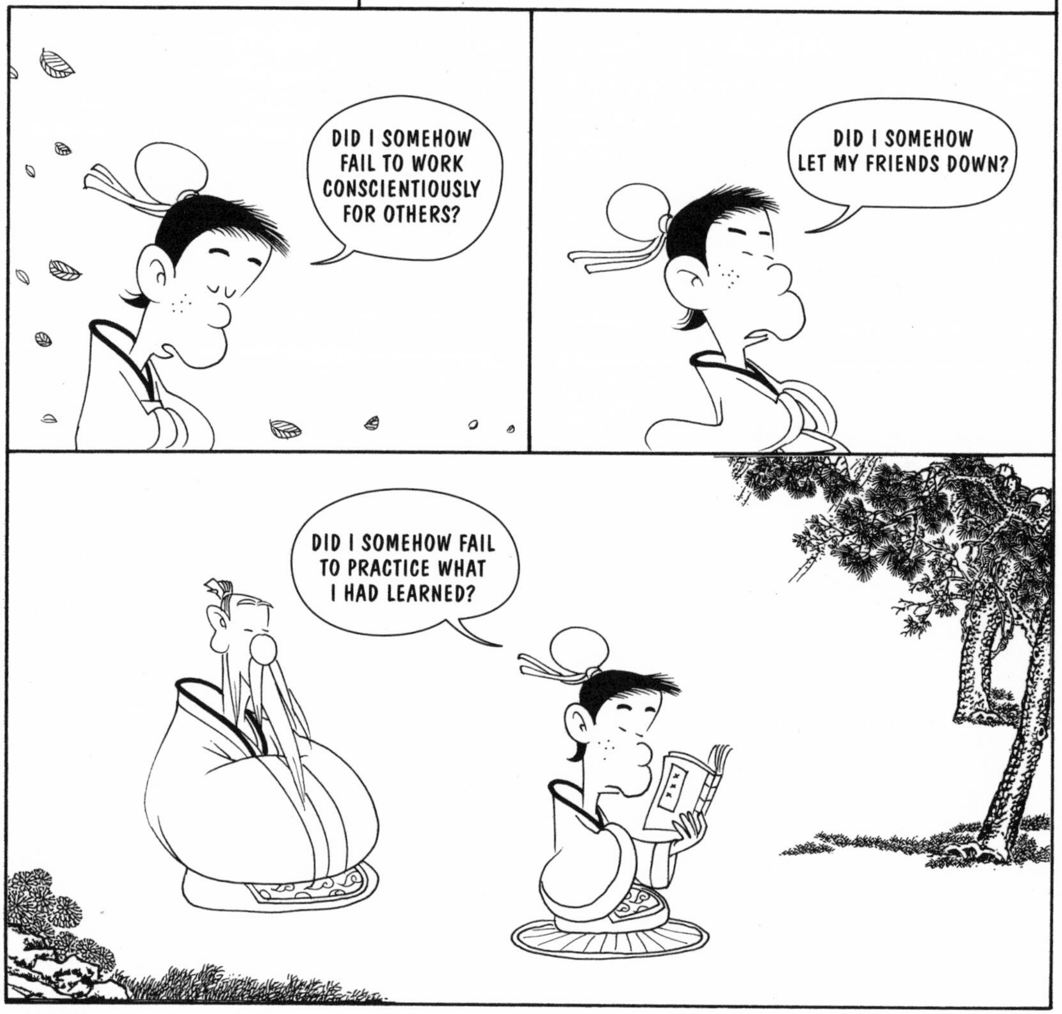
DID I SOMEHOW FAIL TO WORK CONSCIENTIOUSLY FOR OTHERS?
DID I SOMEHOW LET MY FRIENDS DOWN?
DID I SOMEHOW FAIL TO PRACTICE WHAT I HAD LEARNED?

1:5

LEADING A LARGE COUNTRY

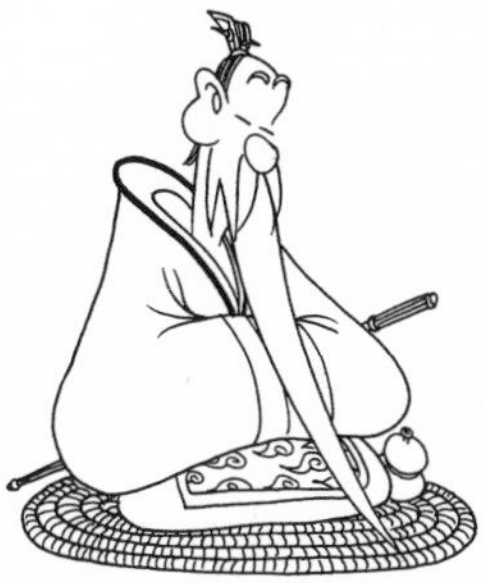

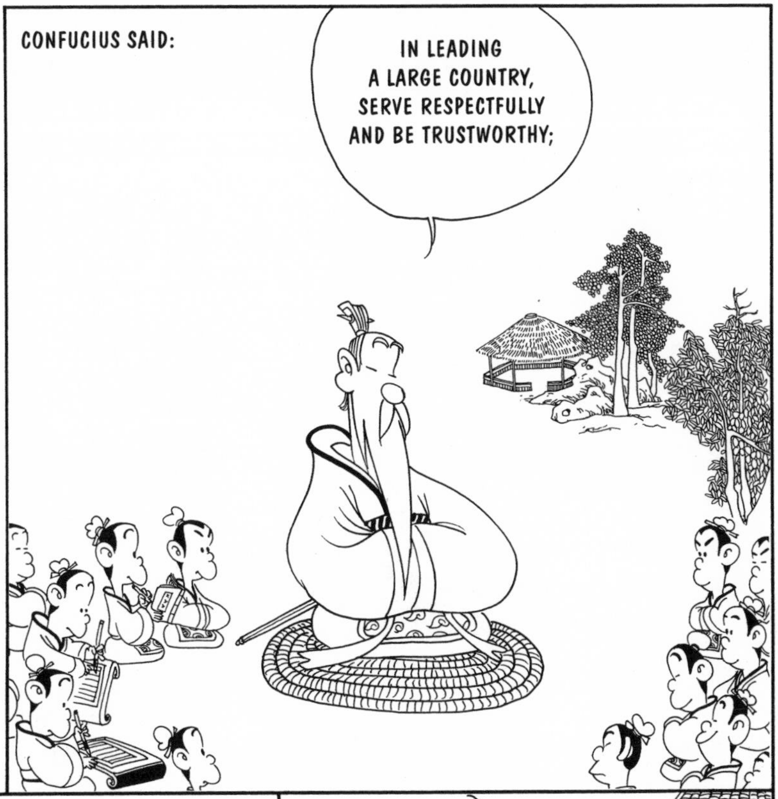
CONFUCIUS SAID:
IN LEADING A LARGE COUNTRY, SERVE RESPECTFULLY AND BE TRUSTWORTHY;

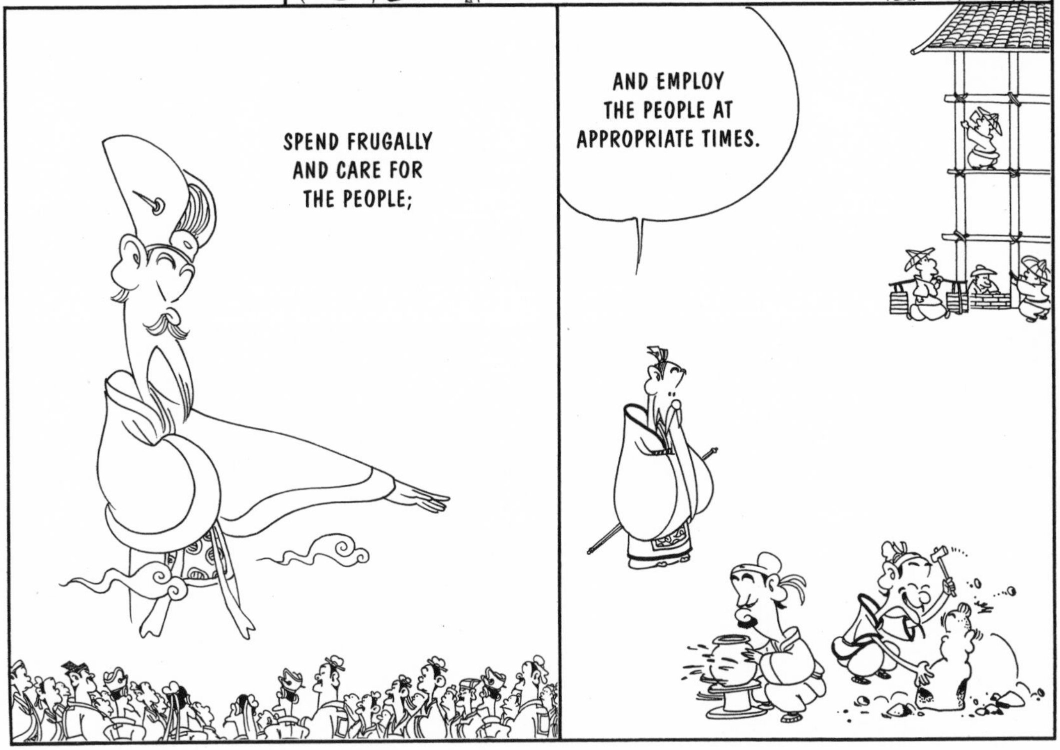
SPEND FRUGALLY AND CARE FOR THE PEOPLE;
AND EMPLOY THE PEOPLE AT APPROPRIATE TIMES.

子曰：「道千乘之國，敬事而信，節用而愛人，使民以時。」

子曰：「弟子入則孝，出則悌，謹而信，汎愛眾，而親仁。行有餘力，則以學文。」

1:6

THE FINE YOUNG MAN

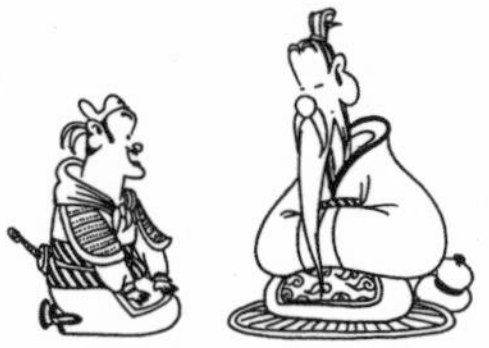

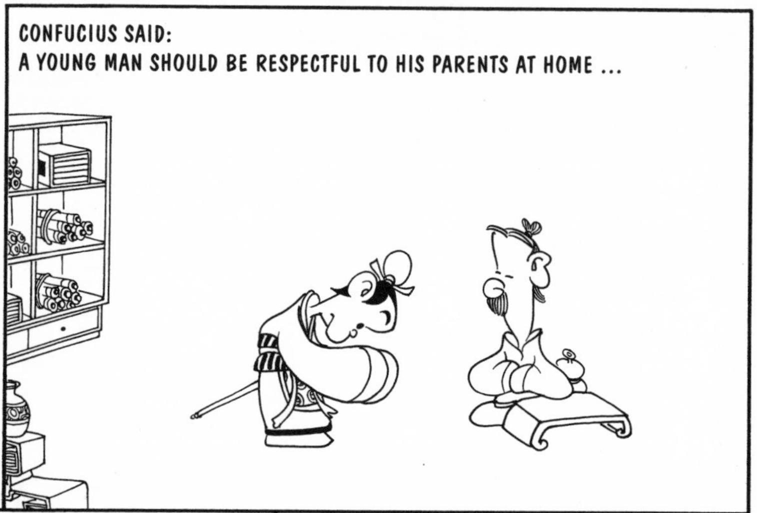
CONFUCIUS SAID:
A YOUNG MAN SHOULD BE RESPECTFUL TO HIS PARENTS AT HOME ...

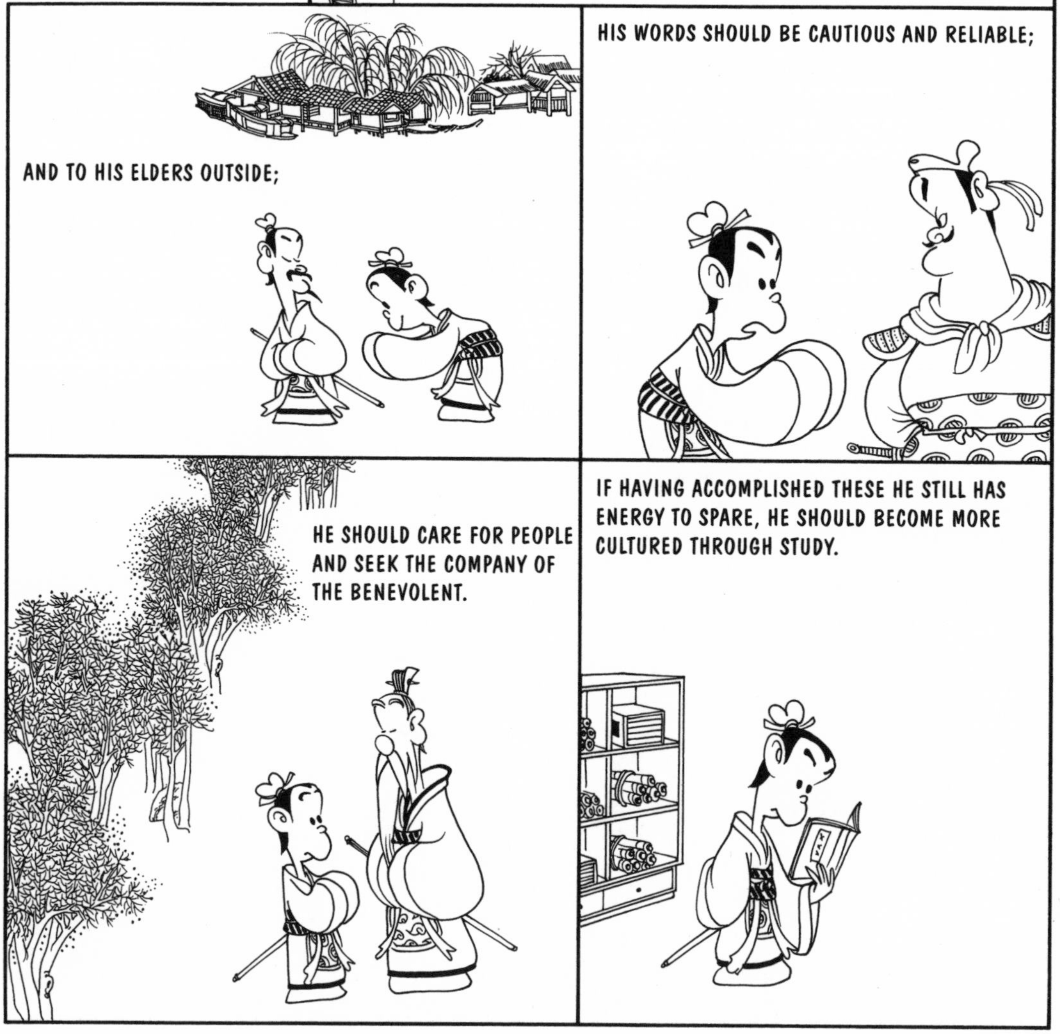
AND TO HIS ELDERS OUTSIDE;
HIS WORDS SHOULD BE CAUTIOUS AND RELIABLE;
HE SHOULD CARE FOR PEOPLE AND SEEK THE COMPANY OF THE BENEVOLENT.
IF HAVING ACCOMPLISHED THESE HE STILL HAS ENERGY TO SPARE, HE SHOULD BECOME MORE CULTURED THROUGH STUDY.

1:8

THE GENTLEMAN

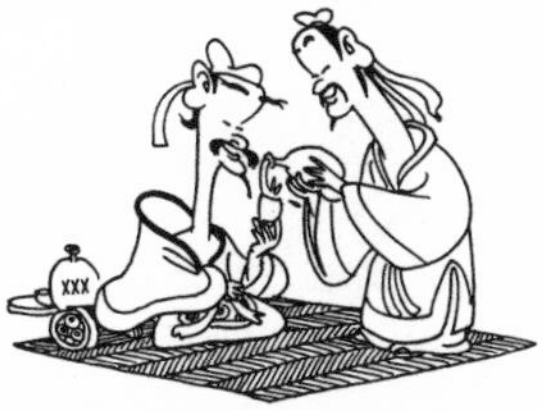

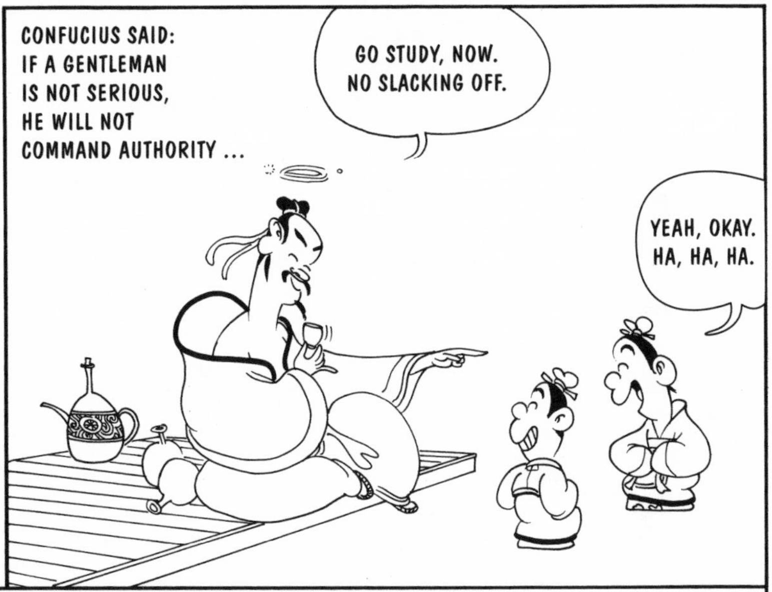
CONFUCIUS SAID: IF A GENTLEMAN IS NOT SERIOUS, HE WILL NOT COMMAND AUTHORITY ...
GO STUDY, NOW. NO SLACKING OFF.
YEAH, OKAY. HA, HA, HA.

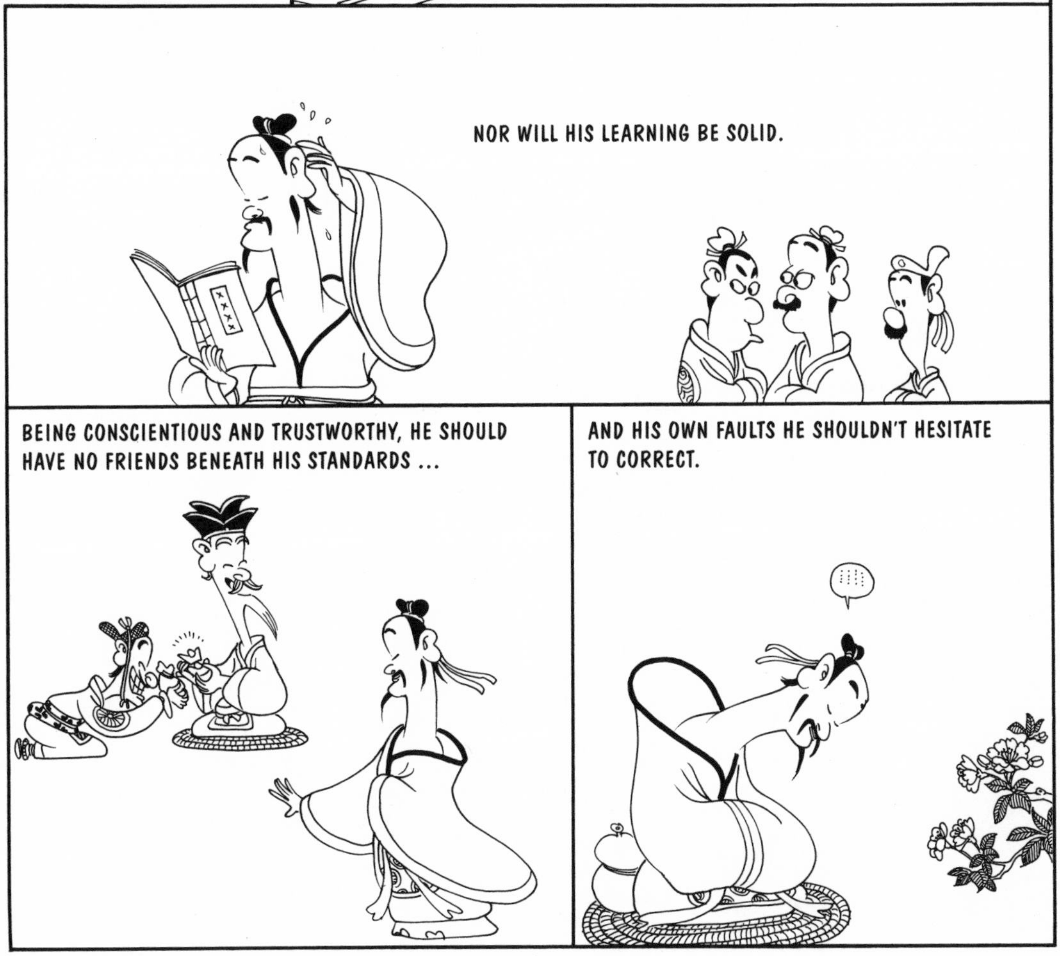
NOR WILL HIS LEARNING BE SOLID.
BEING CONSCIENTIOUS AND TRUSTWORTHY, HE SHOULD HAVE NO FRIENDS BENEATH HIS STANDARDS ...
AND HIS OWN FAULTS HE SHOULDN'T HESITATE TO CORRECT.

子曰：「君子不重則不威，學則不固。主忠信。無友不如己者。過則勿憚改。」

曾子曰：「慎終追遠，民德歸厚矣。」

1:9

VIRTUE AMONG THE PEOPLE

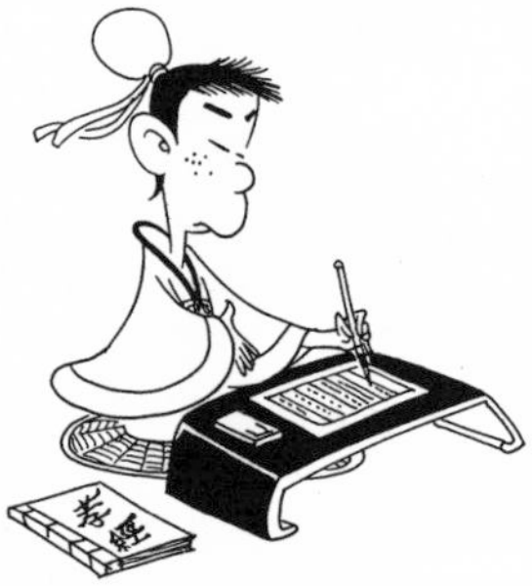
孝經

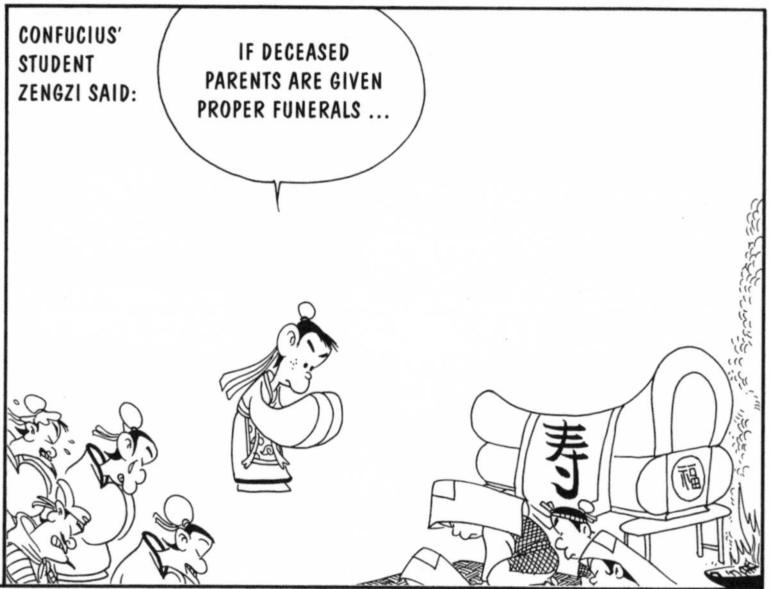
CONFUCIUS' STUDENT ZENGZI SAID:
IF DECEASED PARENTS ARE GIVEN PROPER FUNERALS ...
寿
福

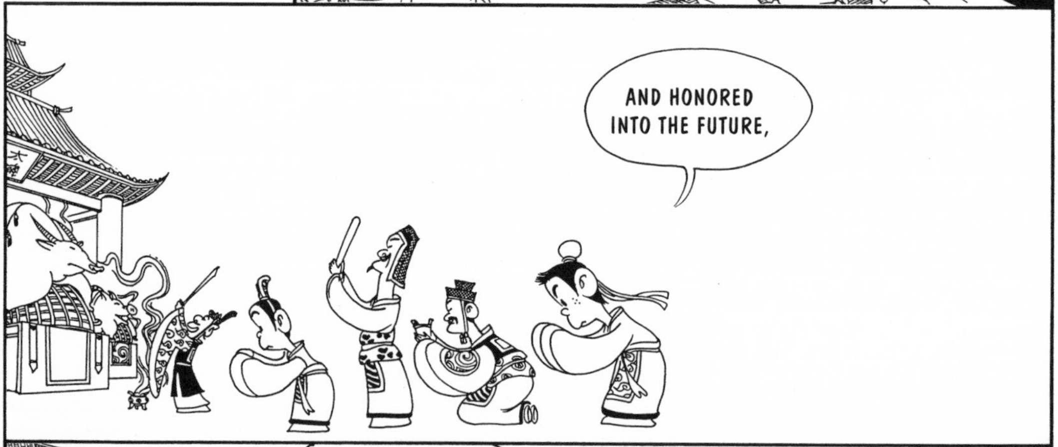
AND HONORED INTO THE FUTURE,

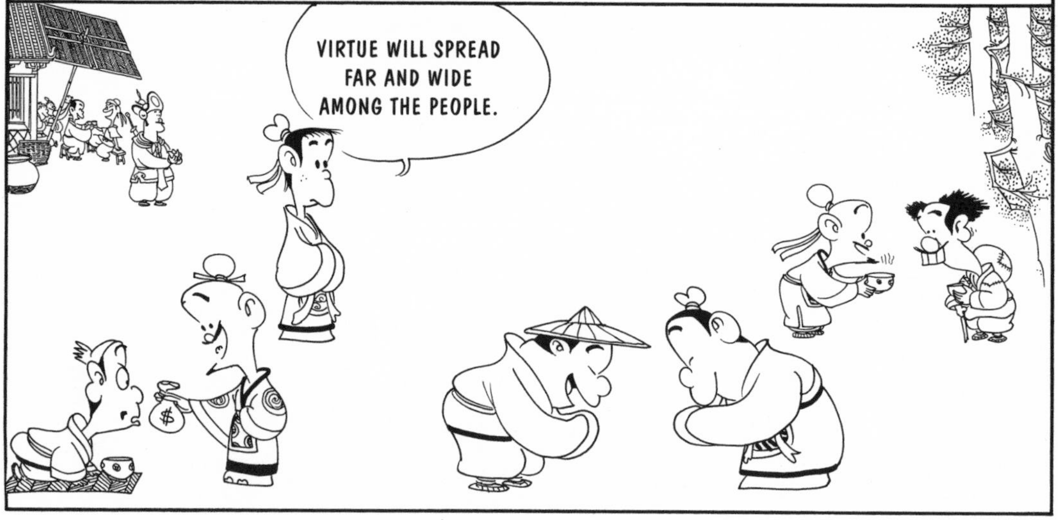
VIRTUE WILL SPREAD FAR AND WIDE AMONG THE PEOPLE.

1:16

RECOGNIZING OTHERS

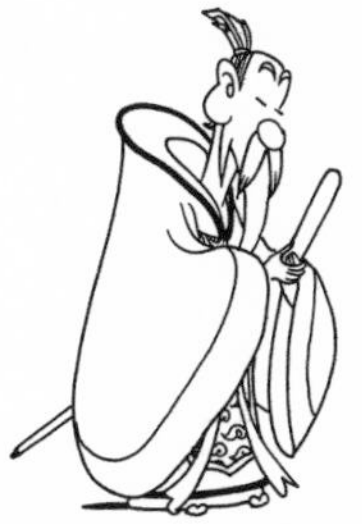

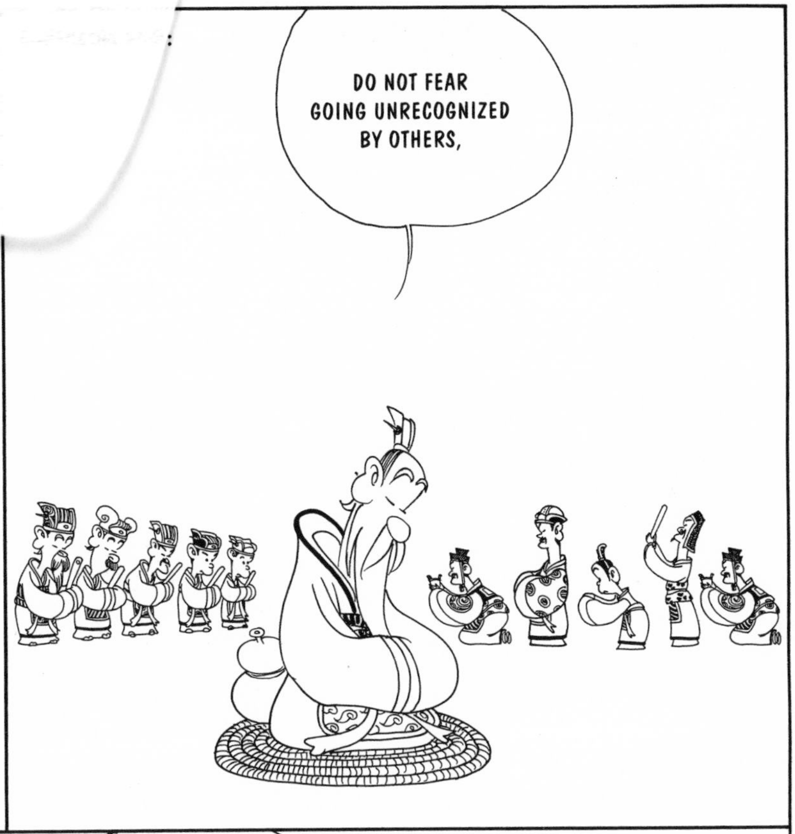
DO NOT FEAR GOING UNRECOGNIZED BY OTHERS,

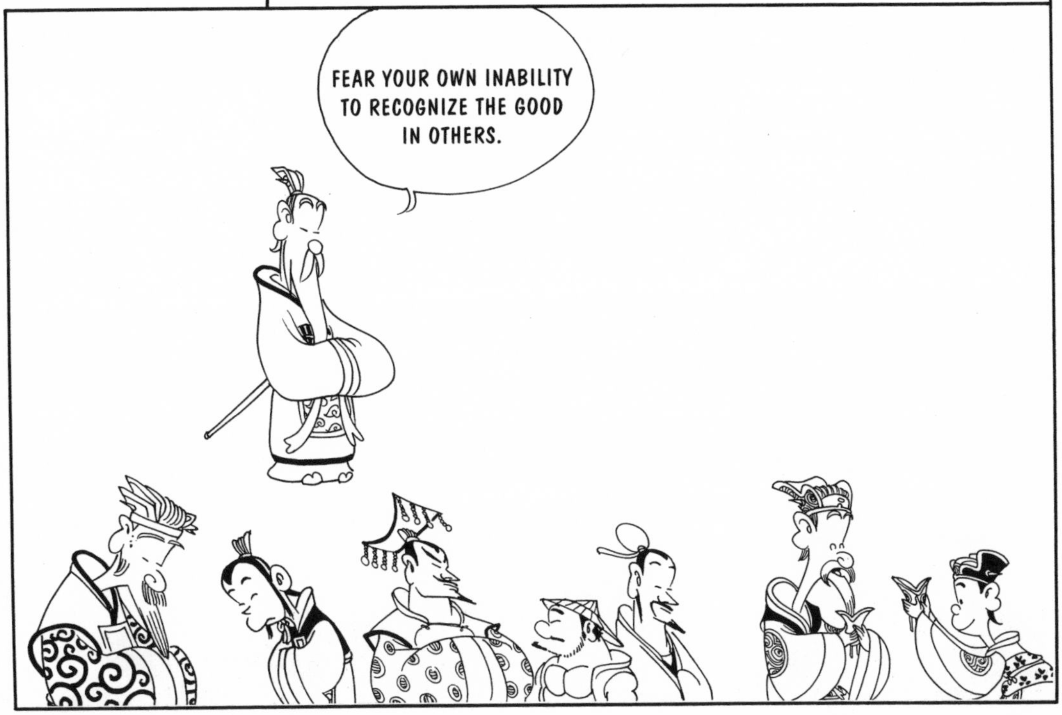
FEAR YOUR OWN INABILITY TO RECOGNIZE THE GOOD IN OTHERS.

子曰：「不患人之不己知，患不知人也。」

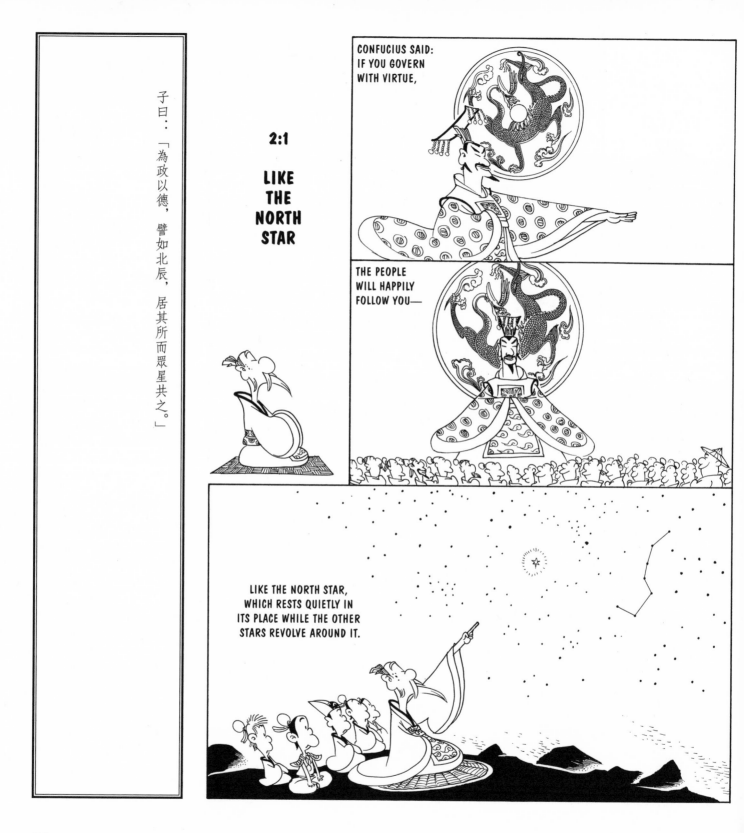

子曰：「為政以德，譬如北辰，居其所而眾星共之。」

2:1

LIKE THE NORTH STAR

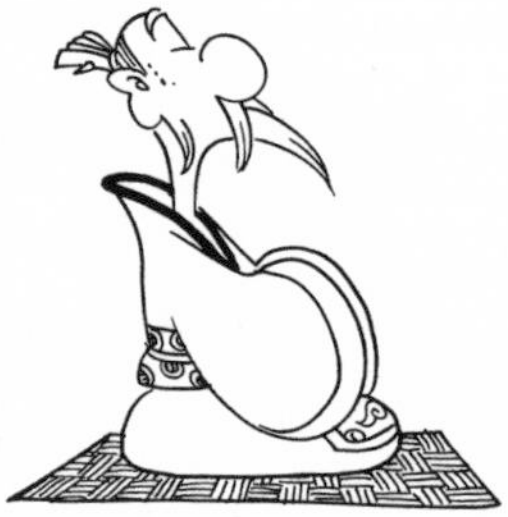

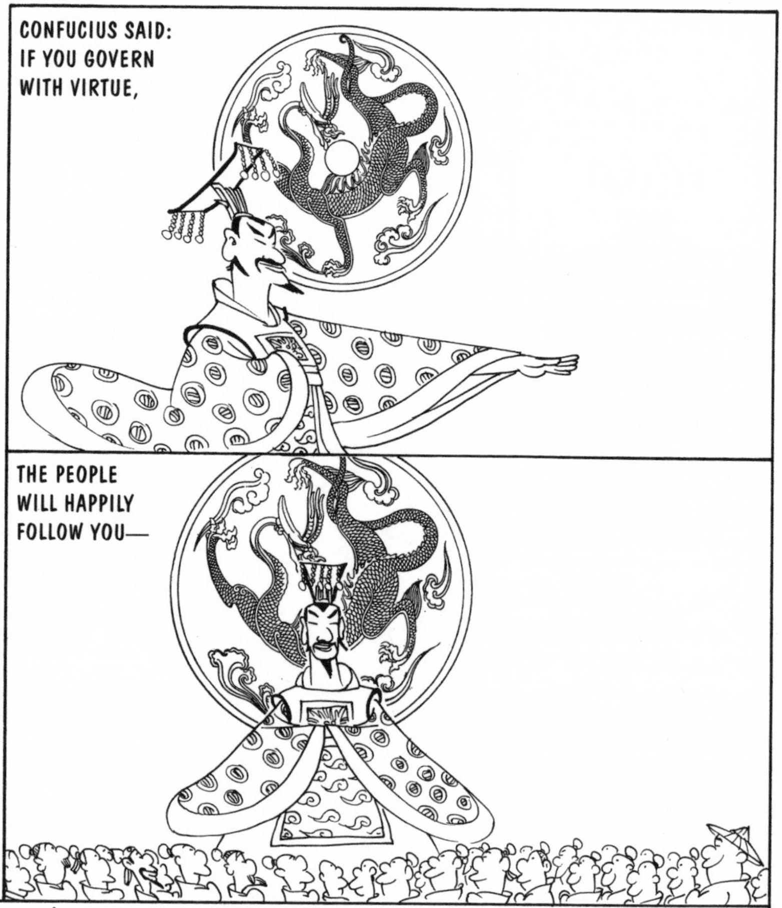
CONFUCIUS SAID: IF YOU GOVERN WITH VIRTUE,
THE PEOPLE WILL HAPPILY FOLLOW YOU—

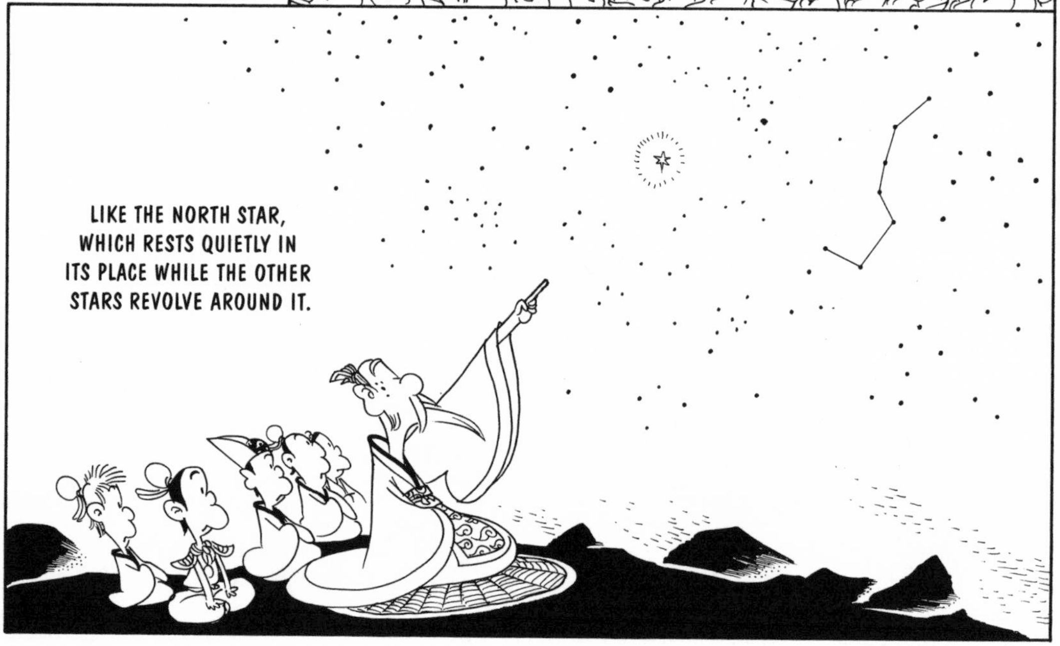
LIKE THE NORTH STAR, WHICH RESTS QUIETLY IN ITS PLACE WHILE THE OTHER STARS REVOLVE AROUND IT.

2:3

FEELING BAD

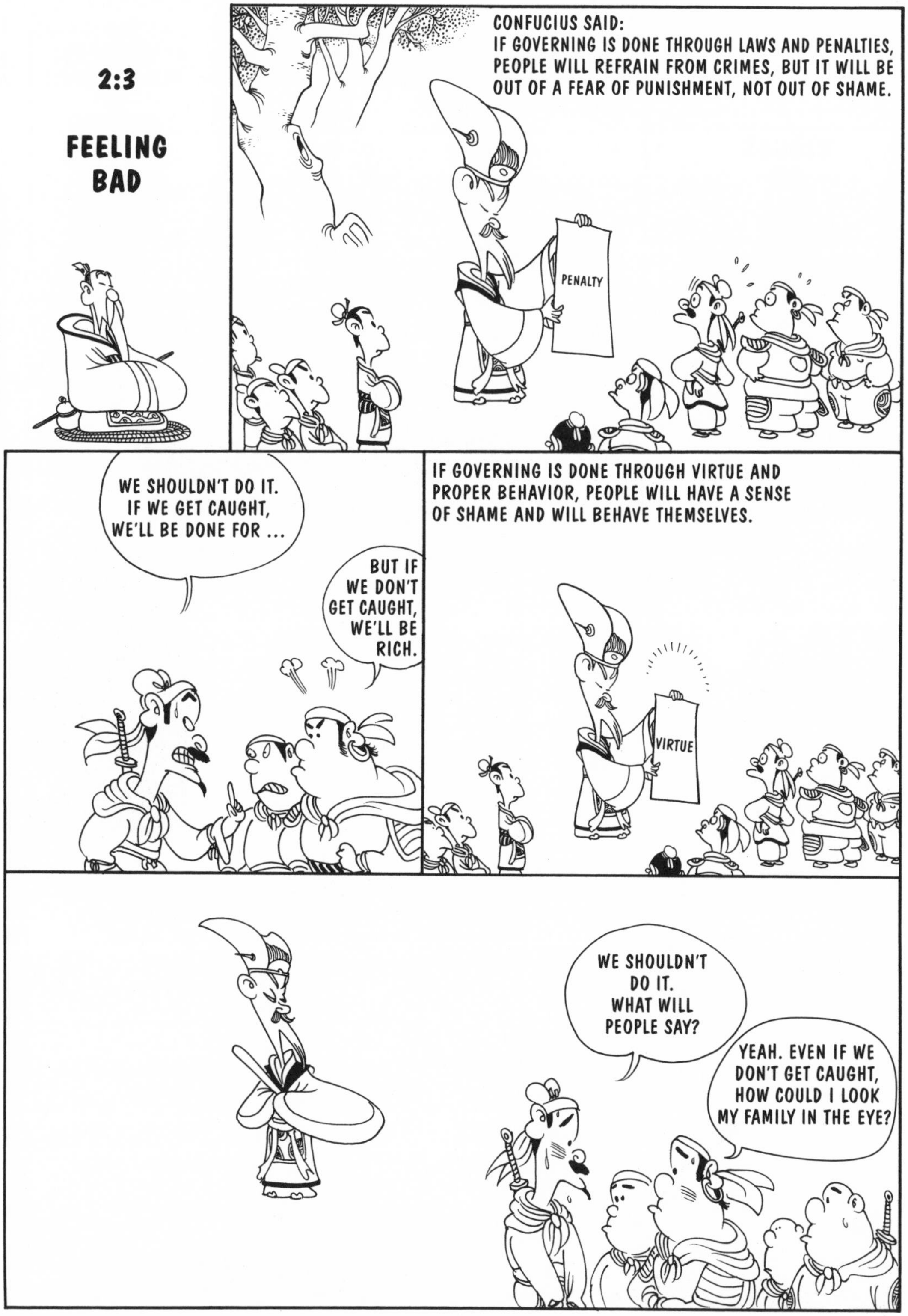
CONFUCIUS SAID:
IF GOVERNING IS DONE THROUGH LAWS AND PENALTIES, PEOPLE WILL REFRAIN FROM CRIMES, BUT IT WILL BE OUT OF A FEAR OF PUNISHMENT, NOT OUT OF SHAME.
PENALTY
WE SHOULDN'T DO IT. IF WE GET CAUGHT, WE'LL BE DONE FOR ...
BUT IF WE DON'T GET CAUGHT, WE'LL BE RICH.
IF GOVERNING IS DONE THROUGH VIRTUE AND PROPER BEHAVIOR, PEOPLE WILL HAVE A SENSE OF SHAME AND WILL BEHAVE THEMSELVES.
VIRTUE
WE SHOULDN'T DO IT. WHAT WILL PEOPLE SAY?
YEAH. EVEN IF WE DON'T GET CAUGHT, HOW COULD I LOOK MY FAMILY IN THE EYE?

子曰：「道之以政，齊之以刑，民免而無恥；道之以德，齊之以禮，有恥且格。」

「吾十有五而志于學，三十而立，四十而不惑，五十而知天命，六十而耳順，七十而從心所欲，不踰矩。」

STAGES OF LIFE

AT FORTY, I WAS IMPERTURBABLE.

AT FIFTY, I UNDERSTOOD MY MISSION IN LIFE.

AT SIXTY, I COULD EASILY JUDGE PEOPLE BY THEIR WORDS

AND AT SEVENTY, I WAS ABLE TO ACT SPONTANEOUSLY, WITHOUT EVER CROSSING THE LINE.

2:7

FEELING FILIAL

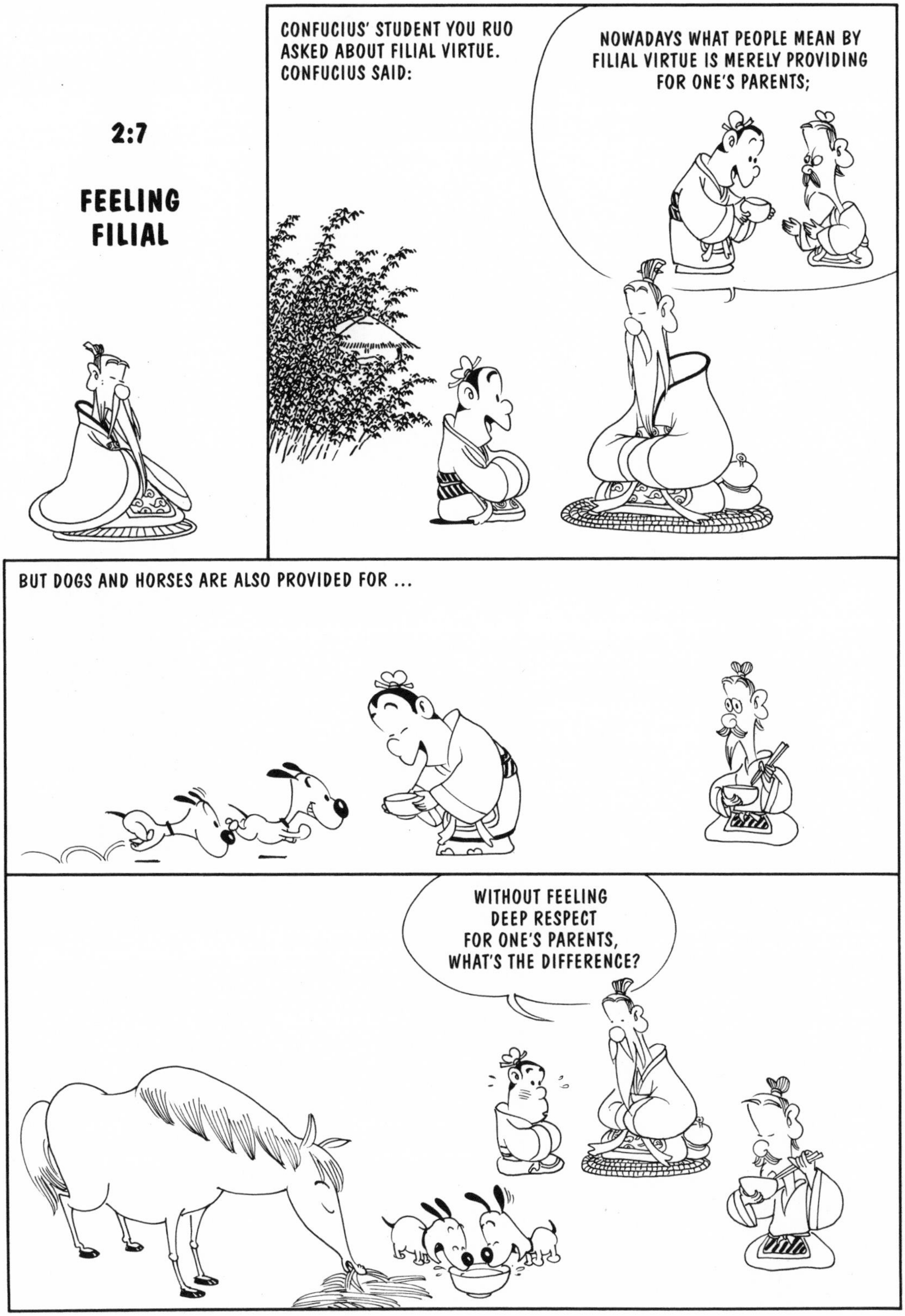
CONFUCIUS' STUDENT YOU RUO ASKED ABOUT FILIAL VIRTUE. CONFUCIUS SAID:
NOWADAYS WHAT PEOPLE MEAN BY FILIAL VIRTUE IS MERELY PROVIDING FOR ONE'S PARENTS;
BUT DOGS AND HORSES ARE ALSO PROVIDED FOR ...
WITHOUT FEELING DEEP RESPECT FOR ONE'S PARENTS, WHAT'S THE DIFFERENCE?

問孝。子曰：「今之孝者，是謂能養。至於犬馬，皆能有養；不敬，何以別乎？」

子曰：「溫故而知新，可以為師矣。」

2:11

BECOMING A TEACHER

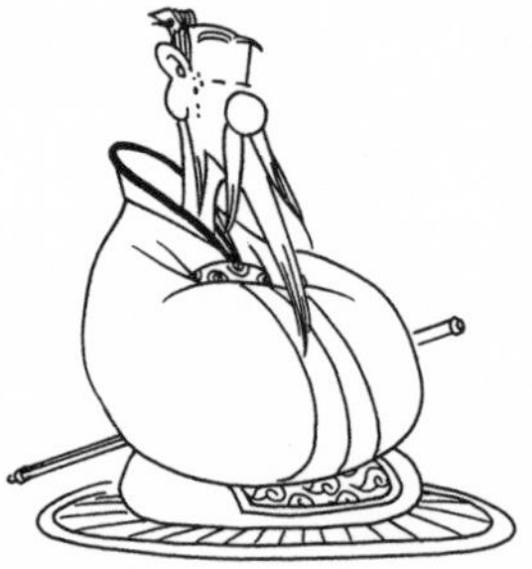

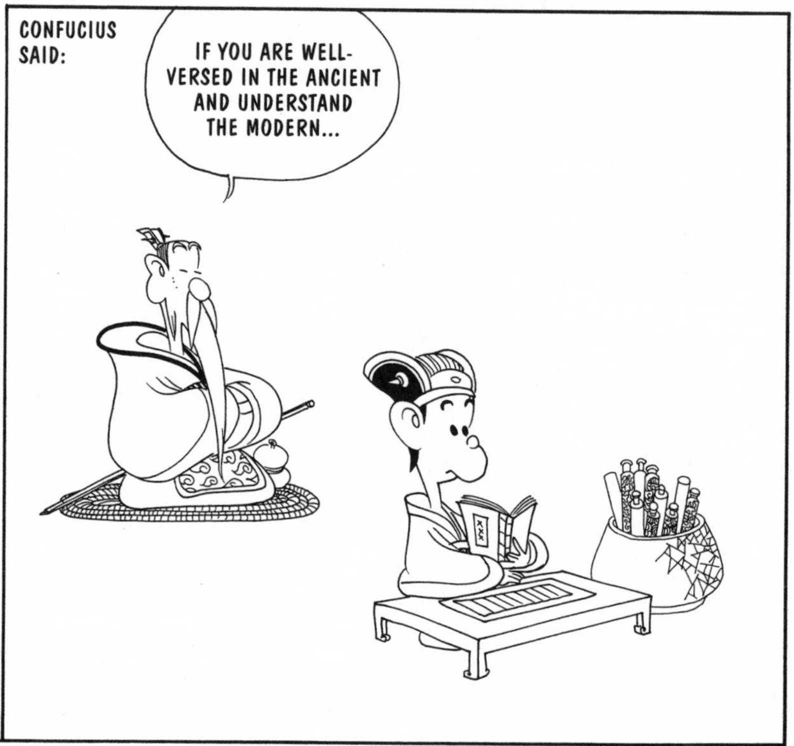
CONFUCIUS SAID:
IF YOU ARE WELL-VERSED IN THE ANCIENT AND UNDERSTAND THE MODERN...

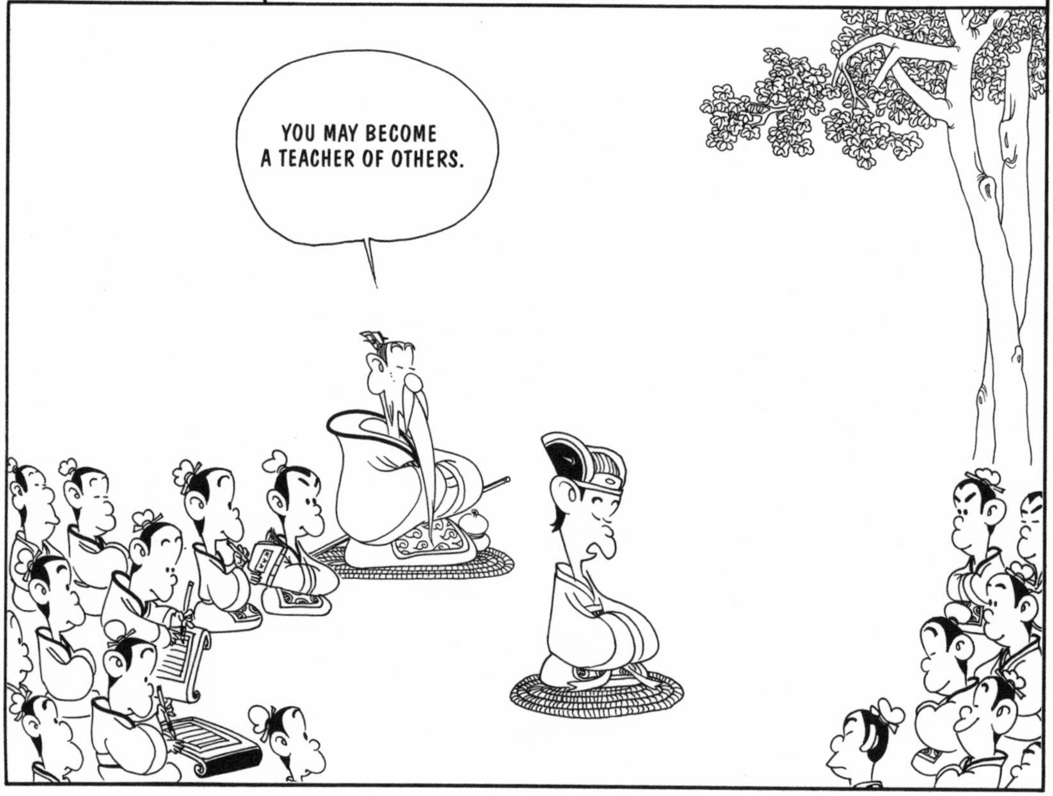
YOU MAY BECOME A TEACHER OF OTHERS.

2:13

WORDS AND ACTIONS

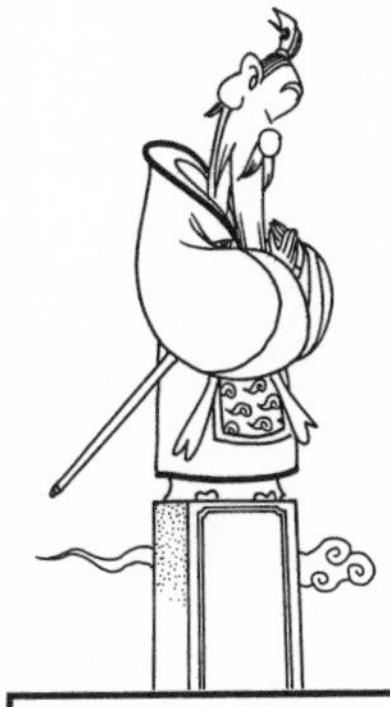

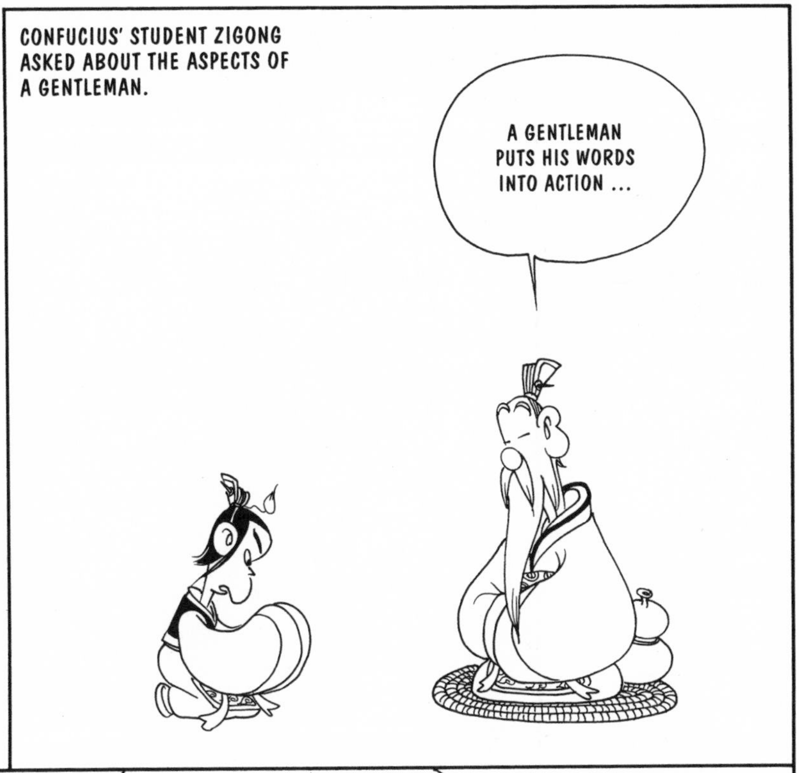
CONFUCIUS' STUDENT ZIGONG ASKED ABOUT THE ASPECTS OF A GENTLEMAN.
A GENTLEMAN PUTS HIS WORDS INTO ACTION ...

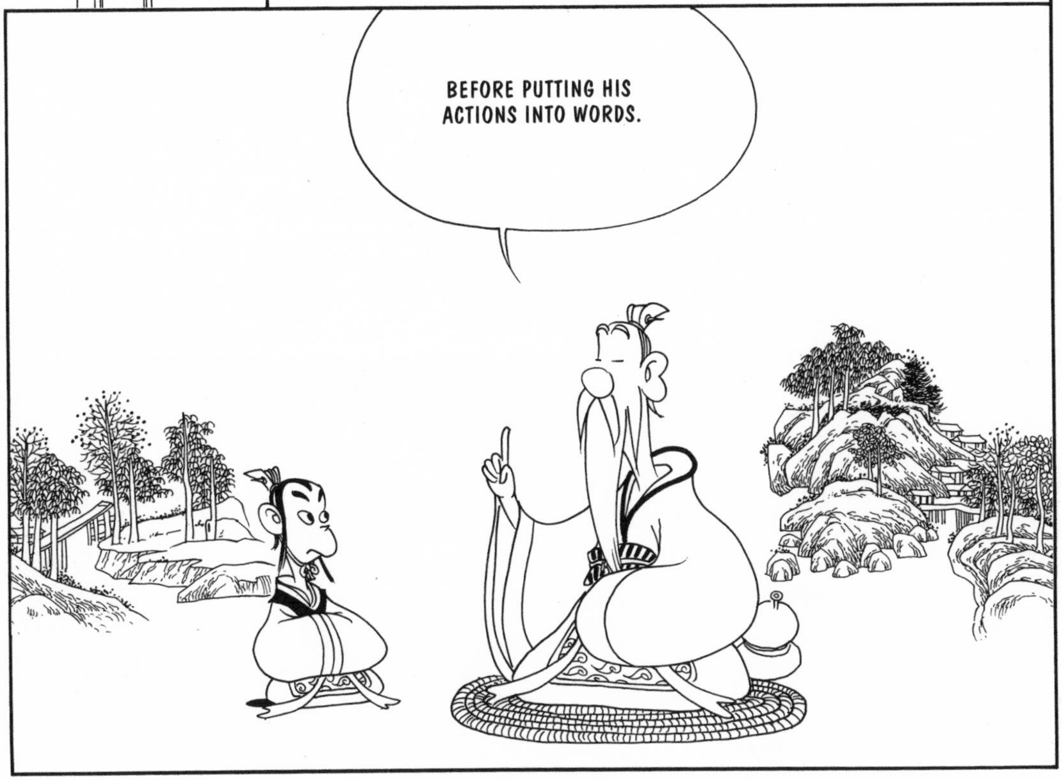
BEFORE PUTTING HIS ACTIONS INTO WORDS.

子貢問君子。子曰：「先行其言而後從之。」

子曰：「君子周而不比，小人比而不周。」

2:14

NON-PARTISAN

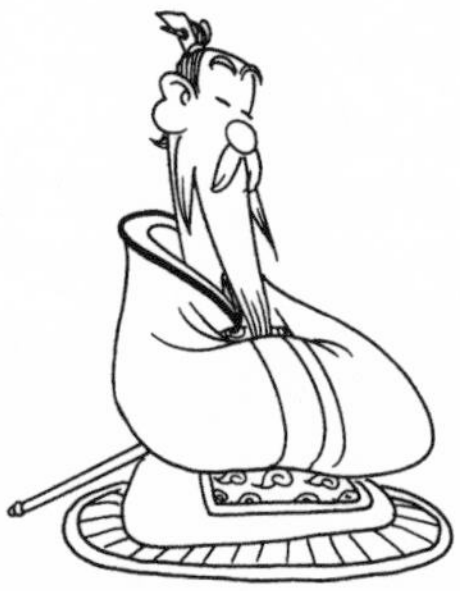

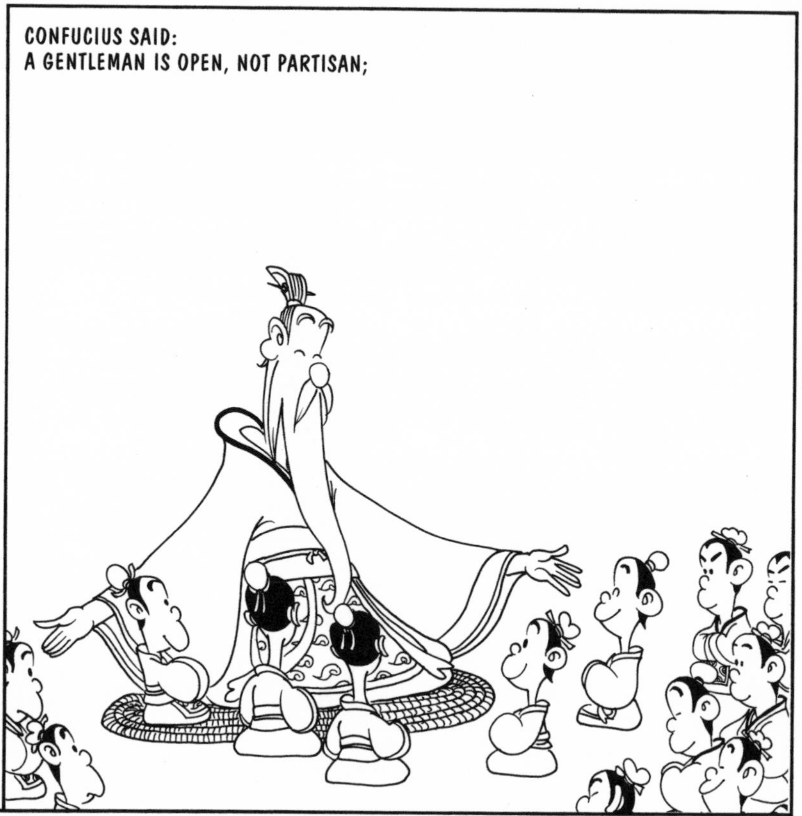
CONFUCIUS SAID:
A GENTLEMAN IS OPEN, NOT PARTISAN;

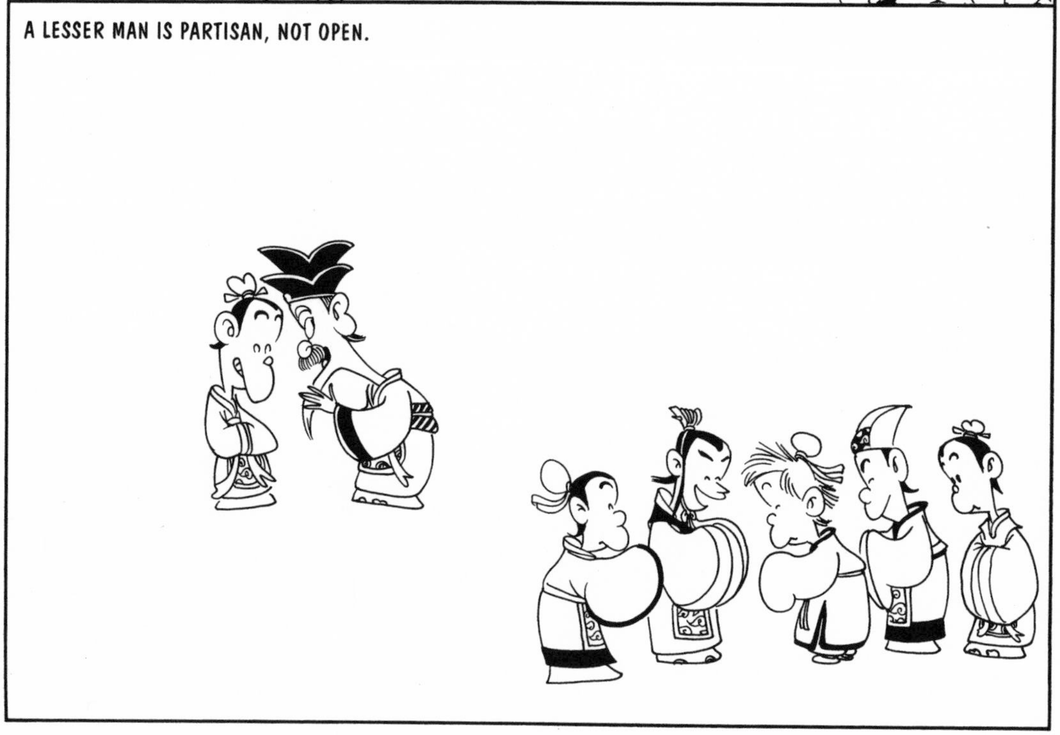
A LESSER MAN IS PARTISAN, NOT OPEN.

2:15

STUDY AND REFLECTION

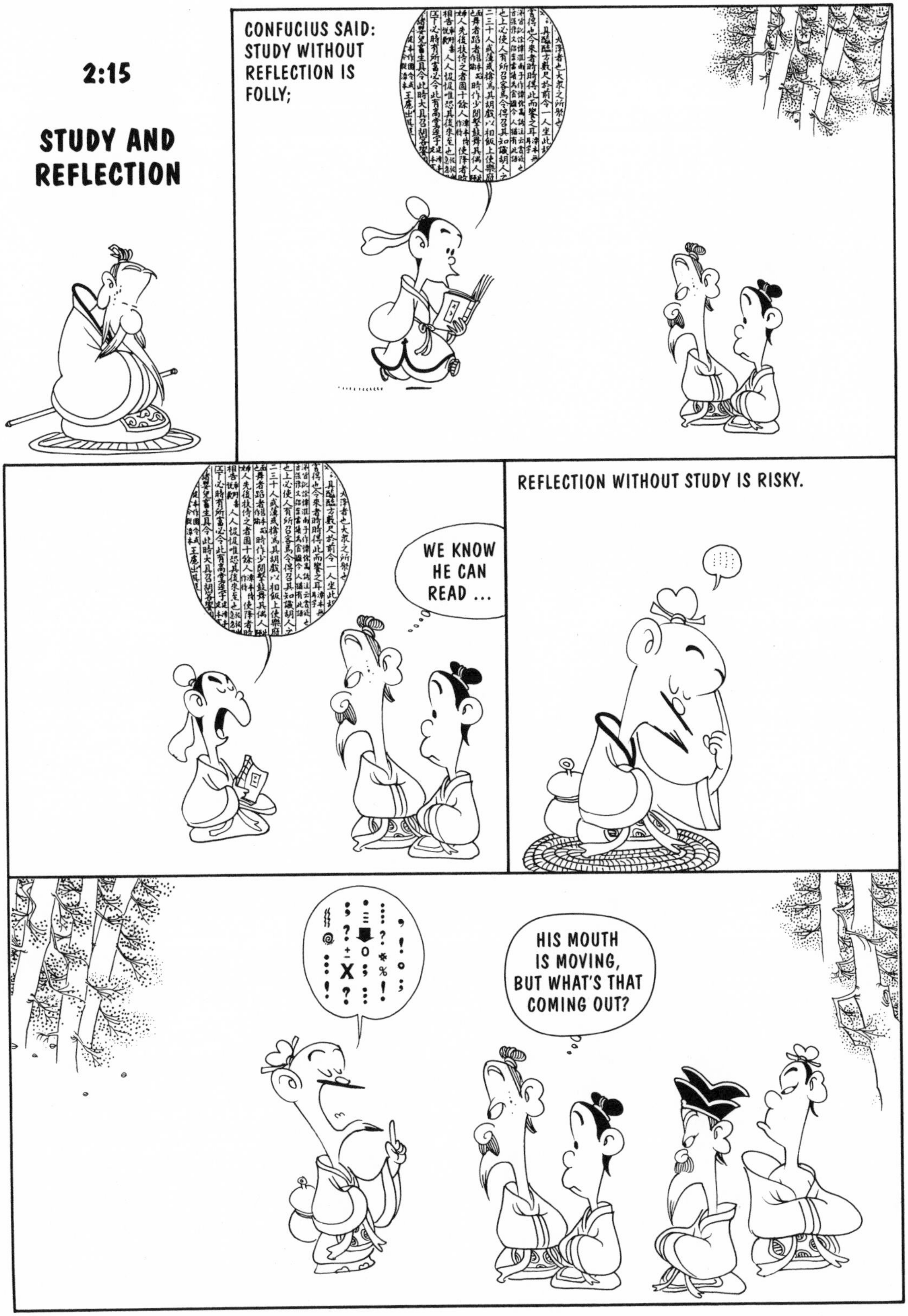

CONFUCIUS SAID: STUDY WITHOUT REFLECTION IS FOLLY;
WE KNOW HE CAN READ ...
REFLECTION WITHOUT STUDY IS RISKY.
HIS MOUTH IS MOVING, BUT WHAT'S THAT COMING OUT?

子曰：「學而不思則罔，思而不學則殆。」

子曰：「攻乎異端，斯害也已。」

2:16

THE CULT FIGURE

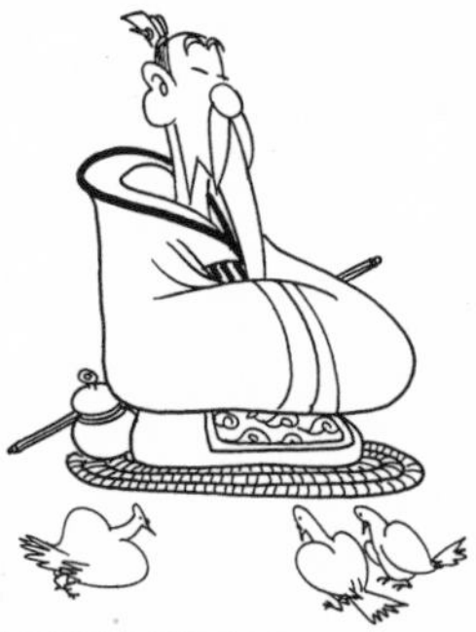

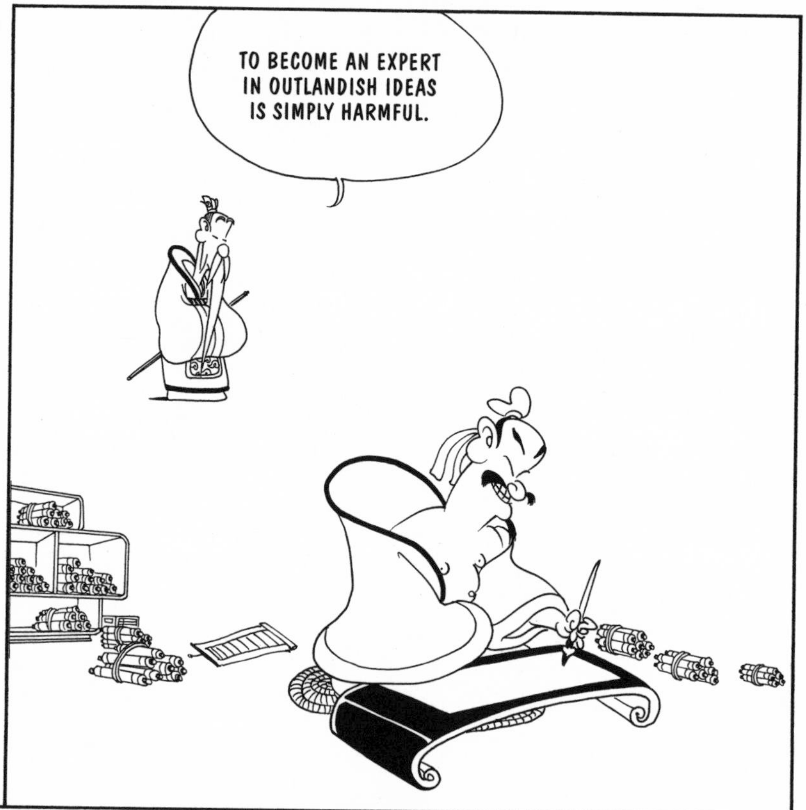
TO BECOME AN EXPERT IN OUTLANDISH IDEAS IS SIMPLY HARMFUL.

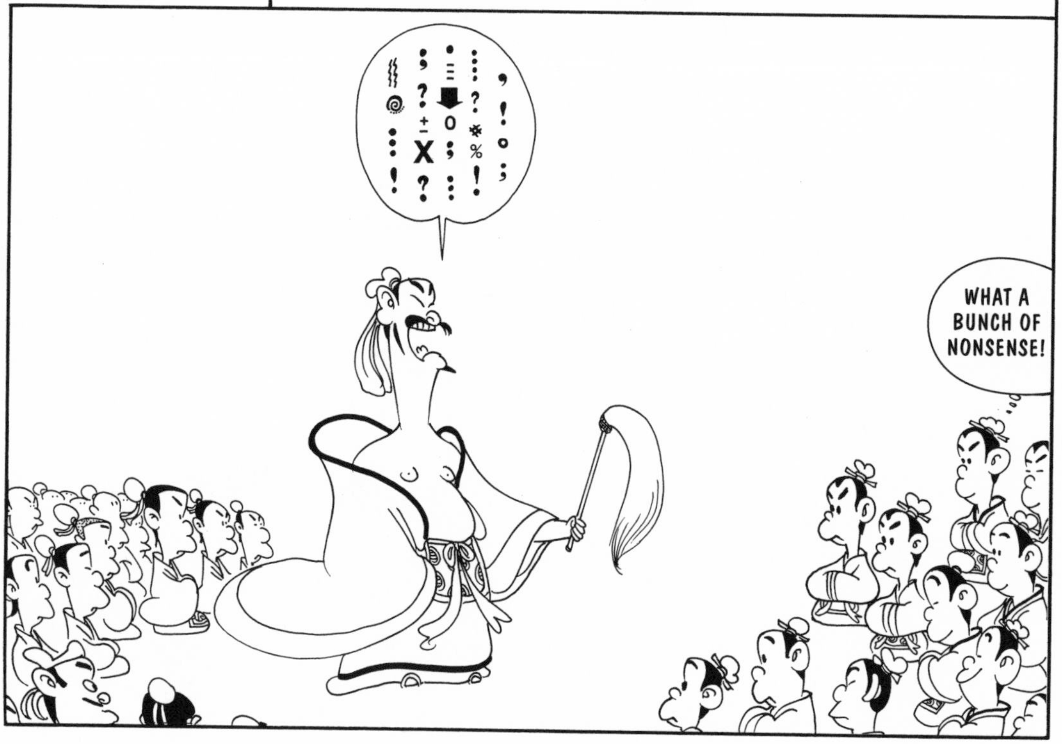
WHAT A BUNCH OF NONSENSE!

2:17

TRUE UNDERSTANDING

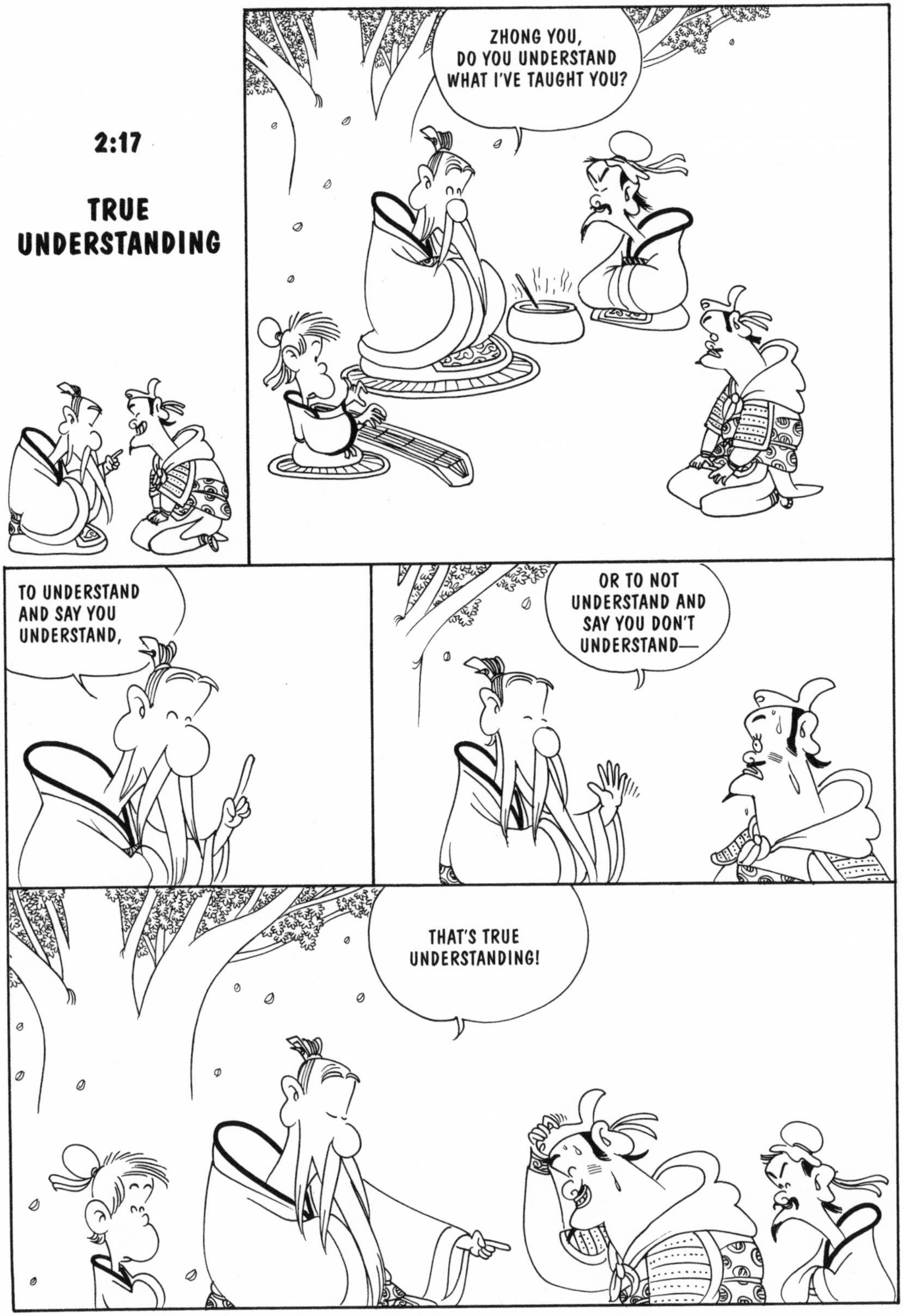
ZHONG YOU, DO YOU UNDERSTAND WHAT I'VE TAUGHT YOU?
TO UNDERSTAND AND SAY YOU UNDERSTAND,
OR TO NOT UNDERSTAND AND SAY YOU DON'T UNDERSTAND—
THAT'S TRUE UNDERSTANDING!

子曰：「由！誨女知之乎！知之為知之，不知為不知，是知也。」

子曰：「君子無所爭。必也射乎！揖讓而升，下而飲。其爭也君子。」

3:7

HOW A GENTLEMAN CONTENDS

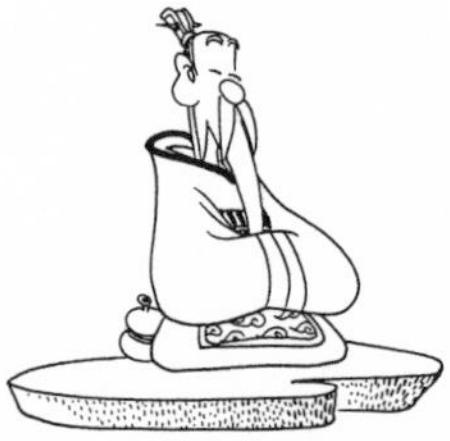

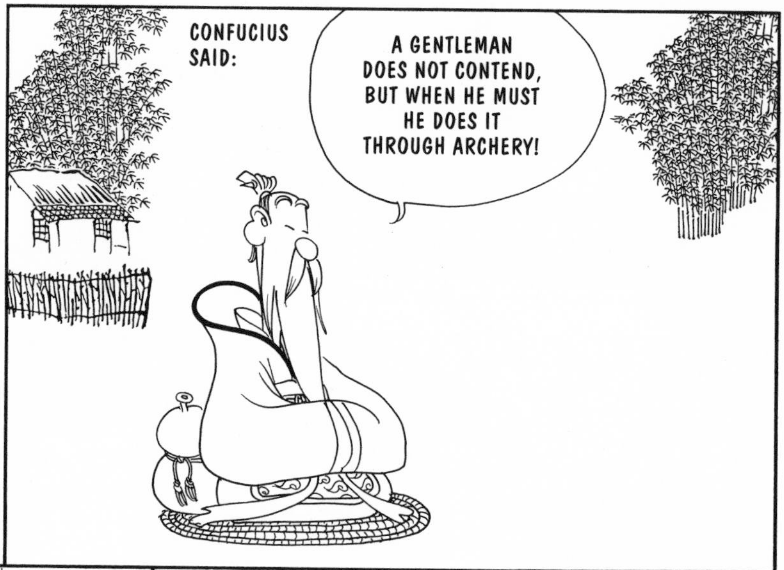
CONFUCIUS SAID:
A GENTLEMAN DOES NOT CONTEND, BUT WHEN HE MUST HE DOES IT THROUGH ARCHERY!

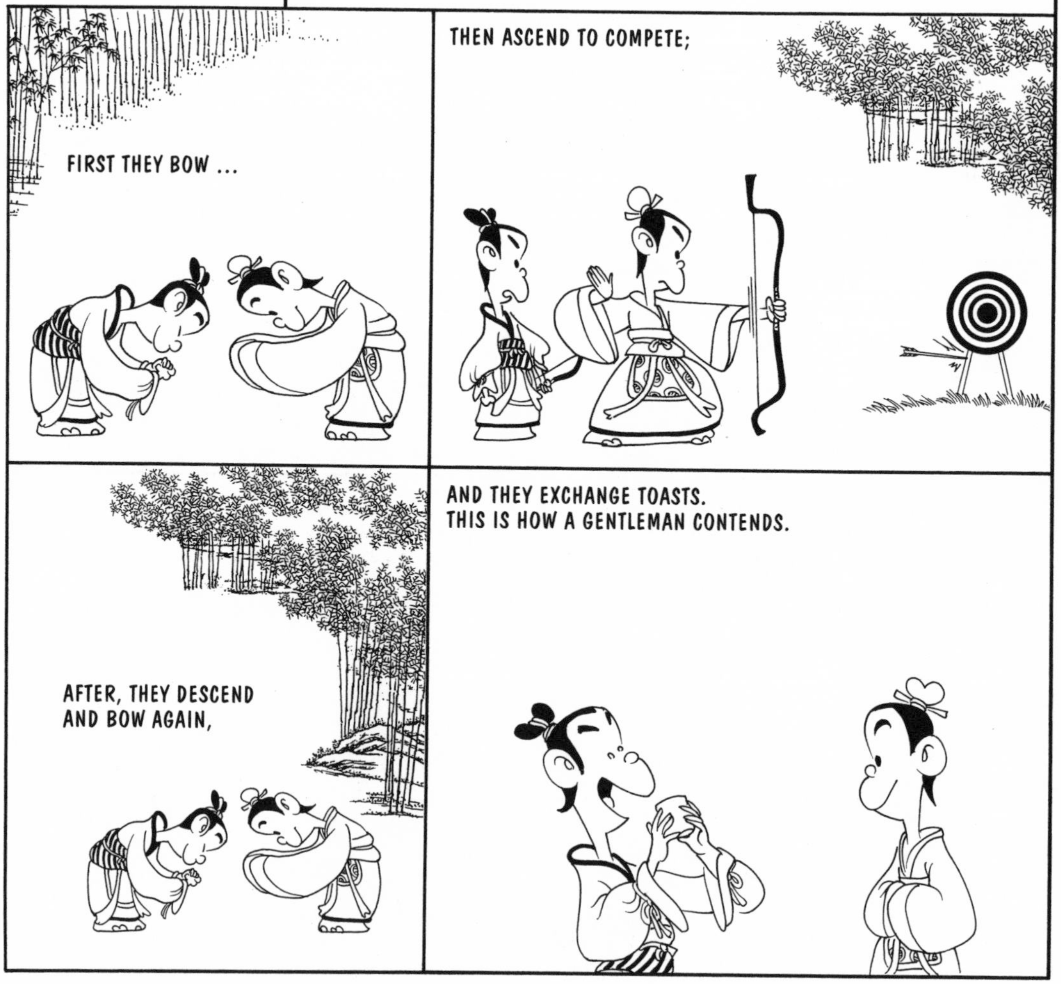
FIRST THEY BOW ...
THEN ASCEND TO COMPETE;
AFTER, THEY DESCEND AND BOW AGAIN,
AND THEY EXCHANGE TOASTS.
THIS IS HOW A GENTLEMAN CONTENDS.

3:15

PROPER CEREMONY

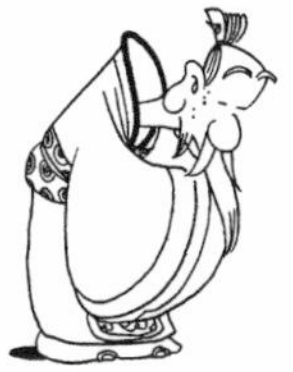

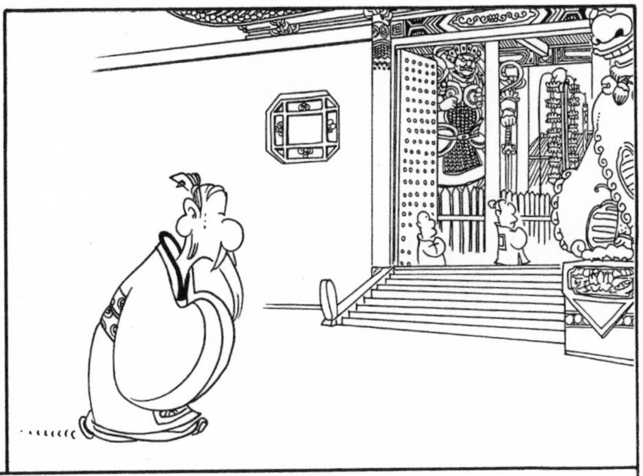

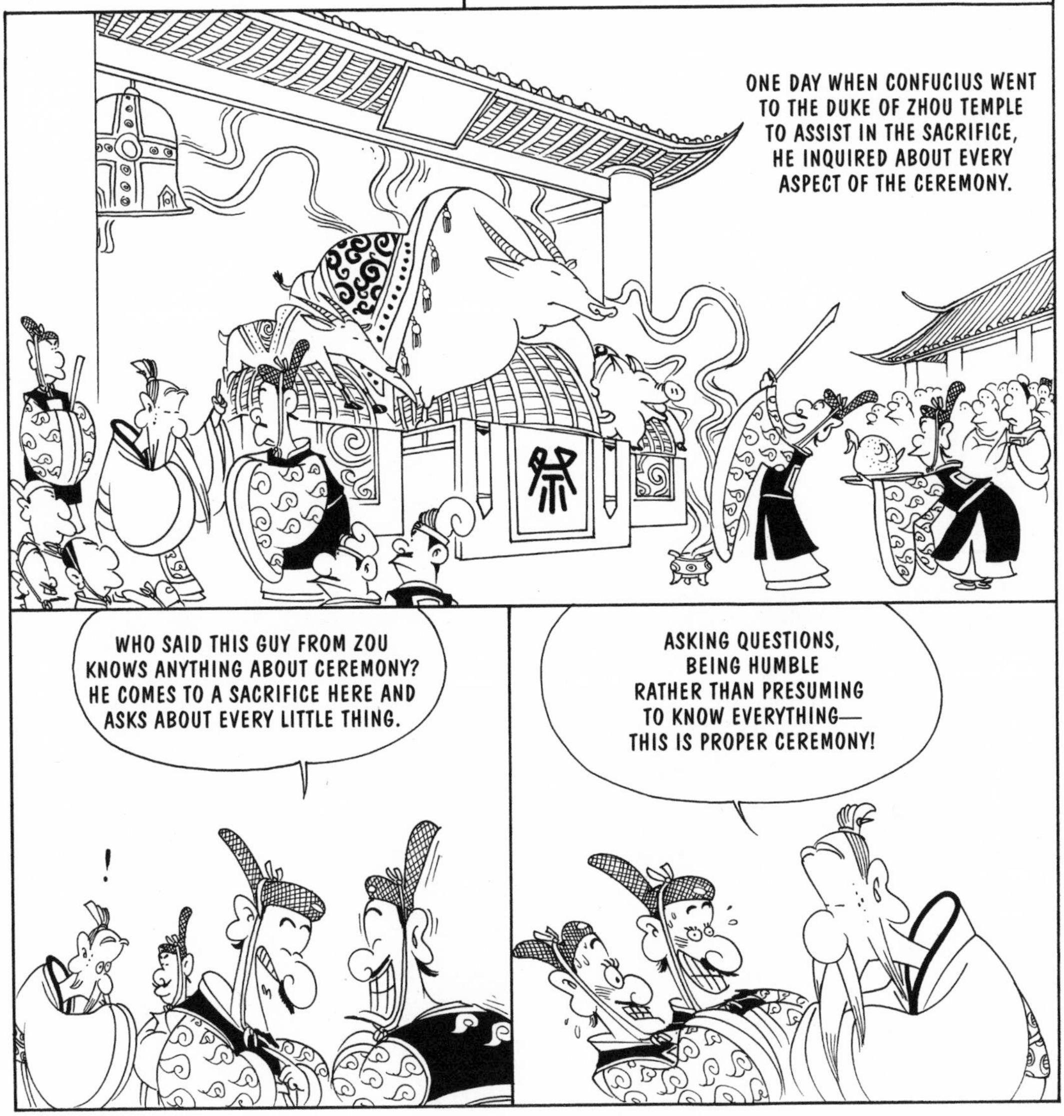
ONE DAY WHEN CONFUCIUS WENT TO THE DUKE OF ZHOU TEMPLE TO ASSIST IN THE SACRIFICE, HE INQUIRED ABOUT EVERY ASPECT OF THE CEREMONY.
祭
WHO SAID THIS GUY FROM ZOU KNOWS ANYTHING ABOUT CEREMONY? HE COMES TO A SACRIFICE HERE AND ASKS ABOUT EVERY LITTLE THING.
!
ASKING QUESTIONS, BEING HUMBLE RATHER THAN PRESUMING TO KNOW EVERYTHING—THIS IS PROPER CEREMONY!

子入太廟，每事問。或曰：「孰謂鄹人之子知禮乎？入太廟，每事問。」子聞之，曰：「是禮也。」

子貢欲去告朔之餼羊。子曰：「賜也！爾愛其羊，我愛其禮。」

3:17

THE SACRIFICIAL GOAT

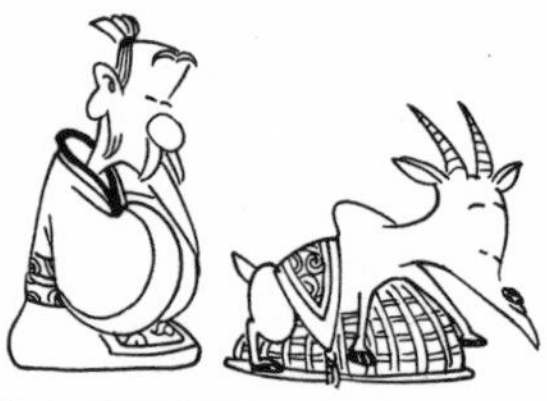

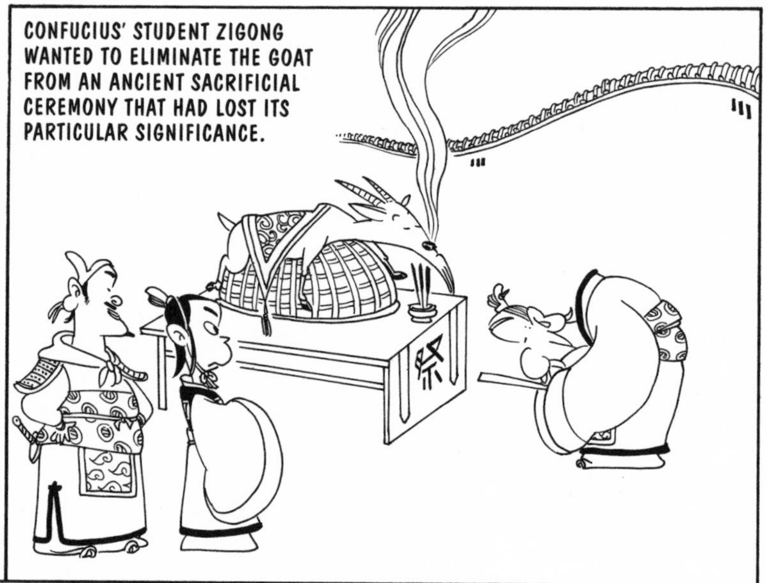
CONFUCIUS' STUDENT ZIGONG WANTED TO ELIMINATE THE GOAT FROM AN ANCIENT SACRIFICIAL CEREMONY THAT HAD LOST ITS PARTICULAR SIGNIFICANCE.
祭

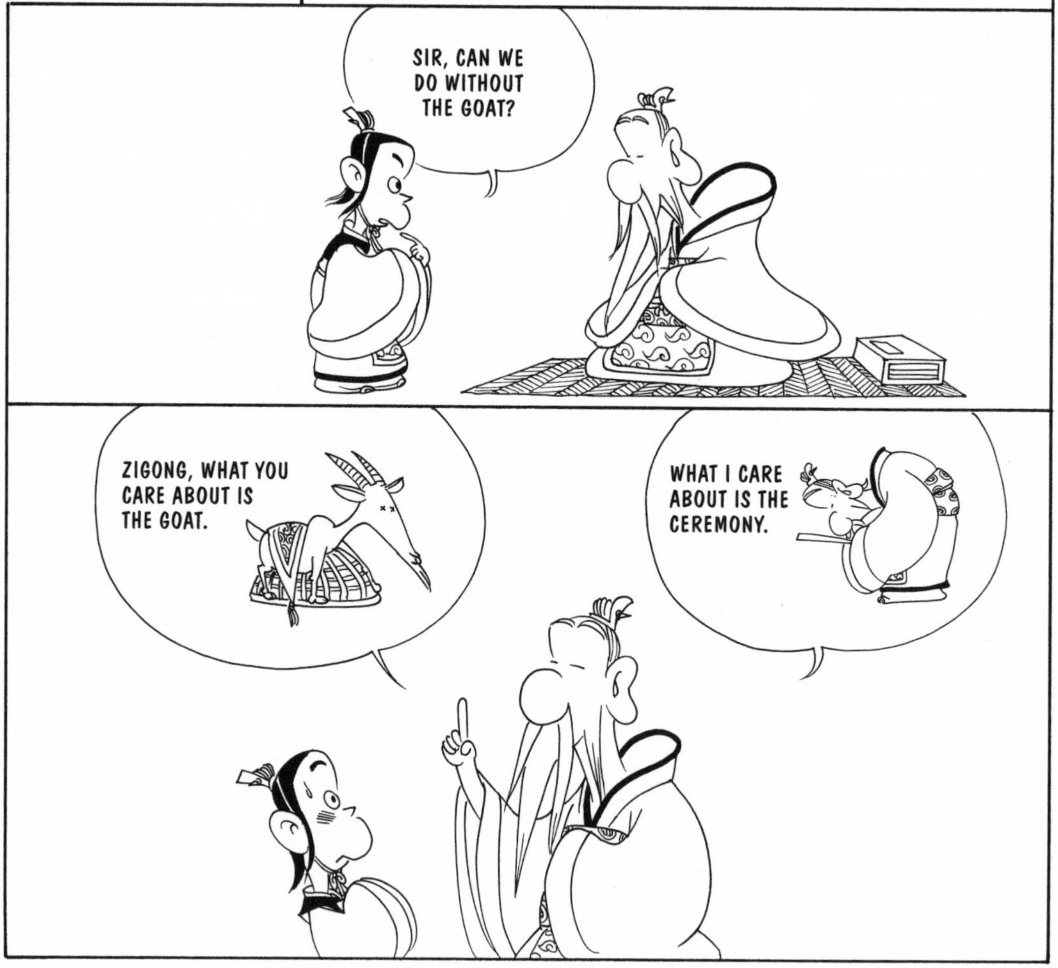
SIR, CAN WE DO WITHOUT THE GOAT?
ZIGONG, WHAT YOU CARE ABOUT IS THE GOAT.
WHAT I CARE ABOUT IS THE CEREMONY.

3:19

SOVEREIGNS AND MINISTERS

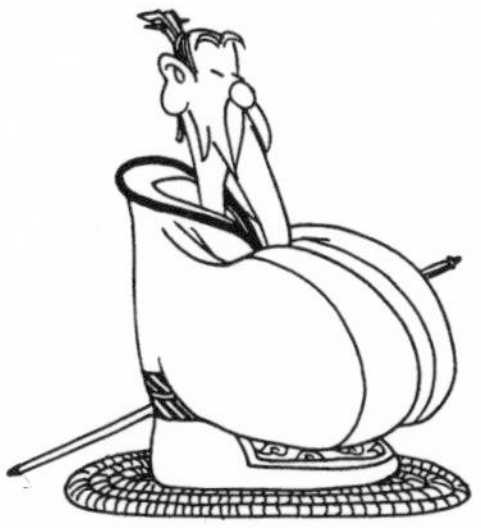

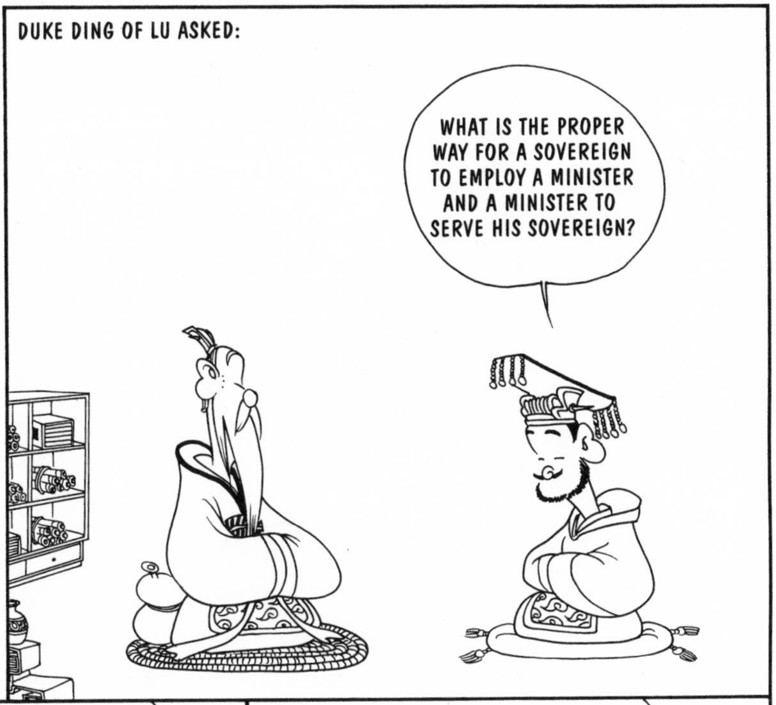
DUKE DING OF LU ASKED:
WHAT IS THE PROPER WAY FOR A SOVEREIGN TO EMPLOY A MINISTER AND A MINISTER TO SERVE HIS SOVEREIGN?

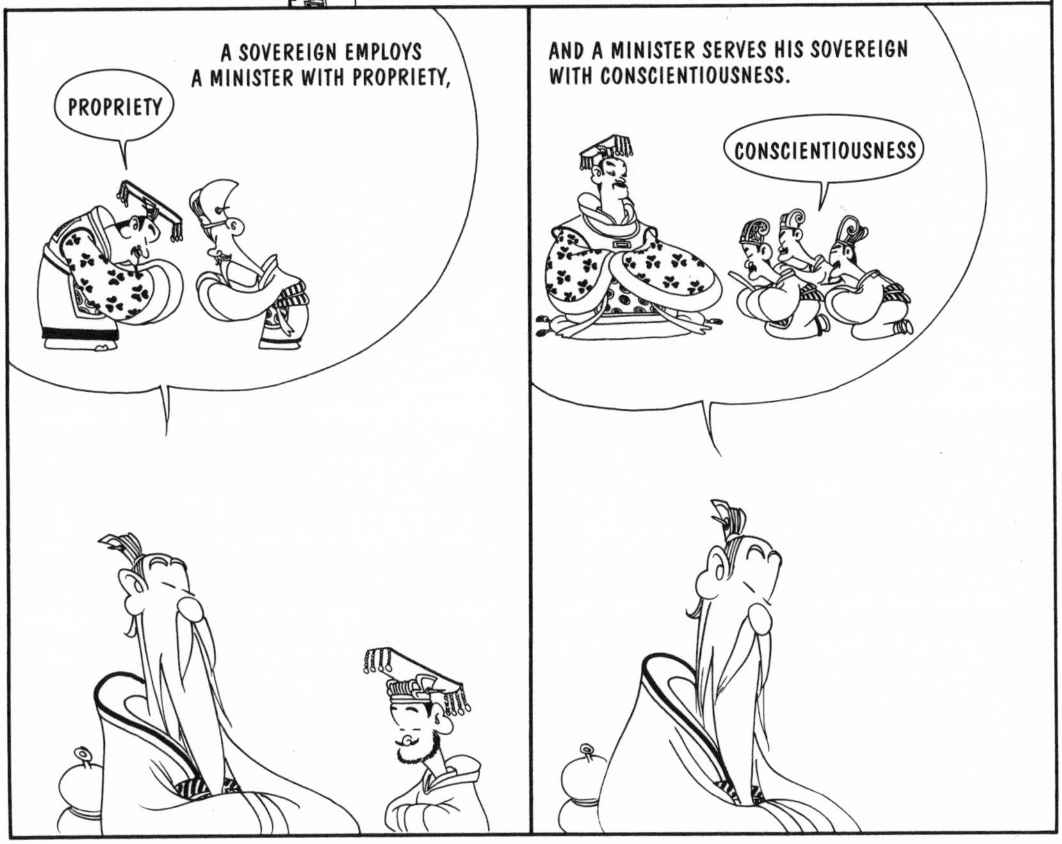
A SOVEREIGN EMPLOYS A MINISTER WITH PROPRIETY,
PROPRIETY
AND A MINISTER SERVES HIS SOVEREIGN WITH CONSCIENTIOUSNESS.
CONSCIENTIOUSNESS

定公問：「君使臣，臣事君，如之何？」孔子對曰：「君使臣以禮，臣事君以忠。」

子曰：「里仁為美。擇不處仁，焉得知？」

4:1

A BENEVOLENT NEIGHBORHOOD

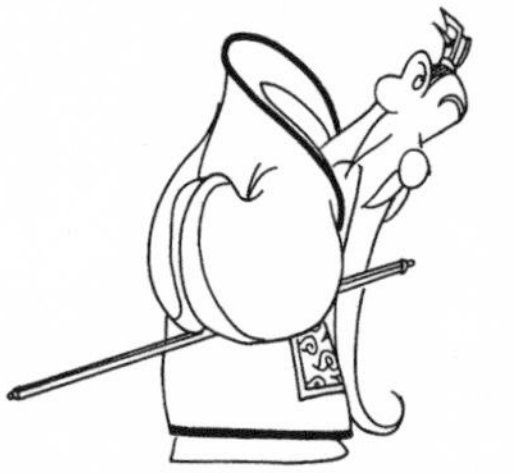

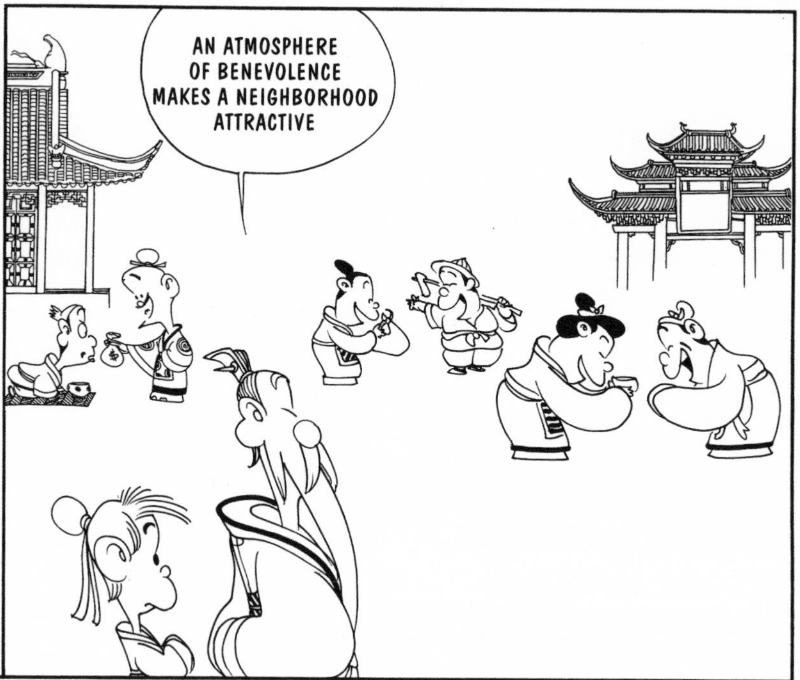
AN ATMOSPHERE OF BENEVOLENCE MAKES A NEIGHBORHOOD ATTRACTIVE

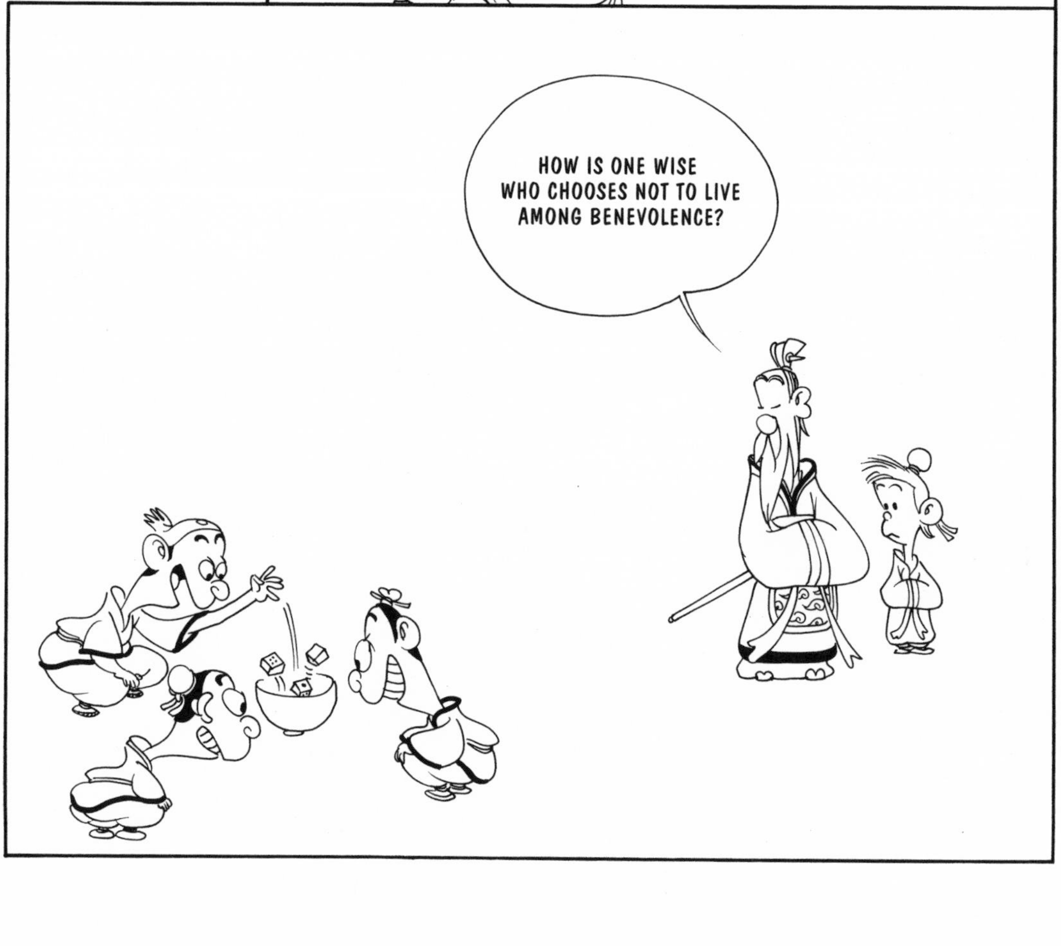
HOW IS ONE WISE WHO CHOOSES NOT TO LIVE AMONG BENEVOLENCE?

4:2

RESIDING IN BENEVOLENCE

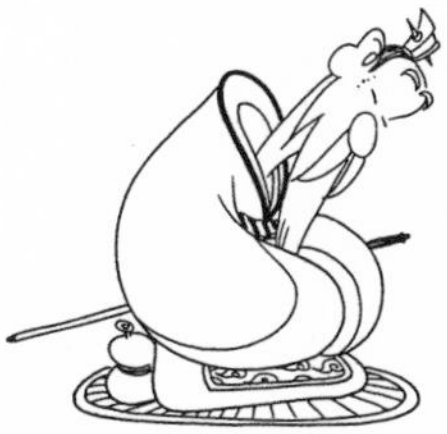

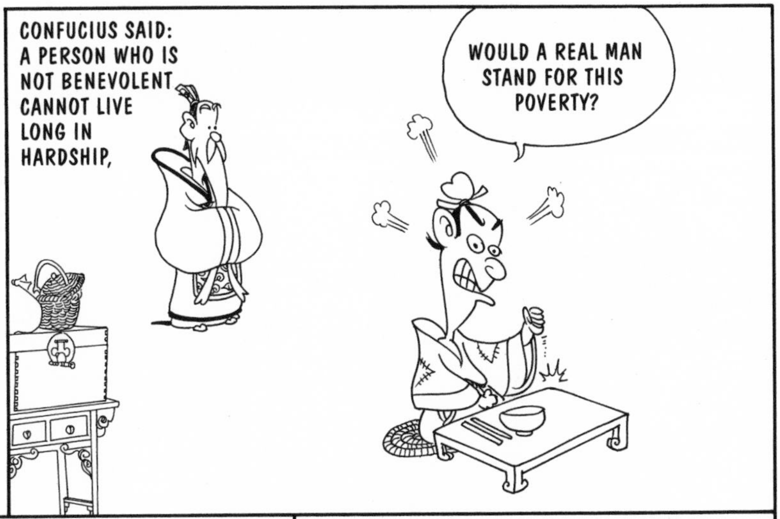
CONFUCIUS SAID: A PERSON WHO IS NOT BENEVOLENT CANNOT LIVE LONG IN HARDSHIP,
WOULD A REAL MAN STAND FOR THIS POVERTY?

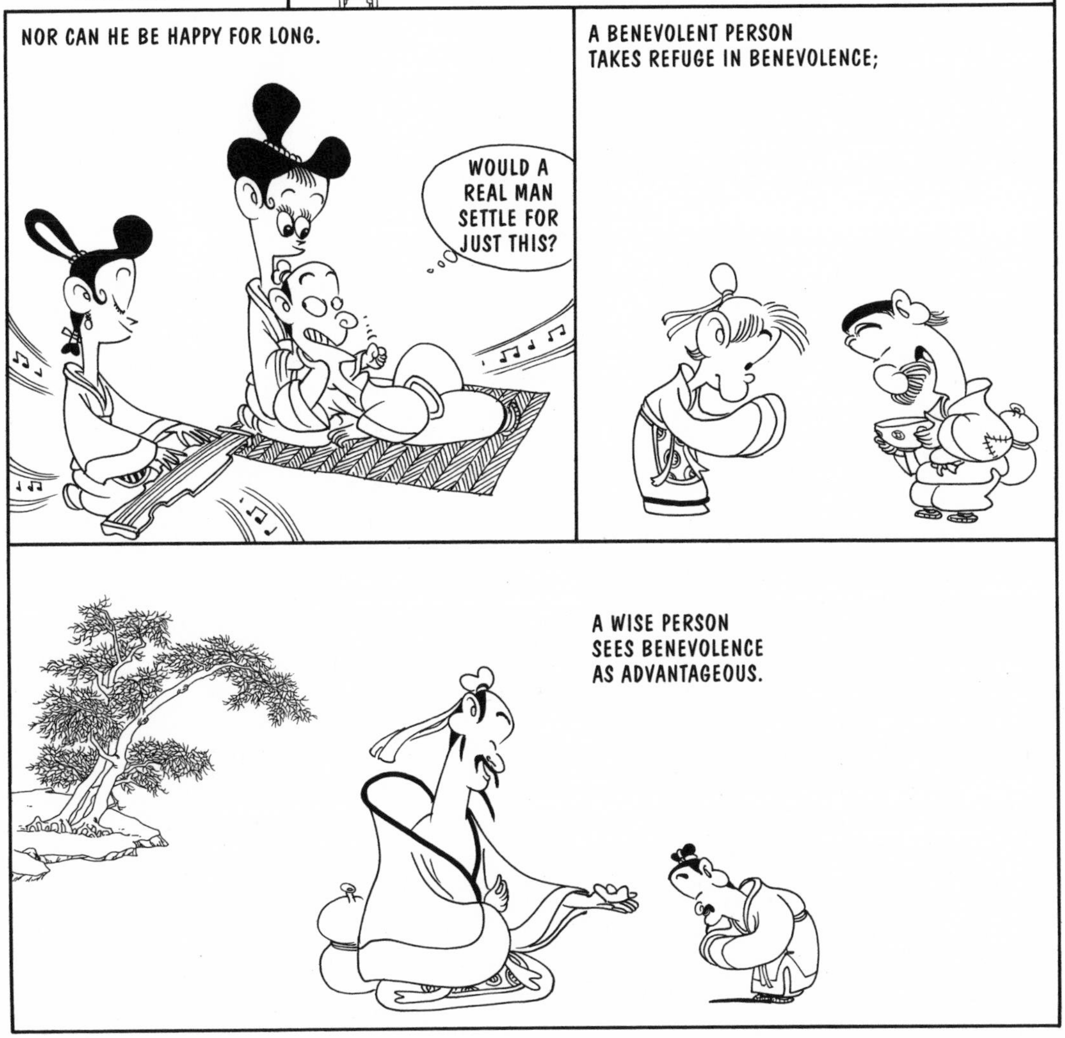
NOR CAN HE BE HAPPY FOR LONG.
WOULD A REAL MAN SETTLE FOR JUST THIS?
A BENEVOLENT PERSON TAKES REFUGE IN BENEVOLENCE;
A WISE PERSON SEES BENEVOLENCE AS ADVANTAGEOUS.

子曰：「不仁者不可以久處約，不可以長處樂。仁者安仁，知者利仁。」

子曰：「唯仁者能好人，能恶人。」

4:3

LIKING PEOPLE

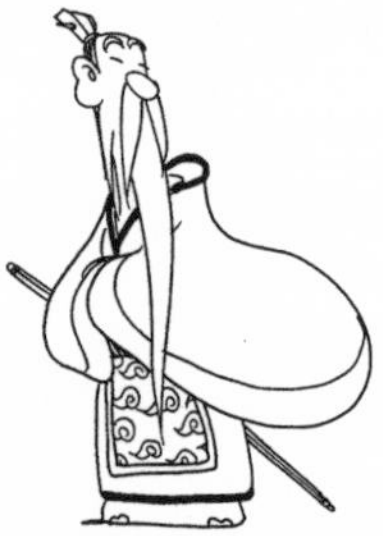

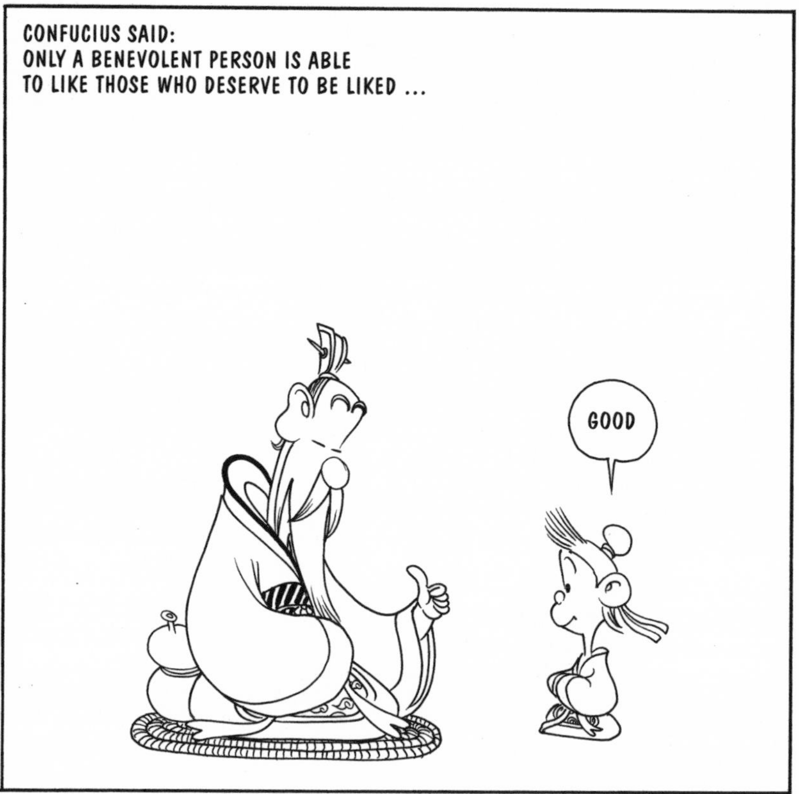
CONFUCIUS SAID:
ONLY A BENEVOLENT PERSON IS ABLE
TO LIKE THOSE WHO DESERVE TO BE LIKED ...
GOOD

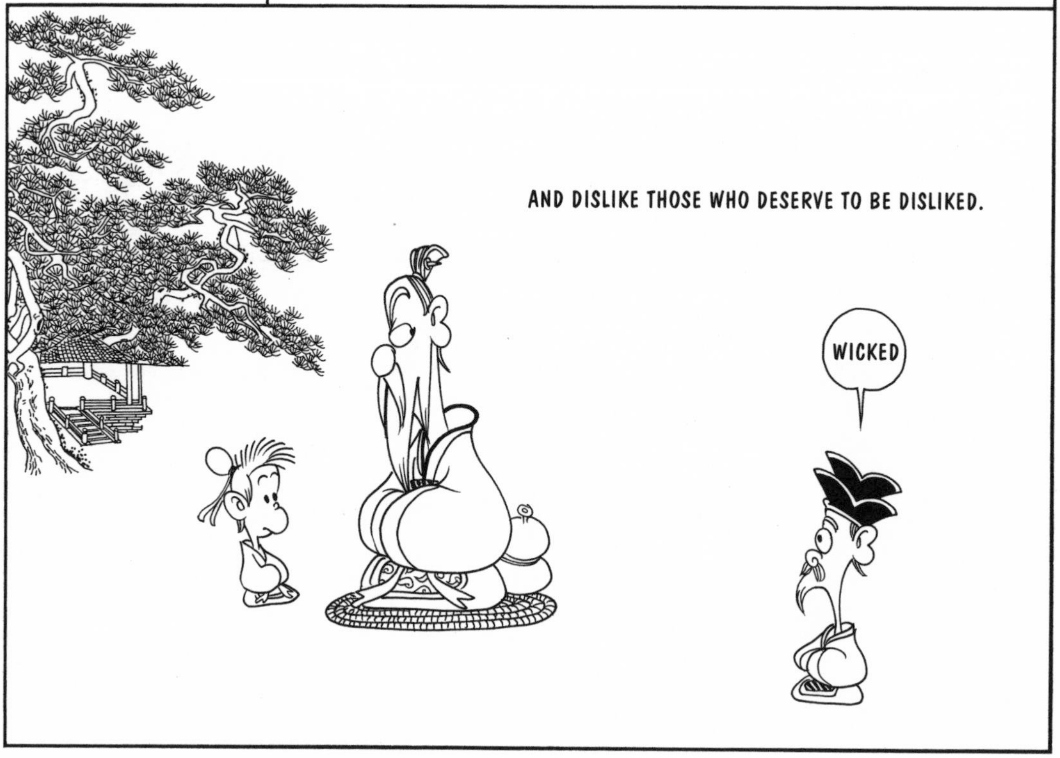
AND DISLIKE THOSE WHO DESERVE TO BE DISLIKED.
WICKED

4:4

MINDFUL BENEVOLENCE

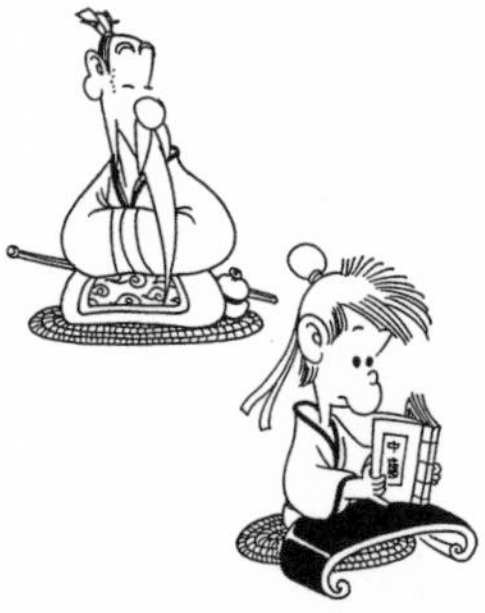

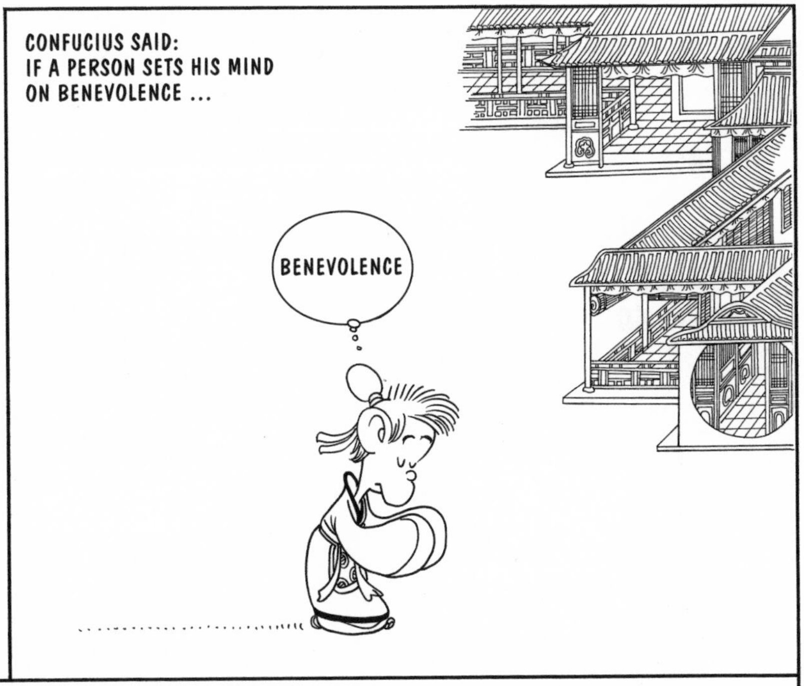

CONFUCIUS SAID:
IF A PERSON SETS HIS MIND
ON BENEVOLENCE ...
BENEVOLENCE

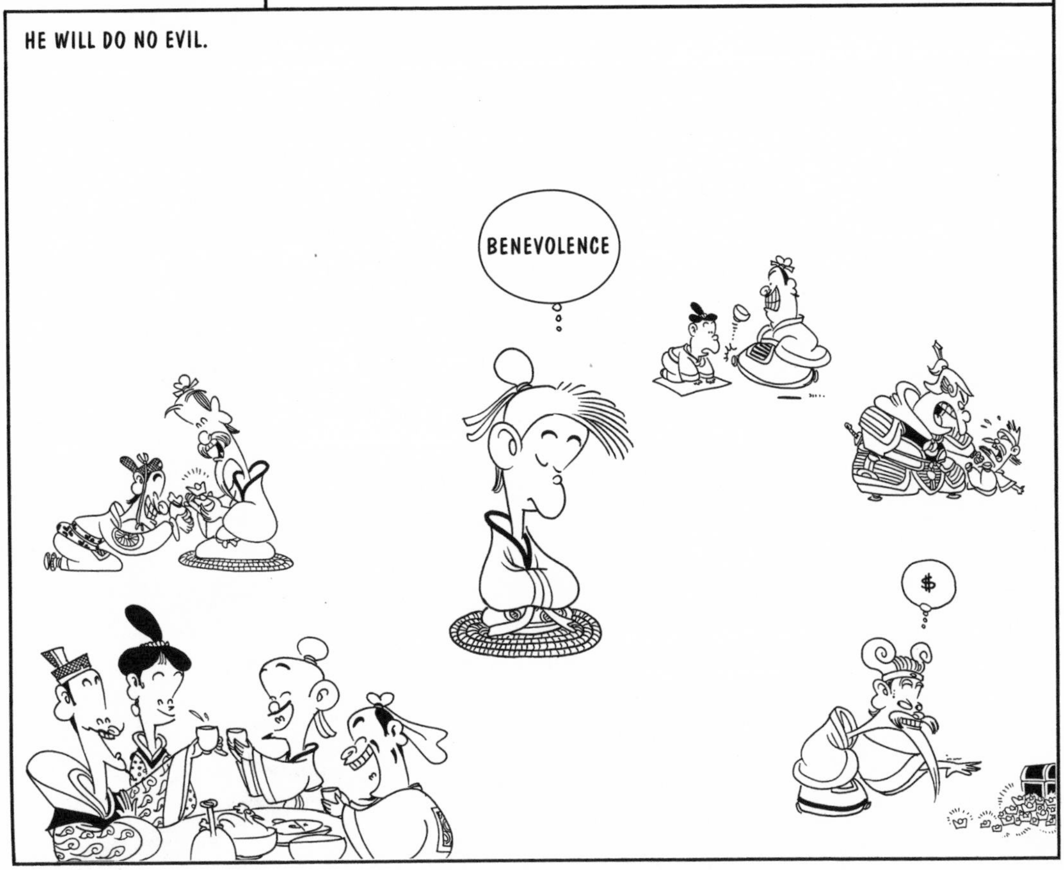

HE WILL DO NO EVIL.
BENEVOLENCE
$

子曰：「苟志於仁矣，無惡也。」

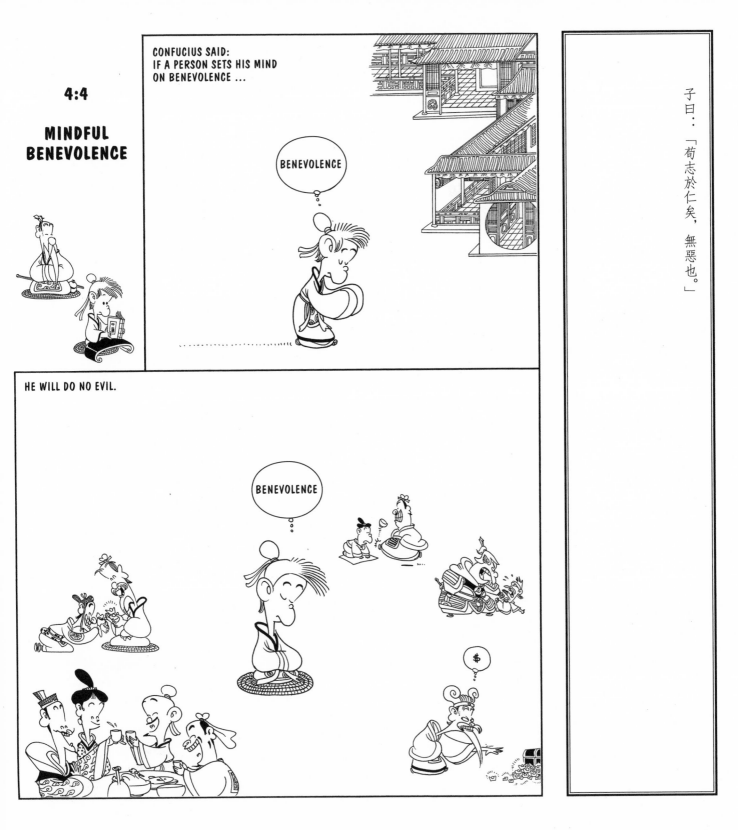

子曰：「朝聞道，夕死可矣。」

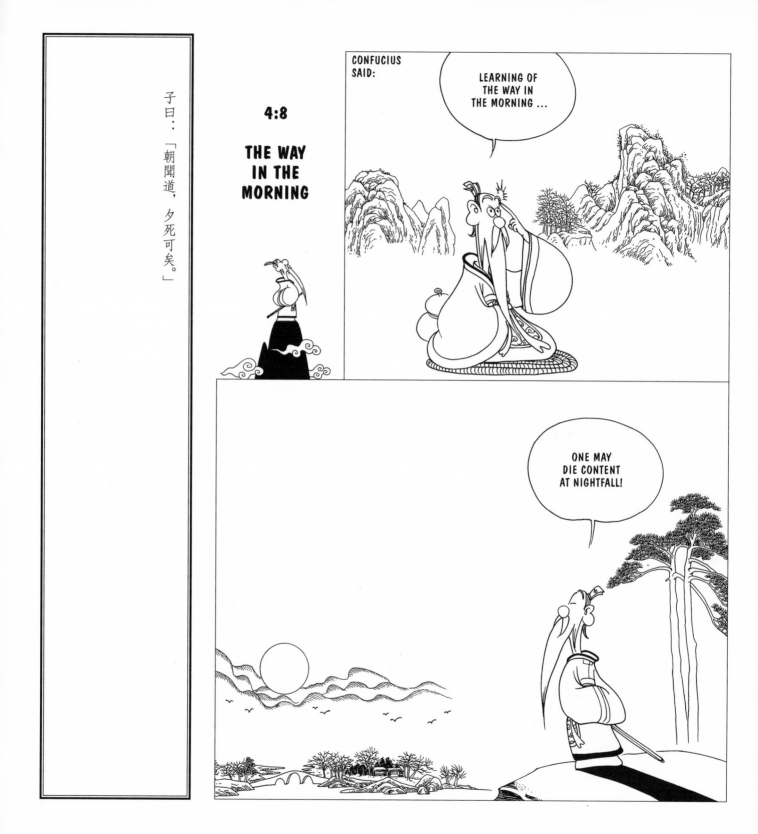

4:8

THE WAY IN THE MORNING

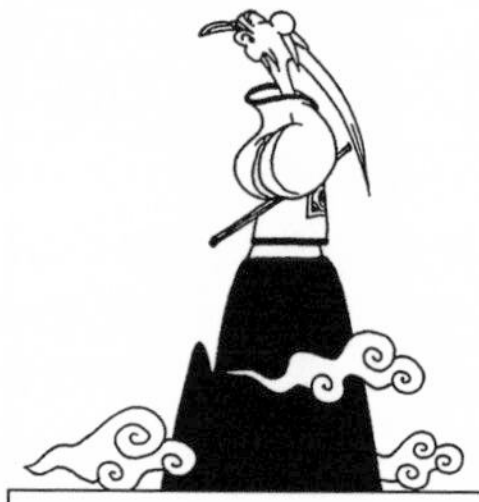

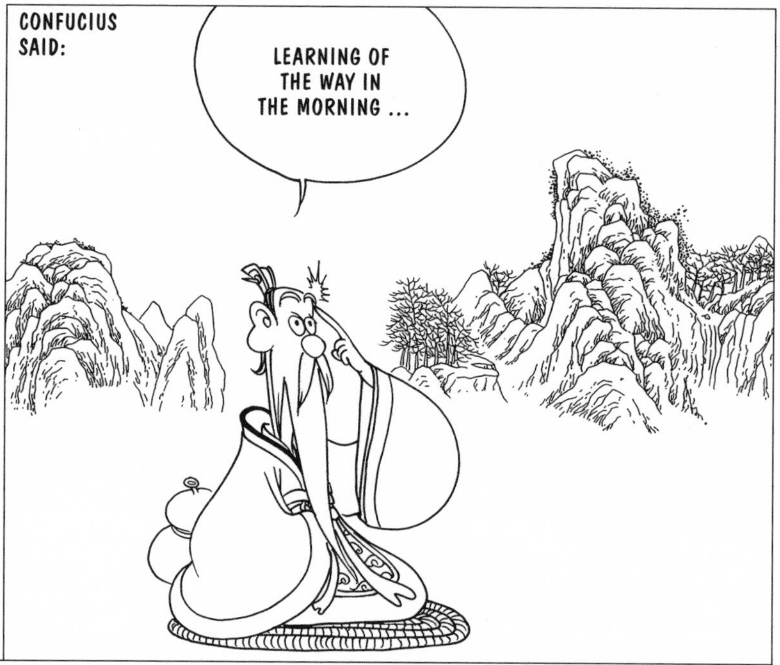
CONFUCIUS SAID:
LEARNING OF THE WAY IN THE MORNING ...

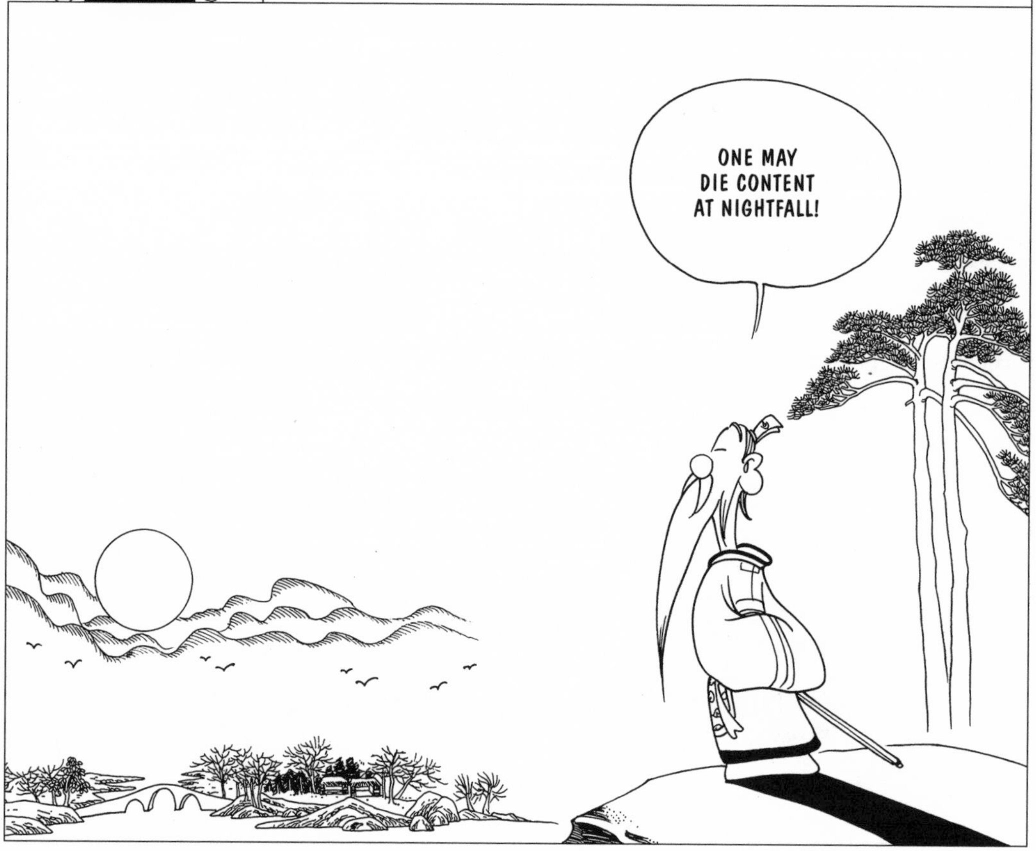
ONE MAY DIE CONTENT AT NIGHTFALL!

4:9

THE WAY OF SELF-RESPECT

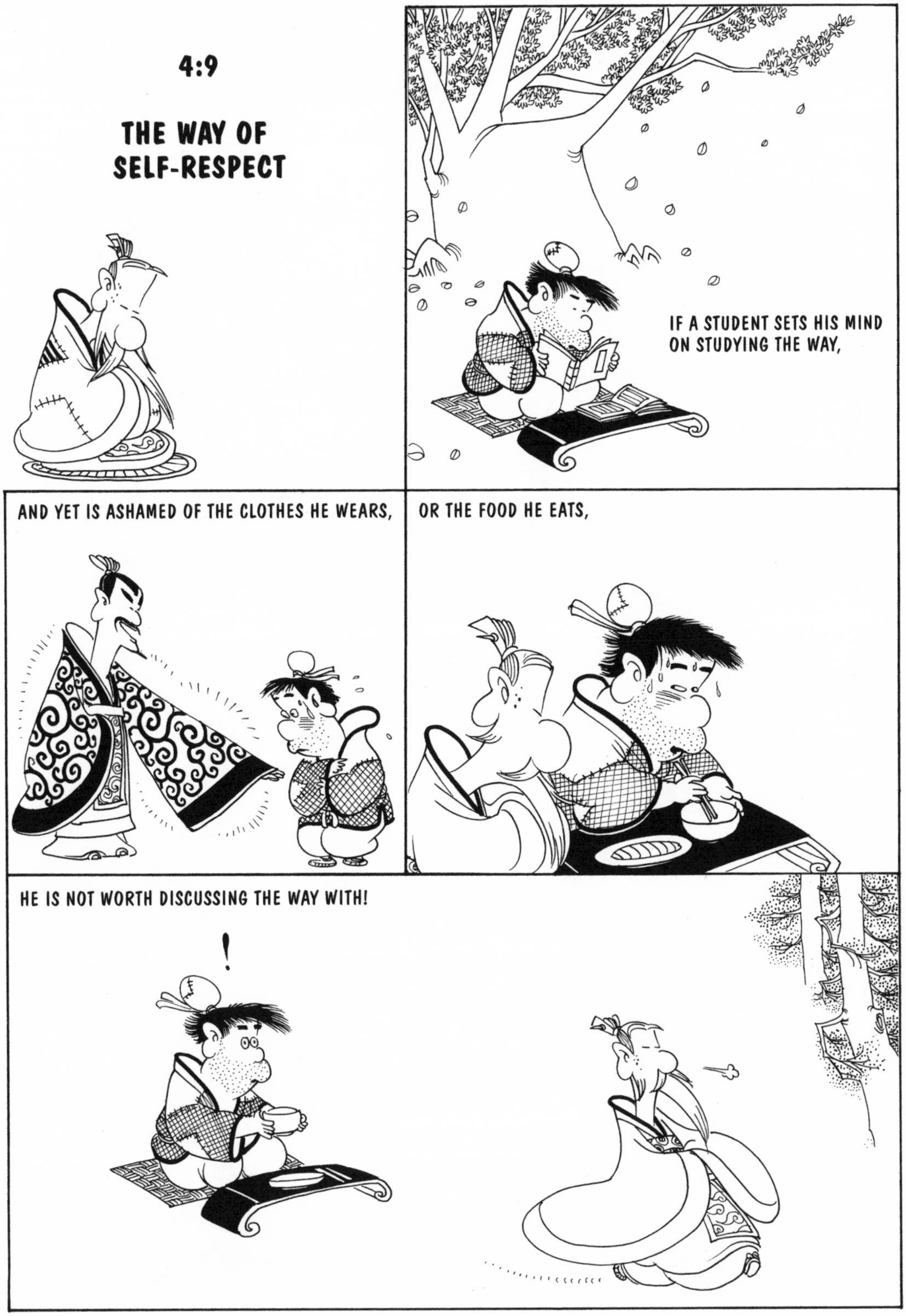
IF A STUDENT SETS HIS MIND ON STUDYING THE WAY,
AND YET IS ASHAMED OF THE CLOTHES HE WEARS,
OR THE FOOD HE EATS,
HE IS NOT WORTH DISCUSSING THE WAY WITH!
!

子曰：「士志於道，而恥惡衣惡食者，未足與議也。」

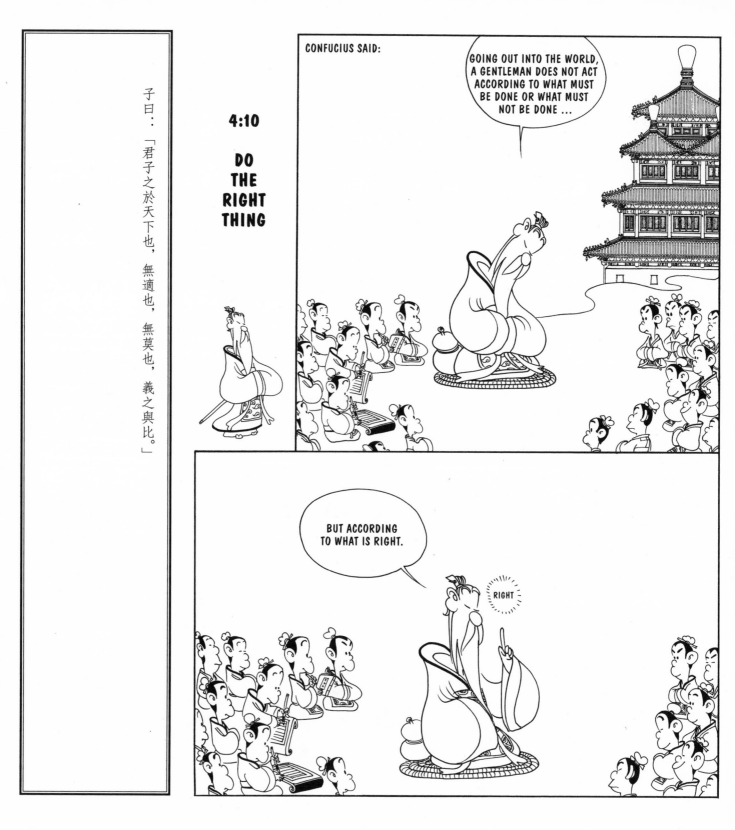

子曰：「君子之於天下也，無適也，無莫也，義之與比。」

4:10

DO THE RIGHT THING

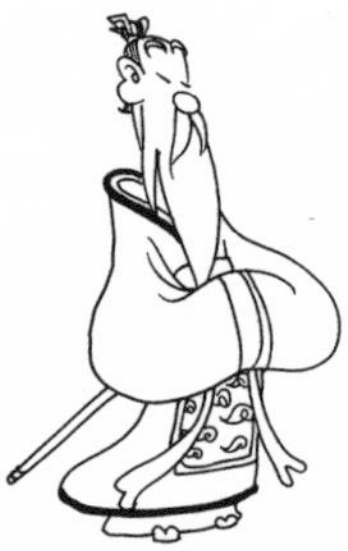

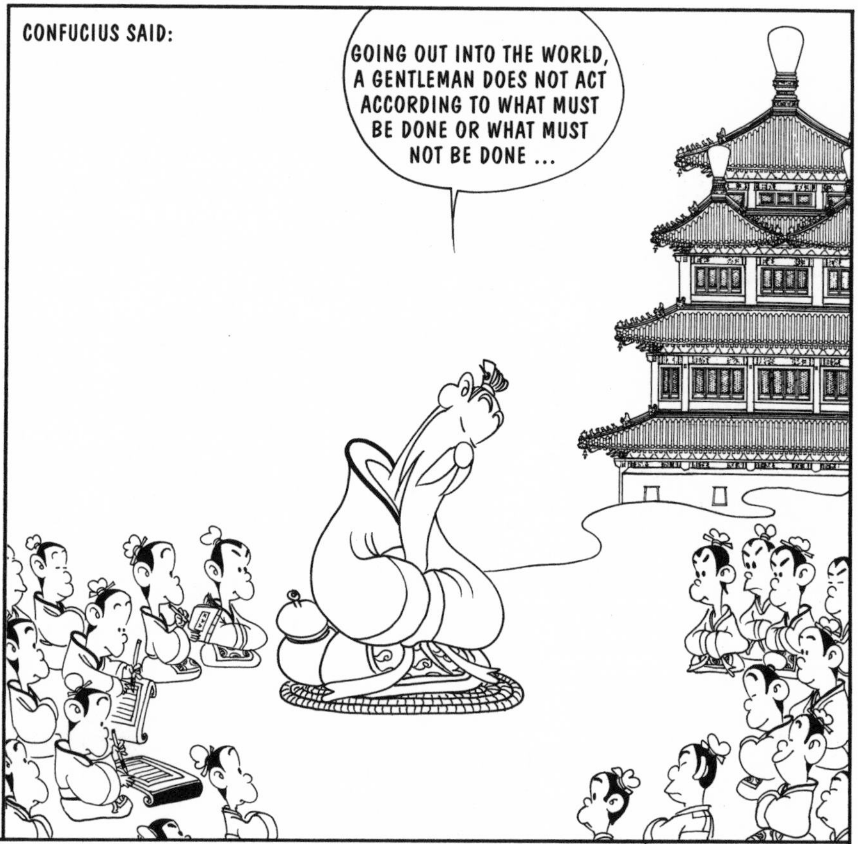

CONFUCIUS SAID:
GOING OUT INTO THE WORLD, A GENTLEMAN DOES NOT ACT ACCORDING TO WHAT MUST BE DONE OR WHAT MUST NOT BE DONE ...

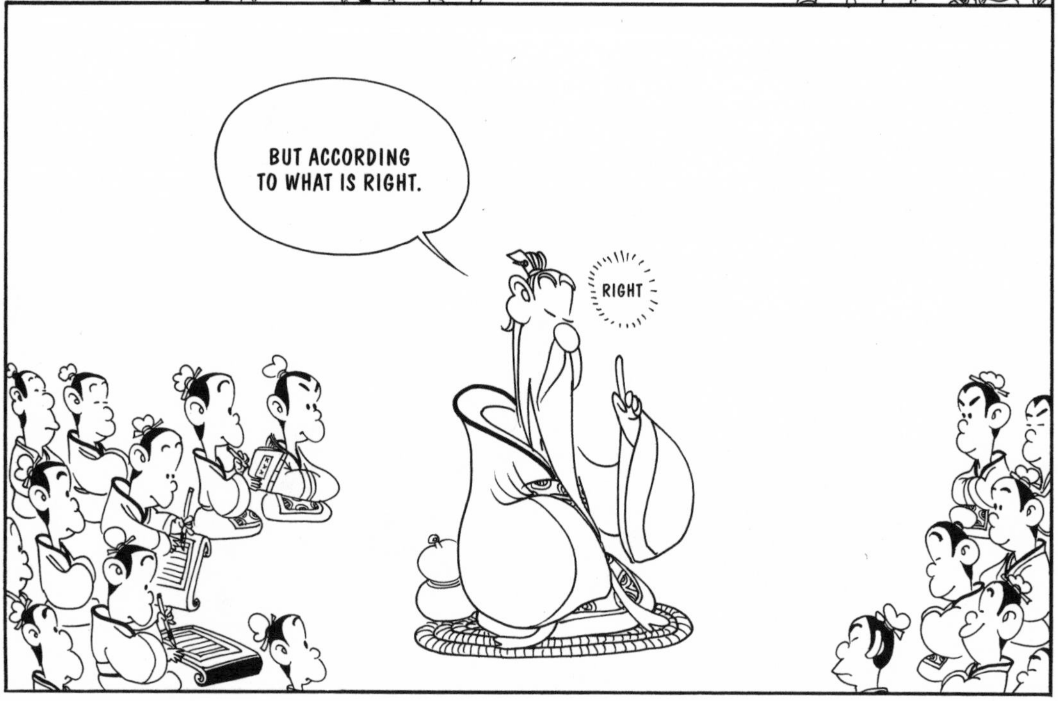

BUT ACCORDING TO WHAT IS RIGHT.
RIGHT

4:12

SELF-INTEREST

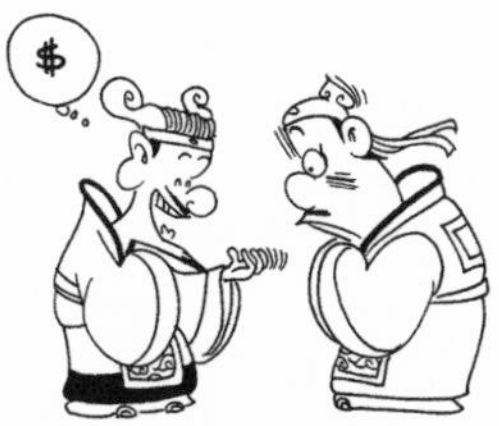

$

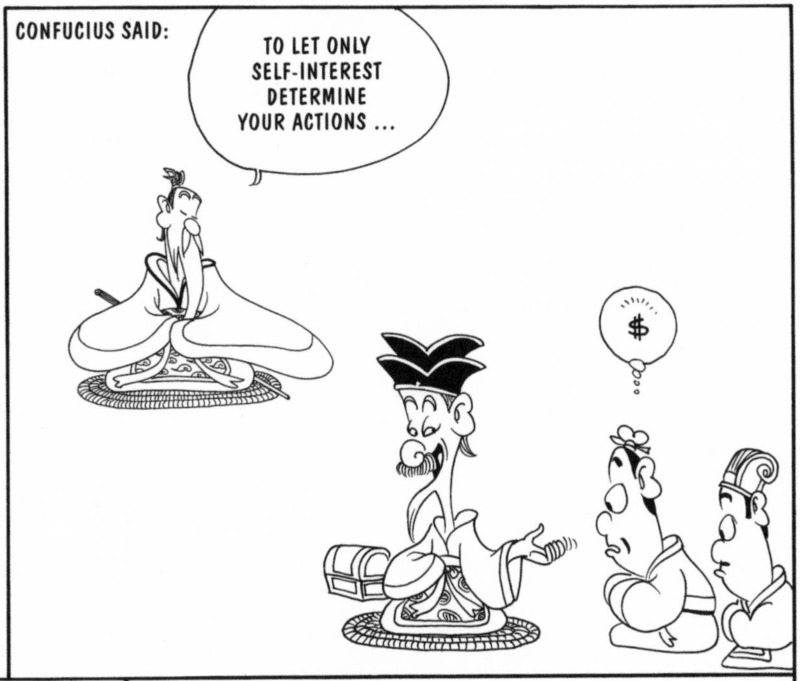

CONFUCIUS SAID:
TO LET ONLY SELF-INTEREST DETERMINE YOUR ACTIONS ...
$

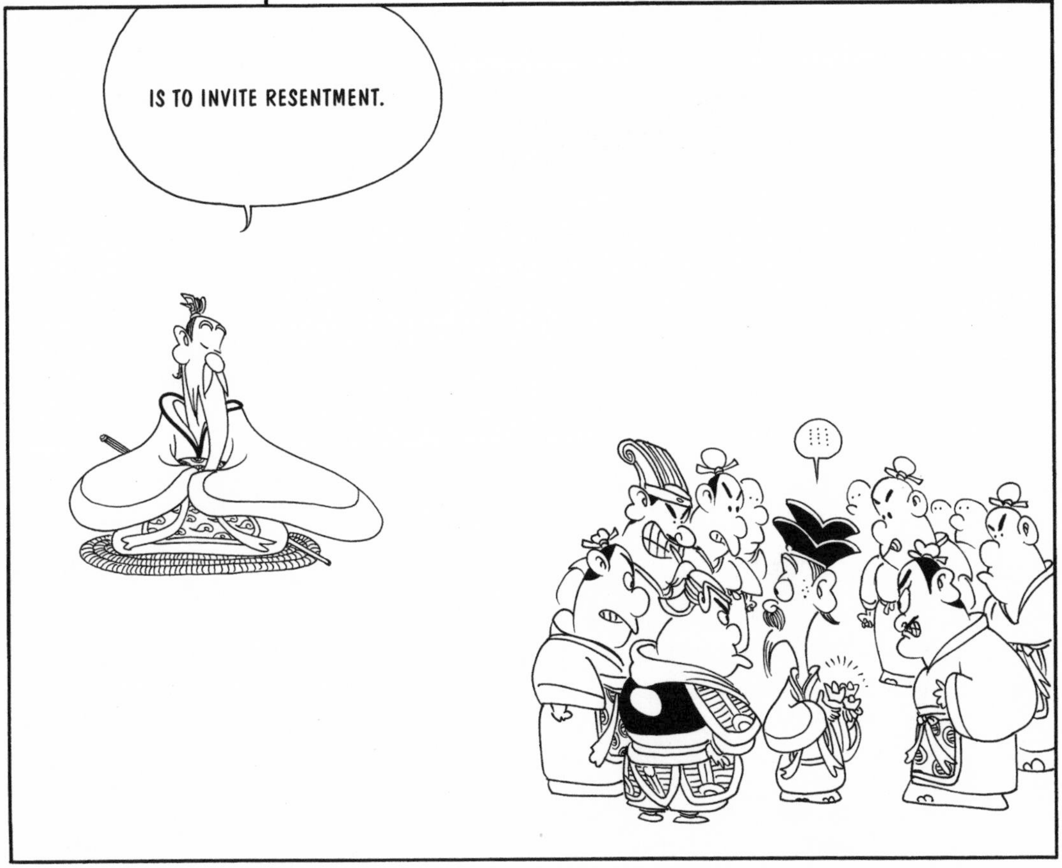

IS TO INVITE RESENTMENT.

子曰：「放於利而行，多怨。」

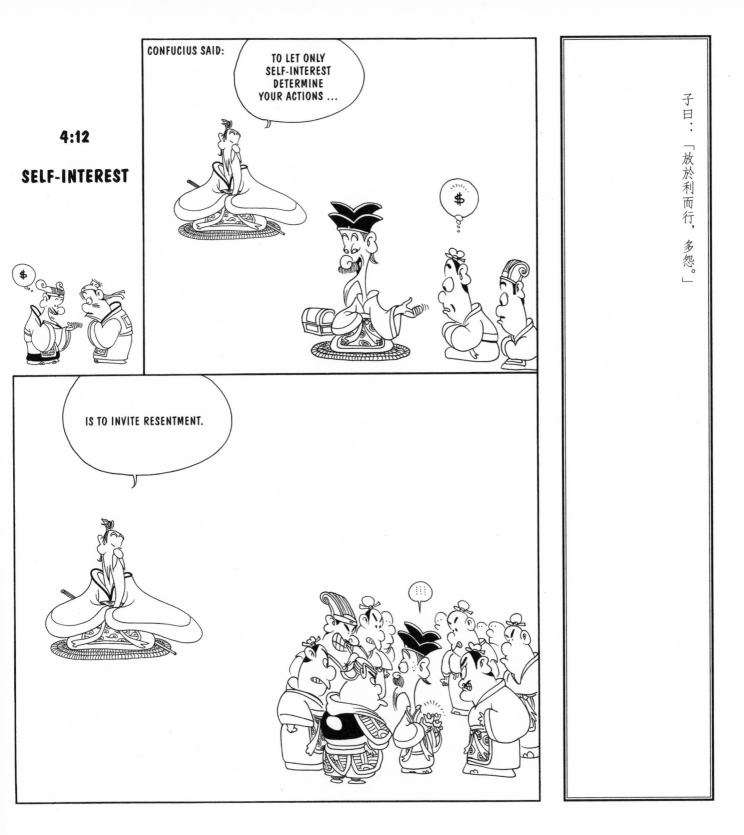

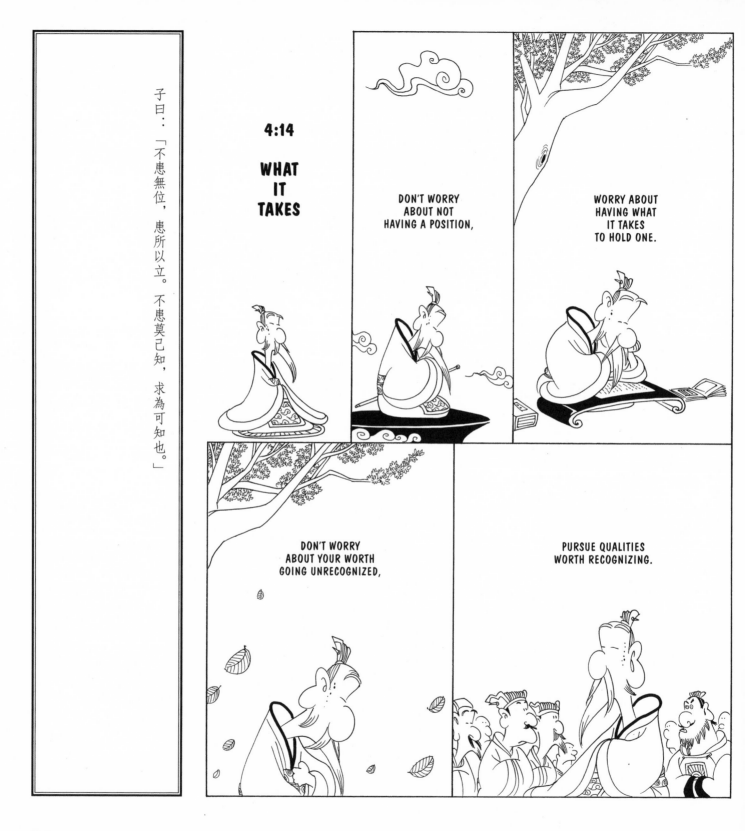

子曰：「不患無位，患所以立。不患莫己知，求為可知也。」

4:14

WHAT IT TAKES

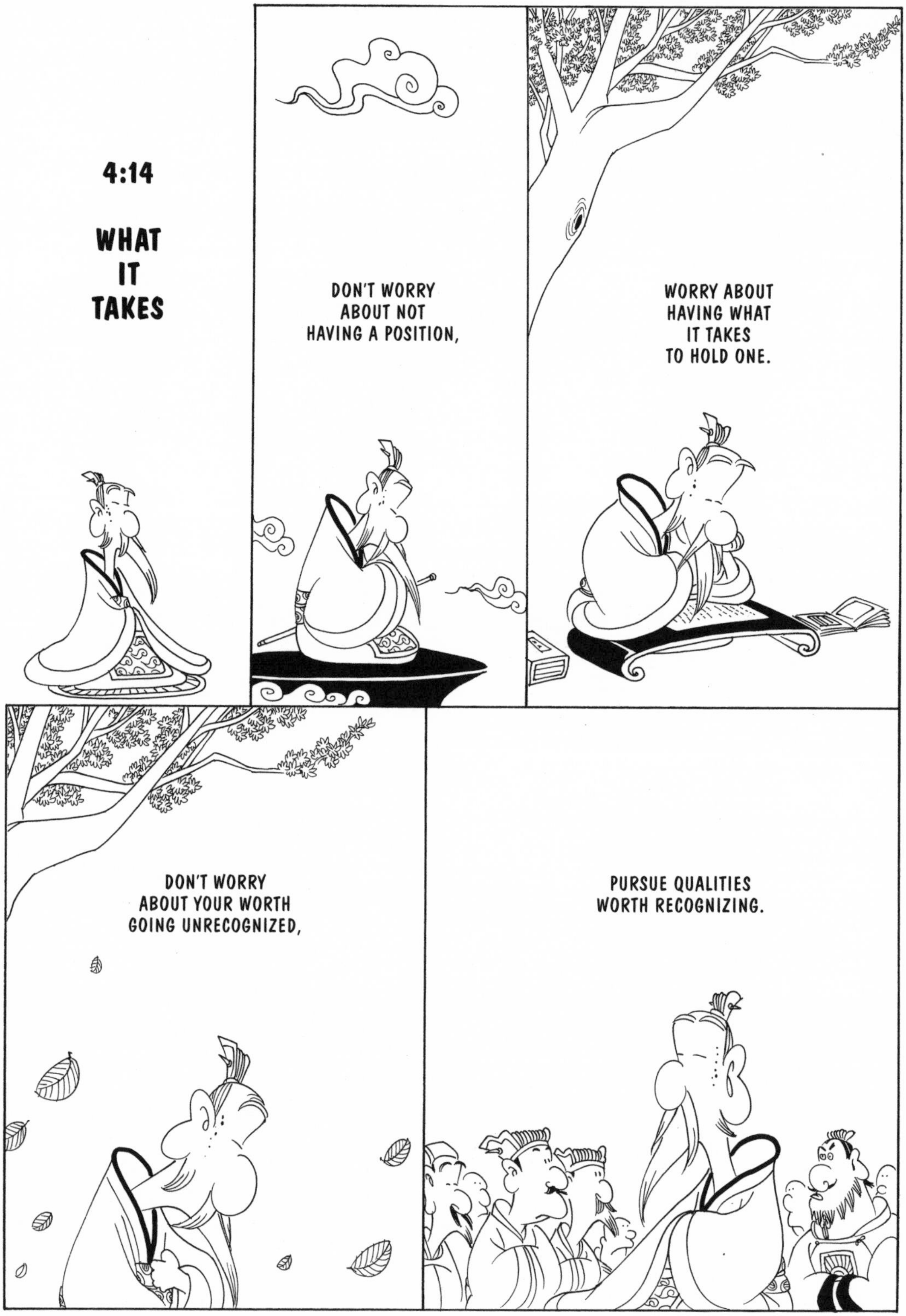

DON'T WORRY ABOUT NOT HAVING A POSITION,
WORRY ABOUT HAVING WHAT IT TAKES TO HOLD ONE.
DON'T WORRY ABOUT YOUR WORTH GOING UNRECOGNIZED,
PURSUE QUALITIES WORTH RECOGNIZING.

4:16

UNDERSTANDING WHAT'S RIGHT

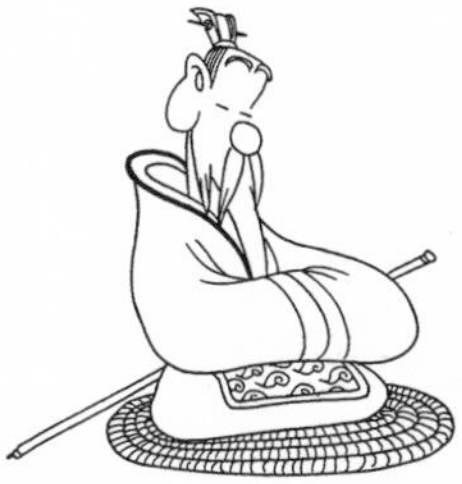

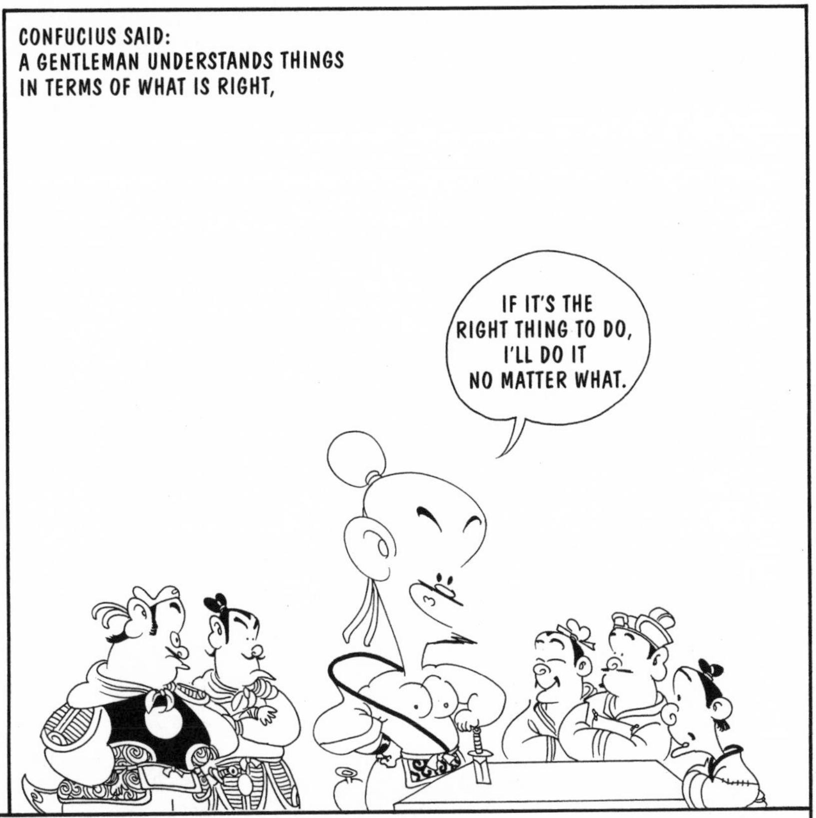
CONFUCIUS SAID:
A GENTLEMAN UNDERSTANDS THINGS IN TERMS OF WHAT IS RIGHT,
IF IT'S THE RIGHT THING TO DO, I'LL DO IT NO MATTER WHAT.

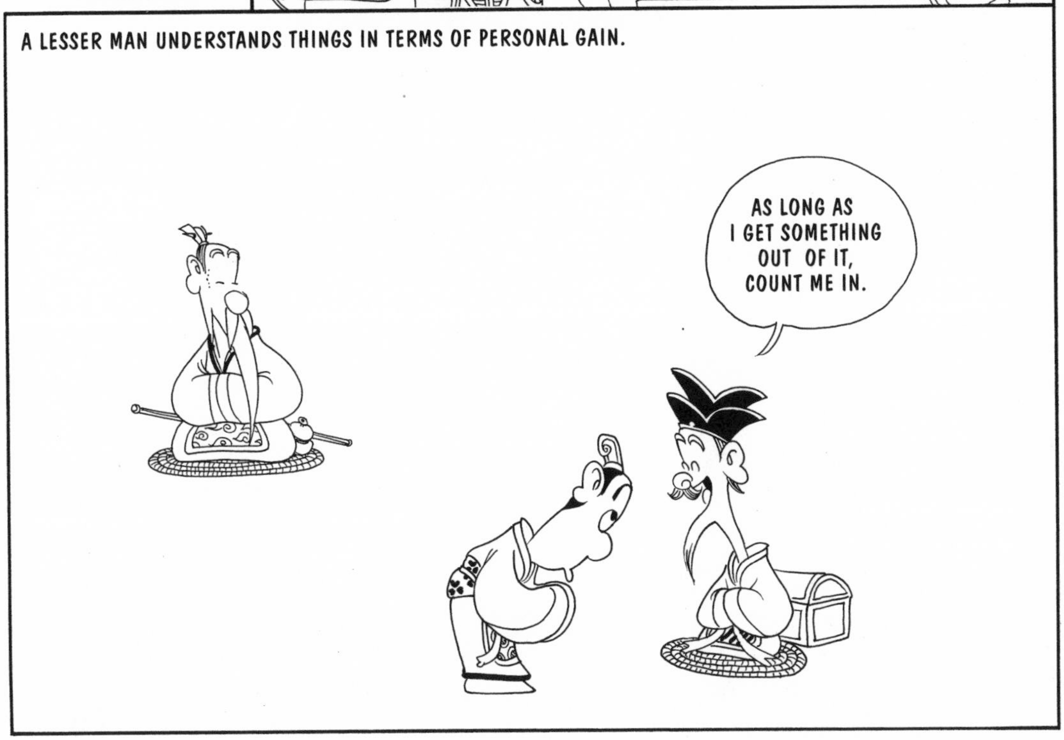
A LESSER MAN UNDERSTANDS THINGS IN TERMS OF PERSONAL GAIN.
AS LONG AS I GET SOMETHING OUT OF IT, COUNT ME IN.

子曰：「君子喻於義，小人喻於利。」

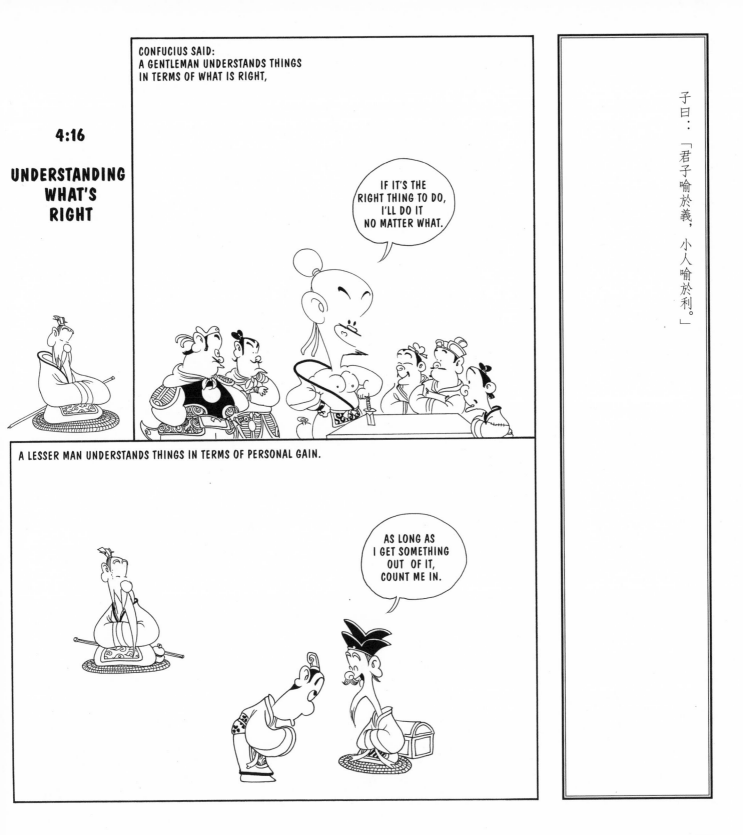

子曰：「見賢思齊焉，見不賢而內自省也。」

4:17

SEEING YOURSELF IN OTHERS

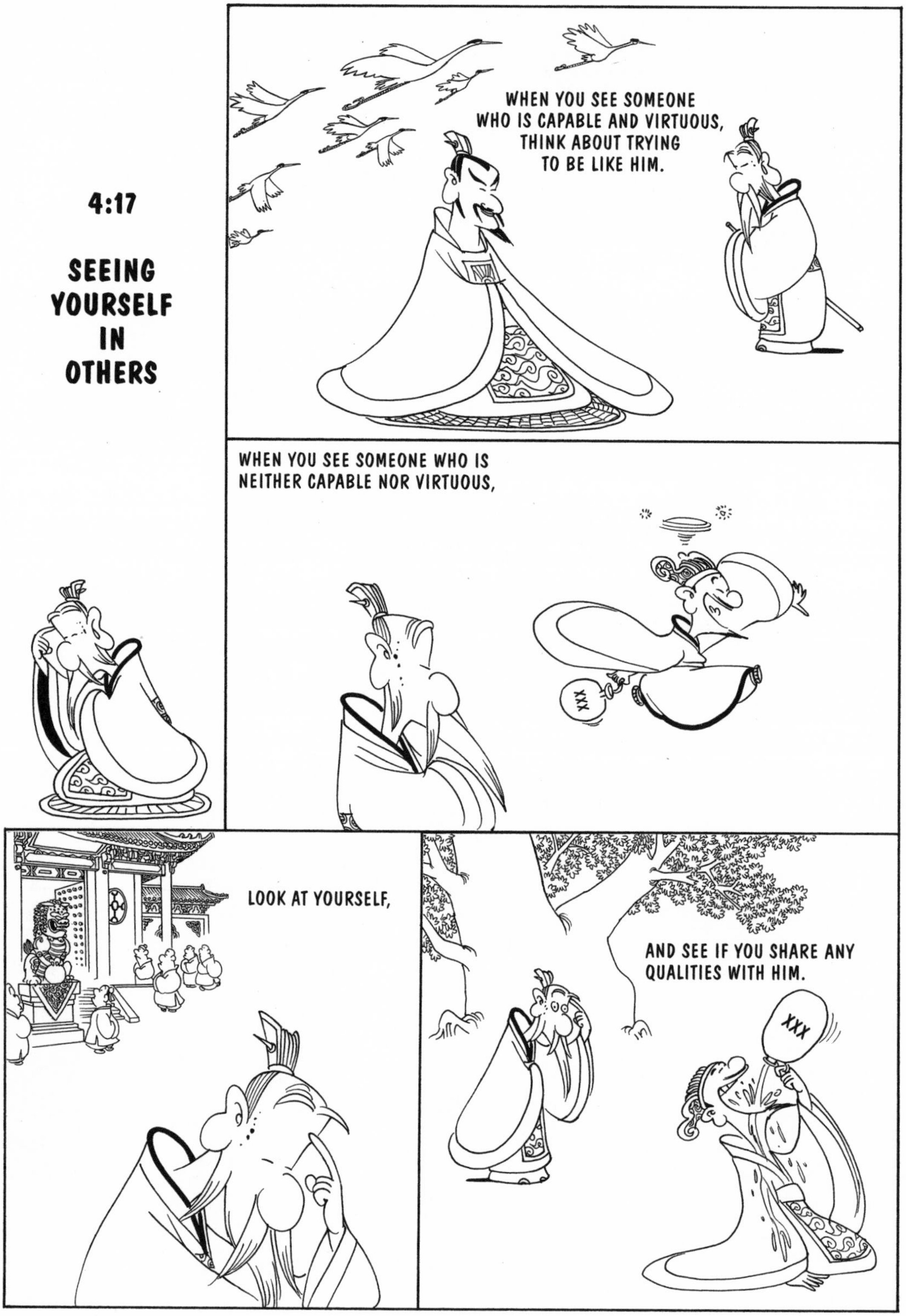

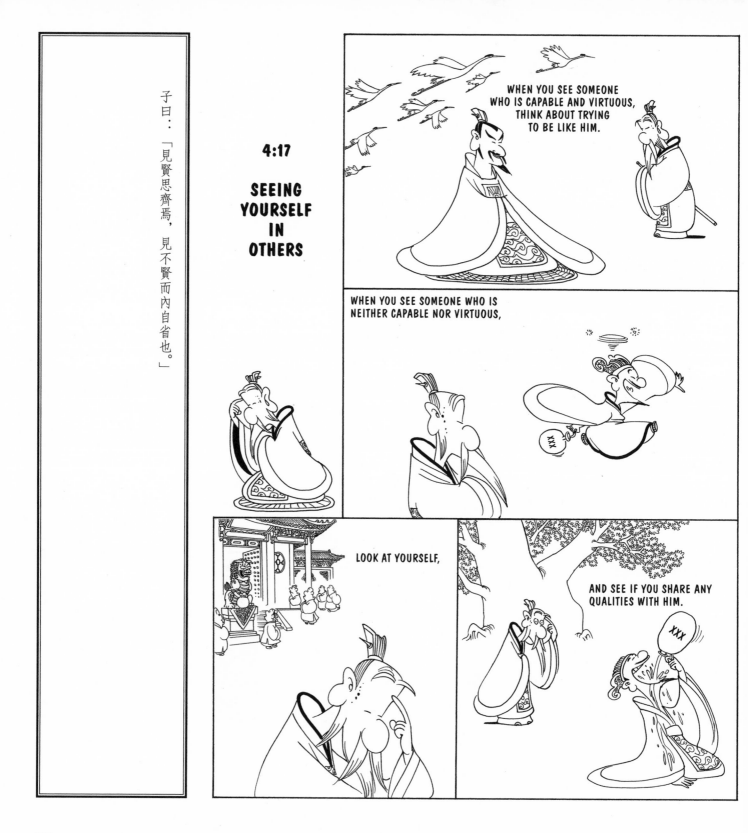

WHEN YOU SEE SOMEONE WHO IS CAPABLE AND VIRTUOUS, THINK ABOUT TRYING TO BE LIKE HIM.
WHEN YOU SEE SOMEONE WHO IS NEITHER CAPABLE NOR VIRTUOUS,
XXX
LOOK AT YOURSELF,
AND SEE IF YOU SHARE ANY QUALITIES WITH HIM.
XXX

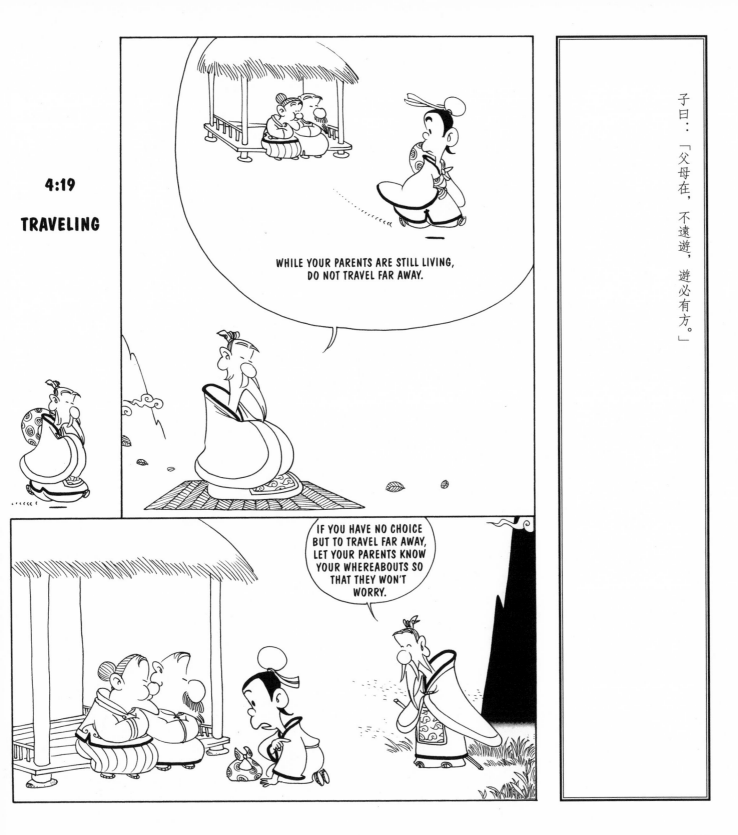

4:19

TRAVELING

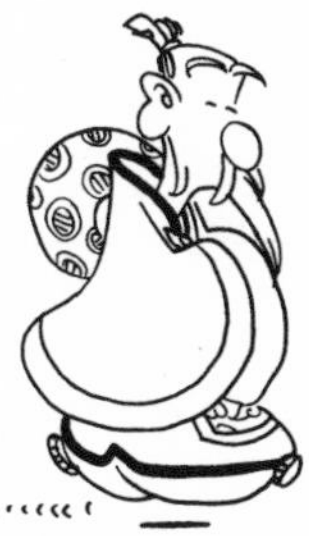

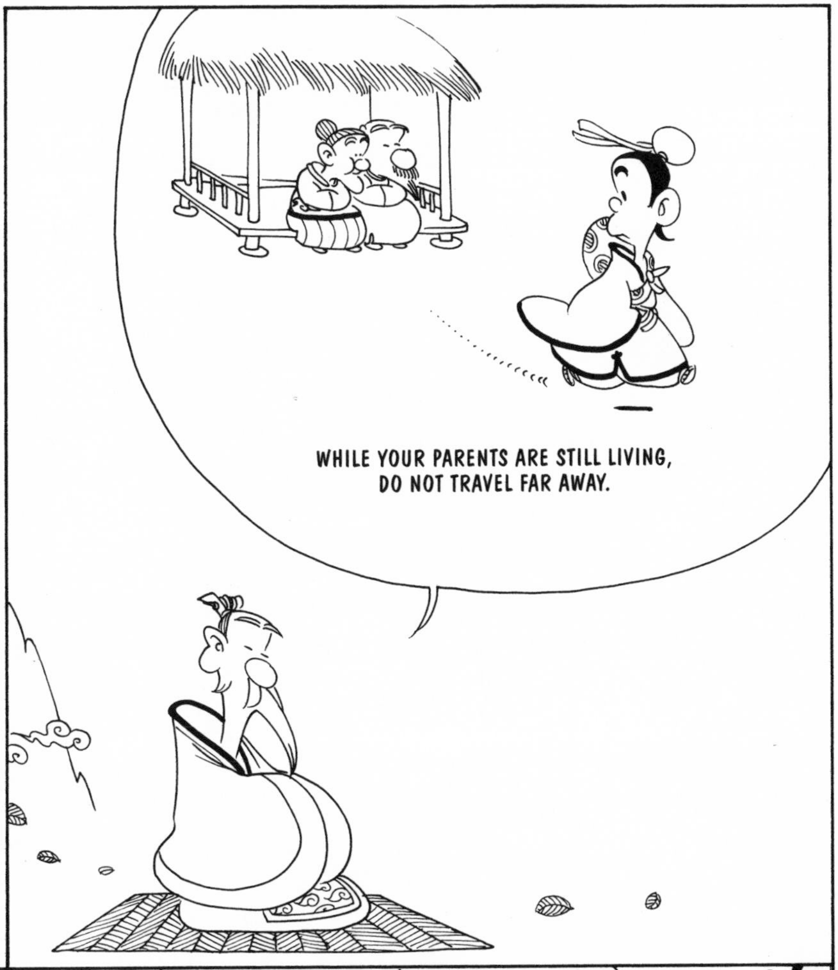

WHILE YOUR PARENTS ARE STILL LIVING, DO NOT TRAVEL FAR AWAY.

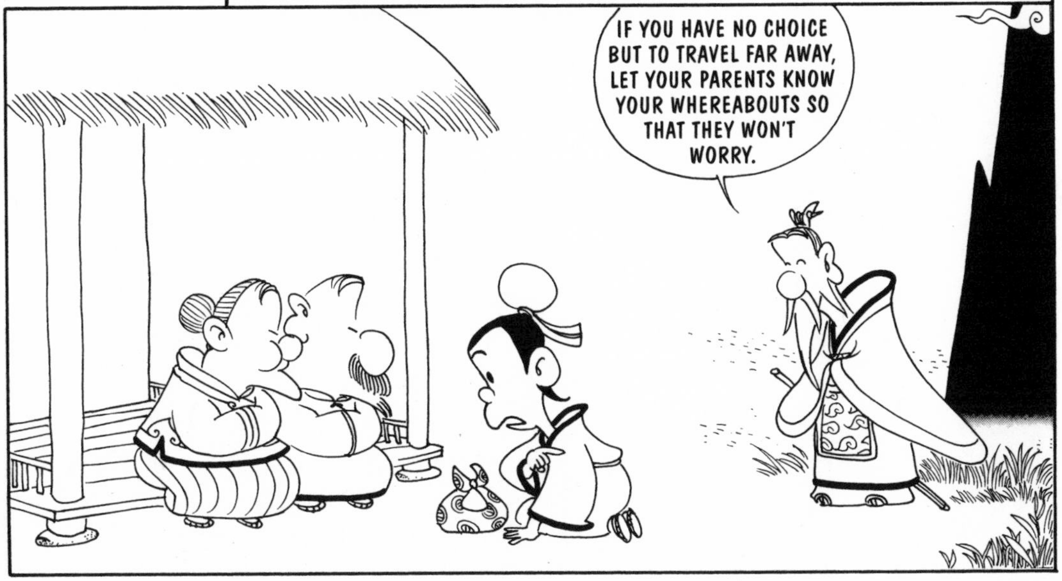

IF YOU HAVE NO CHOICE BUT TO TRAVEL FAR AWAY, LET YOUR PARENTS KNOW YOUR WHEREABOUTS SO THAT THEY WON'T WORRY.

子曰：「父母在，不遠遊，遊必有方。」

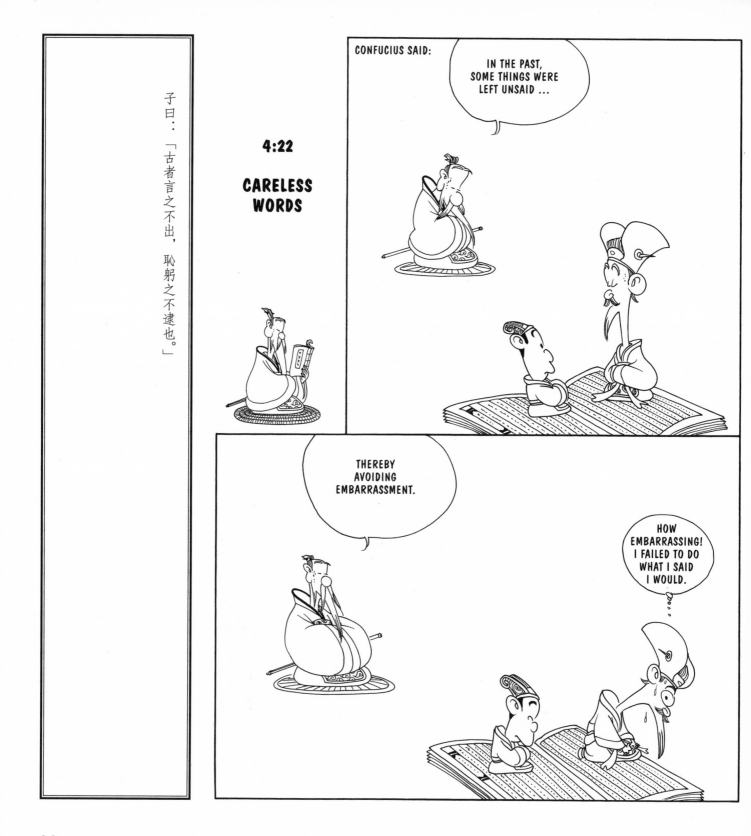

子曰：「古者言之不出，恥躬之不逮也。」

4:22

CARELESS WORDS

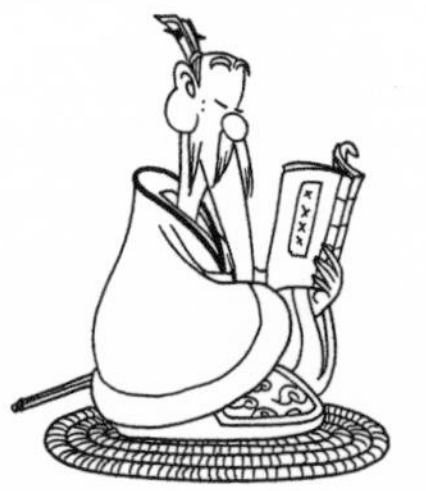

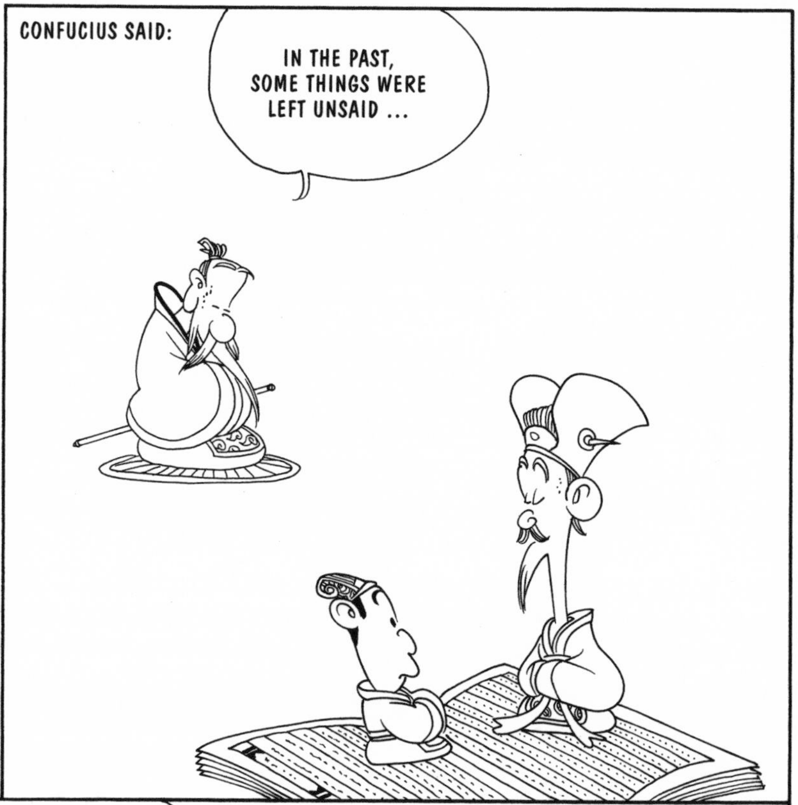
CONFUCIUS SAID:
IN THE PAST, SOME THINGS WERE LEFT UNSAID ...

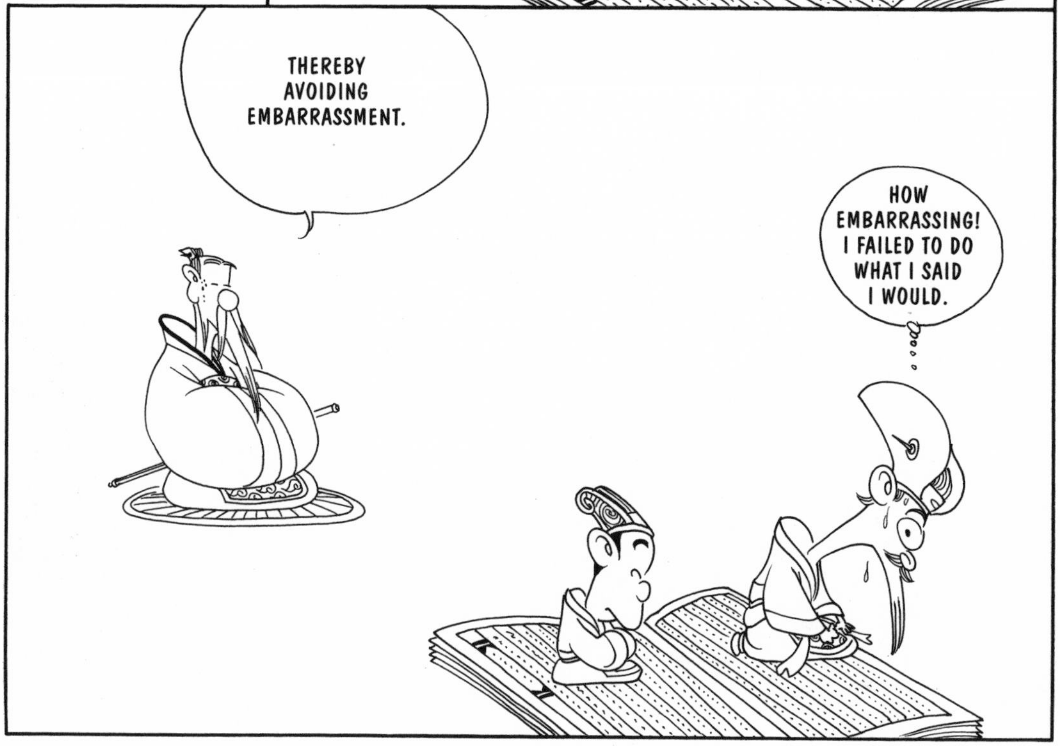
THEREBY AVOIDING EMBARRASSMENT.
HOW EMBARRASSING! I FAILED TO DO WHAT I SAID I WOULD.

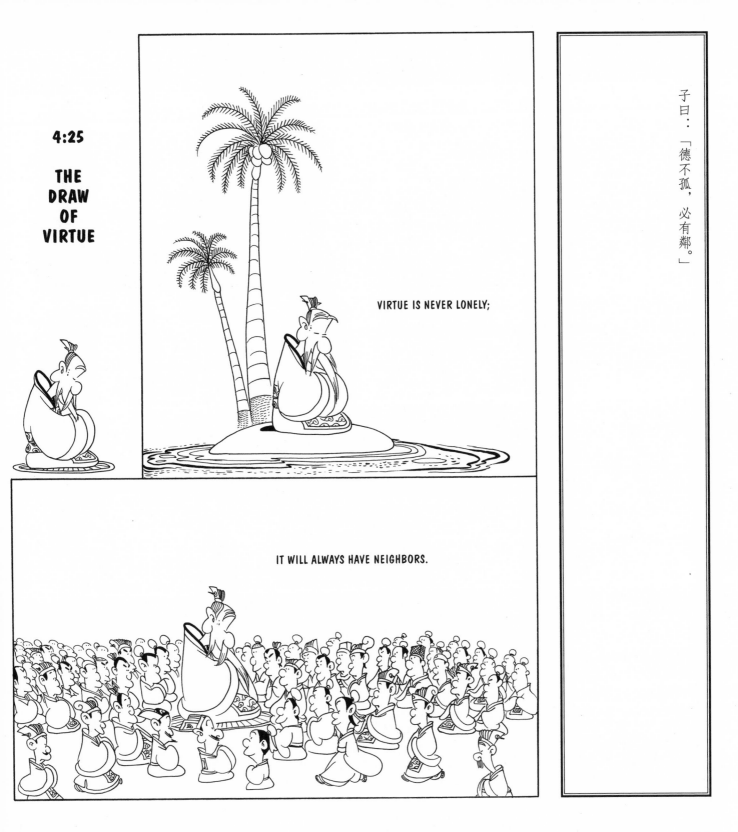

4:25

THE DRAW OF VIRTUE

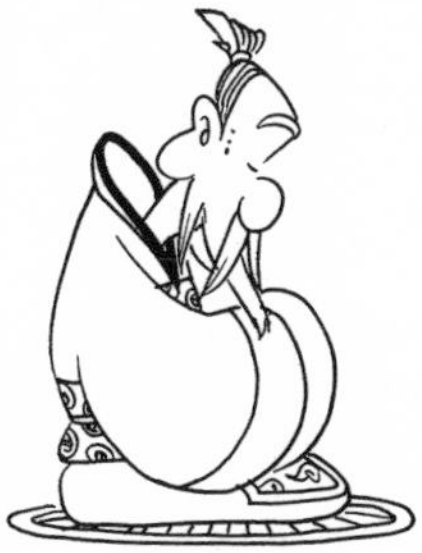

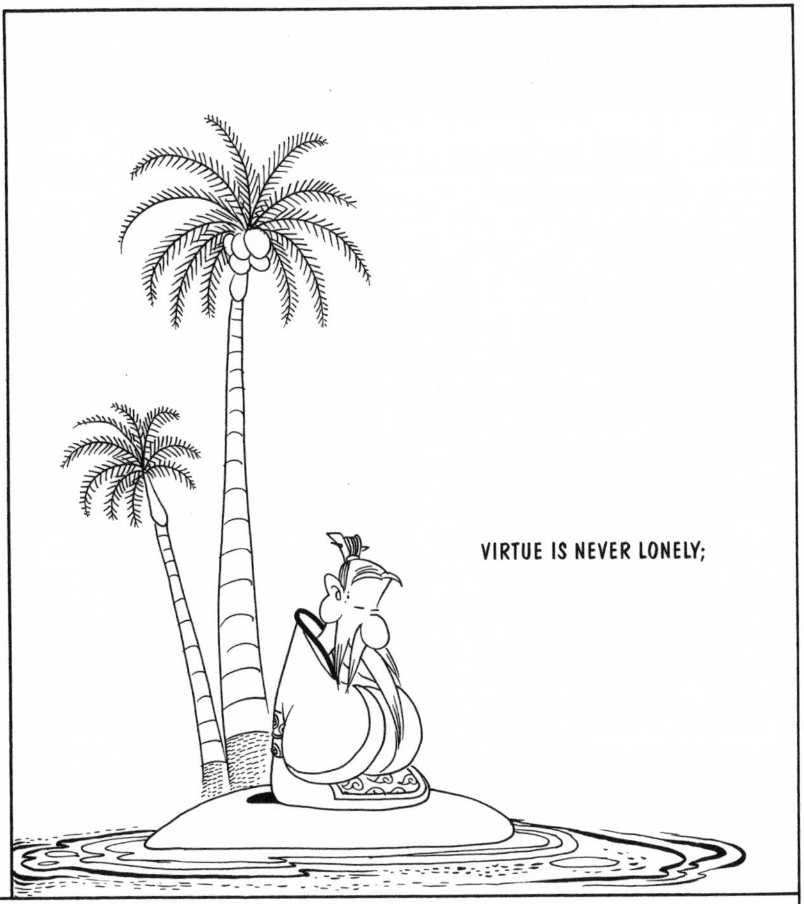
VIRTUE IS NEVER LONELY;

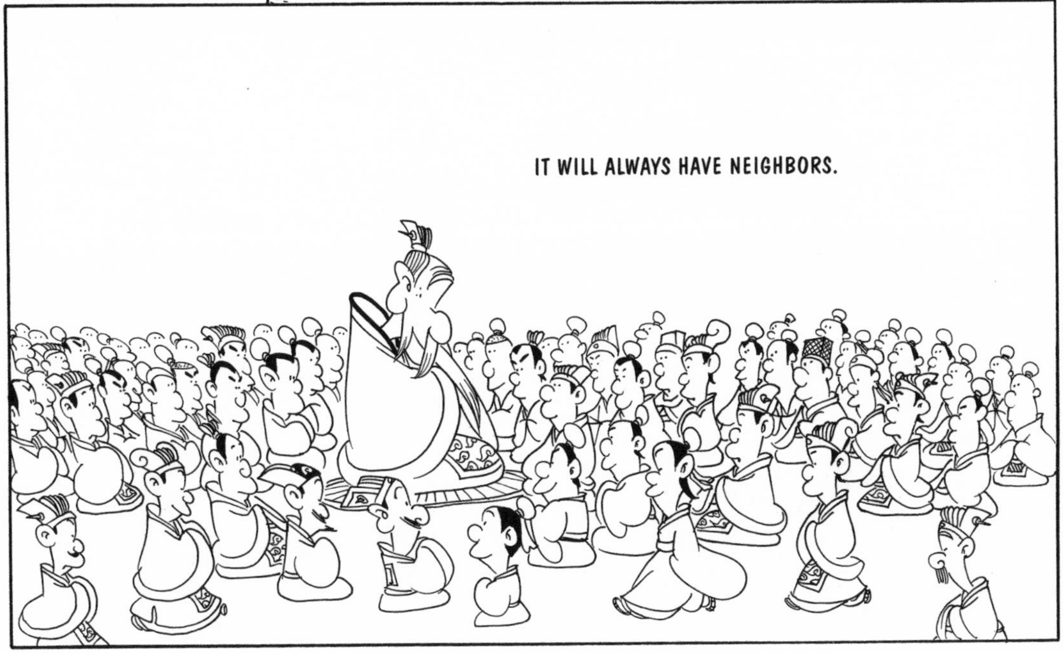
IT WILL ALWAYS HAVE NEIGHBORS.

子曰：「德不孤，必有鄰。」

子謂子貢曰：「女與回也孰愈？」對曰：「賜也何敢望回？回也聞一以知十，賜也聞一以知二。」子曰：「弗如也；吾與女弗如也。」

5:9

BETTER THAN YAN HUI

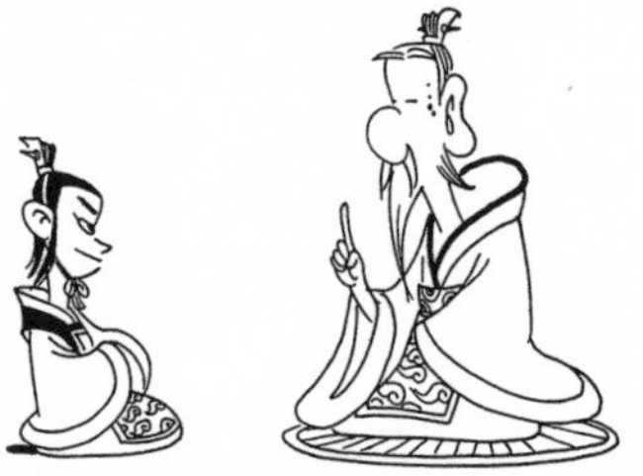

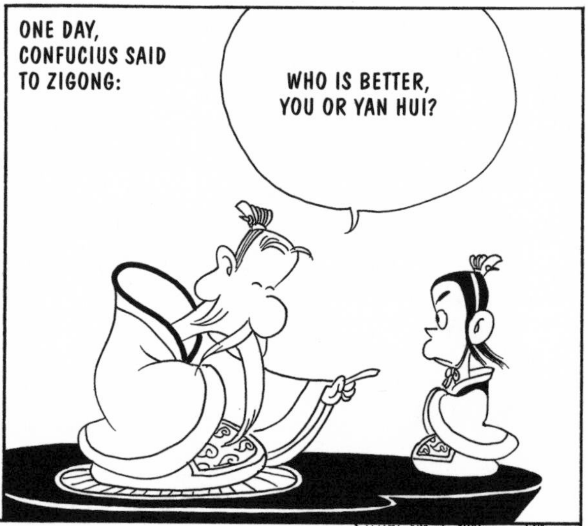
ONE DAY, CONFUCIUS SAID TO ZIGONG:
WHO IS BETTER, YOU OR YAN HUI?

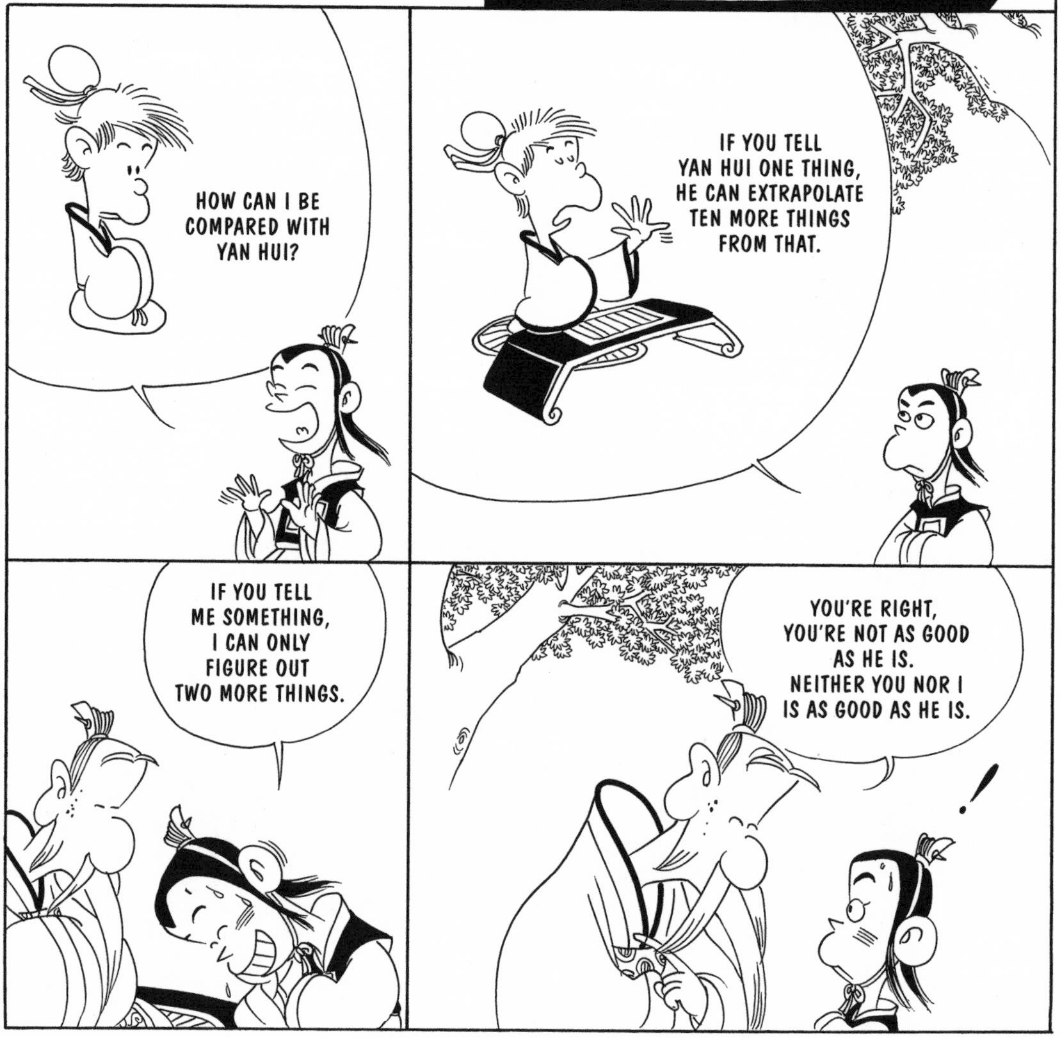
HOW CAN I BE COMPARED WITH YAN HUI?
IF YOU TELL YAN HUI ONE THING, HE CAN EXTRAPOLATE TEN MORE THINGS FROM THAT.
IF YOU TELL ME SOMETHING, I CAN ONLY FIGURE OUT TWO MORE THINGS.
YOU'RE RIGHT, YOU'RE NOT AS GOOD AS HE IS. NEITHER YOU NOR I IS AS GOOD AS HE IS.
!

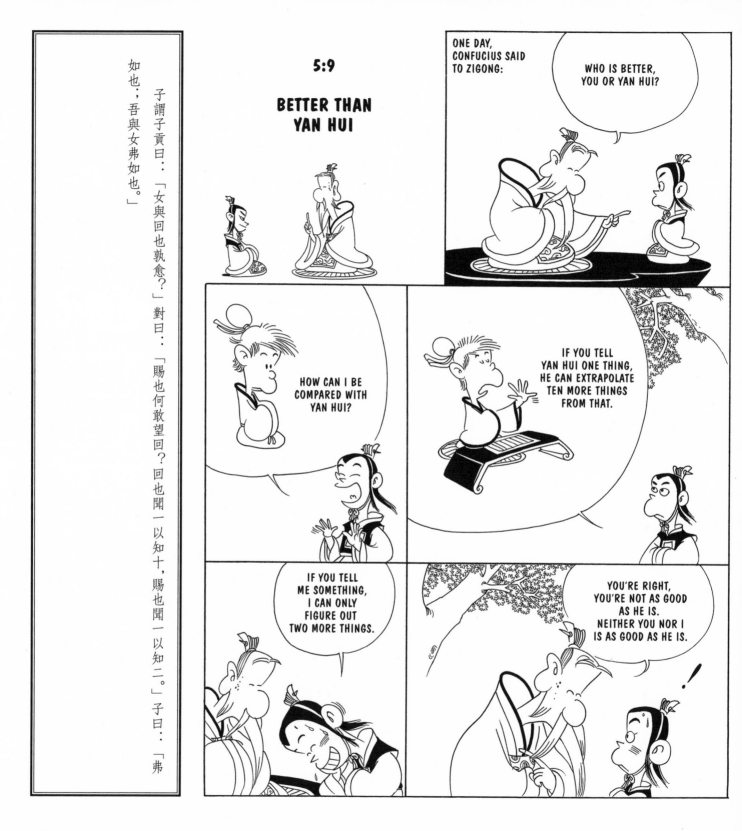

5:10

ZAI YU AND THE FILTHY WALL

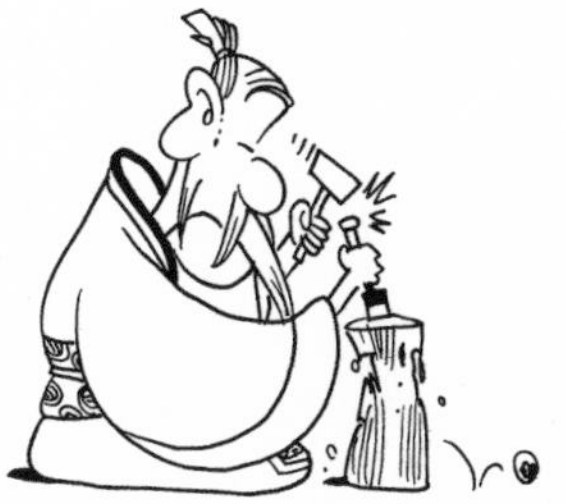

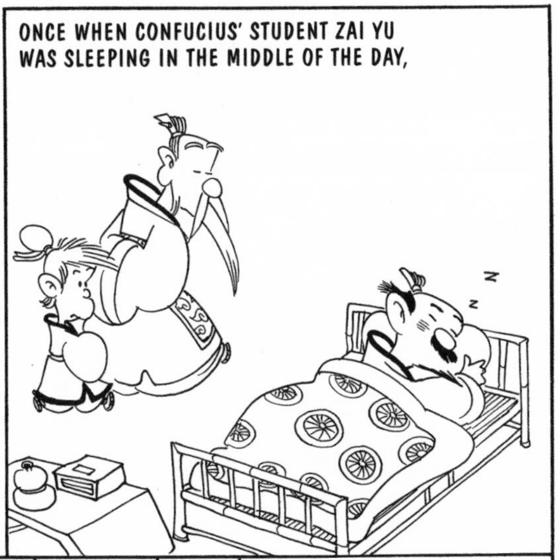
ONCE WHEN CONFUCIUS' STUDENT ZAI YU WAS SLEEPING IN THE MIDDLE OF THE DAY,

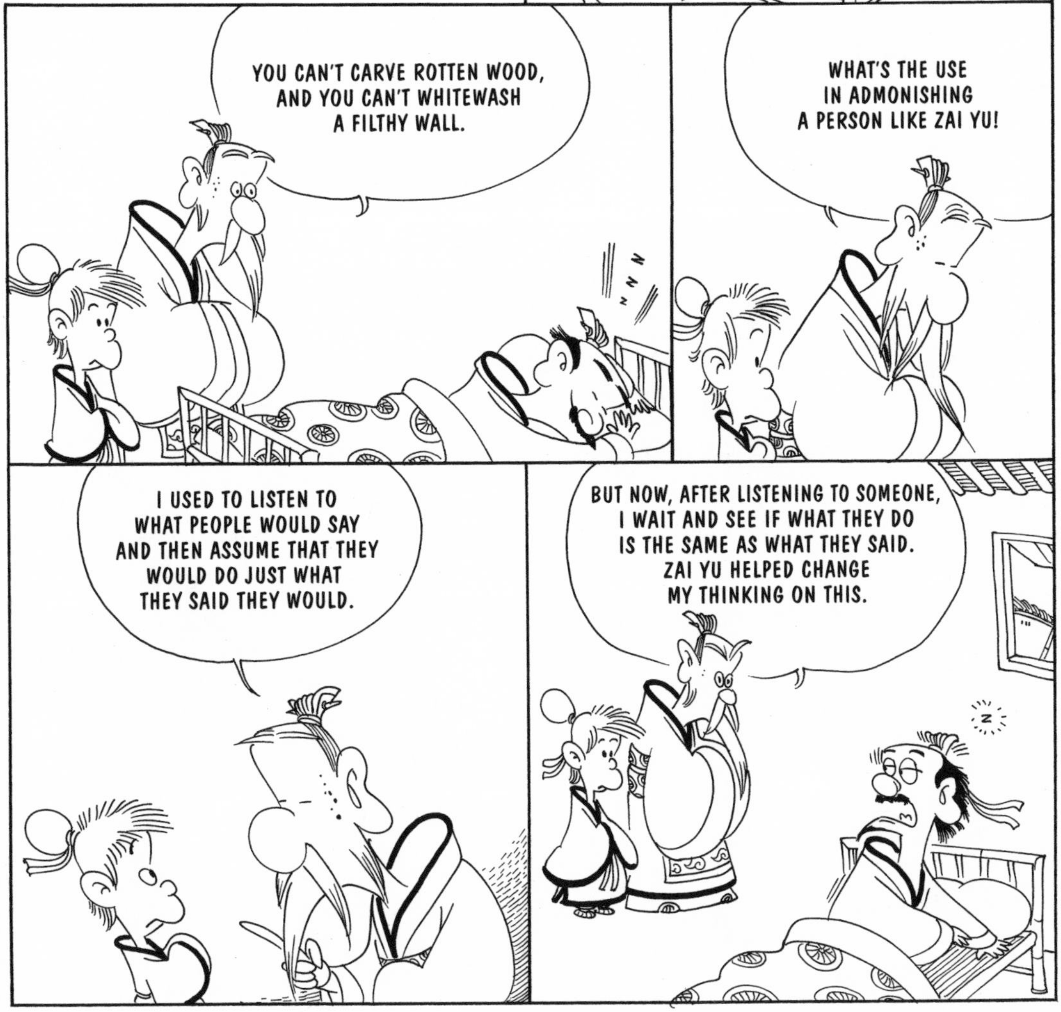
YOU CAN'T CARVE ROTTEN WOOD, AND YOU CAN'T WHITEWASH A FILTHY WALL.
WHAT'S THE USE IN ADMONISHING A PERSON LIKE ZAI YU!
I USED TO LISTEN TO WHAT PEOPLE WOULD SAY AND THEN ASSUME THAT THEY WOULD DO JUST WHAT THEY SAID THEY WOULD.
BUT NOW, AFTER LISTENING TO SOMEONE, I WAIT AND SEE IF WHAT THEY DO IS THE SAME AS WHAT THEY SAID. ZAI YU HELPED CHANGE MY THINKING ON THIS.

宰予晝寢。子曰：「朽木不可雕也，糞土之牆不可杇也；於予與何誅？」子曰：「始吾於人也，聽其言而信其行；今吾於人也，聽其言而觀其行。於予與改是。」

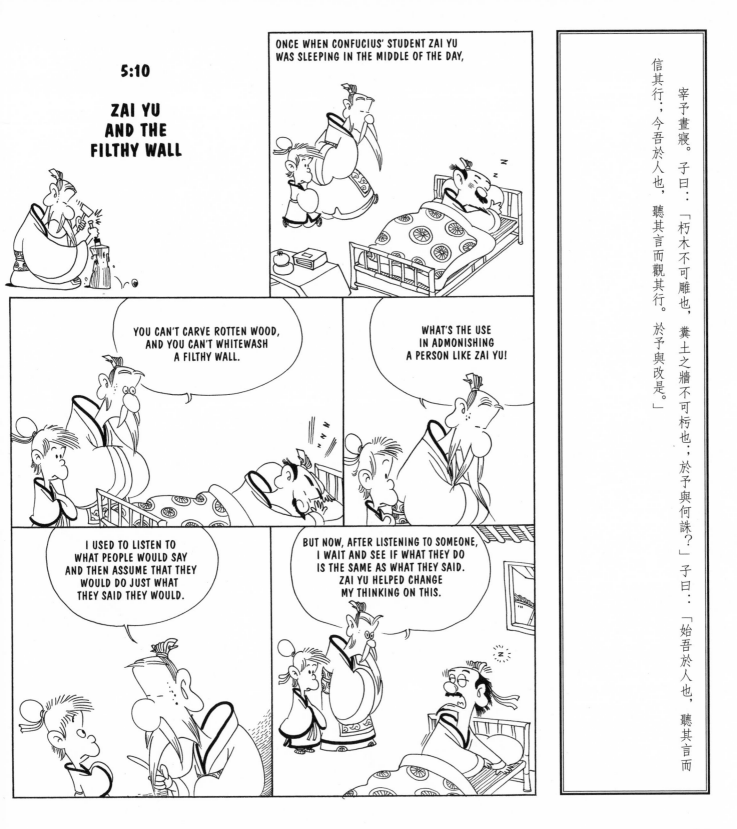

子曰：「吾未見剛者。」或對曰：「申棖。」子曰：「棖也慾，焉得剛？」

5:11

SHEN CHENG'S INFIRMITY

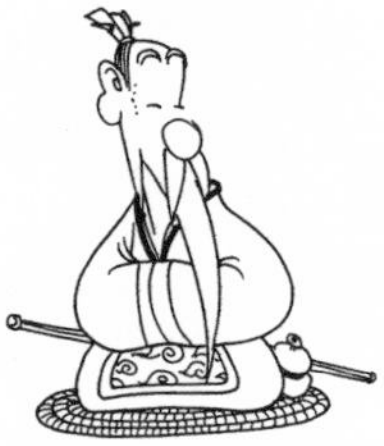

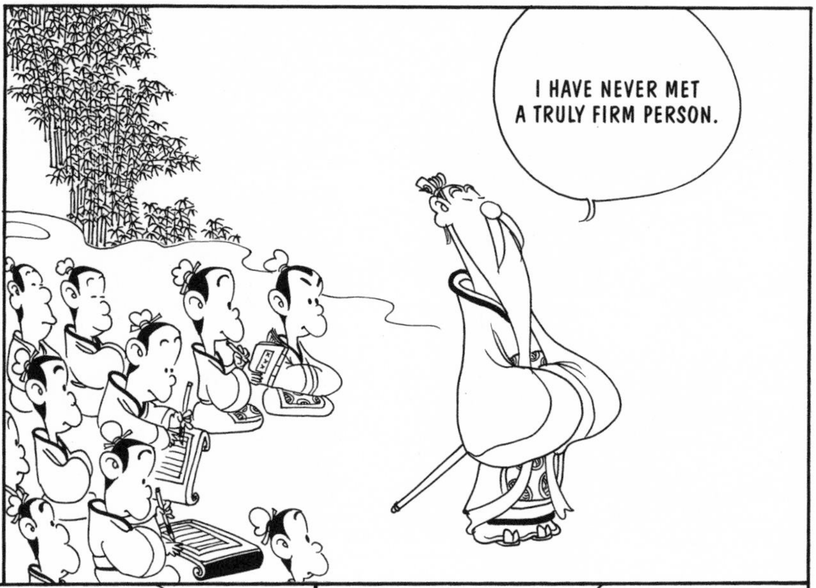
I HAVE NEVER MET A TRULY FIRM PERSON.

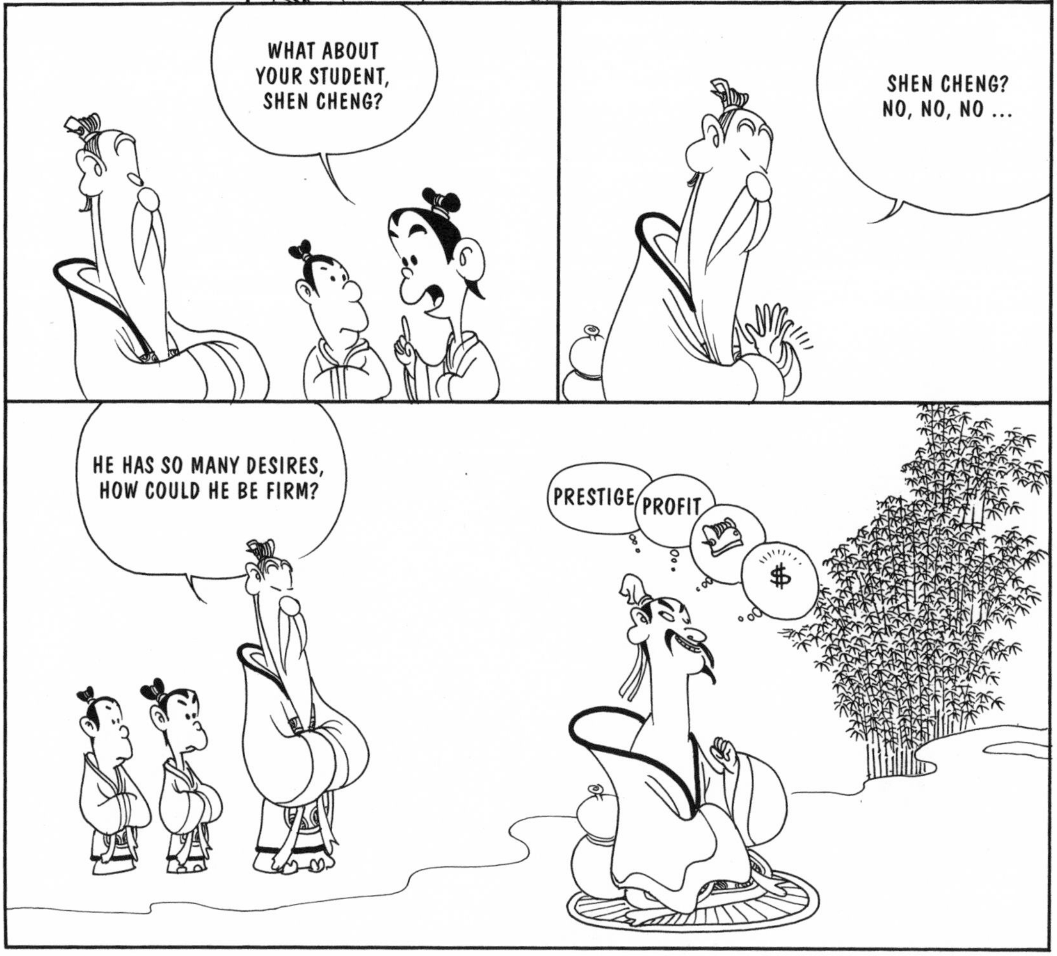
WHAT ABOUT YOUR STUDENT, SHEN CHENG?
SHEN CHENG? NO, NO, NO ...
HE HAS SO MANY DESIRES, HOW COULD HE BE FIRM?
PRESTIGE
PROFIT
$

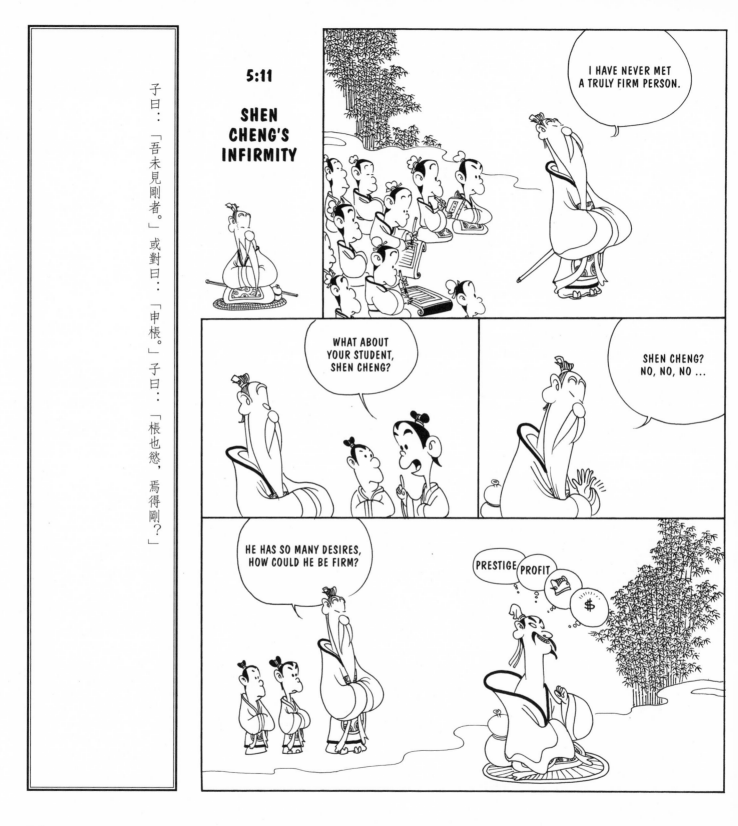

5:15

THE MEANING OF "CULTURED"

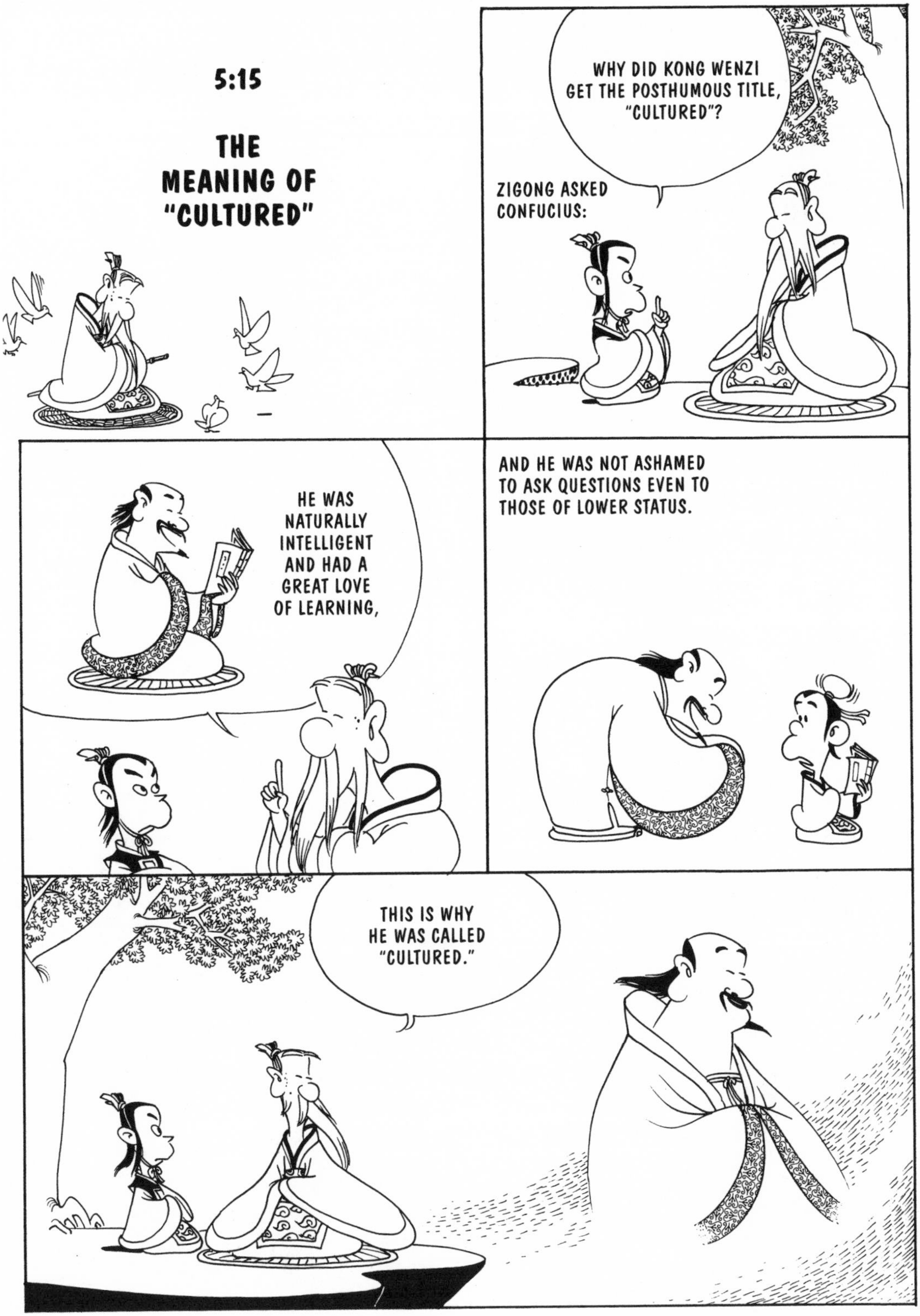
ZIGONG ASKED CONFUCIUS:
WHY DID KONG WENZI GET THE POSTHUMOUS TITLE, "CULTURED"?
HE WAS NATURALLY INTELLIGENT AND HAD A GREAT LOVE OF LEARNING,
AND HE WAS NOT ASHAMED TO ASK QUESTIONS EVEN TO THOSE OF LOWER STATUS.
THIS IS WHY HE WAS CALLED "CULTURED."

子貢問曰：「孔文子何以謂之『文』也？」子曰：「敏而好學，不恥下問，是以謂之『文』也。」

子謂子產，「有君子之道四焉：其行己也恭，其事上也敬，其養民也惠，其使民也義。」

5:16

ZICHAN THE GENTLEMAN

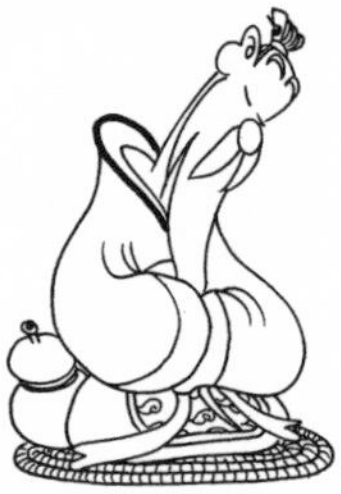

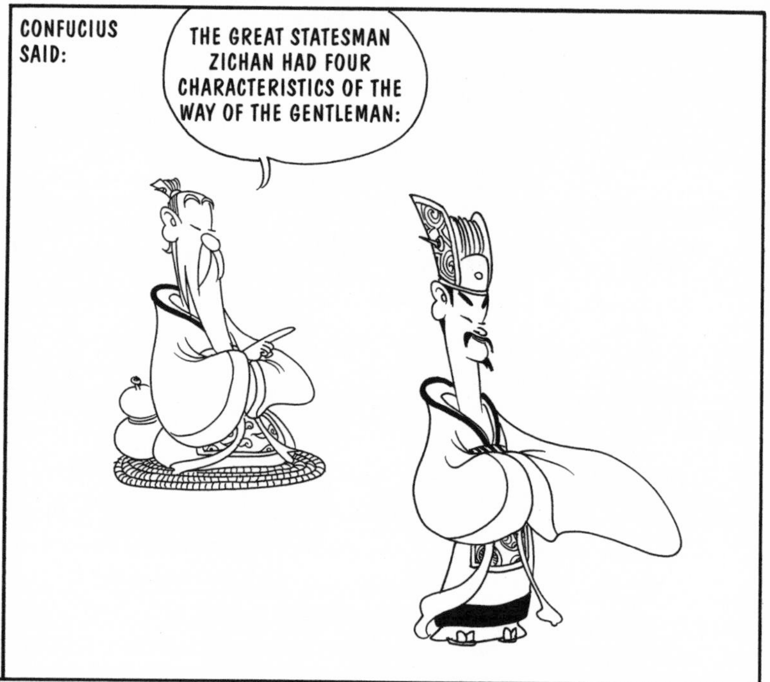

CONFUCIUS SAID:
THE GREAT STATESMAN ZICHAN HAD FOUR CHARACTERISTICS OF THE WAY OF THE GENTLEMAN:

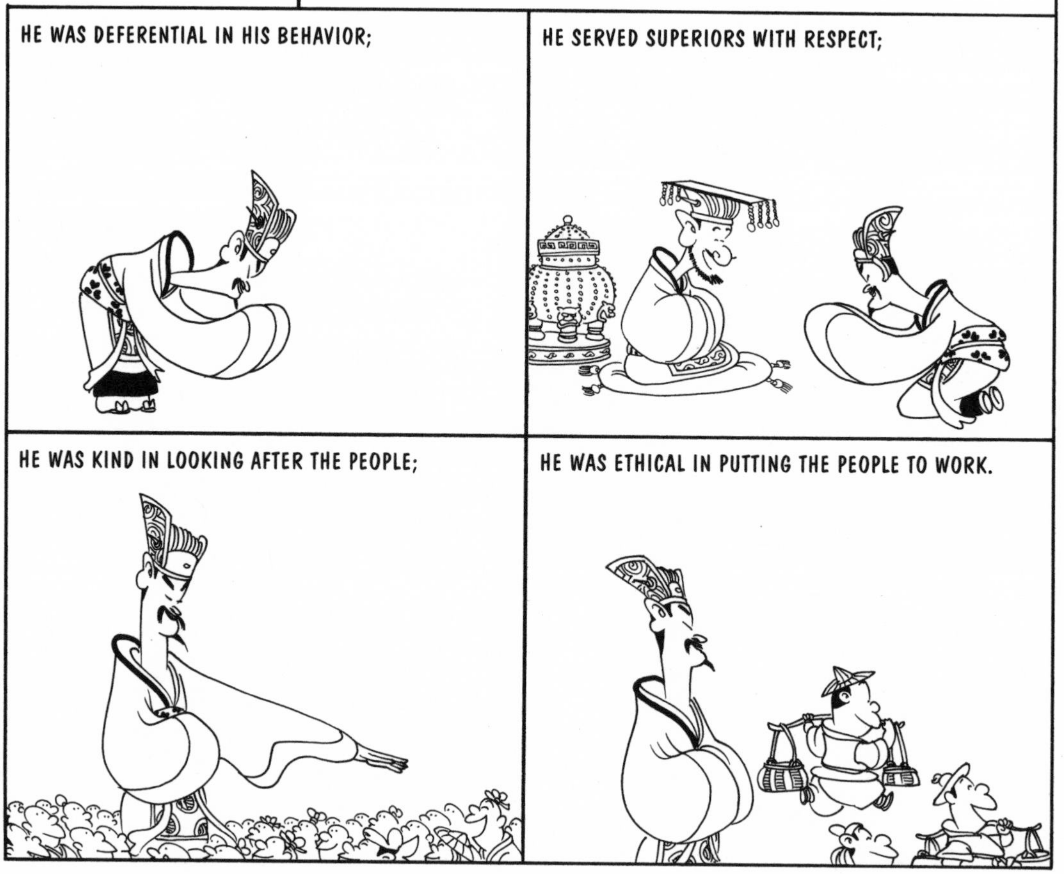

HE WAS DEFERENTIAL IN HIS BEHAVIOR;
HE SERVED SUPERIORS WITH RESPECT;
HE WAS KIND IN LOOKING AFTER THE PEOPLE;
HE WAS ETHICAL IN PUTTING THE PEOPLE TO WORK.

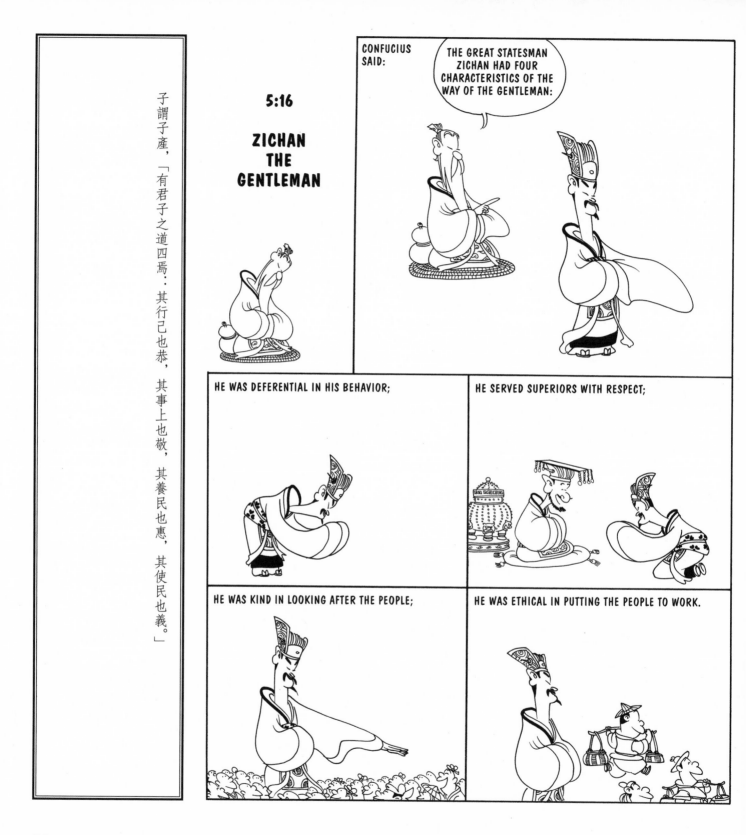

5:23

GRUDGE NOT

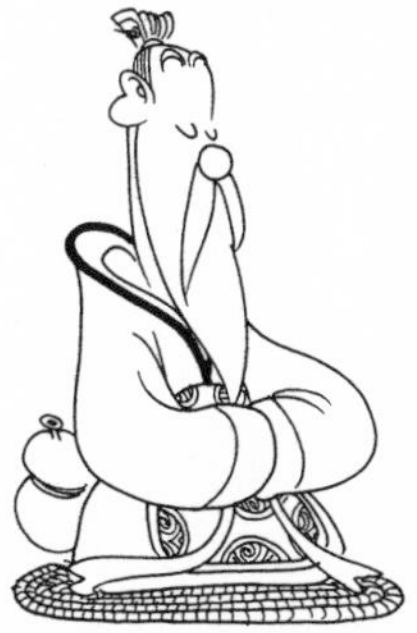

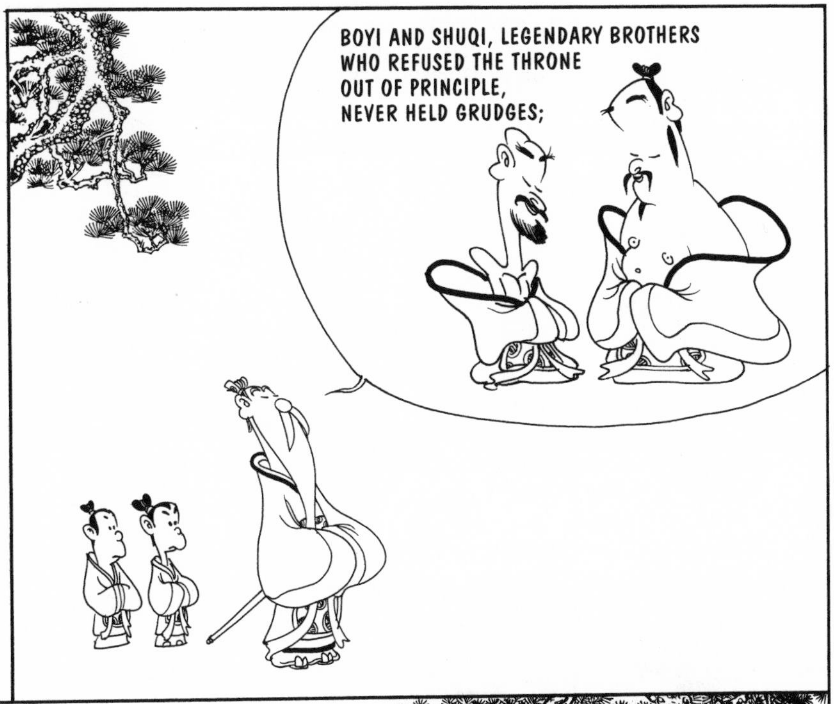
BOYI AND SHUQI, LEGENDARY BROTHERS WHO REFUSED THE THRONE OUT OF PRINCIPLE, NEVER HELD GRUDGES;

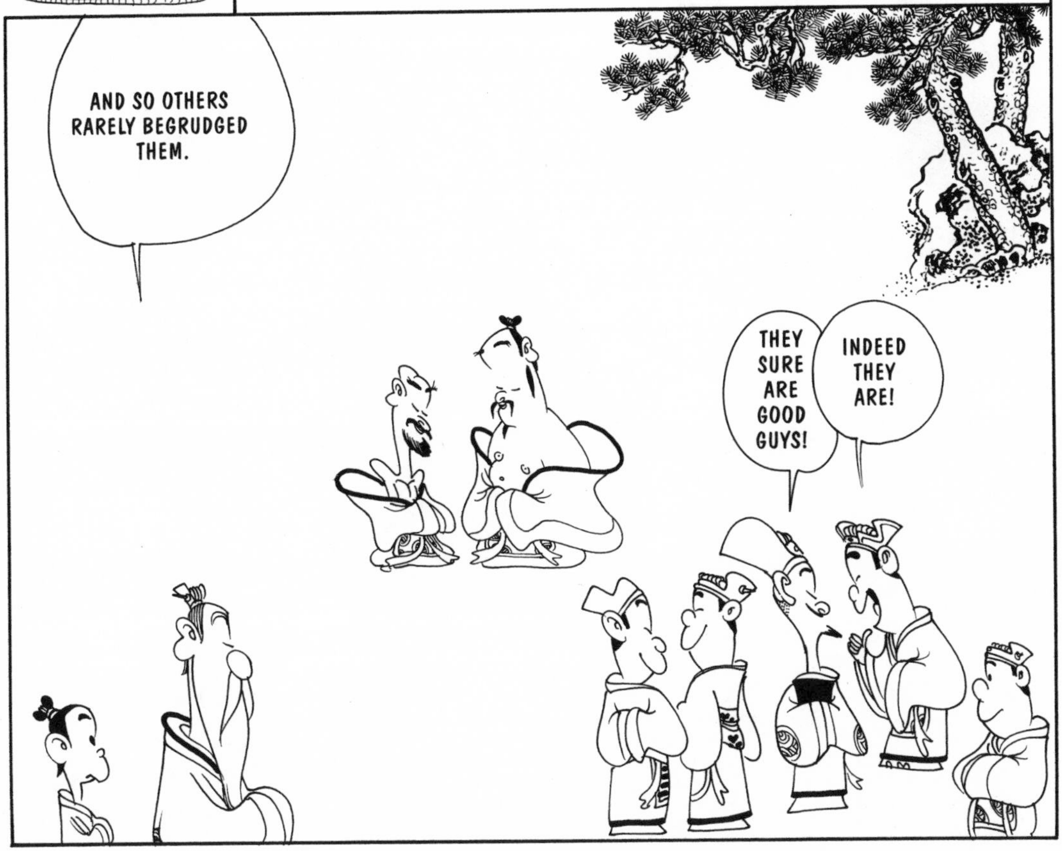
AND SO OTHERS RARELY BEGRUDGED THEM.
THEY SURE ARE GOOD GUYS!
INDEED THEY ARE!

子曰：「伯夷、叔齊不念舊惡，怨是用希。」

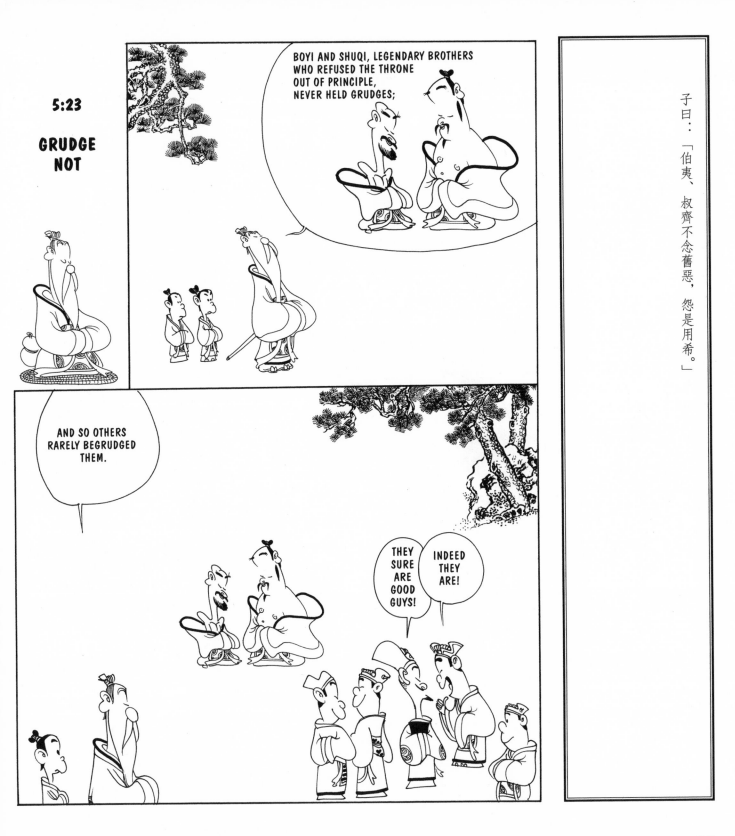

子曰：「巧言、令色、足恭，左丘明恥之，丘亦恥之。匿怨而友其人，左丘明恥之，丘亦恥之。」

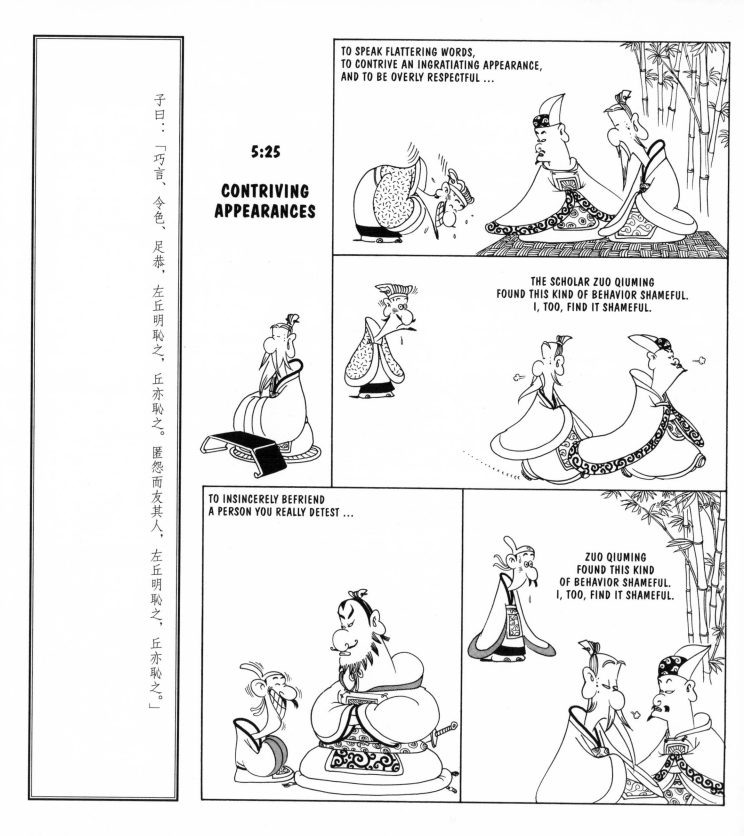

5:25

CONTRIVING APPEARANCES

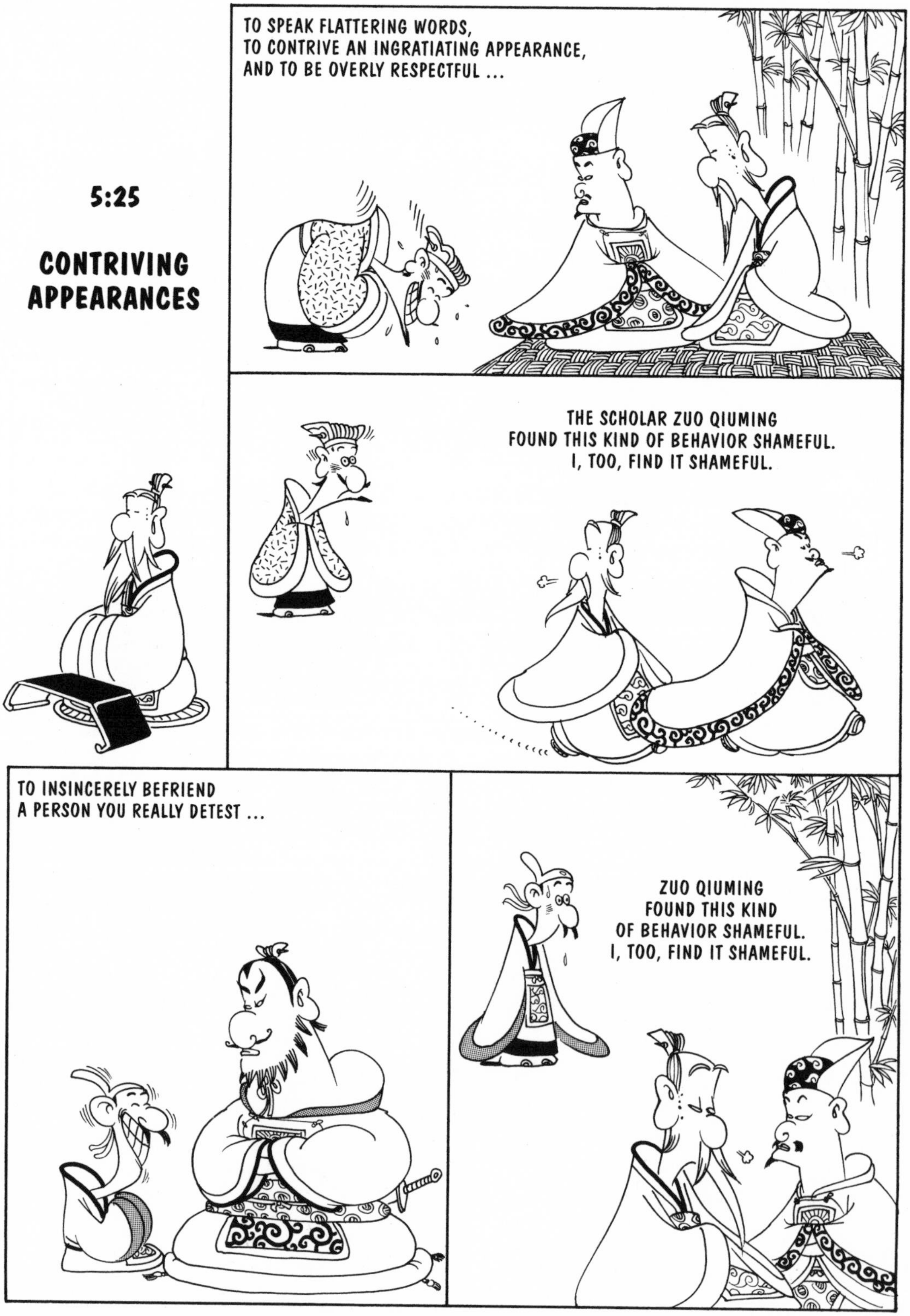

TO SPEAK FLATTERING WORDS, TO CONTRIVE AN INGRATIATING APPEARANCE, AND TO BE OVERLY RESPECTFUL ...
THE SCHOLAR ZUO QIUMING FOUND THIS KIND OF BEHAVIOR SHAMEFUL. I, TOO, FIND IT SHAMEFUL.
TO INSINCERELY BEFRIEND A PERSON YOU REALLY DETEST ...
ZUO QIUMING FOUND THIS KIND OF BEHAVIOR SHAMEFUL. I, TOO, FIND IT SHAMEFUL.

5:26

WISHES

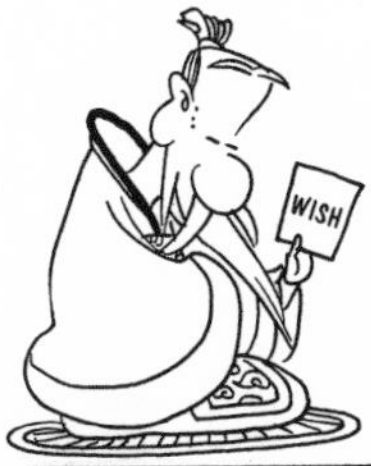
WISH

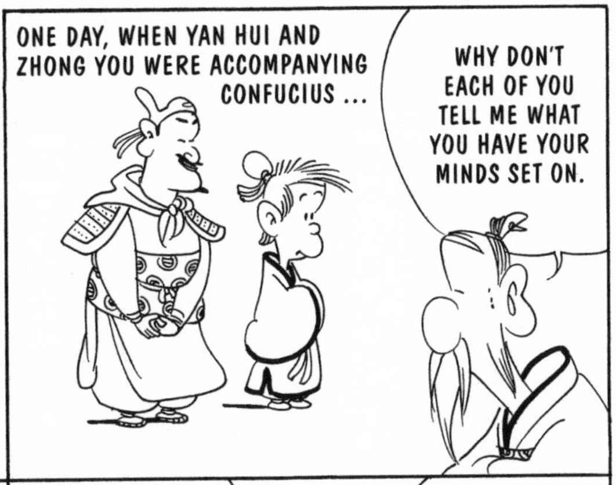
ONE DAY, WHEN YAN HUI AND ZHONG YOU WERE ACCOMPANYING CONFUCIUS ...
WHY DON'T EACH OF YOU TELL ME WHAT YOU HAVE YOUR MINDS SET ON.

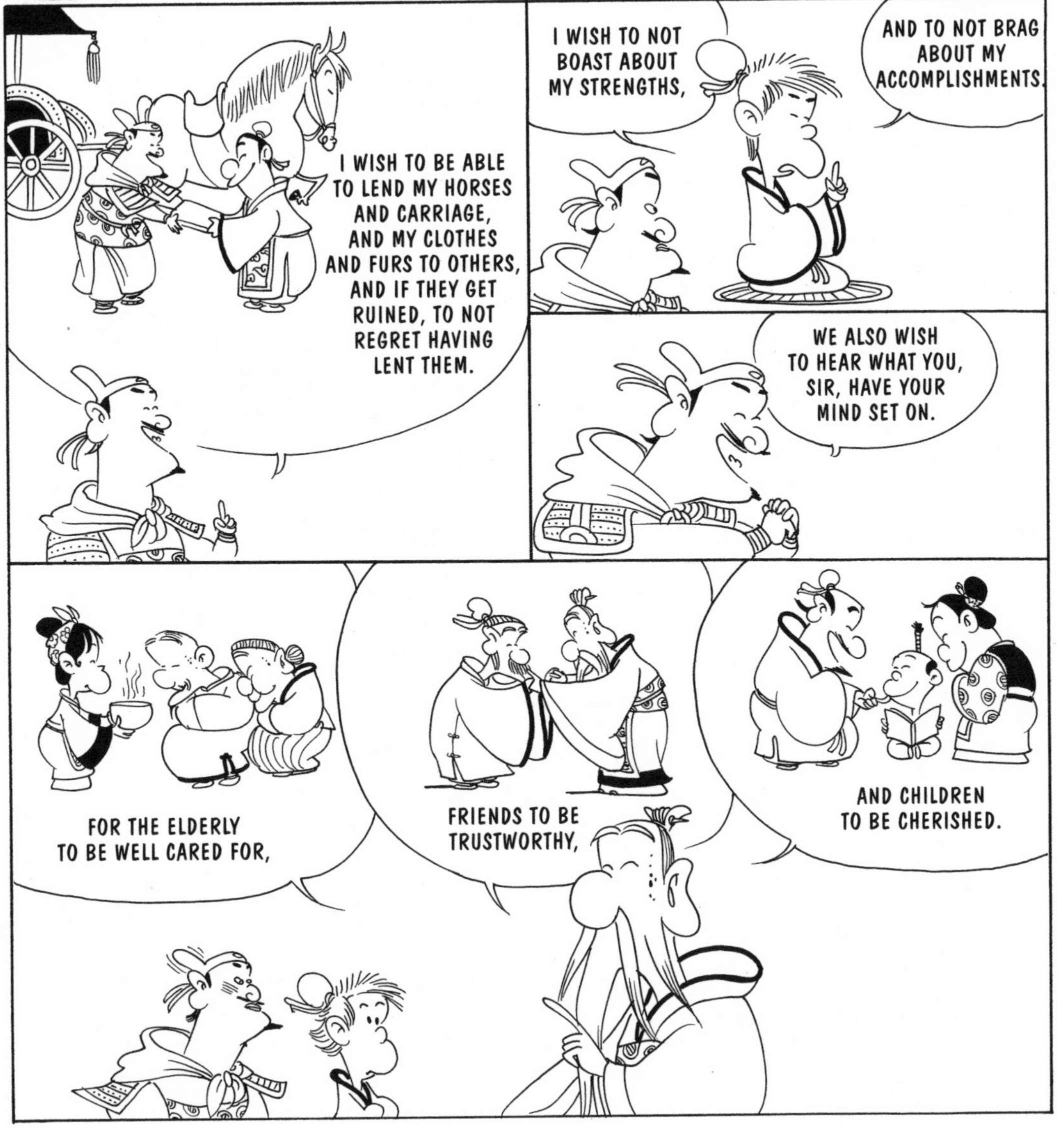

I WISH TO BE ABLE TO LEND MY HORSES AND CARRIAGE, AND MY CLOTHES AND FURS TO OTHERS, AND IF THEY GET RUINED, TO NOT REGRET HAVING LENT THEM.
I WISH TO NOT BOAST ABOUT MY STRENGTHS,
AND TO NOT BRAG ABOUT MY ACCOMPLISHMENTS.
WE ALSO WISH TO HEAR WHAT YOU, SIR, HAVE YOUR MIND SET ON.
FOR THE ELDERLY TO BE WELL CARED FOR,
FRIENDS TO BE TRUSTWORTHY,
AND CHILDREN TO BE CHERISHED.

顏淵季路侍。子曰：「盍各言爾志？」子路曰：「願車馬衣裘與朋友共，敝之而無憾。」顏淵曰：「願無伐善，無施勞。」子路曰：「願聞子之志。」子曰：「老者安之，朋友信之，少者懷之。」

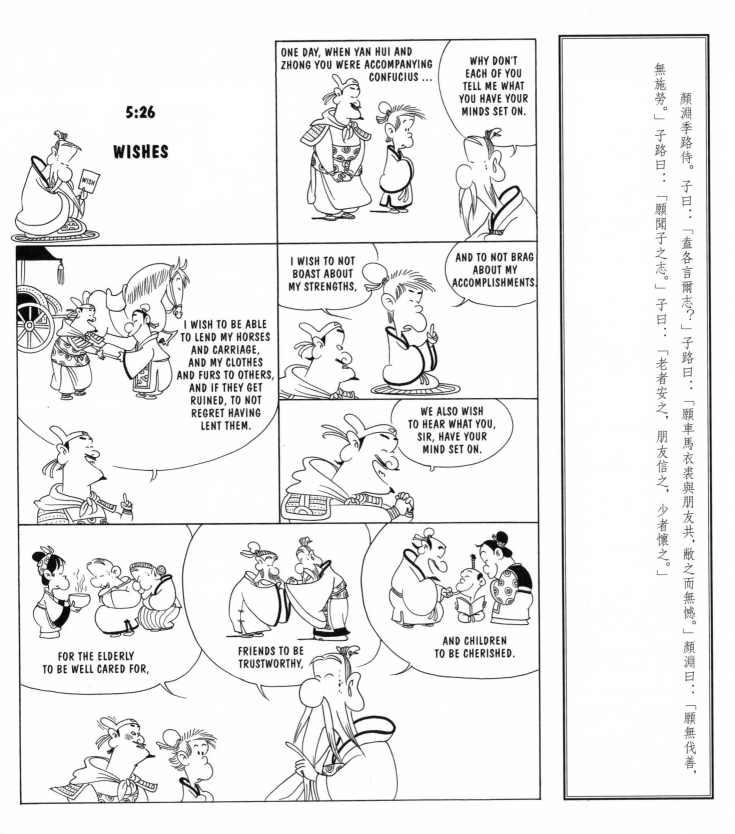

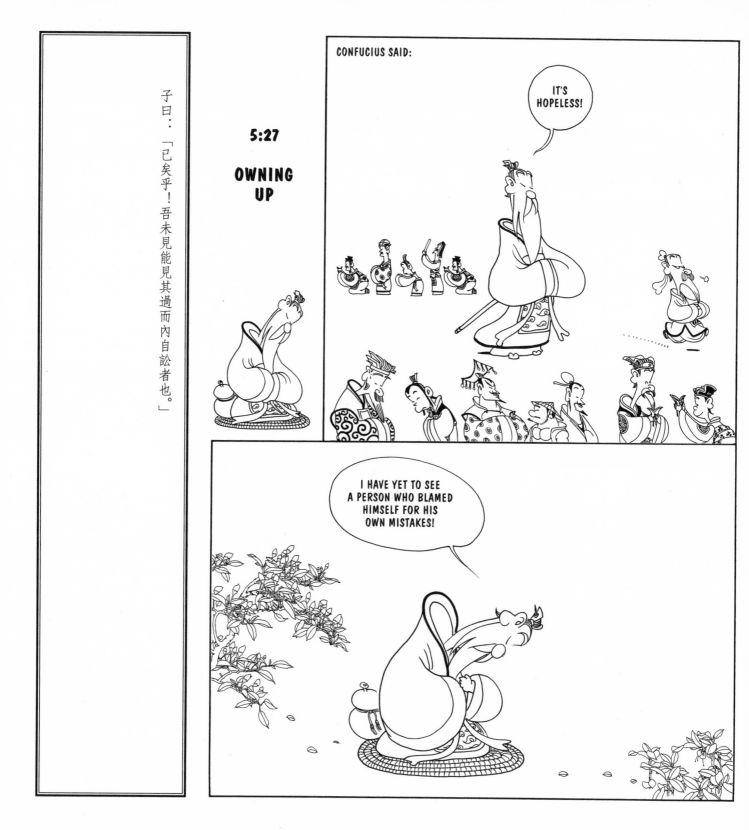

子曰：「已矣乎！吾未見能見其過而內自訟者也。」

5:27

OWNING UP

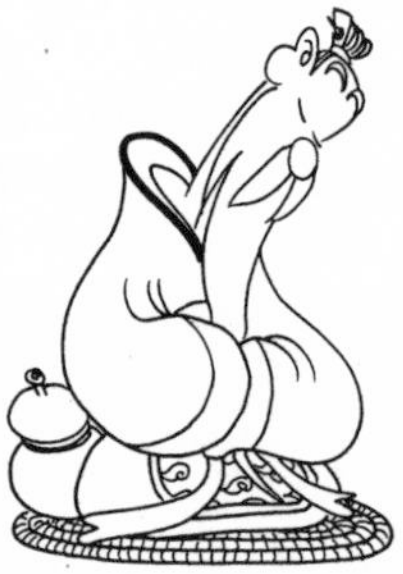

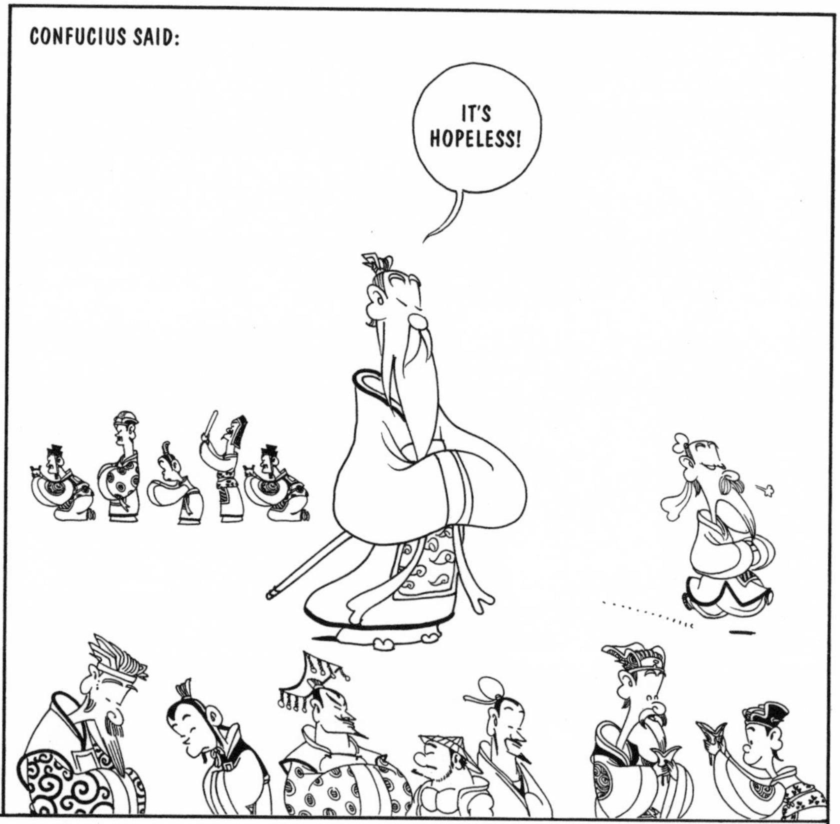
CONFUCIUS SAID:
IT'S HOPELESS!

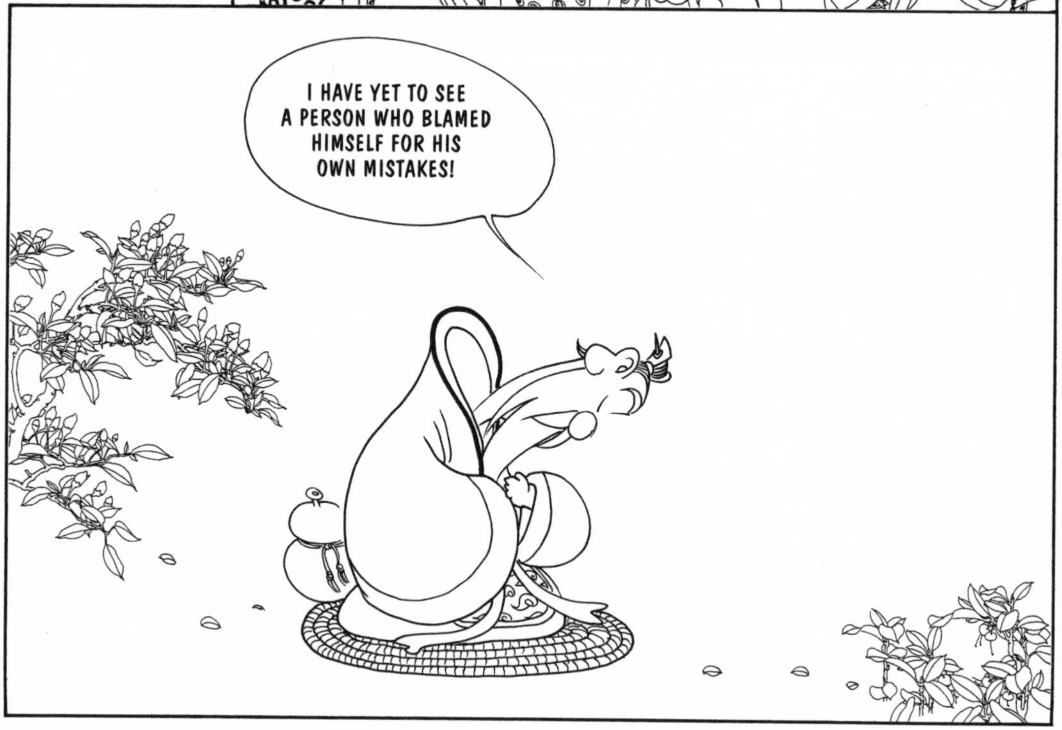
I HAVE YET TO SEE A PERSON WHO BLAMED HIMSELF FOR HIS OWN MISTAKES!

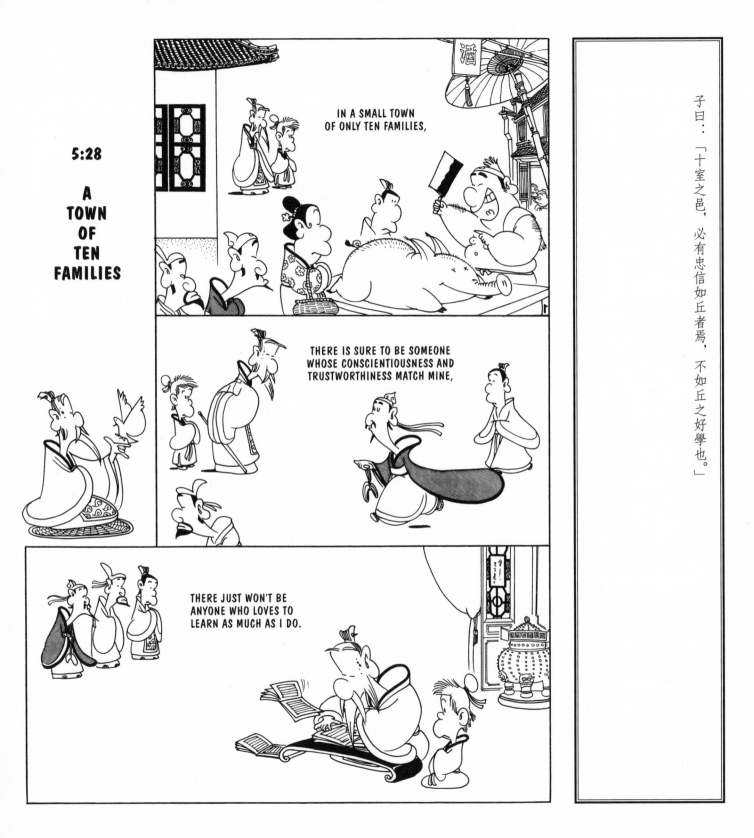

5:28

A TOWN OF TEN FAMILIES

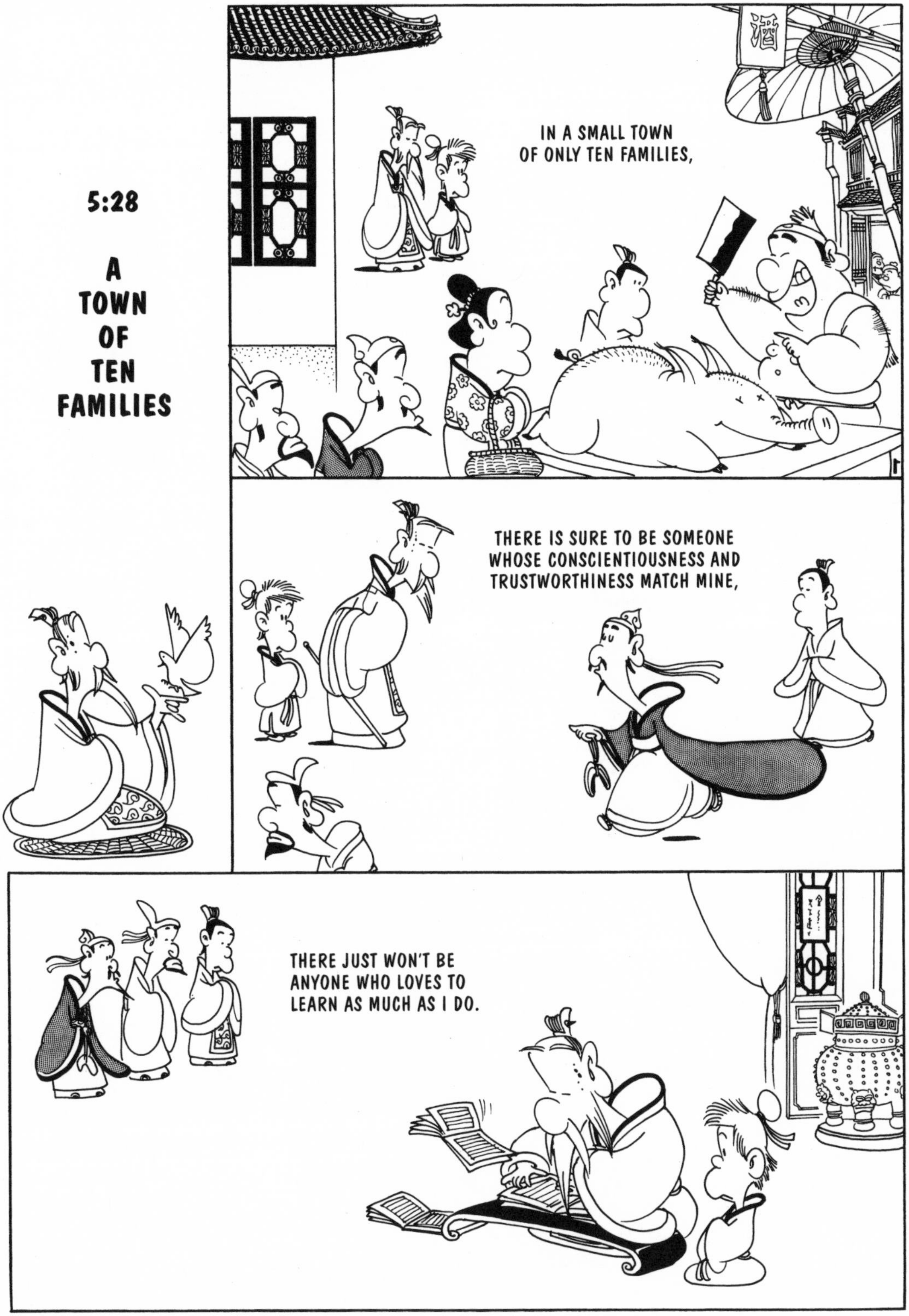

IN A SMALL TOWN OF ONLY TEN FAMILIES,
酒
THERE IS SURE TO BE SOMEONE WHOSE CONSCIENTIOUSNESS AND TRUSTWORTHINESS MATCH MINE,
THERE JUST WON'T BE ANYONE WHO LOVES TO LEARN AS MUCH AS I DO.

子曰：「十室之邑，必有忠信如丘者焉，不如丘之好學也。」

哀公問：「弟子孰為好學？」孔子對曰：「有顏回者好學，不遷怒，不貳過。不幸短命死矣，今也則亡，未聞好學者也。」

6:3

YAN HUI'S LEARNING

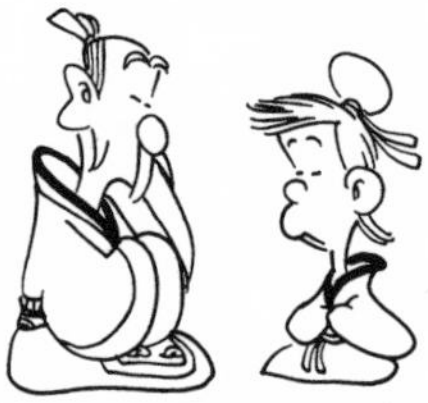

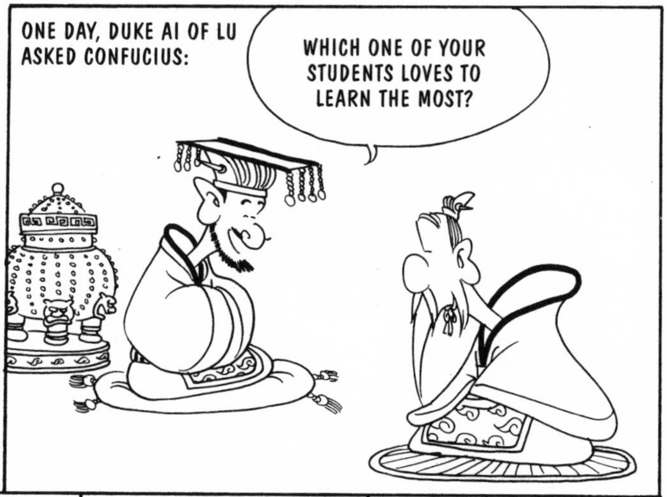
ONE DAY, DUKE AI OF LU ASKED CONFUCIUS:
WHICH ONE OF YOUR STUDENTS LOVES TO LEARN THE MOST?

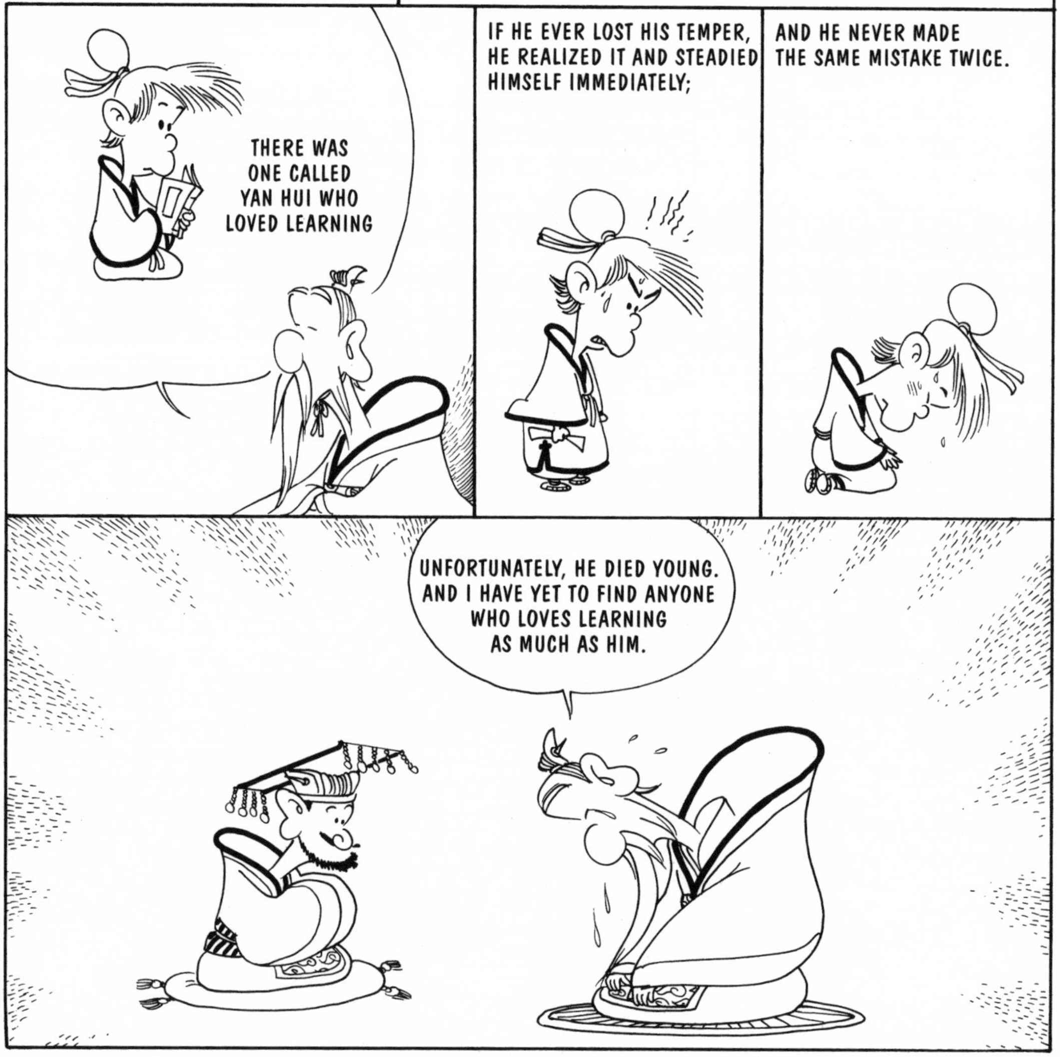
THERE WAS ONE CALLED YAN HUI WHO LOVED LEARNING
IF HE EVER LOST HIS TEMPER, HE REALIZED IT AND STEADIED HIMSELF IMMEDIATELY;
AND HE NEVER MADE THE SAME MISTAKE TWICE.
UNFORTUNATELY, HE DIED YOUNG. AND I HAVE YET TO FIND ANYONE WHO LOVES LEARNING AS MUCH AS HIM.

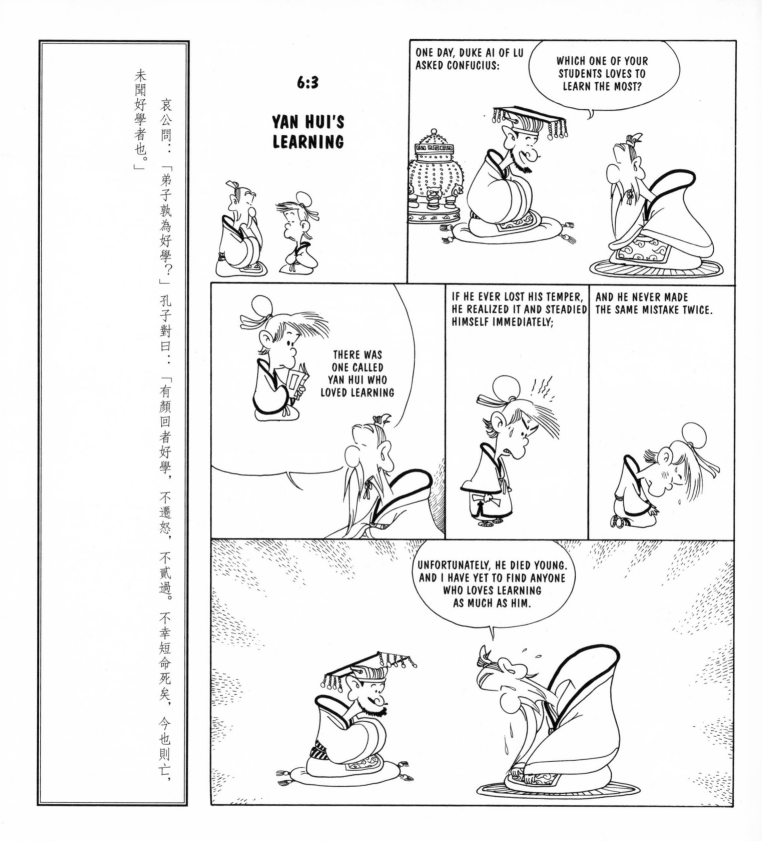

6:11

YAN HUI

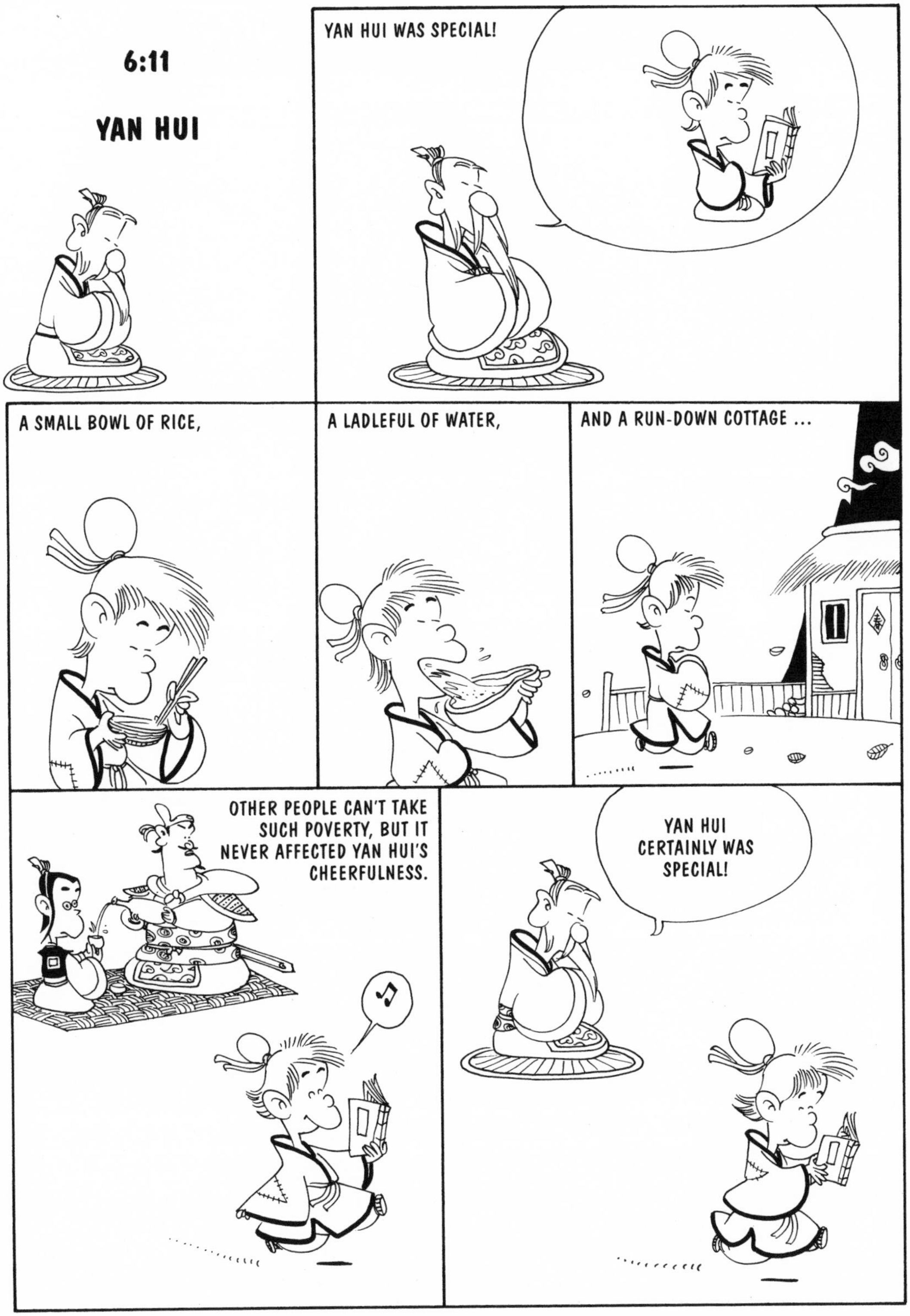

YAN HUI WAS SPECIAL!
A SMALL BOWL OF RICE,
A LADLEFUL OF WATER,
AND A RUN-DOWN COTTAGE ...
OTHER PEOPLE CAN'T TAKE SUCH POVERTY, BUT IT NEVER AFFECTED YAN HUI'S CHEERFULNESS.
YAN HUI CERTAINLY WAS SPECIAL!

子曰：「賢哉回也！一簞食，一瓢飲，在陋巷，人不堪其憂，回也不改其樂。賢哉回也！」

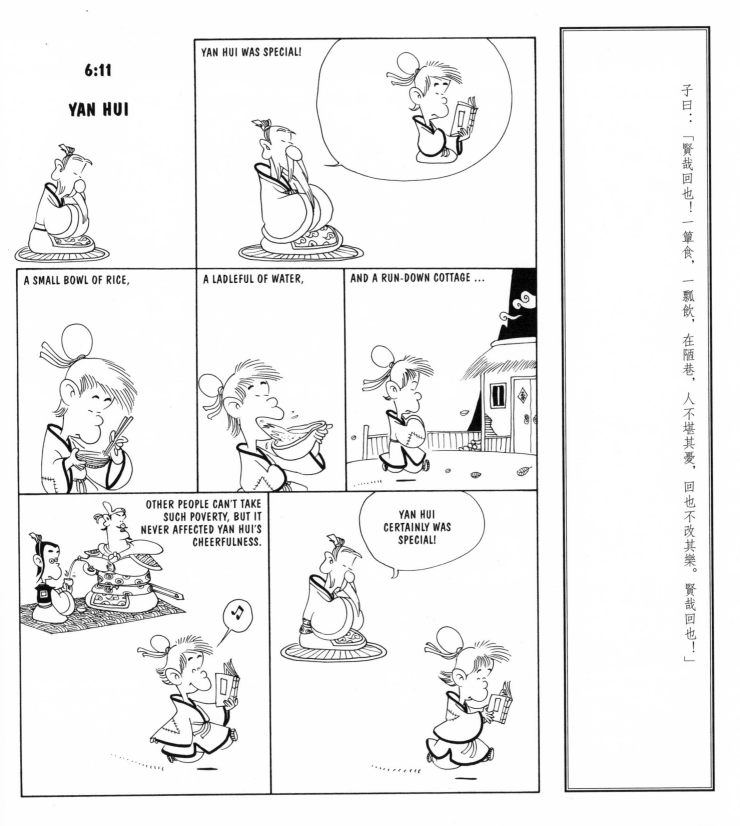

子曰：「質勝文則野，文勝質則史。文質彬彬，然後君子。」

6:18

PEASANTS AND PEDANTS

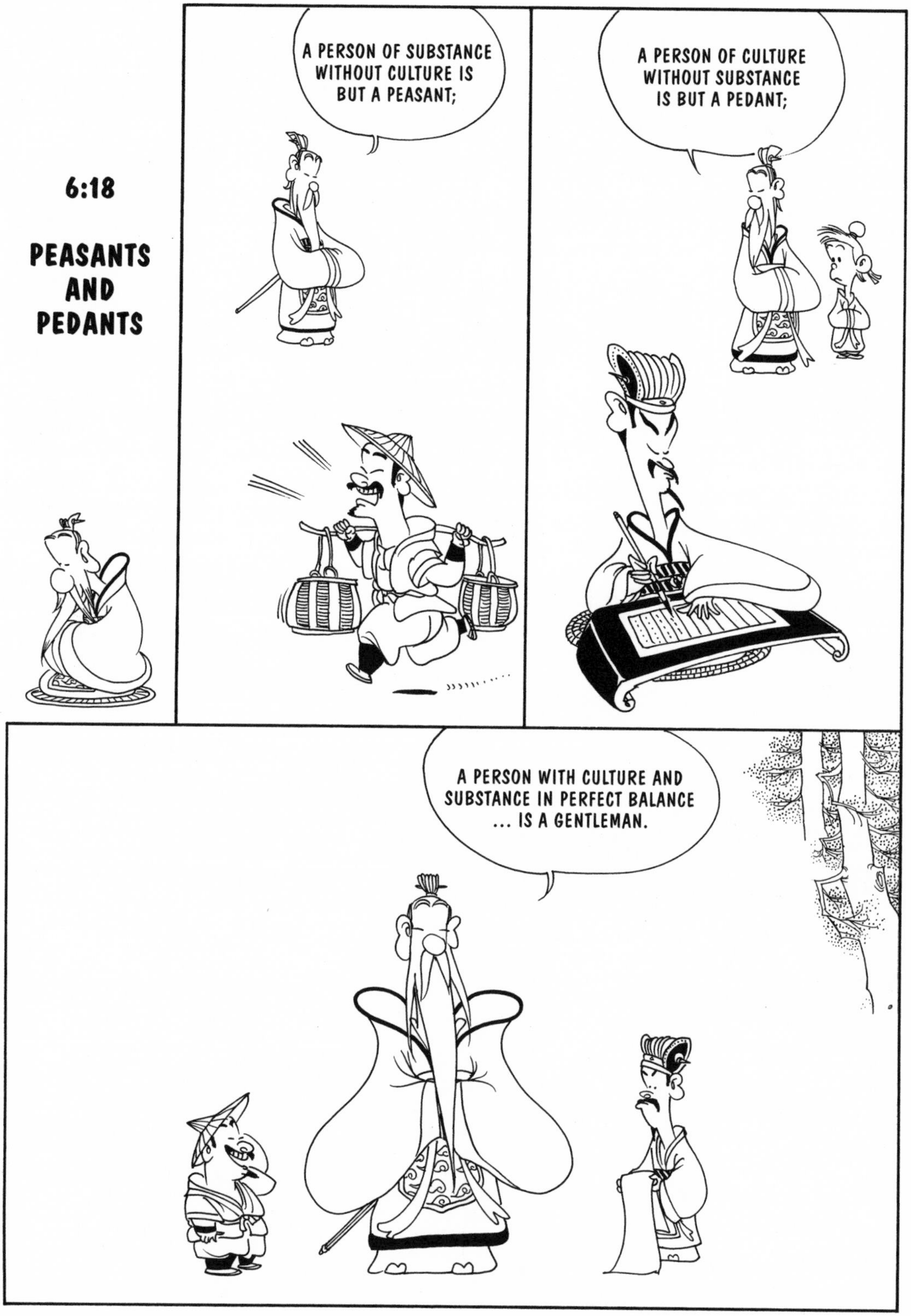
A PERSON OF SUBSTANCE WITHOUT CULTURE IS BUT A PEASANT;
A PERSON OF CULTURE WITHOUT SUBSTANCE IS BUT A PEDANT;
A PERSON WITH CULTURE AND SUBSTANCE IN PERFECT BALANCE ... IS A GENTLEMAN.

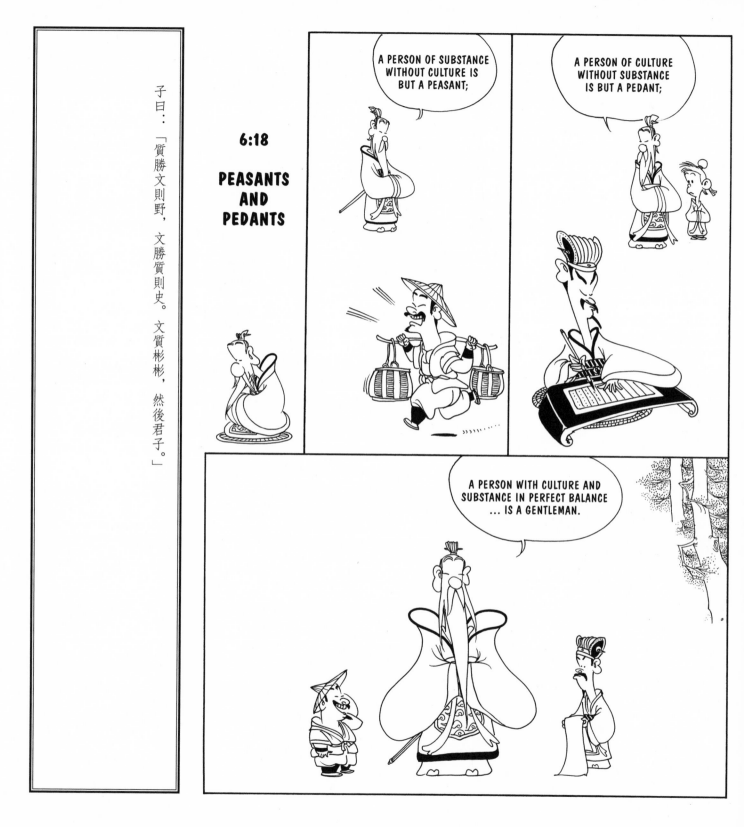

6:20

DELIGHT IS BEST

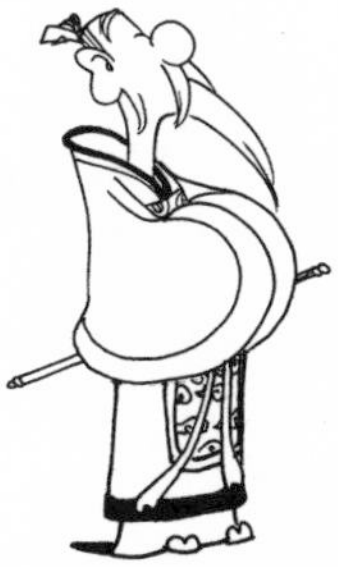

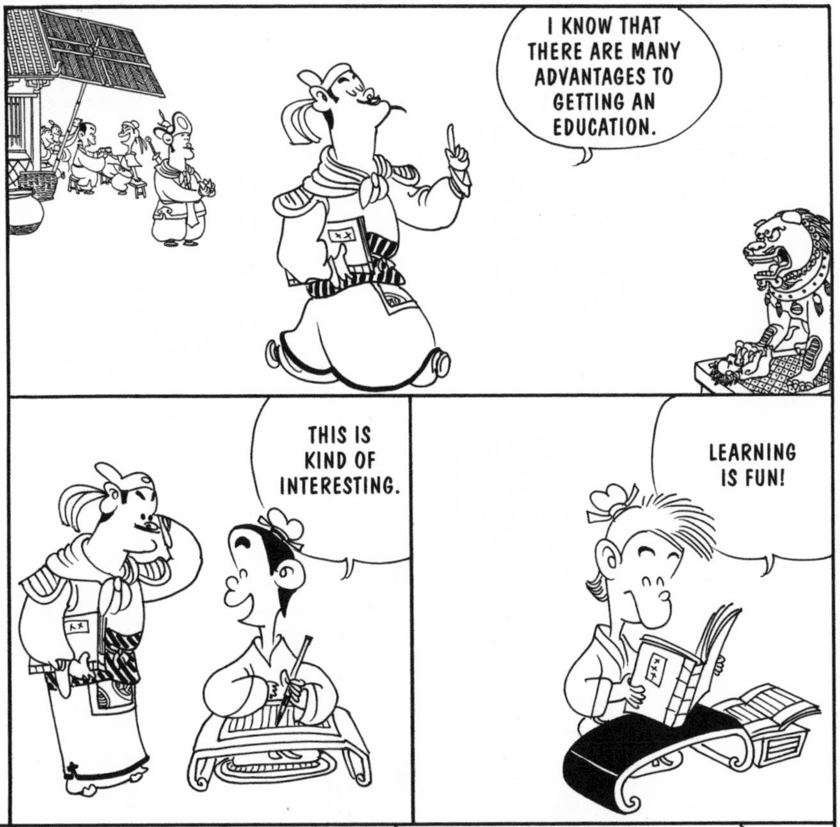
I KNOW THAT THERE ARE MANY ADVANTAGES TO GETTING AN EDUCATION.
THIS IS KIND OF INTERESTING.
LEARNING IS FUN!

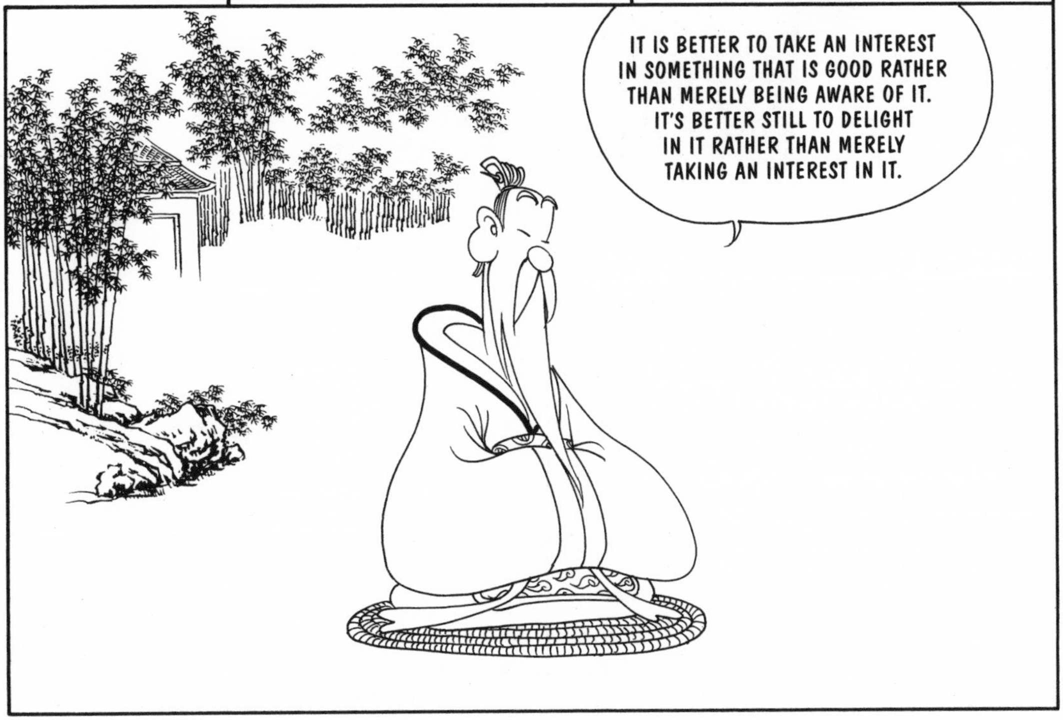

IT IS BETTER TO TAKE AN INTEREST IN SOMETHING THAT IS GOOD RATHER THAN MERELY BEING AWARE OF IT. IT'S BETTER STILL TO DELIGHT IN IT RATHER THAN MERELY TAKING AN INTEREST IN IT.

子曰：「知之者不如好之者，好之者不如樂之者。」

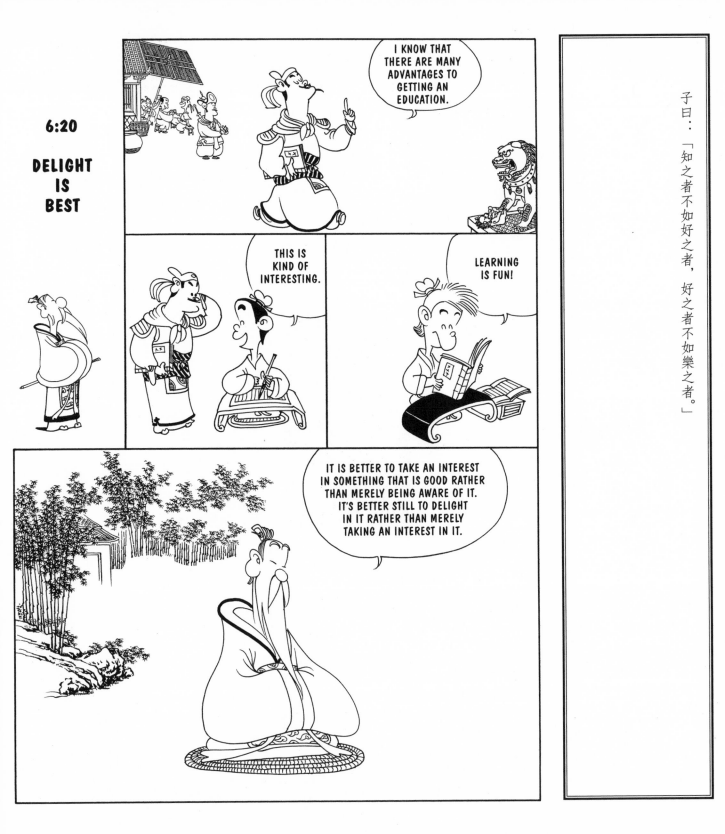

子曰：「知者樂水，仁者樂山。知者動，仁者靜。知者樂，仁者壽。」

6:23

THE WISE AND THE BENEVOLENT

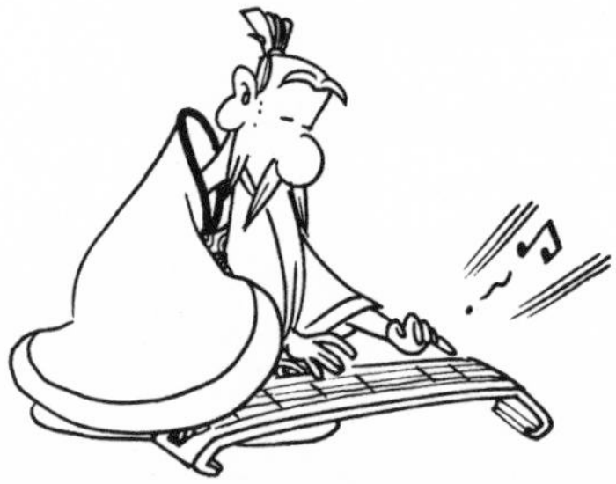

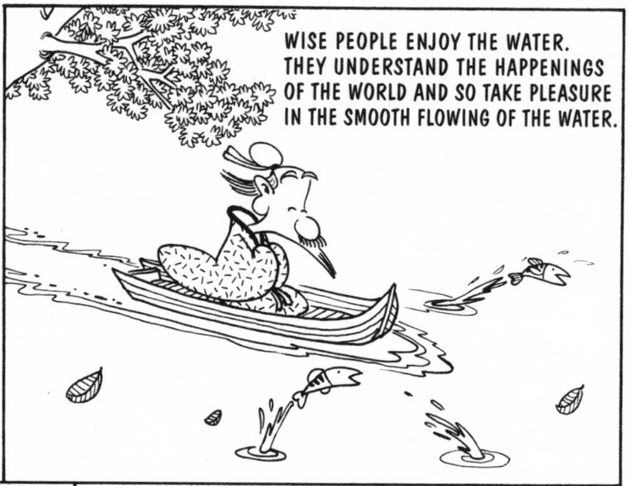
WISE PEOPLE ENJOY THE WATER. THEY UNDERSTAND THE HAPPENINGS OF THE WORLD AND SO TAKE PLEASURE IN THE SMOOTH FLOWING OF THE WATER.

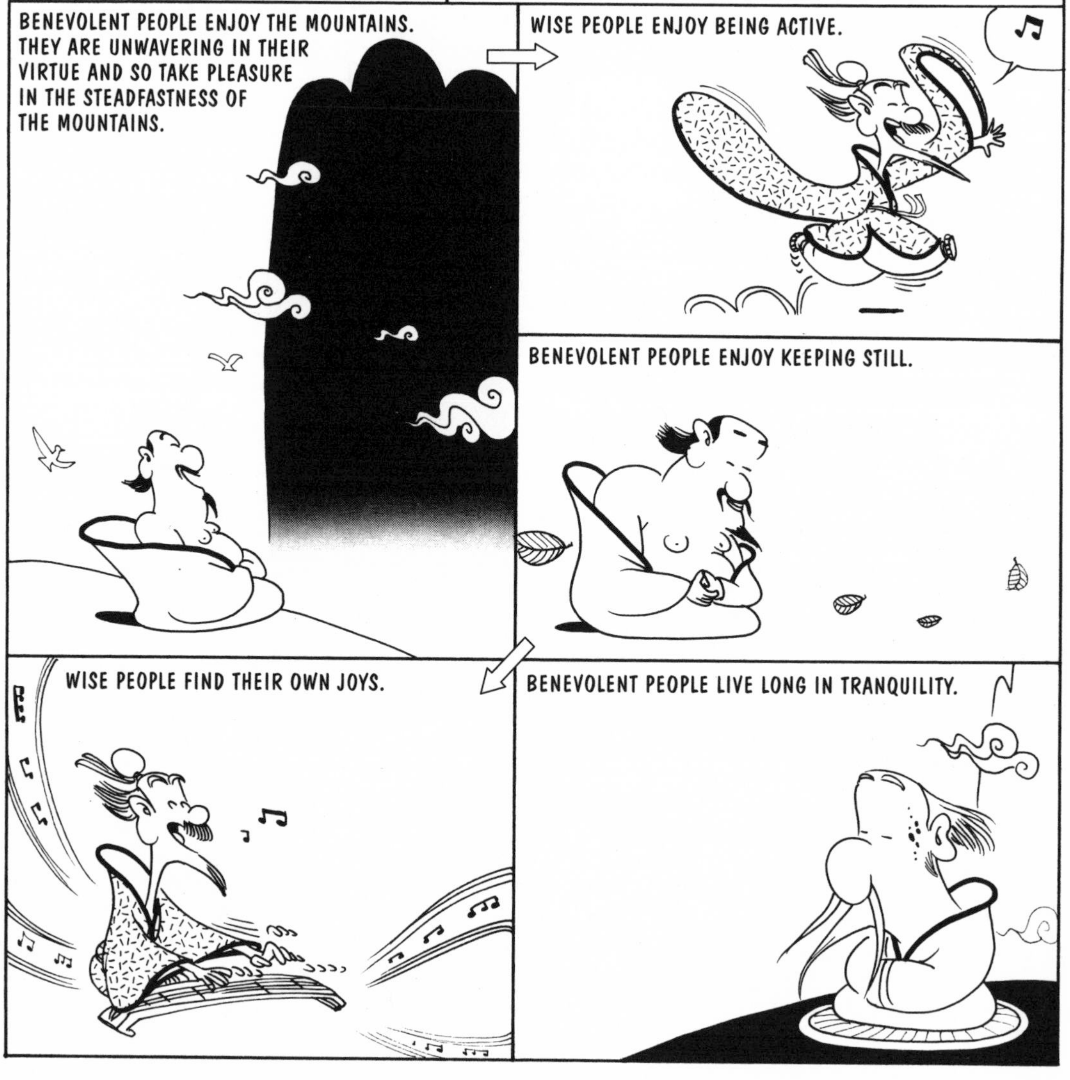
BENEVOLENT PEOPLE ENJOY THE MOUNTAINS. THEY ARE UNWAVERING IN THEIR VIRTUE AND SO TAKE PLEASURE IN THE STEADFASTNESS OF THE MOUNTAINS.
WISE PEOPLE ENJOY BEING ACTIVE.
BENEVOLENT PEOPLE ENJOY KEEPING STILL.
WISE PEOPLE FIND THEIR OWN JOYS.
BENEVOLENT PEOPLE LIVE LONG IN TRANQUILITY.

6:27

THE GENTLEMAN'S WAY

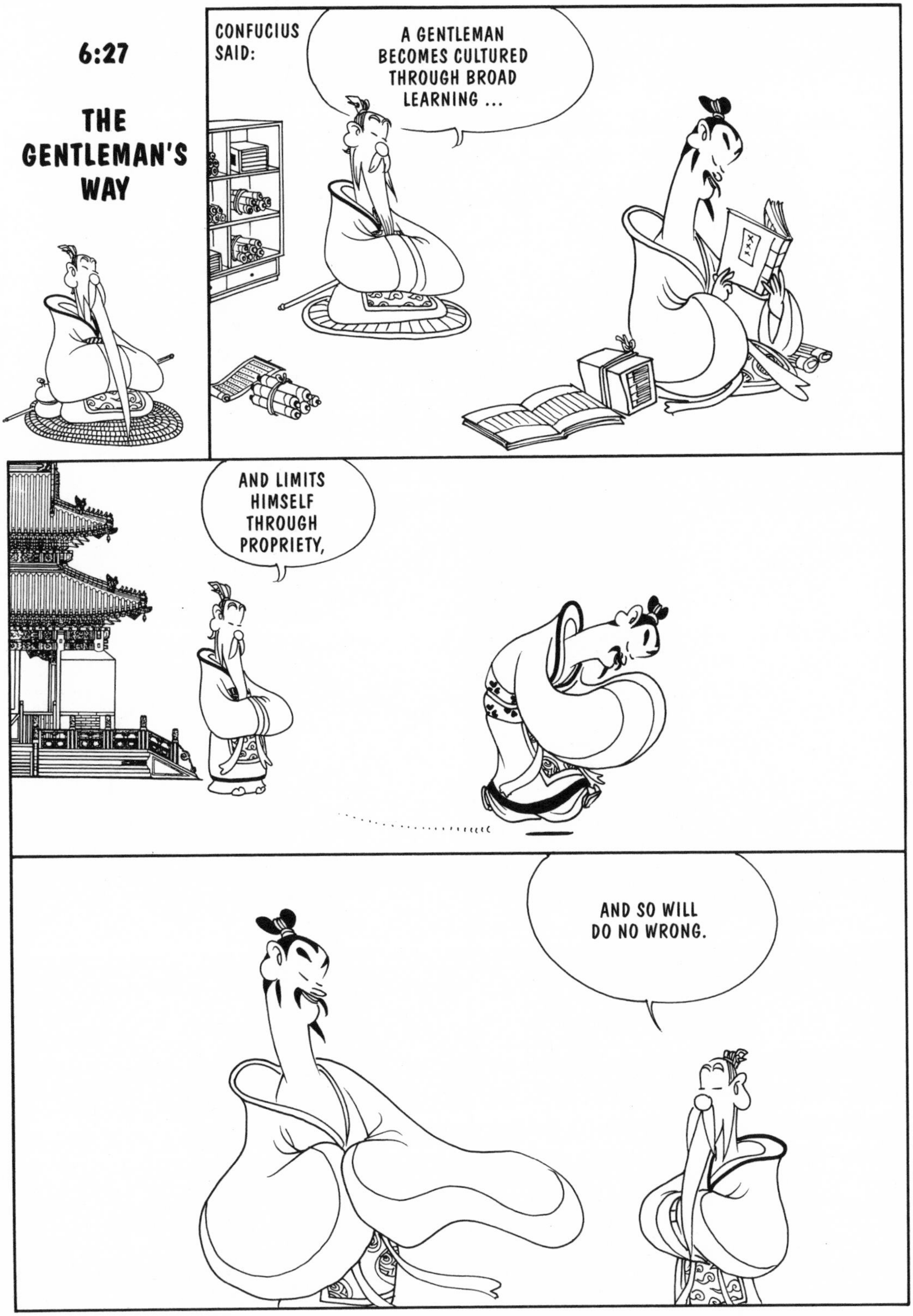
CONFUCIUS SAID:
A GENTLEMAN BECOMES CULTURED THROUGH BROAD LEARNING ...
AND LIMITS HIMSELF THROUGH PROPRIETY,
AND SO WILL DO NO WRONG.

子曰：「君子博學於文，約之以禮，亦可以弗畔矣夫！」

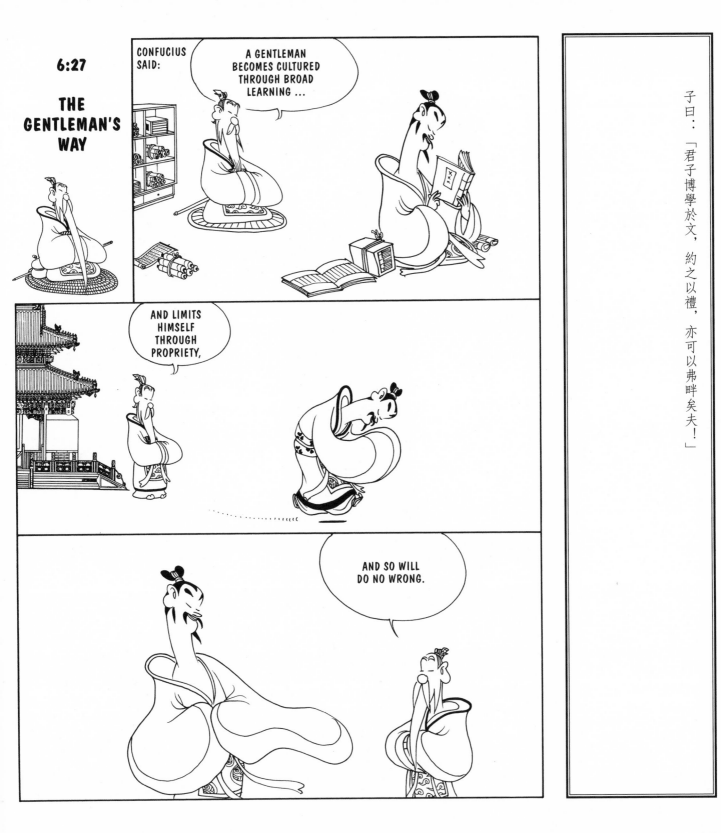

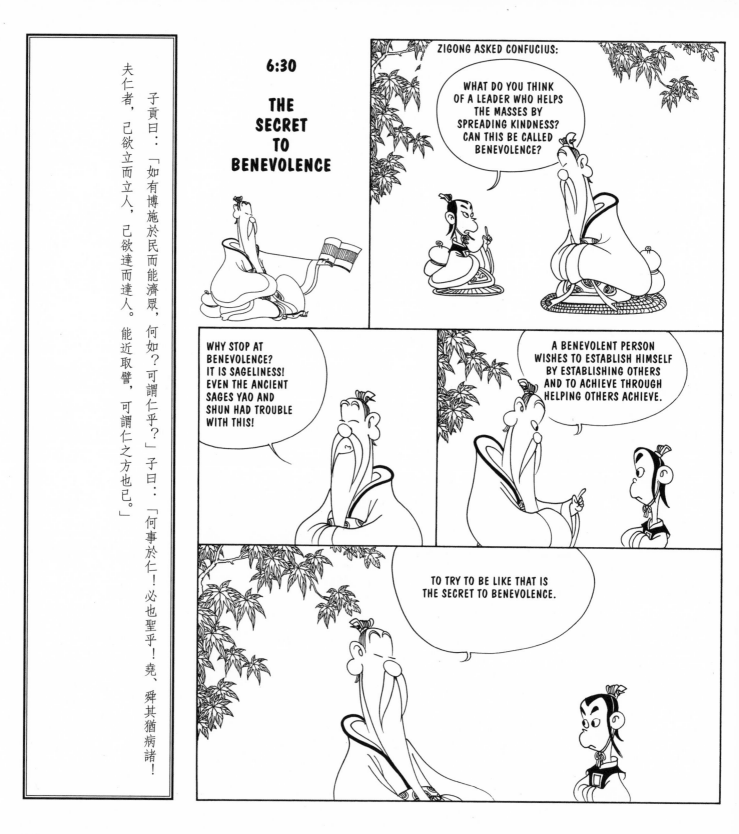

子貢曰：「如有博施於民而能濟眾，何如？可謂仁乎？」子曰：「何事於仁！必也聖乎！堯、舜其猶病諸！夫仁者，己欲立而立人，己欲達而達人。能近取譬，可謂仁之方也已。」

6:30

THE SECRET TO BENEVOLENCE

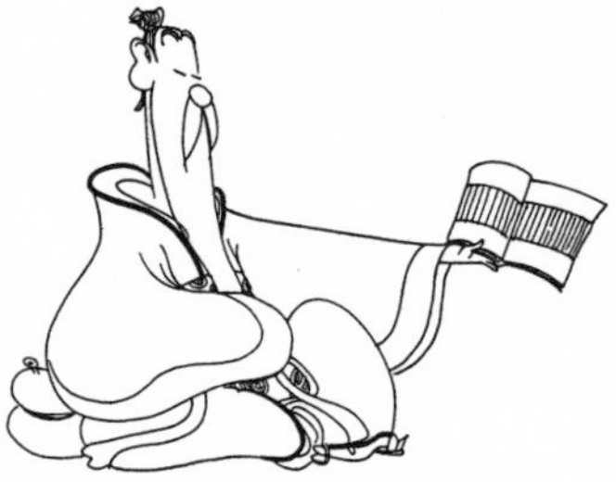

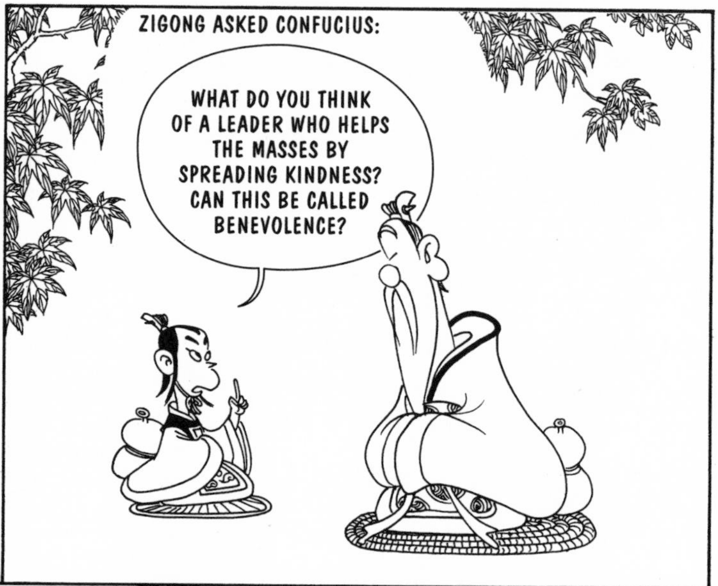
ZIGONG ASKED CONFUCIUS:
WHAT DO YOU THINK OF A LEADER WHO HELPS THE MASSES BY SPREADING KINDNESS? CAN THIS BE CALLED BENEVOLENCE?

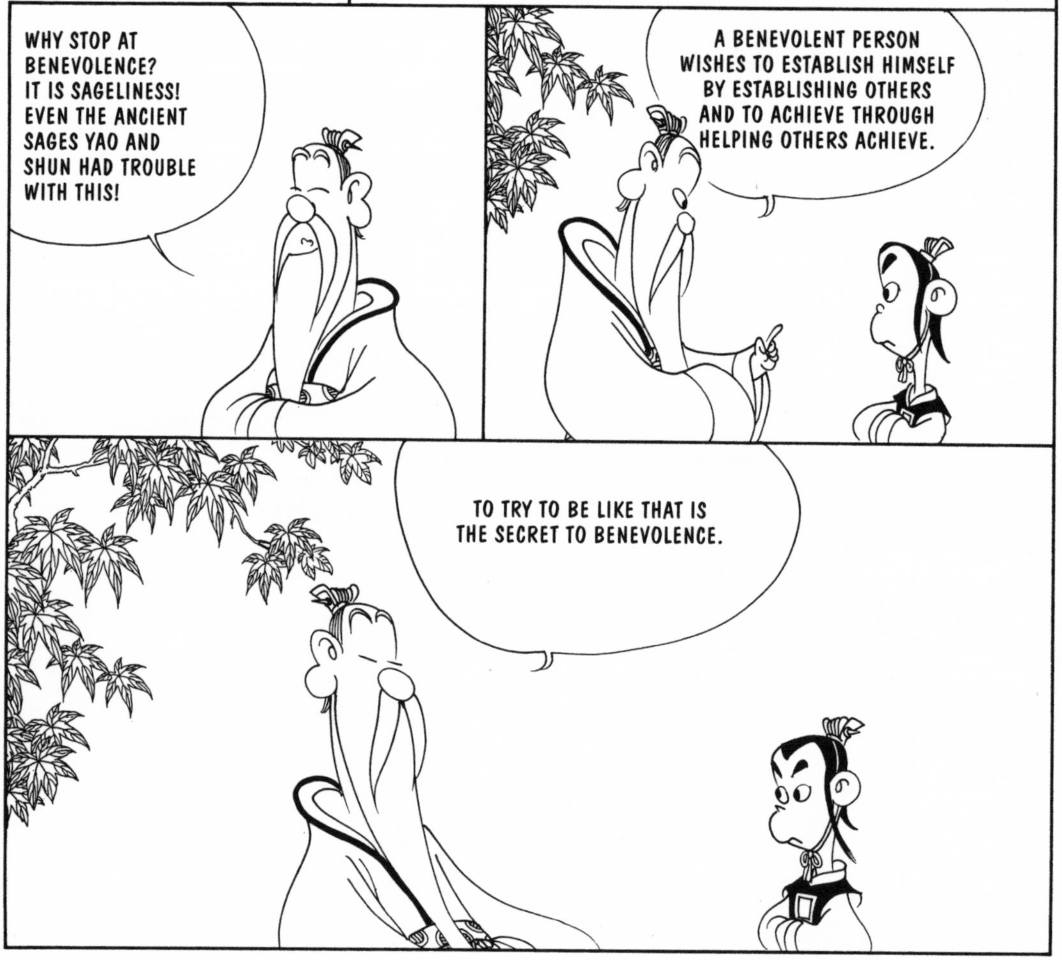
WHY STOP AT BENEVOLENCE? IT IS SAGELINESS! EVEN THE ANCIENT SAGES YAO AND SHUN HAD TROUBLE WITH THIS!
A BENEVOLENT PERSON WISHES TO ESTABLISH HIMSELF BY ESTABLISHING OTHERS AND TO ACHIEVE THROUGH HELPING OTHERS ACHIEVE.
TO TRY TO BE LIKE THAT IS THE SECRET TO BENEVOLENCE.

7:1

TRANSMITTING IDEAS

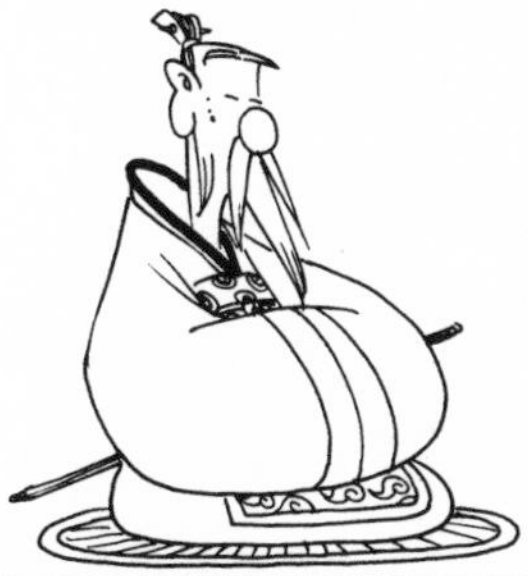

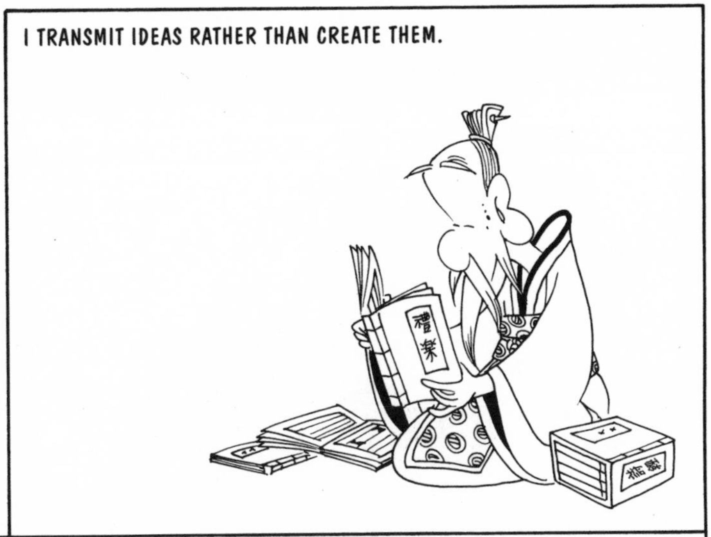
I TRANSMIT IDEAS RATHER THAN CREATE THEM.
禮樂

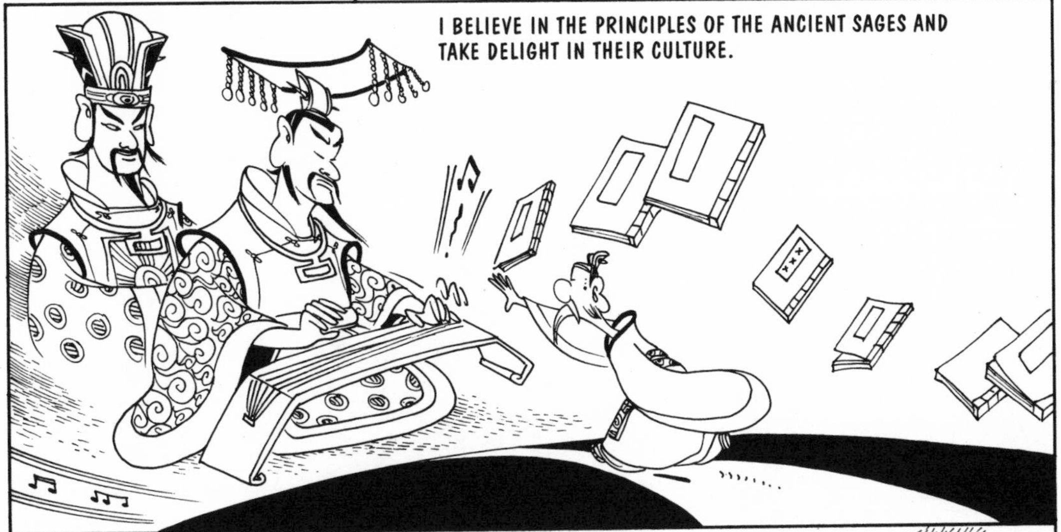
I BELIEVE IN THE PRINCIPLES OF THE ANCIENT SAGES AND TAKE DELIGHT IN THEIR CULTURE.

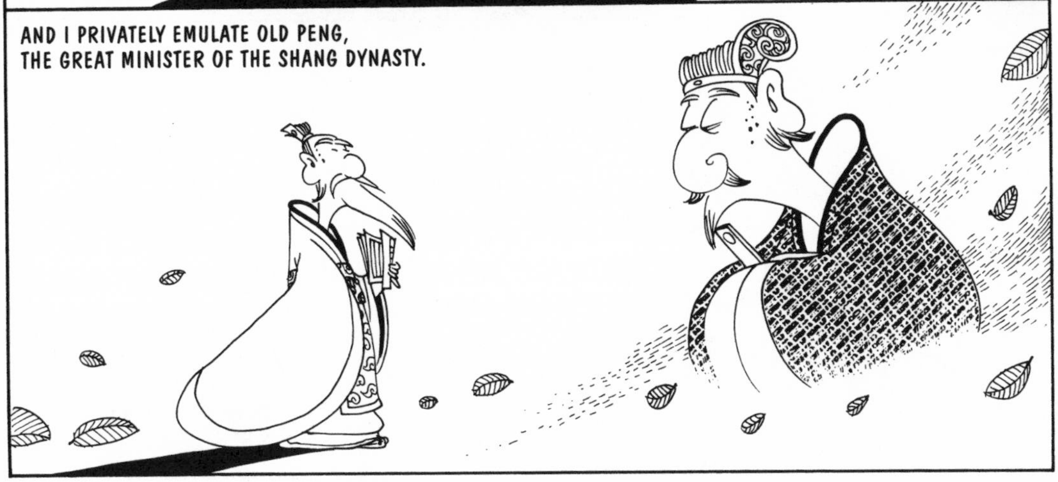
AND I PRIVATELY EMULATE OLD PENG, THE GREAT MINISTER OF THE SHANG DYNASTY.

子曰：「述而不作，信而好古，竊比於我老彭。」

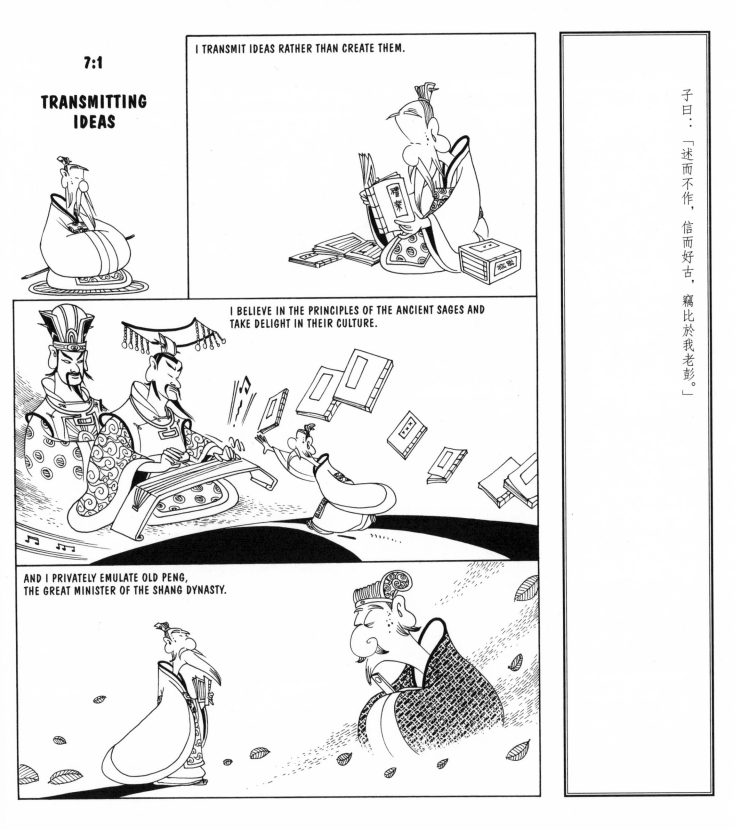

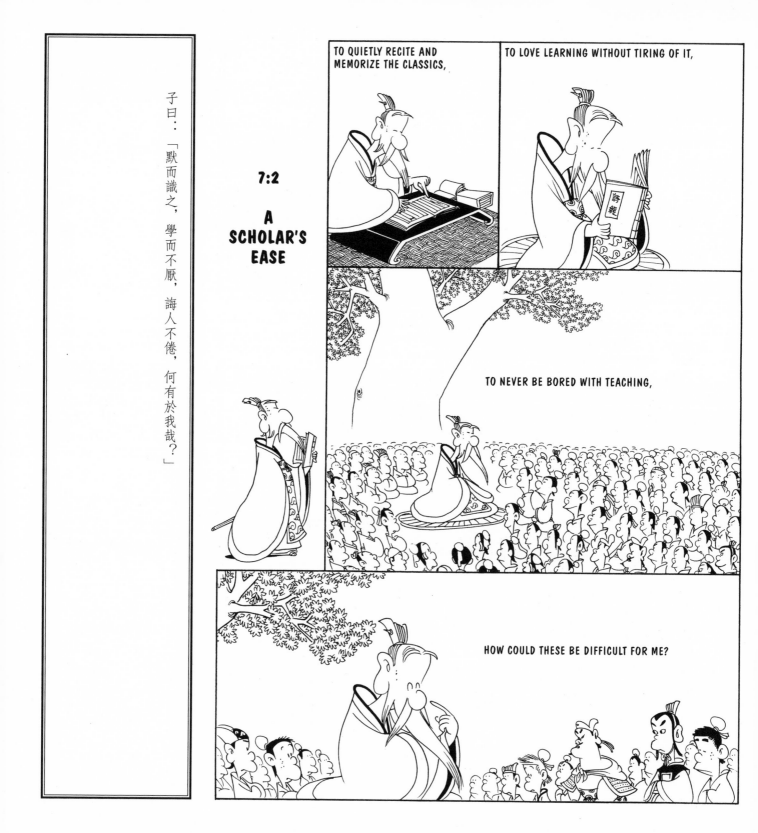

子曰：「默而識之，學而不厭，誨人不倦，何有於我哉？」

7:2

A SCHOLAR'S EASE

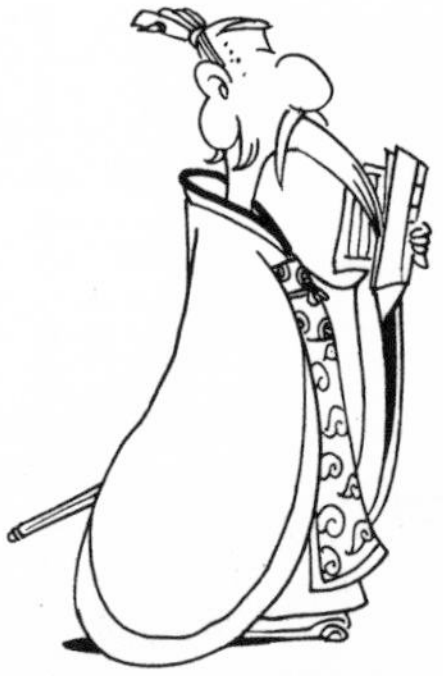

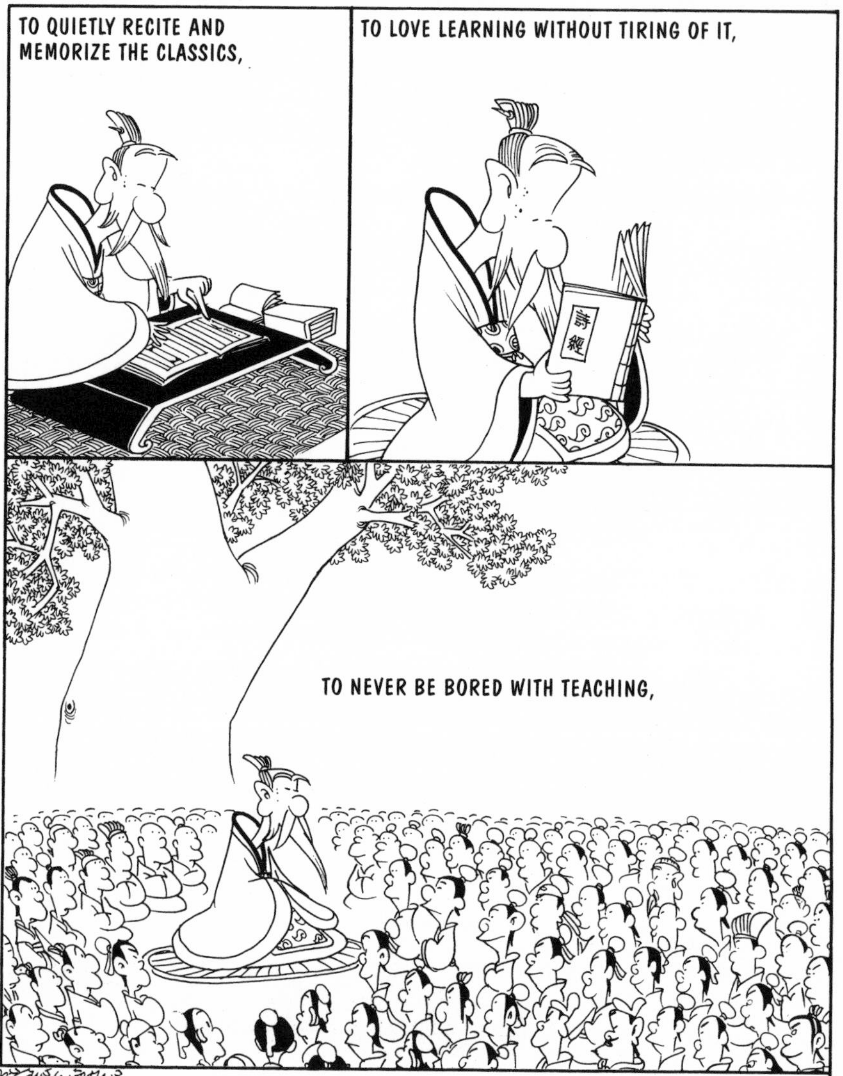

TO QUIETLY RECITE AND MEMORIZE THE CLASSICS,
TO LOVE LEARNING WITHOUT TIRING OF IT,
詩經
TO NEVER BE BORED WITH TEACHING,

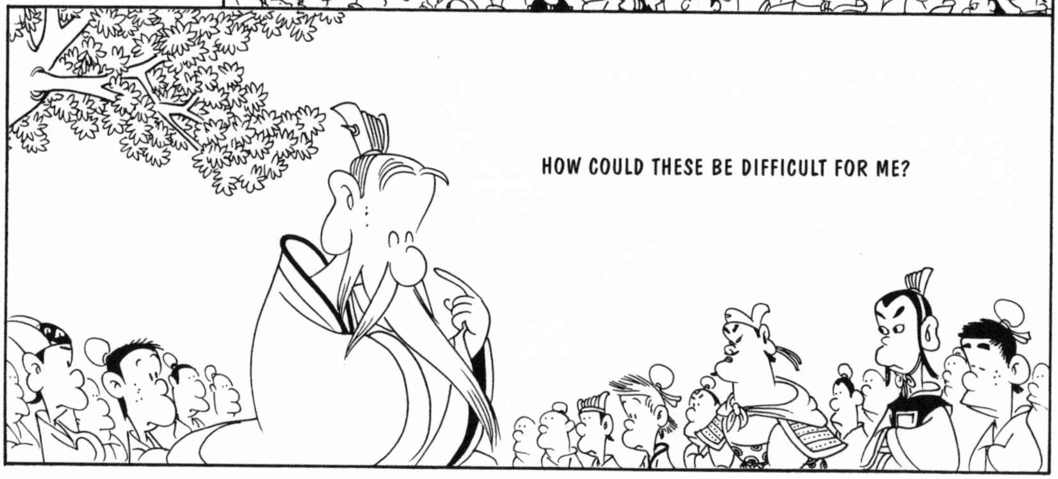

HOW COULD THESE BE DIFFICULT FOR ME?

7:3

A GENTLEMAN'S WORRIES

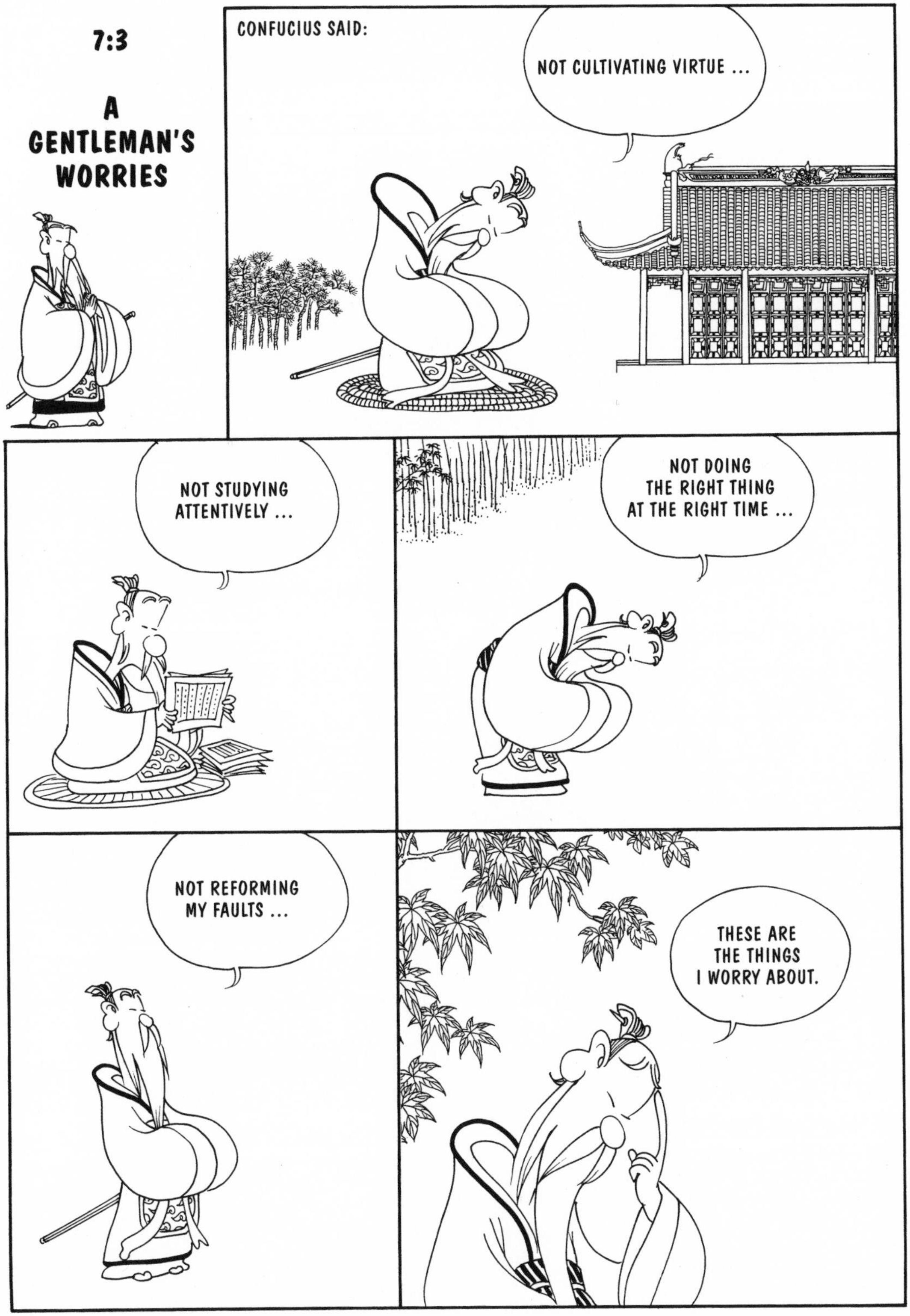
CONFUCIUS SAID:
NOT CULTIVATING VIRTUE ...
NOT STUDYING ATTENTIVELY ...
NOT DOING THE RIGHT THING AT THE RIGHT TIME ...
NOT REFORMING MY FAULTS ...
THESE ARE THE THINGS I WORRY ABOUT.

子曰：「德之不脩，學之不講，聞義不能徙，不善不能改，是吾憂也。」

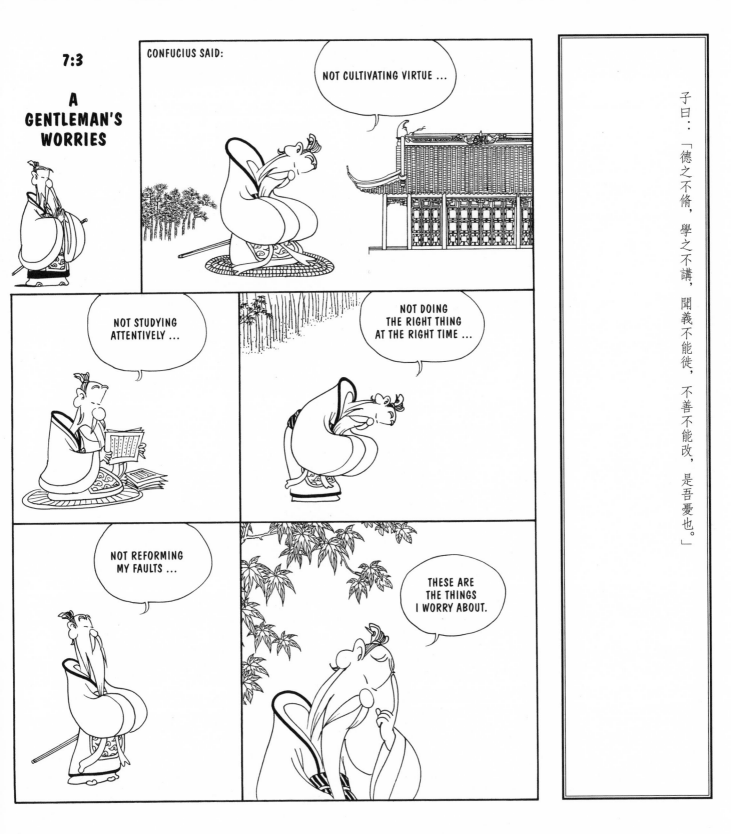

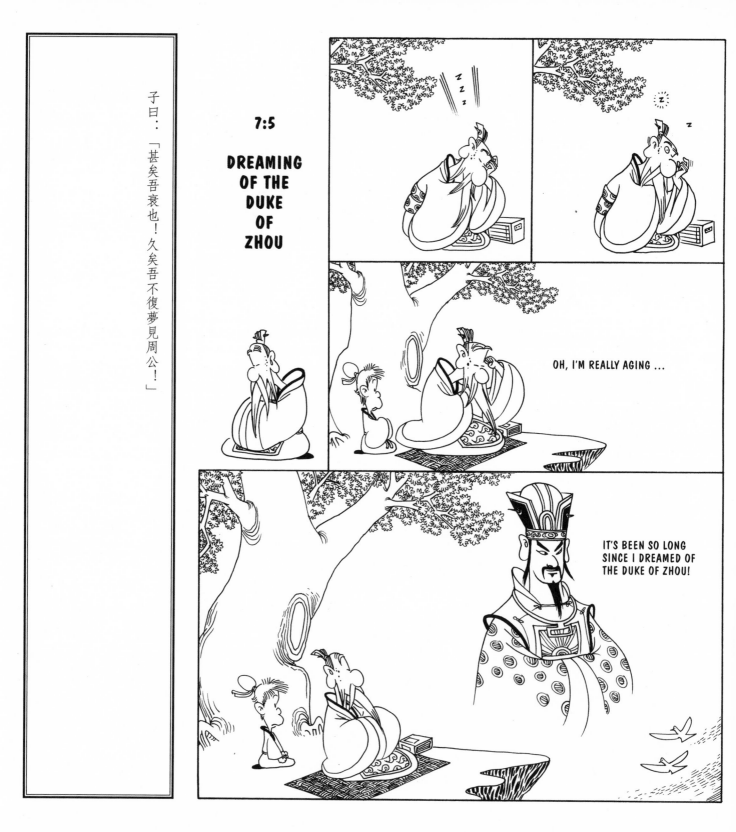

子曰：「甚矣吾衰也！久矣吾不復夢見周公！」

7:5

DREAMING OF THE DUKE OF ZHOU

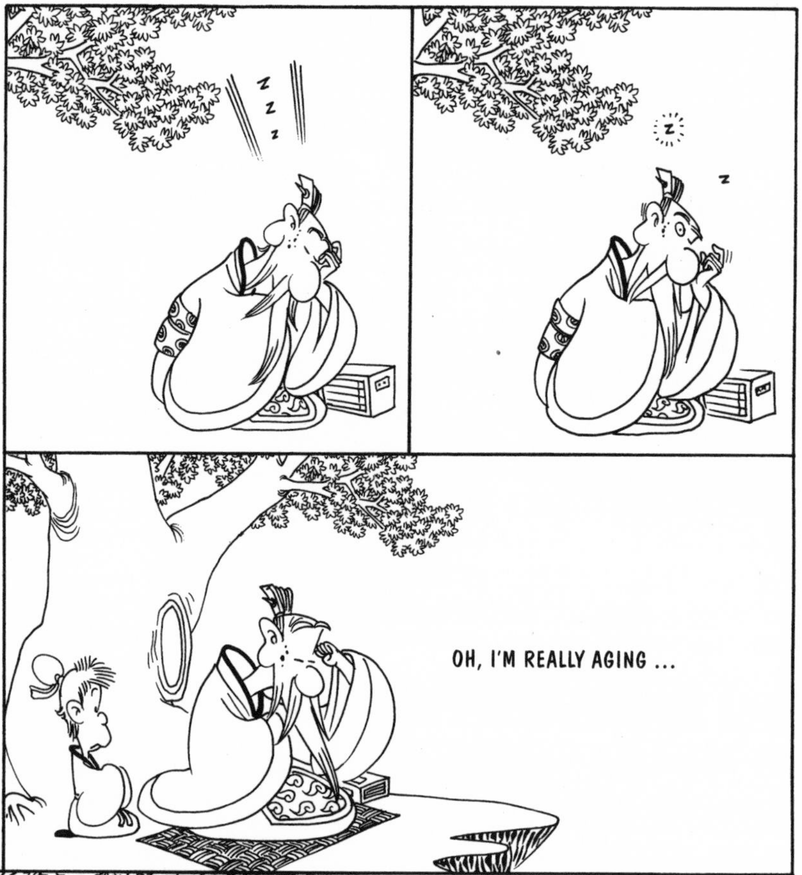

Z Z Z
Z
Z
OH, I'M REALLY AGING ...

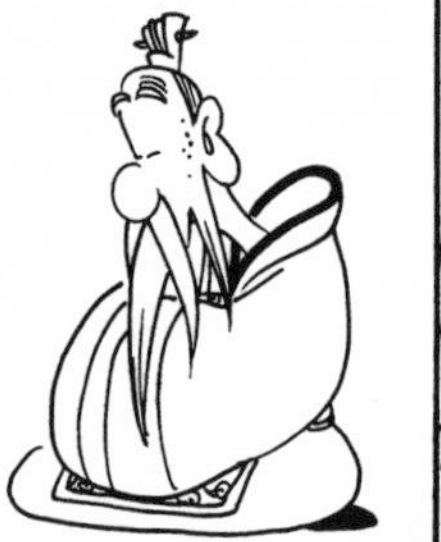

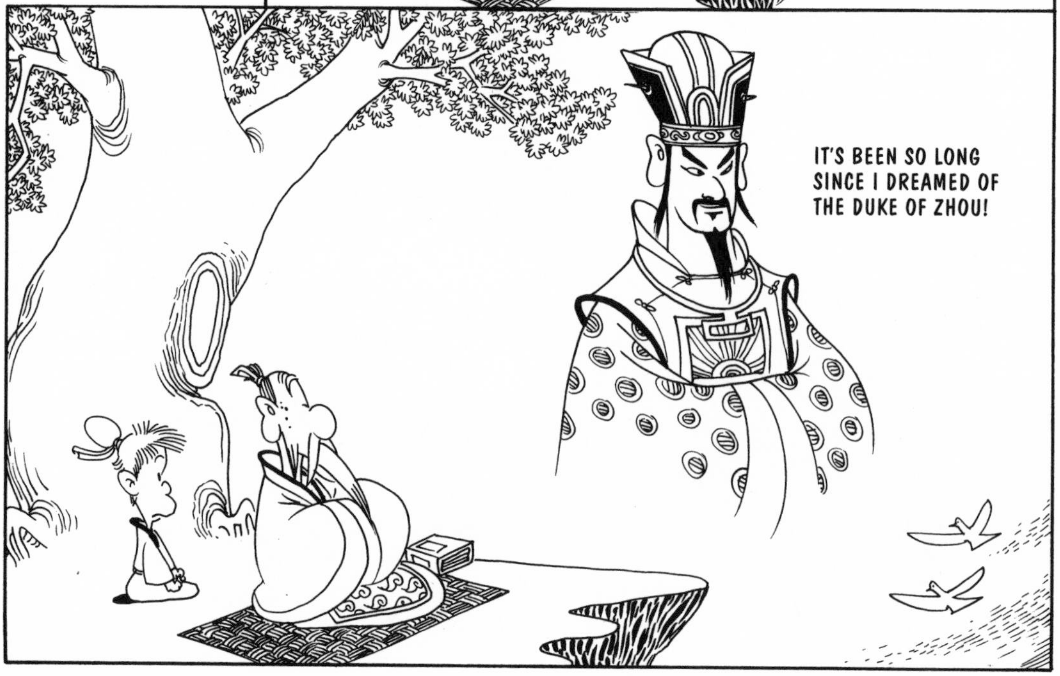

IT'S BEEN SO LONG SINCE I DREAMED OF THE DUKE OF ZHOU!

7:6

THE FOUNDATION OF GOOD CONDUCT

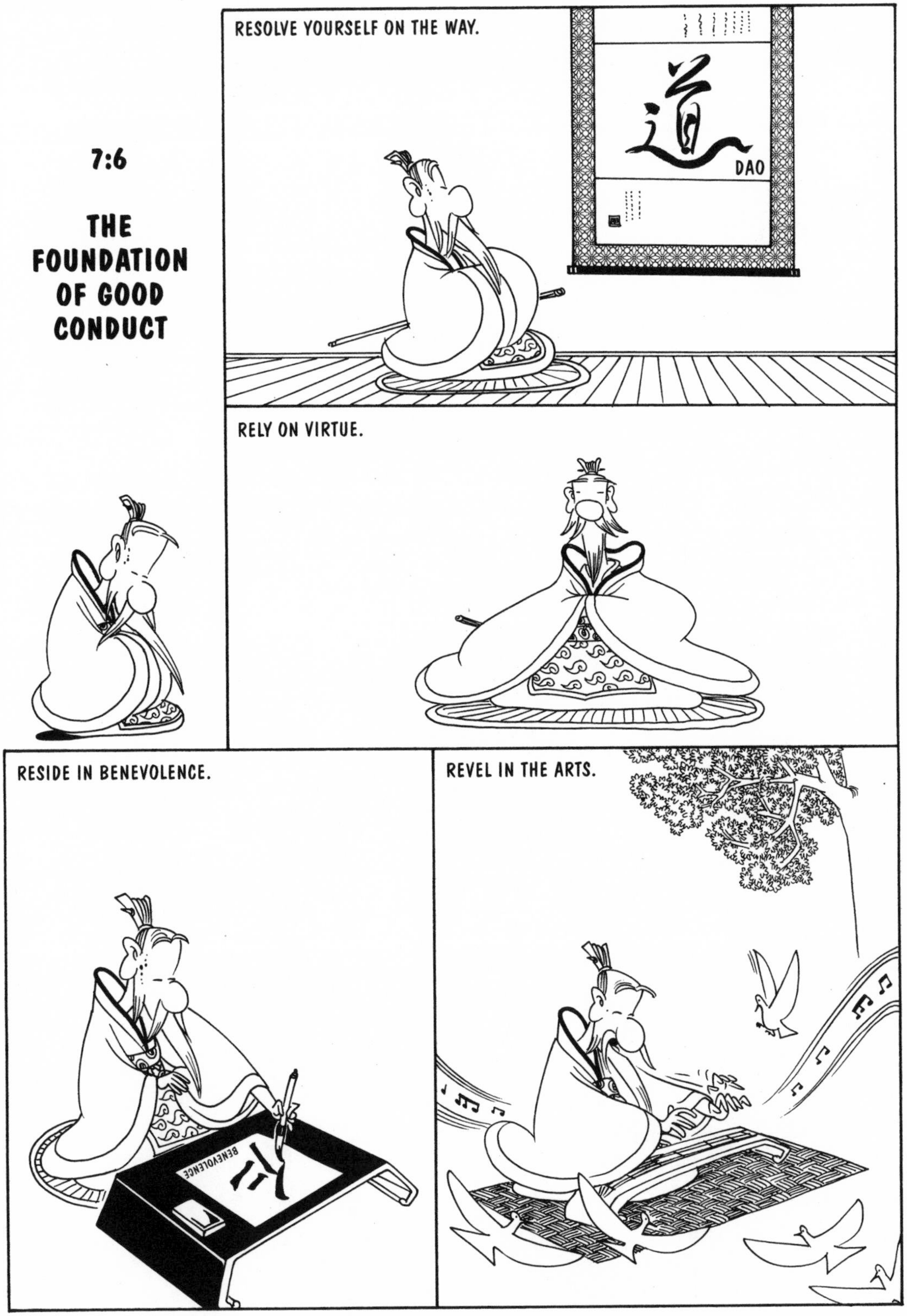

RESOLVE YOURSELF ON THE WAY.
DAO
RELY ON VIRTUE.
RESIDE IN BENEVOLENCE.
BENEVOLENCE
REVEL IN THE ARTS.

子曰：「志於道，據於德，依於仁，遊於藝。」

子曰：「自行束脩以上，吾未嘗無誨焉。」

7:7

UNIVERSAL EDUCATION

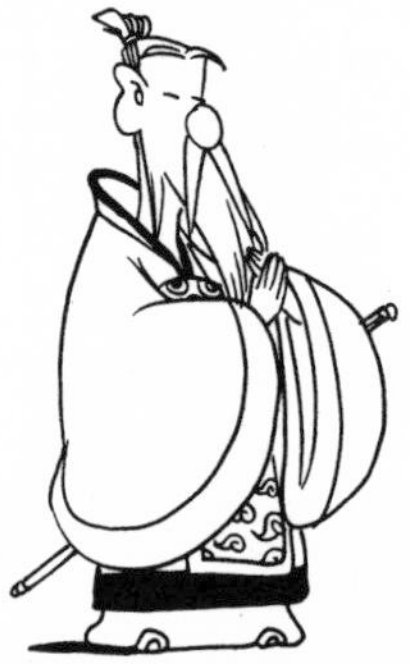

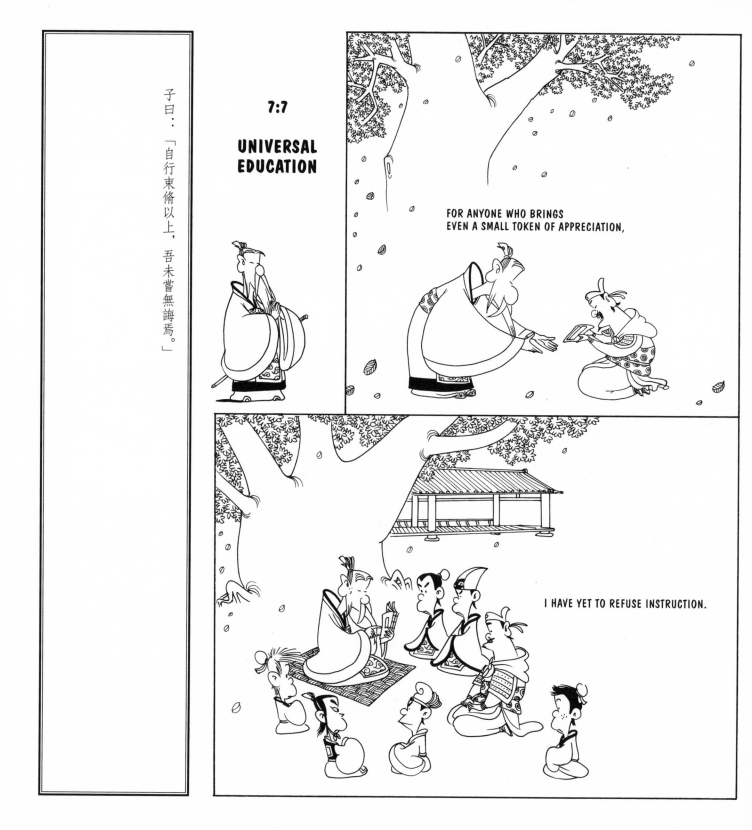

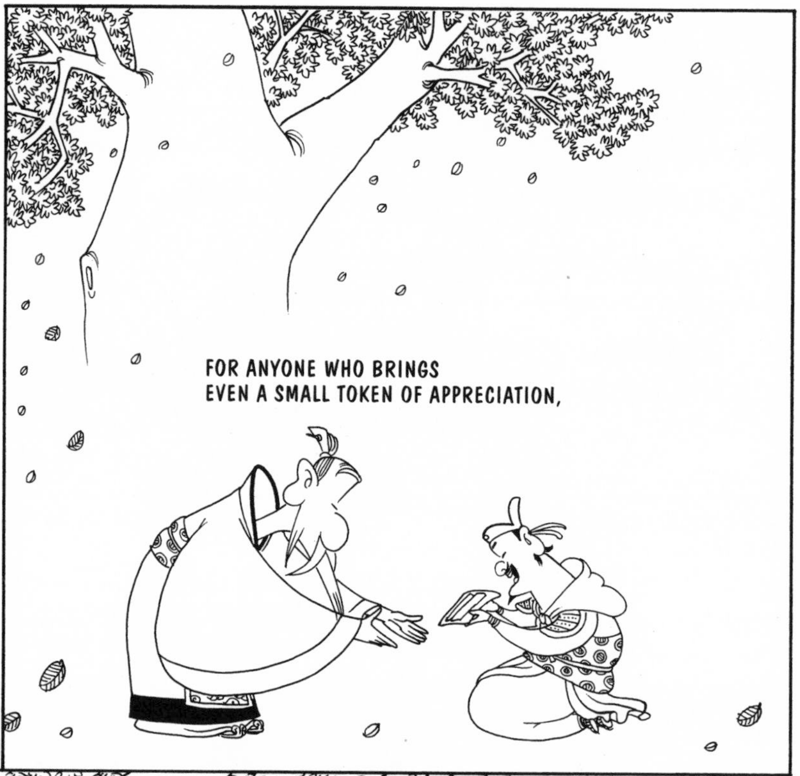
FOR ANYONE WHO BRINGS
EVEN A SMALL TOKEN OF APPRECIATION,

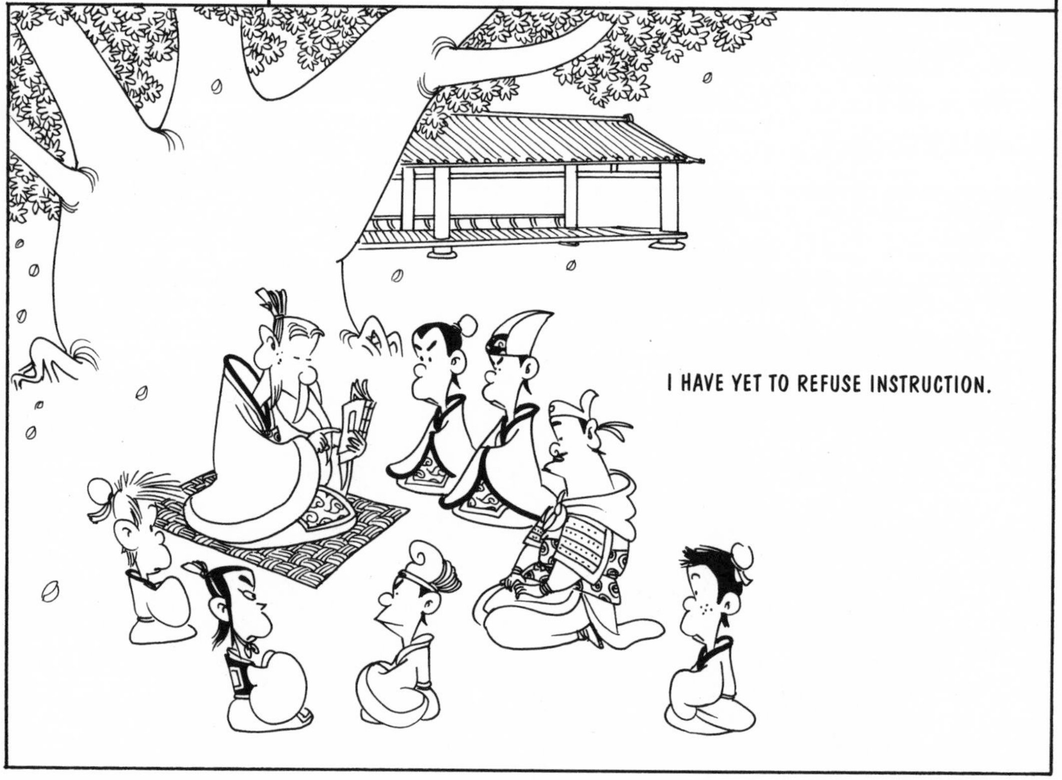
I HAVE YET TO REFUSE INSTRUCTION.

7:8

TEACHING GOOD STUDENTS

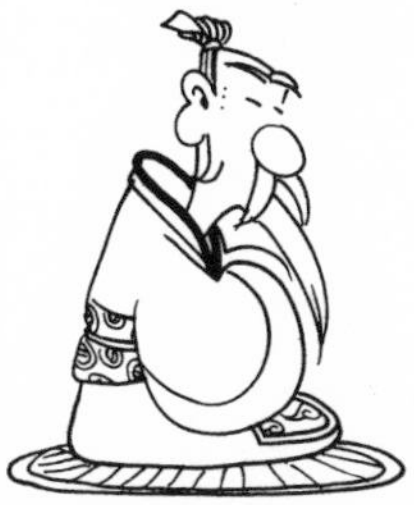

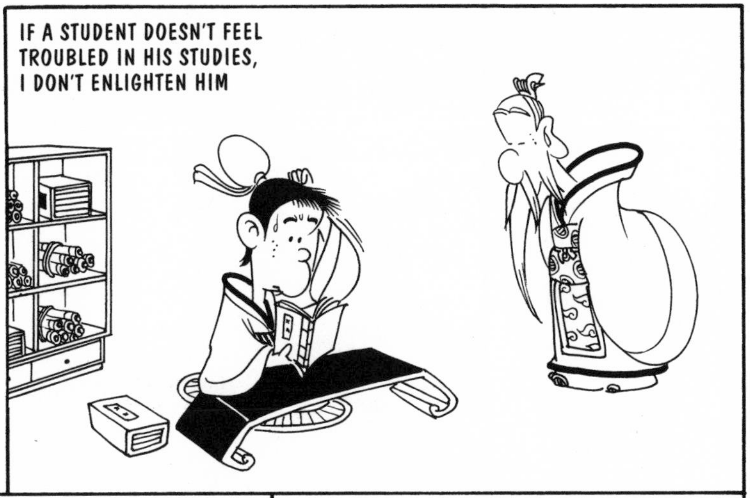
IF A STUDENT DOESN'T FEEL TROUBLED IN HIS STUDIES, I DON'T ENLIGHTEN HIM

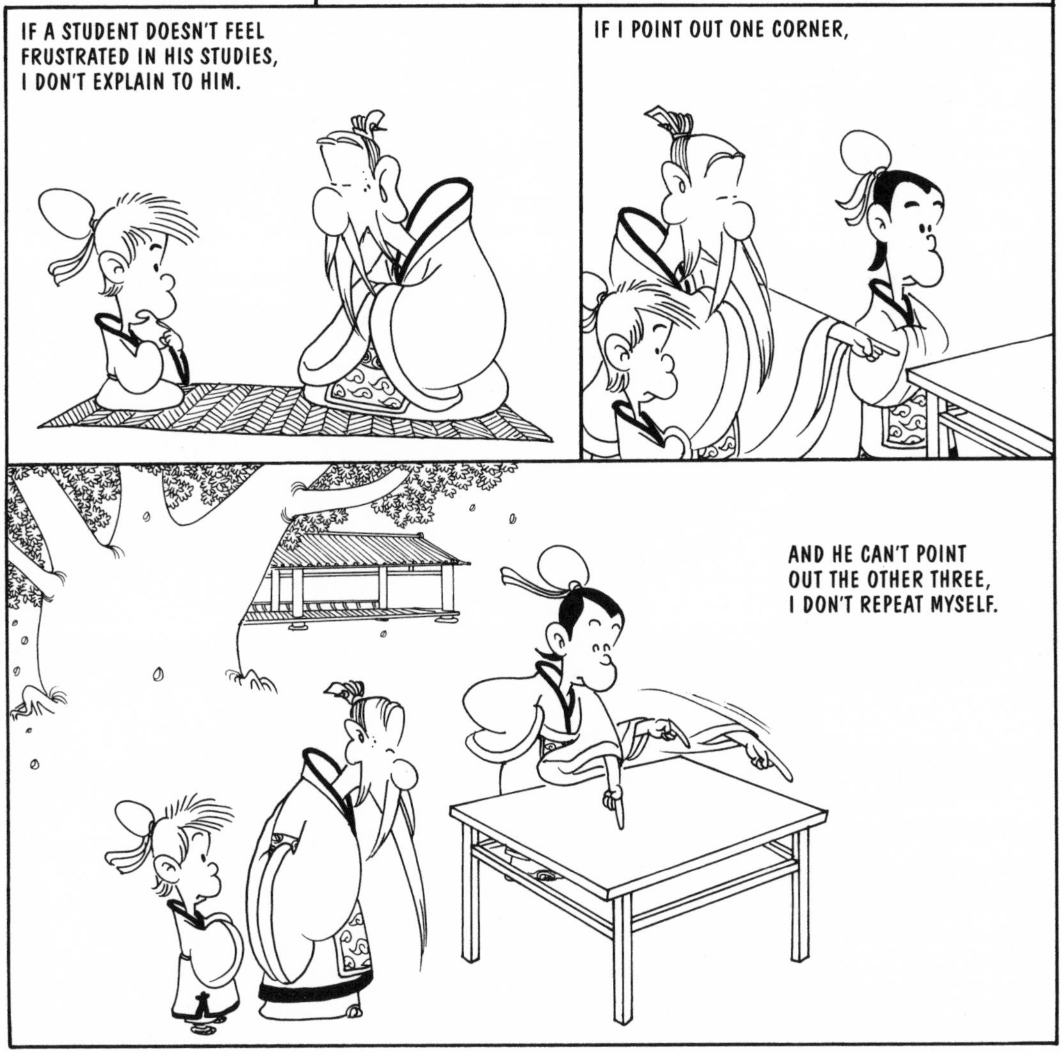
IF A STUDENT DOESN'T FEEL FRUSTRATED IN HIS STUDIES, I DON'T EXPLAIN TO HIM.
IF I POINT OUT ONE CORNER,
AND HE CAN'T POINT OUT THE OTHER THREE, I DON'T REPEAT MYSELF.

子曰：「不憤不啟，不悱不發。舉一隅不以三隅反，則不復也。」

子曰：「富而可求也，雖執鞭之士，吾亦為之。如不可求，從吾所好。」

7:12

WEALTH OR ENJOYMENT

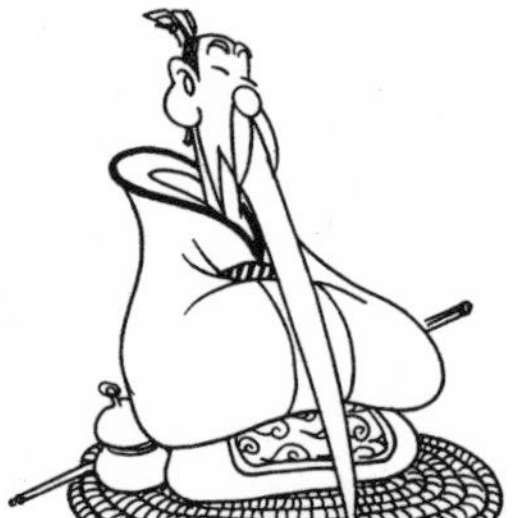

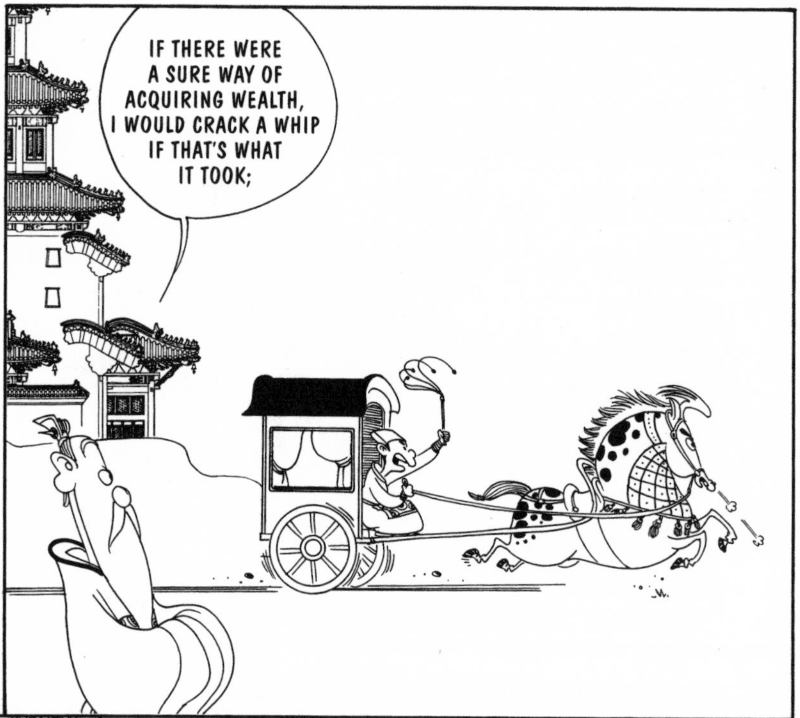
IF THERE WERE A SURE WAY OF ACQUIRING WEALTH, I WOULD CRACK A WHIP IF THAT'S WHAT IT TOOK;

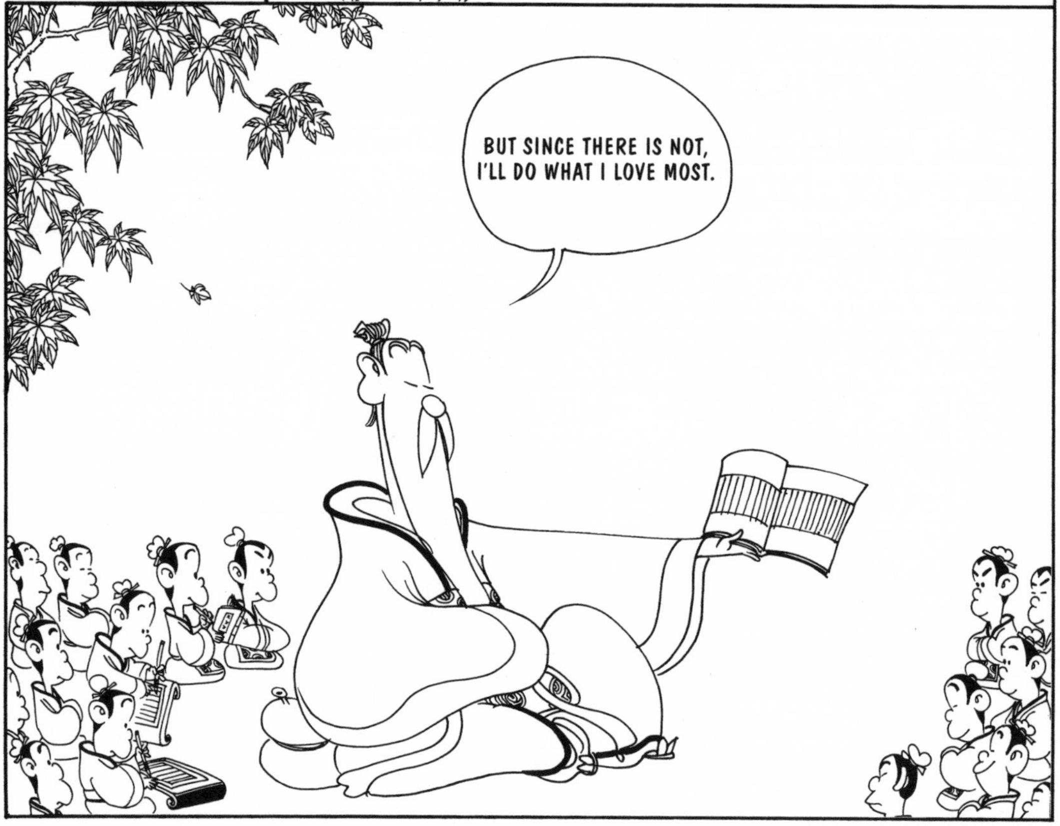
BUT SINCE THERE IS NOT, I'LL DO WHAT I LOVE MOST.

7:16

SIMPLE PLEASURES

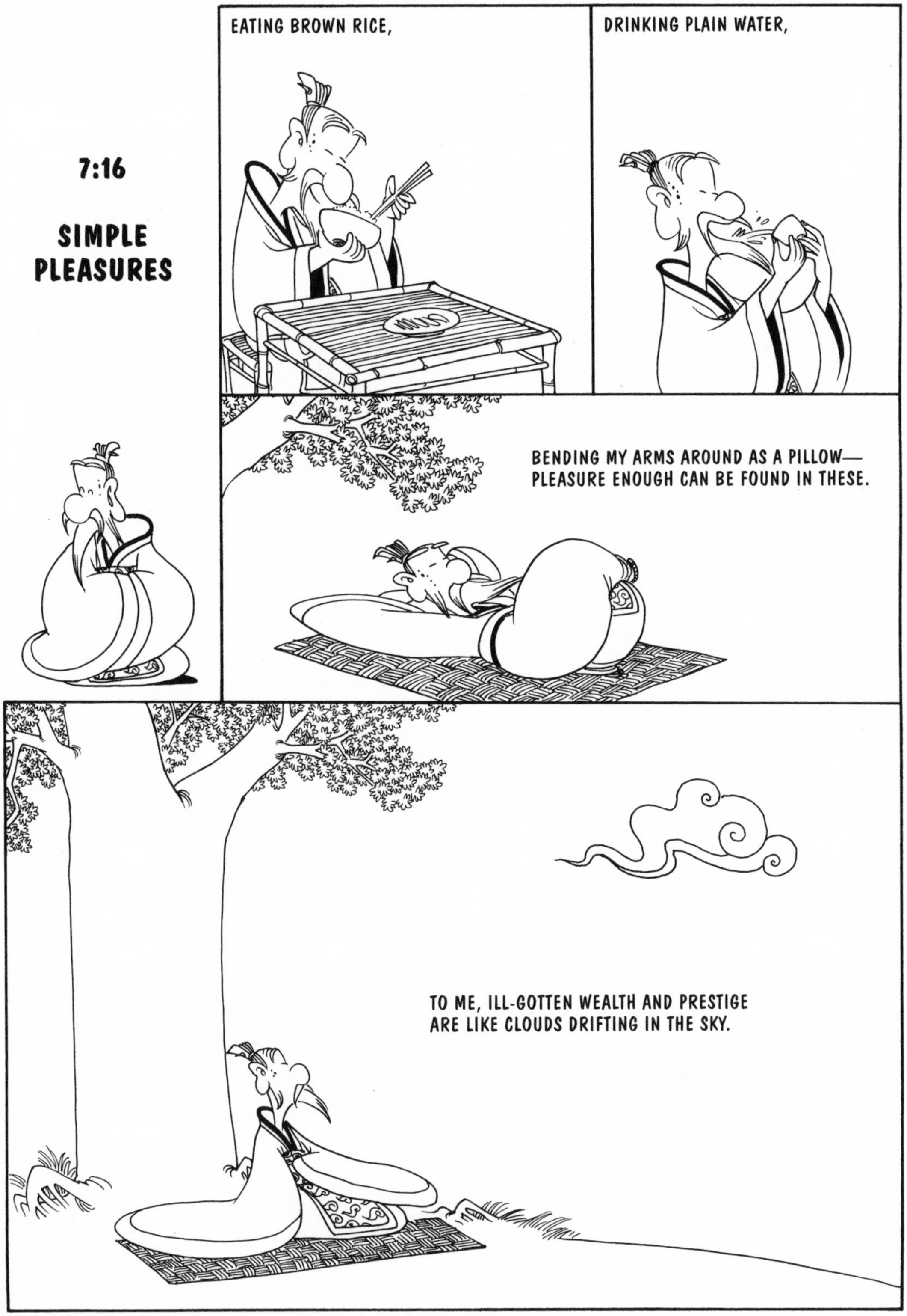
EATING BROWN RICE,
DRINKING PLAIN WATER,
BENDING MY ARMS AROUND AS A PILLOW—PLEASURE ENOUGH CAN BE FOUND IN THESE.
TO ME, ILL-GOTTEN WEALTH AND PRESTIGE ARE LIKE CLOUDS DRIFTING IN THE SKY.

子曰：「飯疏食飲水，曲肱而枕之，樂亦在其中矣。不義而富且貴，於我如浮雲。」

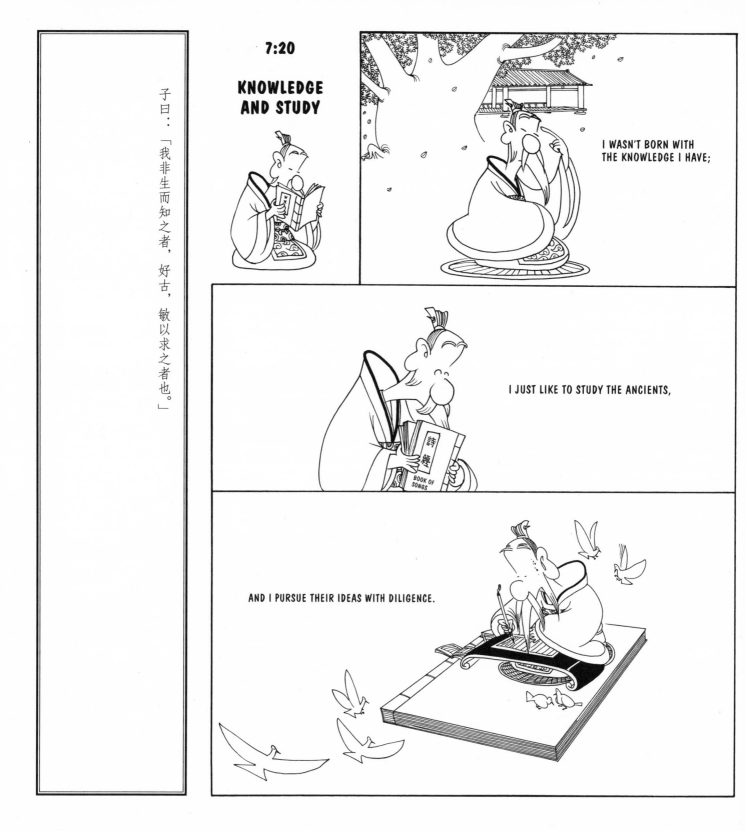

子曰：「我非生而知之者，好古，敏以求之者也。」

7:20

KNOWLEDGE AND STUDY

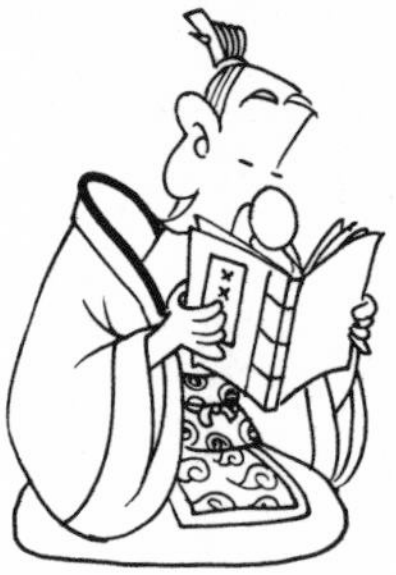

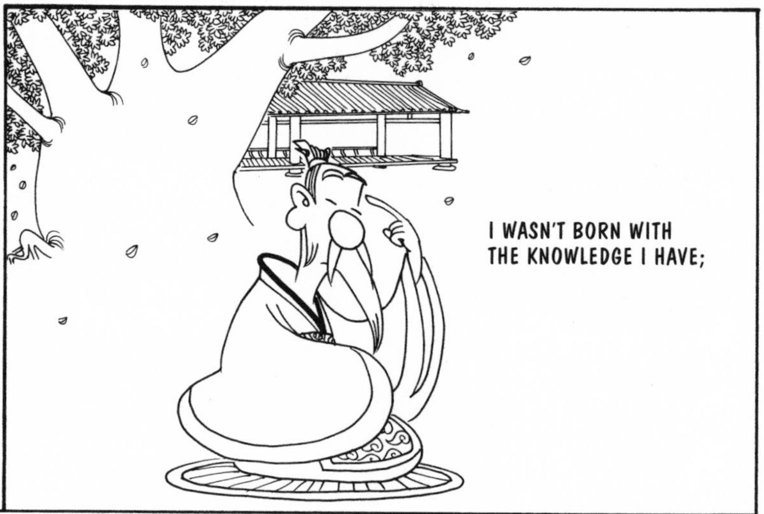
I WASN'T BORN WITH THE KNOWLEDGE I HAVE;

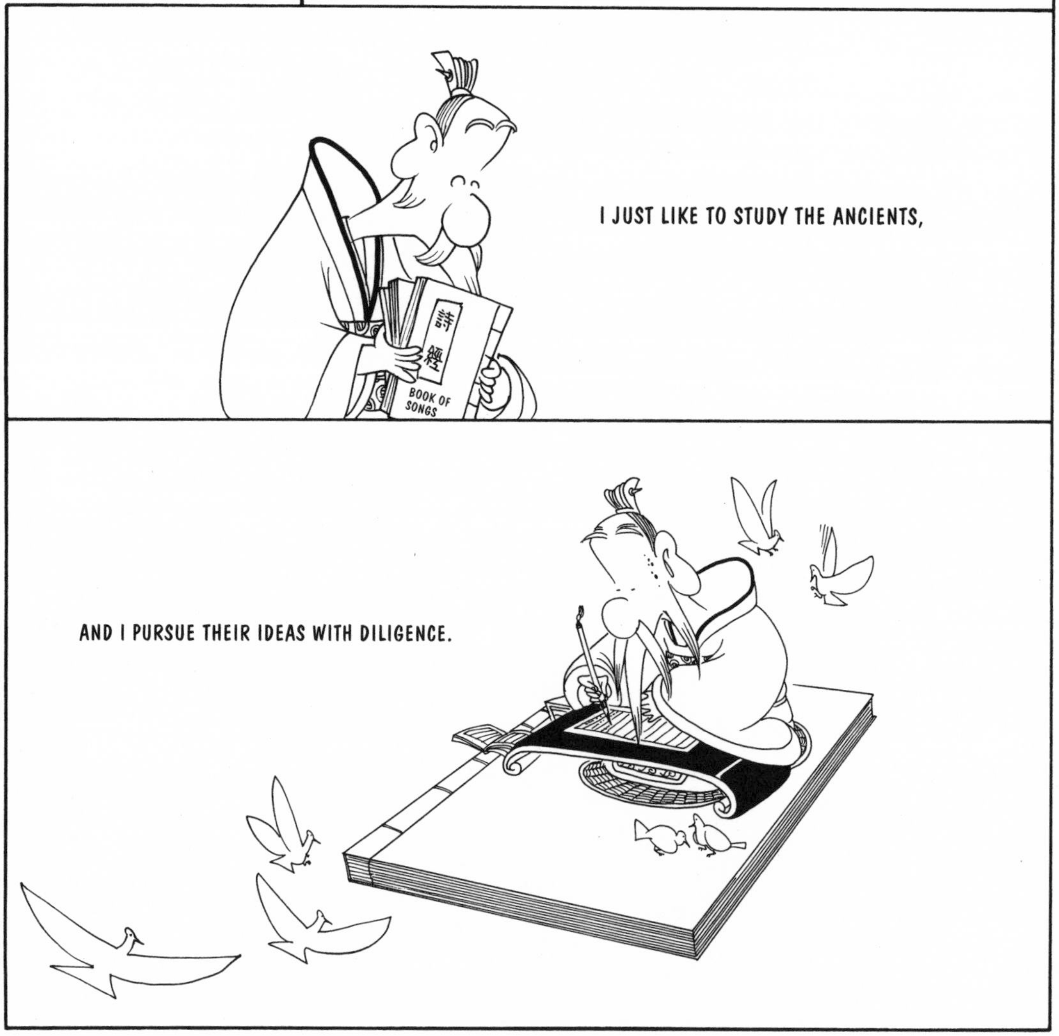
I JUST LIKE TO STUDY THE ANCIENTS,
詩經
BOOK OF SONGS
AND I PURSUE THEIR IDEAS WITH DILIGENCE.

7:22

LEARNING FROM OTHERS

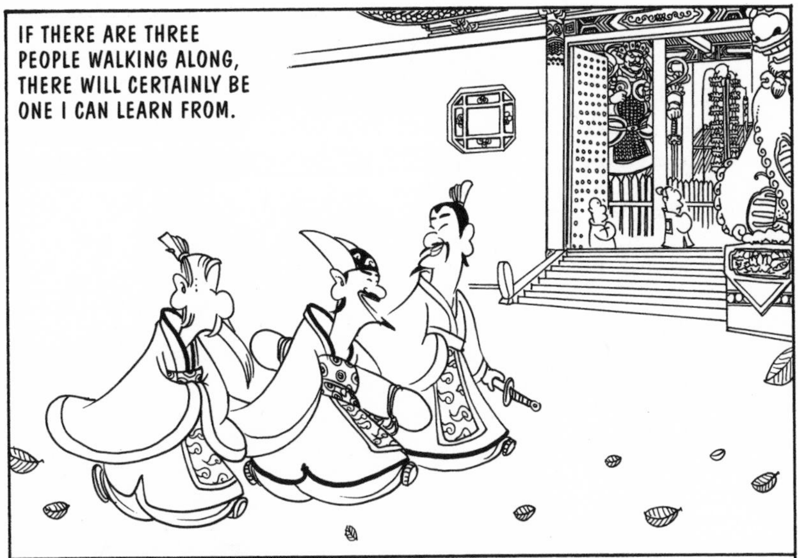
IF THERE ARE THREE PEOPLE WALKING ALONG, THERE WILL CERTAINLY BE ONE I CAN LEARN FROM.

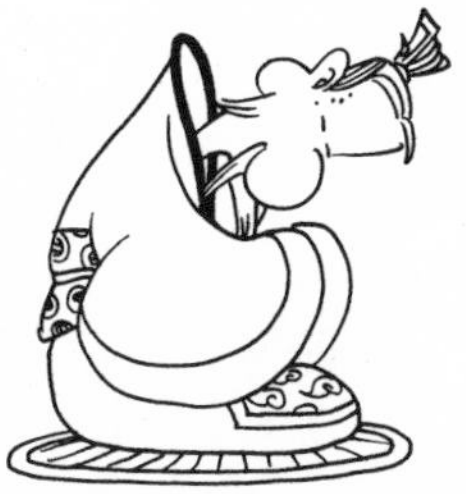

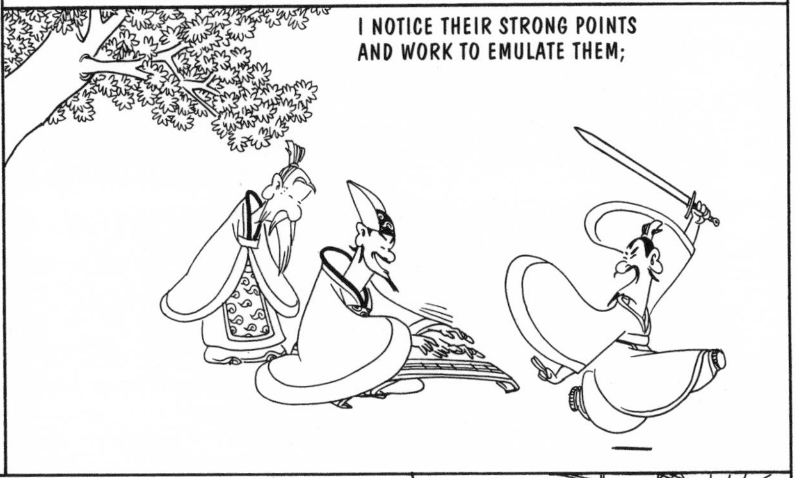
I NOTICE THEIR STRONG POINTS AND WORK TO EMULATE THEM;

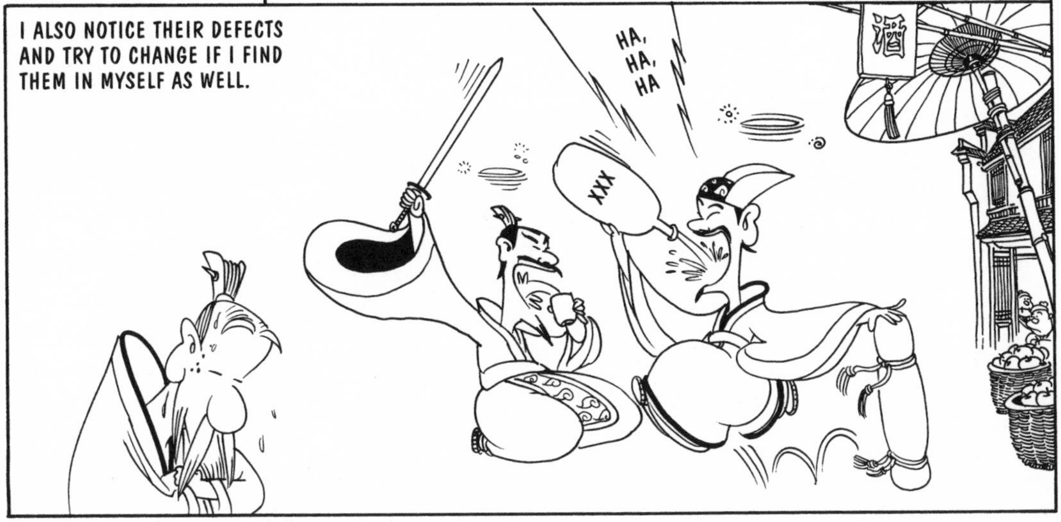
I ALSO NOTICE THEIR DEFECTS AND TRY TO CHANGE IF I FIND THEM IN MYSELF AS WELL.
HA, HA, HA
XXX
酒

子曰：「三人行，必有我師焉，擇其善者而從之，其不善者而改之。」

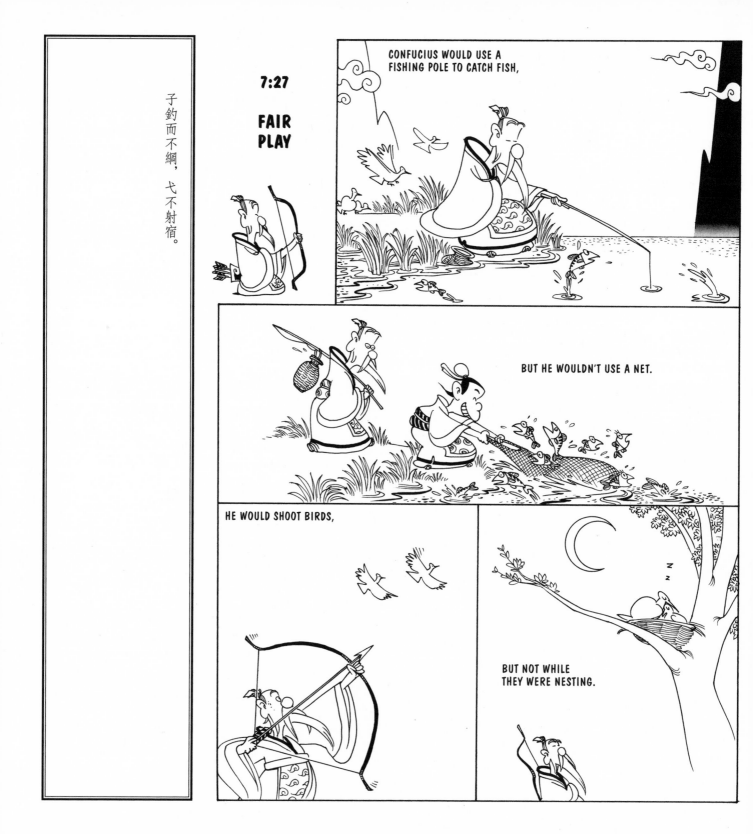

子釣而不綱，弋不射宿。

7:27

FAIR PLAY

CONFUCIUS WOULD USE A FISHING POLE TO CATCH FISH,

BUT HE WOULDN'T USE A NET.

HE WOULD SHOOT BIRDS,

BUT NOT WHILE THEY WERE NESTING.

7:36

EXTRAVAGANCE AND THRIFT

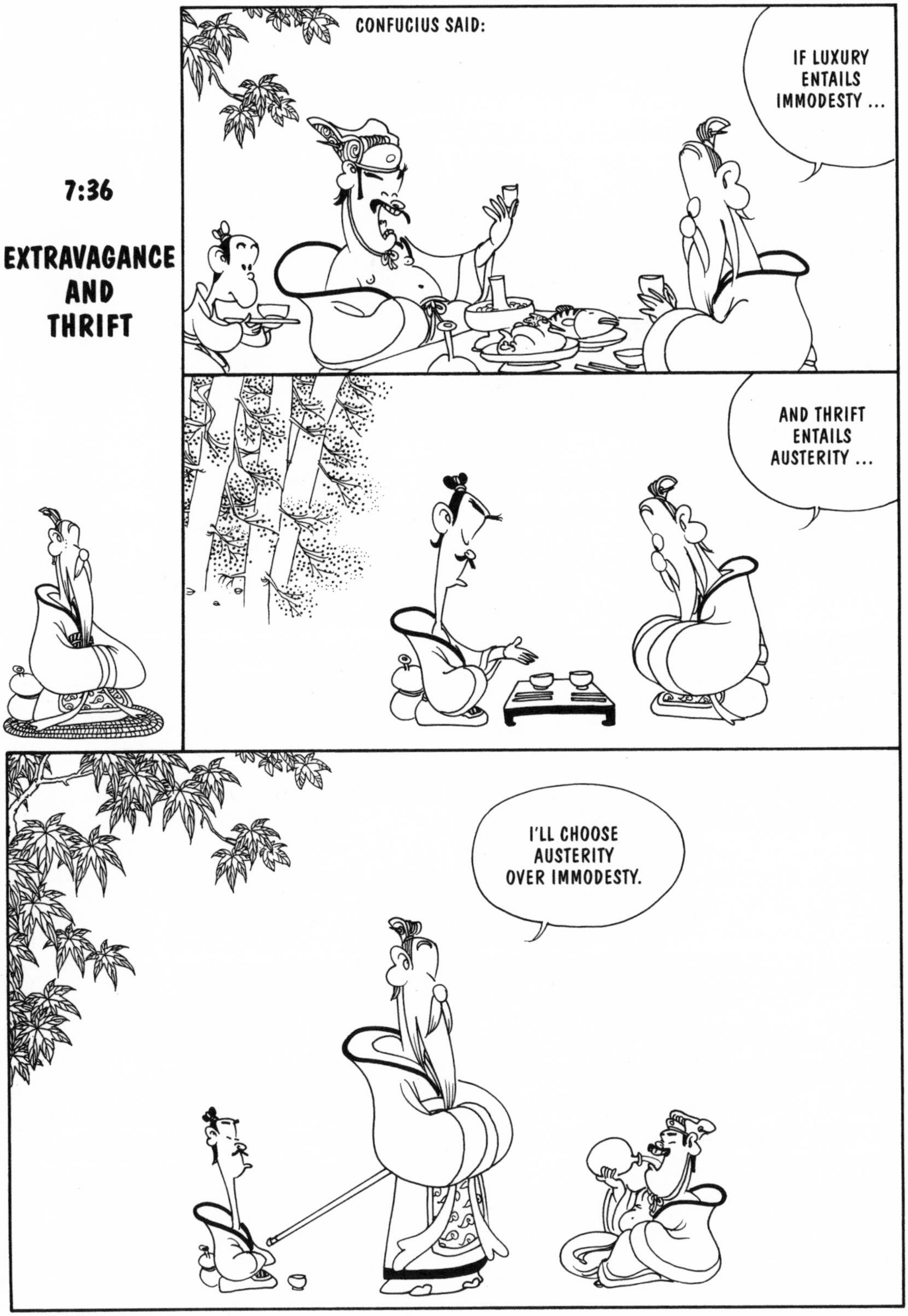
CONFUCIUS SAID:
IF LUXURY ENTAILS IMMODESTY ...
AND THRIFT ENTAILS AUSTERITY ...
I'LL CHOOSE AUSTERITY OVER IMMODESTY.

子曰：「奢則不孫，儉則固。與其不孫也，寧固。」

子曰：「君子坦蕩蕩，小人長戚戚。」

7:37

A GENTLEMAN'S FREEDOM

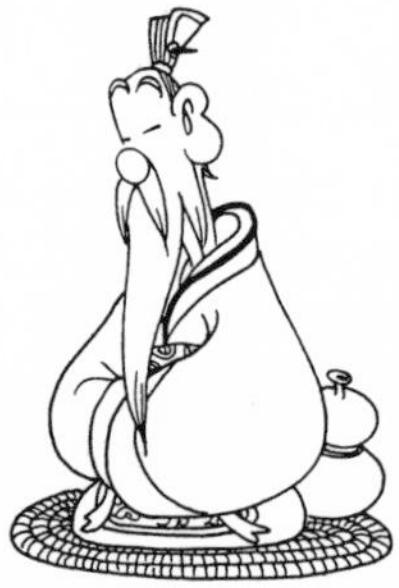

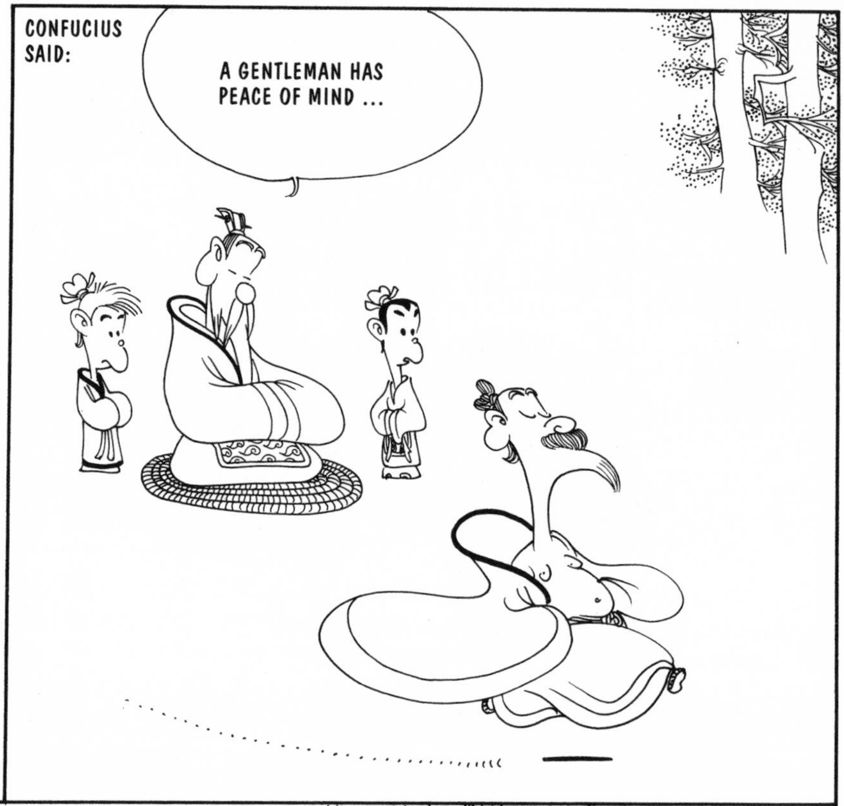
CONFUCIUS SAID:
A GENTLEMAN HAS PEACE OF MIND ...

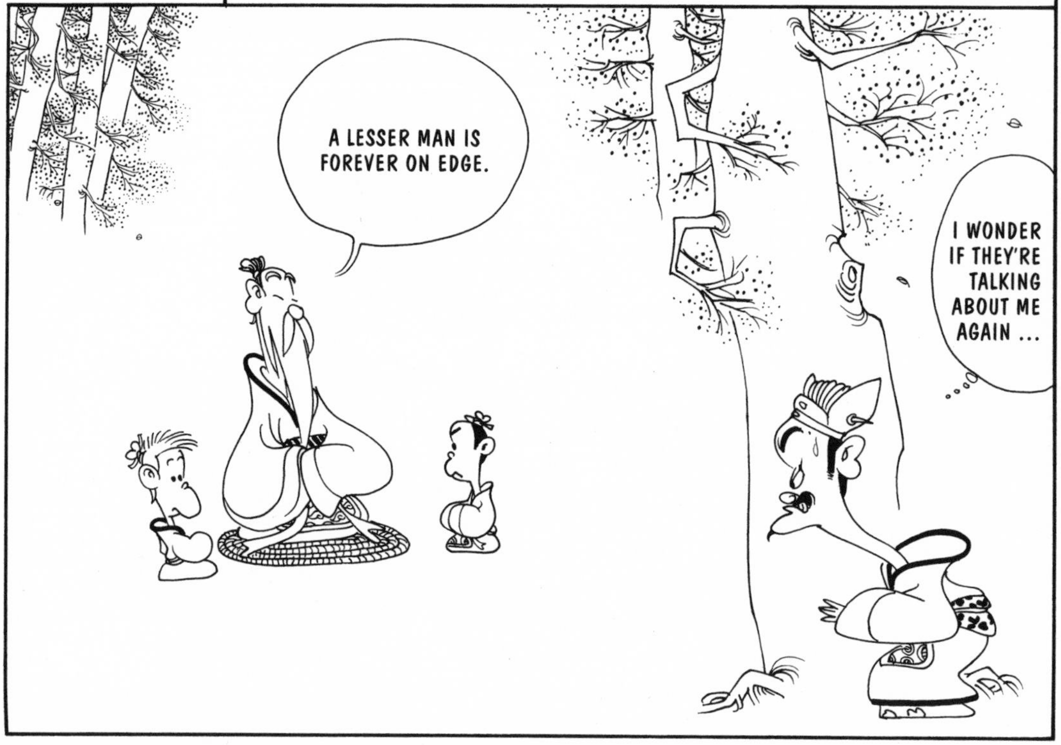
A LESSER MAN IS FOREVER ON EDGE.
I WONDER IF THEY'RE TALKING ABOUT ME AGAIN ...

8:4

DYING MEN TELL NO LIES

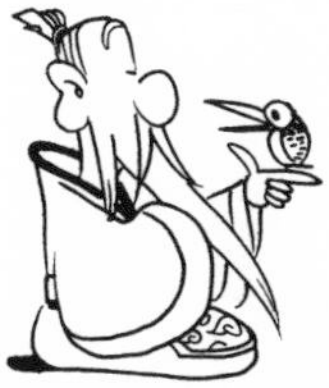

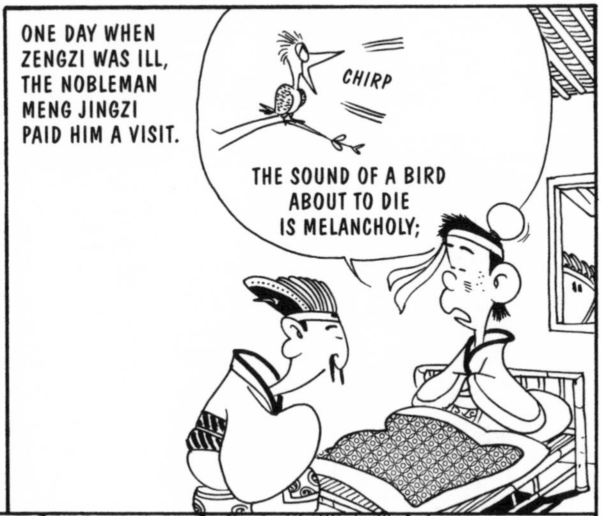

ONE DAY WHEN ZENGZI WAS ILL, THE NOBLEMAN MENG JINGZI PAID HIM A VISIT.
CHIRP
THE SOUND OF A BIRD ABOUT TO DIE IS MELANCHOLY;

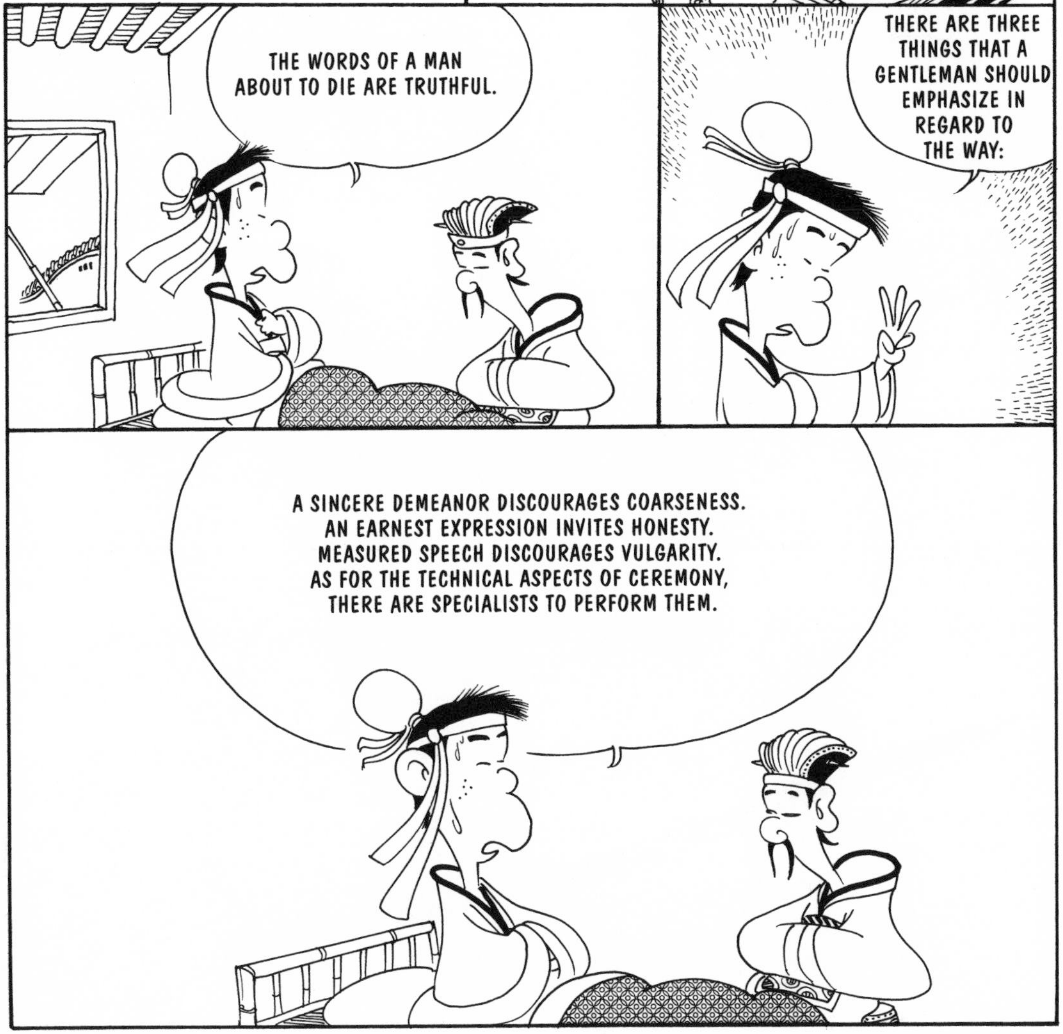

THE WORDS OF A MAN ABOUT TO DIE ARE TRUTHFUL.
THERE ARE THREE THINGS THAT A GENTLEMAN SHOULD EMPHASIZE IN REGARD TO THE WAY:
A SINCERE DEMEANOR DISCOURAGES COARSENESS.
AN EARNEST EXPRESSION INVITES HONESTY.
MEASURED SPEECH DISCOURAGES VULGARITY.
AS FOR THE TECHNICAL ASPECTS OF CEREMONY, THERE ARE SPECIALISTS TO PERFORM THEM.

曾子有疾，孟敬子問之。曾子言曰：「鳥之將死，其鳴也哀；人之將死，其言也善。君子所貴乎道者三：動容貌，斯遠暴慢矣；正顏色，斯近信矣；出辭氣，斯遠鄙倍矣。籩豆之事，則有司存。」

曾子曰：「士不可以不弘毅，任重而道遠。仁以為己任，不亦重乎？死而後已，不亦遠乎？」

8:7

THE BURDEN OF YOUTH

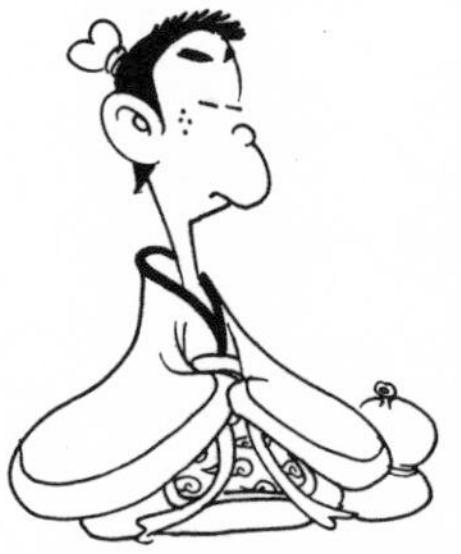

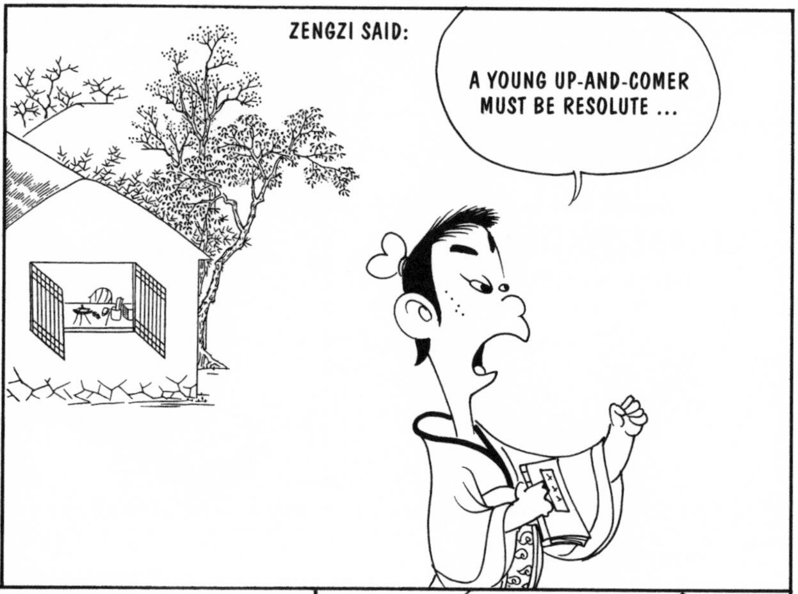
ZENGZI SAID:
A YOUNG UP-AND-COMER MUST BE RESOLUTE ...

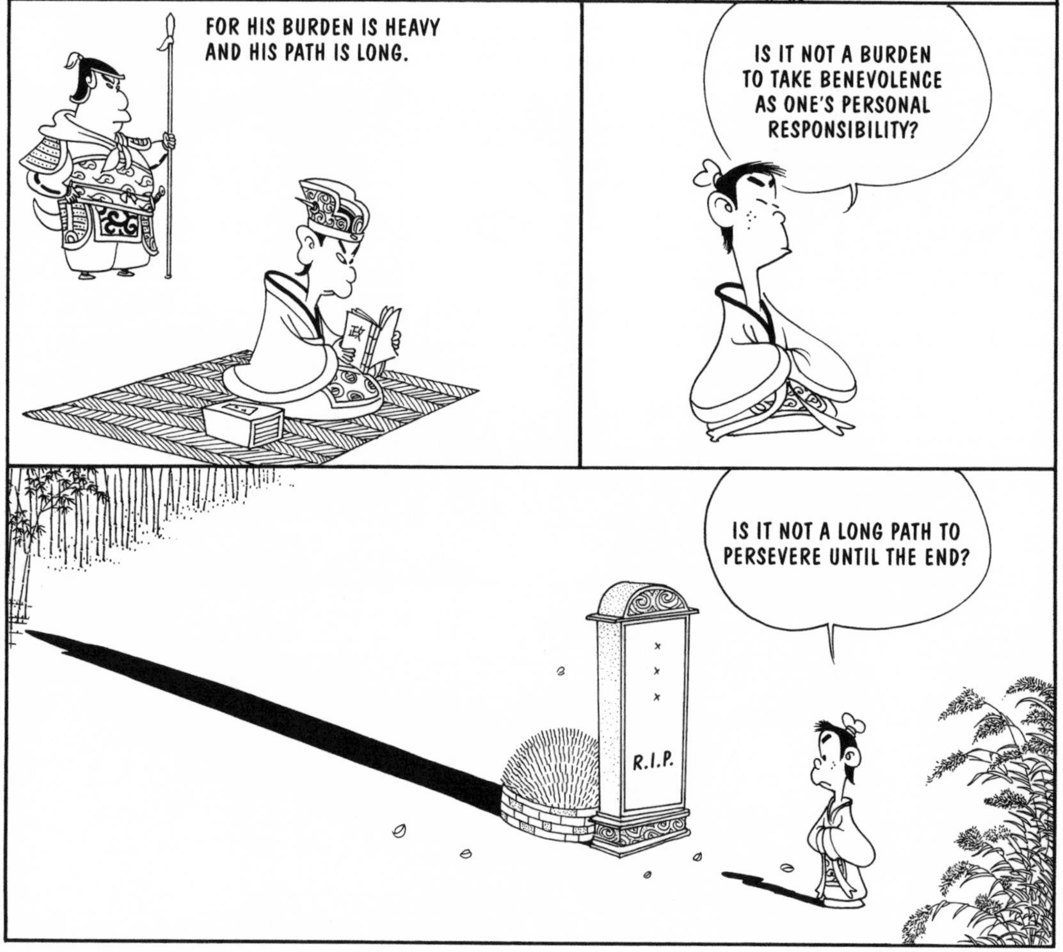
FOR HIS BURDEN IS HEAVY AND HIS PATH IS LONG.
IS IT NOT A BURDEN TO TAKE BENEVOLENCE AS ONE'S PERSONAL RESPONSIBILITY?
IS IT NOT A LONG PATH TO PERSEVERE UNTIL THE END?
R.I.P.

8:17

GOOD STUDENTS FEAR FORGETTING

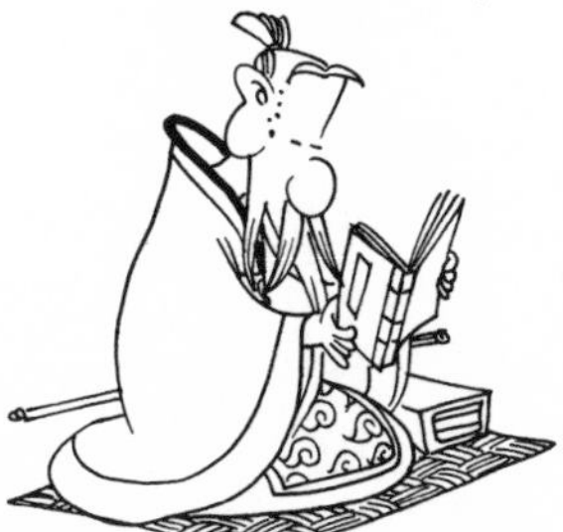

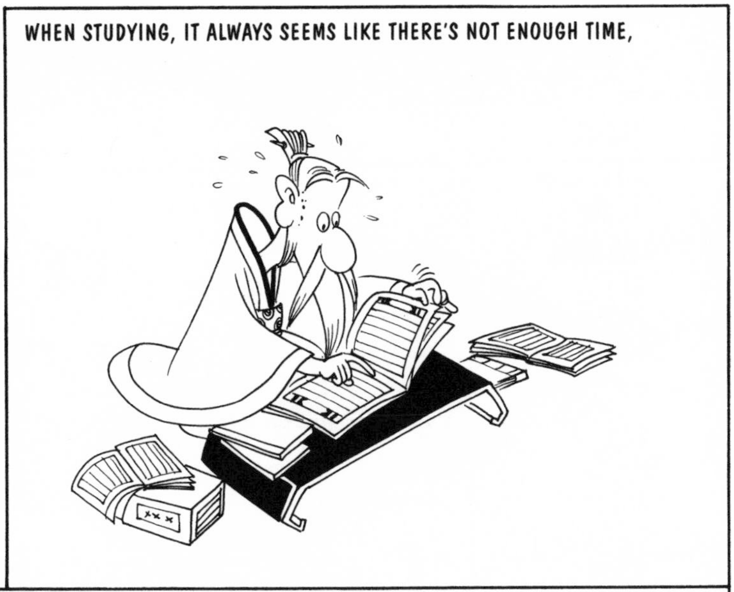
WHEN STUDYING, IT ALWAYS SEEMS LIKE THERE'S NOT ENOUGH TIME,

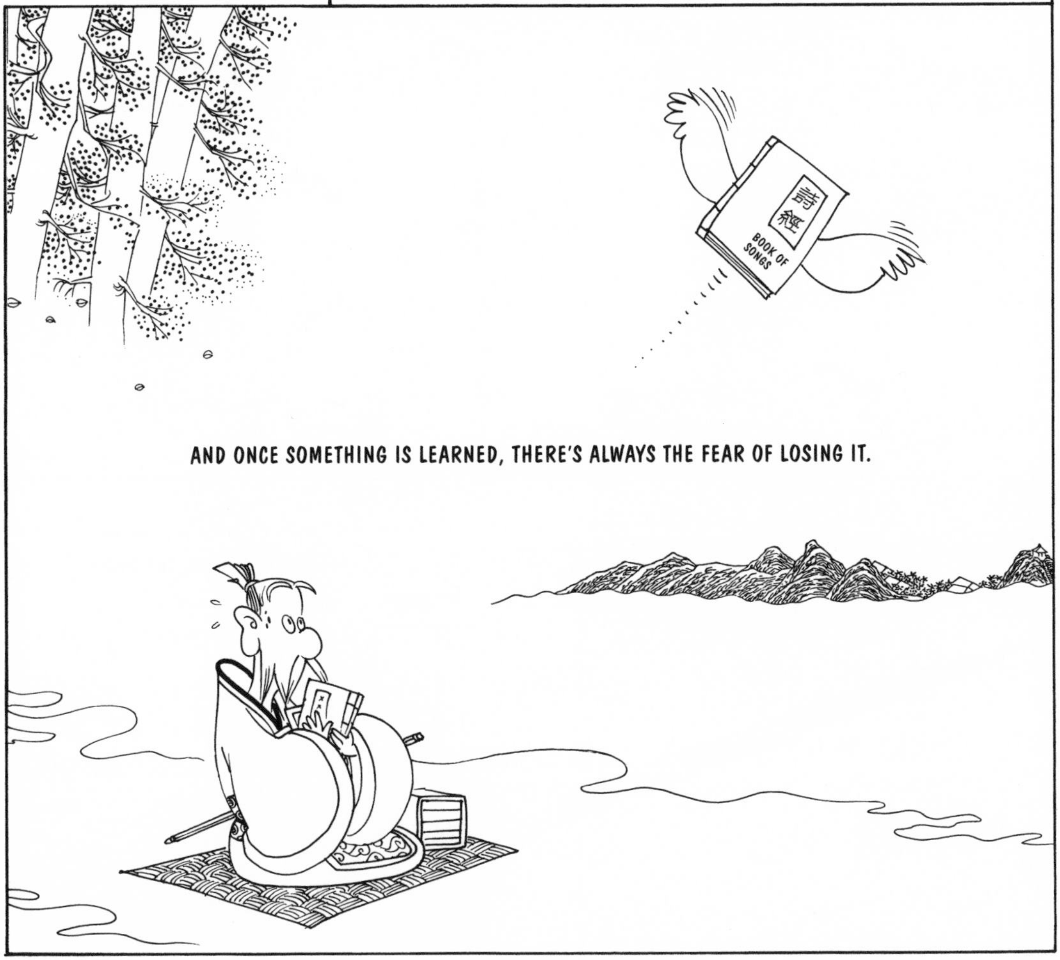
詩經
BOOK OF SONGS
AND ONCE SOMETHING IS LEARNED, THERE'S ALWAYS THE FEAR OF LOSING IT.

子曰：「學如不及，猶恐失之。」

子罕言利與命與仁。

9:1

PERSONAL ADVANTAGE, FATE, BENEVOLENCE

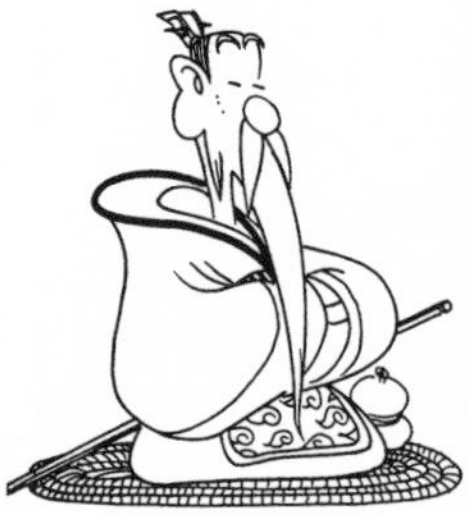

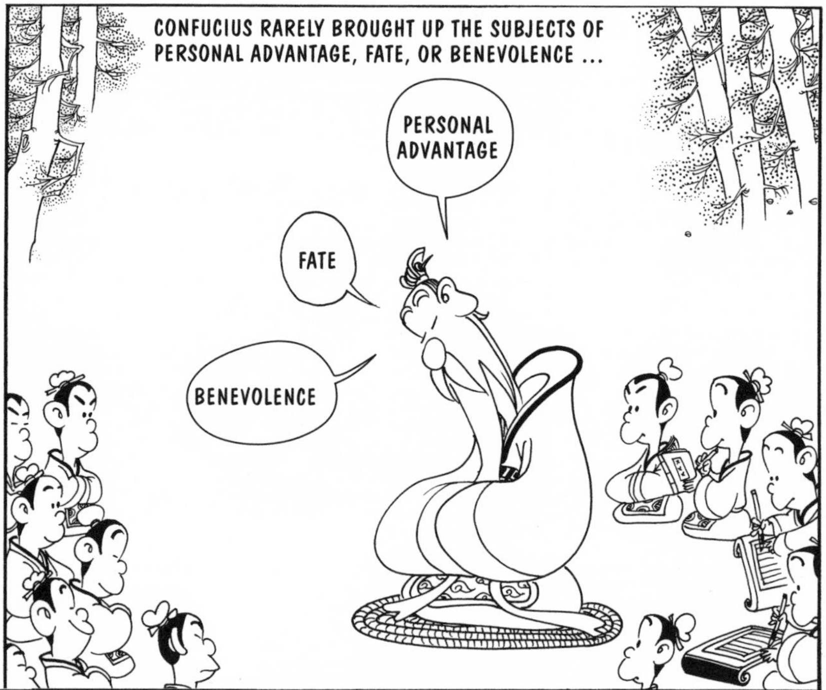

CONFUCIUS RARELY BROUGHT UP THE SUBJECTS OF PERSONAL ADVANTAGE, FATE, OR BENEVOLENCE ...
PERSONAL ADVANTAGE
FATE
BENEVOLENCE

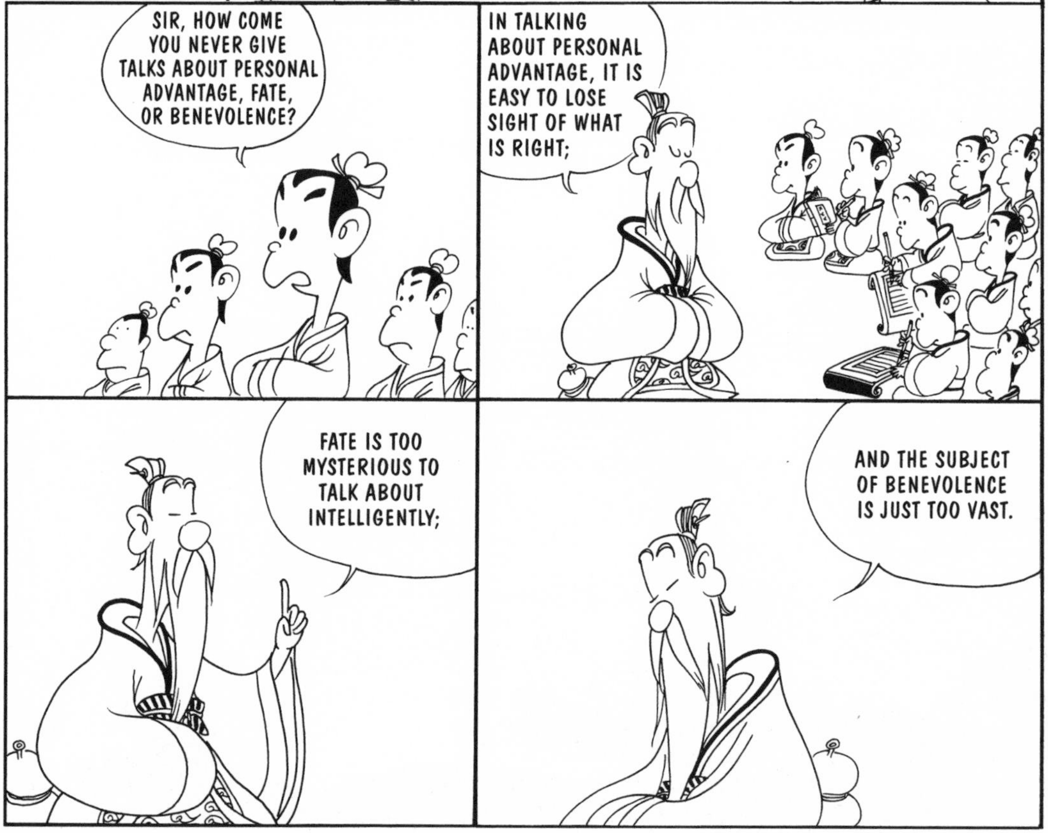

SIR, HOW COME YOU NEVER GIVE TALKS ABOUT PERSONAL ADVANTAGE, FATE, OR BENEVOLENCE?
IN TALKING ABOUT PERSONAL ADVANTAGE, IT IS EASY TO LOSE SIGHT OF WHAT IS RIGHT;
FATE IS TOO MYSTERIOUS TO TALK ABOUT INTELLIGENTLY;
AND THE SUBJECT OF BENEVOLENCE IS JUST TOO VAST.

9:17

THE RIVER OF TIME

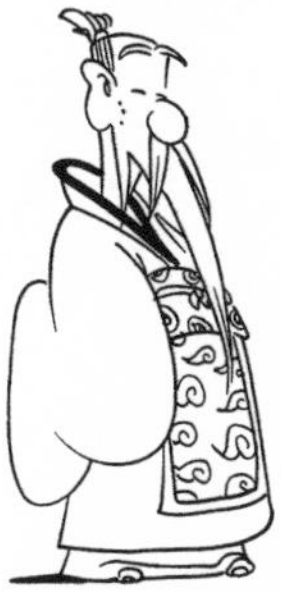

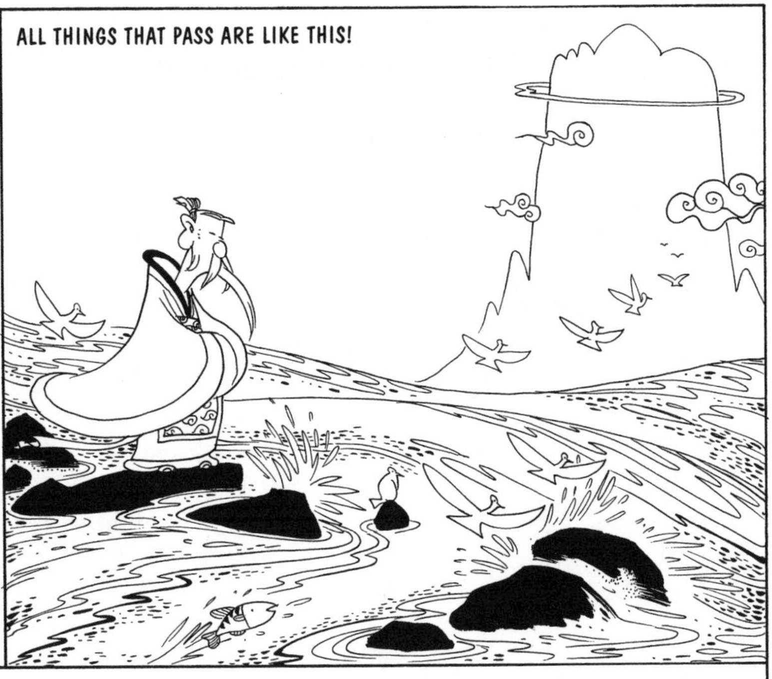
ALL THINGS THAT PASS ARE LIKE THIS!

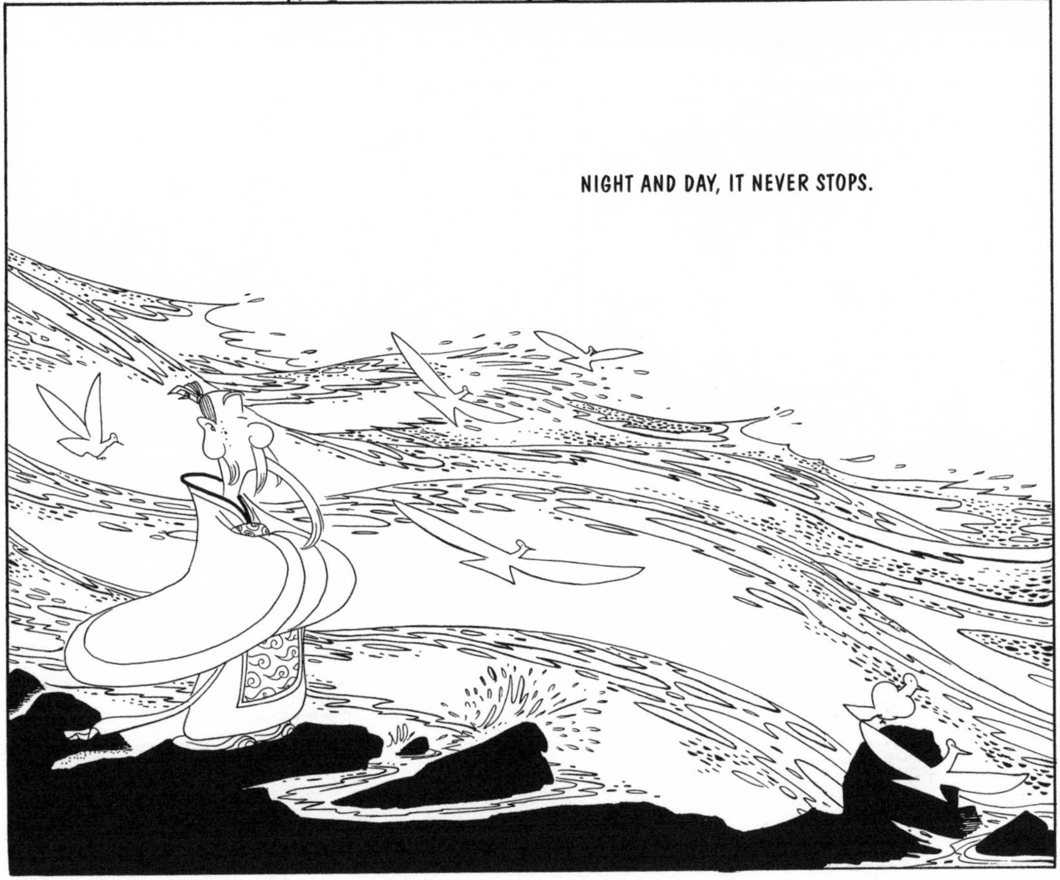
NIGHT AND DAY, IT NEVER STOPS.

子在川上，曰：「逝者如斯夫！不舍晝夜。」

子曰：「後生可畏，焉知來者之不如今也？四十、五十而無聞焉，斯亦不足畏也已。」

9:23

AGE AND RESPECT

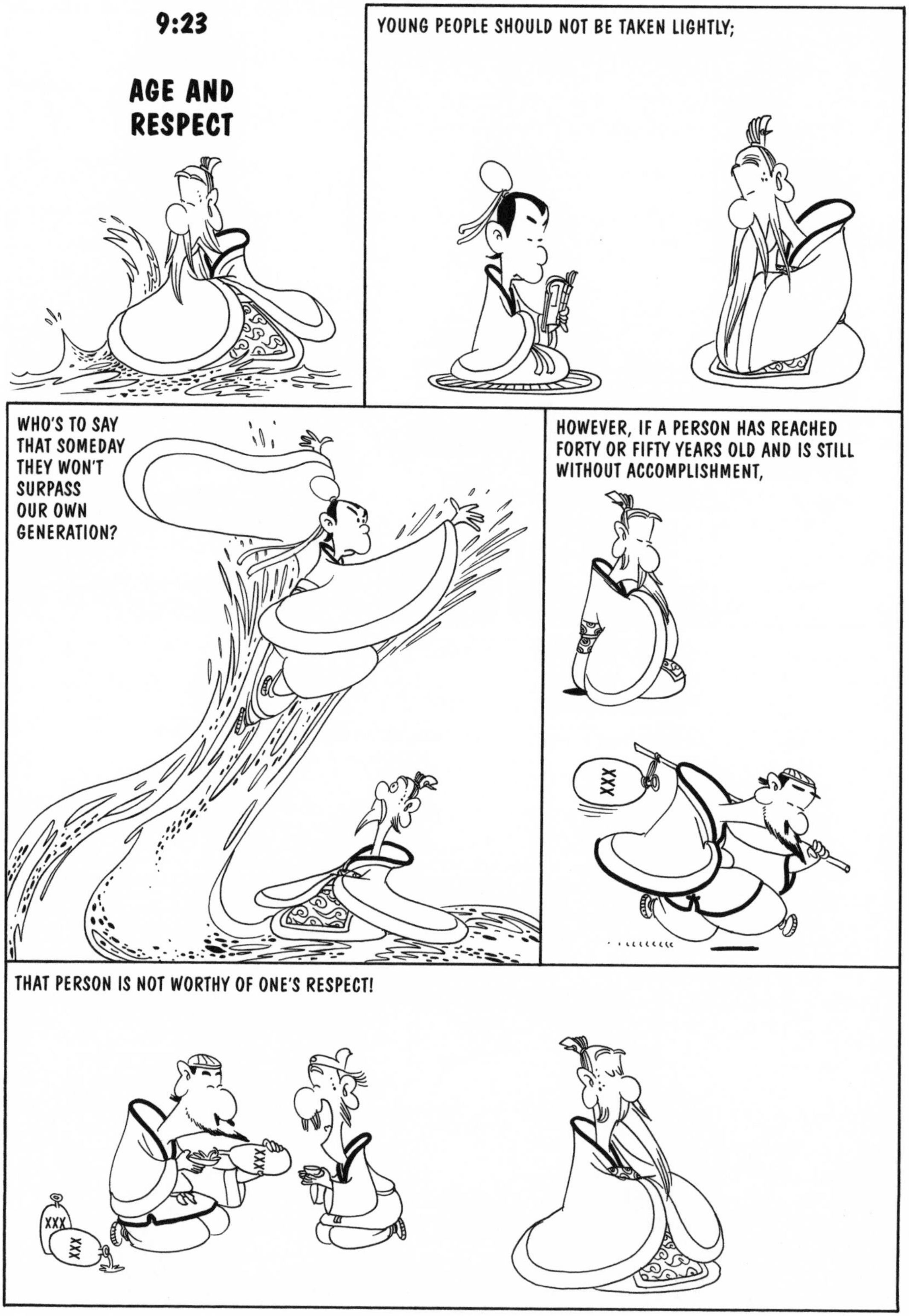
YOUNG PEOPLE SHOULD NOT BE TAKEN LIGHTLY;
WHO'S TO SAY THAT SOMEDAY THEY WON'T SURPASS OUR OWN GENERATION?
HOWEVER, IF A PERSON HAS REACHED FORTY OR FIFTY YEARS OLD AND IS STILL WITHOUT ACCOMPLISHMENT,
XXX
THAT PERSON IS NOT WORTHY OF ONE'S RESPECT!
XXX
XXX
XXX

9:26

UNBREAKABLE WILL

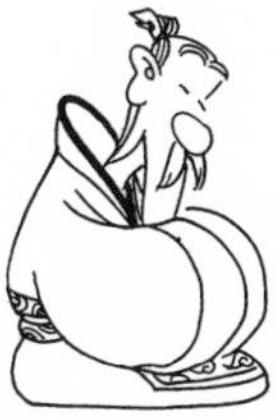

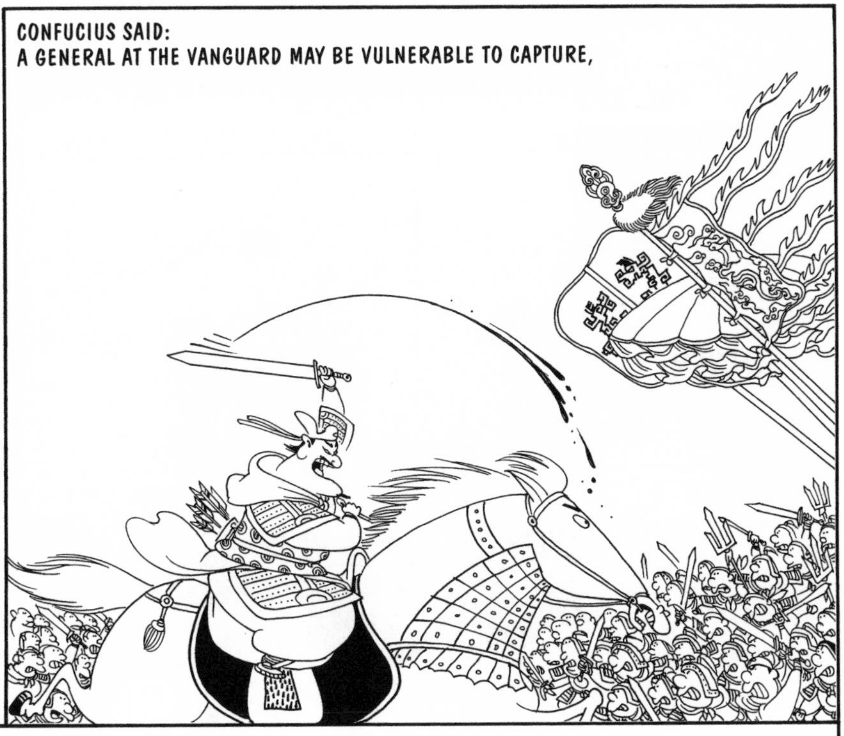
CONFUCIUS SAID:
A GENERAL AT THE VANGUARD MAY BE VULNERABLE TO CAPTURE,

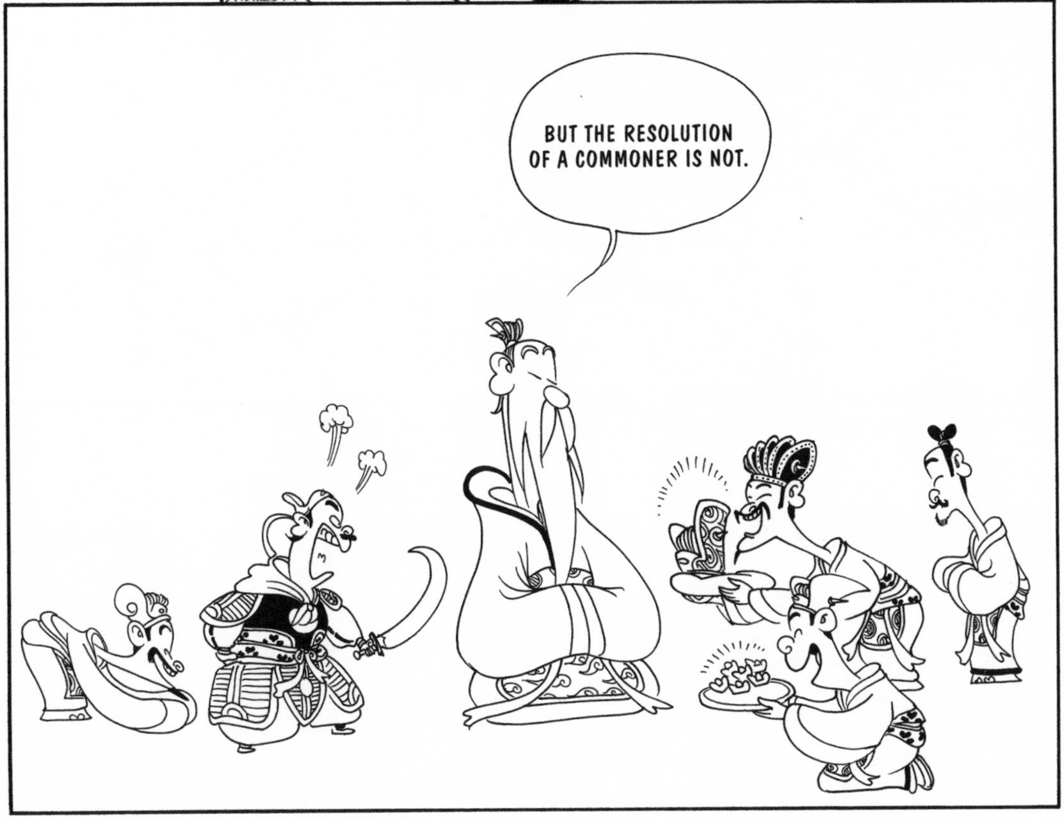
BUT THE RESOLUTION OF A COMMONER IS NOT.

子曰：「三軍可奪帥也，匹夫不可奪志也。」

子曰：「知者不惑，仁者不憂，勇者不懼。」

9:29

NEVER

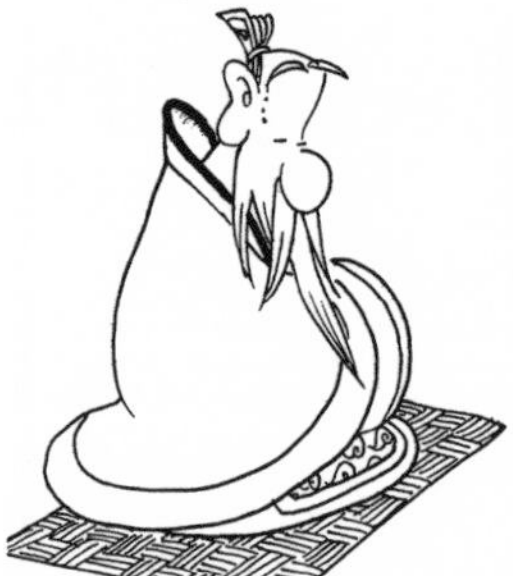

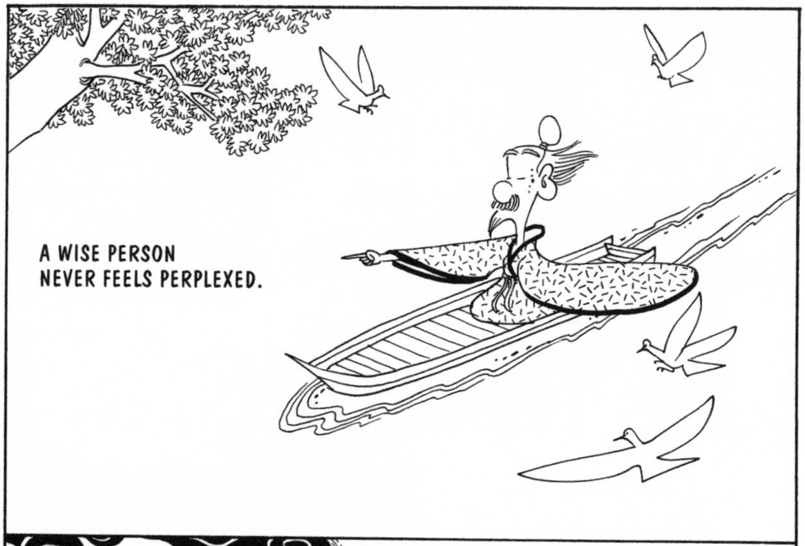
A WISE PERSON
NEVER FEELS PERPLEXED.

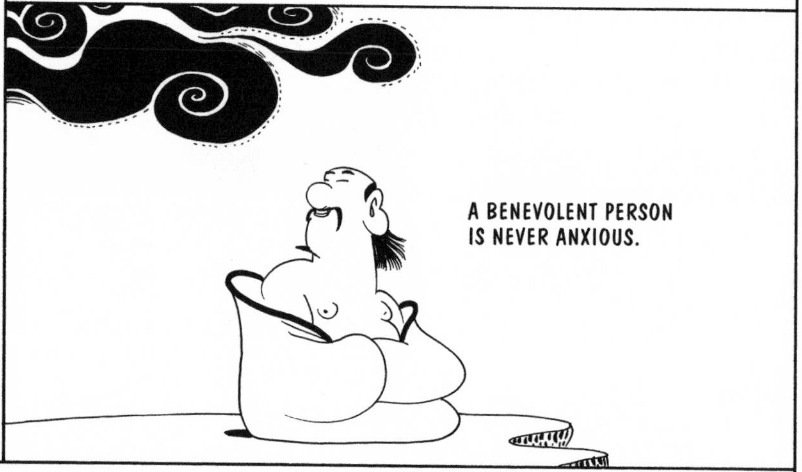
A BENEVOLENT PERSON
IS NEVER ANXIOUS.

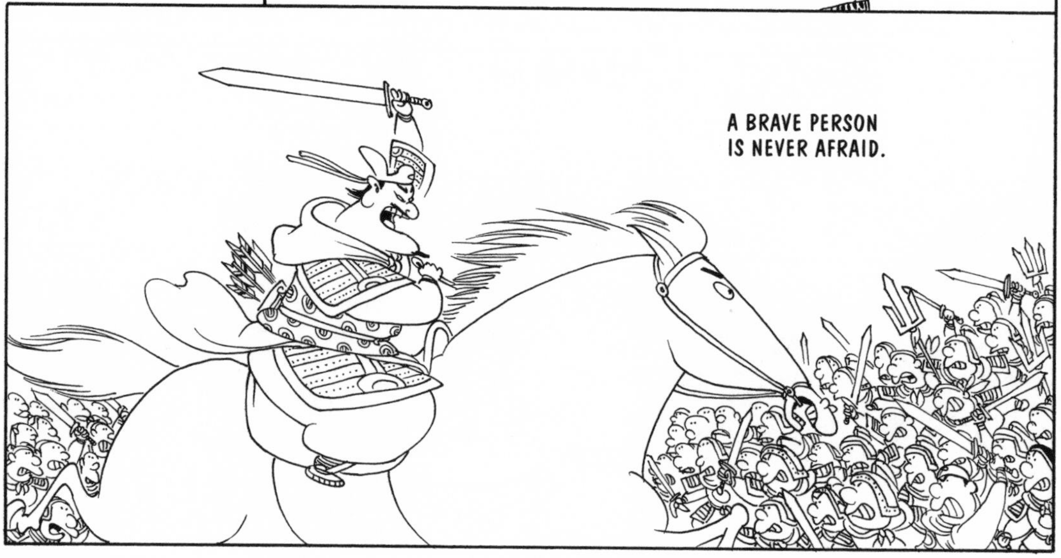
A BRAVE PERSON
IS NEVER AFRAID.

10:17

FIRE IN THE STABLE

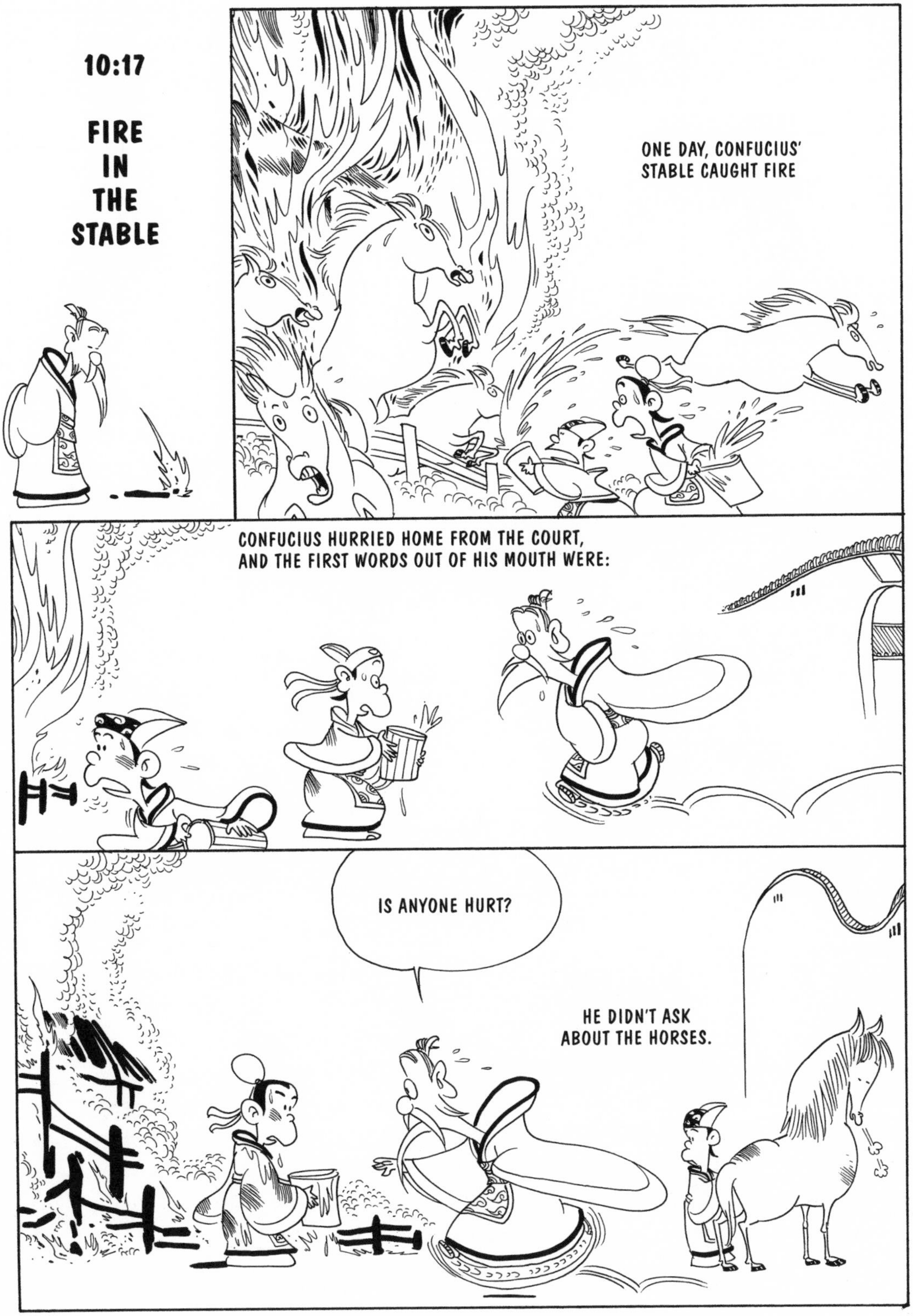

ONE DAY, CONFUCIUS' STABLE CAUGHT FIRE
CONFUCIUS HURRIED HOME FROM THE COURT, AND THE FIRST WORDS OUT OF HIS MOUTH WERE:
IS ANYONE HURT?
HE DIDN'T ASK ABOUT THE HORSES.

廄焚。子退朝，曰：「傷人乎？」不問馬。

季路問事鬼神。子曰：「未能事人，焉能事鬼？」

11:12

SPIRITS AND DEATH

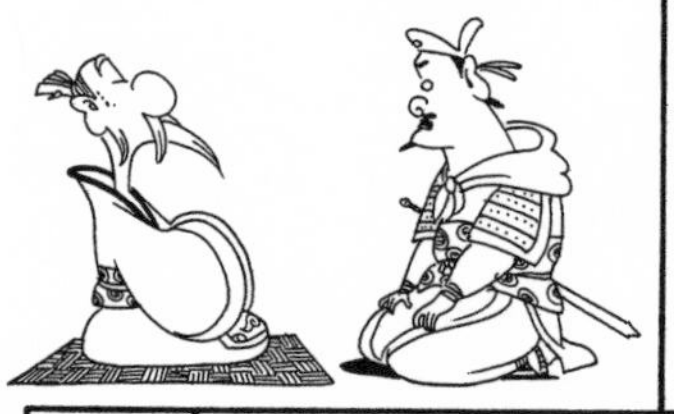

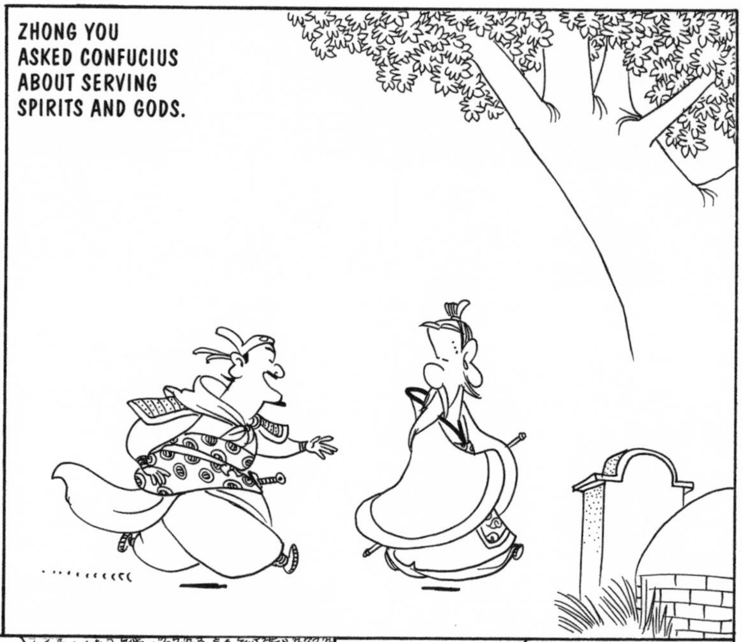
ZHONG YOU ASKED CONFUCIUS ABOUT SERVING SPIRITS AND GODS.

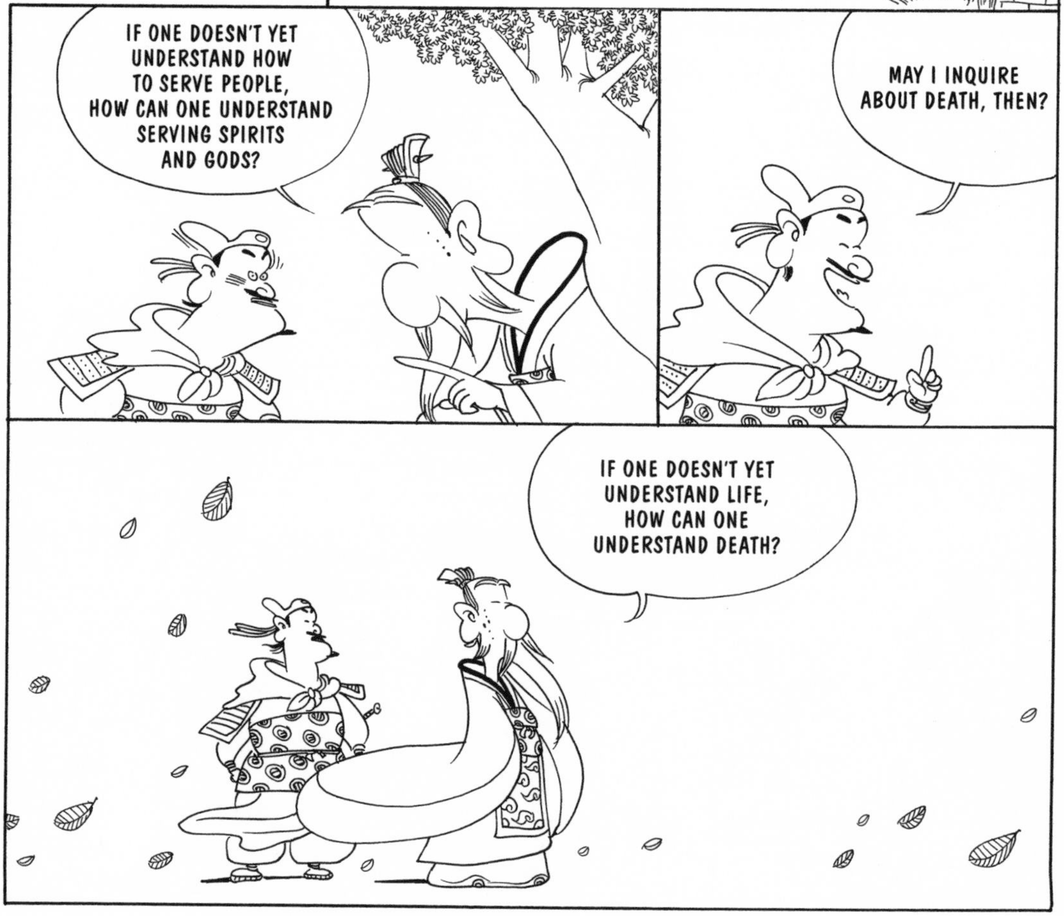
IF ONE DOESN'T YET UNDERSTAND HOW TO SERVE PEOPLE, HOW CAN ONE UNDERSTAND SERVING SPIRITS AND GODS?
MAY I INQUIRE ABOUT DEATH, THEN?
IF ONE DOESN'T YET UNDERSTAND LIFE, HOW CAN ONE UNDERSTAND DEATH?

11:16

OVERDOING IT

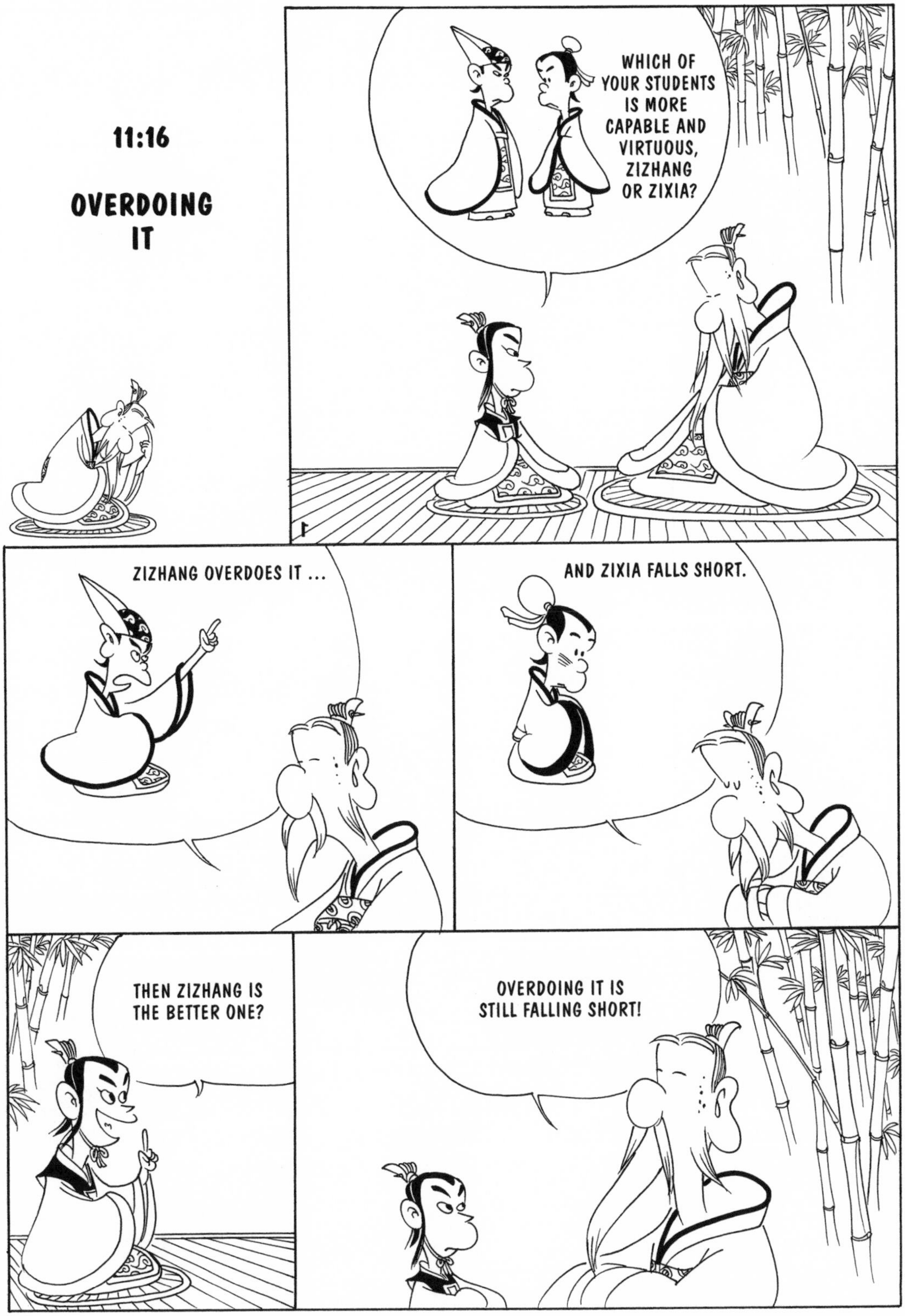
WHICH OF YOUR STUDENTS IS MORE CAPABLE AND VIRTUOUS, ZIZHANG OR ZIXIA?
ZIZHANG OVERDOES IT ...
AND ZIXIA FALLS SHORT.
THEN ZIZHANG IS THE BETTER ONE?
OVERDOING IT IS STILL FALLING SHORT!

子貢問：「師與商也孰賢？」子曰：「師也過，商也不及。」曰：「然則師愈與？」子曰：「過猶不及。」

柴也愚，參也魯，師也辟，由也喭。子曰：「回也其庶乎，屢空。賜不受命，而貨殖焉，億則屢中。」

11:18–19

CHAI IS NAÏVE

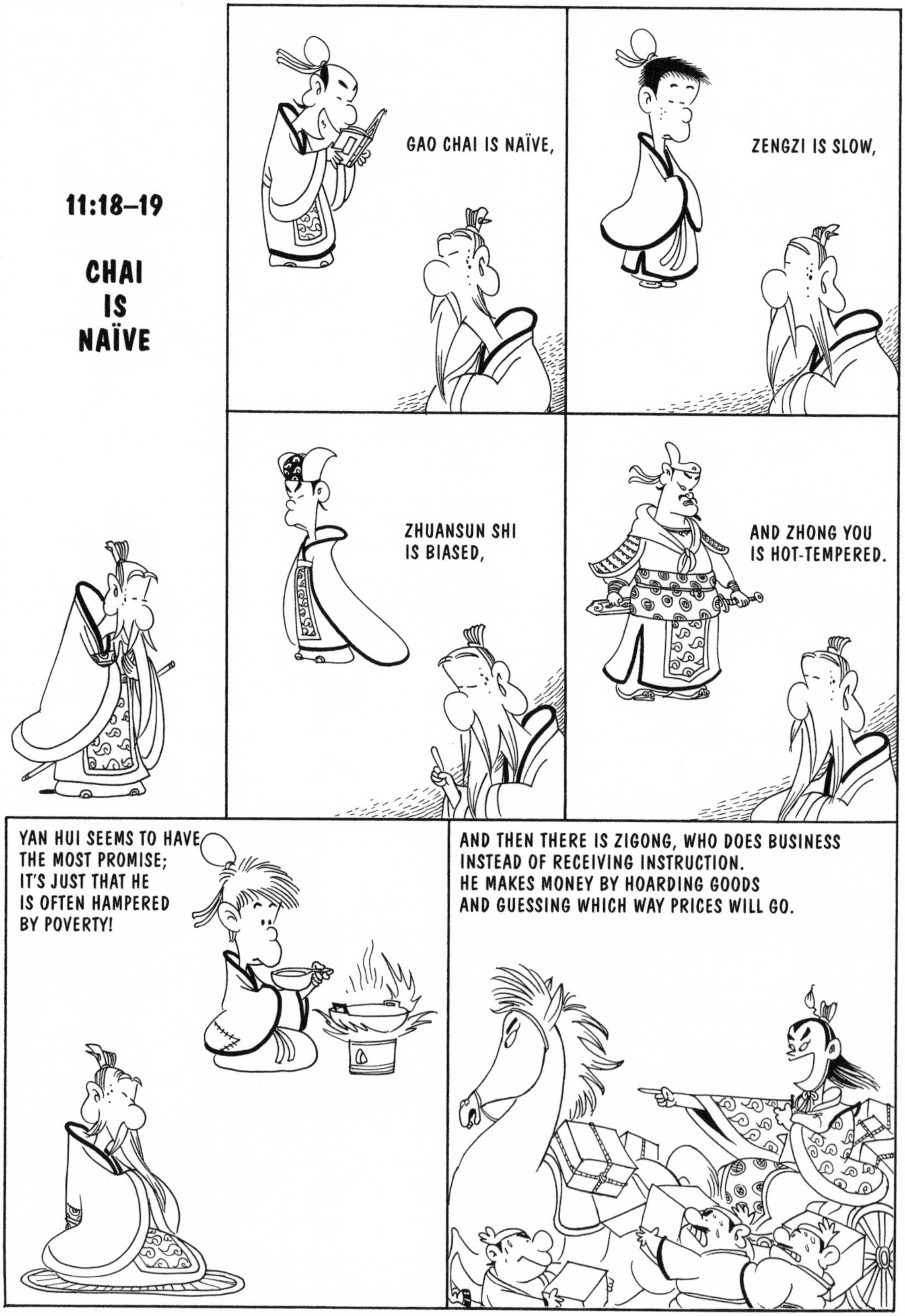
GAO CHAI IS NAÏVE,
ZENGZI IS SLOW,
ZHUANSUN SHI IS BIASED,
AND ZHONG YOU IS HOT-TEMPERED.
YAN HUI SEEMS TO HAVE THE MOST PROMISE; IT'S JUST THAT HE IS OFTEN HAMPERED BY POVERTY!
AND THEN THERE IS ZIGONG, WHO DOES BUSINESS INSTEAD OF RECEIVING INSTRUCTION. HE MAKES MONEY BY HOARDING GOODS AND GUESSING WHICH WAY PRICES WILL GO.

12:1

BENEVOLENCE

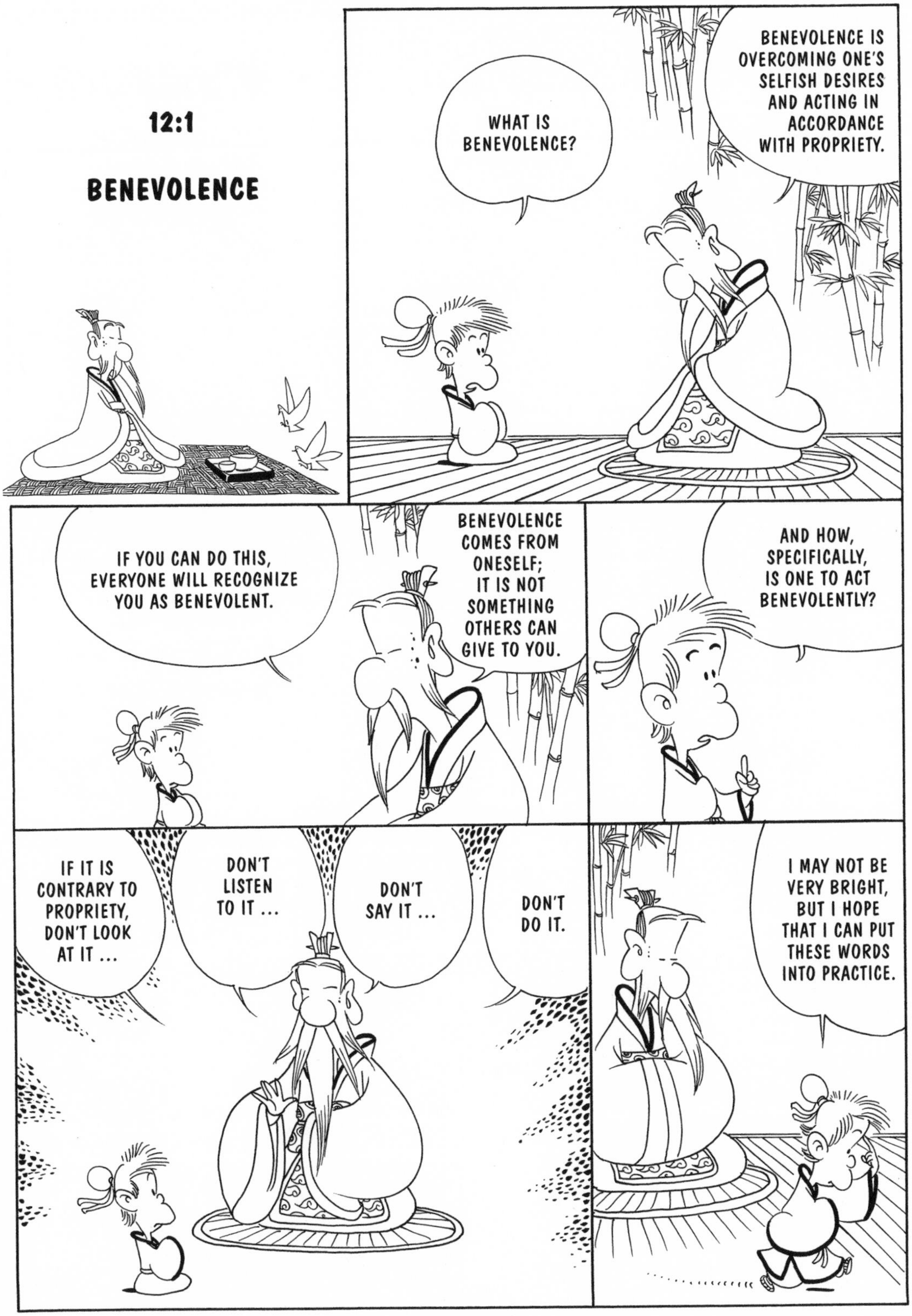

WHAT IS BENEVOLENCE?
BENEVOLENCE IS OVERCOMING ONE'S SELFISH DESIRES AND ACTING IN ACCORDANCE WITH PROPRIETY.
IF YOU CAN DO THIS, EVERYONE WILL RECOGNIZE YOU AS BENEVOLENT.
BENEVOLENCE COMES FROM ONESELF; IT IS NOT SOMETHING OTHERS CAN GIVE TO YOU.
AND HOW, SPECIFICALLY, IS ONE TO ACT BENEVOLENTLY?
IF IT IS CONTRARY TO PROPRIETY, DON'T LOOK AT IT ...
DON'T LISTEN TO IT ...
DON'T SAY IT ...
DON'T DO IT.
I MAY NOT BE VERY BRIGHT, BUT I HOPE THAT I CAN PUT THESE WORDS INTO PRACTICE.

顏淵問仁。子曰：「克己復禮為仁。一日克己復禮，天下歸仁焉。為仁由己，而由人乎哉？」

顏淵曰：「請問其目。」子曰：「非禮勿視，非禮勿聽，非禮勿言，非禮勿動。」

顏淵曰：「回雖不敏，請事斯語矣。」

仲弓問仁。子曰：「出門如見大賓，使民如承大祭。己所不欲，勿施於人。在邦無怨，在家無怨。」
仲弓曰：「雍雖不敏，請事斯語矣。」

12:2

THE GOLDEN RULE

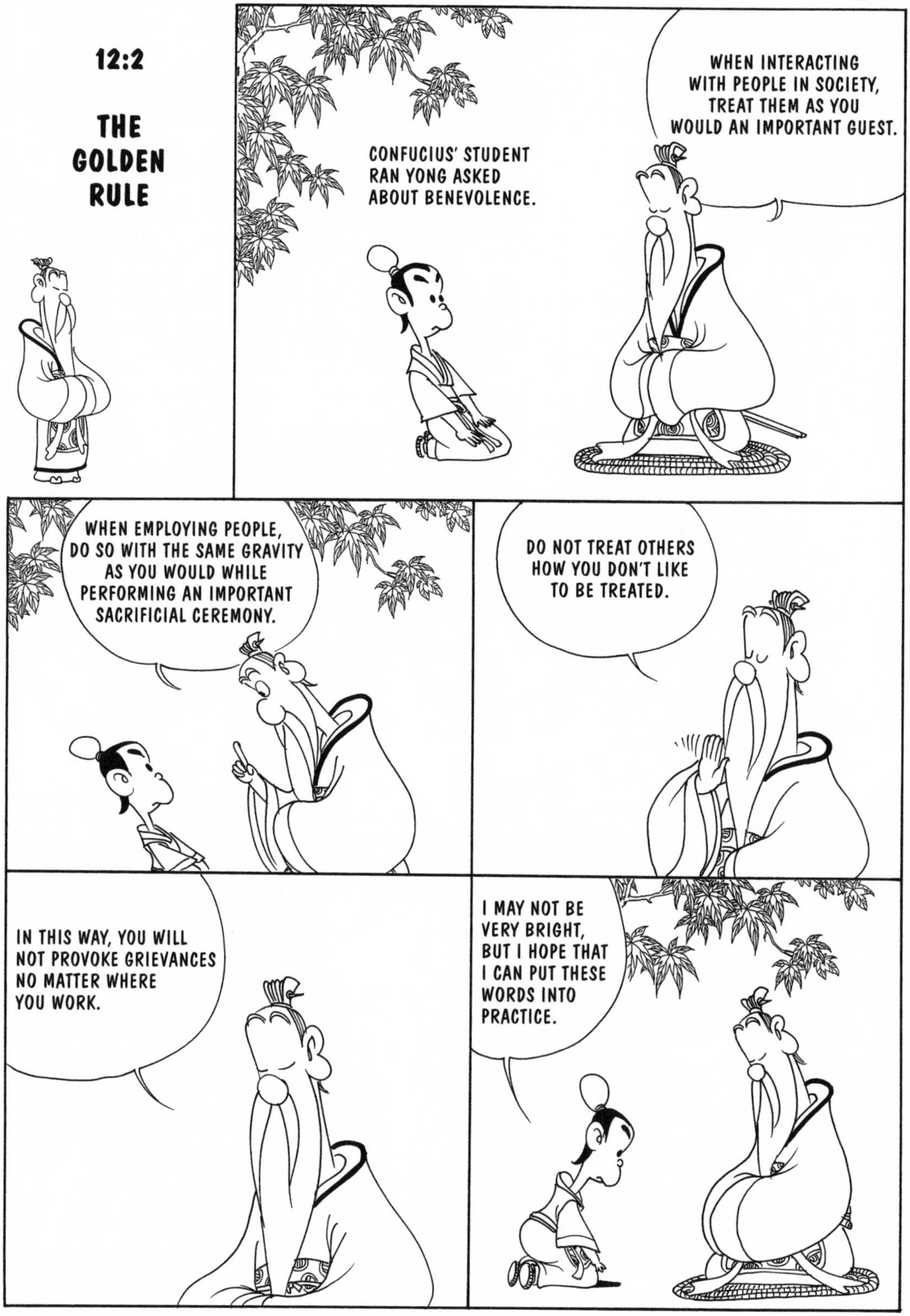
CONFUCIUS' STUDENT RAN YONG ASKED ABOUT BENEVOLENCE.
WHEN INTERACTING WITH PEOPLE IN SOCIETY, TREAT THEM AS YOU WOULD AN IMPORTANT GUEST.
WHEN EMPLOYING PEOPLE, DO SO WITH THE SAME GRAVITY AS YOU WOULD WHILE PERFORMING AN IMPORTANT SACRIFICIAL CEREMONY.
DO NOT TREAT OTHERS HOW YOU DON'T LIKE TO BE TREATED.
IN THIS WAY, YOU WILL NOT PROVOKE GRIEVANCES NO MATTER WHERE YOU WORK.
I MAY NOT BE VERY BRIGHT, BUT I HOPE THAT I CAN PUT THESE WORDS INTO PRACTICE.

12:5

BROTHERS

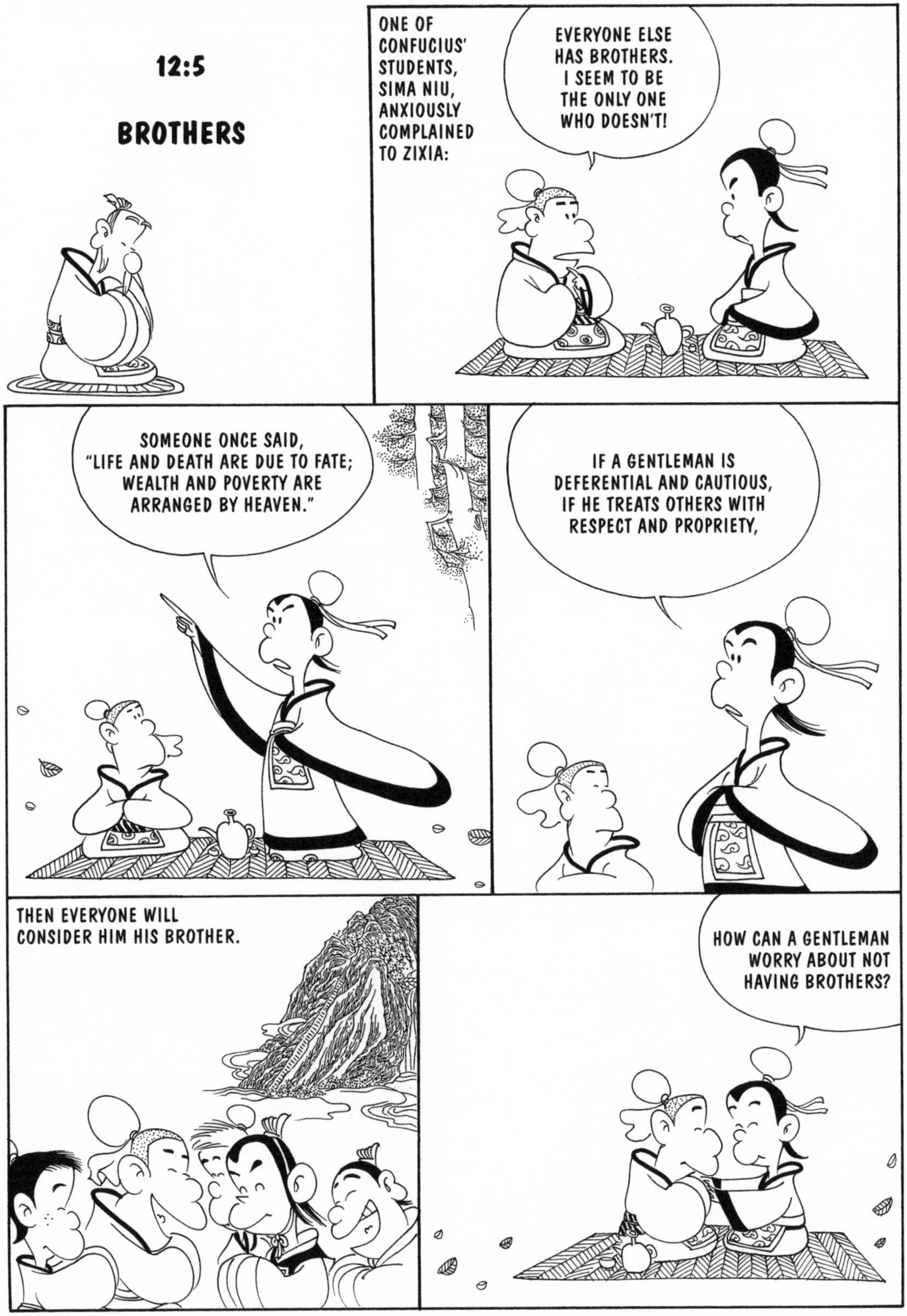
ONE OF CONFUCIUS' STUDENTS, SIMA NIU, ANXIOUSLY COMPLAINED TO ZIXIA:
EVERYONE ELSE HAS BROTHERS. I SEEM TO BE THE ONLY ONE WHO DOESN'T!
SOMEONE ONCE SAID, "LIFE AND DEATH ARE DUE TO FATE; WEALTH AND POVERTY ARE ARRANGED BY HEAVEN."
IF A GENTLEMAN IS DEFERENTIAL AND CAUTIOUS, IF HE TREATS OTHERS WITH RESPECT AND PROPRIETY,
THEN EVERYONE WILL CONSIDER HIM HIS BROTHER.
HOW CAN A GENTLEMAN WORRY ABOUT NOT HAVING BROTHERS?

司馬牛憂曰：「人皆有兄弟，我獨亡。」子夏曰：「商聞之矣：死生有命，富貴在天。君子敬而無失，與人恭而有禮。四海之內，皆兄弟也。君子何患乎無兄弟也？」

12:7

THE PEOPLE'S TRUST

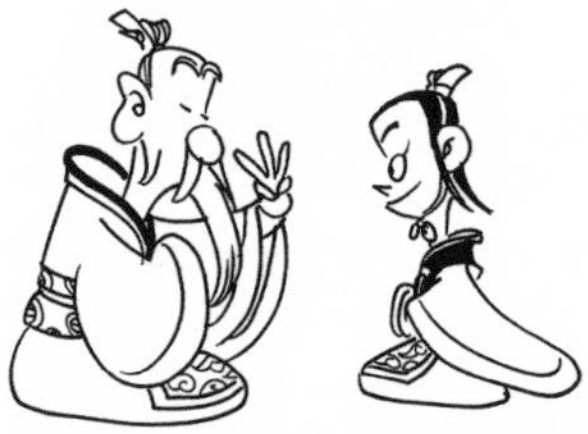

子貢問政。子曰：「足食，足兵，民信之矣。」
子貢曰：「必不得已而去，於斯三者何先？」曰：「去兵。」
子貢曰：「必不得已而去，於斯二者何先？」曰：「去食。自古皆有死，民無信不立。」

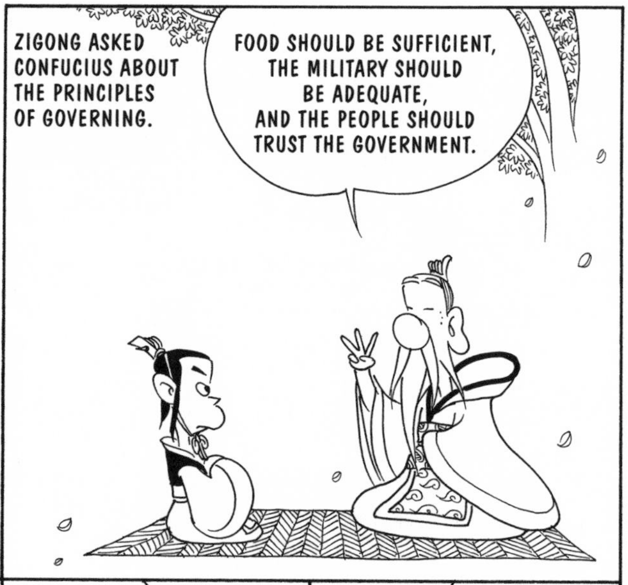
ZIGONG ASKED CONFUCIUS ABOUT THE PRINCIPLES OF GOVERNING.
FOOD SHOULD BE SUFFICIENT, THE MILITARY SHOULD BE ADEQUATE, AND THE PEOPLE SHOULD TRUST THE GOVERNMENT.

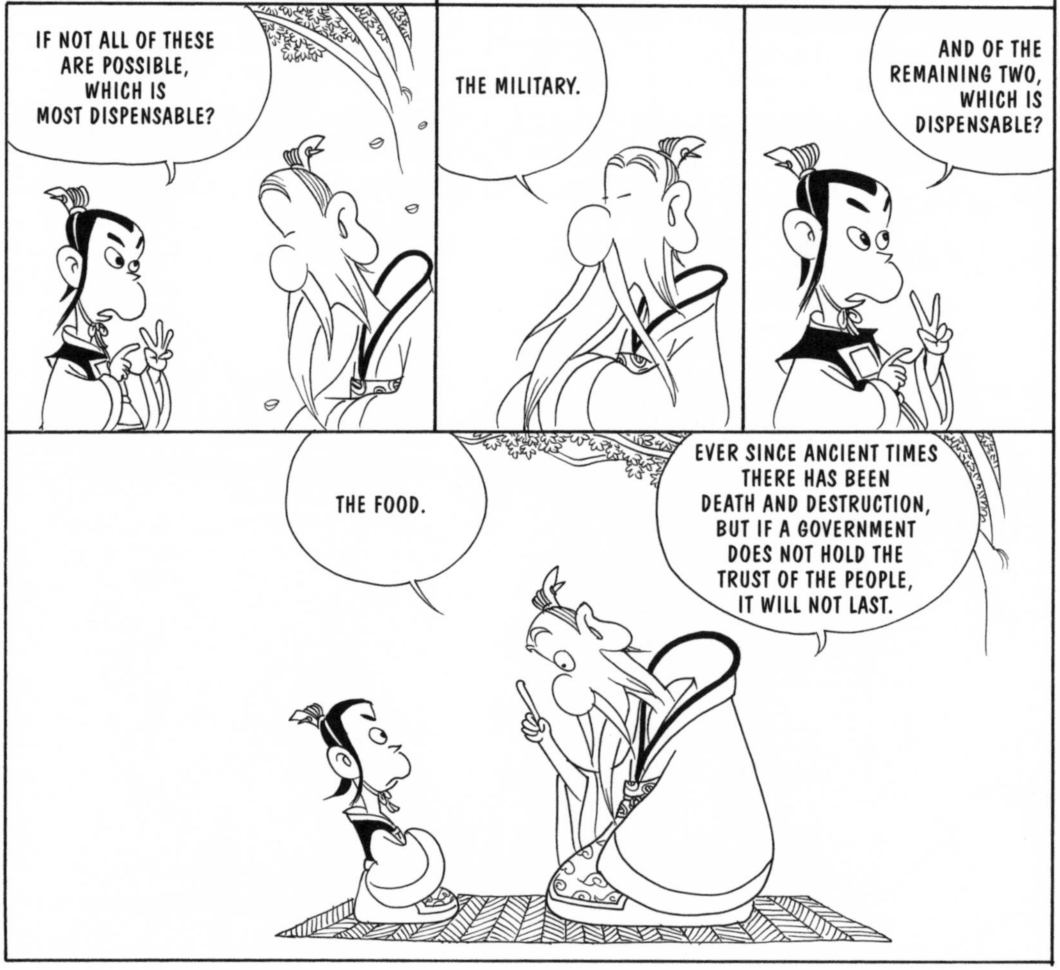
IF NOT ALL OF THESE ARE POSSIBLE, WHICH IS MOST DISPENSABLE?
THE MILITARY.
AND OF THE REMAINING TWO, WHICH IS DISPENSABLE?
THE FOOD.
EVER SINCE ANCIENT TIMES THERE HAS BEEN DEATH AND DESTRUCTION, BUT IF A GOVERNMENT DOES NOT HOLD THE TRUST OF THE PEOPLE, IT WILL NOT LAST.

12:16

SUPPORTING THE GOOD

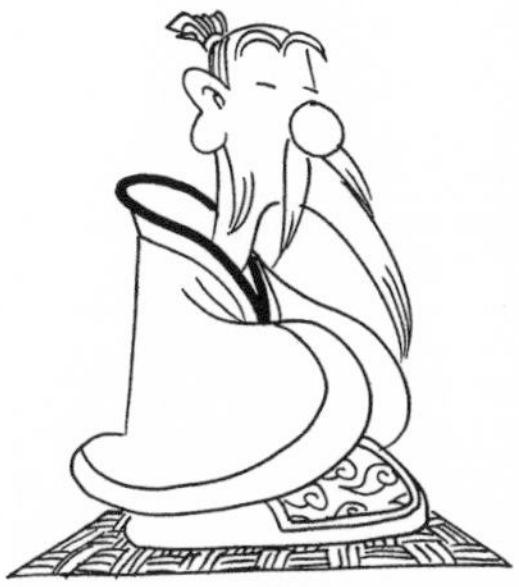

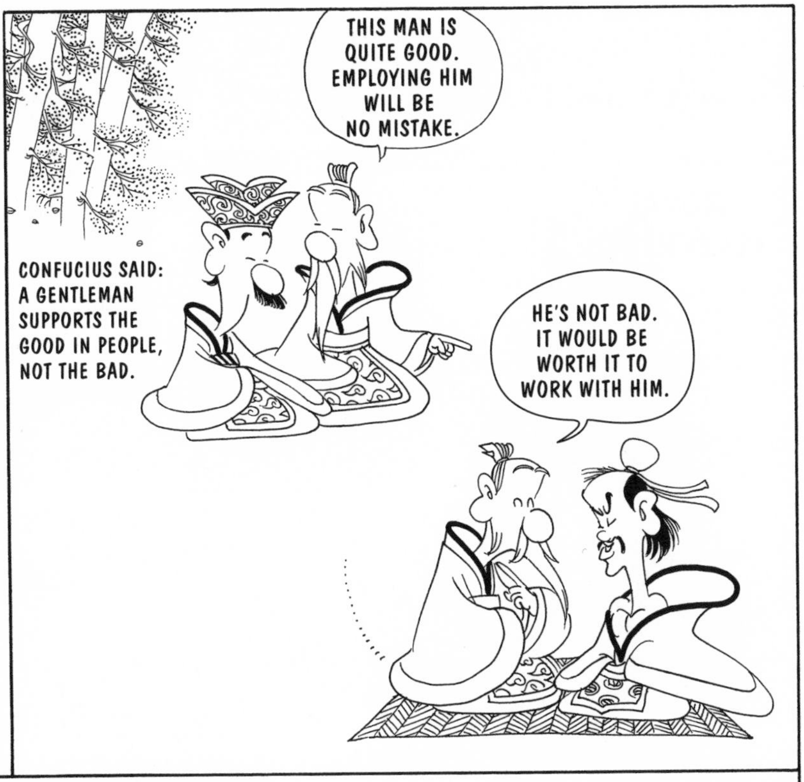
CONFUCIUS SAID: A GENTLEMAN SUPPORTS THE GOOD IN PEOPLE, NOT THE BAD.
THIS MAN IS QUITE GOOD. EMPLOYING HIM WILL BE NO MISTAKE.
HE'S NOT BAD. IT WOULD BE WORTH IT TO WORK WITH HIM.

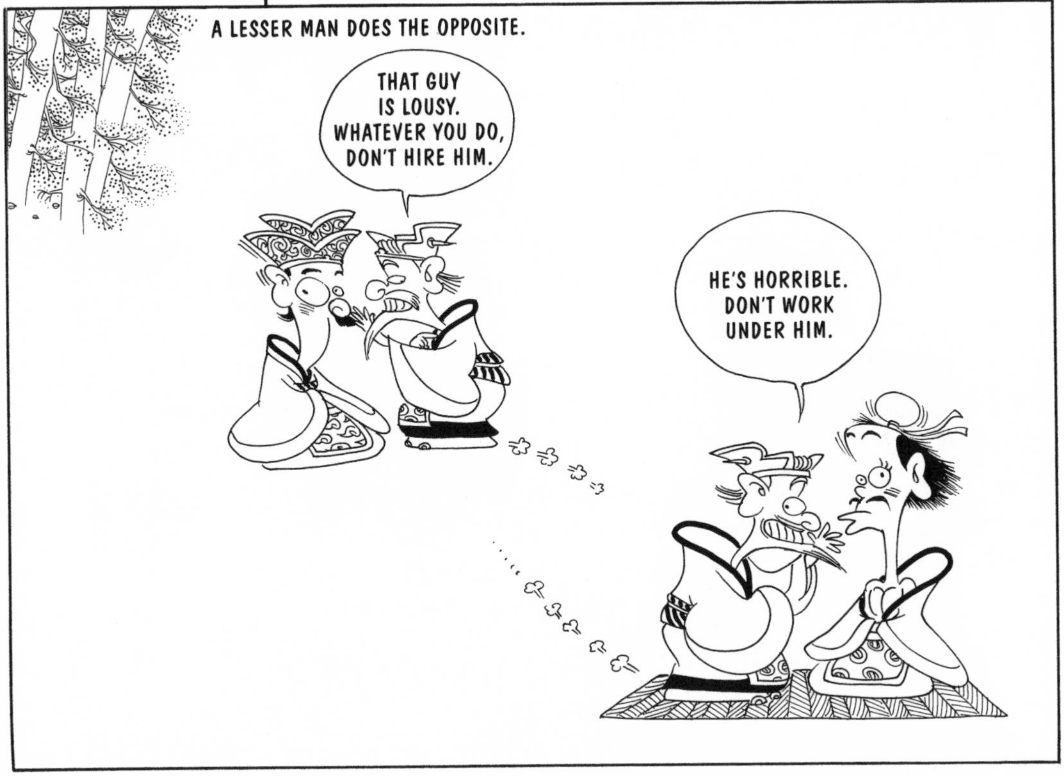
A LESSER MAN DOES THE OPPOSITE.
THAT GUY IS LOUSY. WHATEVER YOU DO, DON'T HIRE HIM.
HE'S HORRIBLE. DON'T WORK UNDER HIM.

子曰：「君子成人之美，不成人之惡。小人反是。」

季康子問政於孔子。孔子對曰：「政者、正也。子帥以正，孰敢不正？」

12:17

MORAL LEADERSHIP

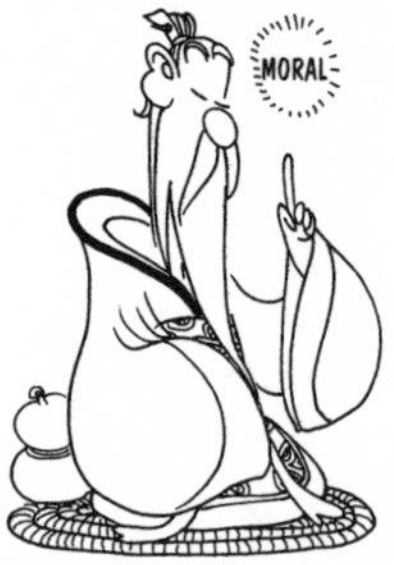
MORAL

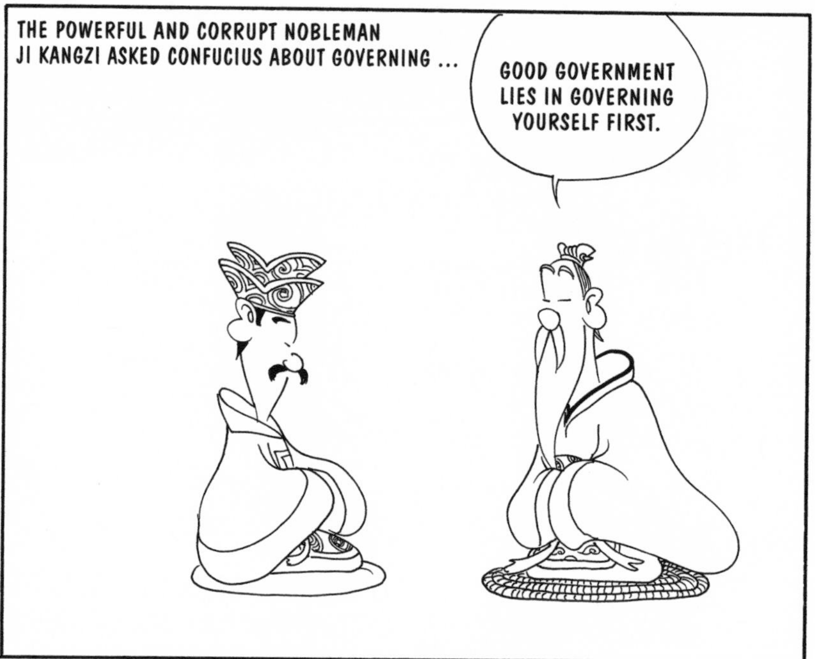
THE POWERFUL AND CORRUPT NOBLEMAN JI KANGZI ASKED CONFUCIUS ABOUT GOVERNING ...
GOOD GOVERNMENT LIES IN GOVERNING YOURSELF FIRST.

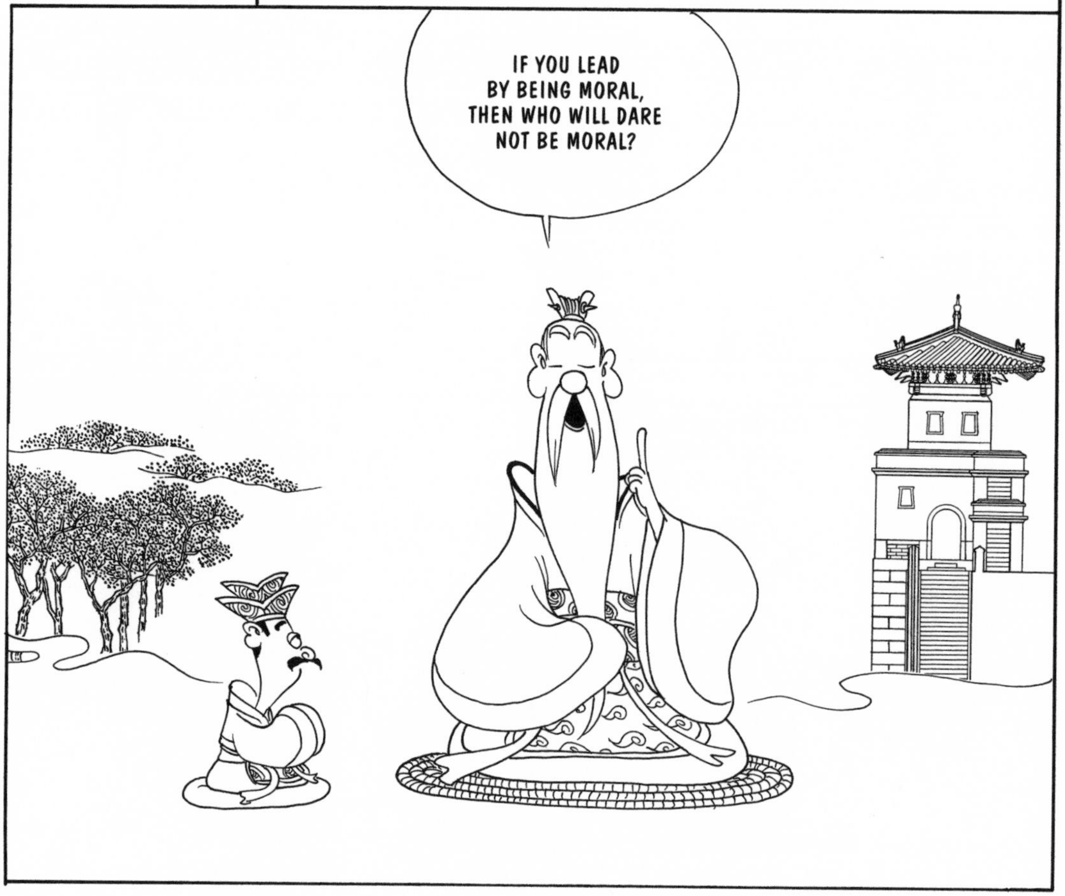
IF YOU LEAD BY BEING MORAL, THEN WHO WILL DARE NOT BE MORAL?

12:23

GIVING ADVICE TO FRIENDS

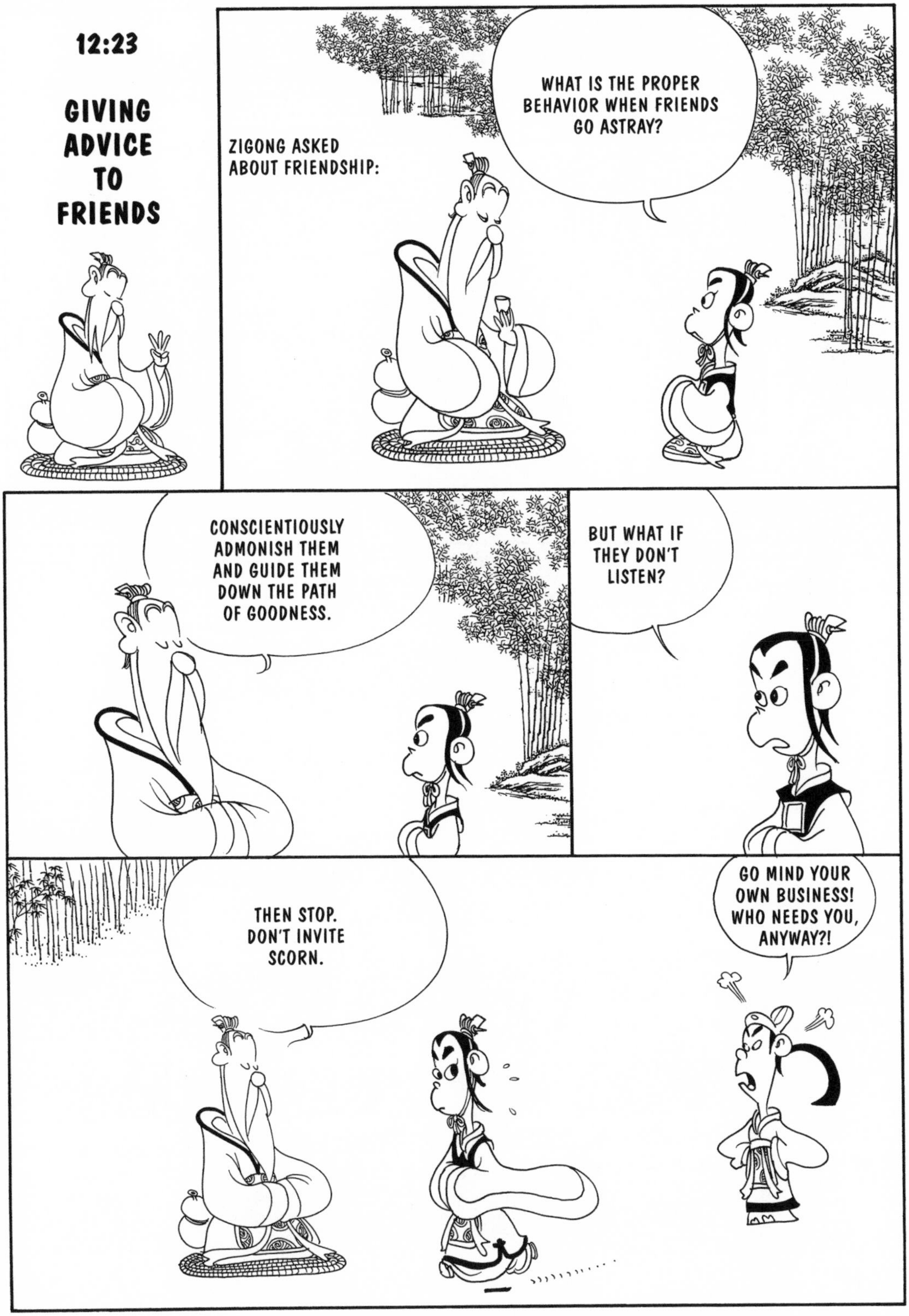
ZIGONG ASKED ABOUT FRIENDSHIP:
WHAT IS THE PROPER BEHAVIOR WHEN FRIENDS GO ASTRAY?
CONSCIENTIOUSLY ADMONISH THEM AND GUIDE THEM DOWN THE PATH OF GOODNESS.
BUT WHAT IF THEY DON'T LISTEN?
THEN STOP. DON'T INVITE SCORN.
GO MIND YOUR OWN BUSINESS! WHO NEEDS YOU, ANYWAY?!

子貢問友。子曰：「忠告而善道之，不可則止，毋自辱焉。」

曾子曰：「君子以文會友，以友輔仁。」

12:24

MAKING FRIENDS

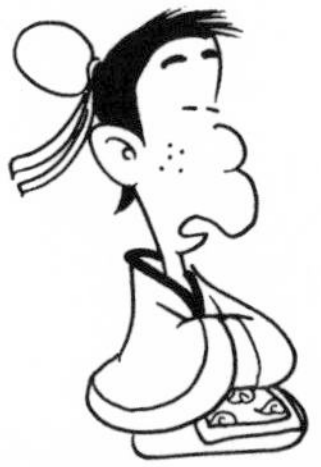

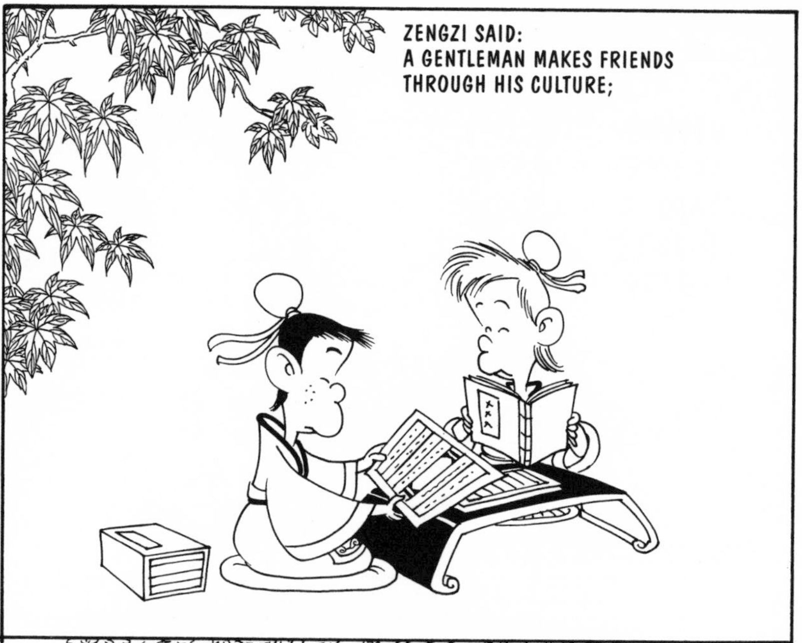
ZENGZI SAID:
A GENTLEMAN MAKES FRIENDS
THROUGH HIS CULTURE;

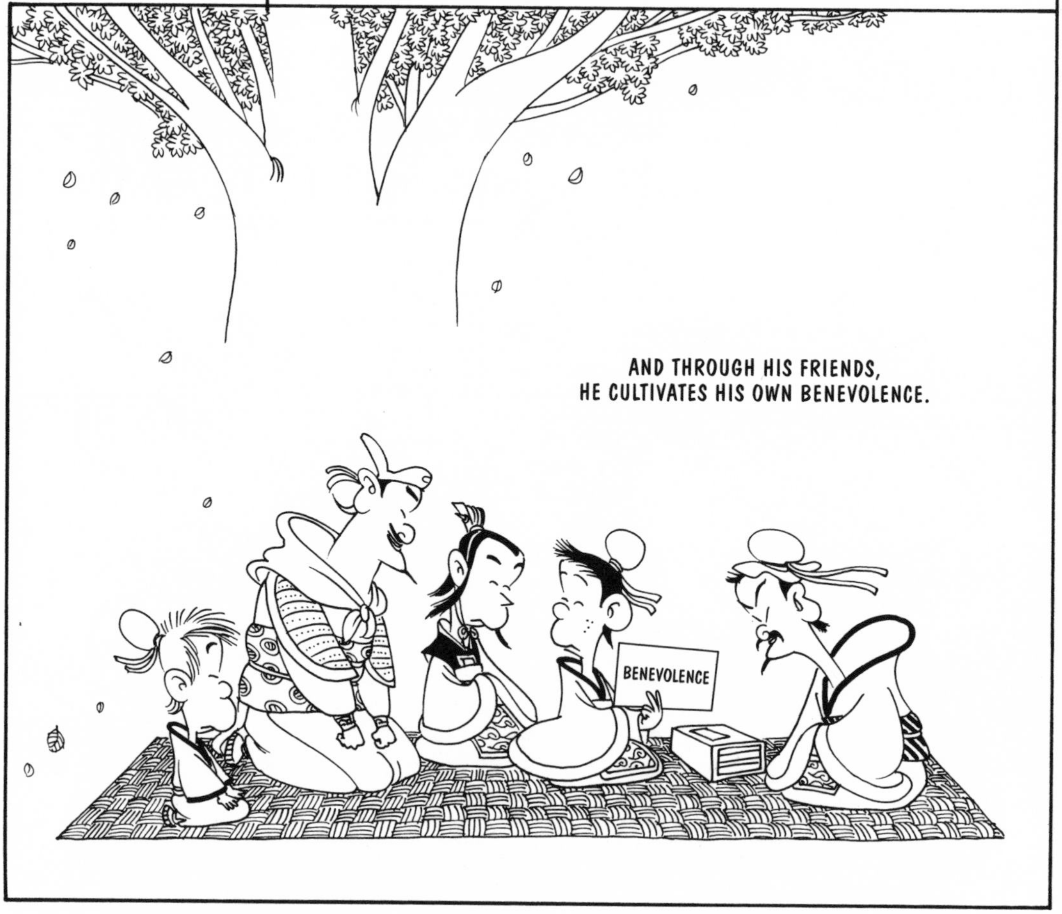
AND THROUGH HIS FRIENDS,
HE CULTIVATES HIS OWN BENEVOLENCE.
BENEVOLENCE

13:1

LEADING FROM BEHIND

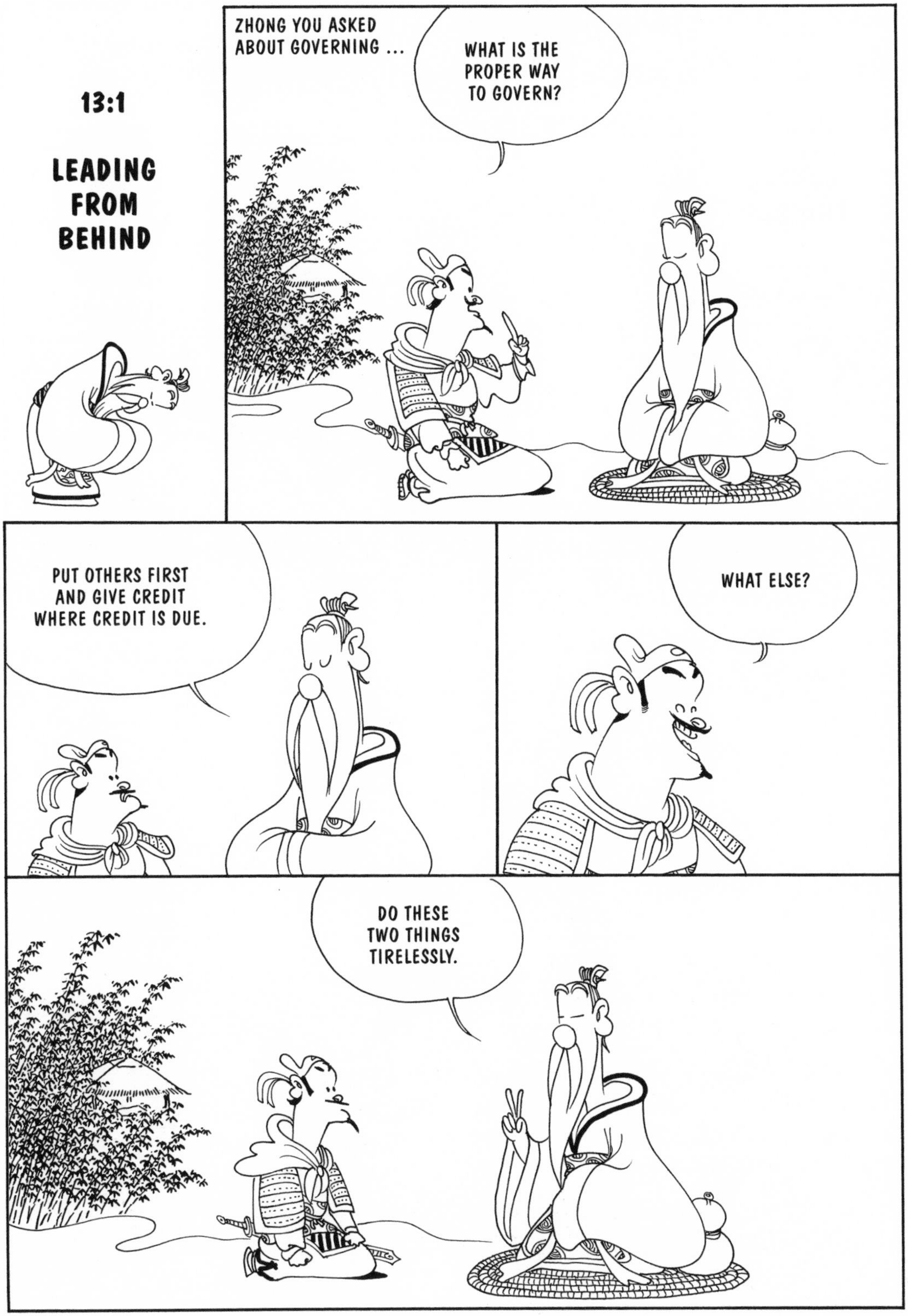
ZHONG YOU ASKED ABOUT GOVERNING ...
WHAT IS THE PROPER WAY TO GOVERN?
PUT OTHERS FIRST AND GIVE CREDIT WHERE CREDIT IS DUE.
WHAT ELSE?
DO THESE TWO THINGS TIRELESSLY.

子路問政。子曰：「先之勞之。」請益。曰：「無倦。」

子曰：「其身正，不令而行；其身不正，雖令不從。」

13:6

THE MORAL LEADER

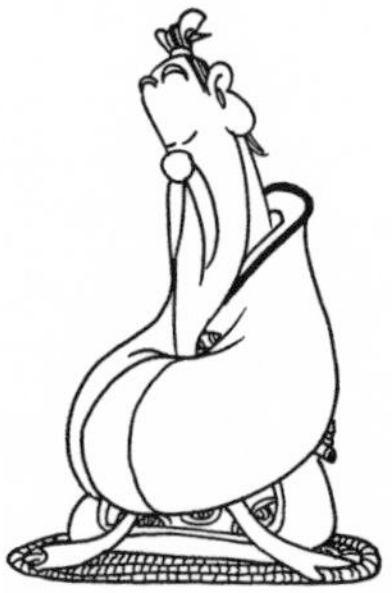

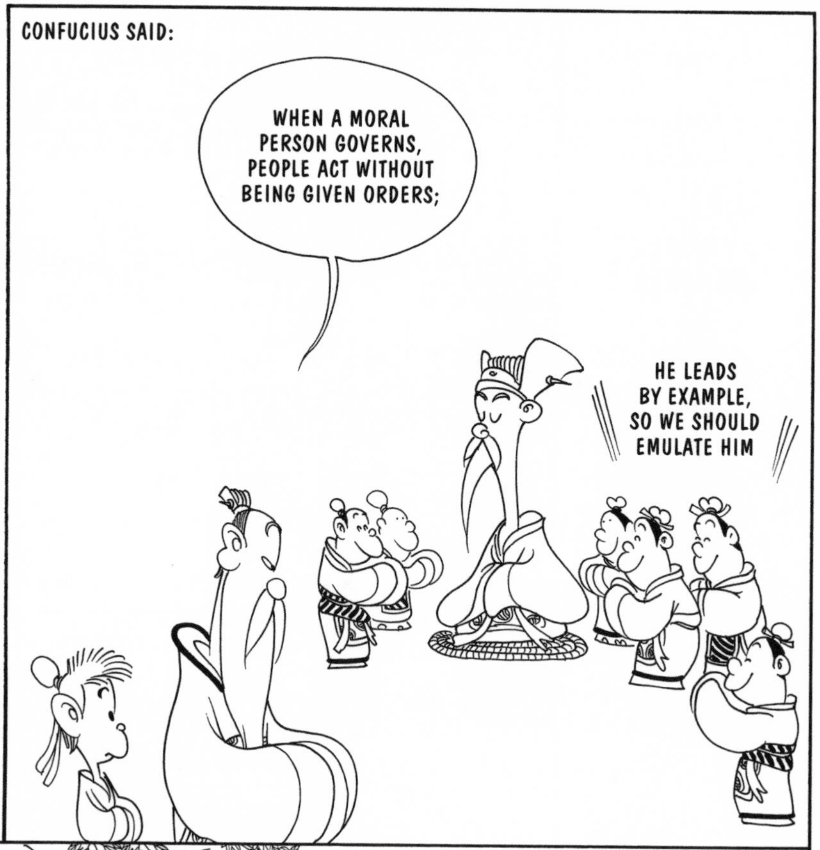
CONFUCIUS SAID:
WHEN A MORAL PERSON GOVERNS, PEOPLE ACT WITHOUT BEING GIVEN ORDERS;
HE LEADS BY EXAMPLE, SO WE SHOULD EMULATE HIM

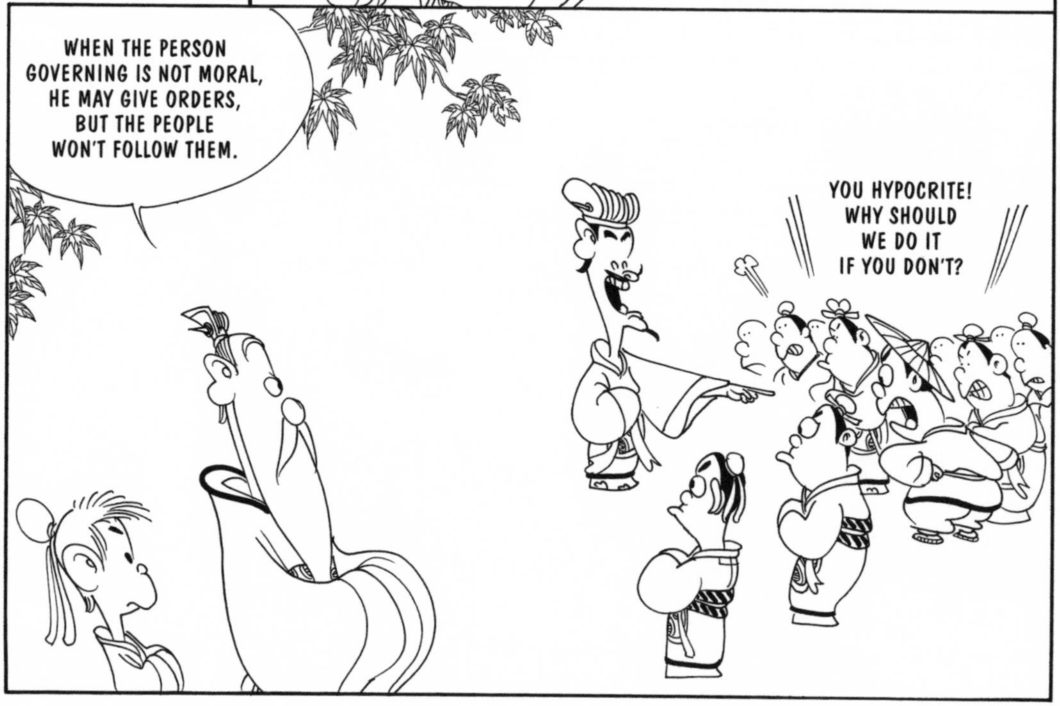
WHEN THE PERSON GOVERNING IS NOT MORAL, HE MAY GIVE ORDERS, BUT THE PEOPLE WON'T FOLLOW THEM.
YOU HYPOCRITE! WHY SHOULD WE DO IT IF YOU DON'T?

13:13

GOVERNING ONESELF TO GOVERN OTHERS

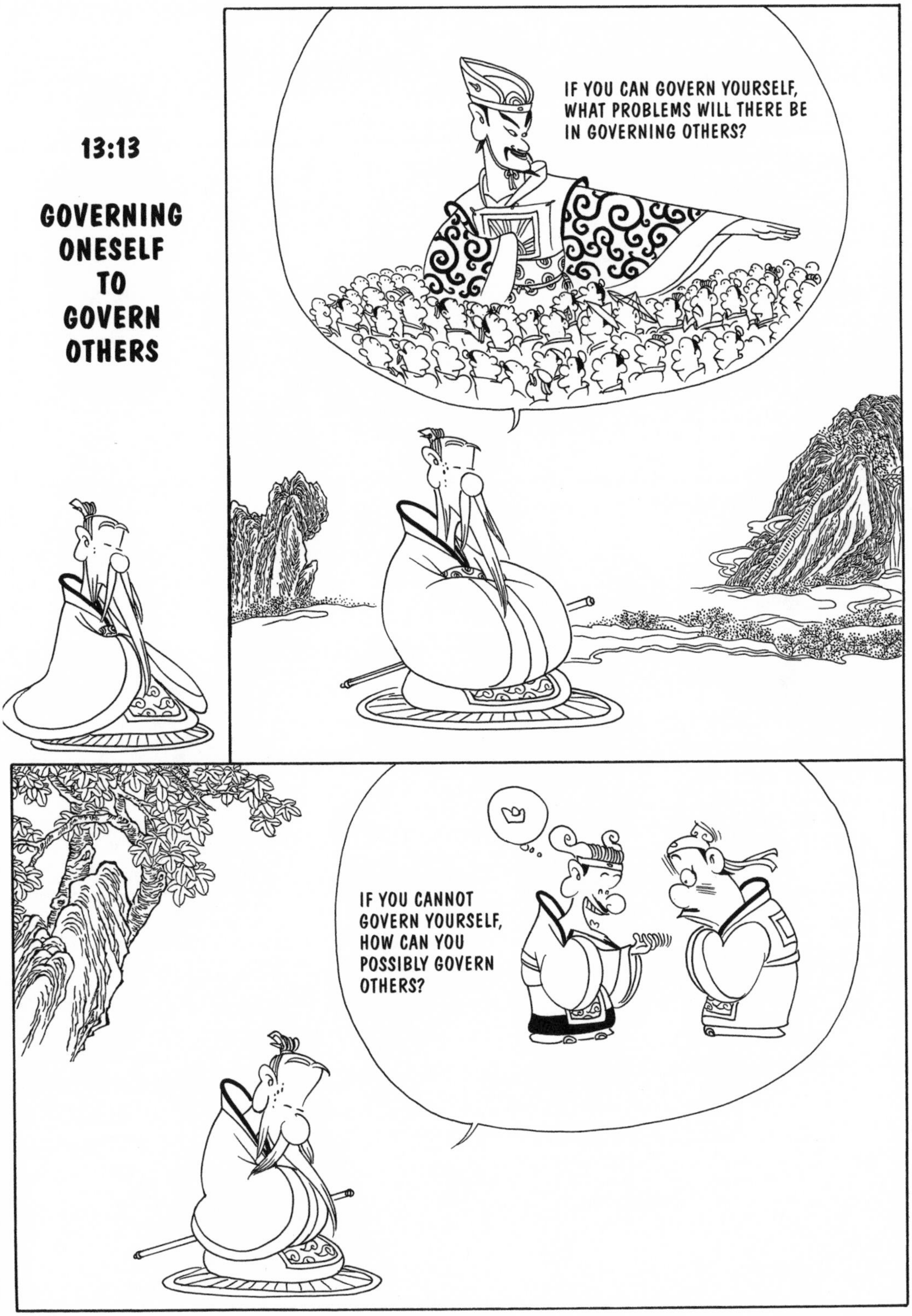

IF YOU CAN GOVERN YOURSELF, WHAT PROBLEMS WILL THERE BE IN GOVERNING OTHERS?
IF YOU CANNOT GOVERN YOURSELF, HOW CAN YOU POSSIBLY GOVERN OTHERS?

子曰：「苟正其身矣，於從政乎何有？不能正其身，如正人何？」

子夏為莒父宰，問政。子曰：「無欲速，無見小利。欲速，則不達；見小利，大事不成。」

13:17

PATIENCE AND PRESCIENCE

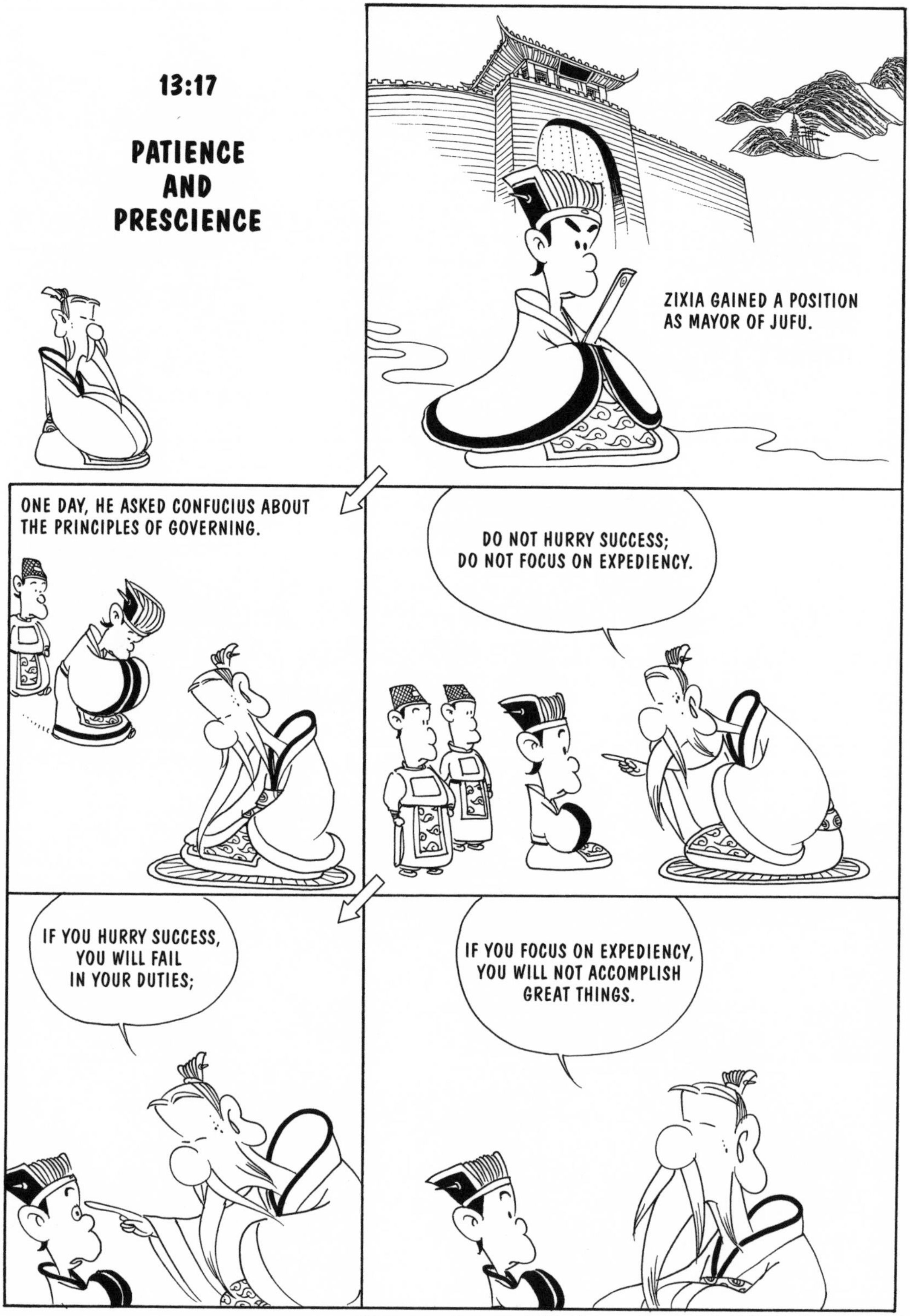

ZIXIA GAINED A POSITION AS MAYOR OF JUFU.
ONE DAY, HE ASKED CONFUCIUS ABOUT THE PRINCIPLES OF GOVERNING.
DO NOT HURRY SUCCESS; DO NOT FOCUS ON EXPEDIENCY.
IF YOU HURRY SUCCESS, YOU WILL FAIL IN YOUR DUTIES;
IF YOU FOCUS ON EXPEDIENCY, YOU WILL NOT ACCOMPLISH GREAT THINGS.

13:19

FAN CHI ASKS ABOUT BENEVOLENCE

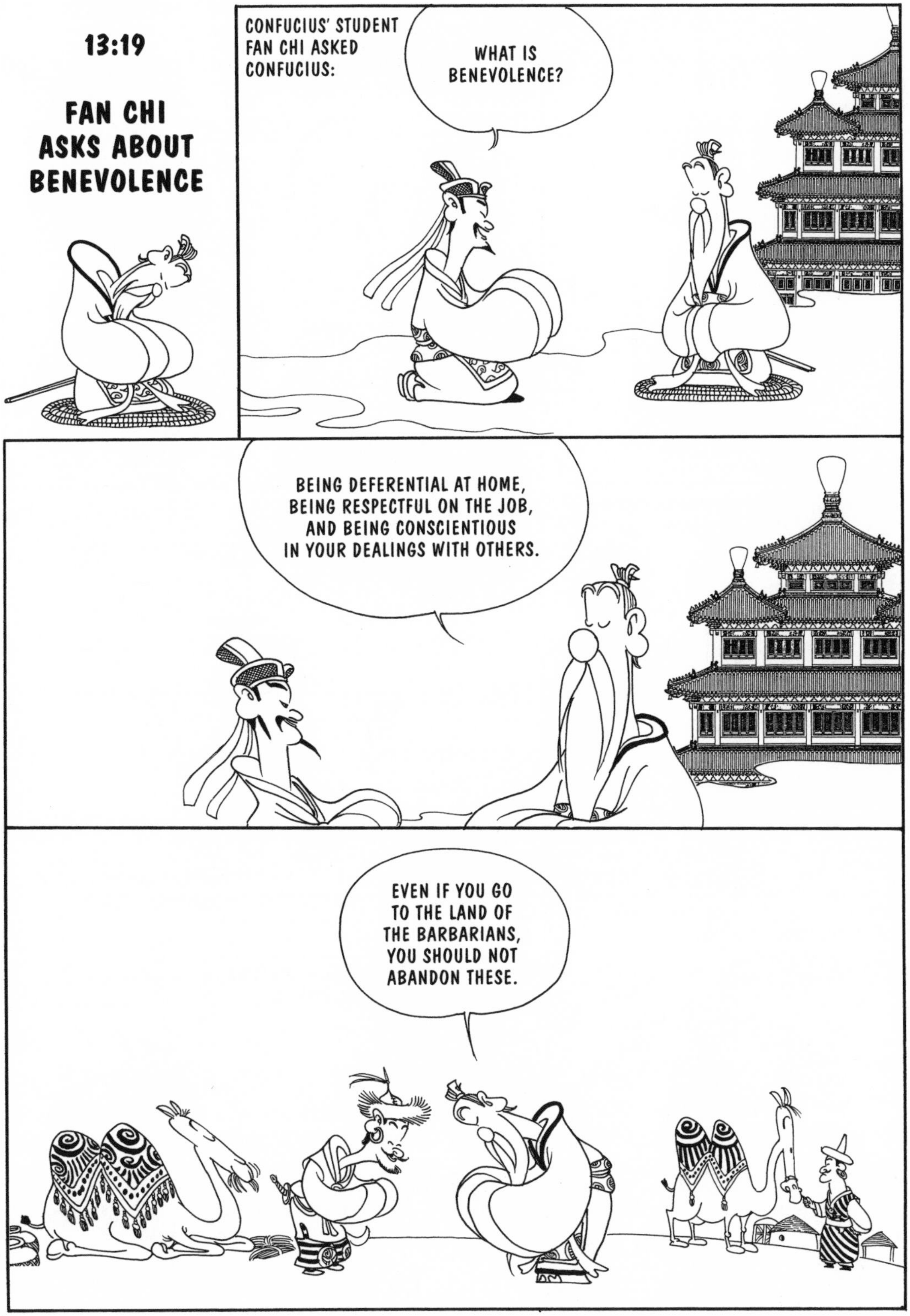
CONFUCIUS' STUDENT FAN CHI ASKED CONFUCIUS:
WHAT IS BENEVOLENCE?
BEING DEFERENTIAL AT HOME, BEING RESPECTFUL ON THE JOB, AND BEING CONSCIENTIOUS IN YOUR DEALINGS WITH OTHERS.
EVEN IF YOU GO TO THE LAND OF THE BARBARIANS, YOU SHOULD NOT ABANDON THESE.

樊遲問仁。子曰：「居處恭，執事敬，與人忠。雖之夷狄，不可棄也。」

子曰：「君子和而不同，小人同而不和。」

13:23

HARMONIZE

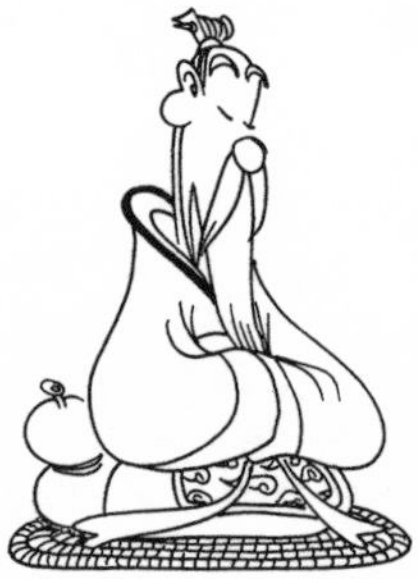

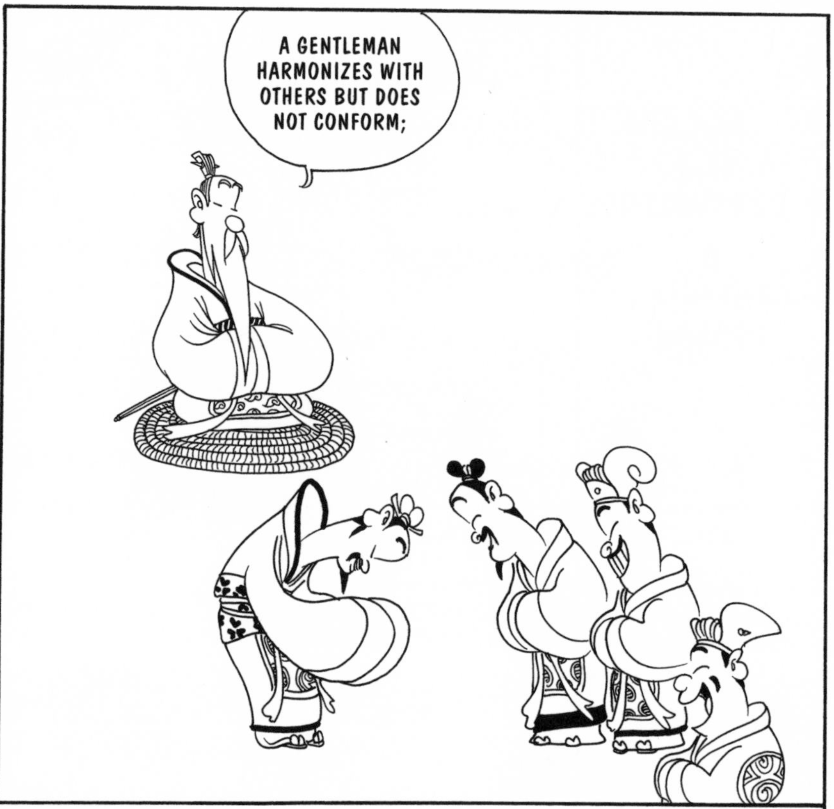
A GENTLEMAN HARMONIZES WITH OTHERS BUT DOES NOT CONFORM;

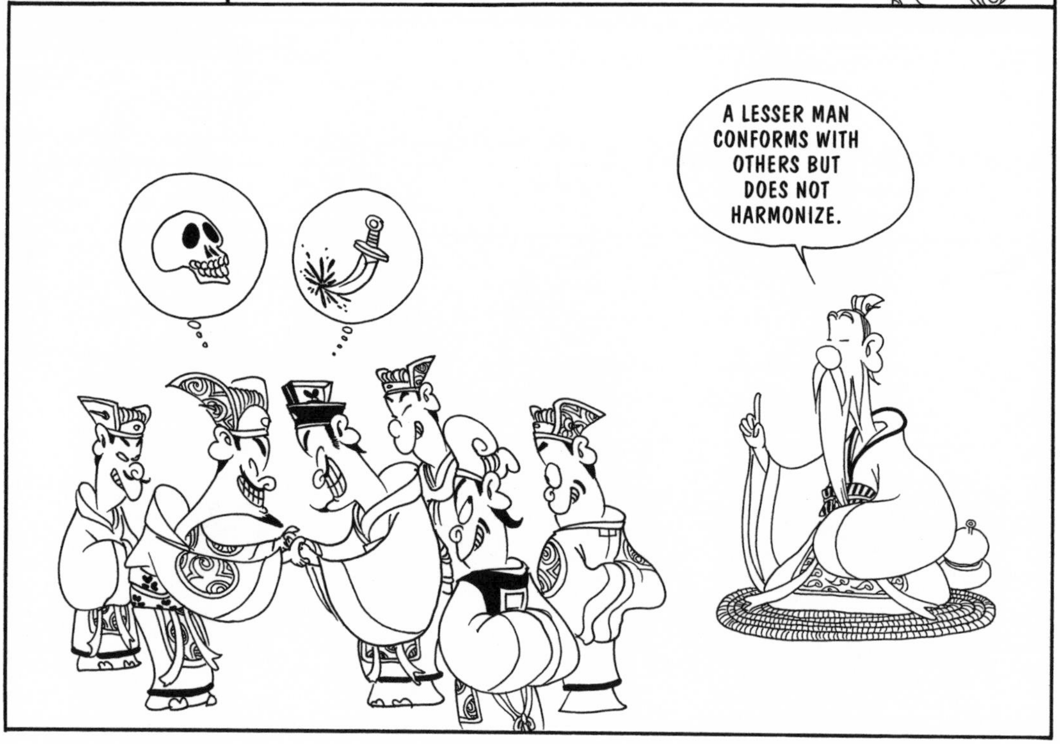
A LESSER MAN CONFORMS WITH OTHERS BUT DOES NOT HARMONIZE.

13:26

A CONTENTED PERSON

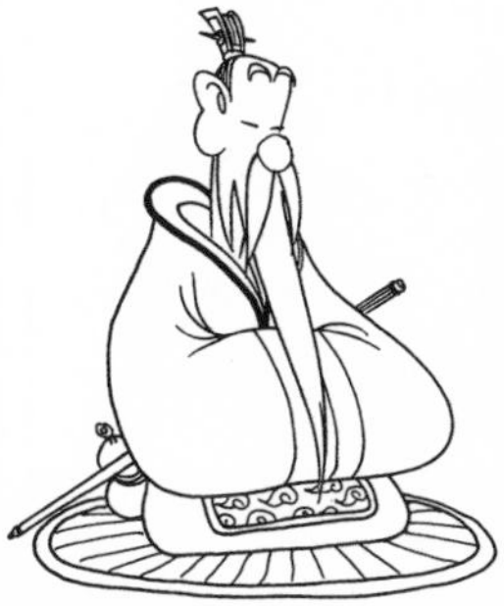

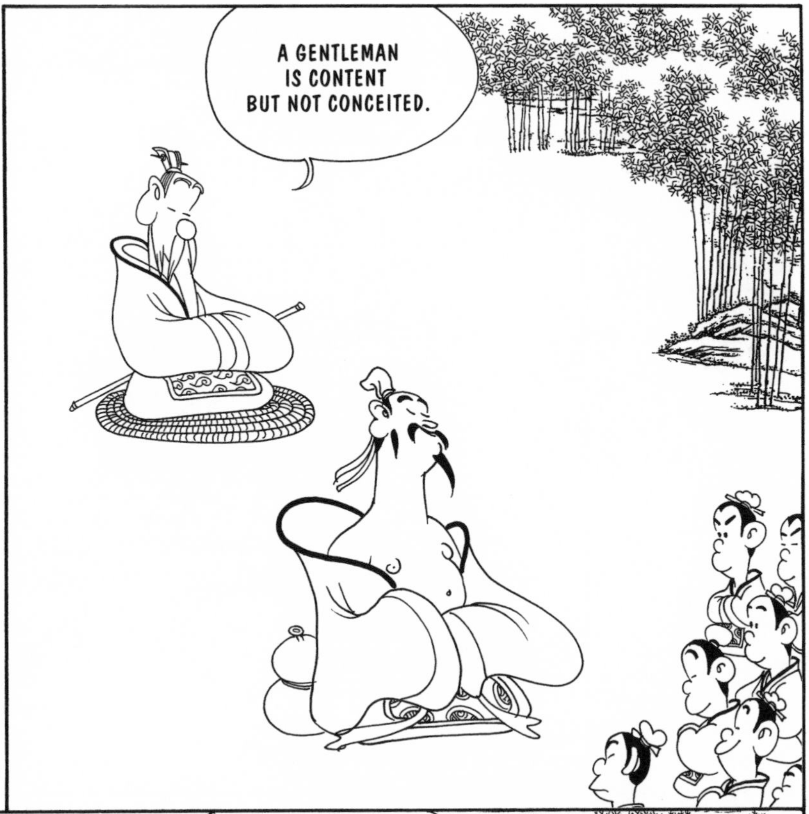
A GENTLEMAN IS CONTENT BUT NOT CONCEITED.

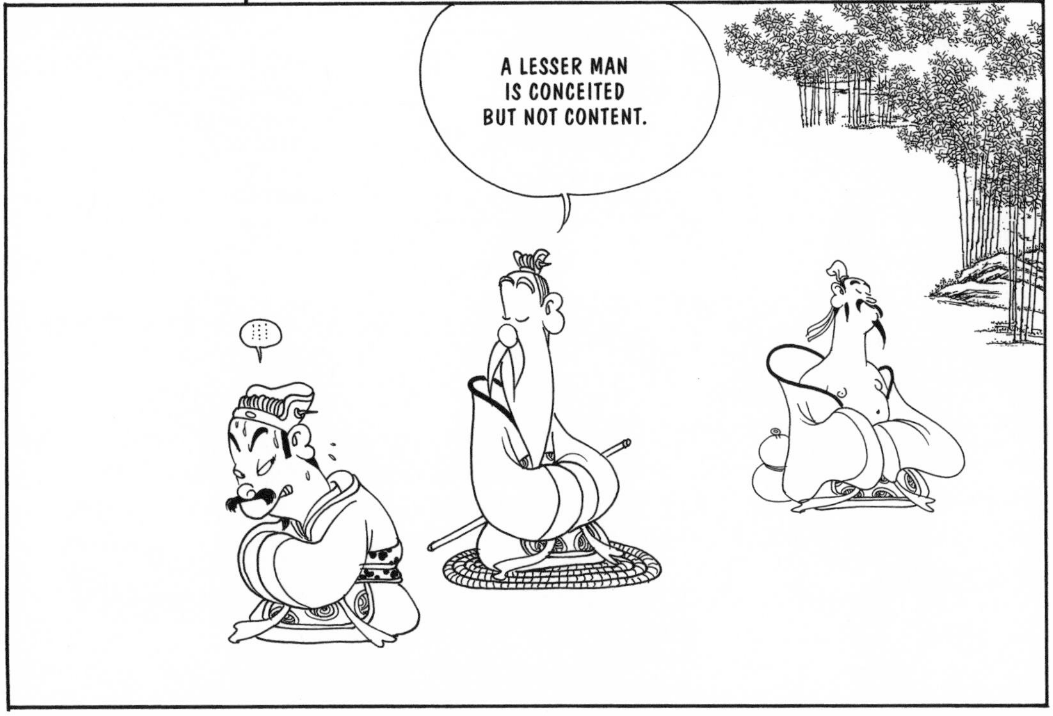
A LESSER MAN IS CONCEITED BUT NOT CONTENT.

子曰：「君子泰而不驕，小人驕而不泰。」

憲問恥。子曰：「邦有道、穀，邦無道、穀，恥也。」

14:1

WORKING FOR A CORRUPT GOVERNMENT

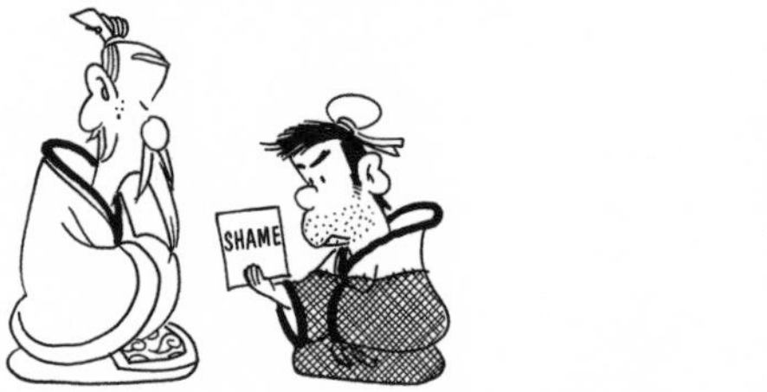
SHAME

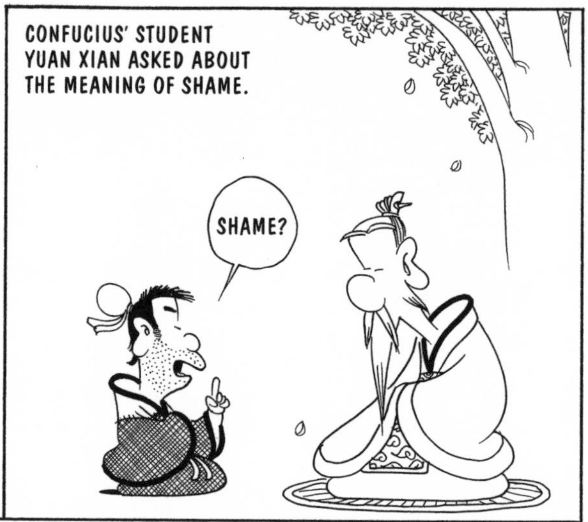
CONFUCIUS' STUDENT YUAN XIAN ASKED ABOUT THE MEANING OF SHAME.
SHAME?

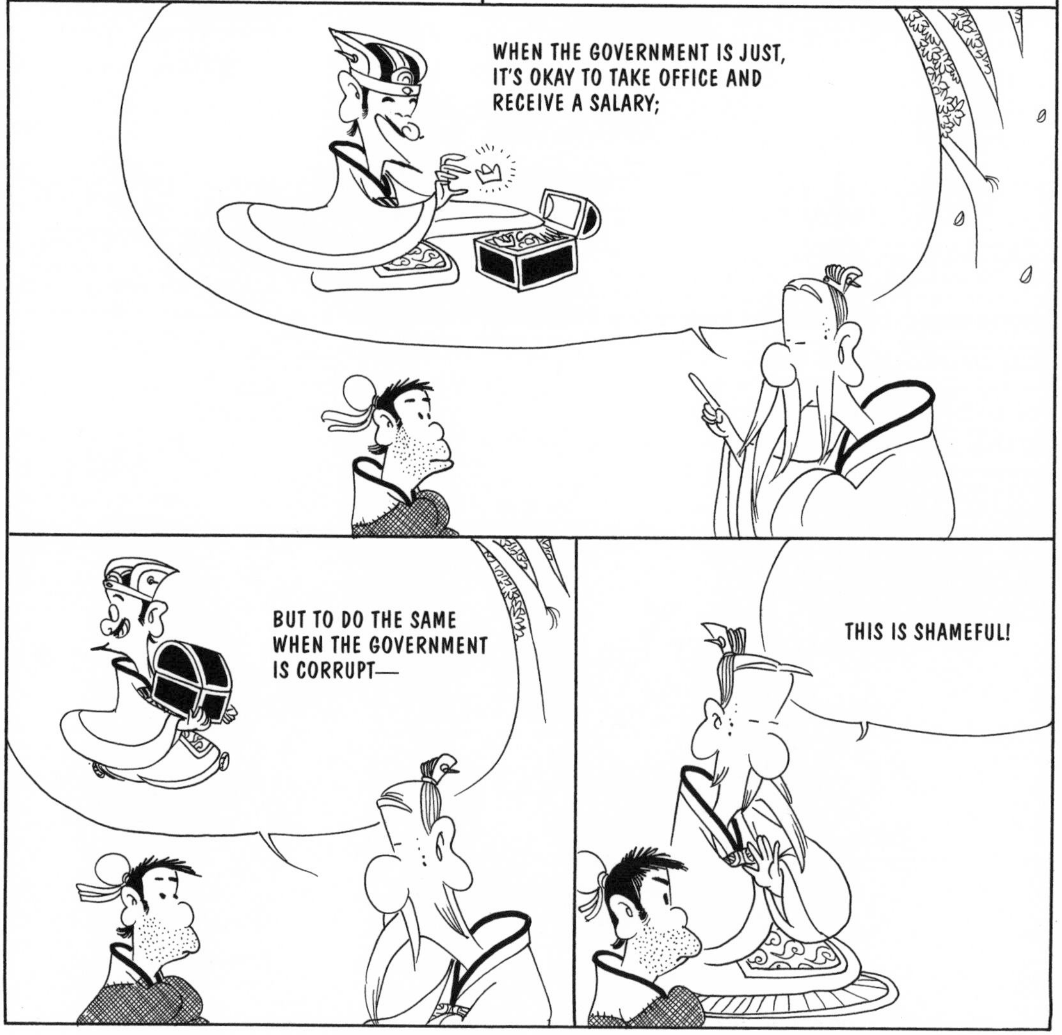
WHEN THE GOVERNMENT IS JUST, IT'S OKAY TO TAKE OFFICE AND RECEIVE A SALARY;
BUT TO DO THE SAME WHEN THE GOVERNMENT IS CORRUPT—
THIS IS SHAMEFUL!

14:10

POOR WITHOUT COMPLAINT

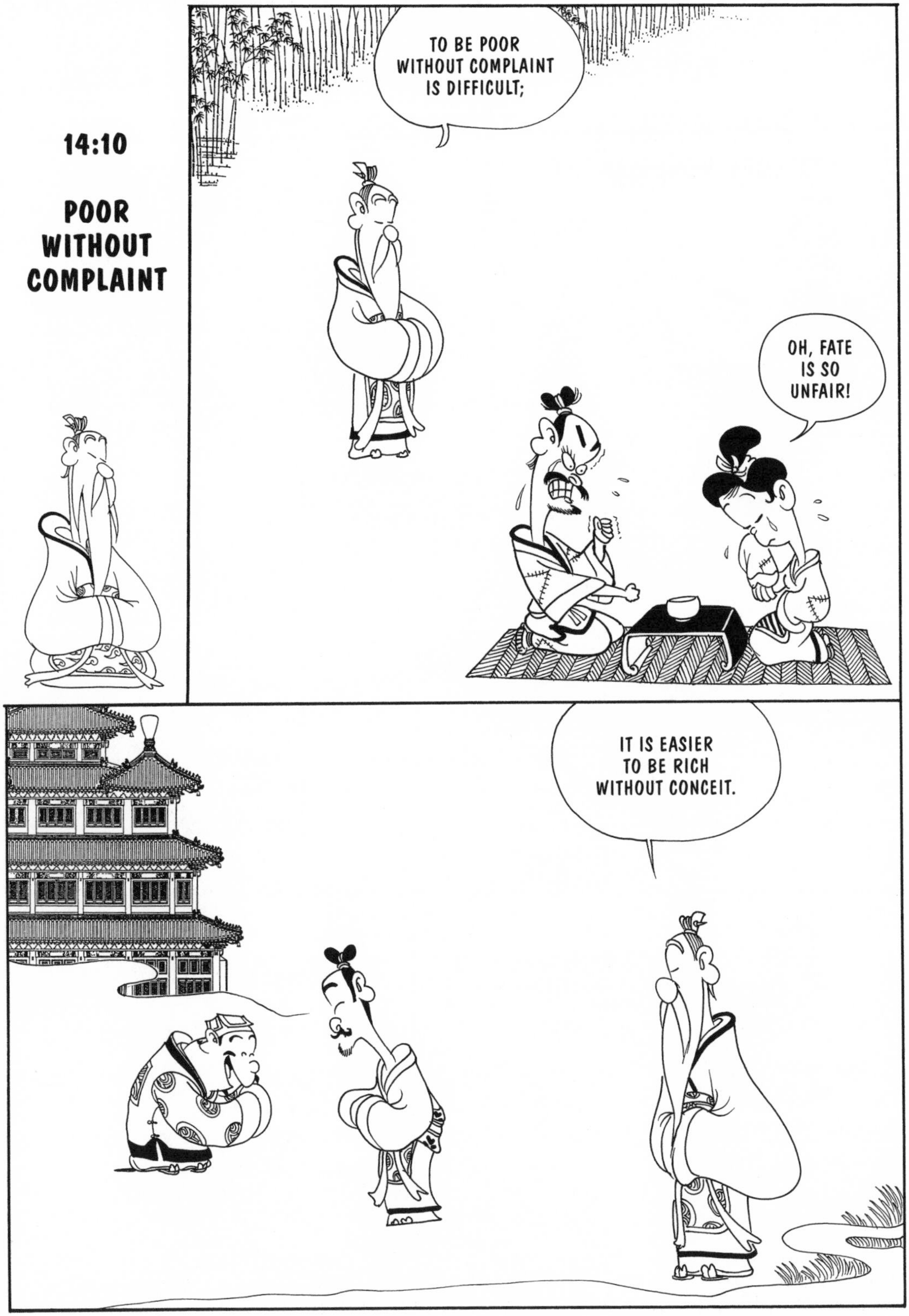
TO BE POOR WITHOUT COMPLAINT IS DIFFICULT;
OH, FATE IS SO UNFAIR!
IT IS EASIER TO BE RICH WITHOUT CONCEIT.

子曰：「貧而無怨難，富而無驕易。」

子路問成人。子曰：「若臧武仲之知，公綽之不欲，卞莊子之勇，冉求之藝，文之以禮樂，亦可以為成人矣。」曰：「今之成人者何必然？見利思義，見危授命，久要不忘平生之言，亦可以為成人矣。」

14:12

THE COMPLETE PERSON

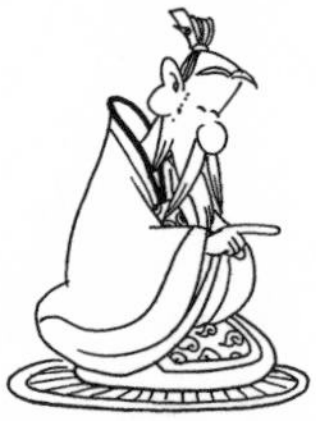

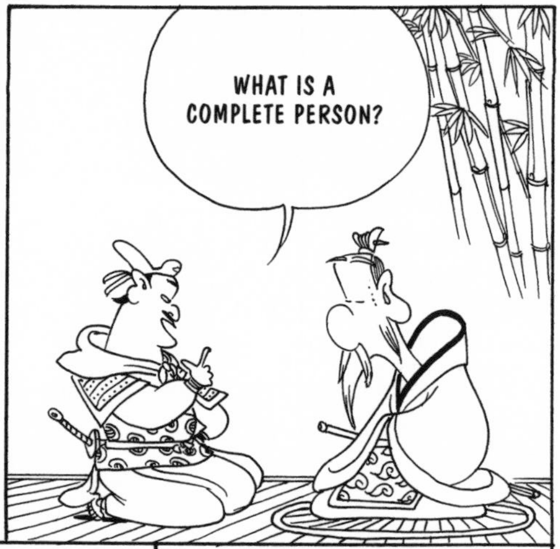
WHAT IS A COMPLETE PERSON?

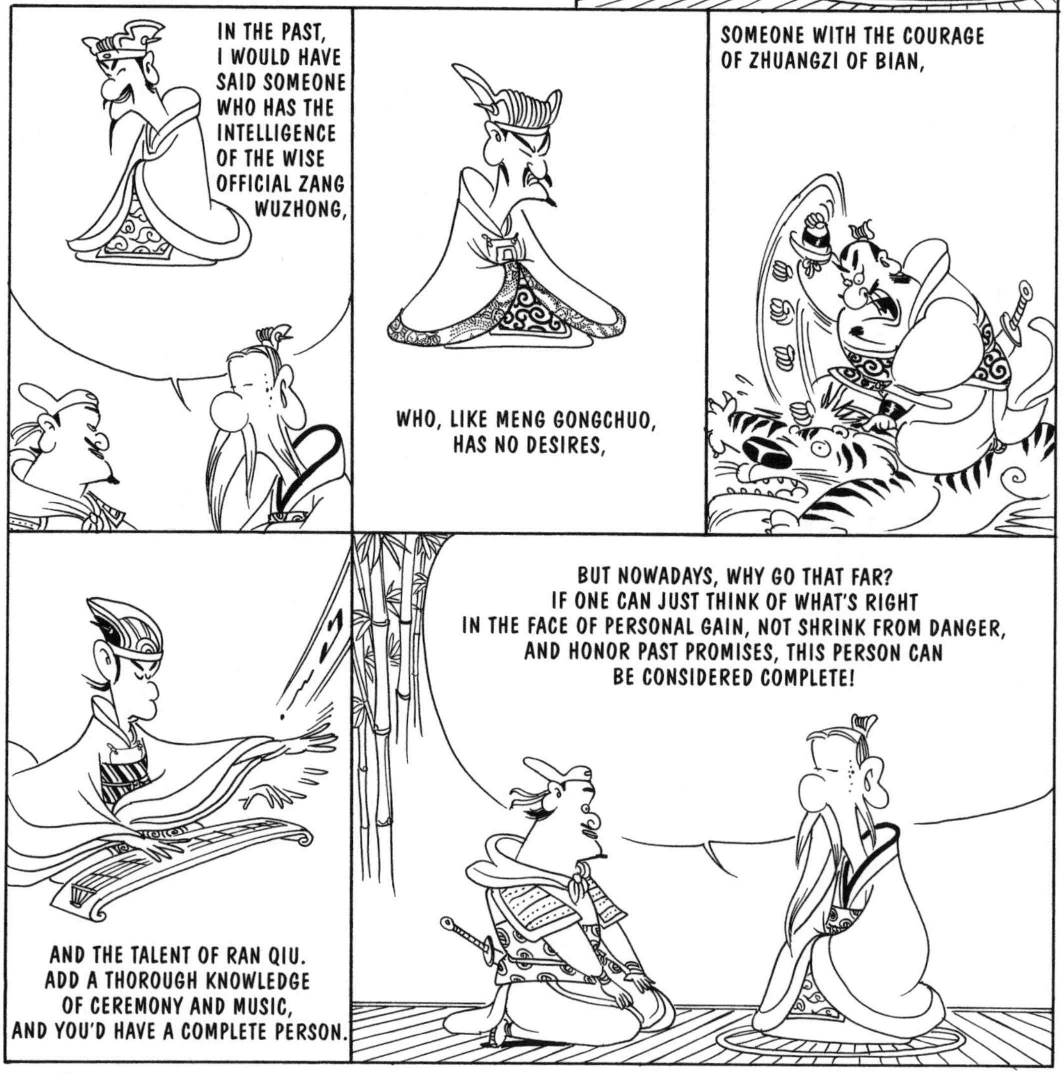
IN THE PAST, I WOULD HAVE SAID SOMEONE WHO HAS THE INTELLIGENCE OF THE WISE OFFICIAL ZANG WUZHONG,
WHO, LIKE MENG GONGCHUO, HAS NO DESIRES,
SOMEONE WITH THE COURAGE OF ZHUANGZI OF BIAN,
AND THE TALENT OF RAN QIU. ADD A THOROUGH KNOWLEDGE OF CEREMONY AND MUSIC, AND YOU'D HAVE A COMPLETE PERSON.
BUT NOWADAYS, WHY GO THAT FAR? IF ONE CAN JUST THINK OF WHAT'S RIGHT IN THE FACE OF PERSONAL GAIN, NOT SHRINK FROM DANGER, AND HONOR PAST PROMISES, THIS PERSON CAN BE CONSIDERED COMPLETE!

14:20

IMMODEST WORDS

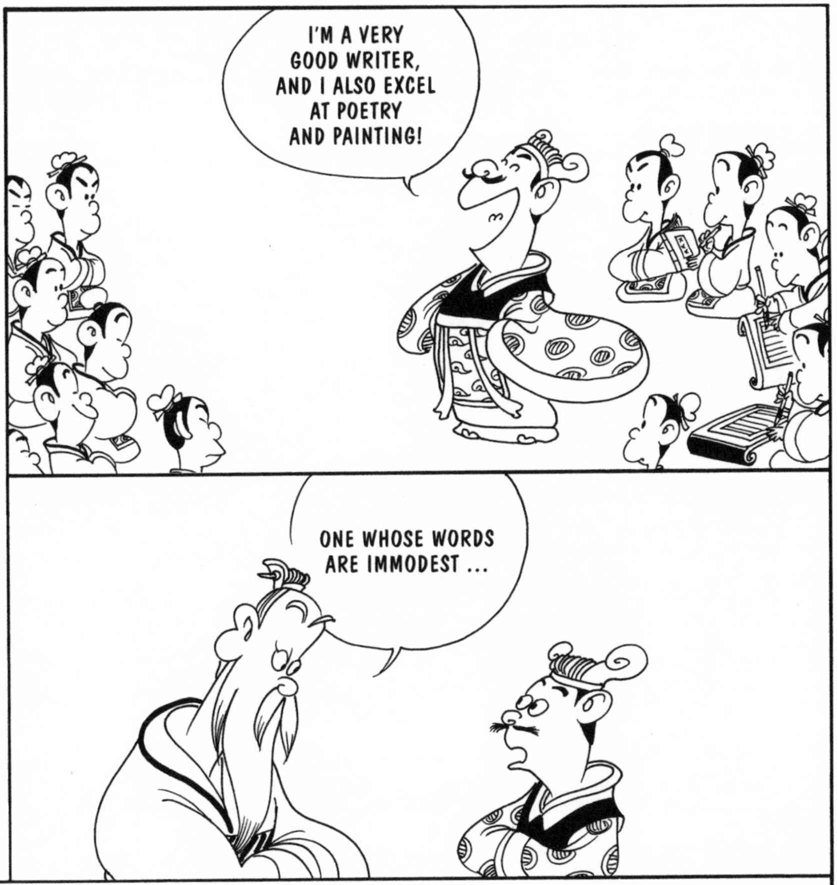
I'M A VERY GOOD WRITER, AND I ALSO EXCEL AT POETRY AND PAINTING!
ONE WHOSE WORDS ARE IMMODEST ...

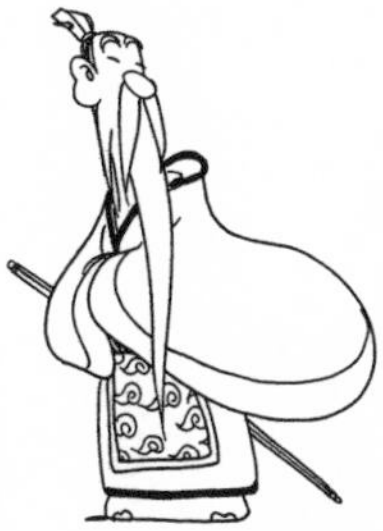

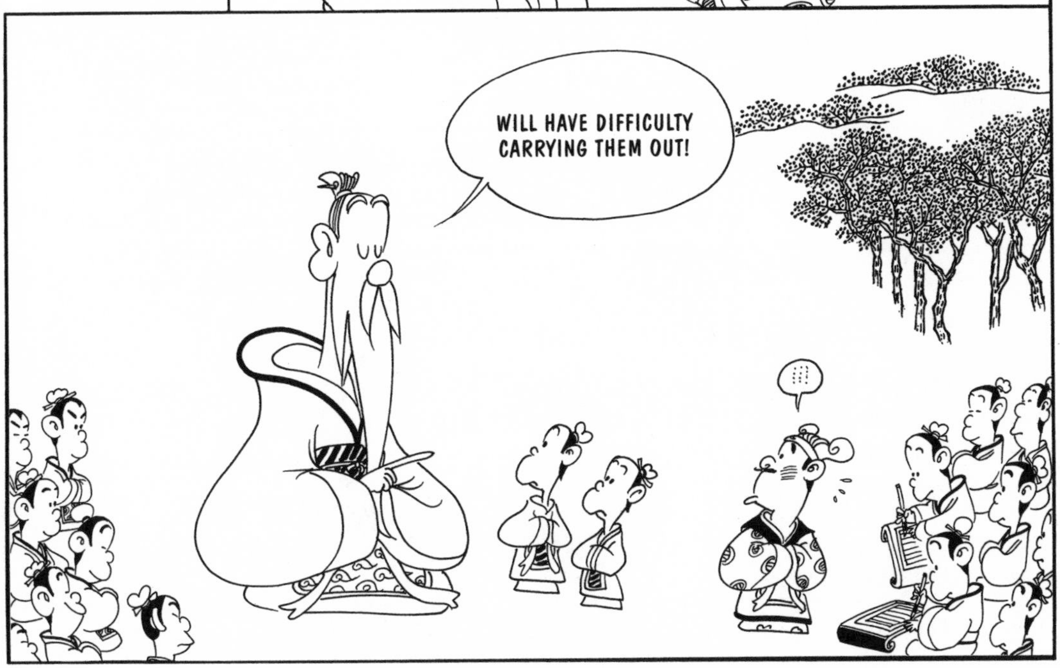
WILL HAVE DIFFICULTY CARRYING THEM OUT!

子曰：「其言之不怍，則為之也難。」

子曰：「古之學者為己，今之學者為人。」

14:24

STUDY FOR THE SAKE OF LEARNING

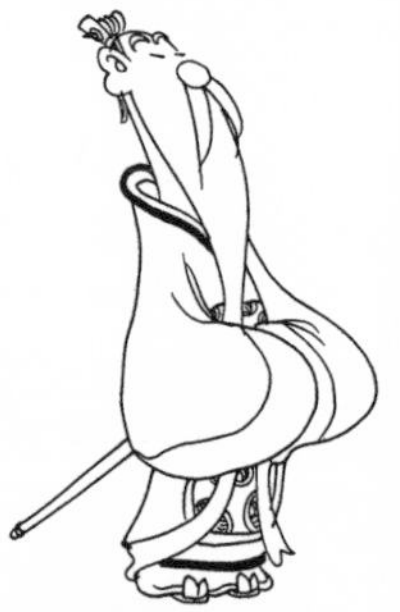

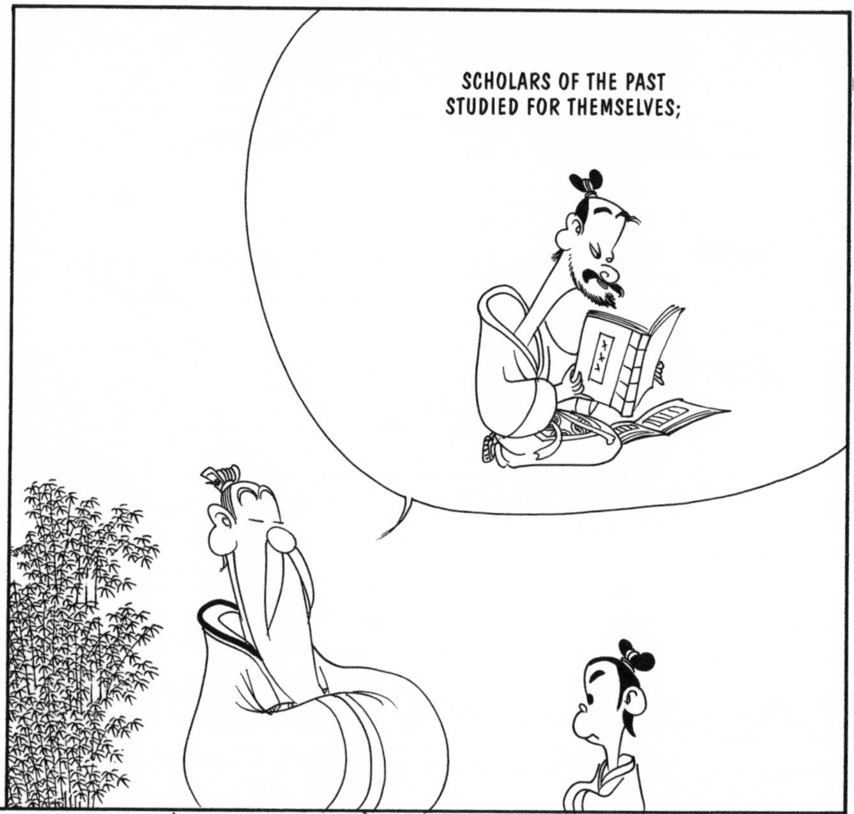
SCHOLARS OF THE PAST STUDIED FOR THEMSELVES;

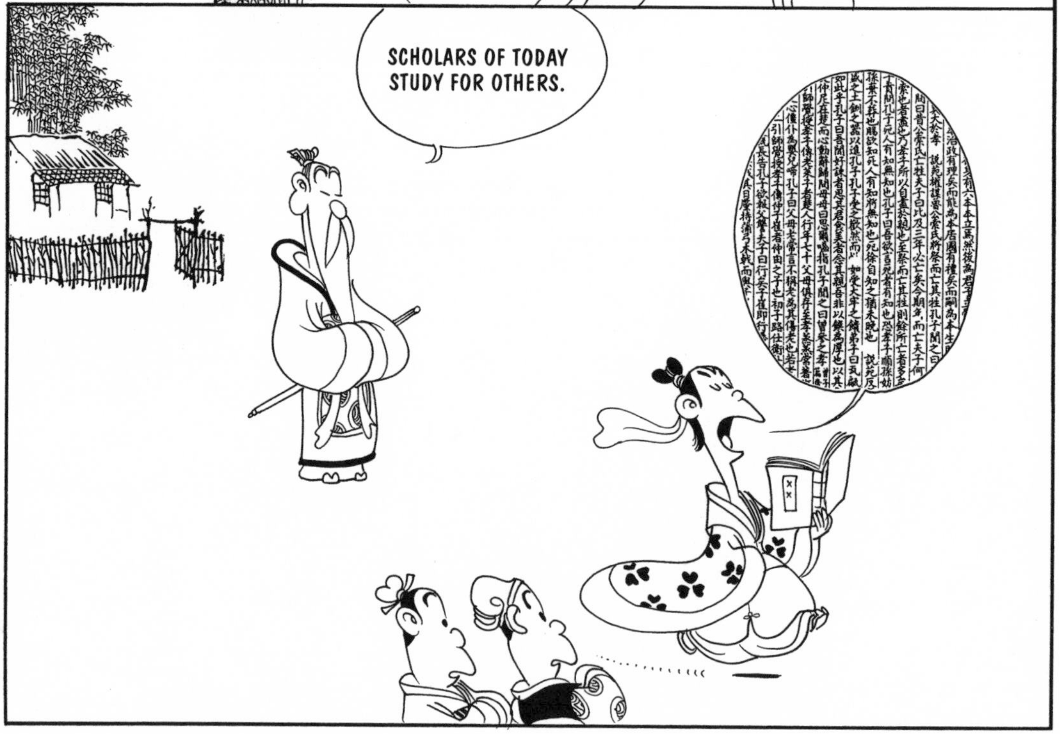
SCHOLARS OF TODAY STUDY FOR OTHERS.

14:27

EXTRAVAGANT IN DEEDS

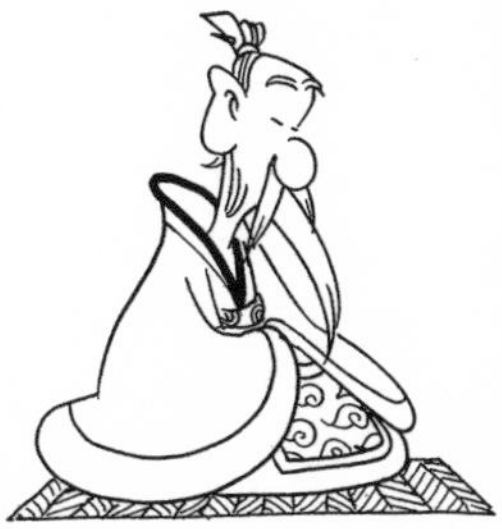

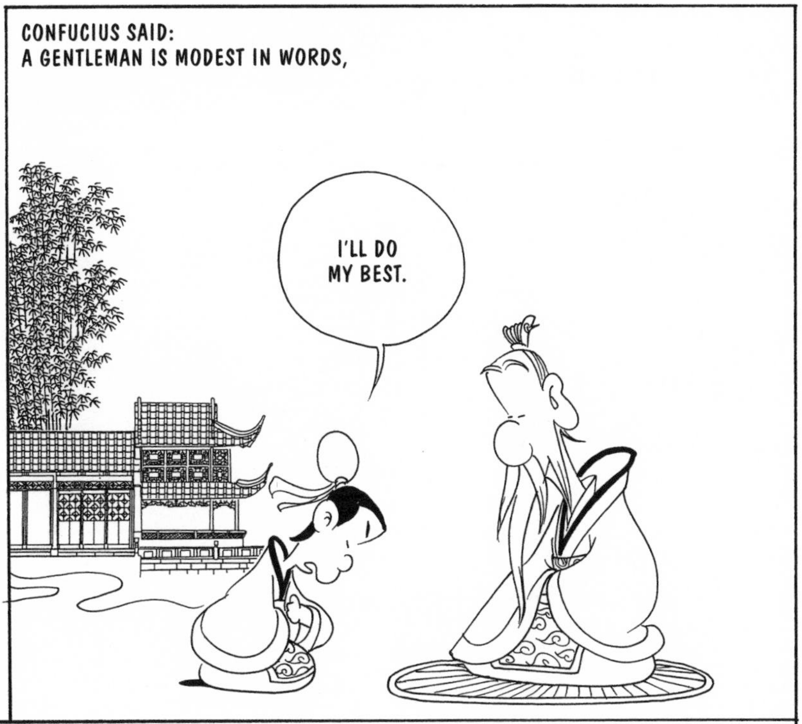
CONFUCIUS SAID:
A GENTLEMAN IS MODEST IN WORDS,
I'LL DO MY BEST.

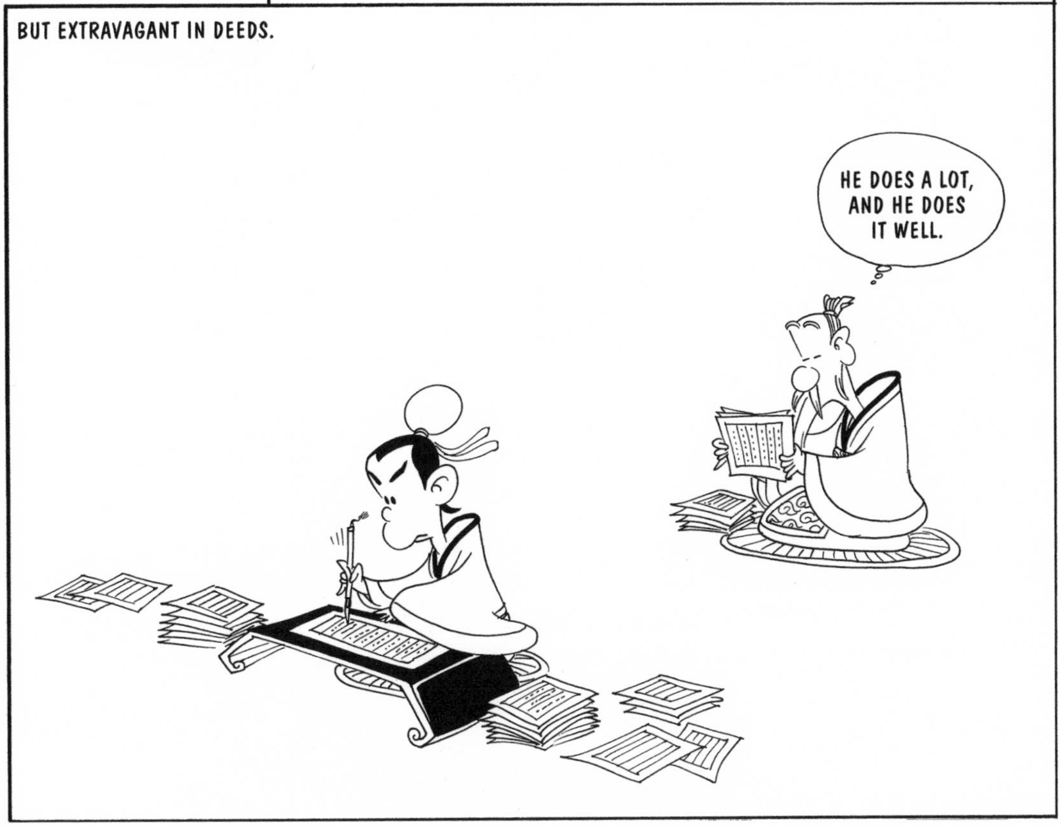
BUT EXTRAVAGANT IN DEEDS.
HE DOES A LOT, AND HE DOES IT WELL.

子曰：「君子恥其言而過其行。」

子貢方人。子曰：「賜也賢乎哉？夫我則不暇。」

14:29

THROWING STONES

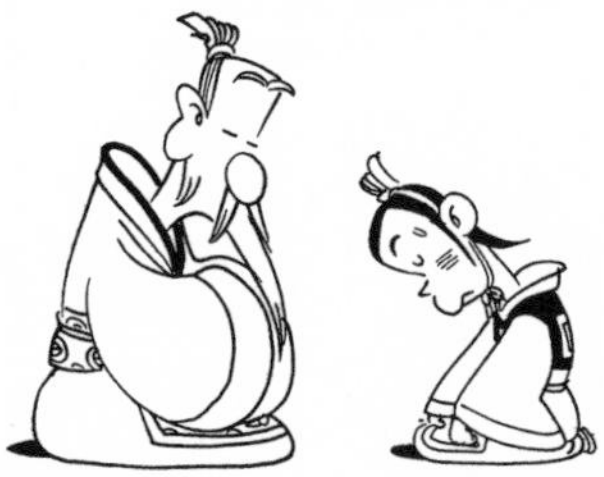

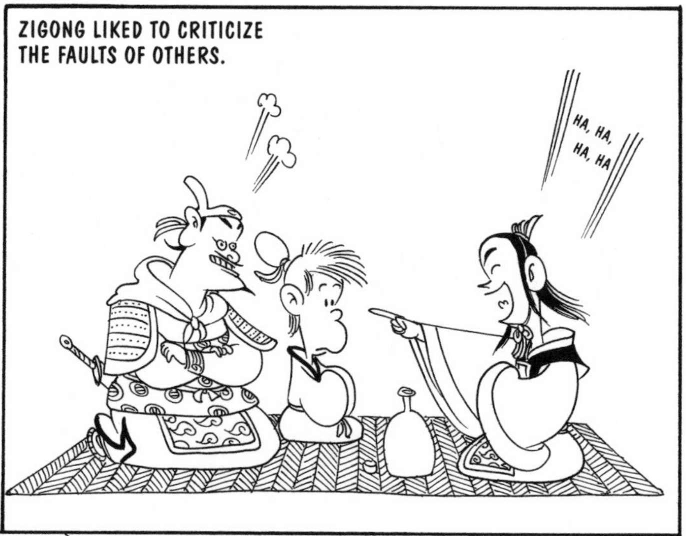
ZIGONG LIKED TO CRITICIZE THE FAULTS OF OTHERS.
HA, HA, HA, HA

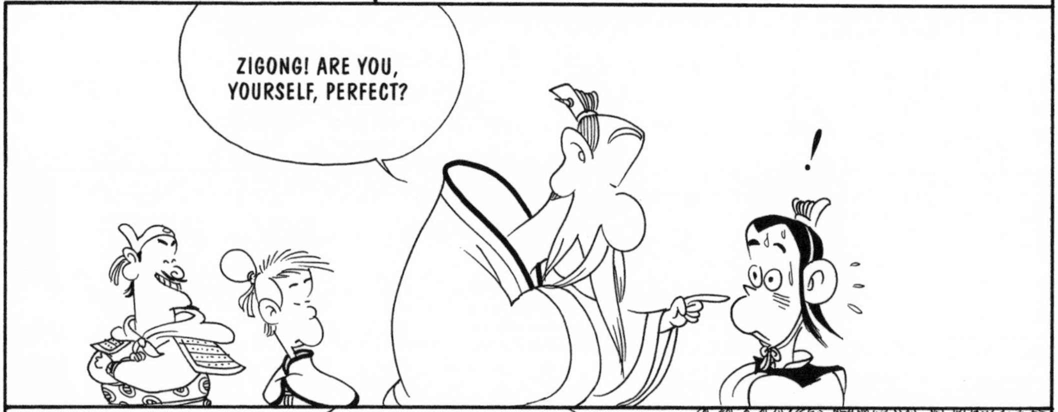
ZIGONG! ARE YOU, YOURSELF, PERFECT?
!

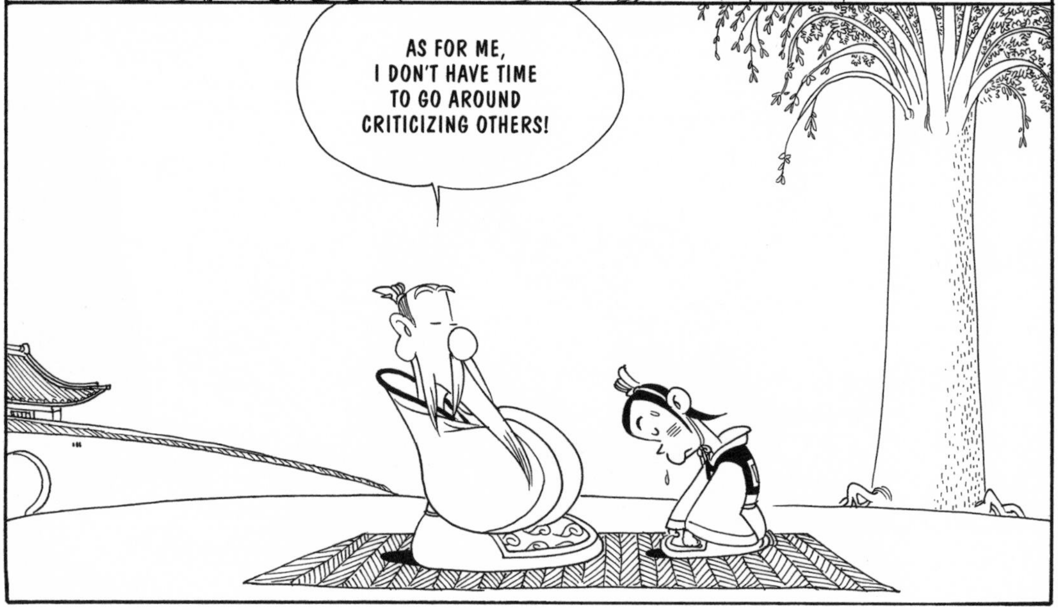
AS FOR ME, I DON'T HAVE TIME TO GO AROUND CRITICIZING OTHERS!

14:33

A GOOD HORSE

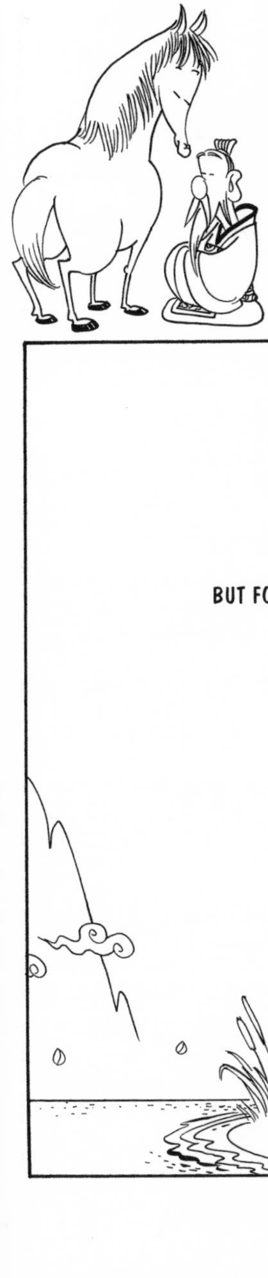

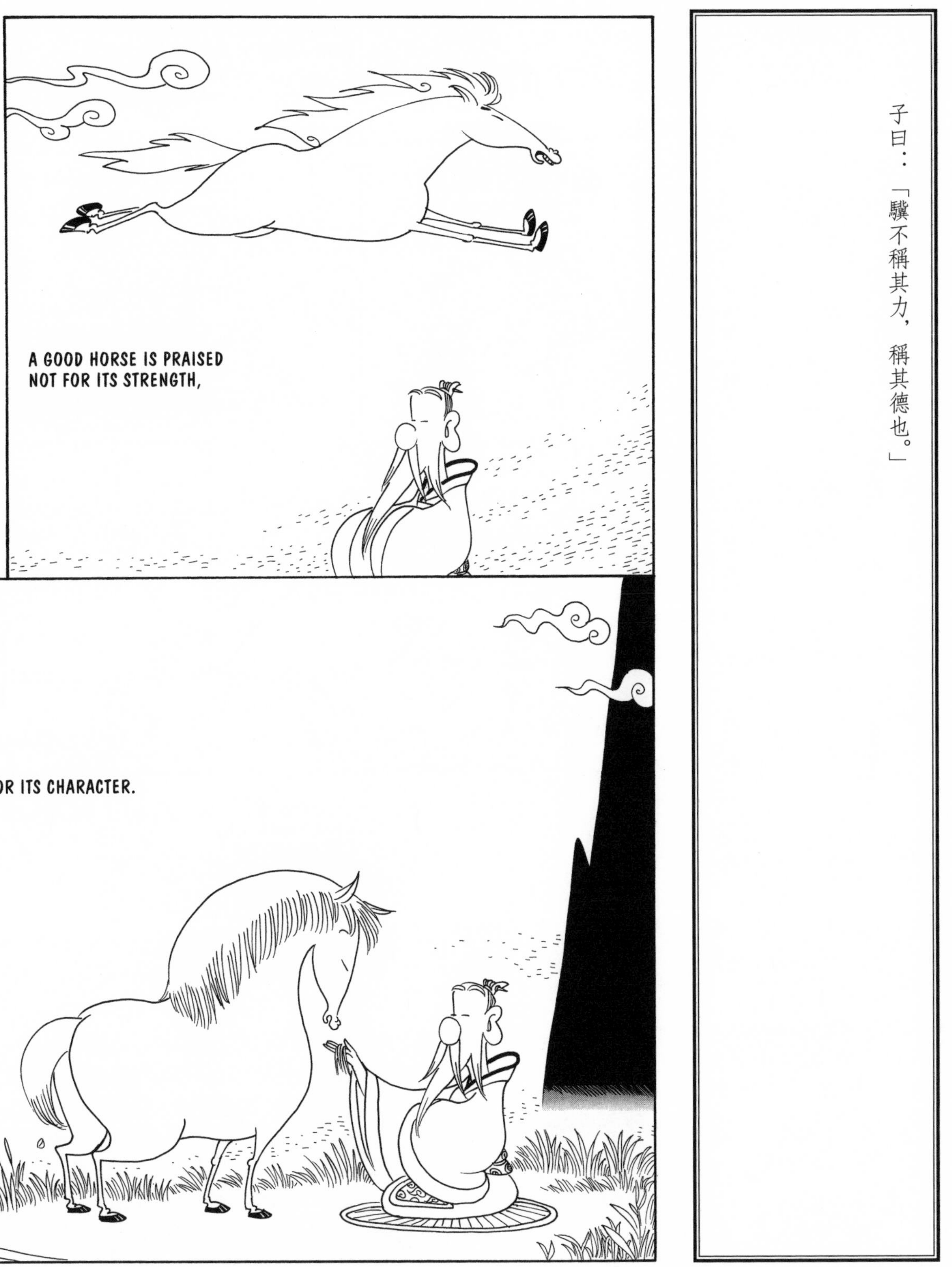
A GOOD HORSE IS PRAISED NOT FOR ITS STRENGTH,
BUT FOR ITS CHARACTER.

子曰：「驥不稱其力，稱其德也。」

或曰：「『以德報怨』，何如？」子曰：「何以報德？『以直報怨，以德報德。』」

14:34

HOW TO TREAT ONE'S ENEMIES

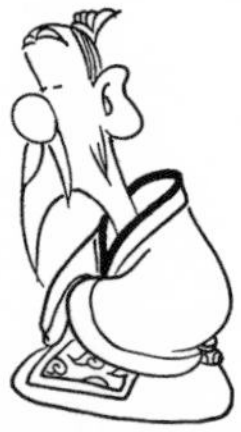

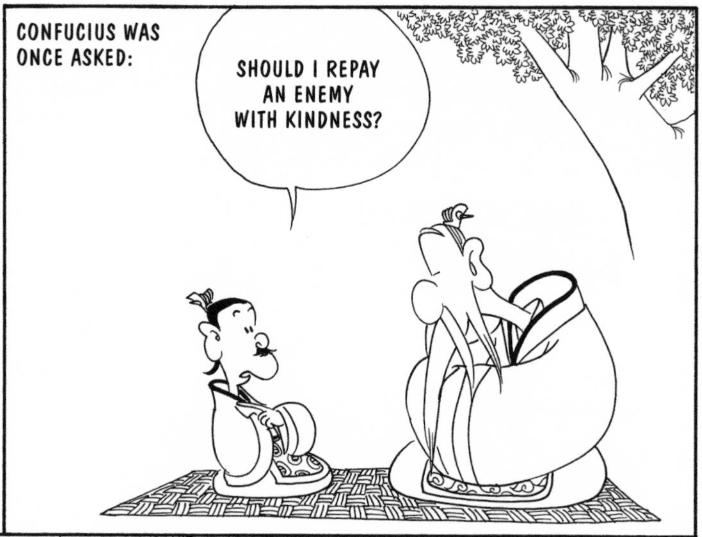
CONFUCIUS WAS ONCE ASKED:
SHOULD I REPAY AN ENEMY WITH KINDNESS?

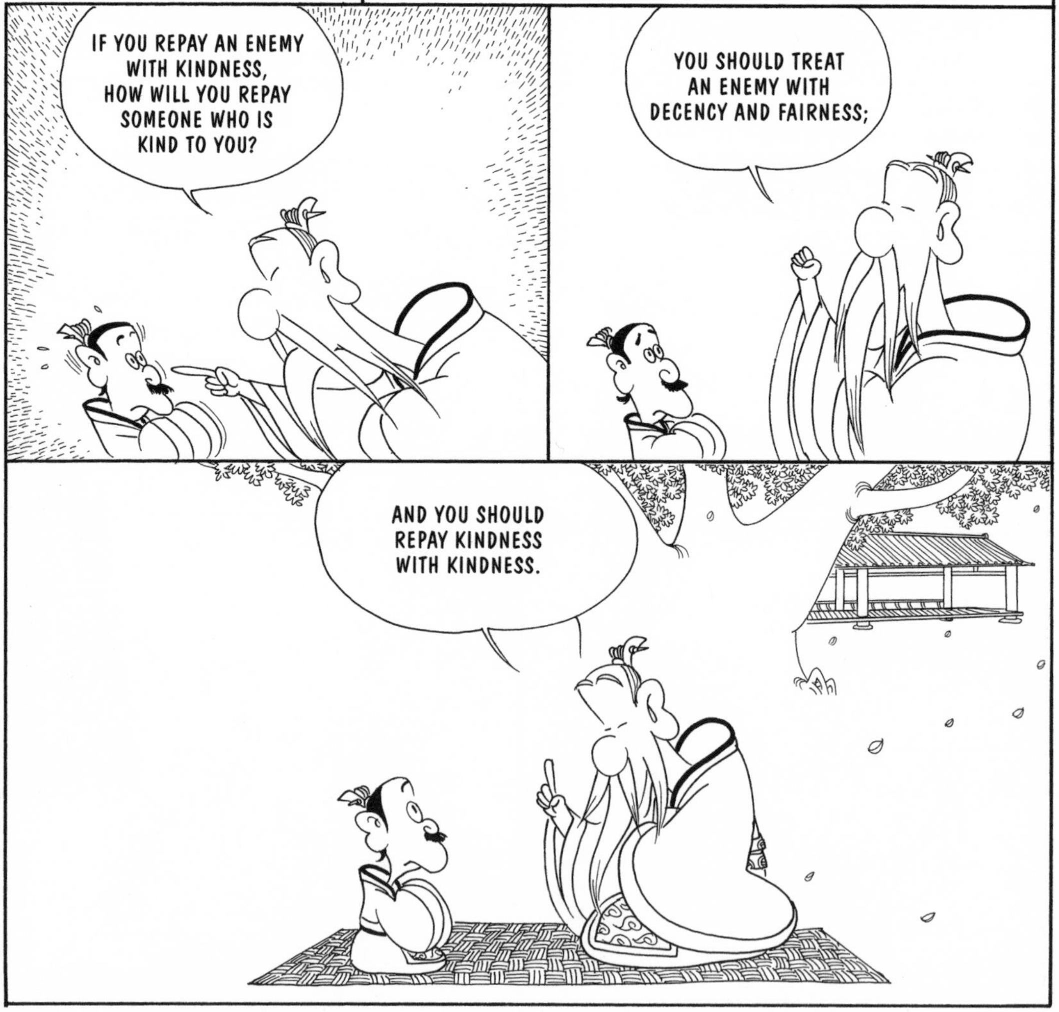
IF YOU REPAY AN ENEMY WITH KINDNESS, HOW WILL YOU REPAY SOMEONE WHO IS KIND TO YOU?
YOU SHOULD TREAT AN ENEMY WITH DECENCY AND FAIRNESS;
AND YOU SHOULD REPAY KINDNESS WITH KINDNESS.

14:35

UNDERSTANDING CONFUCIUS

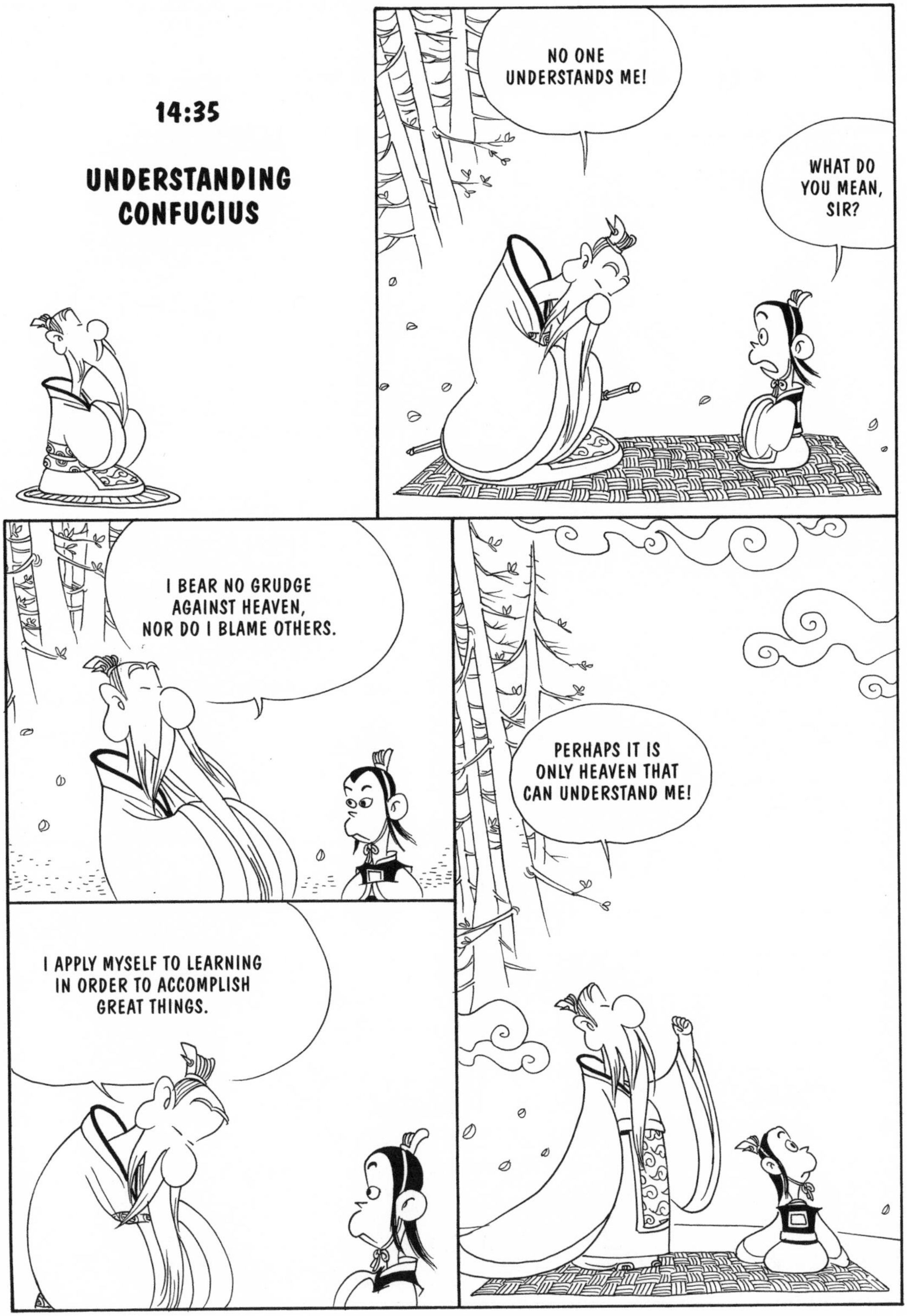
NO ONE UNDERSTANDS ME!
WHAT DO YOU MEAN, SIR?
I BEAR NO GRUDGE AGAINST HEAVEN, NOR DO I BLAME OTHERS.
I APPLY MYSELF TO LEARNING IN ORDER TO ACCOMPLISH GREAT THINGS.
PERHAPS IT IS ONLY HEAVEN THAT CAN UNDERSTAND ME!

子曰：「莫我知也夫！」子貢曰：「何為其莫知子也？」子曰：「不怨天，不尤人，下學而上達。知我者其天乎！」

子路宿於石門。晨門曰：「奚自？」子路曰：「自孔氏。」曰：「是知其不可而為之者與？」

14:38

STUBBORN

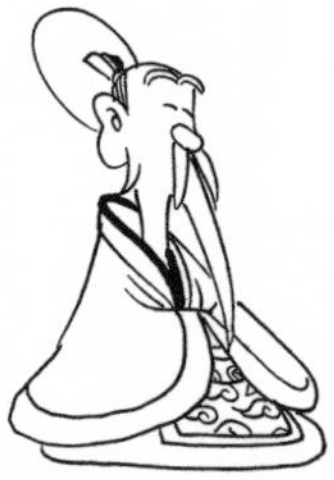

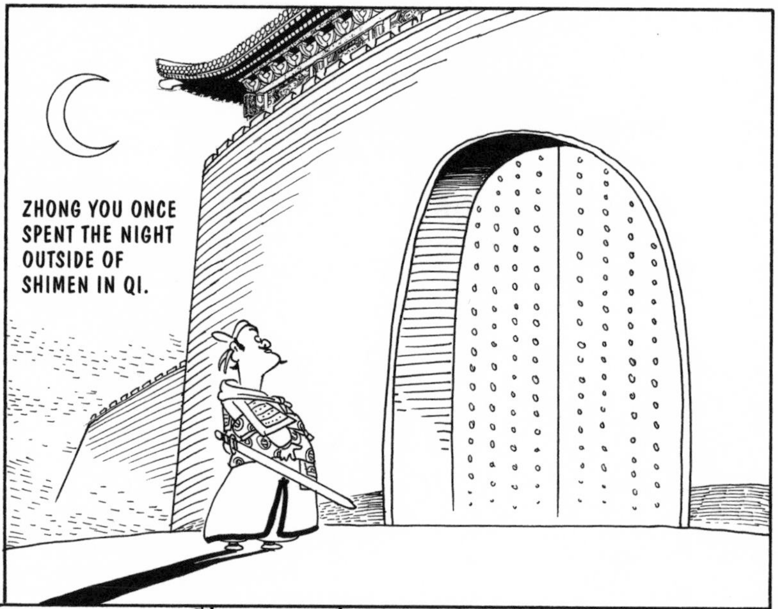
ZHONG YOU ONCE SPENT THE NIGHT OUTSIDE OF SHIMEN IN QI.

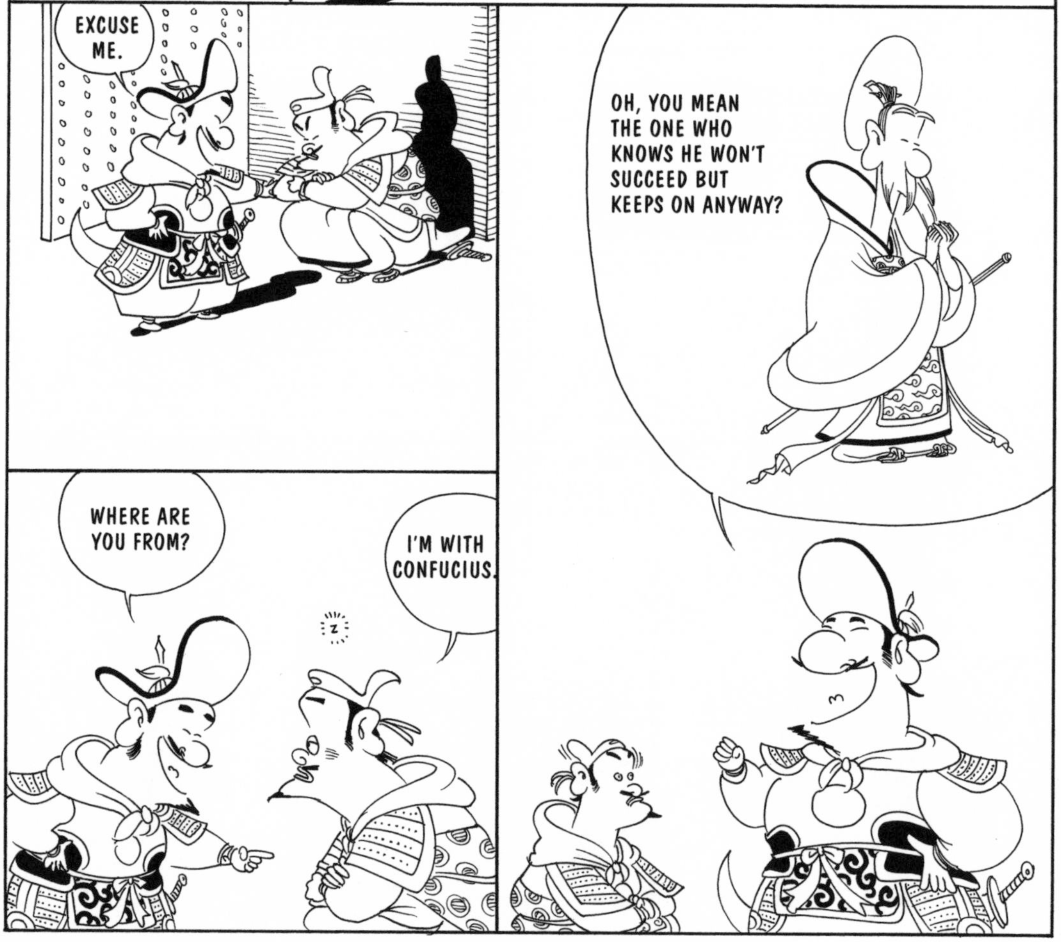
EXCUSE ME.
WHERE ARE YOU FROM?
I'M WITH CONFUCIUS.
Z
OH, YOU MEAN THE ONE WHO KNOWS HE WON'T SUCCEED BUT KEEPS ON ANYWAY?

14:43

A WASTED LIFE

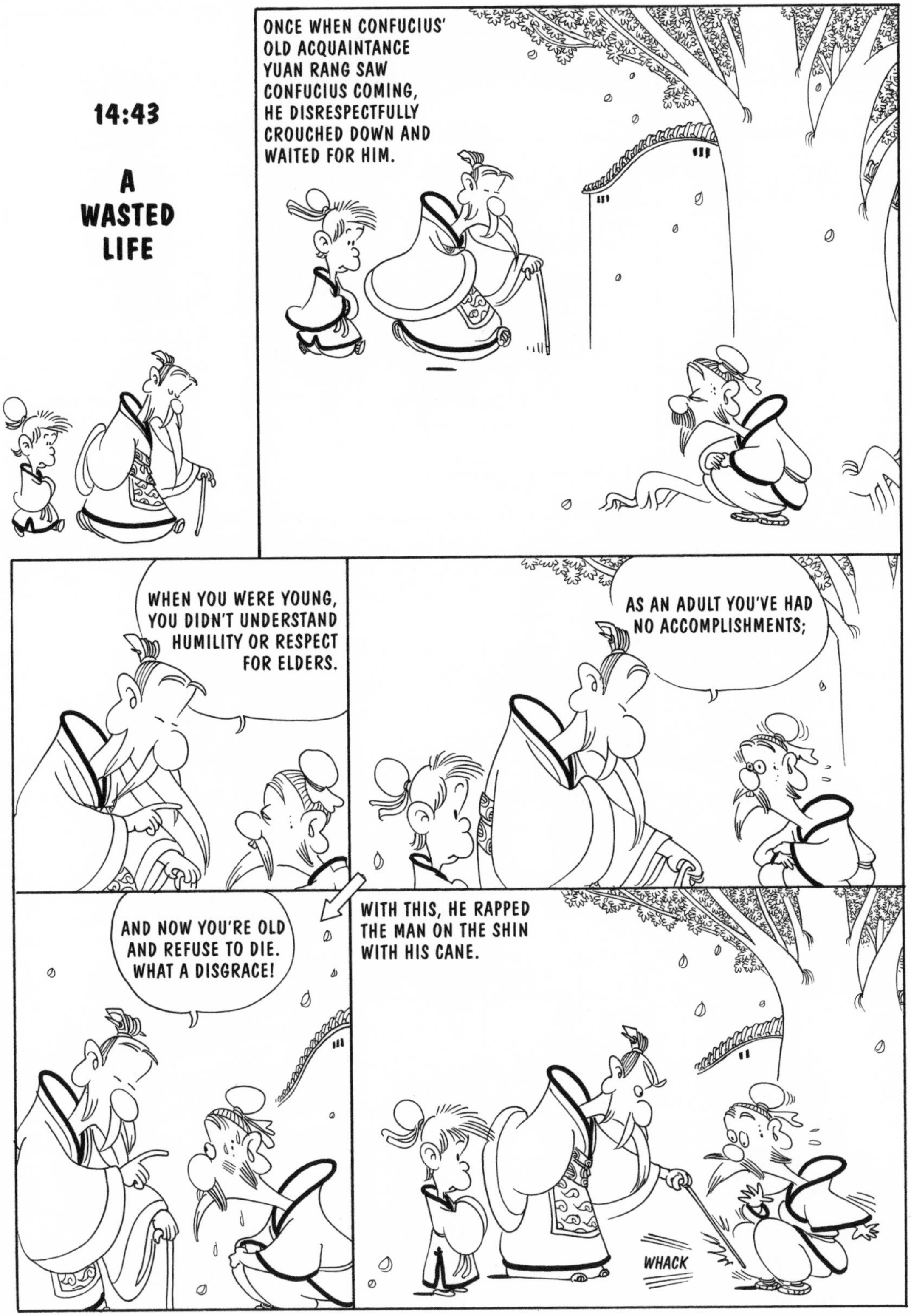
ONCE WHEN CONFUCIUS' OLD ACQUAINTANCE YUAN RANG SAW CONFUCIUS COMING, HE DISRESPECTFULLY CROUCHED DOWN AND WAITED FOR HIM.
WHEN YOU WERE YOUNG, YOU DIDN'T UNDERSTAND HUMILITY OR RESPECT FOR ELDERS.
AS AN ADULT YOU'VE HAD NO ACCOMPLISHMENTS;
AND NOW YOU'RE OLD AND REFUSE TO DIE. WHAT A DISGRACE!
WITH THIS, HE RAPPED THE MAN ON THE SHIN WITH HIS CANE.
WHACK

原壤夷俟。子曰：「幼而不孫弟，長而無述焉，老而不死，是為賊。」以杖叩其脛。

子曰：「直哉史魚！邦有道，如矢；邦無道，如矢。君子哉蘧伯玉！邦有道，則仕；邦無道，則可卷而懷之。」

15:7

CONDITIONAL SERVICE

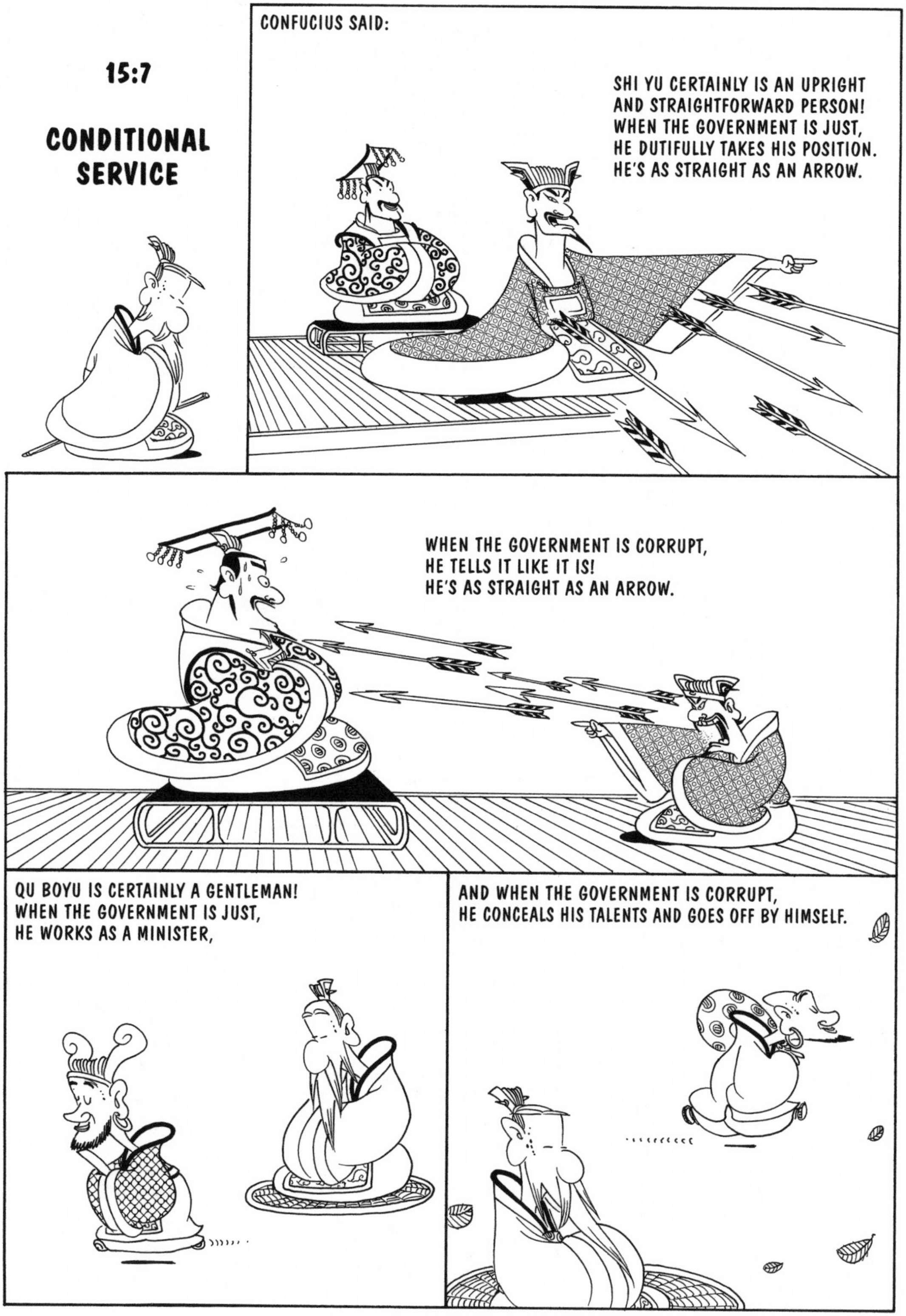
CONFUCIUS SAID:
SHI YU CERTAINLY IS AN UPRIGHT AND STRAIGHTFORWARD PERSON! WHEN THE GOVERNMENT IS JUST, HE DUTIFULLY TAKES HIS POSITION. HE'S AS STRAIGHT AS AN ARROW.
WHEN THE GOVERNMENT IS CORRUPT, HE TELLS IT LIKE IT IS! HE'S AS STRAIGHT AS AN ARROW.
QU BOYU IS CERTAINLY A GENTLEMAN! WHEN THE GOVERNMENT IS JUST, HE WORKS AS A MINISTER,
AND WHEN THE GOVERNMENT IS CORRUPT, HE CONCEALS HIS TALENTS AND GOES OFF BY HIMSELF.

15:8

MISSPEAKING

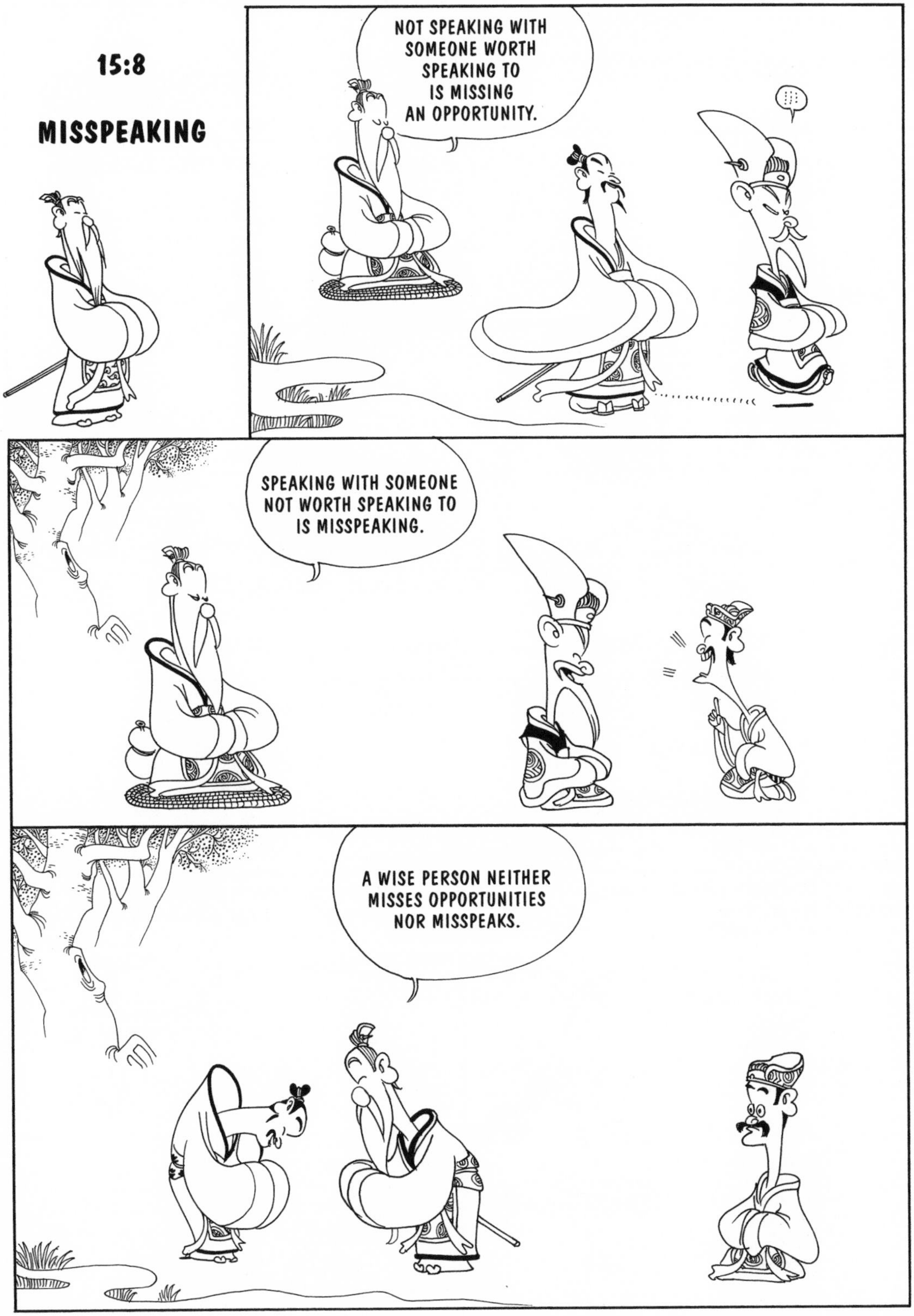
NOT SPEAKING WITH SOMEONE WORTH SPEAKING TO IS MISSING AN OPPORTUNITY.
SPEAKING WITH SOMEONE NOT WORTH SPEAKING TO IS MISSPEAKING.
A WISE PERSON NEITHER MISSES OPPORTUNITIES NOR MISSPEAKS.

子曰：「可與言而不與言，失人；不可與言而與之言，失言。知者不失人，亦不失言。」

子貢問為仁。子曰：「工欲善其事，必先利其器。居是邦也，事其大夫之賢者，友其士之仁者。」

15:10

CULTIVATING BENEVOLENCE

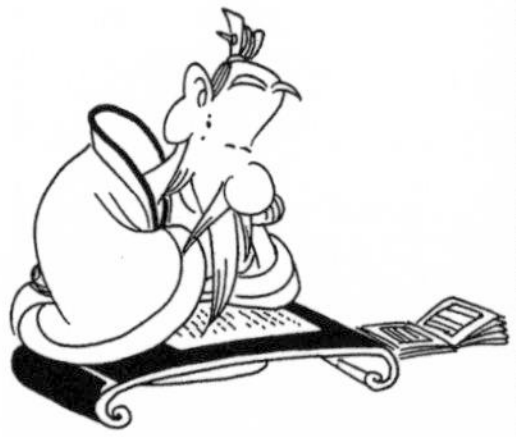

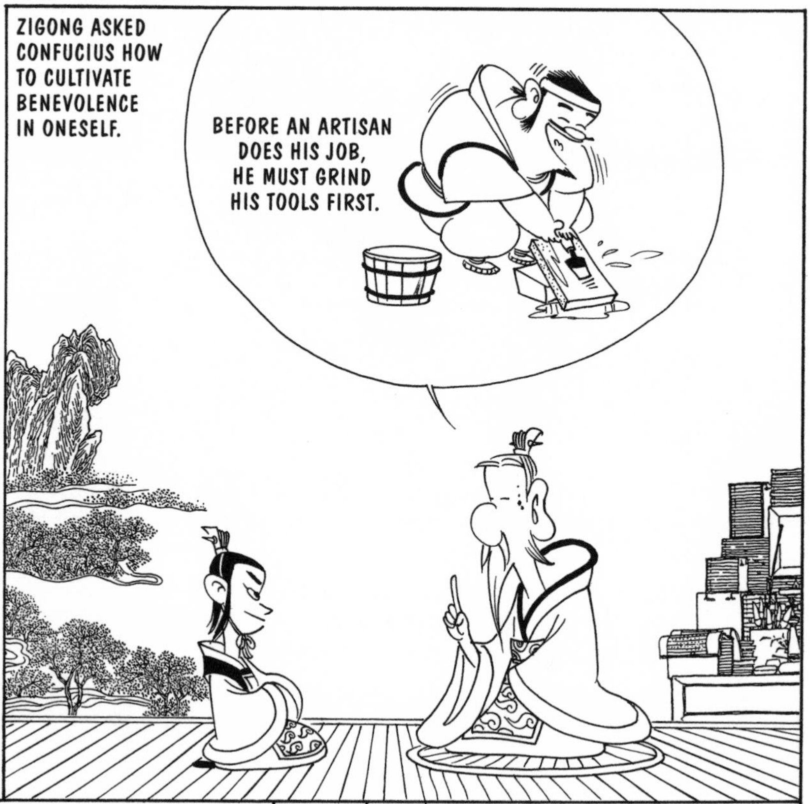
ZIGONG ASKED CONFUCIUS HOW TO CULTIVATE BENEVOLENCE IN ONESELF.
BEFORE AN ARTISAN DOES HIS JOB, HE MUST GRIND HIS TOOLS FIRST.

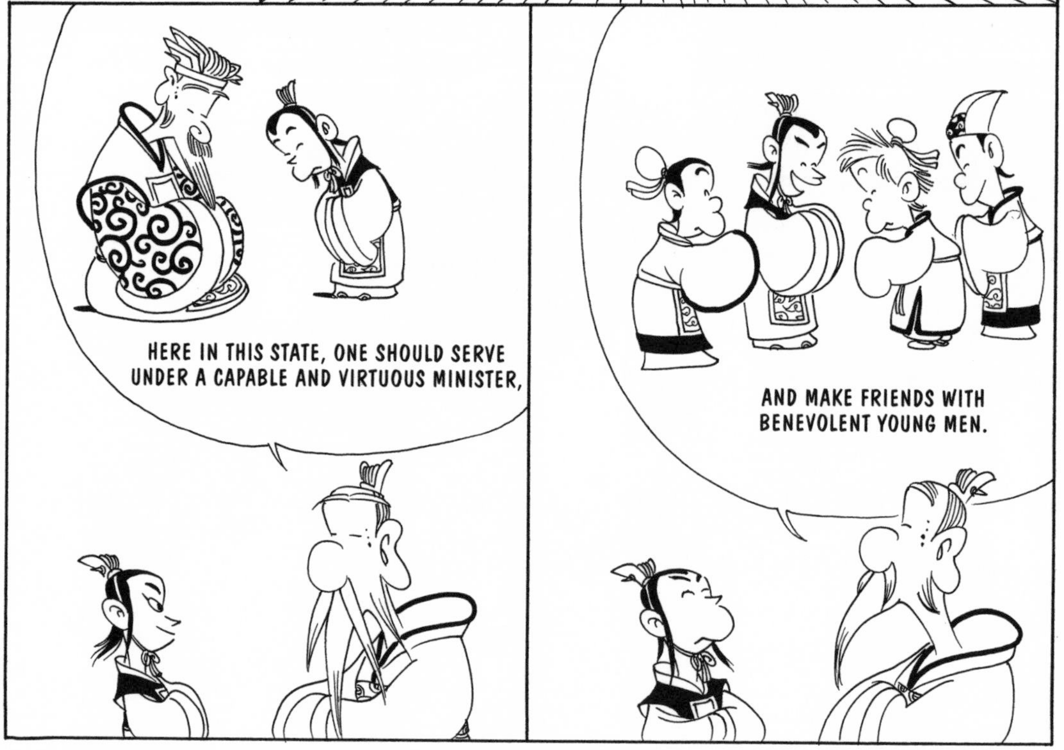
HERE IN THIS STATE, ONE SHOULD SERVE UNDER A CAPABLE AND VIRTUOUS MINISTER,
AND MAKE FRIENDS WITH BENEVOLENT YOUNG MEN.

15:12

THINKING AHEAD

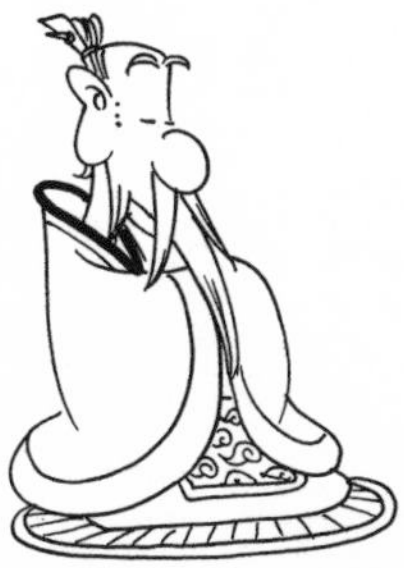

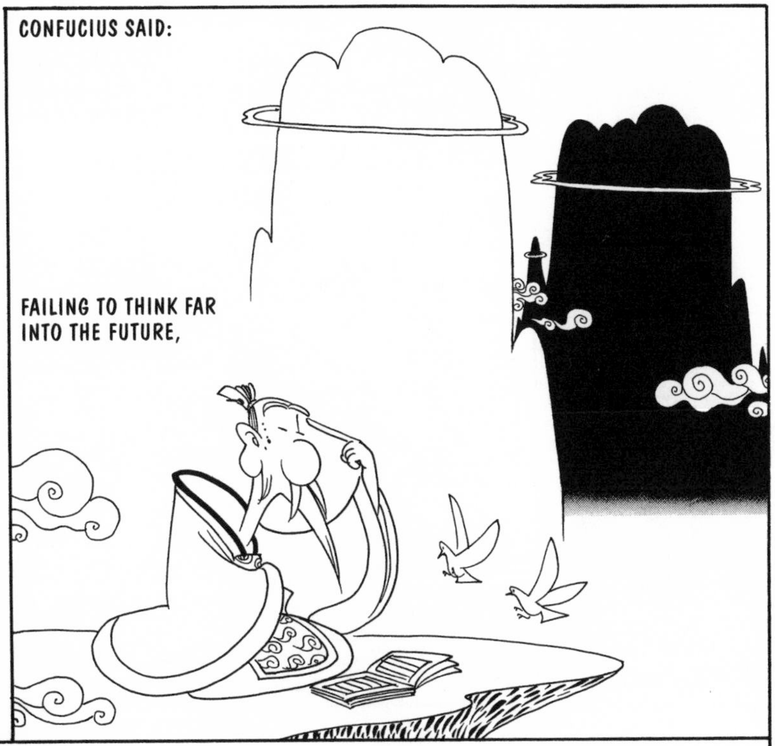
CONFUCIUS SAID:
FAILING TO THINK FAR INTO THE FUTURE,

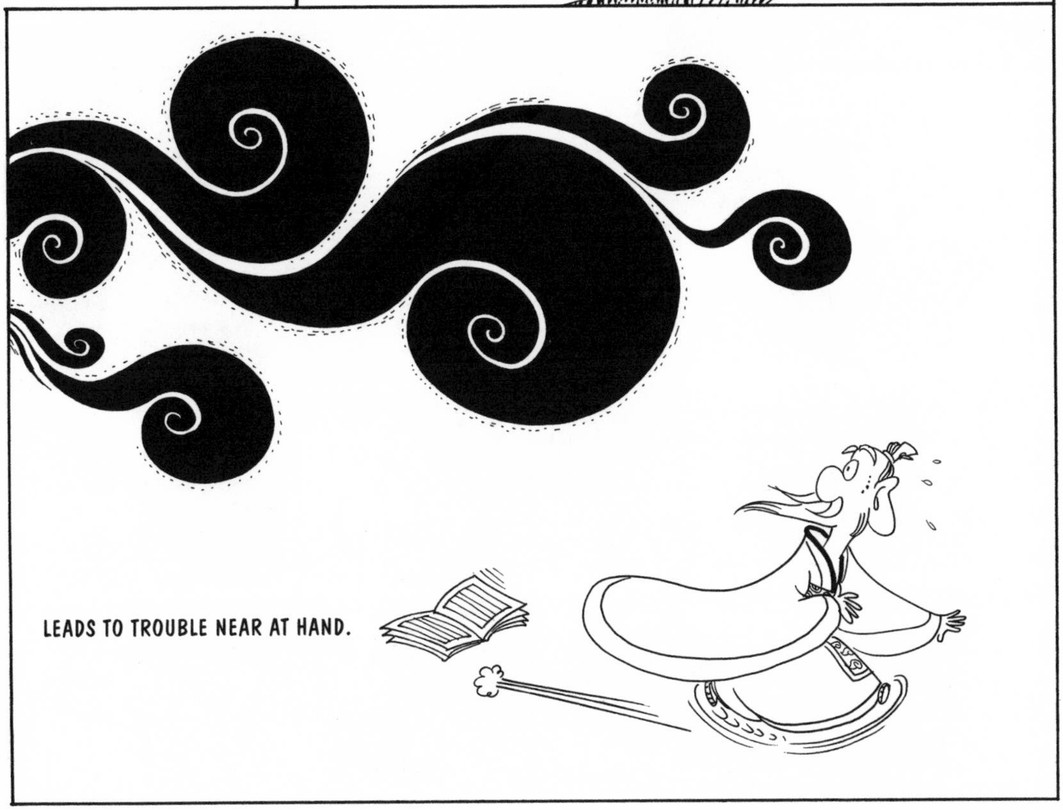
LEADS TO TROUBLE NEAR AT HAND.

子曰：「人無遠慮，必有近憂。」

子曰：「群居終日，言不及義，好行小慧，難矣哉！」

15:17

THE DIFFICULT ONES

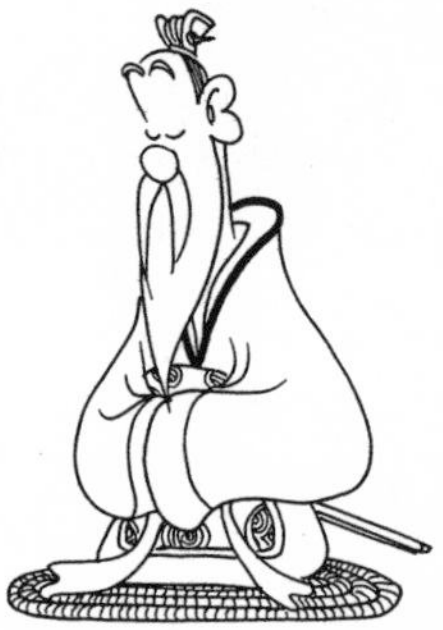

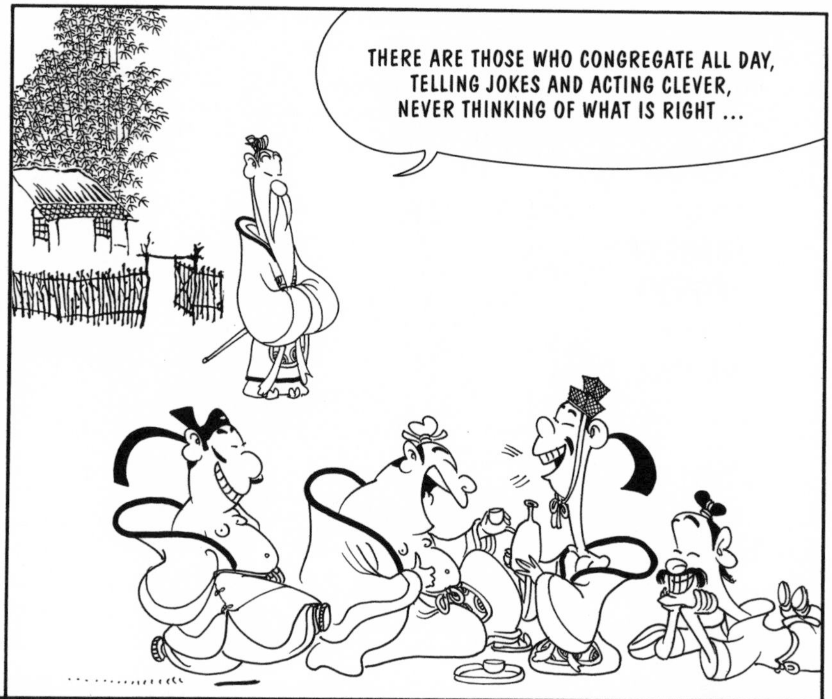
THERE ARE THOSE WHO CONGREGATE ALL DAY, TELLING JOKES AND ACTING CLEVER, NEVER THINKING OF WHAT IS RIGHT ...

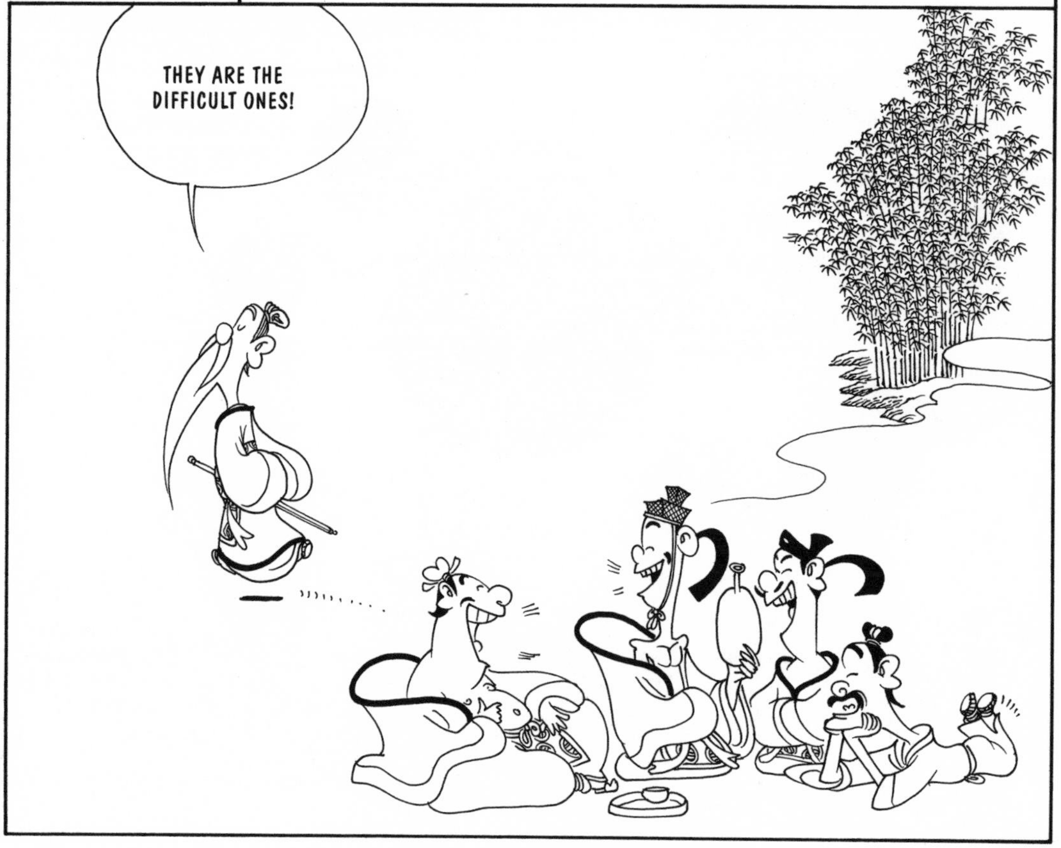
THEY ARE THE DIFFICULT ONES!

15:23

JUDGING WORDS AND PEOPLE

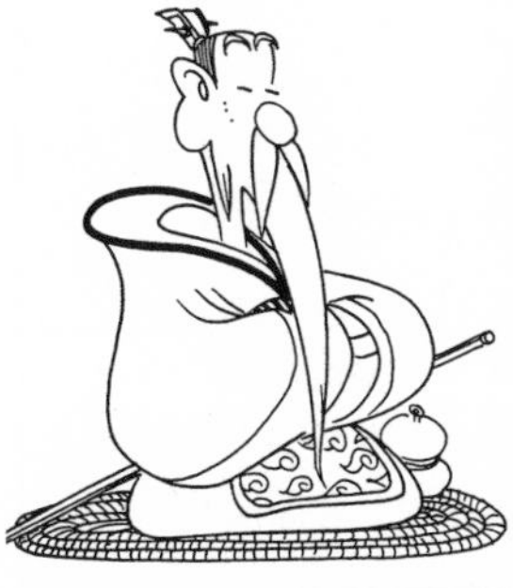

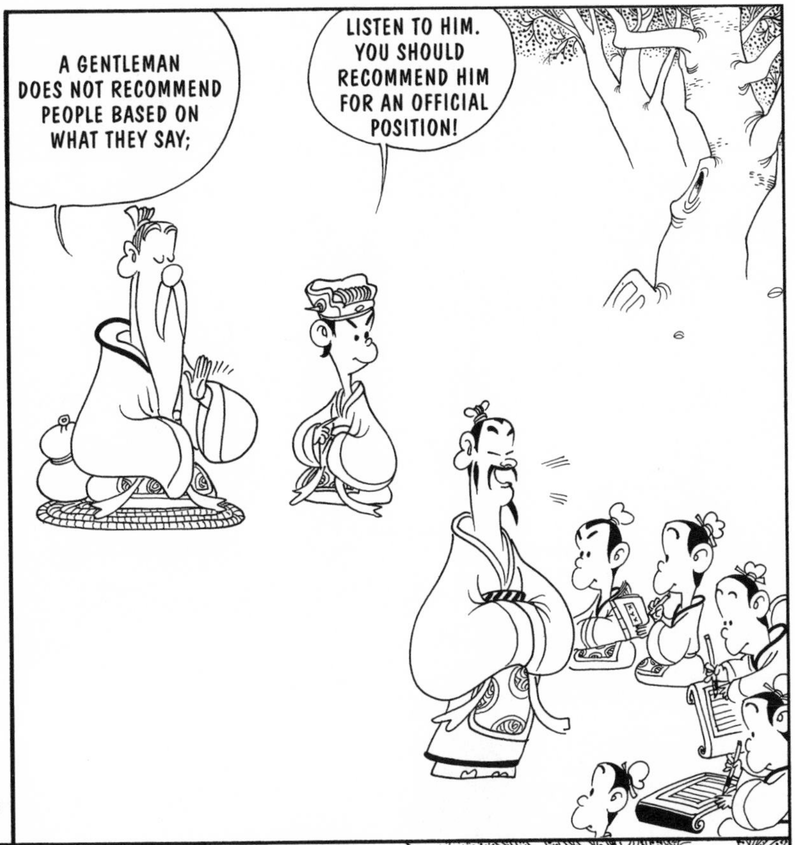
LISTEN TO HIM. YOU SHOULD RECOMMEND HIM FOR AN OFFICIAL POSITION!
A GENTLEMAN DOES NOT RECOMMEND PEOPLE BASED ON WHAT THEY SAY;

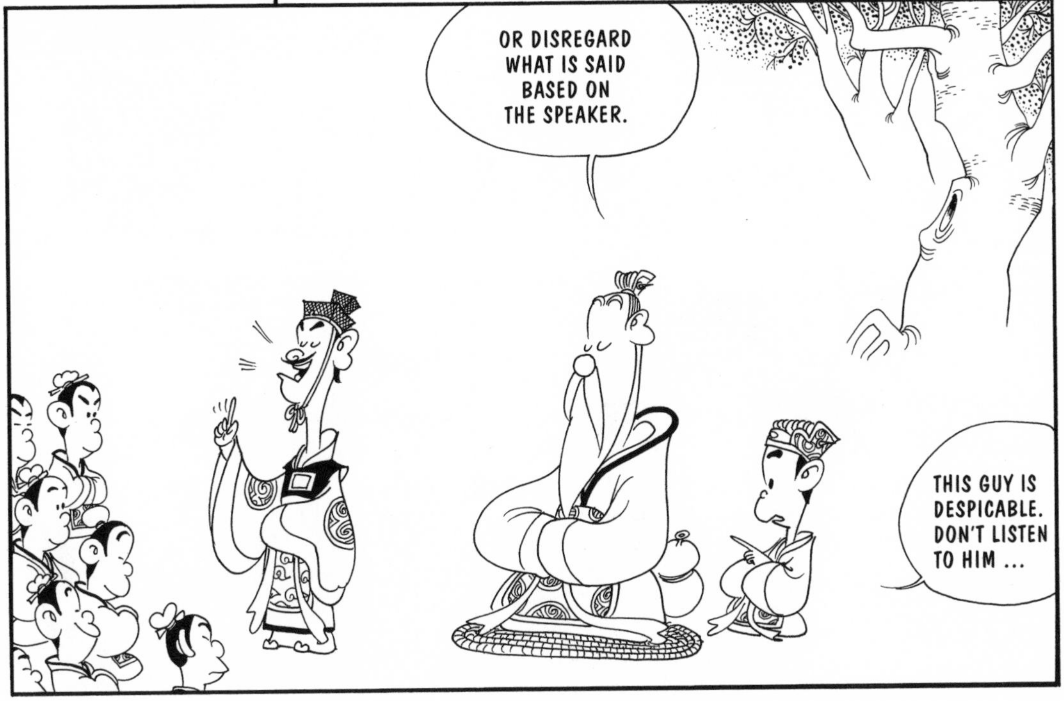
THIS GUY IS DESPICABLE. DON'T LISTEN TO HIM ...
OR DISREGARD WHAT IS SAID BASED ON THE SPEAKER.

子曰：「君子不以言舉人，不以人廢言。」

子貢問曰：「有一言而可以終身行之者乎？」子曰：「其恕乎！己所不欲，勿施於人。」

15:24

BE THOUGHTFUL

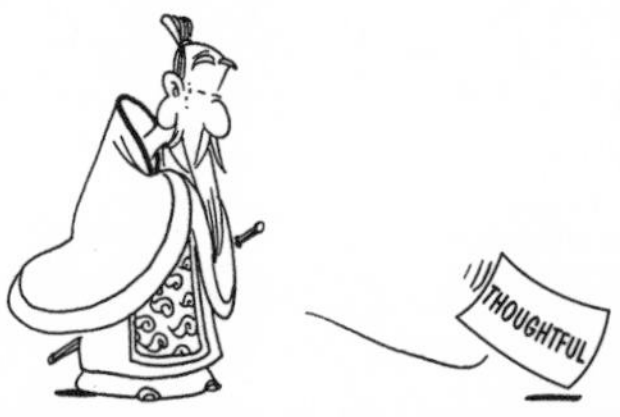
THOUGHTFUL

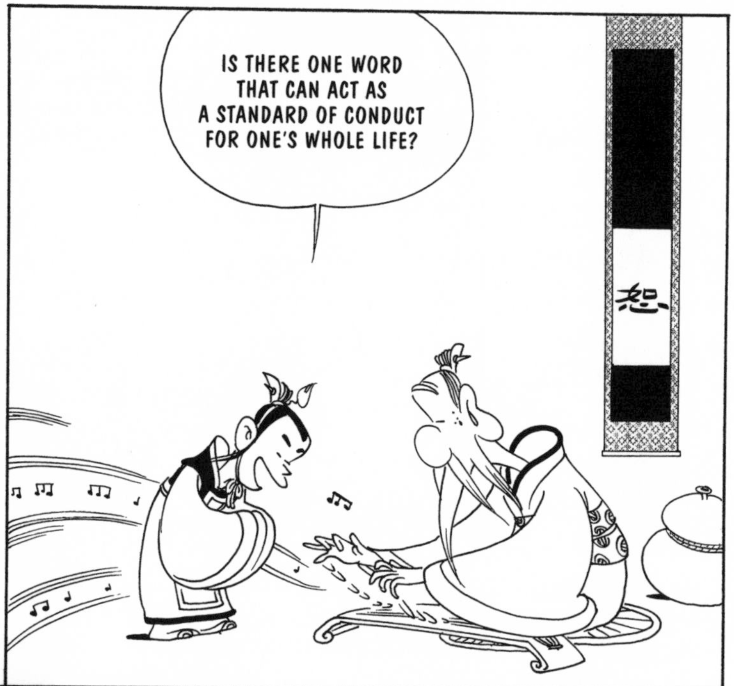
IS THERE ONE WORD THAT CAN ACT AS A STANDARD OF CONDUCT FOR ONE'S WHOLE LIFE?

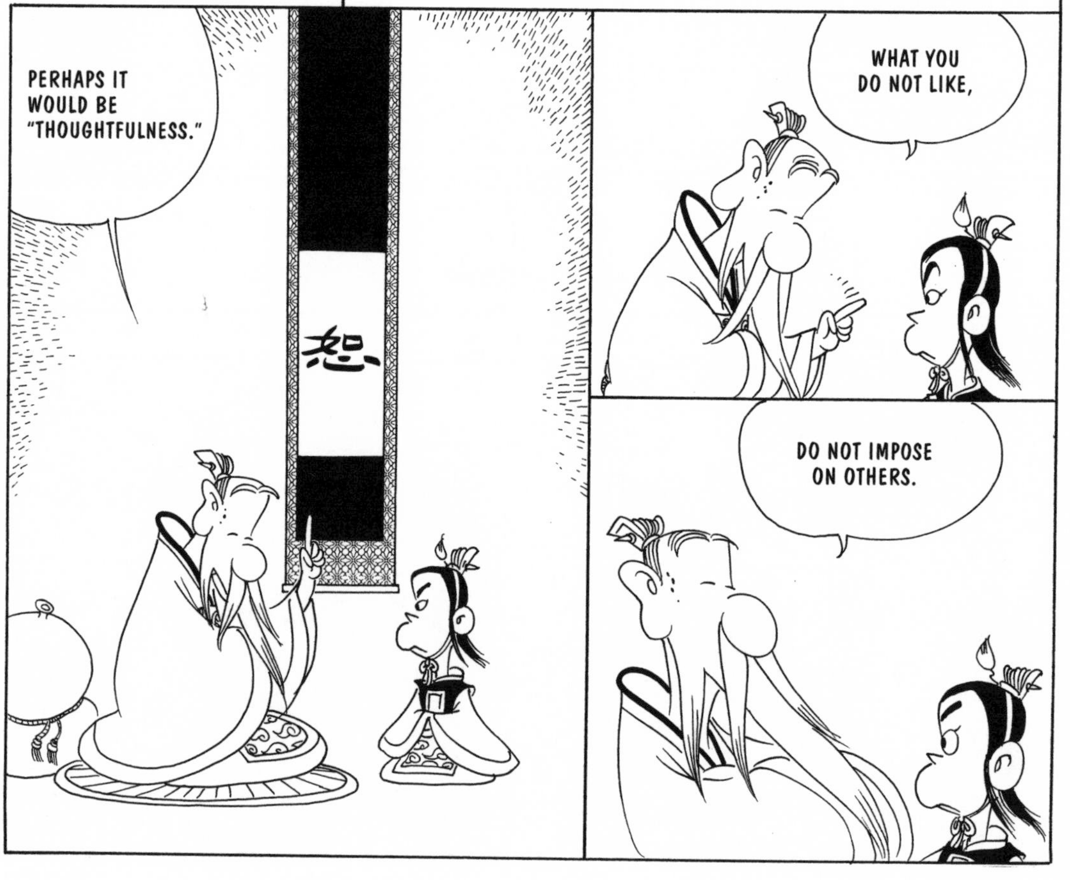
PERHAPS IT WOULD BE "THOUGHTFULNESS."
WHAT YOU DO NOT LIKE,
DO NOT IMPOSE ON OTHERS.

15:27

PATIENCE AND DISCRETION

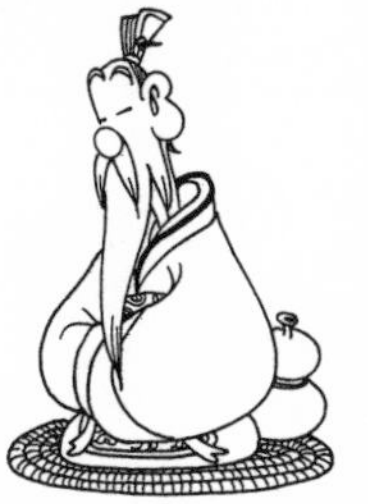

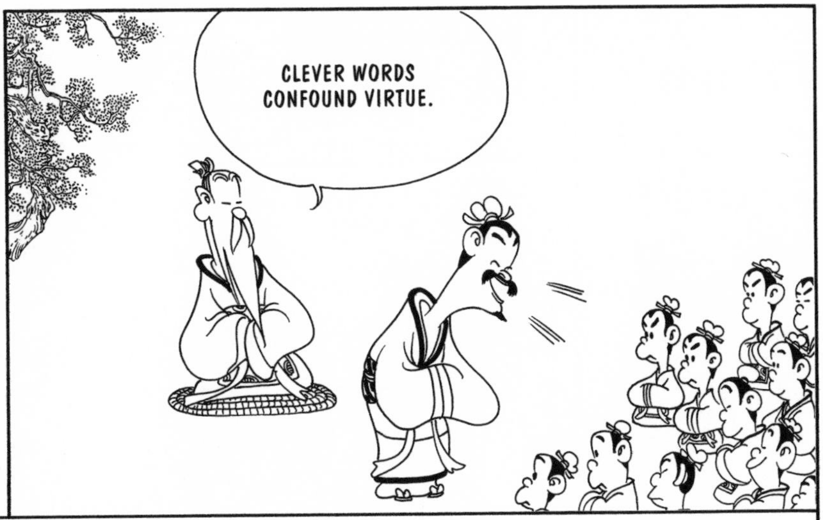
CLEVER WORDS CONFOUND VIRTUE.

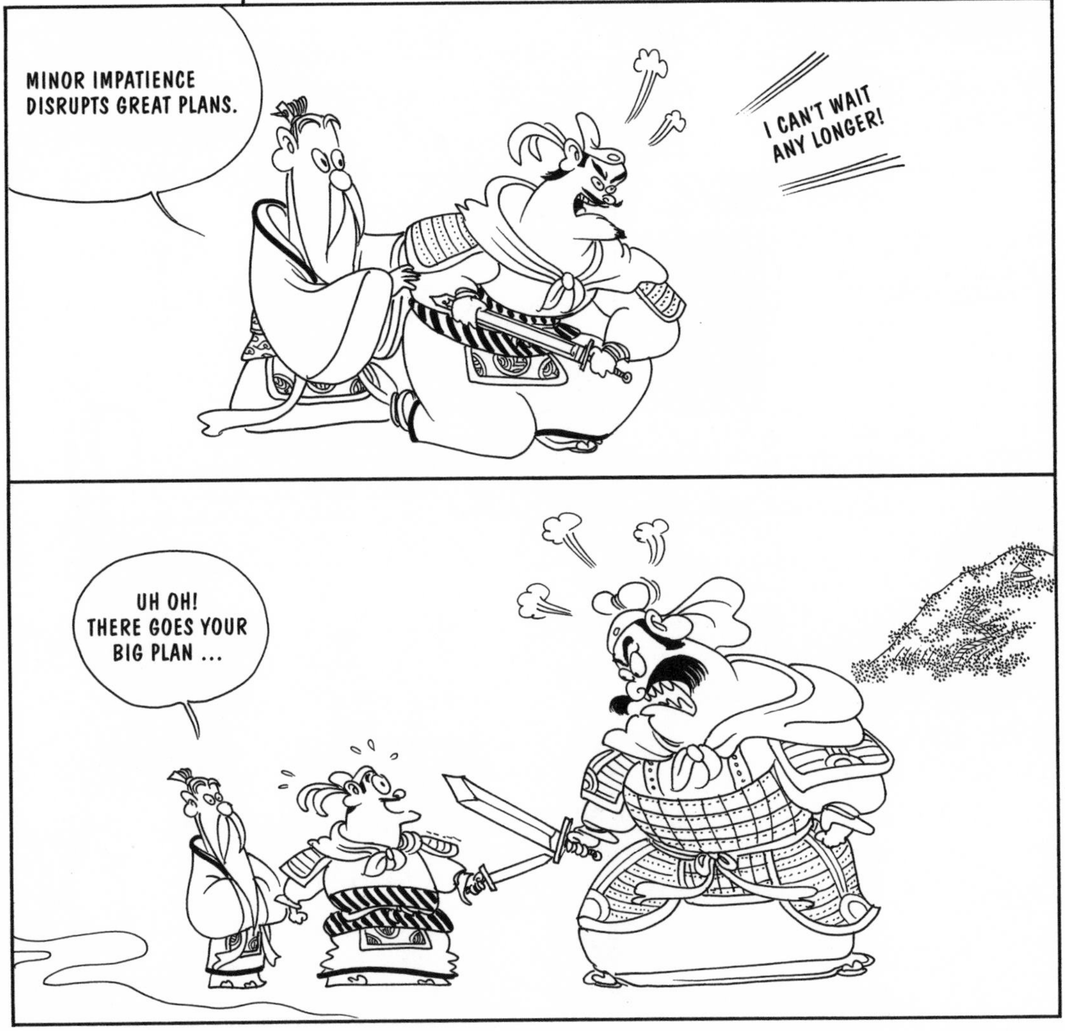
MINOR IMPATIENCE DISRUPTS GREAT PLANS.
I CAN'T WAIT ANY LONGER!
UH OH! THERE GOES YOUR BIG PLAN ...

子曰：「巧言亂德。小不忍，則亂大謀。」

子曰：「眾惡之，必察焉；眾好之，必察焉。」

15:28

BE SKEPTICAL

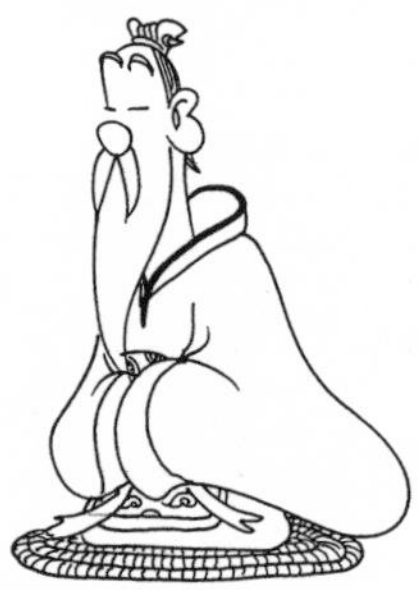

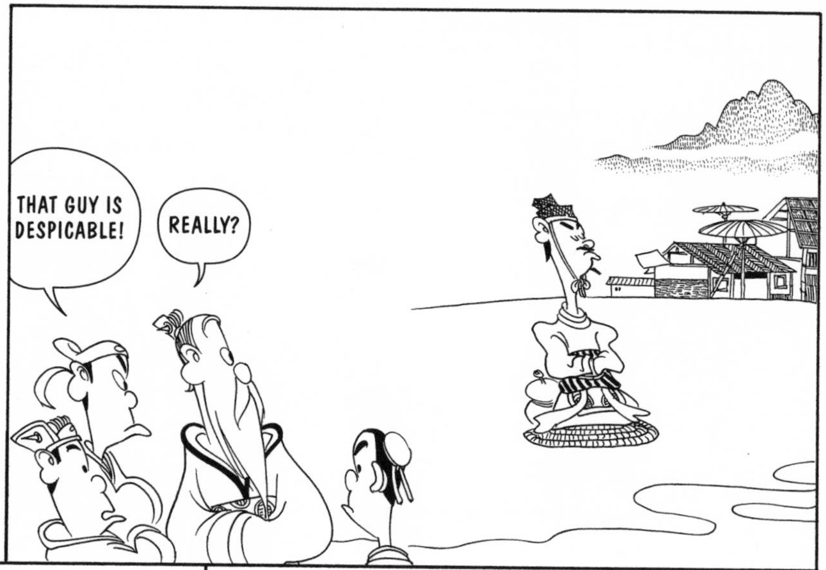
THAT GUY IS DESPICABLE!
REALLY?

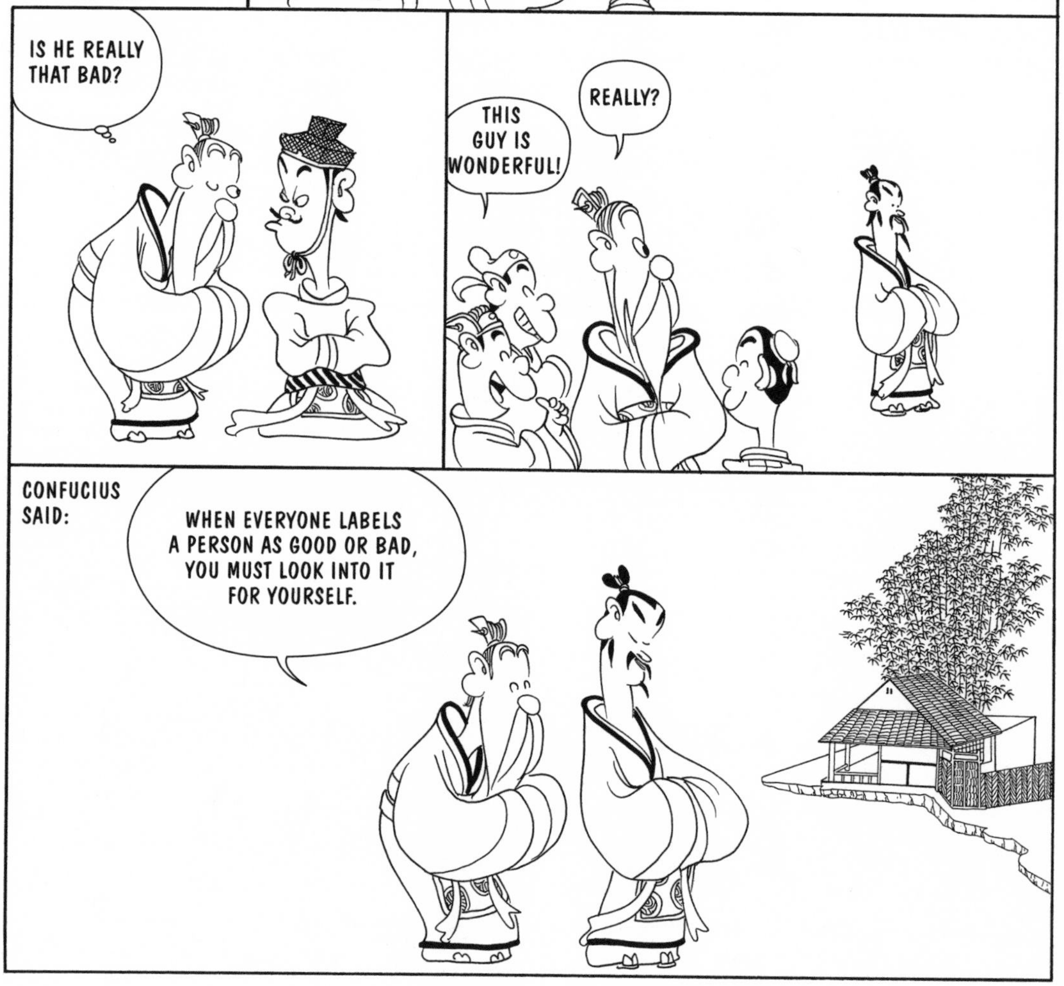
IS HE REALLY THAT BAD?
THIS GUY IS WONDERFUL!
REALLY?
CONFUCIUS SAID:
WHEN EVERYONE LABELS A PERSON AS GOOD OR BAD, YOU MUST LOOK INTO IT FOR YOURSELF.

15:29

THE DAO

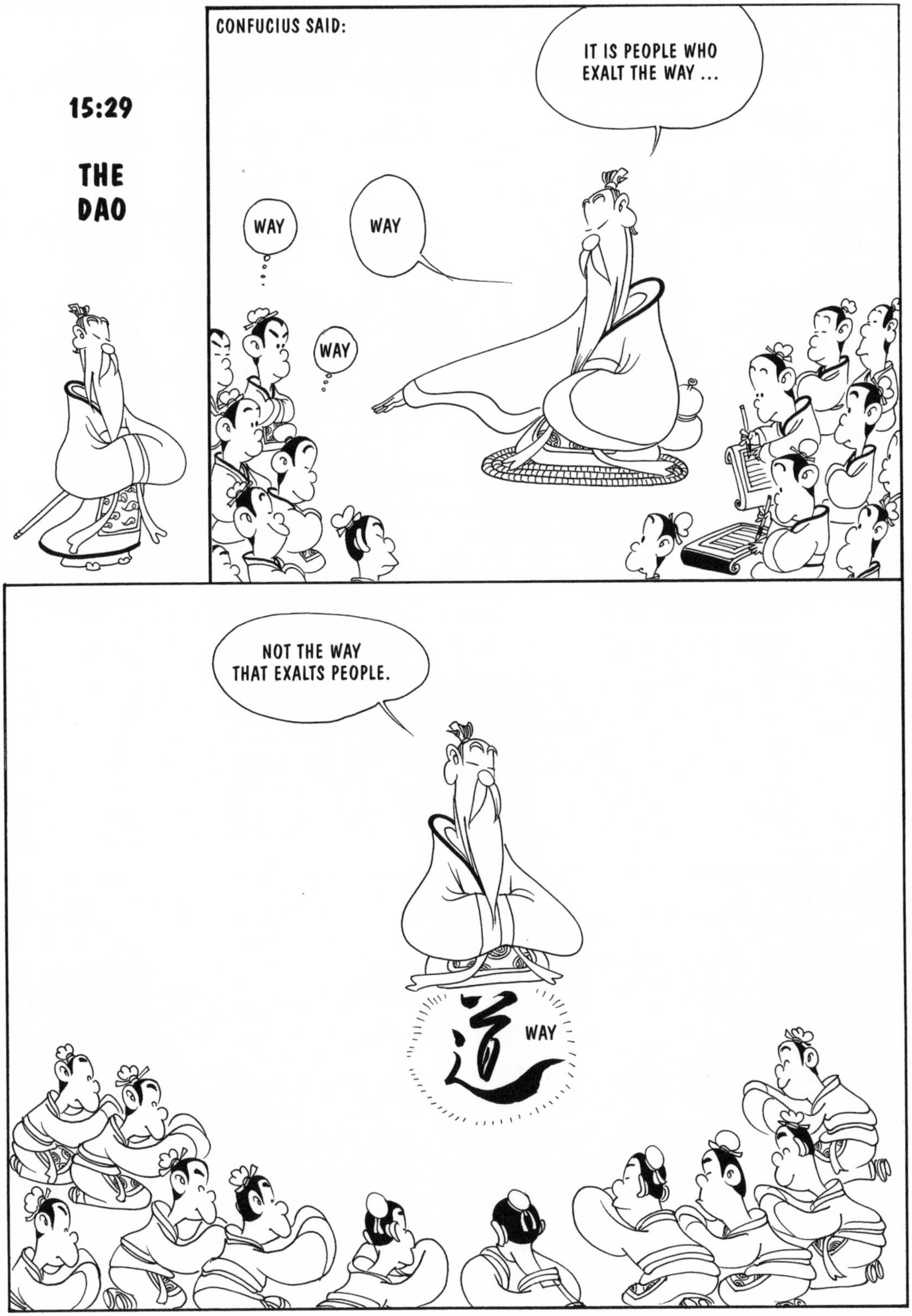
CONFUCIUS SAID:
IT IS PEOPLE WHO EXALT THE WAY ...
WAY
WAY
WAY
NOT THE WAY THAT EXALTS PEOPLE.
道
WAY

子曰：「人能弘道，非道弘人。」

子曰：「過而不改，是謂過矣。」

15:30

THE REAL TRANSGRESSION

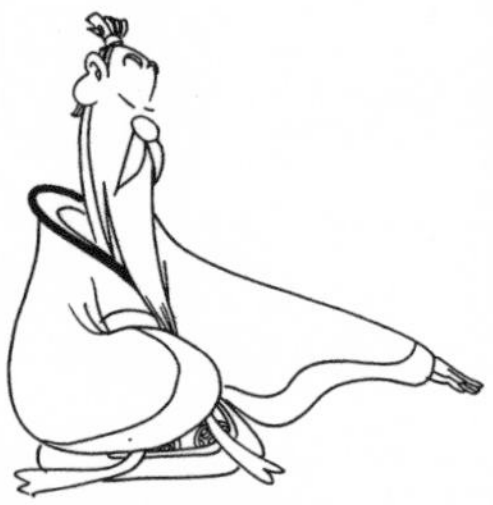

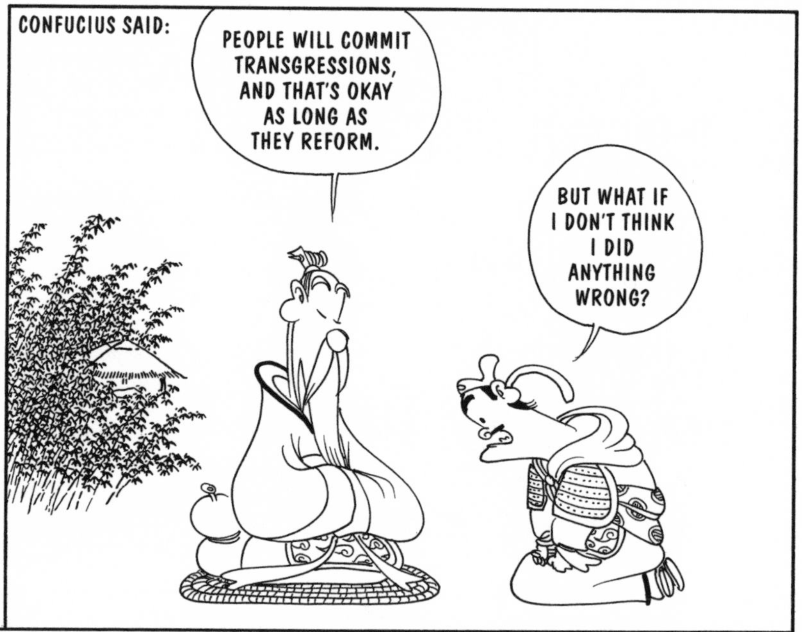
CONFUCIUS SAID:
PEOPLE WILL COMMIT TRANSGRESSIONS, AND THAT'S OKAY AS LONG AS THEY REFORM.
BUT WHAT IF I DON'T THINK I DID ANYTHING WRONG?

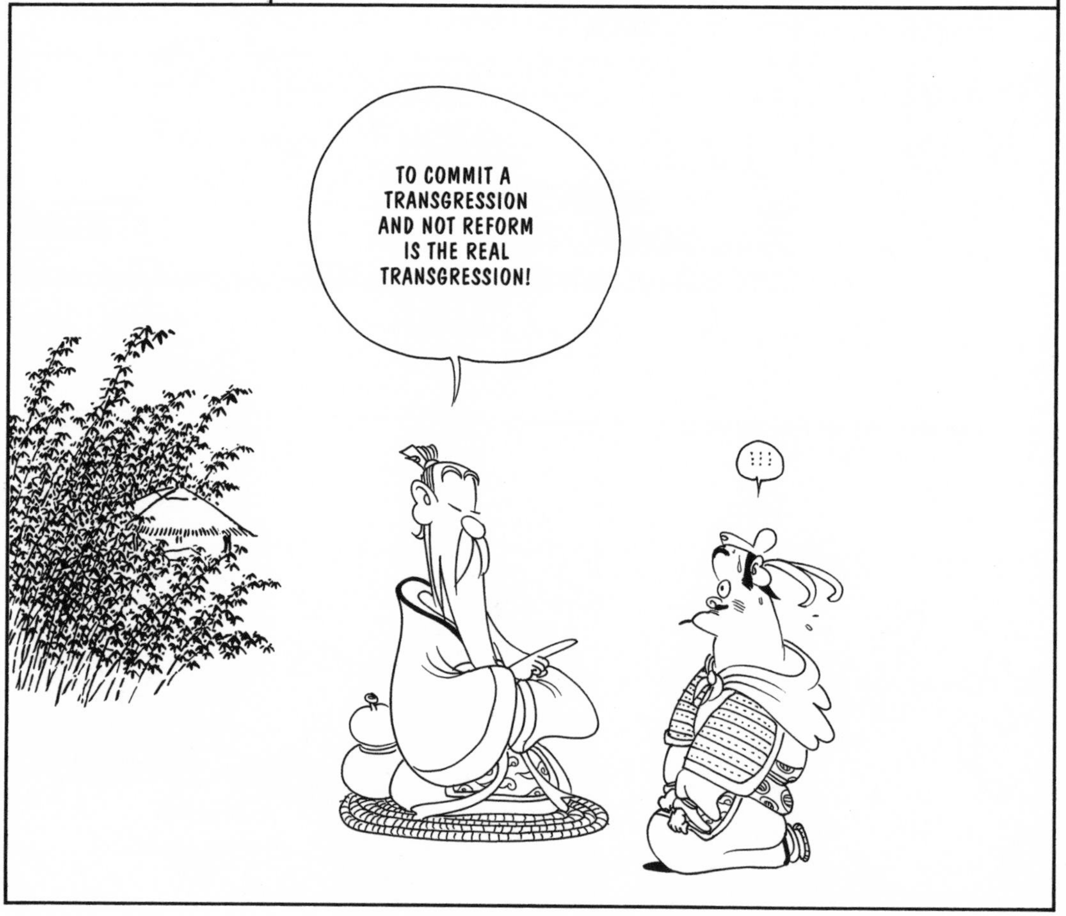
TO COMMIT A TRANSGRESSION AND NOT REFORM IS THE REAL TRANSGRESSION!

15:31

THINKING VS. STUDYING

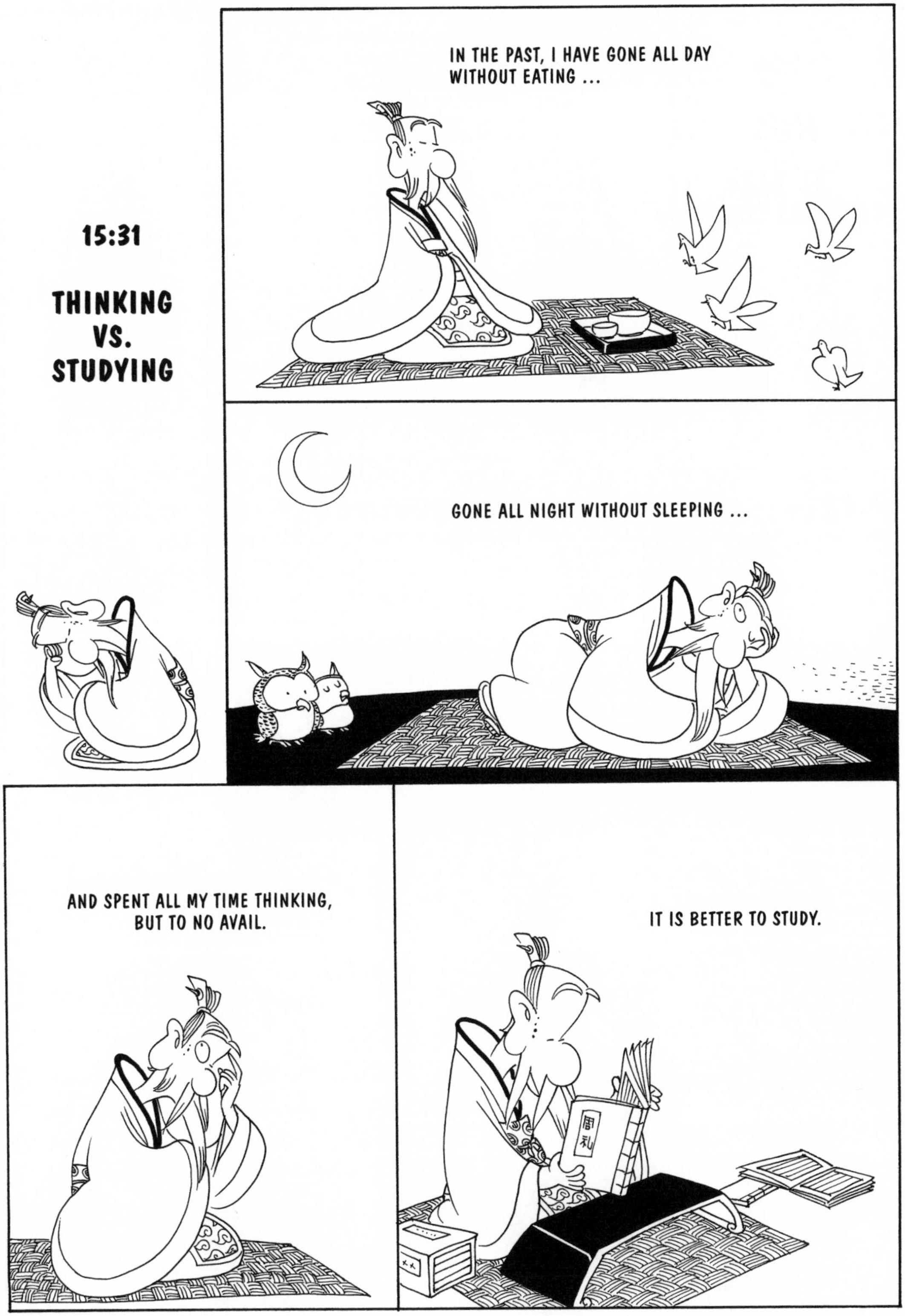
IN THE PAST, I HAVE GONE ALL DAY WITHOUT EATING ...
GONE ALL NIGHT WITHOUT SLEEPING ...
AND SPENT ALL MY TIME THINKING, BUT TO NO AVAIL.
IT IS BETTER TO STUDY.

子曰：「吾嘗終日不食，終夜不寢，以思，無益，不如學也。」

子曰：「當仁，不讓於師。」

15:36

YIELD TO NO ONE

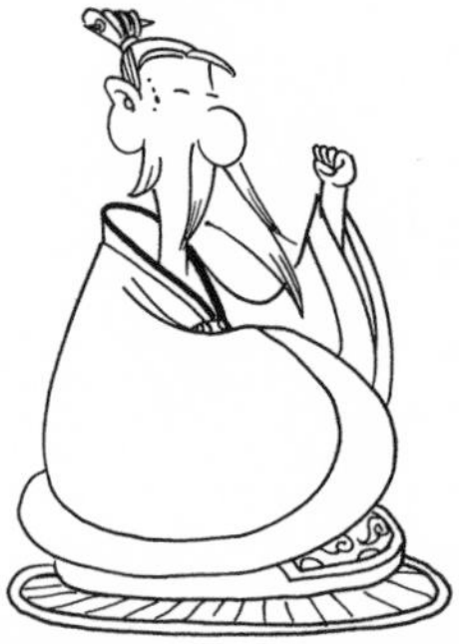

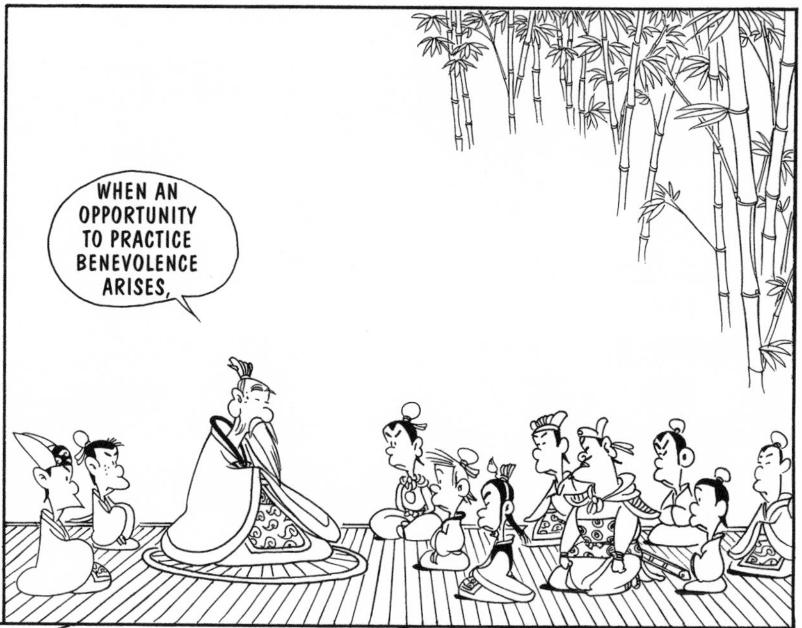
WHEN AN OPPORTUNITY TO PRACTICE BENEVOLENCE ARISES,

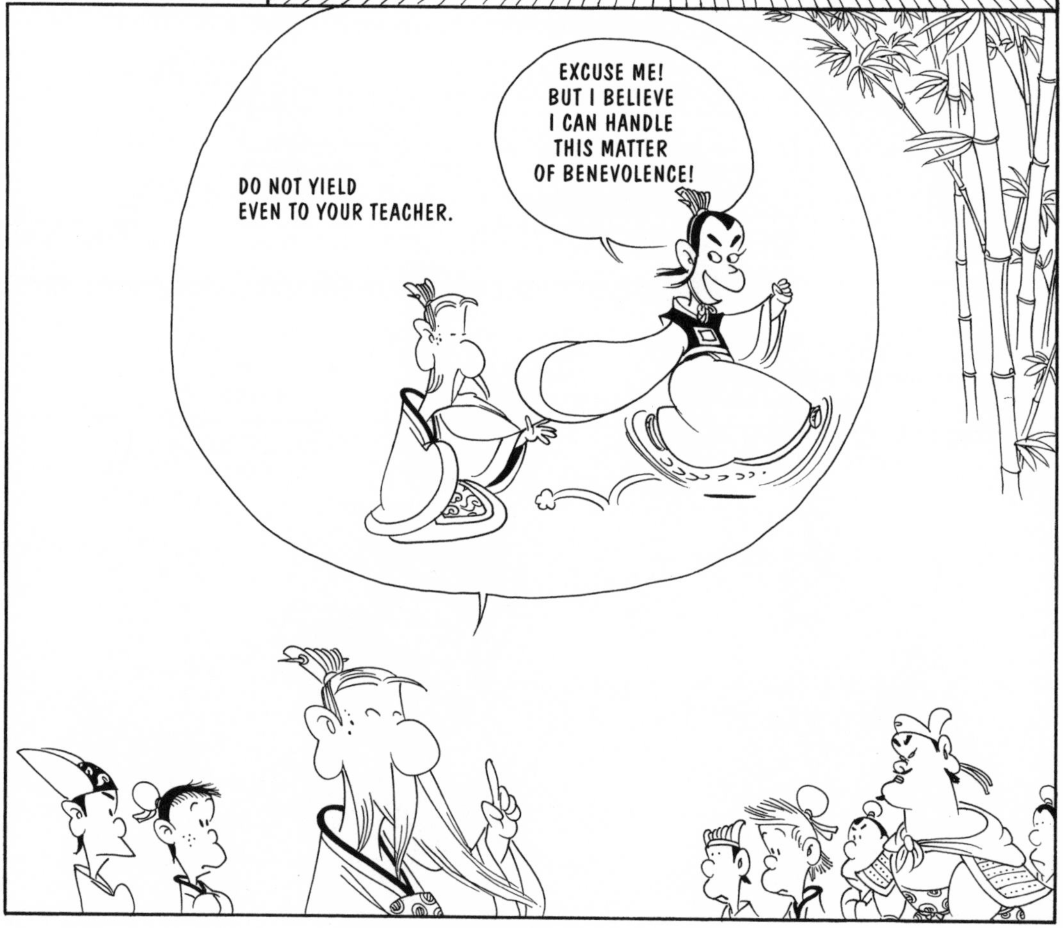
DO NOT YIELD EVEN TO YOUR TEACHER.
EXCUSE ME! BUT I BELIEVE I CAN HANDLE THIS MATTER OF BENEVOLENCE!

15:37

THE PROPER WAY

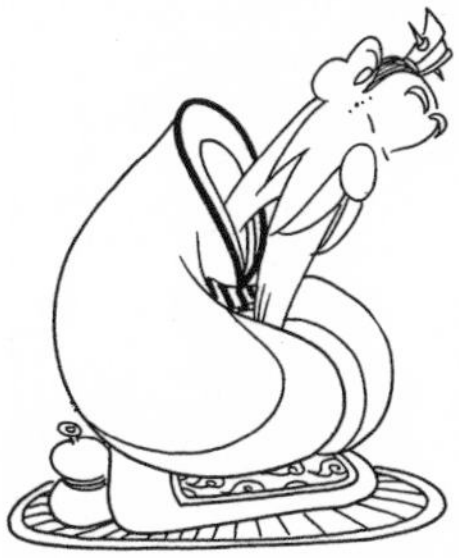

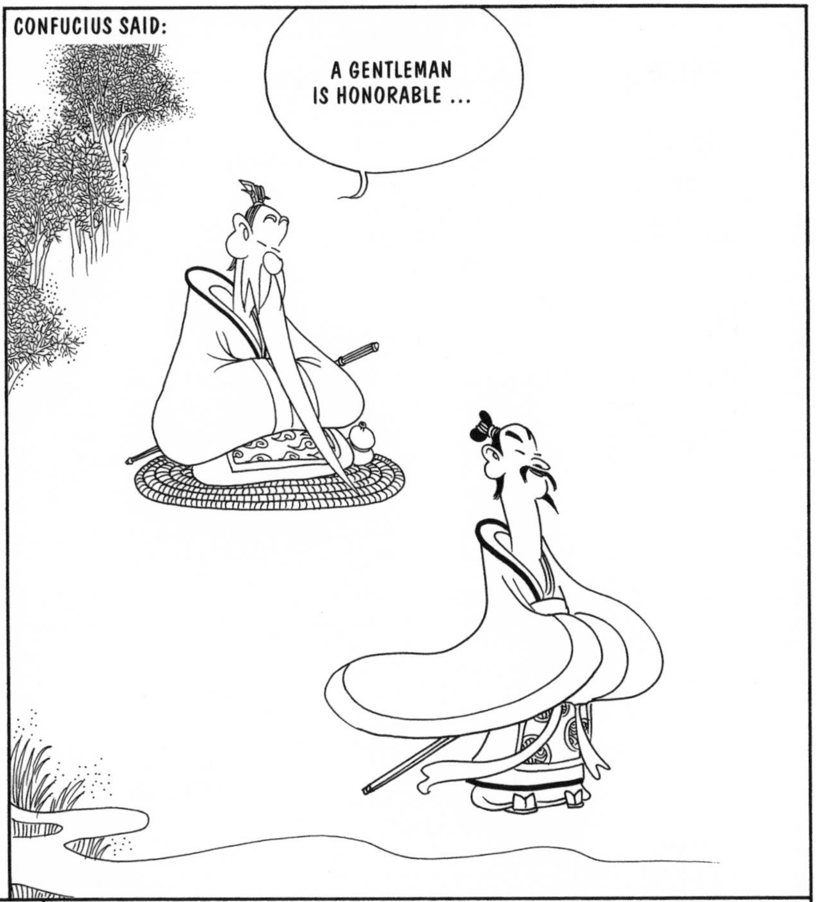
CONFUCIUS SAID:
A GENTLEMAN IS HONORABLE ...

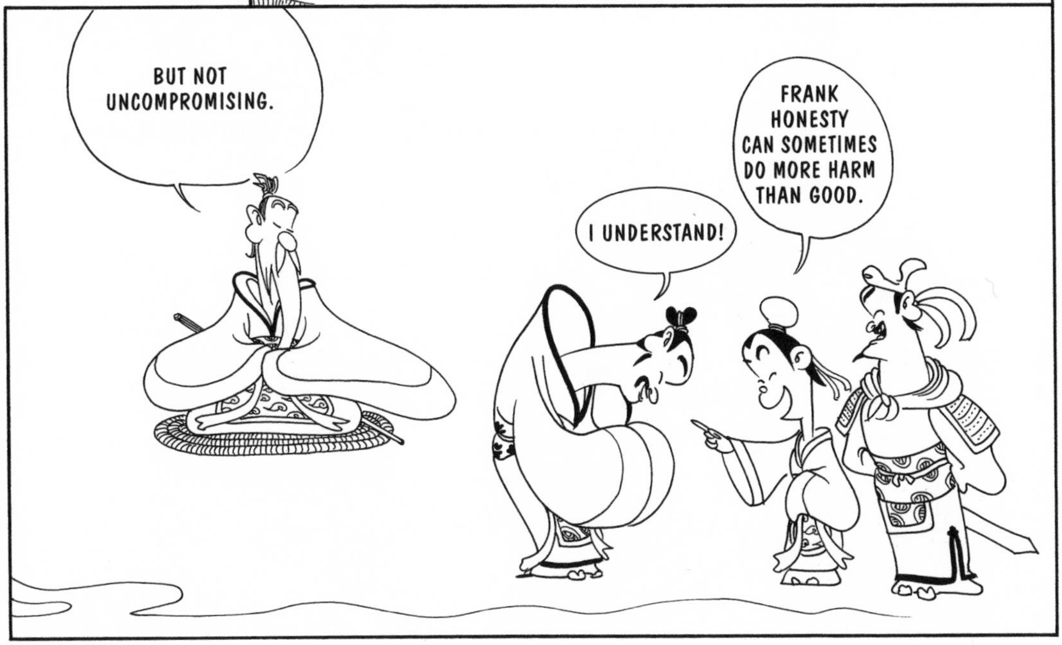
BUT NOT UNCOMPROMISING.
FRANK HONESTY CAN SOMETIMES DO MORE HARM THAN GOOD.
I UNDERSTAND!

子曰：「君子貞而不諒。」

16:4

MAKING FRIENDS

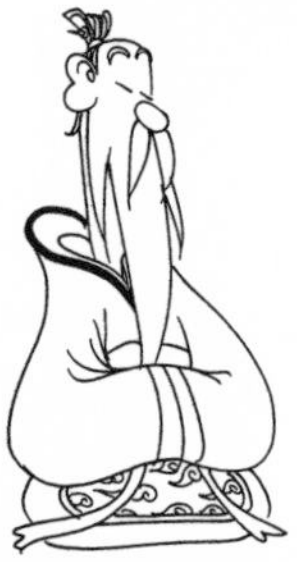

孔子曰：「益者三友，損者三友。友直，友諒，友多聞，益矣。友便辟，友善柔，友便佞，損矣。」

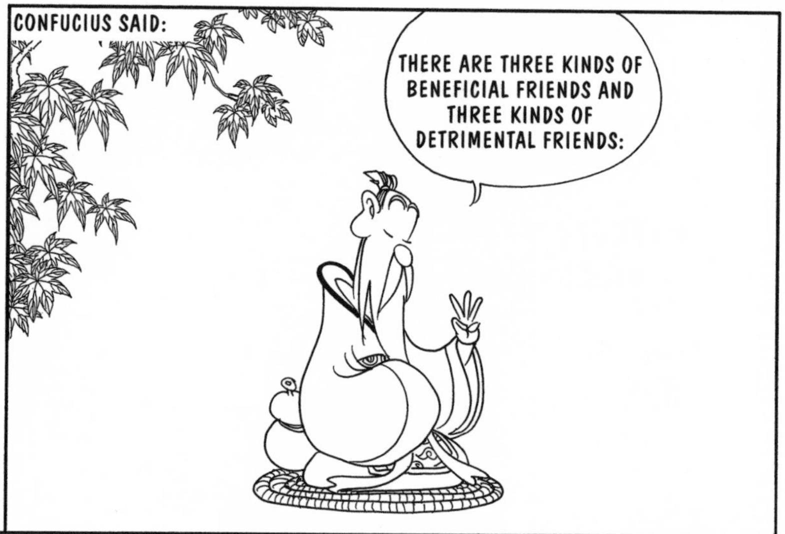
CONFUCIUS SAID:
THERE ARE THREE KINDS OF BENEFICIAL FRIENDS AND THREE KINDS OF DETRIMENTAL FRIENDS:

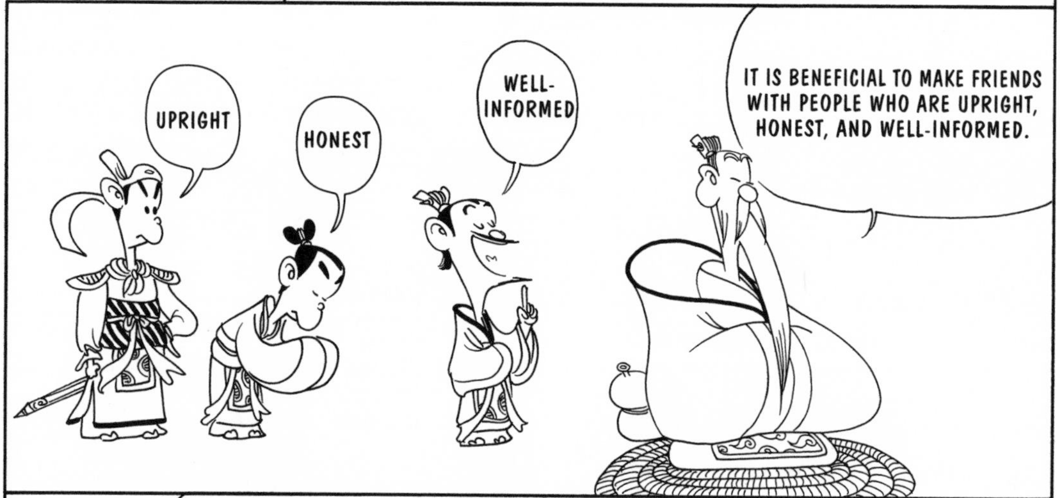
IT IS BENEFICIAL TO MAKE FRIENDS WITH PEOPLE WHO ARE UPRIGHT, HONEST, AND WELL-INFORMED.
UPRIGHT
HONEST
WELL-INFORMED

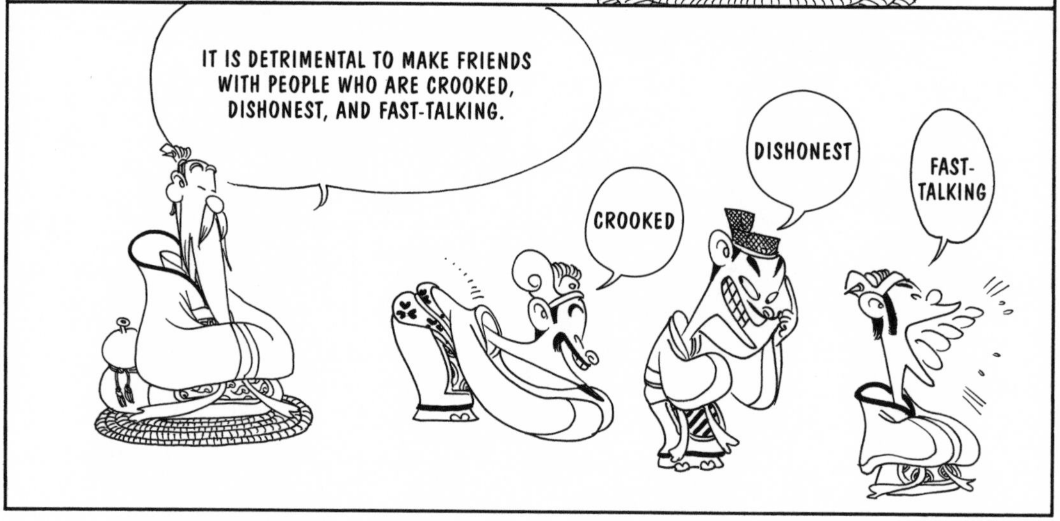
IT IS DETRIMENTAL TO MAKE FRIENDS WITH PEOPLE WHO ARE CROOKED, DISHONEST, AND FAST-TALKING.
CROOKED
DISHONEST
FAST-TALKING

16:7

THREE VICES

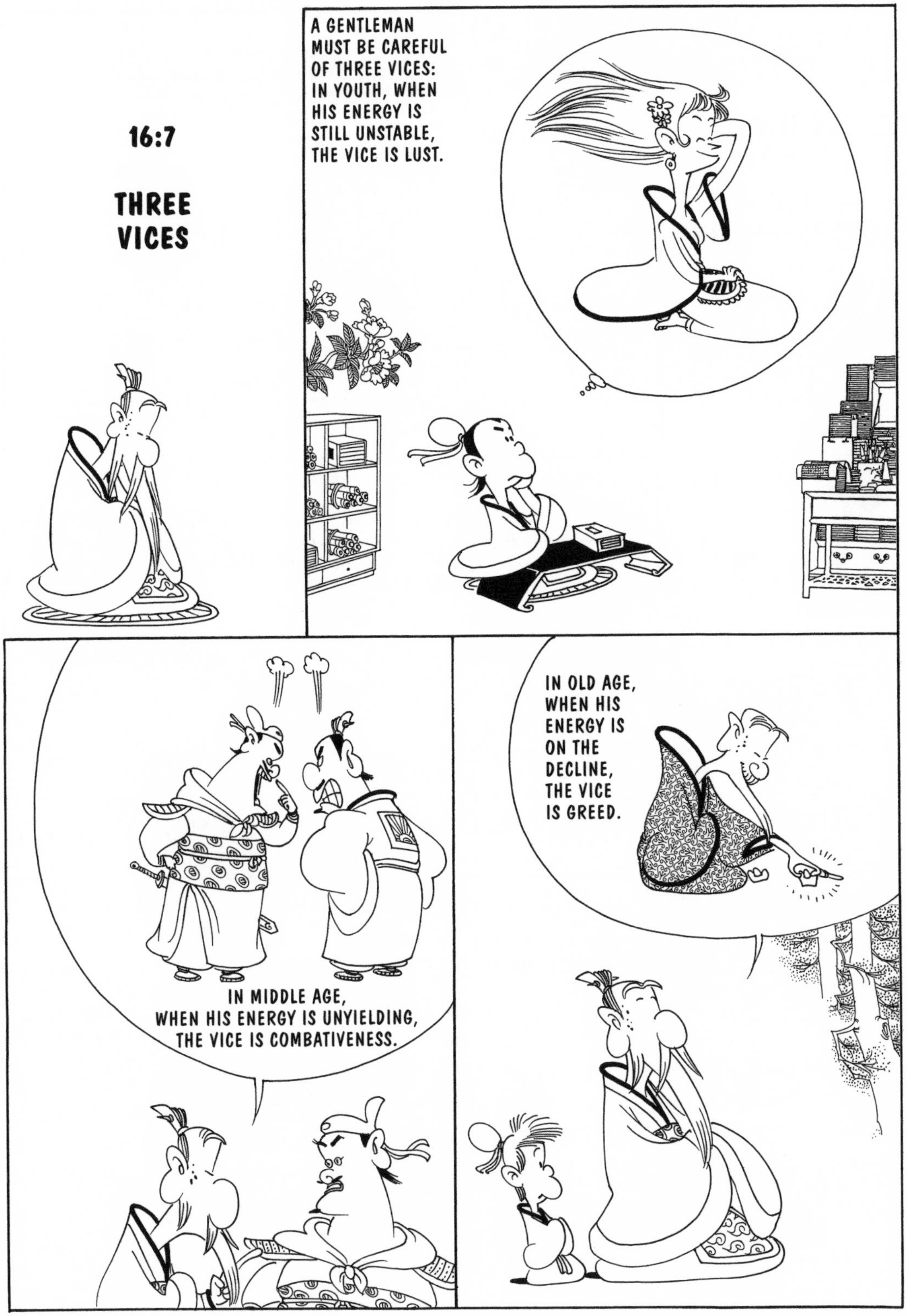
A GENTLEMAN MUST BE CAREFUL OF THREE VICES: IN YOUTH, WHEN HIS ENERGY IS STILL UNSTABLE, THE VICE IS LUST.
IN MIDDLE AGE, WHEN HIS ENERGY IS UNYIELDING, THE VICE IS COMBATIVENESS.
IN OLD AGE, WHEN HIS ENERGY IS ON THE DECLINE, THE VICE IS GREED.

孔子曰：「君子有三戒：少之時，血氣未定，戒之在色；及其壯也，血氣方剛，戒之在鬭；及其老也，血氣既衰，戒之在得。」

孔子曰：「生而知之者上也，學而知之者次也；困而學之，又其次也；困而不學，民斯為下矣。」

16:9

NATURAL UNDERSTANDING

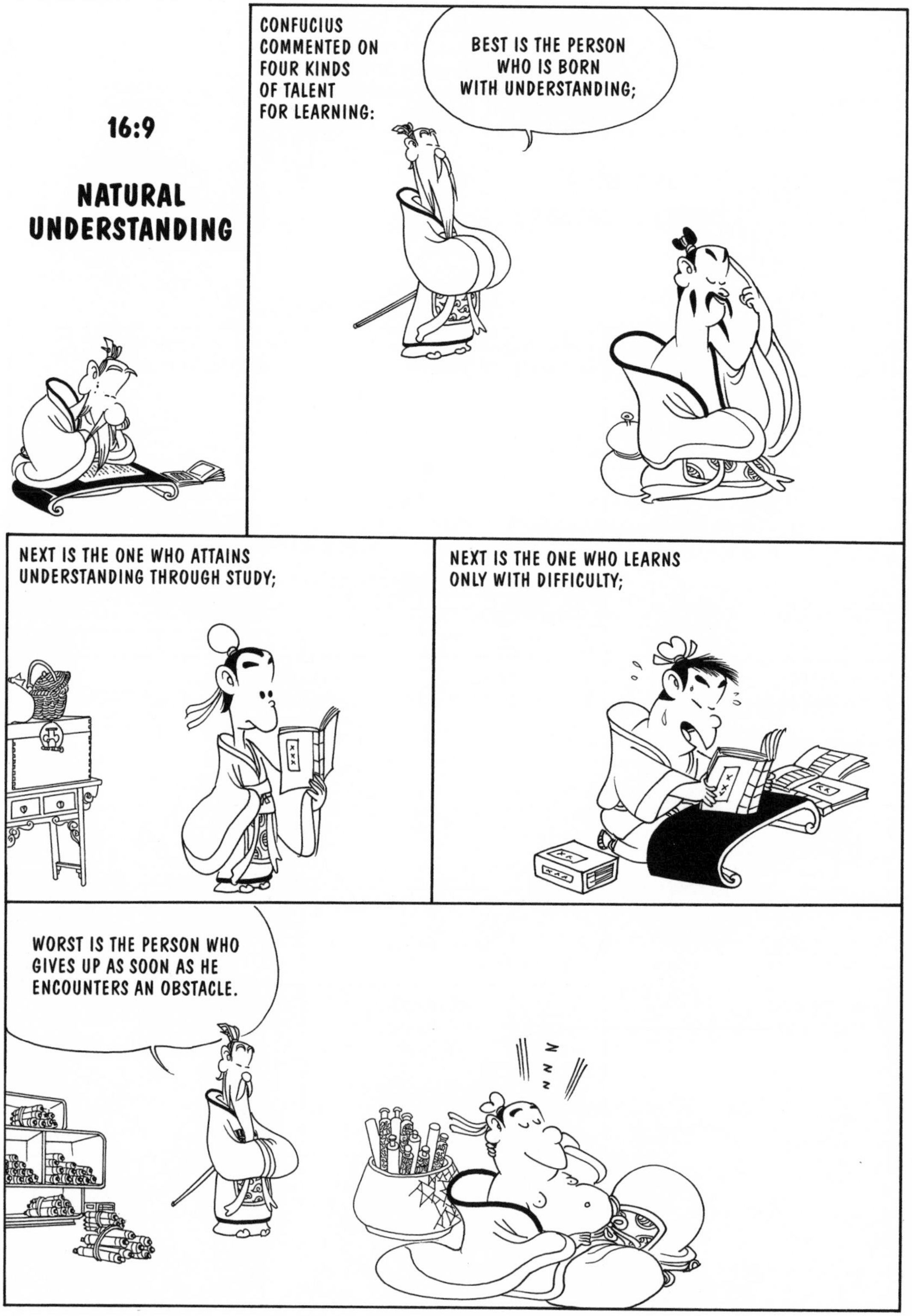
CONFUCIUS COMMENTED ON FOUR KINDS OF TALENT FOR LEARNING:
BEST IS THE PERSON WHO IS BORN WITH UNDERSTANDING;
NEXT IS THE ONE WHO ATTAINS UNDERSTANDING THROUGH STUDY;
NEXT IS THE ONE WHO LEARNS ONLY WITH DIFFICULTY;
WORST IS THE PERSON WHO GIVES UP AS SOON AS HE ENCOUNTERS AN OBSTACLE.
Z Z Z

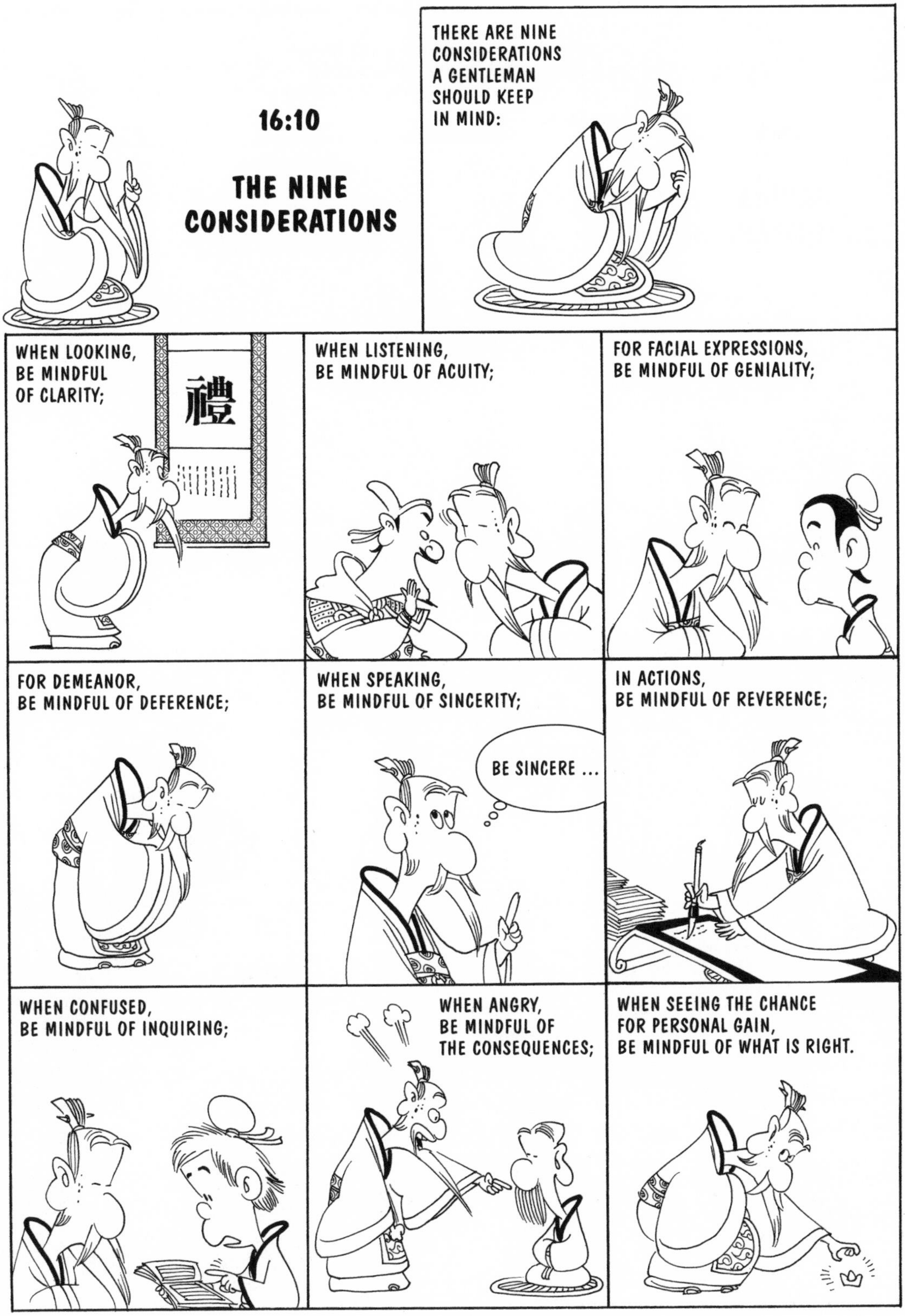
16:10
THE NINE CONSIDERATIONS
THERE ARE NINE CONSIDERATIONS A GENTLEMAN SHOULD KEEP IN MIND:
WHEN LOOKING, BE MINDFUL OF CLARITY;
禮
WHEN LISTENING, BE MINDFUL OF ACUITY;
FOR FACIAL EXPRESSIONS, BE MINDFUL OF GENIALITY;
FOR DEMEANOR, BE MINDFUL OF DEFERENCE;
WHEN SPEAKING, BE MINDFUL OF SINCERITY;
BE SINCERE ...
IN ACTIONS, BE MINDFUL OF REVERENCE;
WHEN CONFUSED, BE MINDFUL OF INQUIRING;
WHEN ANGRY, BE MINDFUL OF THE CONSEQUENCES;
WHEN SEEING THE CHANCE FOR PERSONAL GAIN, BE MINDFUL OF WHAT IS RIGHT.

孔子曰：「君子有九思：視思明，聽思聰，色思溫，貌思恭，言思忠，事思敬，疑思問，忿思難，見得思義。」

齊景公有馬千駟，死之日，民無德而稱焉。伯夷、叔齊餓于首陽之下，民到于今稱之。其斯之謂與？

16:12

PRAISING DEEDS

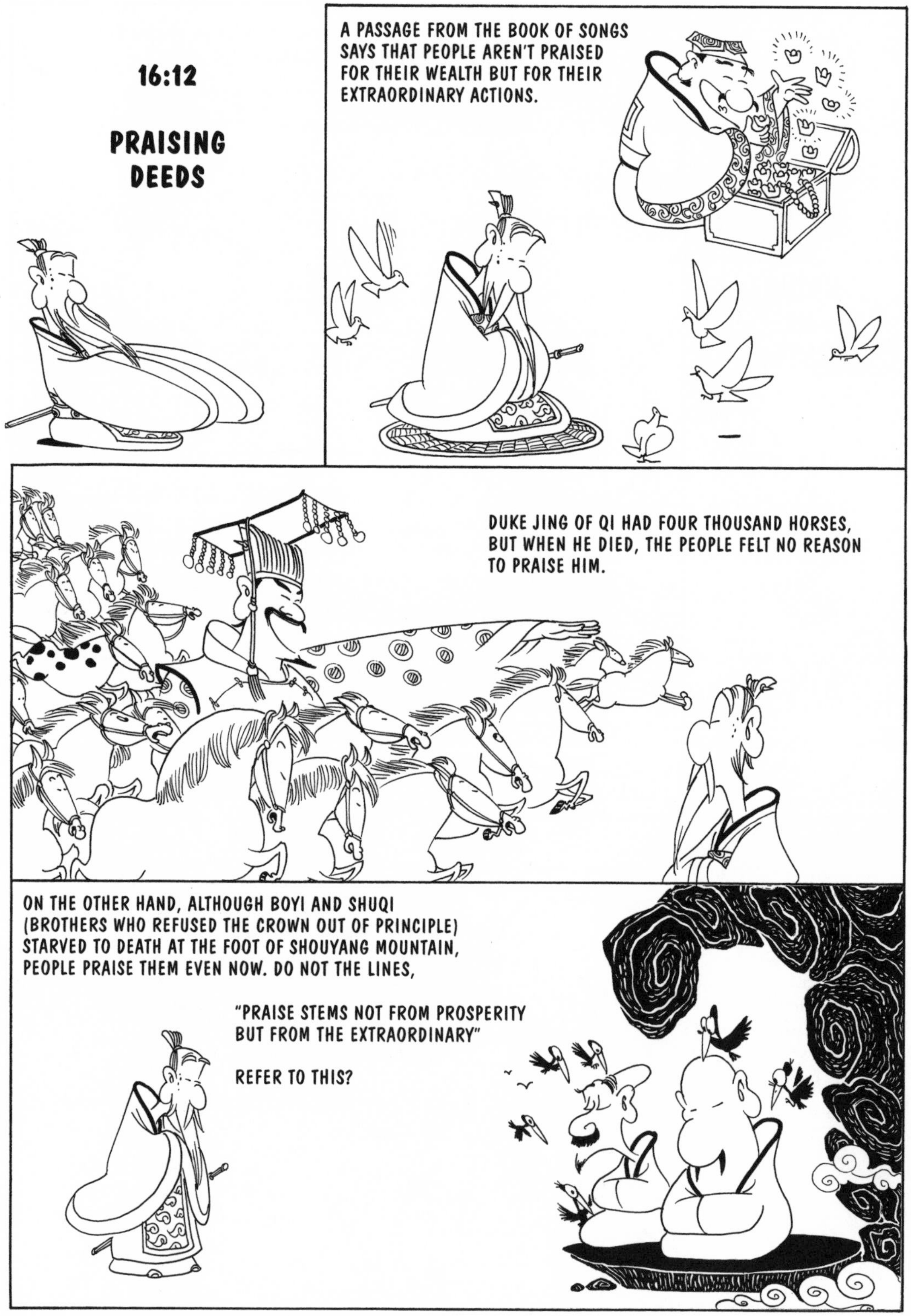

A PASSAGE FROM THE BOOK OF SONGS SAYS THAT PEOPLE AREN'T PRAISED FOR THEIR WEALTH BUT FOR THEIR EXTRAORDINARY ACTIONS.
DUKE JING OF QI HAD FOUR THOUSAND HORSES, BUT WHEN HE DIED, THE PEOPLE FELT NO REASON TO PRAISE HIM.
ON THE OTHER HAND, ALTHOUGH BOYI AND SHUQI (BROTHERS WHO REFUSED THE CROWN OUT OF PRINCIPLE) STARVED TO DEATH AT THE FOOT OF SHOUYANG MOUNTAIN, PEOPLE PRAISE THEM EVEN NOW. DO NOT THE LINES,
"PRAISE STEMS NOT FROM PROSPERITY BUT FROM THE EXTRAORDINARY"
REFER TO THIS?

17:2

NATURE VS. NURTURE

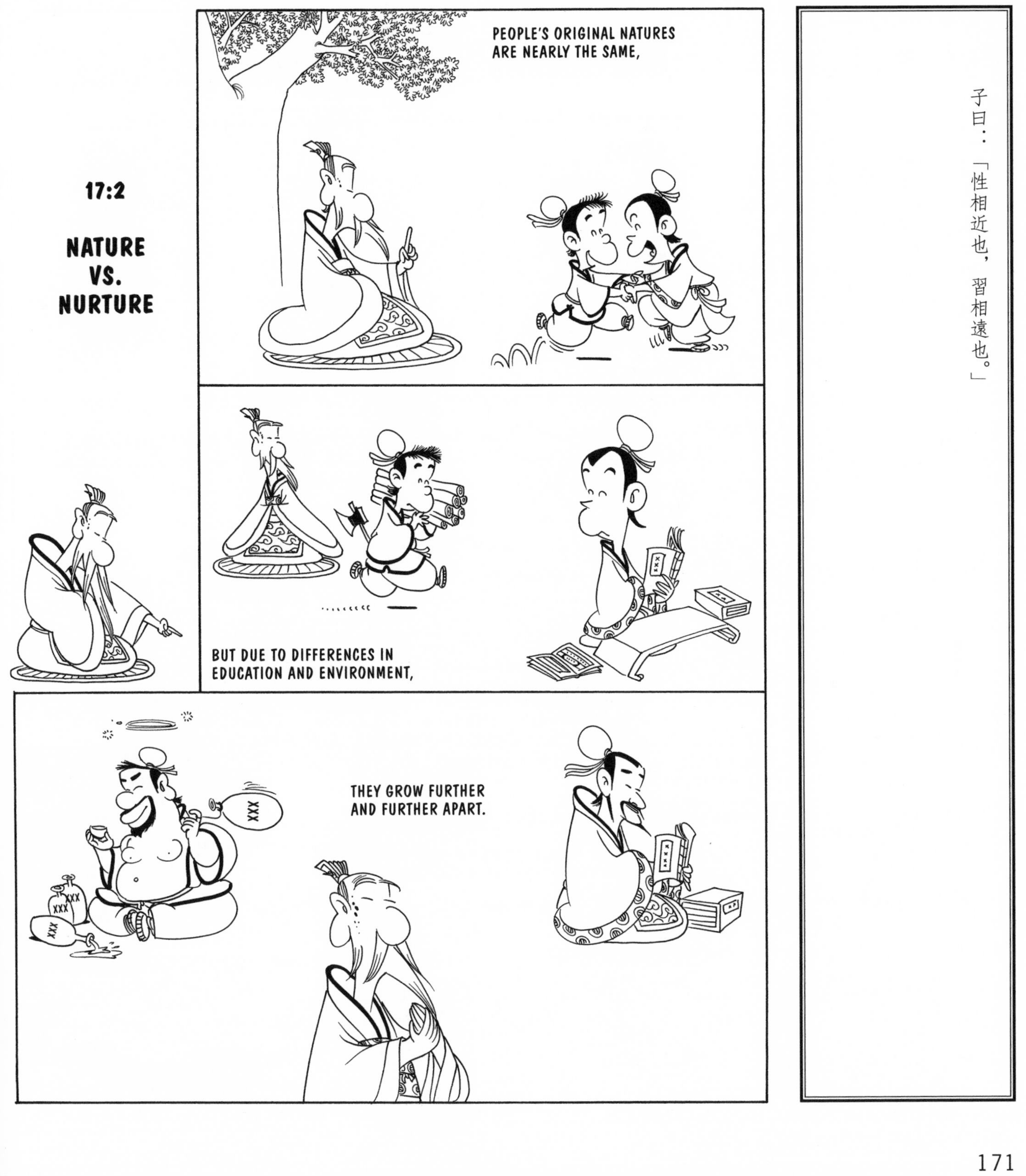

PEOPLE'S ORIGINAL NATURES ARE NEARLY THE SAME,
BUT DUE TO DIFFERENCES IN EDUCATION AND ENVIRONMENT,
THEY GROW FURTHER AND FURTHER APART.

子曰：「性相近也，習相遠也。」

子曰：「由也！女聞六言六蔽矣乎？」對曰：「未也。」
「居！吾語女。好仁不好學，其蔽也愚；好知不好學，其蔽也蕩；好信不好學，其蔽也賊；好直不好學，其蔽也絞；好勇不好學，其蔽也亂；好剛不好學，其蔽也狂。」

17:8

THE SIX DEFECTS

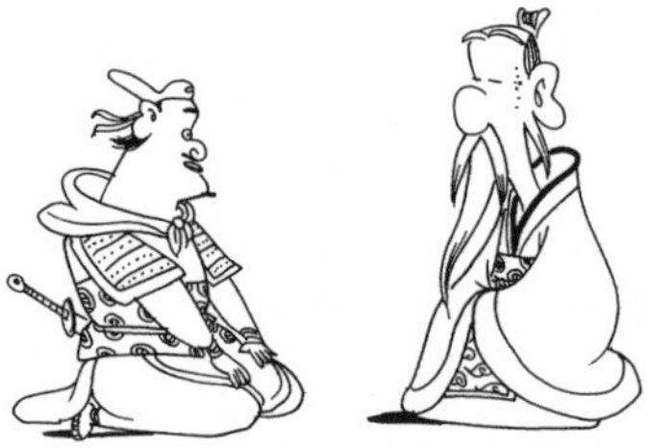

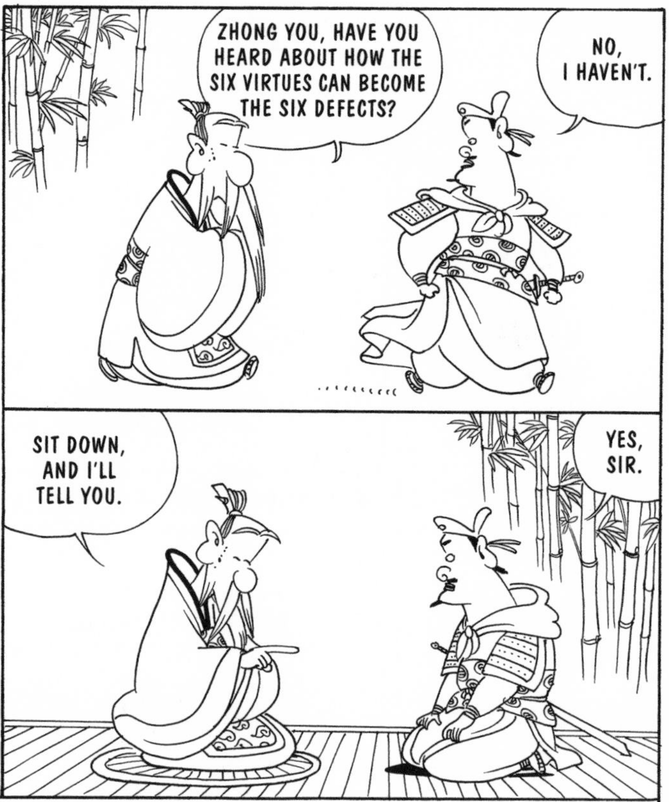
ZHONG YOU, HAVE YOU HEARD ABOUT HOW THE SIX VIRTUES CAN BECOME THE SIX DEFECTS?
NO, I HAVEN'T.
SIT DOWN, AND I'LL TELL YOU.
YES, SIR.

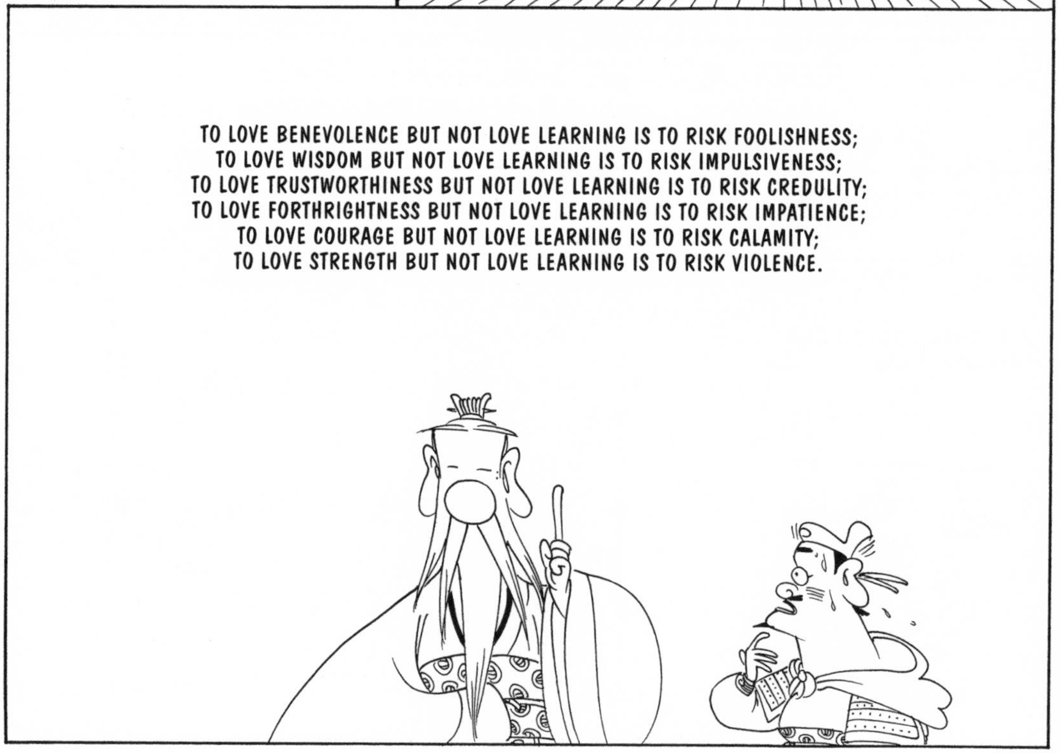
TO LOVE BENEVOLENCE BUT NOT LOVE LEARNING IS TO RISK FOOLISHNESS;
TO LOVE WISDOM BUT NOT LOVE LEARNING IS TO RISK IMPULSIVENESS;
TO LOVE TRUSTWORTHINESS BUT NOT LOVE LEARNING IS TO RISK CREDULITY;
TO LOVE FORTHRIGHTNESS BUT NOT LOVE LEARNING IS TO RISK IMPATIENCE;
TO LOVE COURAGE BUT NOT LOVE LEARNING IS TO RISK CALAMITY;
TO LOVE STRENGTH BUT NOT LOVE LEARNING IS TO RISK VIOLENCE.

17:12

THE BRAZEN BURGLAR

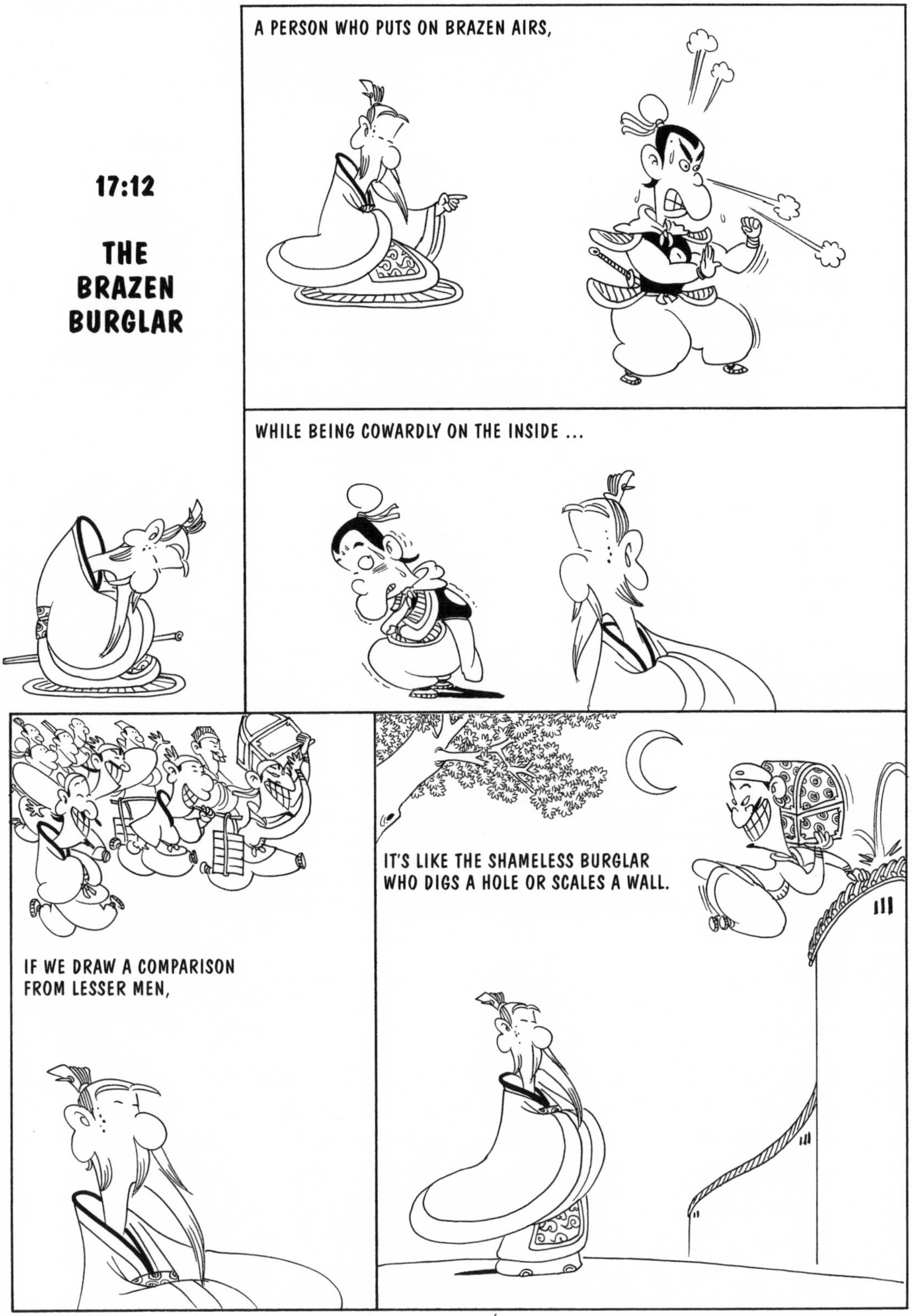

A PERSON WHO PUTS ON BRAZEN AIRS,
WHILE BEING COWARDLY ON THE INSIDE ...
IF WE DRAW A COMPARISON FROM LESSER MEN,
IT'S LIKE THE SHAMELESS BURGLAR WHO DIGS A HOLE OR SCALES A WALL.

子曰：「色厲而內荏，譬諸小人，其猶穿窬之盜也與？」

子曰：「鄉原、德之賊也。」

17:13

THE HOMETOWN BANDIT

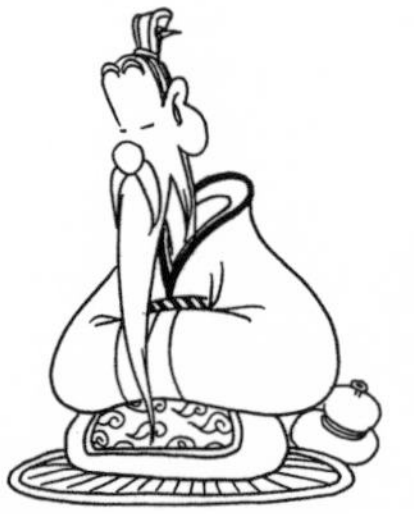

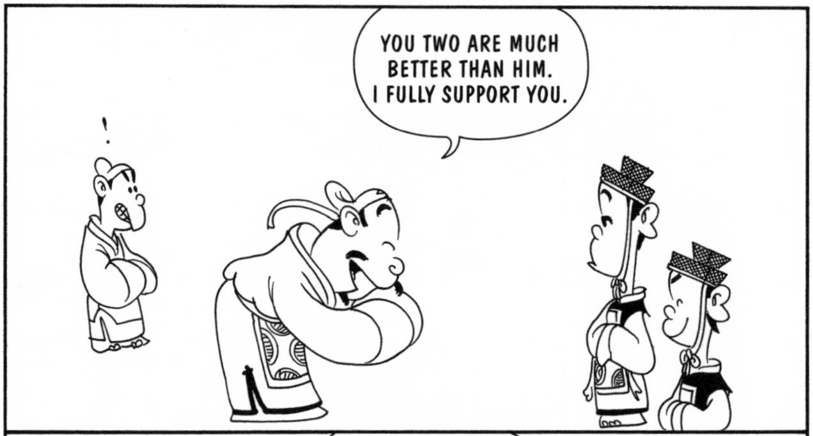
YOU TWO ARE MUCH BETTER THAN HIM. I FULLY SUPPORT YOU.
!

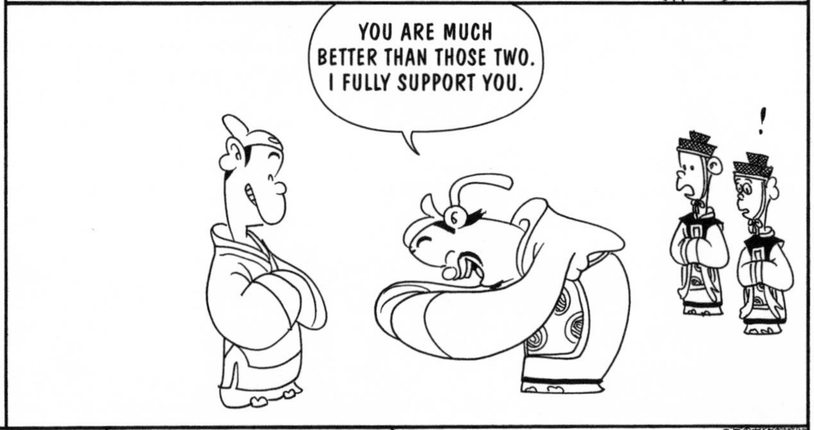
YOU ARE MUCH BETTER THAN THOSE TWO. I FULLY SUPPORT YOU.
!

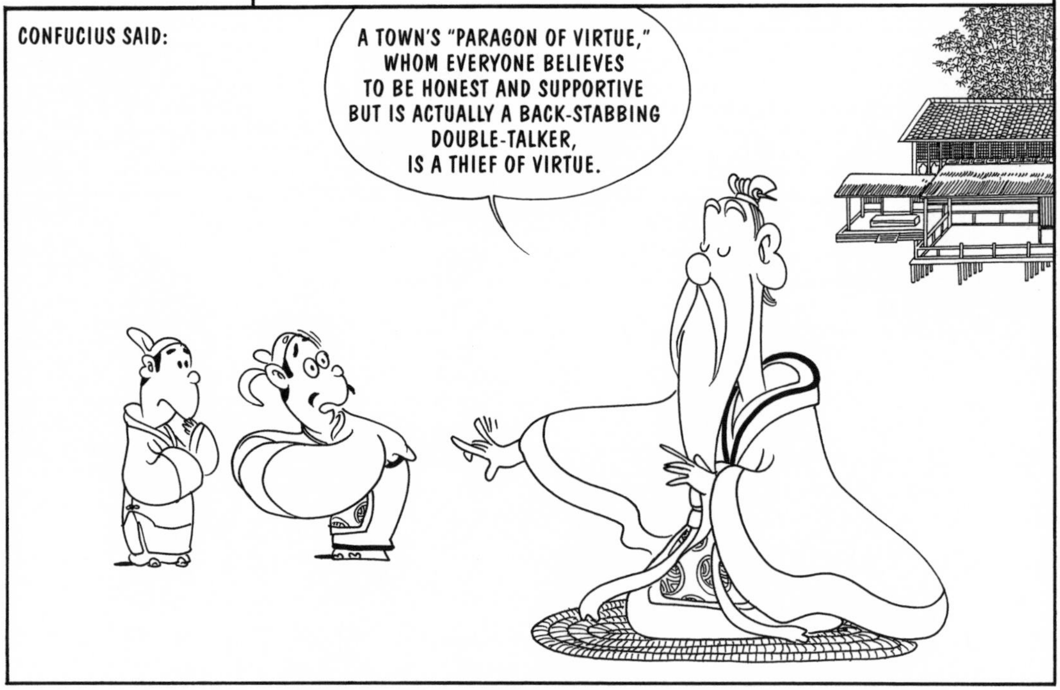
CONFUCIUS SAID:
A TOWN'S "PARAGON OF VIRTUE," WHOM EVERYONE BELIEVES TO BE HONEST AND SUPPORTIVE BUT IS ACTUALLY A BACK-STABBING DOUBLE-TALKER, IS A THIEF OF VIRTUE.

17:14

GOSSIP

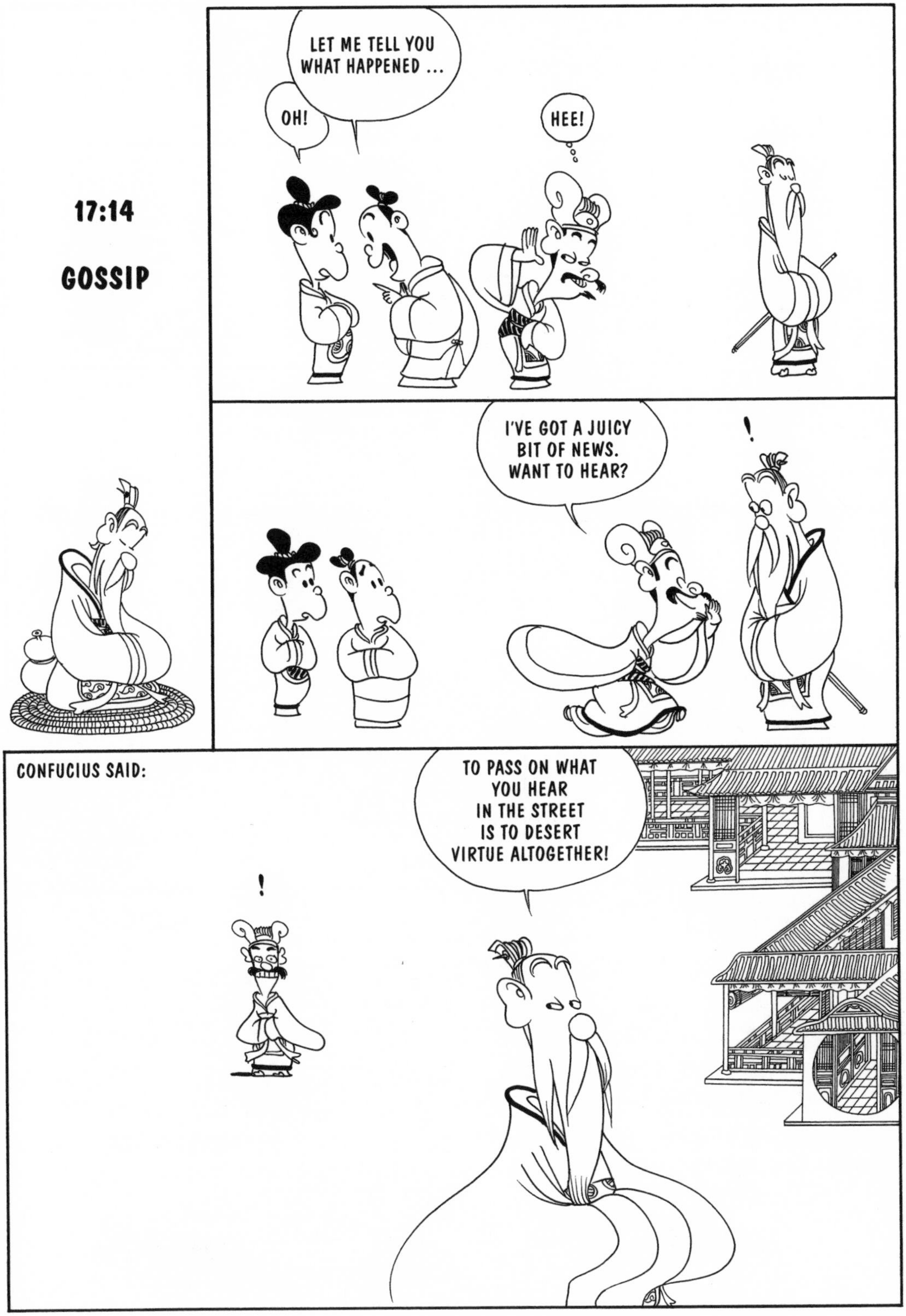
LET ME TELL YOU WHAT HAPPENED ...
OH!
HEE!
I'VE GOT A JUICY BIT OF NEWS. WANT TO HEAR?
!
CONFUCIUS SAID:
TO PASS ON WHAT YOU HEAR IN THE STREET IS TO DESERT VIRTUE ALTOGETHER!
!

子曰：「道聽而塗說，德之棄也。」

子曰：「鄙夫可與事君也與哉？其未得之也，患得之。既得之，患失之。苟患失之，無所不至矣。」

17:15

THE CORRUPT OFFICIAL

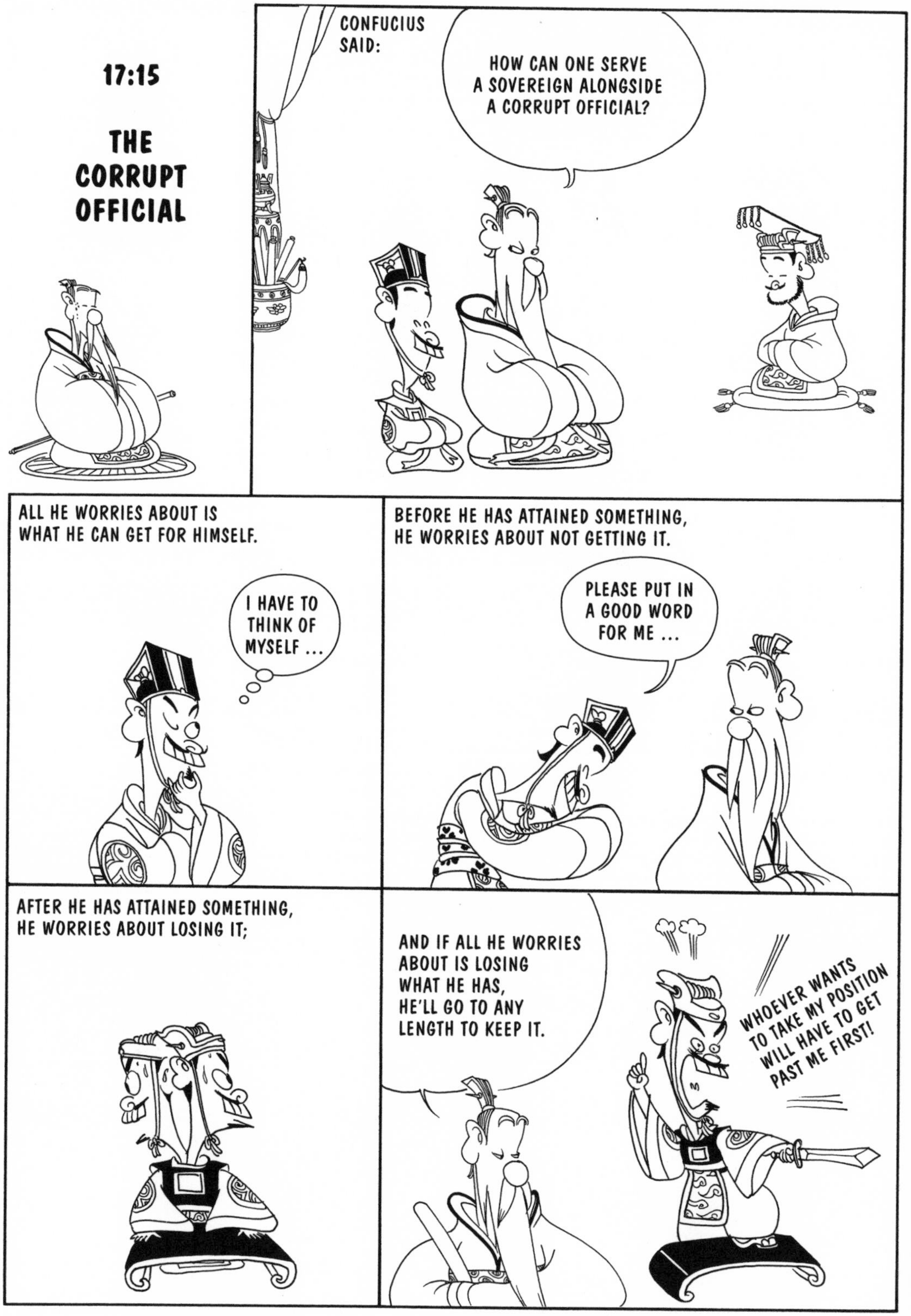
CONFUCIUS SAID:
HOW CAN ONE SERVE A SOVEREIGN ALONGSIDE A CORRUPT OFFICIAL?
ALL HE WORRIES ABOUT IS WHAT HE CAN GET FOR HIMSELF.
I HAVE TO THINK OF MYSELF ...
BEFORE HE HAS ATTAINED SOMETHING, HE WORRIES ABOUT NOT GETTING IT.
PLEASE PUT IN A GOOD WORD FOR ME ...
AFTER HE HAS ATTAINED SOMETHING, HE WORRIES ABOUT LOSING IT;
AND IF ALL HE WORRIES ABOUT IS LOSING WHAT HE HAS, HE'LL GO TO ANY LENGTH TO KEEP IT.
WHOEVER WANTS TO TAKE MY POSITION WILL HAVE TO GET PAST ME FIRST!

17:18

DETESTABLE CHANGES

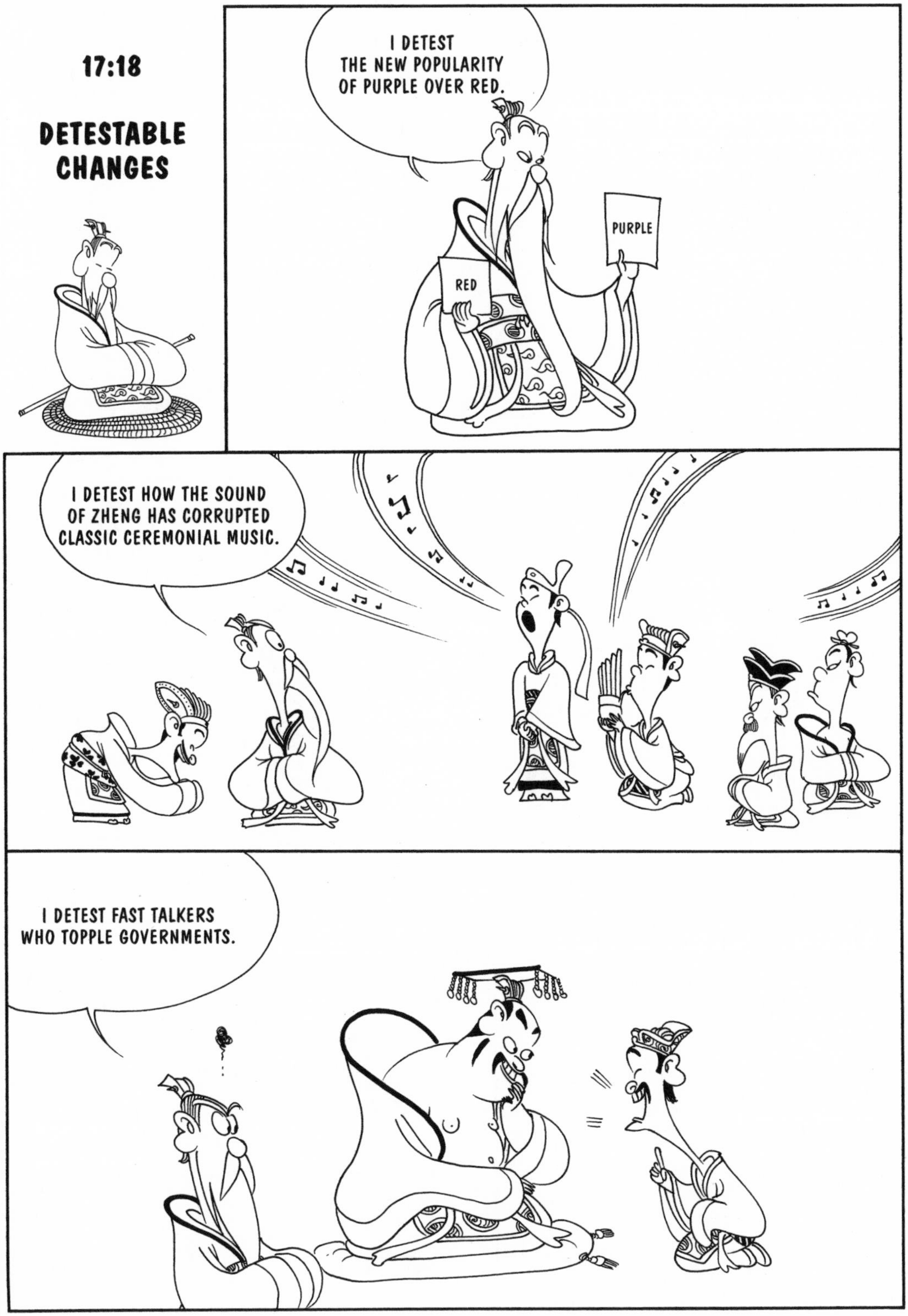

I DETEST THE NEW POPULARITY OF PURPLE OVER RED.
RED
PURPLE
I DETEST HOW THE SOUND OF ZHENG HAS CORRUPTED CLASSIC CEREMONIAL MUSIC.
I DETEST FAST TALKERS WHO TOPPLE GOVERNMENTS.

子曰：「惡紫之奪朱也，惡鄭聲之亂雅樂也，惡利口之覆邦家者。」

孺悲欲見孔子，孔子辭以疾。將命者出戶，取瑟而歌，使之聞之。

17:20

INDIRECT COMMUNICATION

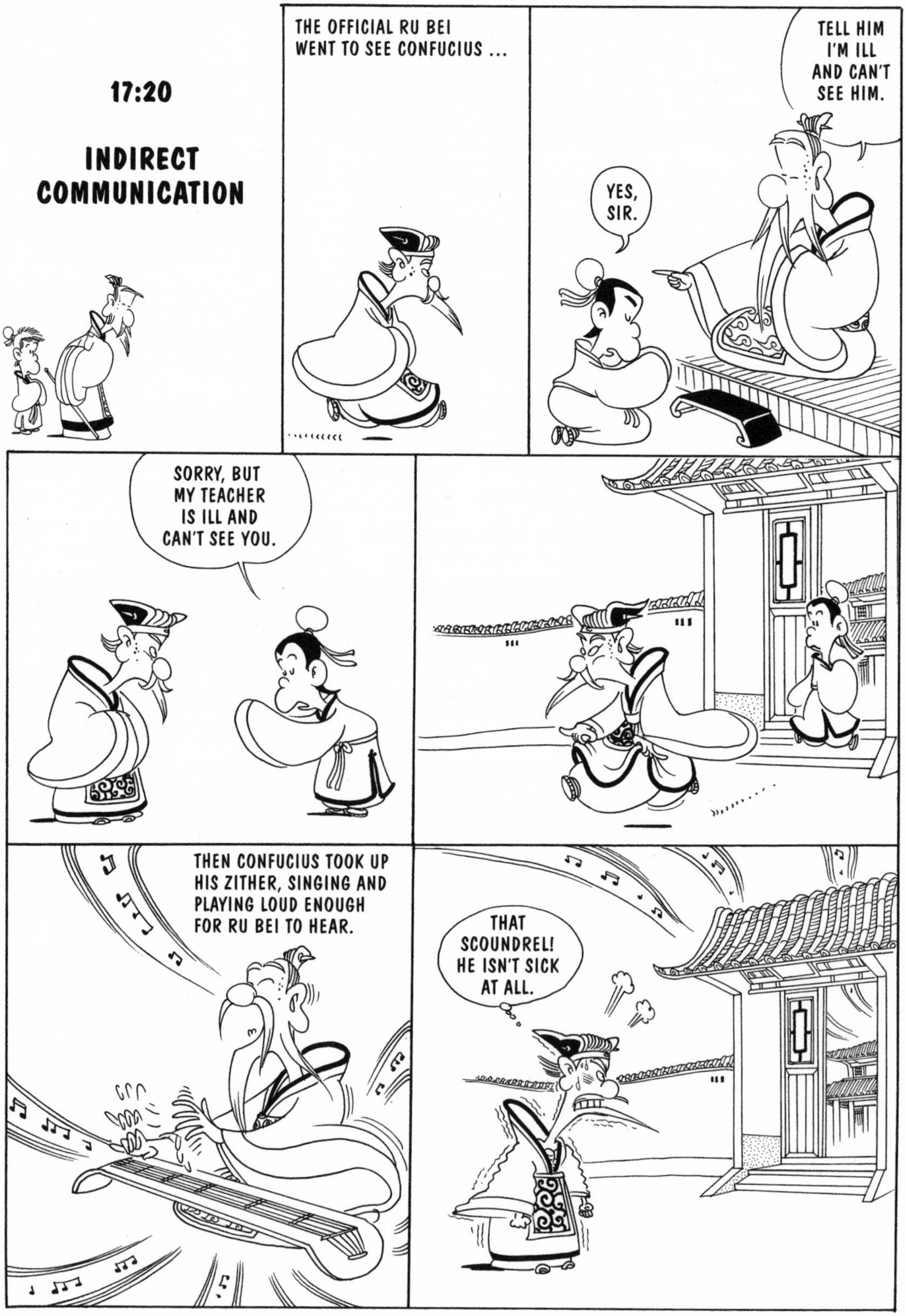

THE OFFICIAL RU BEI WENT TO SEE CONFUCIUS ...
TELL HIM I'M ILL AND CAN'T SEE HIM.
YES, SIR.
SORRY, BUT MY TEACHER IS ILL AND CAN'T SEE YOU.
THEN CONFUCIUS TOOK UP HIS ZITHER, SINGING AND PLAYING LOUD ENOUGH FOR RU BEI TO HEAR.
THAT SCOUNDREL! HE ISN'T SICK AT ALL.

17:22

PLAY GAMES

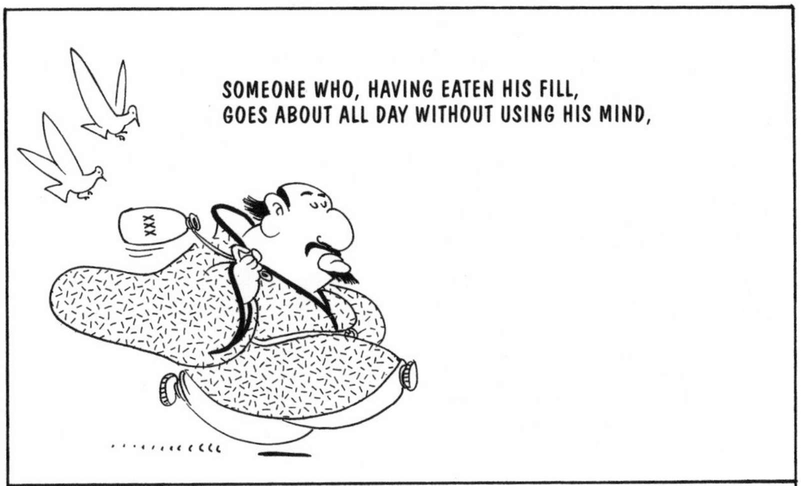
SOMEONE WHO, HAVING EATEN HIS FILL,
GOES ABOUT ALL DAY WITHOUT USING HIS MIND,
XXX

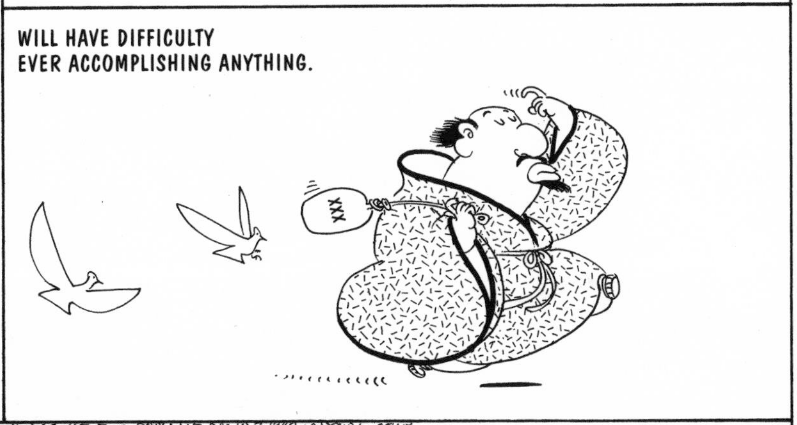
WILL HAVE DIFFICULTY
EVER ACCOMPLISHING ANYTHING.
XXX

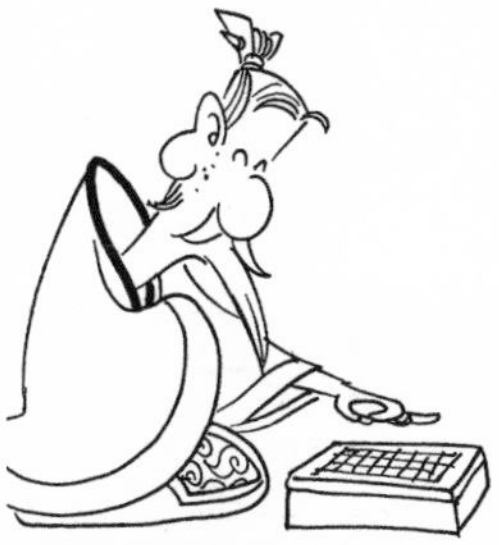

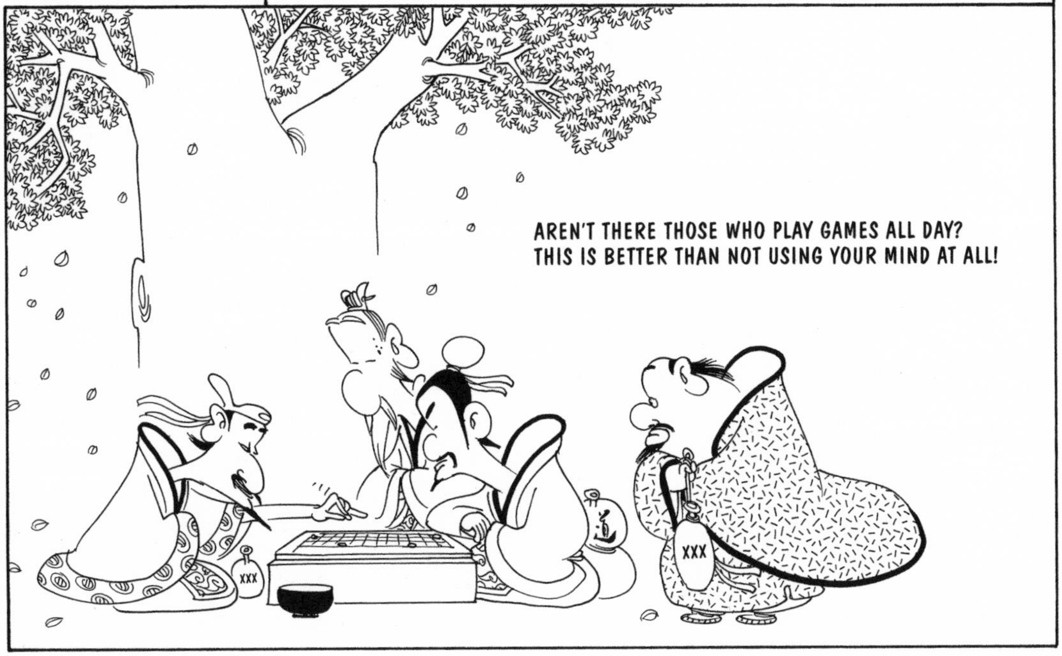
AREN'T THERE THOSE WHO PLAY GAMES ALL DAY?
THIS IS BETTER THAN NOT USING YOUR MIND AT ALL!
XXX
XXX

子曰：「飽食終日，無所用心，難矣哉！不有博弈者乎？為之，猶賢乎已。」

子曰：「唯女子與小人為難養也，近之則不孫，遠之則怨。」

17:25

MAIDS AND VALETS

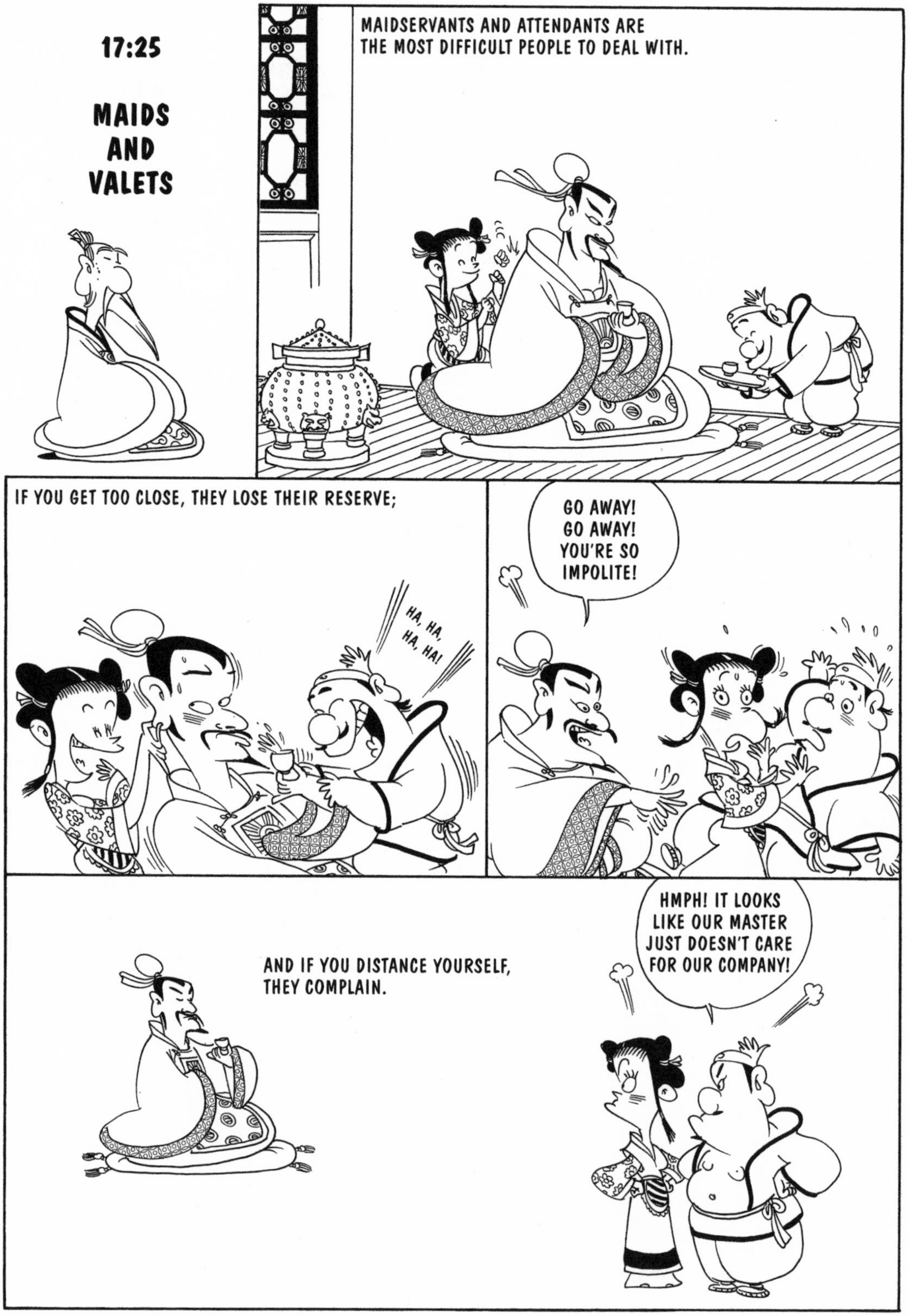
MAIDSERVANTS AND ATTENDANTS ARE THE MOST DIFFICULT PEOPLE TO DEAL WITH.
IF YOU GET TOO CLOSE, THEY LOSE THEIR RESERVE;
HA, HA, HA, HA!
GO AWAY! GO AWAY! YOU'RE SO IMPOLITE!
AND IF YOU DISTANCE YOURSELF, THEY COMPLAIN.
HMPH! IT LOOKS LIKE OUR MASTER JUST DOESN'T CARE FOR OUR COMPANY!

17:26

AN IMMATURE FORTY

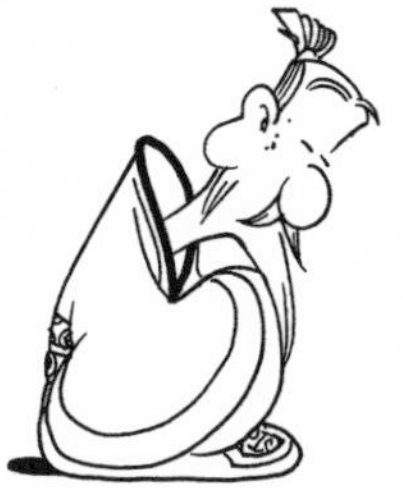

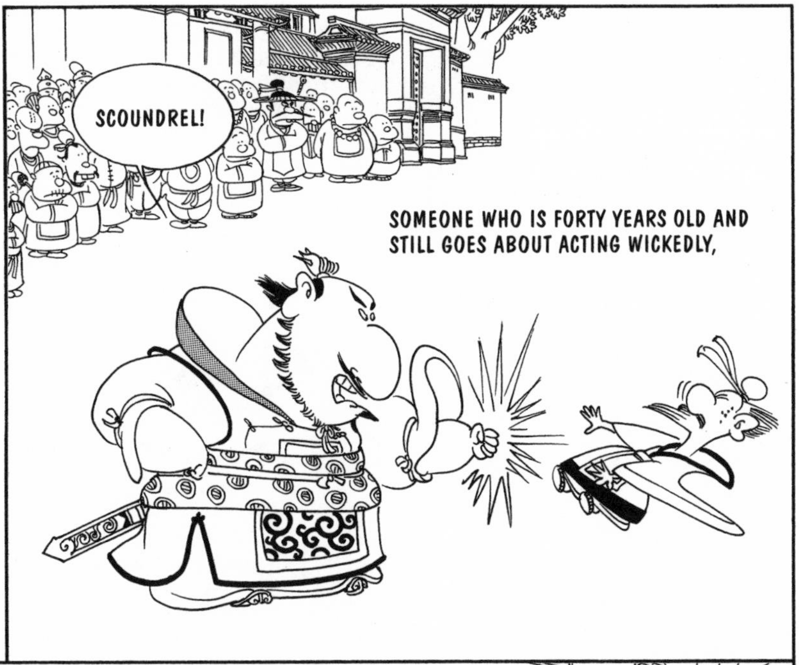
SCOUNDREL!
SOMEONE WHO IS FORTY YEARS OLD AND STILL GOES ABOUT ACTING WICKEDLY,

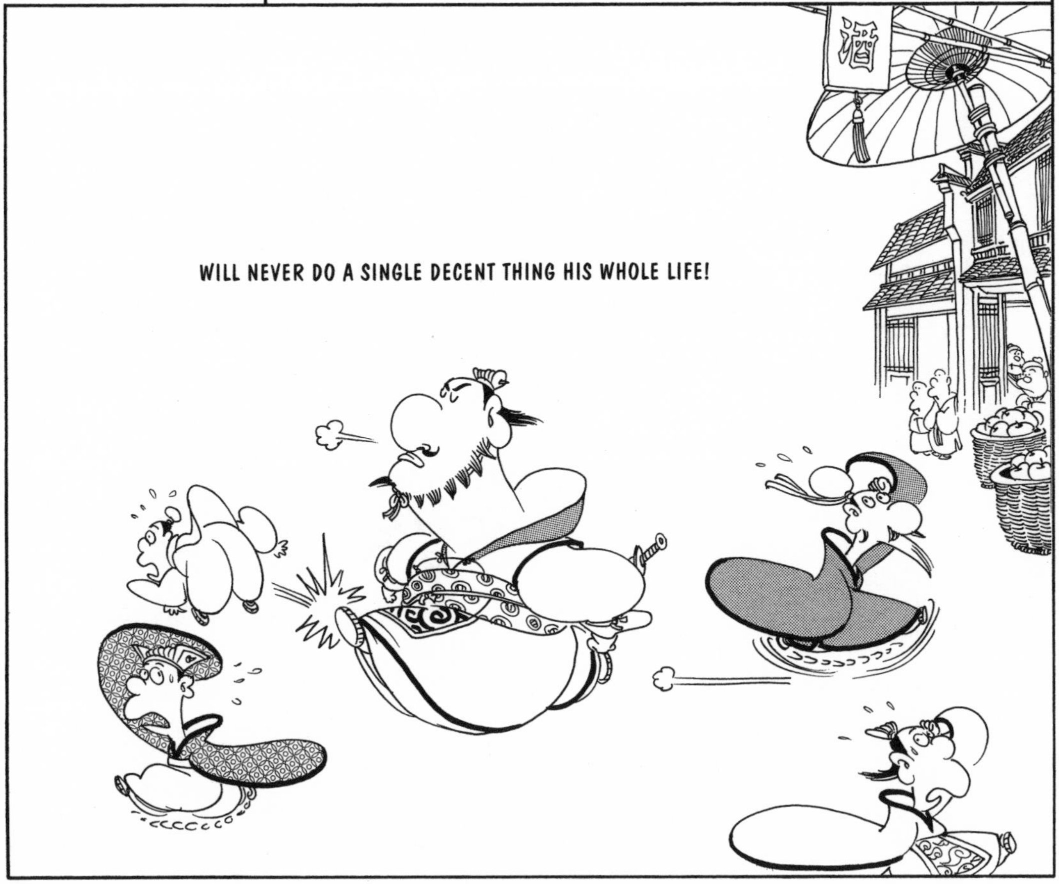
WILL NEVER DO A SINGLE DECENT THING HIS WHOLE LIFE!

子曰：「年四十而見惡焉，其終也已。」

微子去之，箕子為之奴，比干諫而死。孔子曰：「殷有三仁焉。」

18:1

SPEAKING TRUTH TO POWER

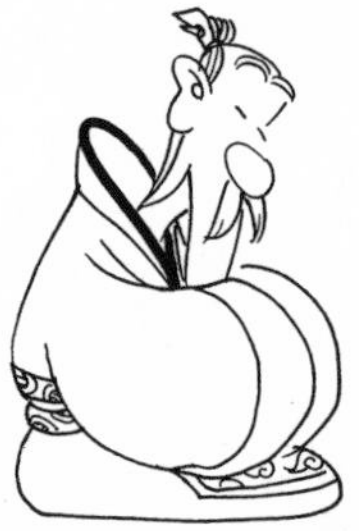

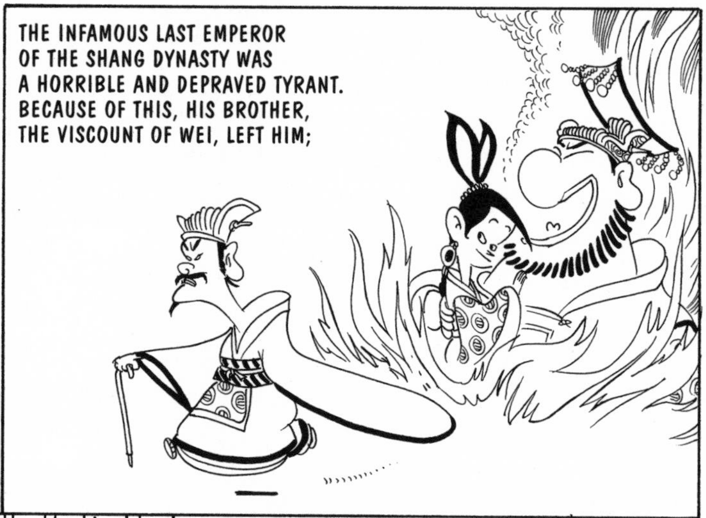
THE INFAMOUS LAST EMPEROR OF THE SHANG DYNASTY WAS A HORRIBLE AND DEPRAVED TYRANT. BECAUSE OF THIS, HIS BROTHER, THE VISCOUNT OF WEI, LEFT HIM;

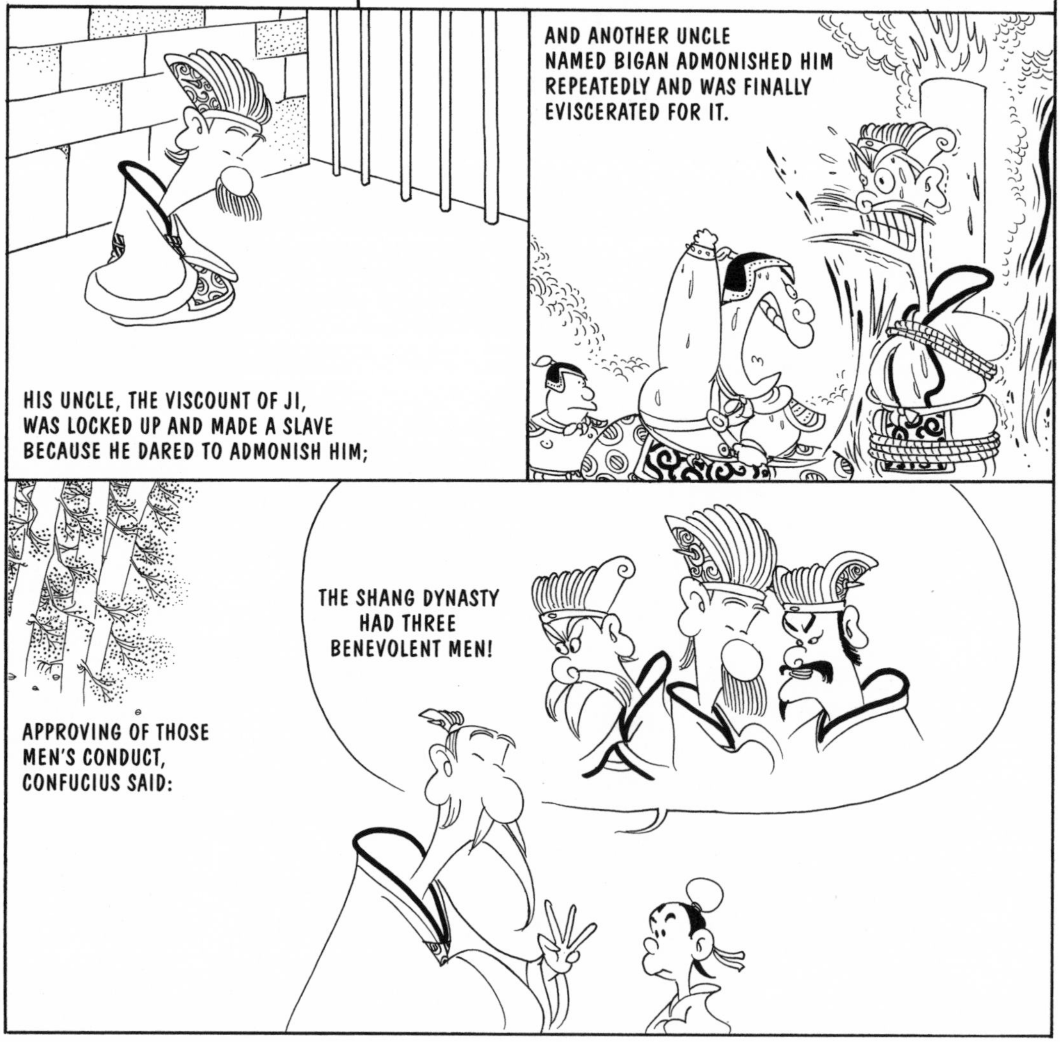
HIS UNCLE, THE VISCOUNT OF JI, WAS LOCKED UP AND MADE A SLAVE BECAUSE HE DARED TO ADMONISH HIM;
AND ANOTHER UNCLE NAMED BIGAN ADMONISHED HIM REPEATEDLY AND WAS FINALLY EVISCERATED FOR IT.
APPROVING OF THOSE MEN'S CONDUCT, CONFUCIUS SAID:
THE SHANG DYNASTY HAD THREE BENEVOLENT MEN!

18:5

CRAZY JIEYU

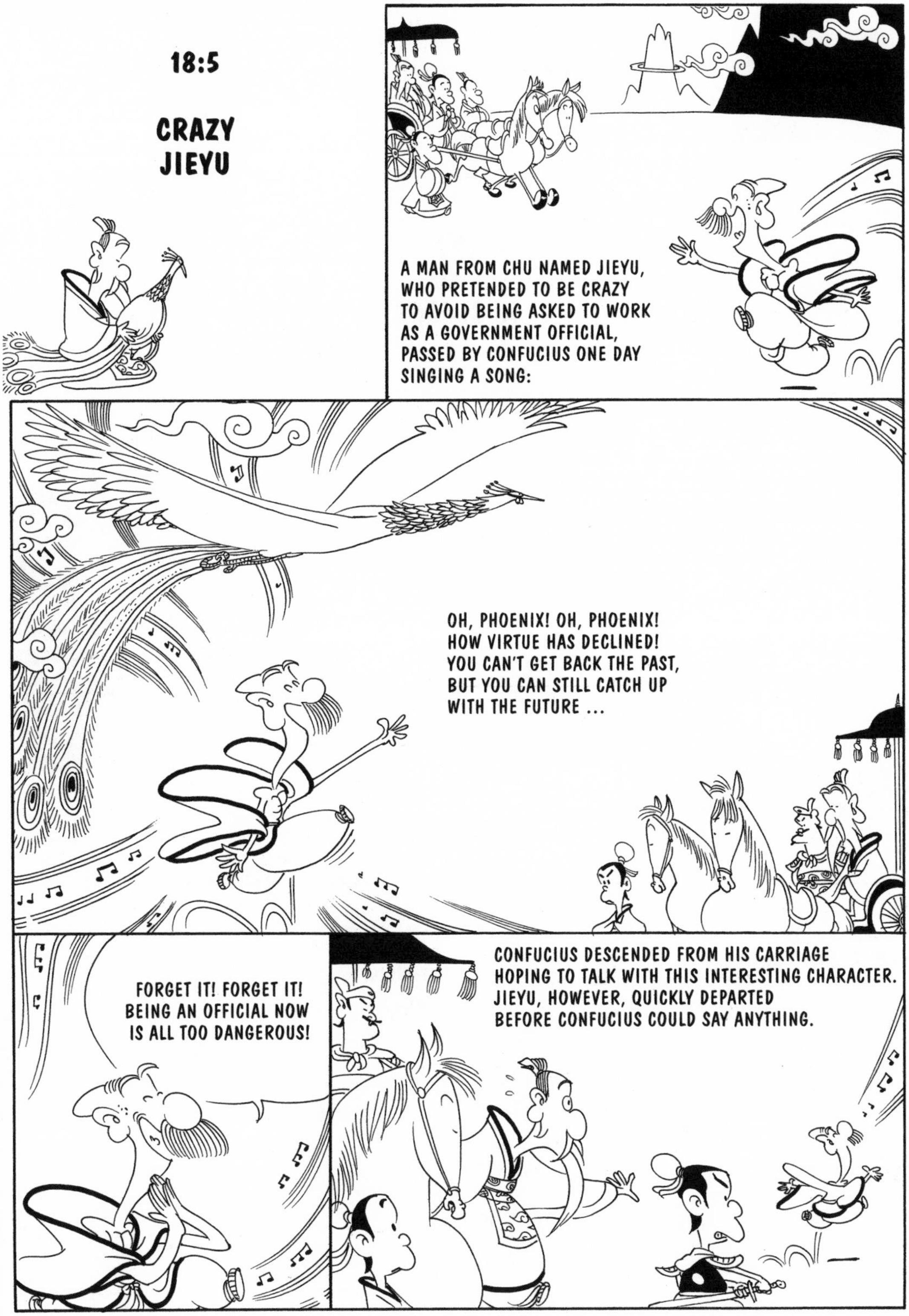
A MAN FROM CHU NAMED JIEYU, WHO PRETENDED TO BE CRAZY TO AVOID BEING ASKED TO WORK AS A GOVERNMENT OFFICIAL, PASSED BY CONFUCIUS ONE DAY SINGING A SONG:
OH, PHOENIX! OH, PHOENIX! HOW VIRTUE HAS DECLINED! YOU CAN'T GET BACK THE PAST, BUT YOU CAN STILL CATCH UP WITH THE FUTURE ...
FORGET IT! FORGET IT! BEING AN OFFICIAL NOW IS ALL TOO DANGEROUS!
CONFUCIUS DESCENDED FROM HIS CARRIAGE HOPING TO TALK WITH THIS INTERESTING CHARACTER. JIEYU, HOWEVER, QUICKLY DEPARTED BEFORE CONFUCIUS COULD SAY ANYTHING.

楚狂接輿歌而過孔子曰：「鳳兮鳳兮！何德之衰？往者不可諫，來者猶可追。已而，已而！今之從政者殆而！」

孔子下，欲與之言。趨而辟之，不得與之言。

長沮、桀溺耦而耕，孔子過之，使子路問津焉。
長沮曰：「夫執輿者為誰？」

18:6

THE TWO RECLUSES

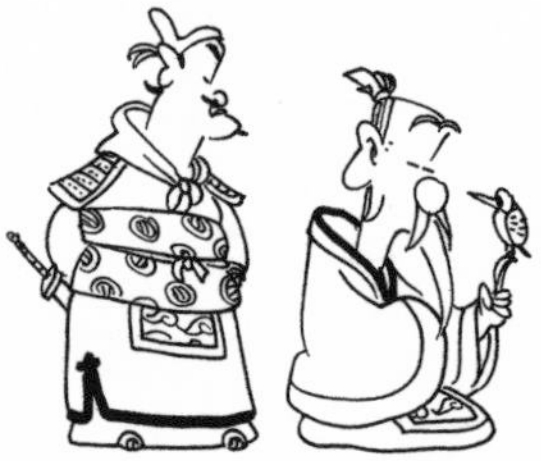

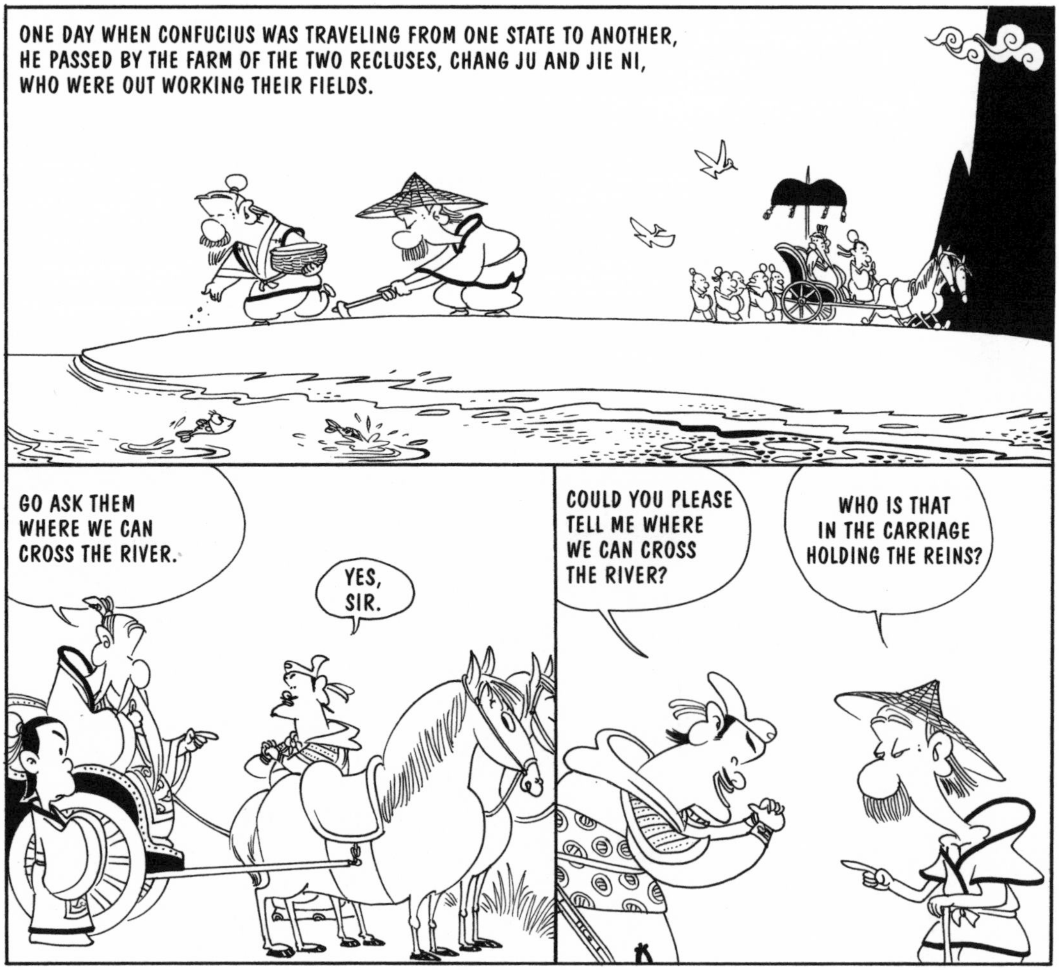

ONE DAY WHEN CONFUCIUS WAS TRAVELING FROM ONE STATE TO ANOTHER, HE PASSED BY THE FARM OF THE TWO RECLUSES, CHANG JU AND JIE NI, WHO WERE OUT WORKING THEIR FIELDS.
GO ASK THEM WHERE WE CAN CROSS THE RIVER.
YES, SIR.
COULD YOU PLEASE TELL ME WHERE WE CAN CROSS THE RIVER?
WHO IS THAT IN THE CARRIAGE HOLDING THE REINS?

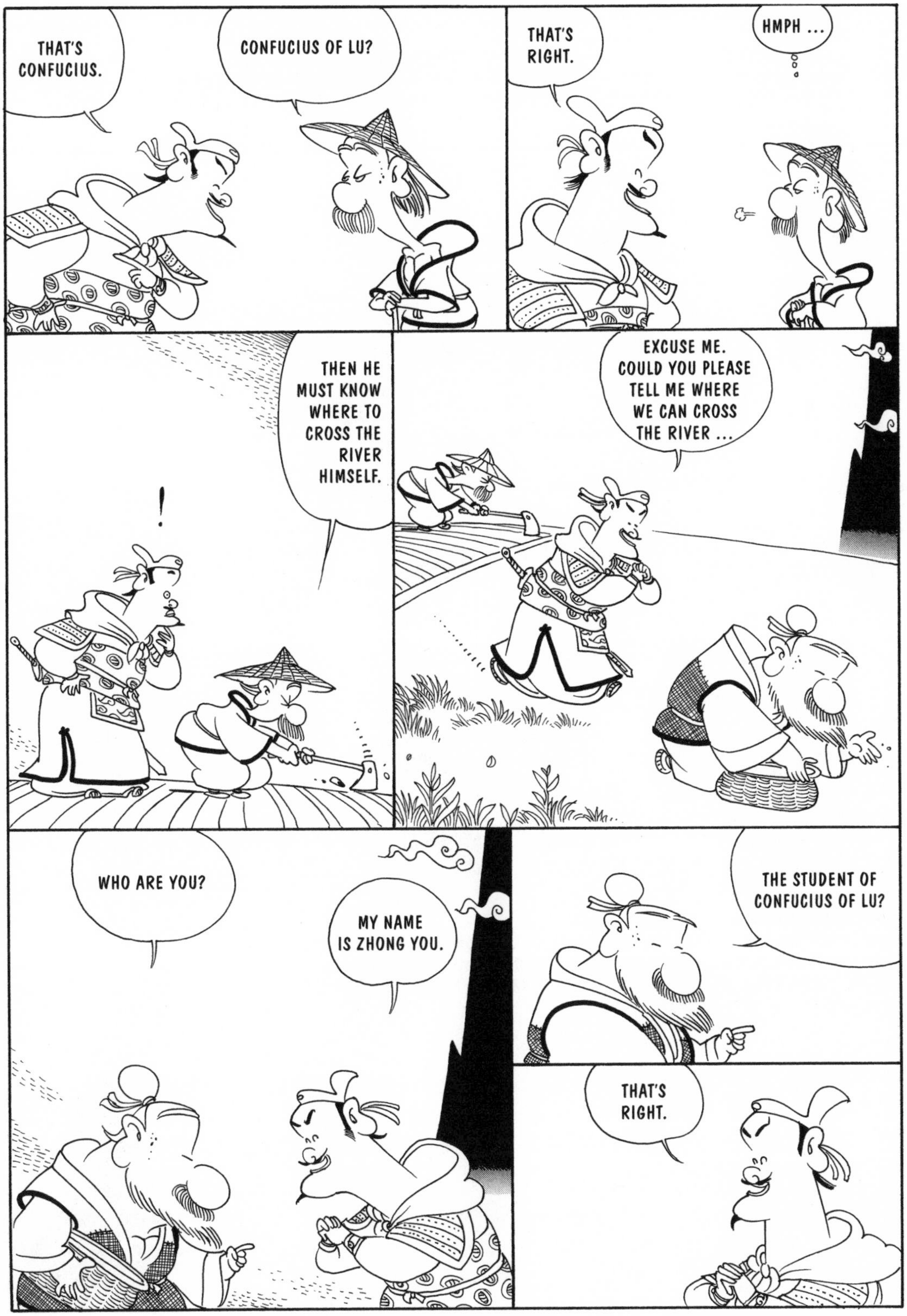
THAT'S CONFUCIUS.
CONFUCIUS OF LU?
THAT'S RIGHT.
HMPH ...
THEN HE MUST KNOW WHERE TO CROSS THE RIVER HIMSELF.
!
EXCUSE ME. COULD YOU PLEASE TELL ME WHERE WE CAN CROSS THE RIVER ...
WHO ARE YOU?
MY NAME IS ZHONG YOU.
THE STUDENT OF CONFUCIUS OF LU?
THAT'S RIGHT.

子路曰：「為孔丘。」曰：「是魯孔丘與？」曰：「是也。」曰：「是知津矣。」
問於桀溺。桀溺曰：「子為誰？」曰：「為仲由。」曰：「是魯孔丘之徒與？」對曰：「然。」

曰：「滔滔者天下皆是也，而誰以易之？且而與其從辟人之士也，豈若從辟世之士哉？」耰而不輟。
子路行以告。
夫子憮然曰：「鳥獸不可與同群，吾非斯人之徒與而誰與？天下有道，丘不與易也。」

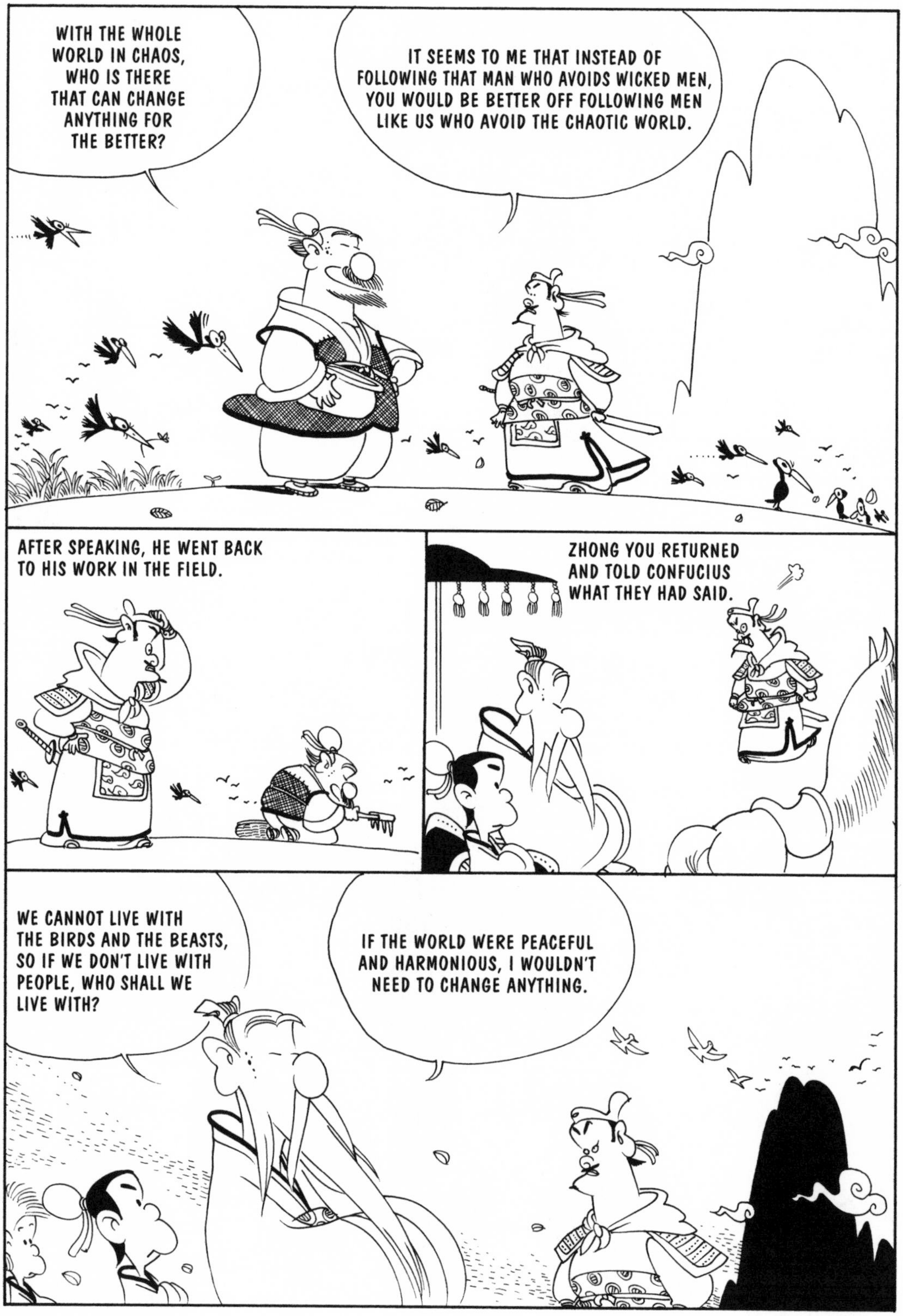

WITH THE WHOLE WORLD IN CHAOS, WHO IS THERE THAT CAN CHANGE ANYTHING FOR THE BETTER?
IT SEEMS TO ME THAT INSTEAD OF FOLLOWING THAT MAN WHO AVOIDS WICKED MEN, YOU WOULD BE BETTER OFF FOLLOWING MEN LIKE US WHO AVOID THE CHAOTIC WORLD.
AFTER SPEAKING, HE WENT BACK TO HIS WORK IN THE FIELD.
ZHONG YOU RETURNED AND TOLD CONFUCIUS WHAT THEY HAD SAID.
WE CANNOT LIVE WITH THE BIRDS AND THE BEASTS, SO IF WE DON'T LIVE WITH PEOPLE, WHO SHALL WE LIVE WITH?
IF THE WORLD WERE PEACEFUL AND HARMONIOUS, I WOULDN'T NEED TO CHANGE ANYTHING.

19:1

BE MINDFUL

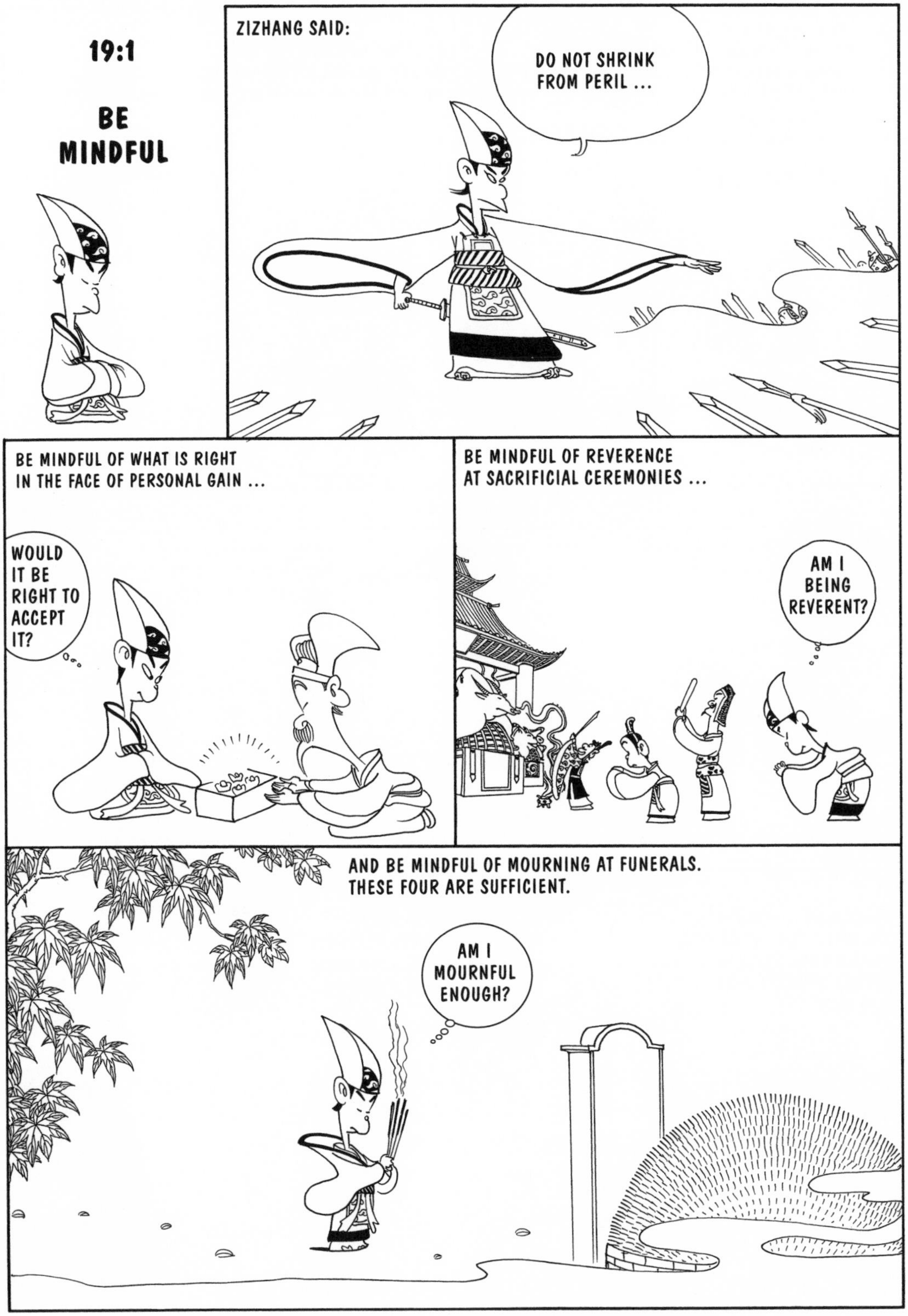
ZIZHANG SAID:
DO NOT SHRINK FROM PERIL ...
BE MINDFUL OF WHAT IS RIGHT IN THE FACE OF PERSONAL GAIN ...
WOULD IT BE RIGHT TO ACCEPT IT?
BE MINDFUL OF REVERENCE AT SACRIFICIAL CEREMONIES ...
AM I BEING REVERENT?
AND BE MINDFUL OF MOURNING AT FUNERALS. THESE FOUR ARE SUFFICIENT.
AM I MOURNFUL ENOUGH?

子張曰：「士見危致命，見得思義，祭思敬，喪思哀，其可已矣。」

子夏曰：「日知其所亡，月無忘其所能，可謂好學也已矣。」

19:5

LOVE OF LEARNING

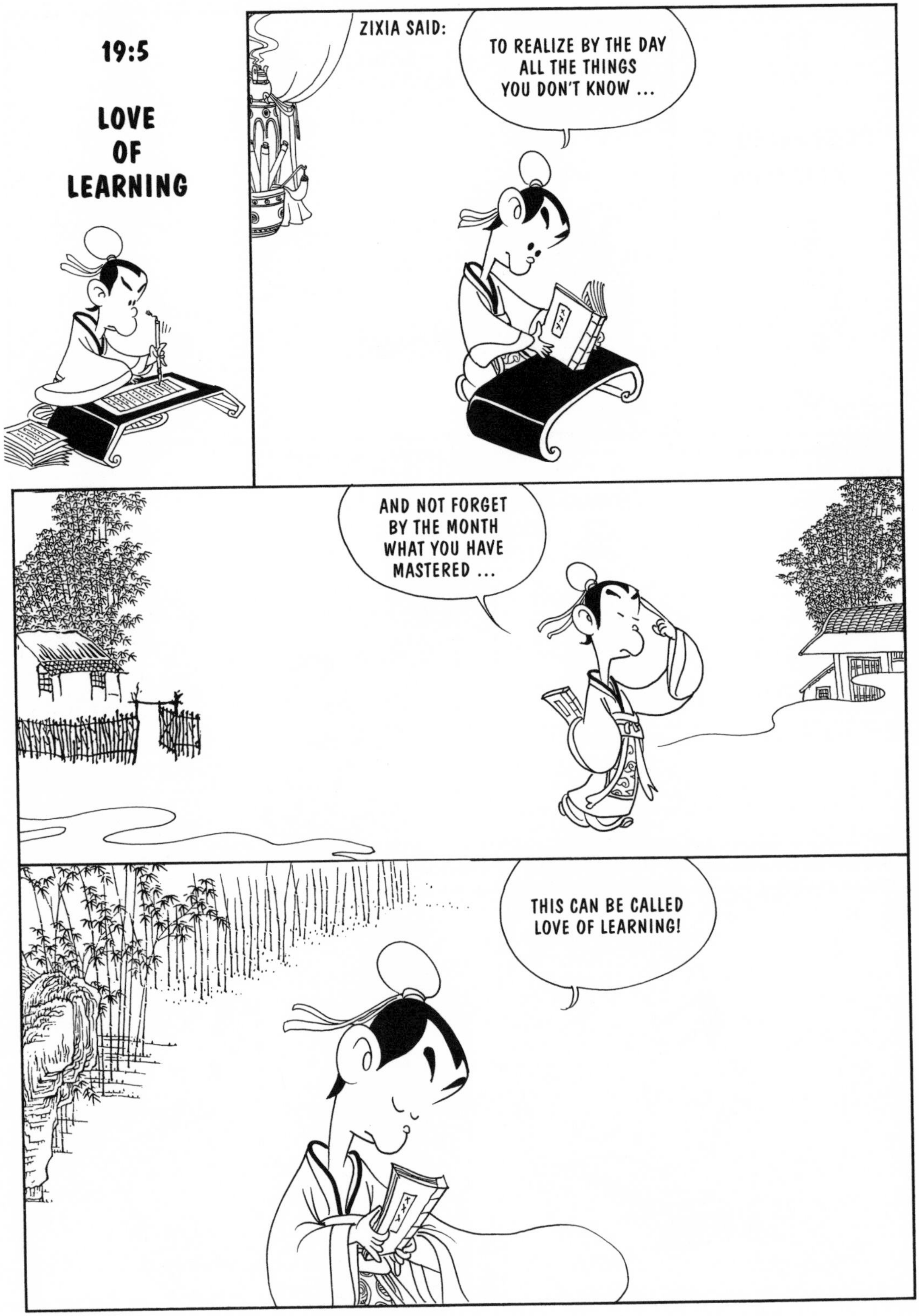

ZIXIA SAID:
TO REALIZE BY THE DAY ALL THE THINGS YOU DON'T KNOW ...
AND NOT FORGET BY THE MONTH WHAT YOU HAVE MASTERED ...
THIS CAN BE CALLED LOVE OF LEARNING!

19:6

BENEVOLENCE REALIZED

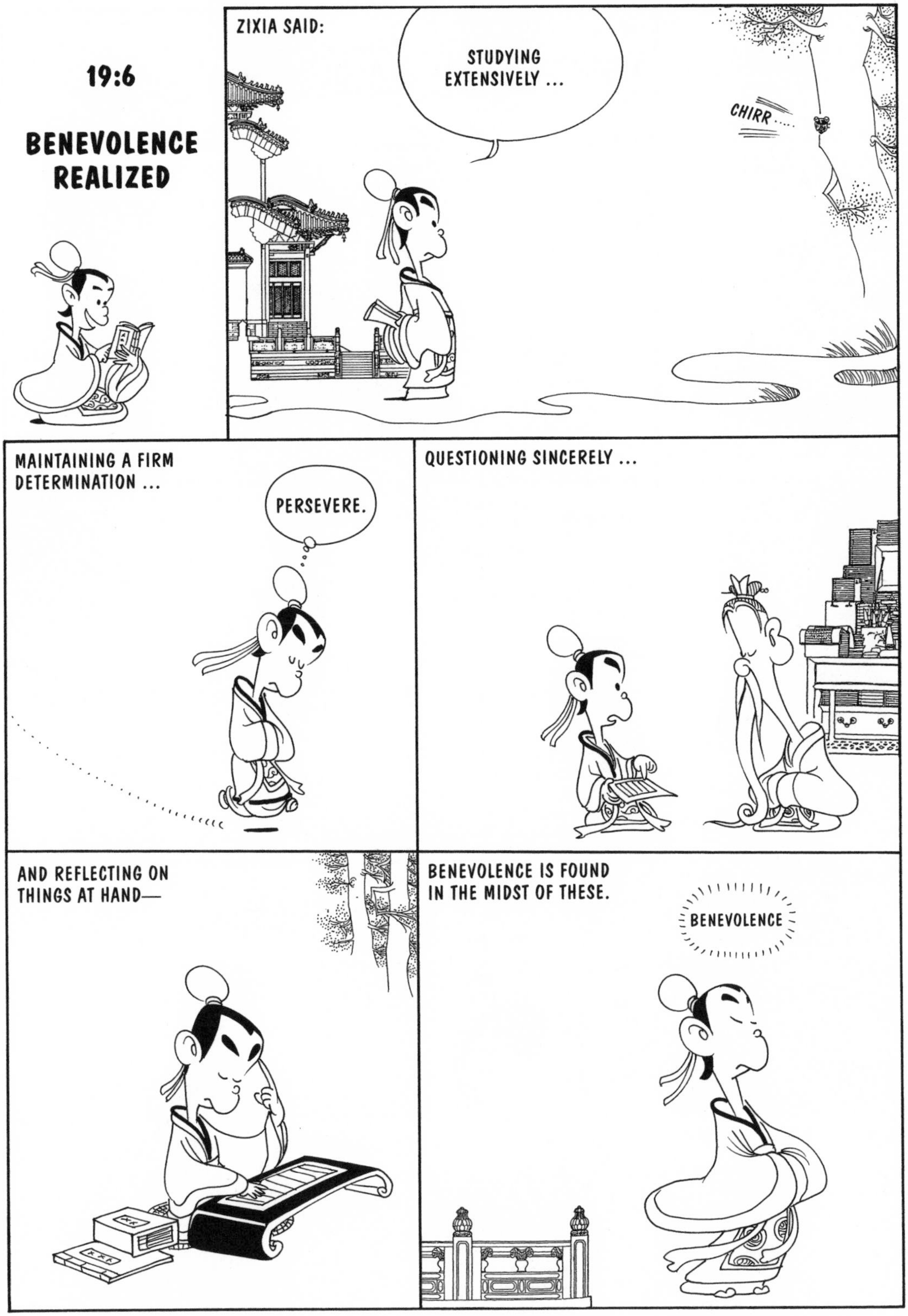
ZIXIA SAID:
STUDYING EXTENSIVELY ...
CHIRR ...
MAINTAINING A FIRM DETERMINATION ...
PERSEVERE.
QUESTIONING SINCERELY ...
AND REFLECTING ON THINGS AT HAND—
BENEVOLENCE IS FOUND IN THE MIDST OF THESE.
BENEVOLENCE

子夏曰：「博學而篤志，切問而近思，仁在其中矣。」

子夏曰：「君子信而後勞其民；未信，則以為厲己也。信而後諫；未信，則以為謗己也。」

19:10

EARNING TRUST

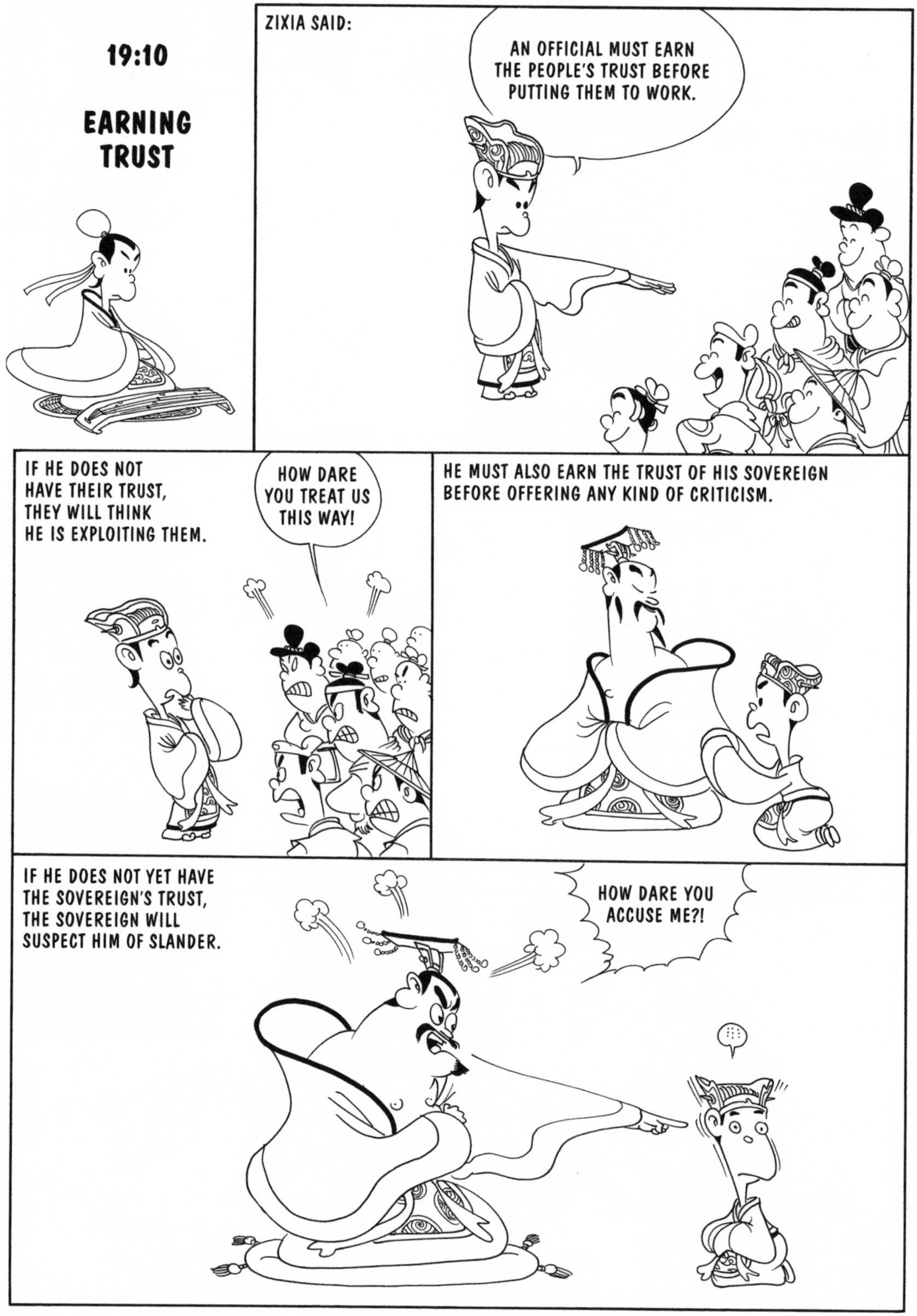
ZIXIA SAID:
AN OFFICIAL MUST EARN THE PEOPLE'S TRUST BEFORE PUTTING THEM TO WORK.
IF HE DOES NOT HAVE THEIR TRUST, THEY WILL THINK HE IS EXPLOITING THEM.
HOW DARE YOU TREAT US THIS WAY!
HE MUST ALSO EARN THE TRUST OF HIS SOVEREIGN BEFORE OFFERING ANY KIND OF CRITICISM.
IF HE DOES NOT YET HAVE THE SOVEREIGN'S TRUST, THE SOVEREIGN WILL SUSPECT HIM OF SLANDER.
HOW DARE YOU ACCUSE ME?!

19:11

CROSSING THE LINE

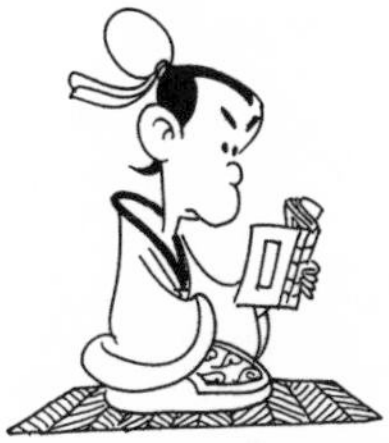

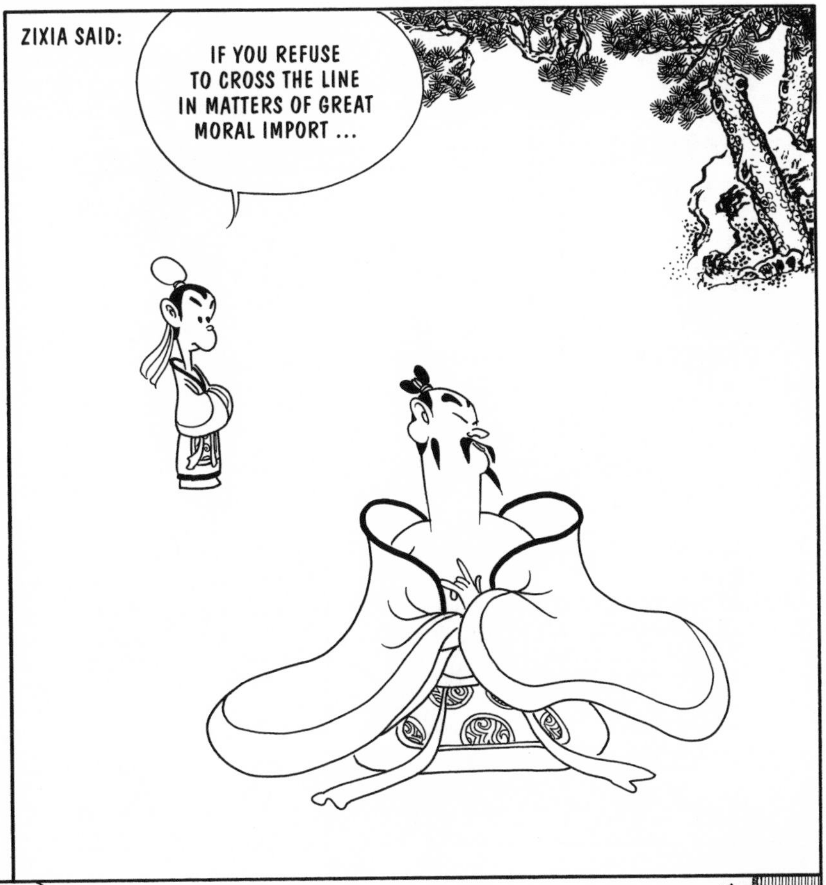
ZIXIA SAID:
IF YOU REFUSE TO CROSS THE LINE IN MATTERS OF GREAT MORAL IMPORT ...

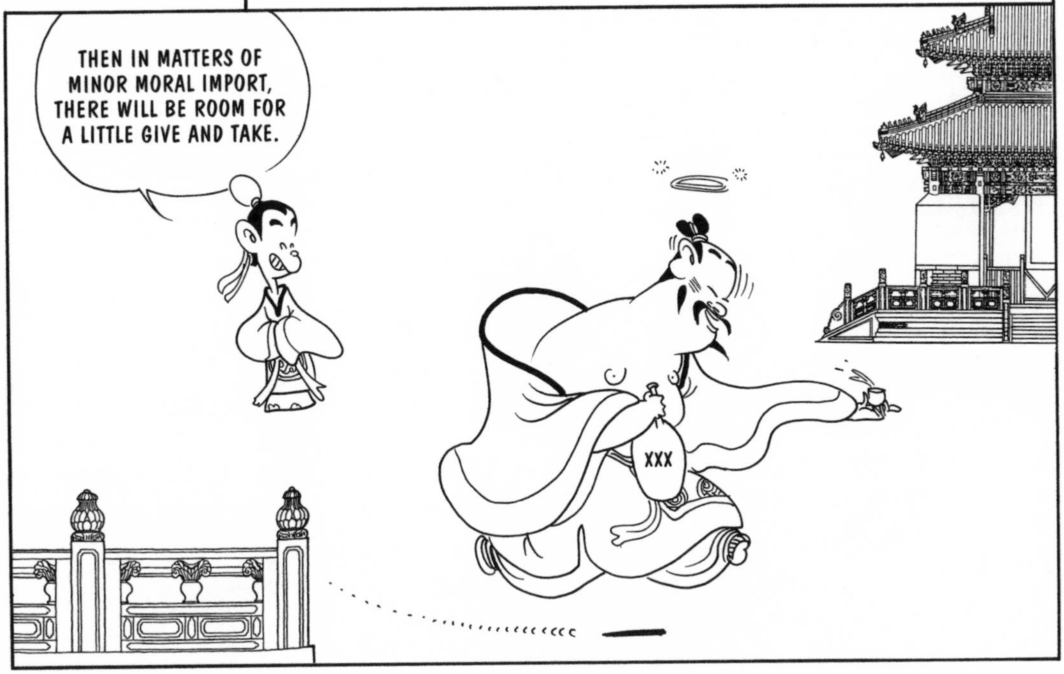
THEN IN MATTERS OF MINOR MORAL IMPORT, THERE WILL BE ROOM FOR A LITTLE GIVE AND TAKE.
XXX

子夏曰：「大德不踰閑，小德出入可也。」

子貢曰：「君子之過也，如日月之食焉：過也，人皆見之；更也，人皆仰之。」

19:21

BEING AN EXAMPLE

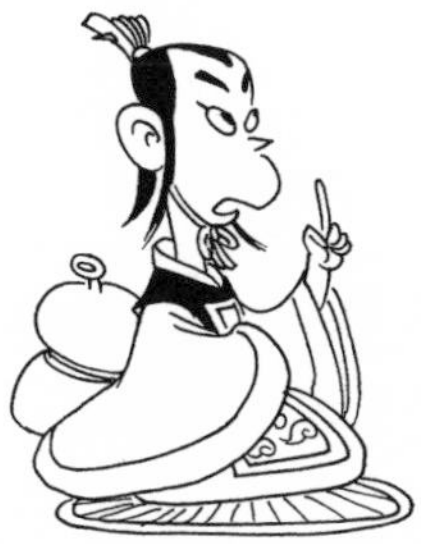

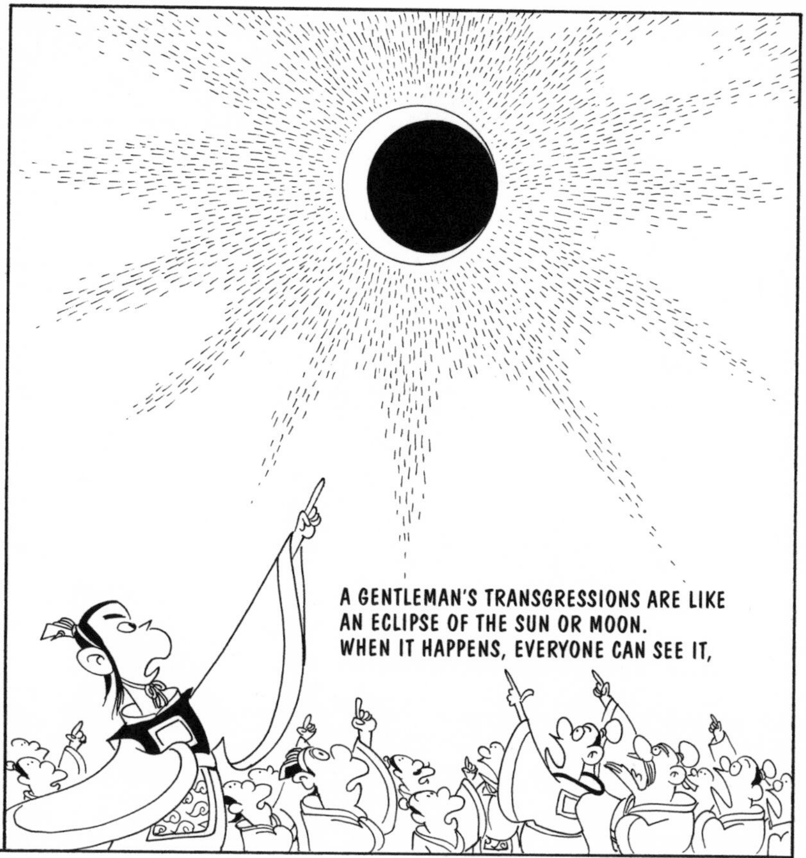
A GENTLEMAN'S TRANSGRESSIONS ARE LIKE AN ECLIPSE OF THE SUN OR MOON. WHEN IT HAPPENS, EVERYONE CAN SEE IT,

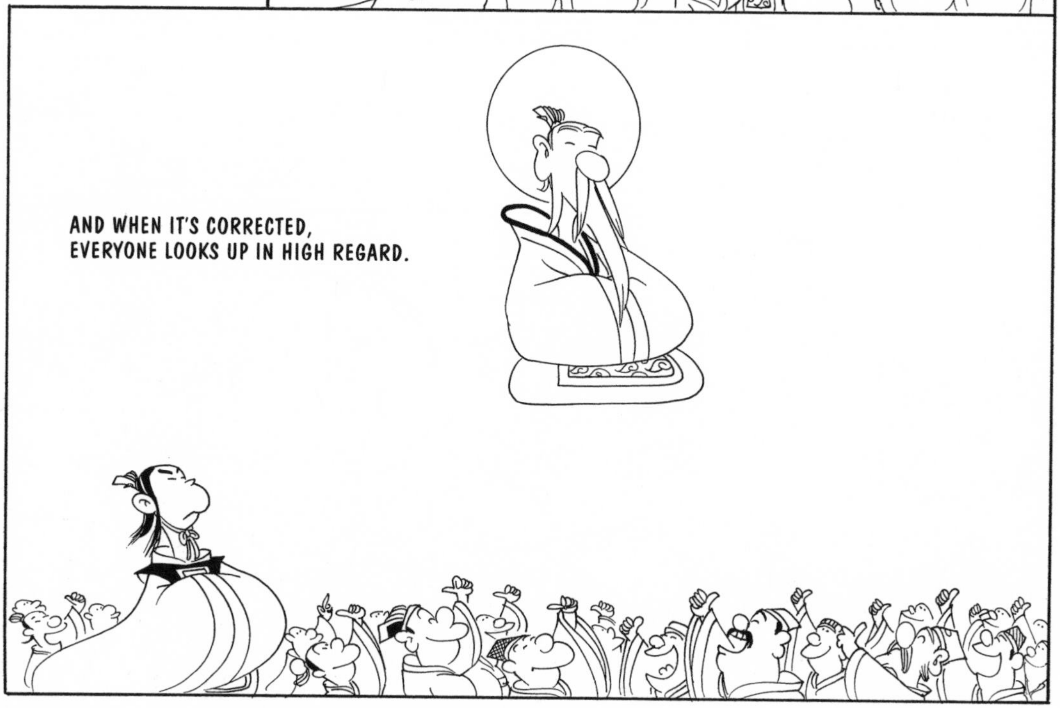
AND WHEN IT'S CORRECTED, EVERYONE LOOKS UP IN HIGH REGARD.

After Confucius

孔子葬魯城北泗上，弟子皆服三年。三年心喪畢，相訣而去，則哭，各復盡哀；或復留。

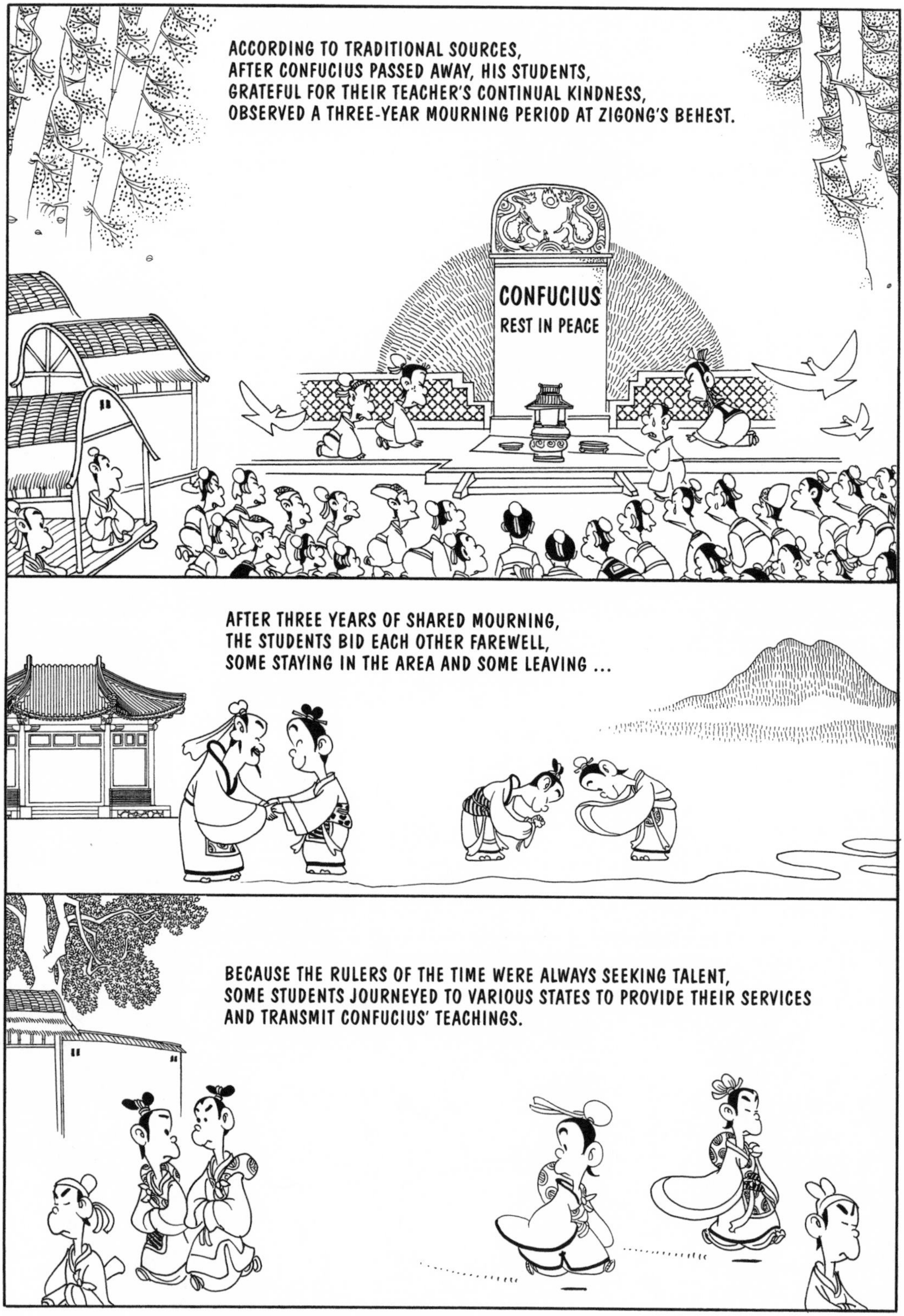
ACCORDING TO TRADITIONAL SOURCES,
AFTER CONFUCIUS PASSED AWAY, HIS STUDENTS,
GRATEFUL FOR THEIR TEACHER'S CONTINUAL KINDNESS,
OBSERVED A THREE-YEAR MOURNING PERIOD AT ZIGONG'S BEHEST.
CONFUCIUS
REST IN PEACE
AFTER THREE YEARS OF SHARED MOURNING,
THE STUDENTS BID EACH OTHER FAREWELL,
SOME STAYING IN THE AREA AND SOME LEAVING ...
BECAUSE THE RULERS OF THE TIME WERE ALWAYS SEEKING TALENT,
SOME STUDENTS JOURNEYED TO VARIOUS STATES TO PROVIDE THEIR SERVICES
AND TRANSMIT CONFUCIUS' TEACHINGS.

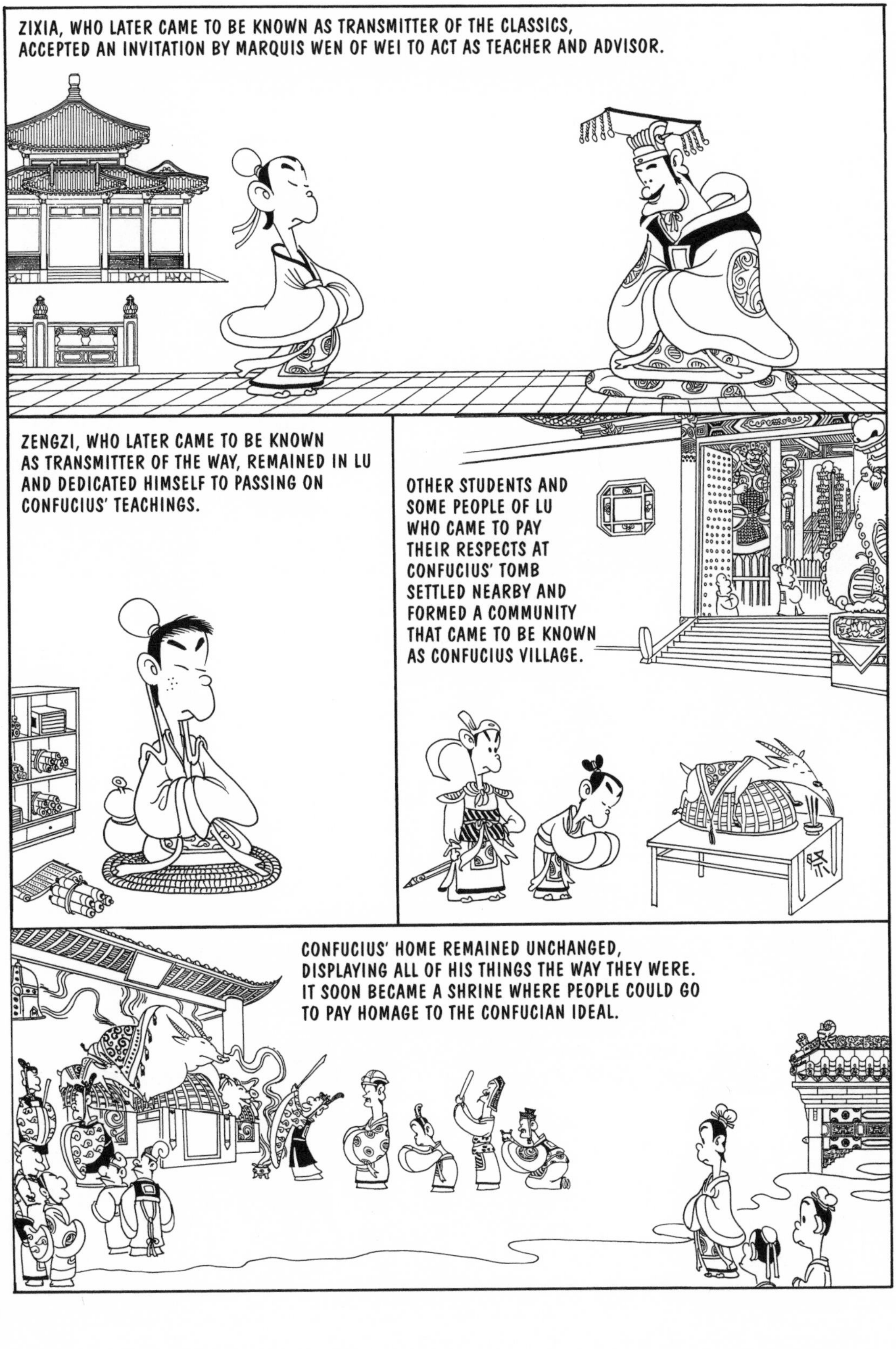
ZIXIA, WHO LATER CAME TO BE KNOWN AS TRANSMITTER OF THE CLASSICS, ACCEPTED AN INVITATION BY MARQUIS WEN OF WEI TO ACT AS TEACHER AND ADVISOR.
ZENGZI, WHO LATER CAME TO BE KNOWN AS TRANSMITTER OF THE WAY, REMAINED IN LU AND DEDICATED HIMSELF TO PASSING ON CONFUCIUS' TEACHINGS.
OTHER STUDENTS AND SOME PEOPLE OF LU WHO CAME TO PAY THEIR RESPECTS AT CONFUCIUS' TOMB SETTLED NEARBY AND FORMED A COMMUNITY THAT CAME TO BE KNOWN AS CONFUCIUS VILLAGE.
祭
CONFUCIUS' HOME REMAINED UNCHANGED, DISPLAYING ALL OF HIS THINGS THE WAY THEY WERE. IT SOON BECAME A SHRINE WHERE PEOPLE COULD GO TO PAY HOMAGE TO THE CONFUCIAN IDEAL.

弟子及魯人往從冢而家者百有餘室，因命曰孔里。魯世世相傳以歲時奉祠孔子冢，而諸儒亦講禮鄉飲大射於孔子冢。孔子冢大一頃。故所居堂弟子內，後世因廟藏孔子衣冠琴車書，至于漢二百餘年不絕。

【史記・孔子世家】

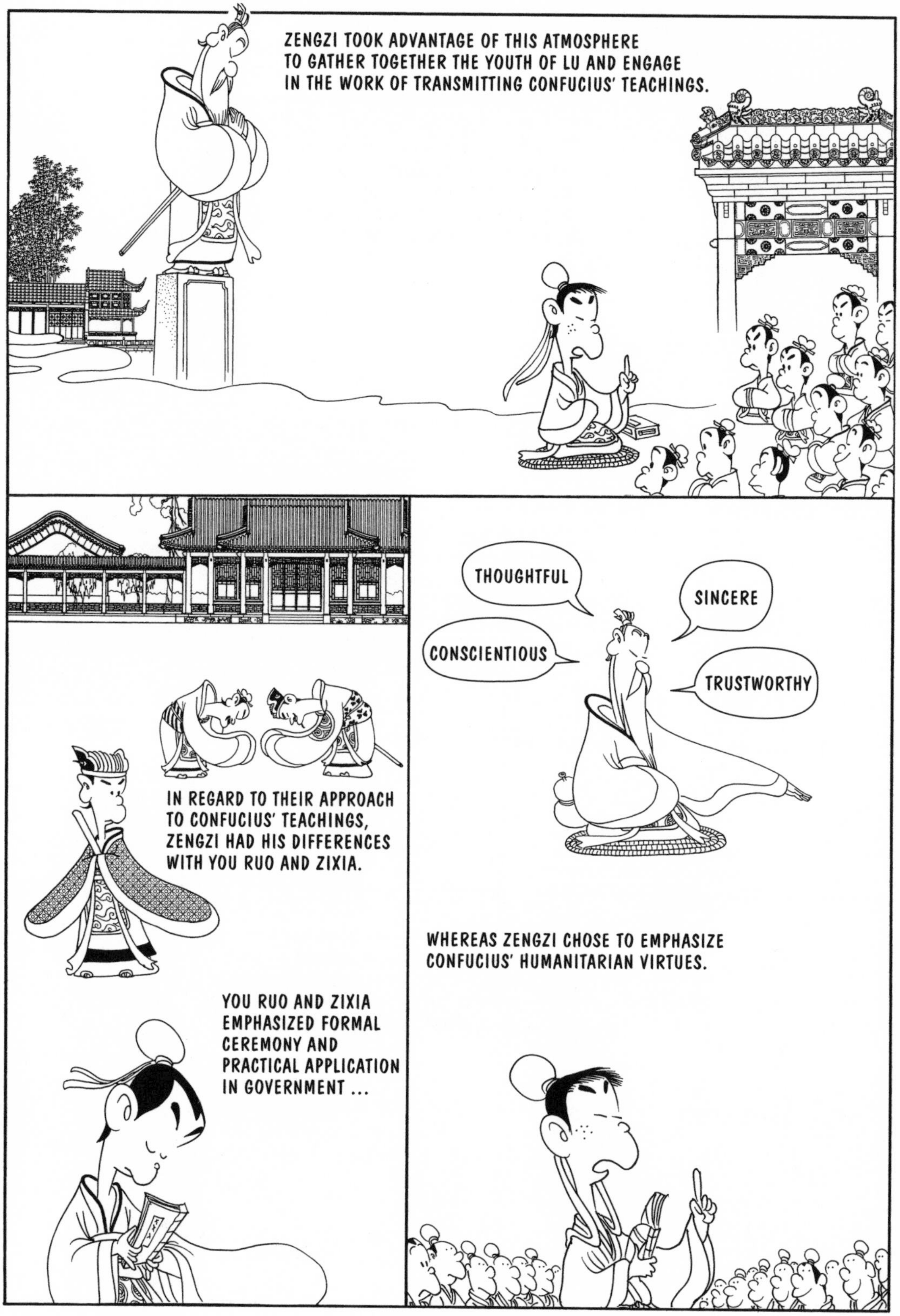
ZENGZI TOOK ADVANTAGE OF THIS ATMOSPHERE TO GATHER TOGETHER THE YOUTH OF LU AND ENGAGE IN THE WORK OF TRANSMITTING CONFUCIUS' TEACHINGS.
IN REGARD TO THEIR APPROACH TO CONFUCIUS' TEACHINGS, ZENGZI HAD HIS DIFFERENCES WITH YOU RUO AND ZIXIA.
YOU RUO AND ZIXIA EMPHASIZED FORMAL CEREMONY AND PRACTICAL APPLICATION IN GOVERNMENT ...
THOUGHTFUL
SINCERE
CONSCIENTIOUS
TRUSTWORTHY
WHEREAS ZENGZI CHOSE TO EMPHASIZE CONFUCIUS' HUMANITARIAN VIRTUES.

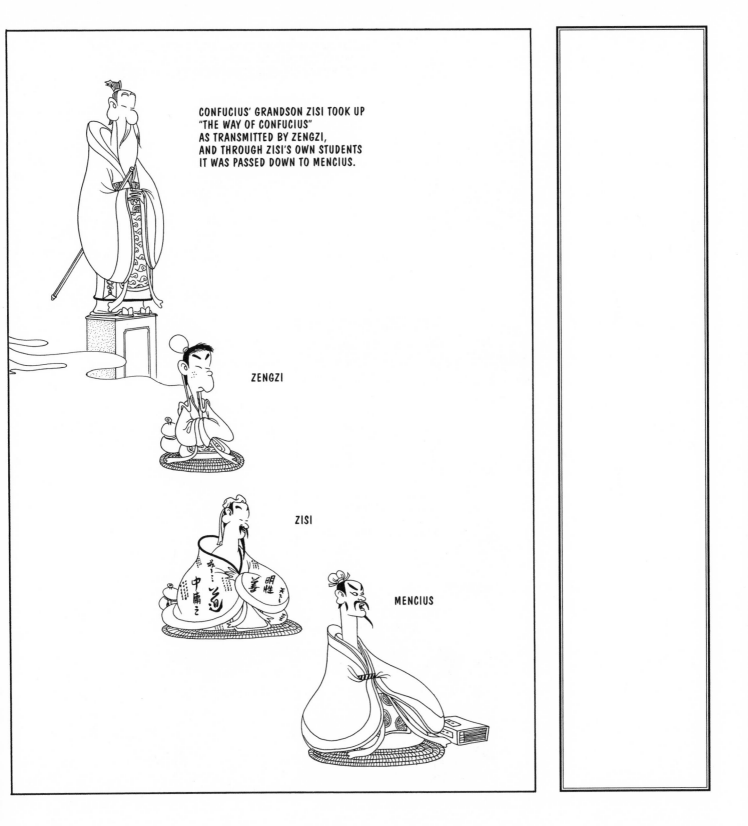

CONFUCIUS' GRANDSON ZISI TOOK UP
"THE WAY OF CONFUCIUS"
AS TRANSMITTED BY ZENGZI,
AND THROUGH ZISI'S OWN STUDENTS
IT WAS PASSED DOWN TO MENCIUS.

ZENGZI

ZISI

MENCIUS

The Students
of Confucius

孔子曰「受業身通者七十有七人」，皆異能之士也。德行：顏淵，閔子騫，冉伯牛，仲弓。政事：冉有，季路。言語：宰我，子貢。文學：子游，子夏。師也辟，參也魯，柴也愚，由也喭，回也屢空。賜不受命而貨殖焉，億則屢中。

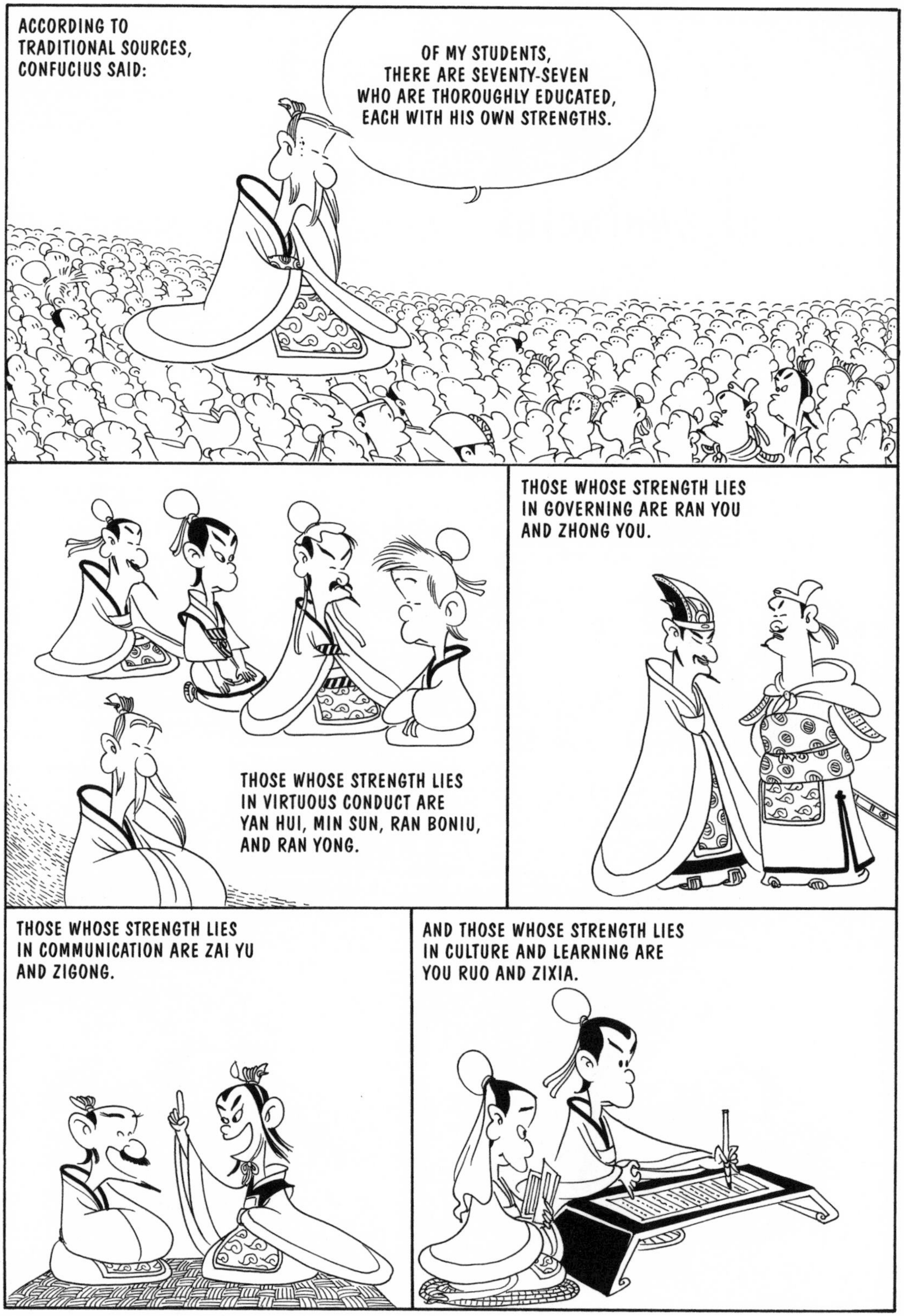

ACCORDING TO TRADITIONAL SOURCES, CONFUCIUS SAID:
OF MY STUDENTS, THERE ARE SEVENTY-SEVEN WHO ARE THOROUGHLY EDUCATED, EACH WITH HIS OWN STRENGTHS.
THOSE WHOSE STRENGTH LIES IN VIRTUOUS CONDUCT ARE YAN HUI, MIN SUN, RAN BONIU, AND RAN YONG.
THOSE WHOSE STRENGTH LIES IN GOVERNING ARE RAN YOU AND ZHONG YOU.
THOSE WHOSE STRENGTH LIES IN COMMUNICATION ARE ZAI YU AND ZIGONG.
AND THOSE WHOSE STRENGTH LIES IN CULTURE AND LEARNING ARE YOU RUO AND ZIXIA.

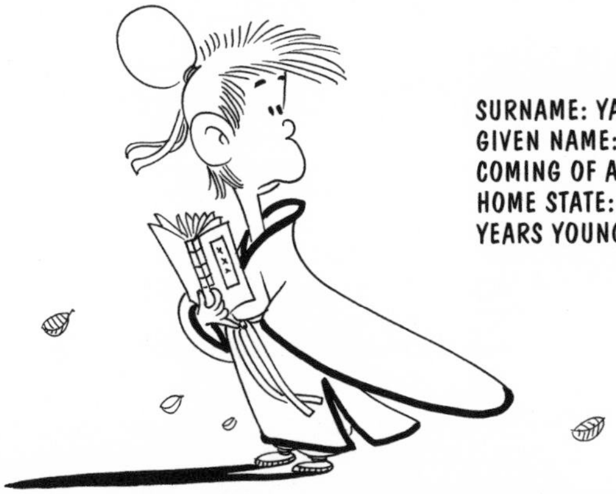

SURNAME: YAN
GIVEN NAME: HUI
COMING OF AGE NAME: ZIYUAN
HOME STATE: LU
YEARS YOUNGER THAN CONFUCIUS: THIRTY

顏回者，魯人也，字子淵。少孔子三十歲。顏淵問仁，孔子曰：「克己復禮，天下歸仁焉。」孔子曰：「賢哉回也！一簞食，一瓢飲，在陋巷，人不堪其憂，回也不改其樂。」「回也如愚，退而省其私，亦足以發，回也不愚。」「用之則行，捨之則藏，唯我與爾有是夫！」

回年二十九，髮盡白，蚤死。孔子哭之慟，曰：「自吾有回，門人益親。」魯哀公問：「弟子孰為好學？」孔子對曰：「有顏回者好學，不遷怒，不貳過。不幸短命死矣，今也則亡。」

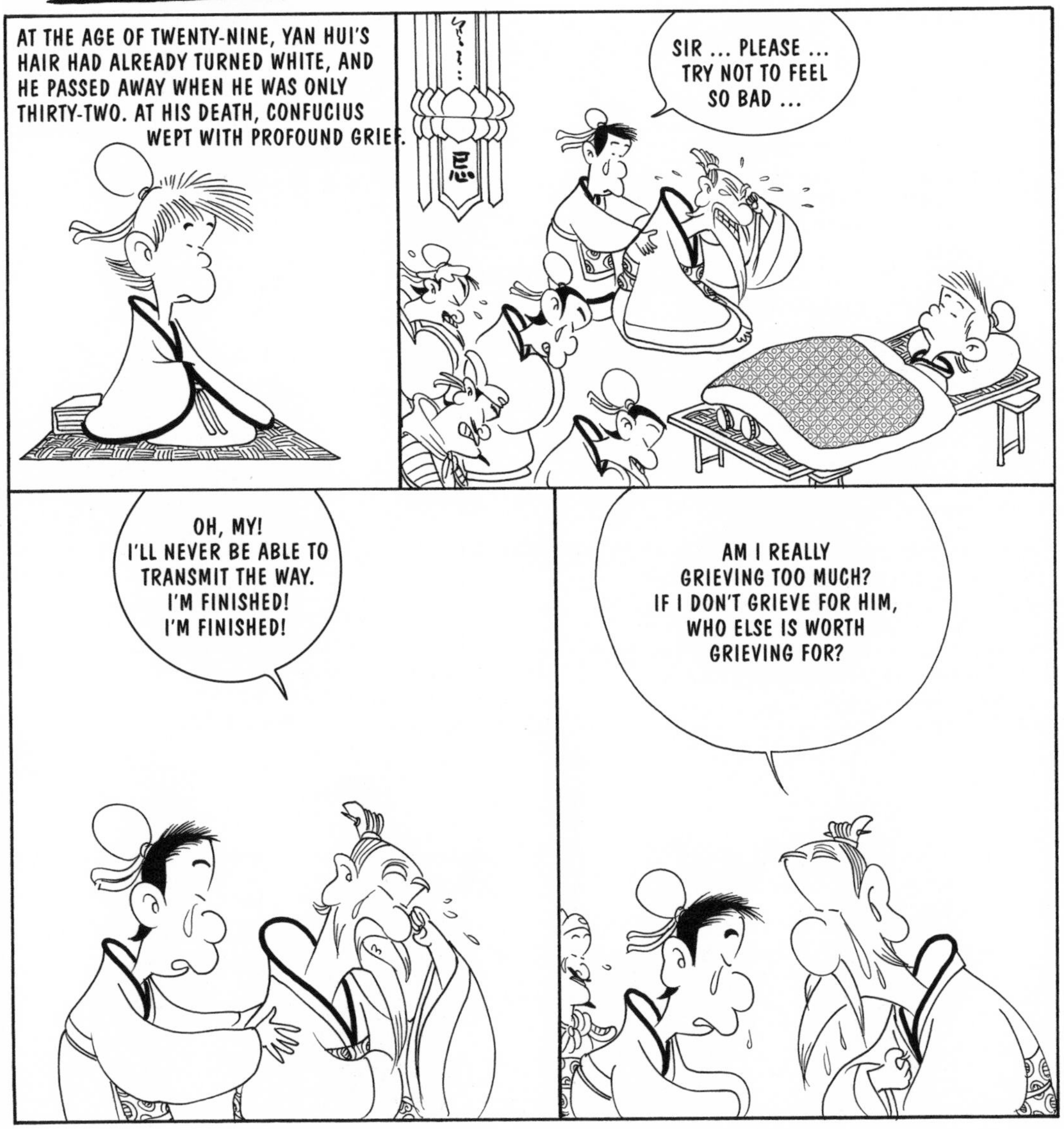
AT THE AGE OF TWENTY-NINE, YAN HUI'S HAIR HAD ALREADY TURNED WHITE, AND HE PASSED AWAY WHEN HE WAS ONLY THIRTY-TWO. AT HIS DEATH, CONFUCIUS WEPT WITH PROFOUND GRIEF.
SIR ... PLEASE ... TRY NOT TO FEEL SO BAD ...
OH, MY! I'LL NEVER BE ABLE TO TRANSMIT THE WAY. I'M FINISHED! I'M FINISHED!
AM I REALLY GRIEVING TOO MUCH? IF I DON'T GRIEVE FOR HIM, WHO ELSE IS WORTH GRIEVING FOR?

閔損字子騫。少孔子十五歲。
孔子曰：「孝哉閔子騫！人不閒於其父母昆弟之言。」不仕大夫，不食汙君之祿。「如有復我者，必在汶上矣。」

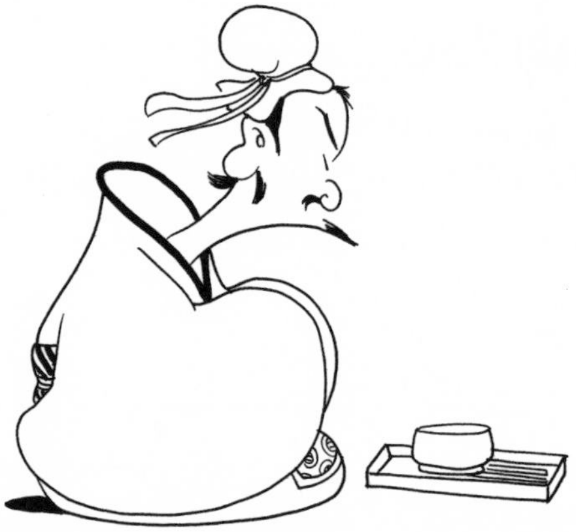

SURNAME: MIN
GIVEN NAME: SUN
COMING OF AGE NAME: ZIQIAN
HOME STATE: LU
YEARS YOUNGER THAN CONFUCIUS: FIFTEEN

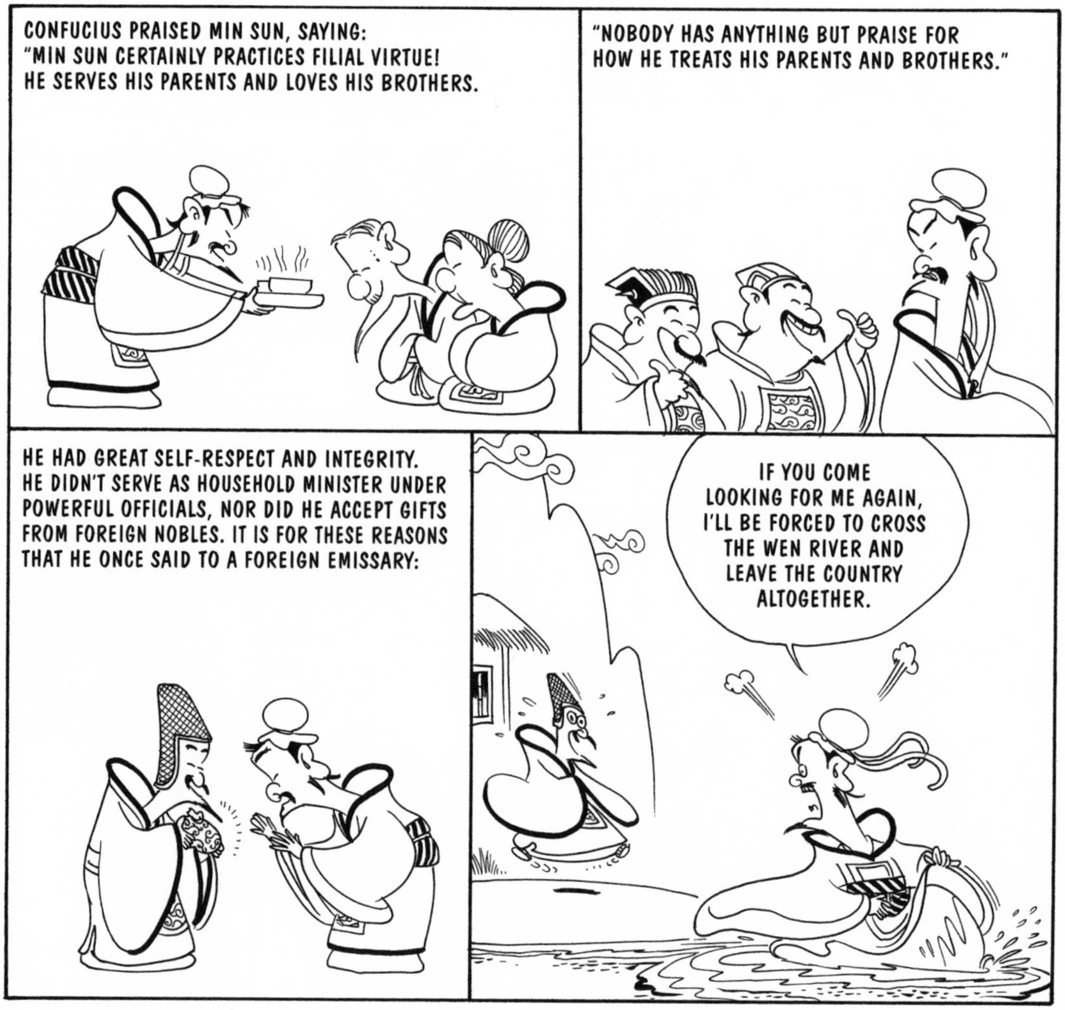
CONFUCIUS PRAISED MIN SUN, SAYING: "MIN SUN CERTAINLY PRACTICES FILIAL VIRTUE! HE SERVES HIS PARENTS AND LOVES HIS BROTHERS.
"NOBODY HAS ANYTHING BUT PRAISE FOR HOW HE TREATS HIS PARENTS AND BROTHERS."
HE HAD GREAT SELF-RESPECT AND INTEGRITY. HE DIDN'T SERVE AS HOUSEHOLD MINISTER UNDER POWERFUL OFFICIALS, NOR DID HE ACCEPT GIFTS FROM FOREIGN NOBLES. IT IS FOR THESE REASONS THAT HE ONCE SAID TO A FOREIGN EMISSARY:
IF YOU COME LOOKING FOR ME AGAIN, I'LL BE FORCED TO CROSS THE WEN RIVER AND LEAVE THE COUNTRY ALTOGETHER.

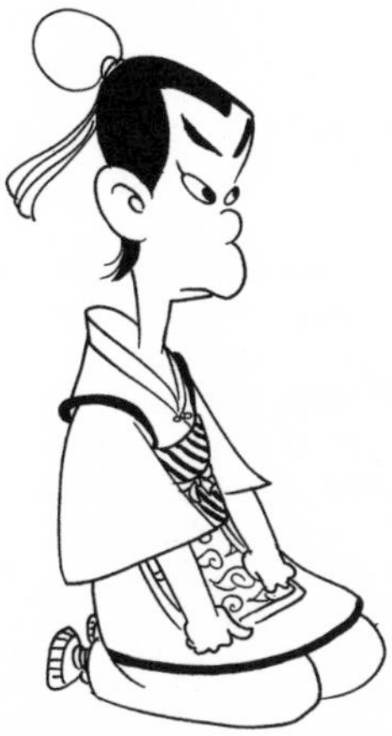

SURNAME: RAN
GIVEN NAME: YONG
COMING OF AGE NAME: ZHONGGONG
HOME STATE: LU
YEARS YOUNGER THAN CONFUCIUS: TWENTY-NINE

CAME FROM A FAMILY OF COMMONERS

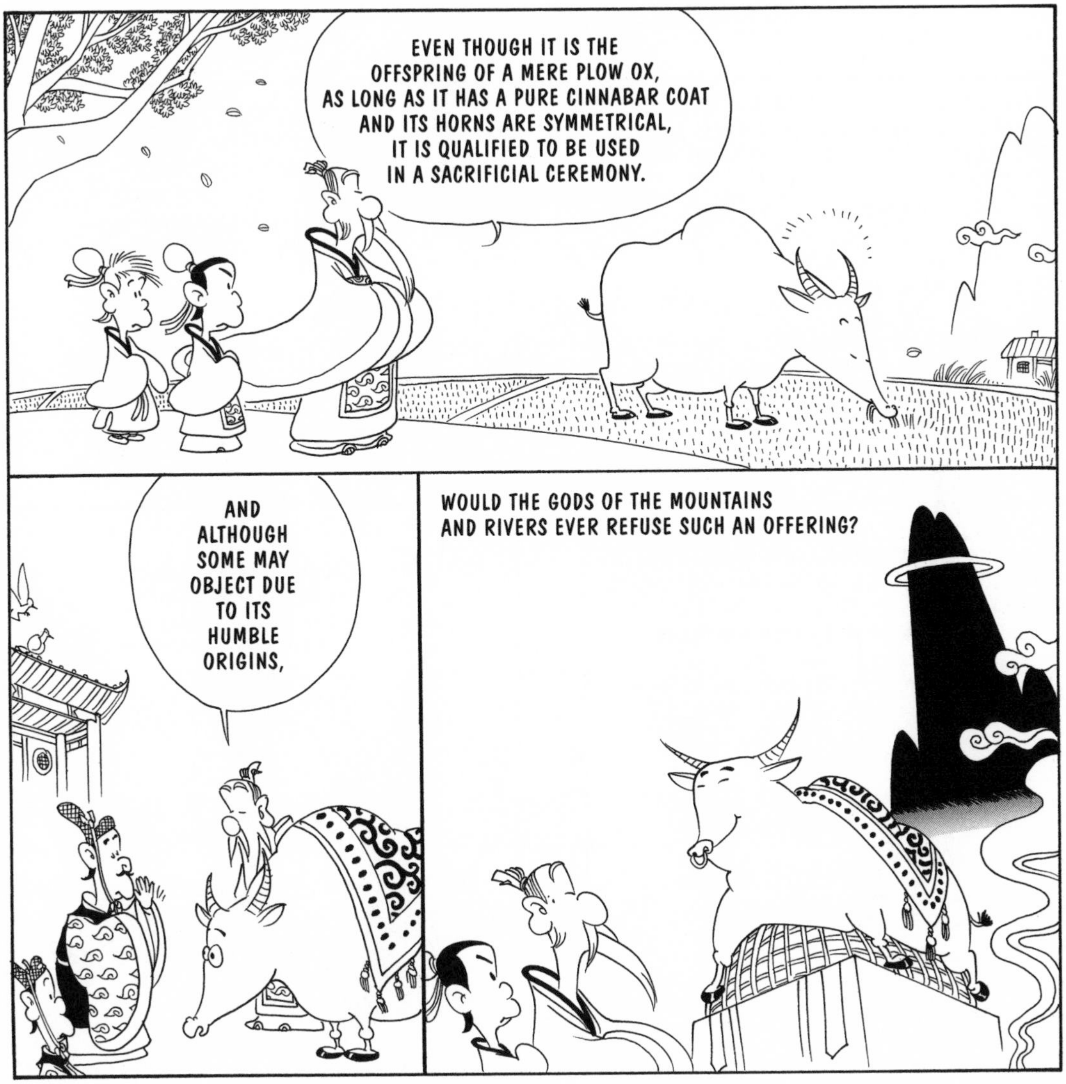
EVEN THOUGH IT IS THE OFFSPRING OF A MERE PLOW OX, AS LONG AS IT HAS A PURE CINNABAR COAT AND ITS HORNS ARE SYMMETRICAL, IT IS QUALIFIED TO BE USED IN A SACRIFICIAL CEREMONY.
AND ALTHOUGH SOME MAY OBJECT DUE TO ITS HUMBLE ORIGINS,
WOULD THE GODS OF THE MOUNTAINS AND RIVERS EVER REFUSE SUCH AN OFFERING?

冉雍字仲弓。

仲弓問政，孔子曰：「出門如見大賓，使民如承大祭。在邦無怨，在家無怨。」

孔子以仲弓為有德行，曰：「雍也可使南面。」

仲弓父，賤人。孔子曰：「犁牛之子騂且角，雖欲勿用，山川其舍諸？」

SURNAME: ZHONG
GIVEN NAME: YOU
COMING OF AGE NAME: ZILU
HOME STATE: LU, BIAN COUNTY
YEARS YOUNGER THAN CONFUCIUS: NINE

STUBBORN AND STRAIGHTFORWARD,
ZHONG YOU WAS ORIGINALLY A COARSE
AND UNREFINED MAN WHO ENJOYED
FIGHTING AND EXHIBITING HIS BRAVERY.
HE WAS TRANSFORMED BY CONFUCIUS.
IN HIS LATER YEARS, HE WAS A SENIOR
OFFICIAL IN THE CITY OF PU IN WEI.
HE WAS KILLED DURING A REBELLION
THAT SWEPT THROUGH WEI.

仲由字子路，卞人也。少孔子九歲。子路性鄙，好勇力，志伉直，冠雄雞，佩豭豚，陵暴孔子。孔子設禮稍誘子路，子路後儒服委質，因門人請為弟子。子路問政，孔子曰：「先之，勞之。」請益。曰：「無倦。」

孔子曰：「片言可以折獄者，其由也與！」「由也好勇過我，無所取材。」「若由也，不得其死然。」「衣敝縕袍與衣狐貉者立而不恥者，其由也與！」「由也升堂矣，未入於室也。」

ZHONG YOU'S STUDIES HAVE ACHIEVED A CERTAIN LEVEL OF ENLIGHTENMENT; IT'S JUST THAT THEY HAVE YET TO ATTAIN THAT REALM OF PROFUNDITY.

TO WEAR WORN CLOTHES AND STAND NEXT TO SOMEONE WEARING FURS AND LEATHER, YET NOT FEEL THE LEAST BIT ASHAMED— I'M AFRAID ONLY ZHONG YOU WOULD BE CAPABLE OF THAT!

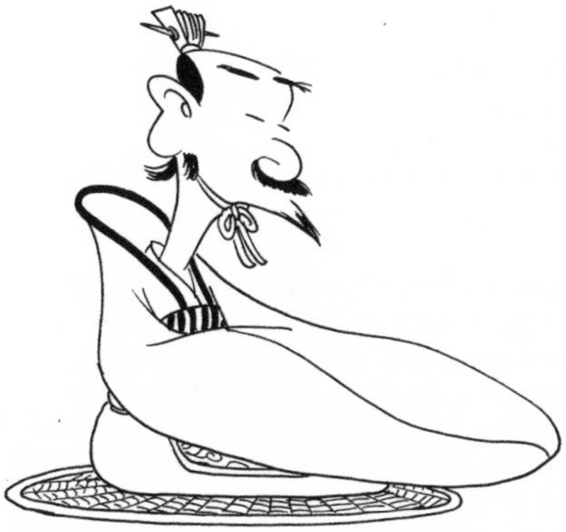

SURNAME: ZAI
GIVEN NAME: YU
COMING OF AGE NAME: ZIWO
HOME STATE: LU
AGE DIFFERENCE WITH CONFUCIUS: UNKNOWN

WITH A SHARP TONGUE AND QUICK WIT, ZAI YU WAS A FINE SPEAKER AND A GOOD DEBATER. HE BECAME A SENIOR OFFICIAL IN THE QI CITY OF LINZI AND PARTICIPATED IN THE TIAN CHANG UPRISING, BY WHICH HE HARMED HIS EXTENDED FAMILY. CONFUCIUS WAS ASHAMED OF HIM.

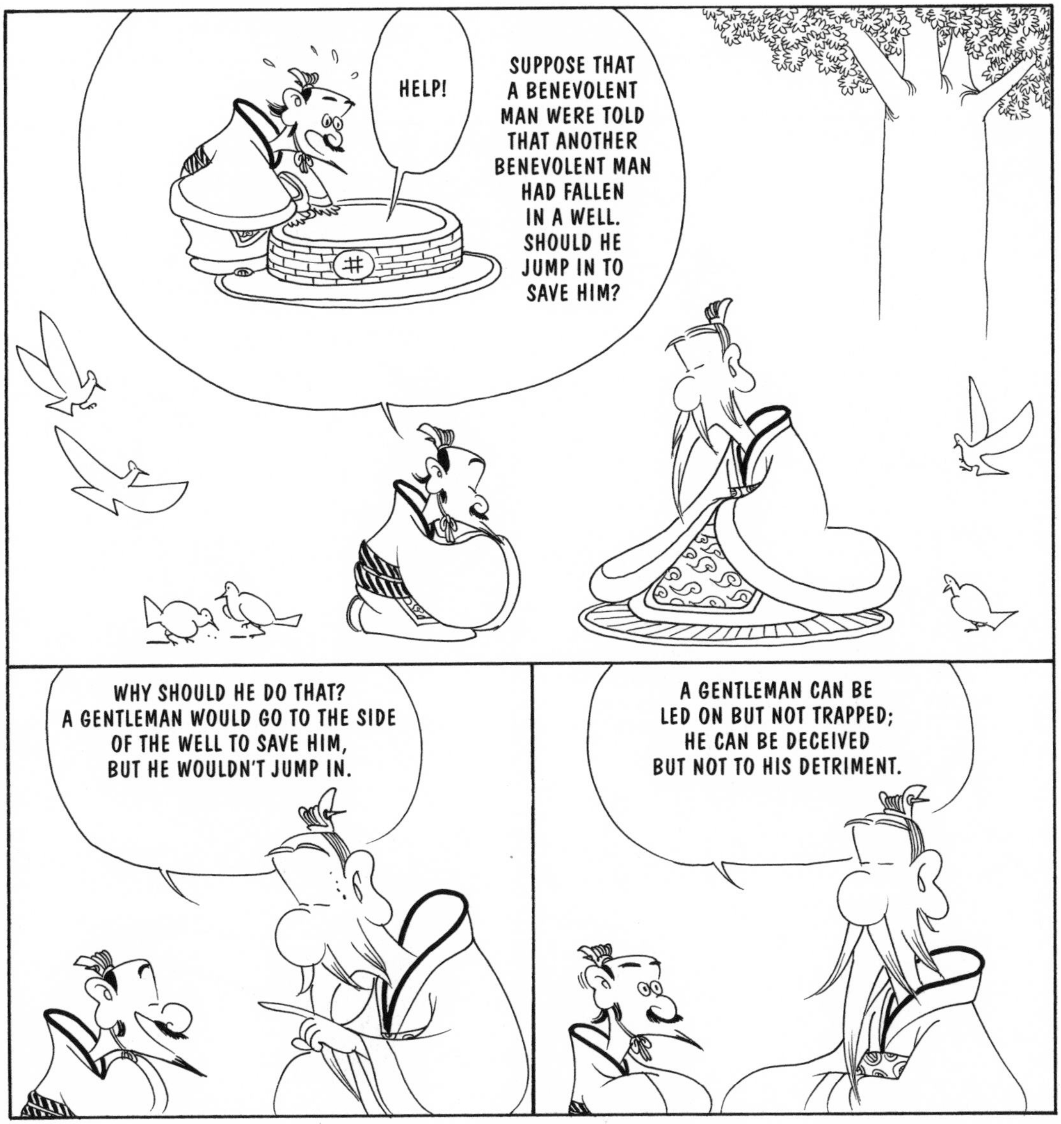
HELP!
SUPPOSE THAT A BENEVOLENT MAN WERE TOLD THAT ANOTHER BENEVOLENT MAN HAD FALLEN IN A WELL. SHOULD HE JUMP IN TO SAVE HIM?
WHY SHOULD HE DO THAT? A GENTLEMAN WOULD GO TO THE SIDE OF THE WELL TO SAVE HIM, BUT HE WOULDN'T JUMP IN.
A GENTLEMAN CAN BE LED ON BUT NOT TRAPPED; HE CAN BE DECEIVED BUT NOT TO HIS DETRIMENT.

宰予字子我。利口辯辭。既受業。問：「三年之喪不已久乎？君子三年不為禮，禮必壞；三年不為樂，樂必崩。舊穀既沒，新穀既升，鑽燧改火，期可已矣。」子曰：「於汝安乎？」曰：「安。」「汝安則為之。君子居喪，食旨不甘，聞樂不樂，故弗為也。」宰我出，子曰：「予之不仁也！子生三年然後免於父母之懷。夫三年之喪，天下之通義也。」

端沐賜，衛人，字子貢。少孔子三十一歲。

子貢利口巧辭，孔子常黜其辯。問曰：「汝與回也孰愈？」對曰：「賜也何敢望回！回也聞一以知十，賜也聞一以知二。」

子貢既已受業，問曰：「賜何人也？」孔子曰：「汝器也。」曰：「何器也？」曰：「瑚璉也。」

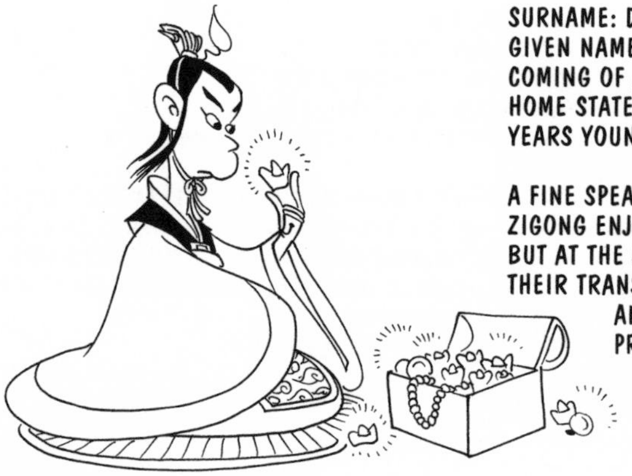

SURNAME: DUANMU
GIVEN NAME: SI
COMING OF AGE NAME: ZIGONG
HOME STATE: WEI
YEARS YOUNGER THAN CONFUCIUS: THIRTY-ONE

A FINE SPEAKER AND A GOOD DEBATER, ZIGONG ENJOYED PRAISING OTHER PEOPLE'S MERITS, BUT AT THE SAME TIME, HE WOULD NOT IGNORE THEIR TRANSGRESSIONS. MORE THAN ONCE HE HELPED LU AND WEI RESOLVE STALEMATES. HE CAME FROM A PROSPEROUS FAMILY, AND BEING GOOD AT BUSINESS, HE ACCUMULATED VAST WEALTH. HE DIED AT AN OLD AGE IN THE STATE OF QI.

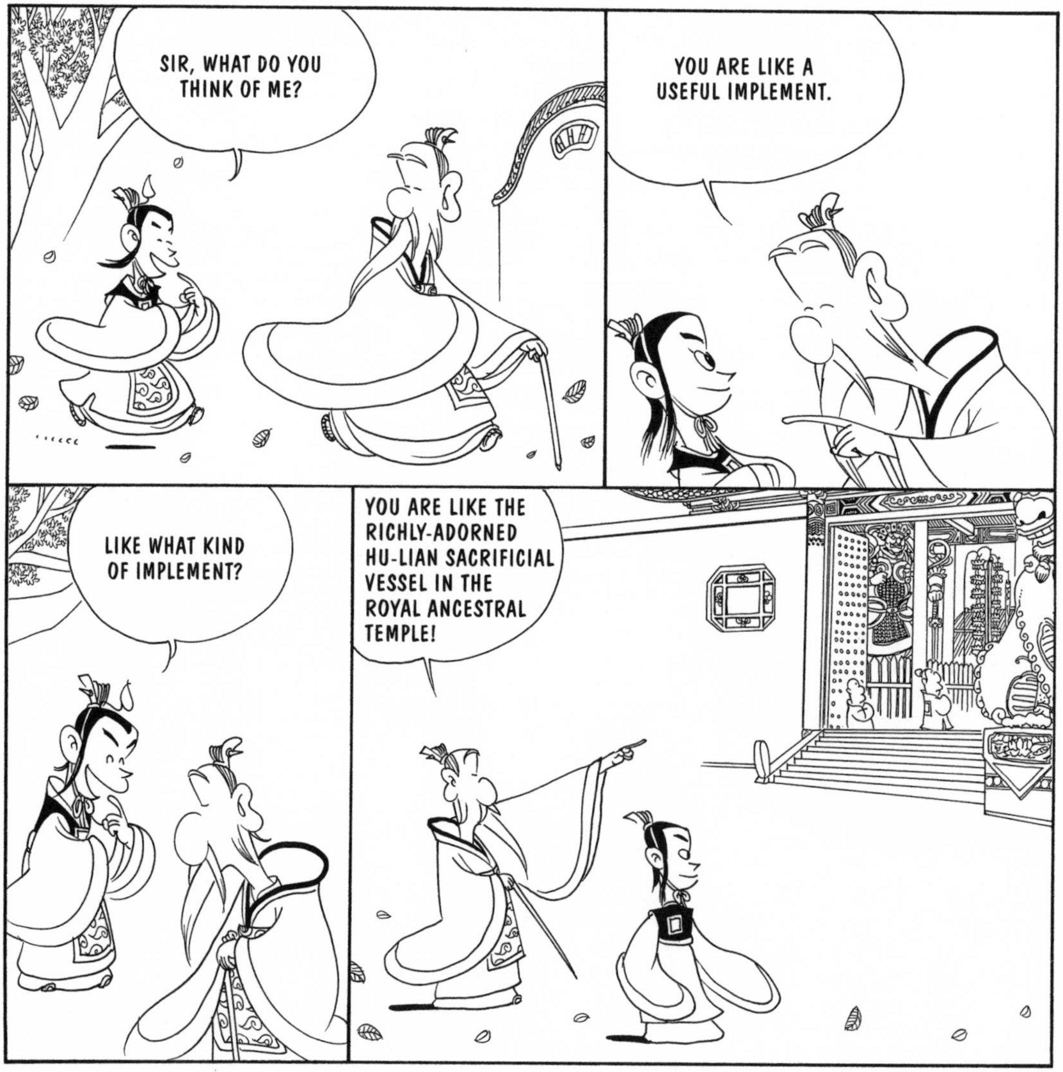

SIR, WHAT DO YOU THINK OF ME?
YOU ARE LIKE A USEFUL IMPLEMENT.
LIKE WHAT KIND OF IMPLEMENT?
YOU ARE LIKE THE RICHLY-ADORNED HU-LIAN SACRIFICIAL VESSEL IN THE ROYAL ANCESTRAL TEMPLE!

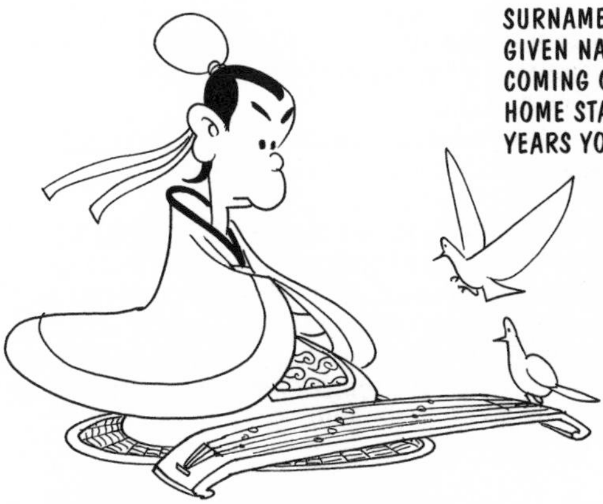

SURNAME: BU
GIVEN NAME: SHANG
COMING OF AGE NAME: ZIXIA
HOME STATE: WEI, WEN REGION
YEARS YOUNGER THAN CONFUCIUS: FORTY-FIVE

AFTER CONFUCIUS DIED, ZIXIA TOOK UP RESIDENCE IN THE XIHE REGION OF WEI, WHERE HE BEGAN TEACHING AND ATTRACTING STUDENTS OF HIS OWN. HE ALSO BECAME THE PERSONAL TUTOR TO MARQUIS WEN OF WEI.

HIS SON DIED YOUNG, AND HIS GRIEF OVER IT CAUSED HIM TO CRY HIMSELF BLIND.

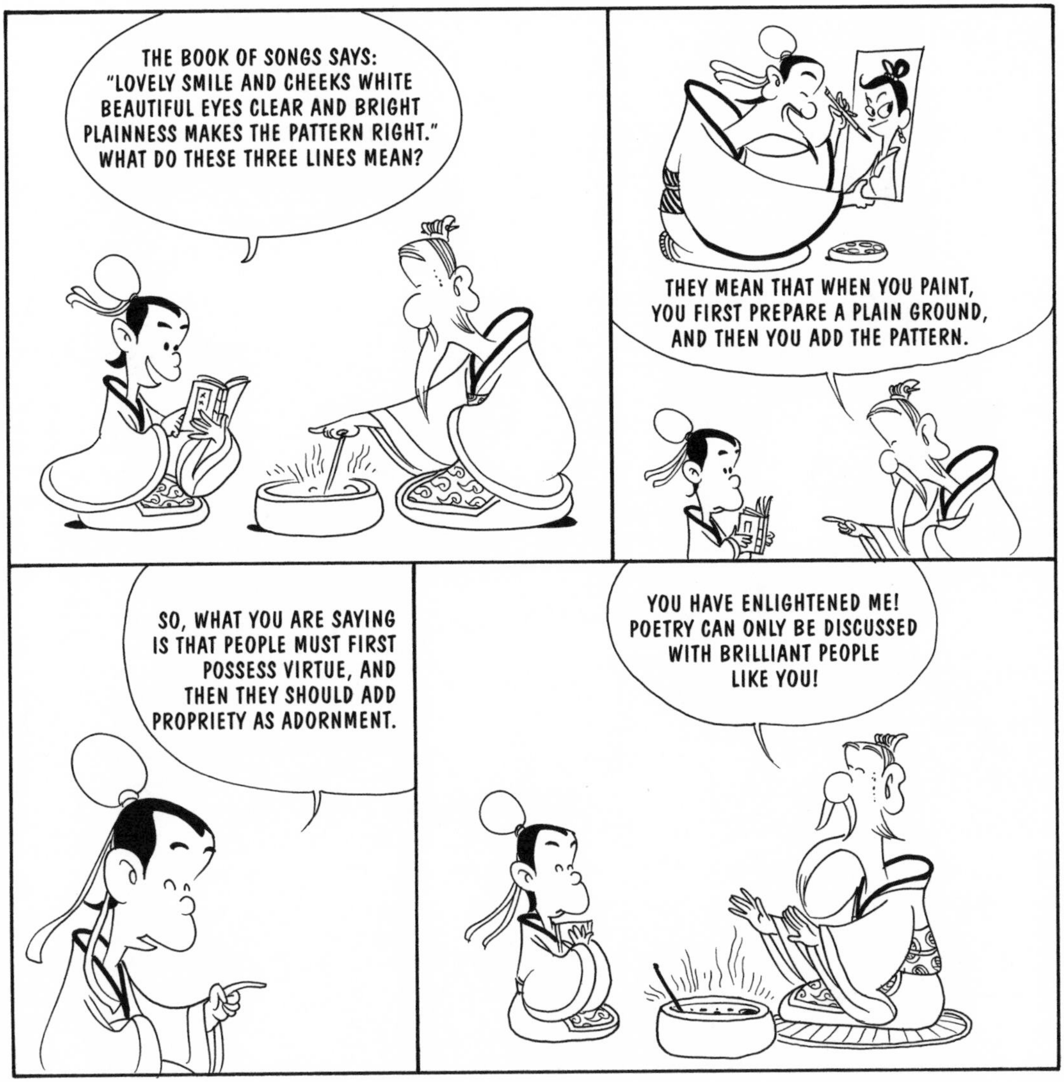
THE BOOK OF SONGS SAYS: "LOVELY SMILE AND CHEEKS WHITE BEAUTIFUL EYES CLEAR AND BRIGHT PLAINNESS MAKES THE PATTERN RIGHT." WHAT DO THESE THREE LINES MEAN?
THEY MEAN THAT WHEN YOU PAINT, YOU FIRST PREPARE A PLAIN GROUND, AND THEN YOU ADD THE PATTERN.
SO, WHAT YOU ARE SAYING IS THAT PEOPLE MUST FIRST POSSESS VIRTUE, AND THEN THEY SHOULD ADD PROPRIETY AS ADORNMENT.
YOU HAVE ENLIGHTENED ME! POETRY CAN ONLY BE DISCUSSED WITH BRILLIANT PEOPLE LIKE YOU!

卜商字子夏。少孔子四十四歲。

子夏問：「『巧笑倩兮，美目盼兮，素以為絢兮』，何謂也？」子曰：「繪事後素。」曰：「禮後乎？」孔子曰：「商始可與言《詩》已矣。」

子謂子夏曰：「汝為君子儒，無為小人儒。」

孔子既沒，子夏居西河教授，為魏文侯師。其子死，哭之失明。

澹臺滅明，武城人，字子羽。少孔子三十九歲。狀貌甚惡。欲事孔子，孔子以為材薄。既已受業，退而修行，行不由徑，非公事不見卿大夫。南游至江，從弟子三百人，設取予去就，名施乎諸侯。孔子聞之，曰：「吾以言取人，失之宰予；以貌取人，失之子羽。」

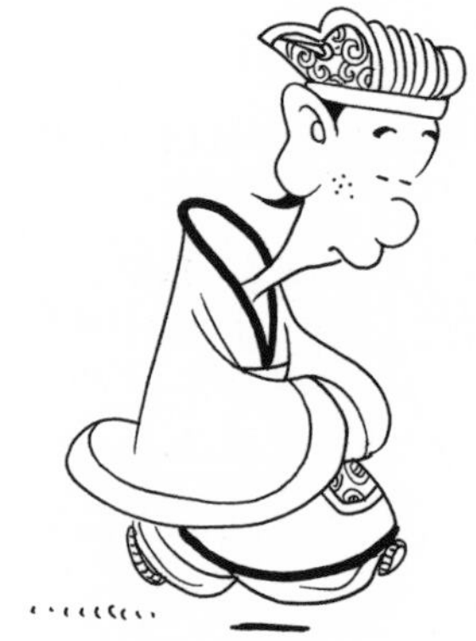

SURNAME: TANTAI
GIVEN NAME: MIEMING
COMING OF AGE NAME: ZIYU
HOME STATE: LU, CITY OF WU
YEARS YOUNGER THAN CONFUCIUS: THIRTY-NINE

TANTAI MIEMING WAS KNOWN TO BE QUITE UGLY. HE TRAVELED TO SOUTHERN CHINA WITH A FOLLOWING OF ABOUT THREE HUNDRED STUDENTS. A MAN OF HIGH INTEGRITY, HE ESTABLISHED A CODE OF CONDUCT FOR THEM, WHICH HE HIMSELF NEVER VIOLATED. HIS STERLING REPUTATION SPREAD TO NOBLEMEN IN THE FOUR CORNERS OF THE LAND.

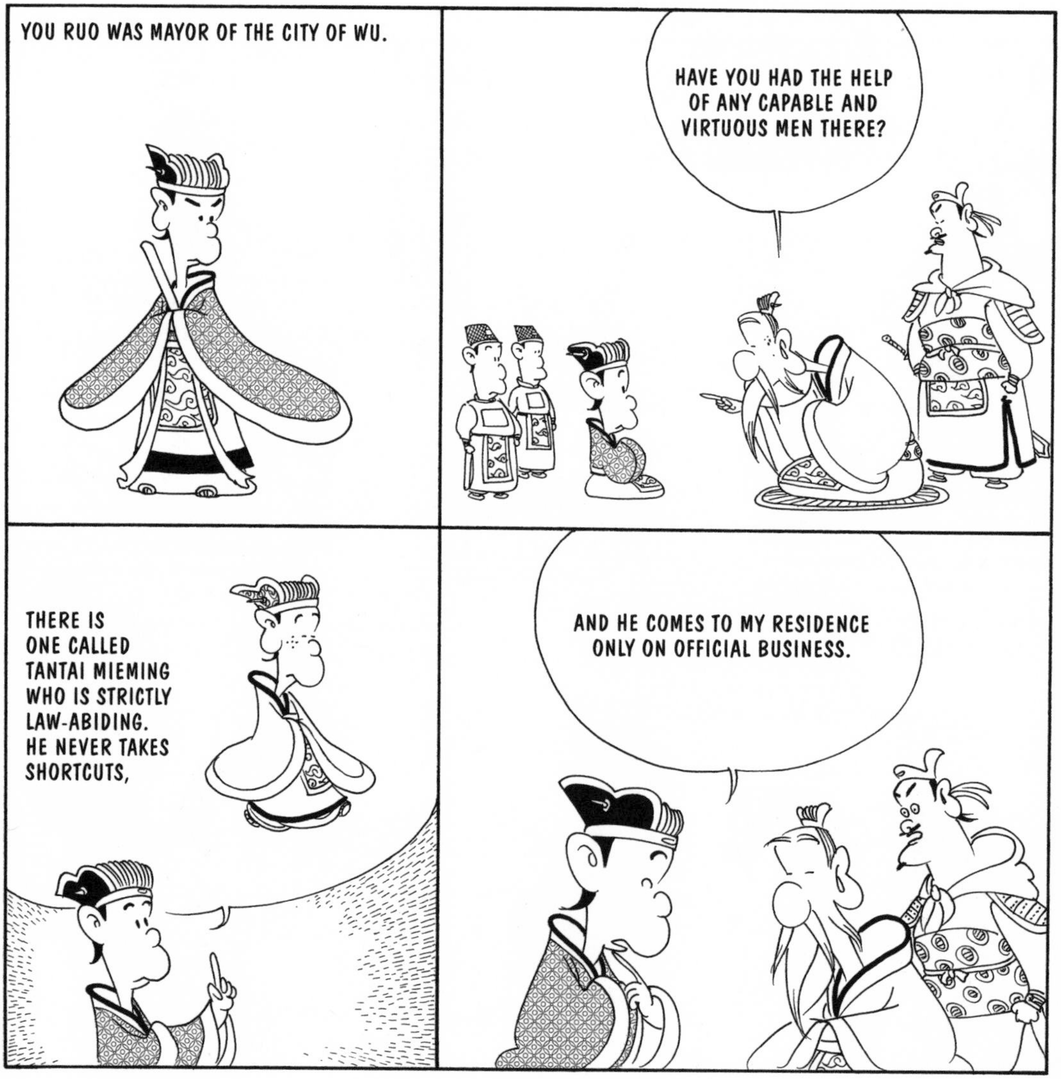
YOU RUO WAS MAYOR OF THE CITY OF WU.
HAVE YOU HAD THE HELP OF ANY CAPABLE AND VIRTUOUS MEN THERE?
THERE IS ONE CALLED TANTAI MIEMING WHO IS STRICTLY LAW-ABIDING. HE NEVER TAKES SHORTCUTS,
AND HE COMES TO MY RESIDENCE ONLY ON OFFICIAL BUSINESS.

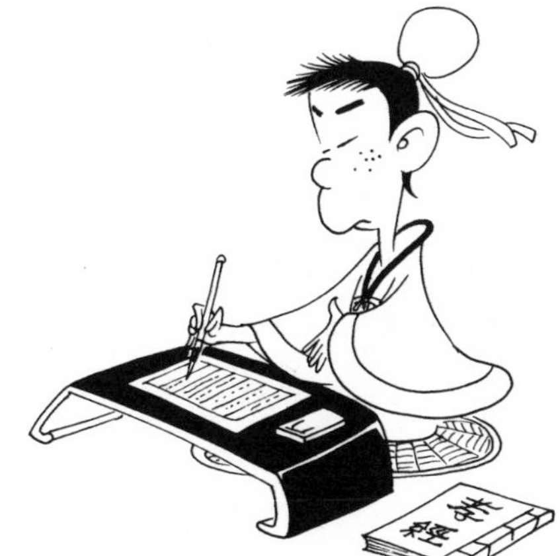
孝經

SURNAME: ZENG
GIVEN NAME: SHEN
COMING OF AGE NAME: ZIYU
HOME STATE: LU, SOUTHERN PART OF THE CITY OF WU
YEARS YOUNGER THAN CONFUCIUS: FORTY-SIX

CONFUCIUS SAW IN ZENGZI A GREAT PROPENSITY TOWARD FILIAL VIRTUE AND SO TRANSMITTED TO HIM ALL THAT HE KNEW ABOUT THE SUBJECT. ZENGZI THEN WROTE THE BOOK OF FILIAL VIRTUE. HE DIED AT AN OLD AGE IN THE STATE OF LU.

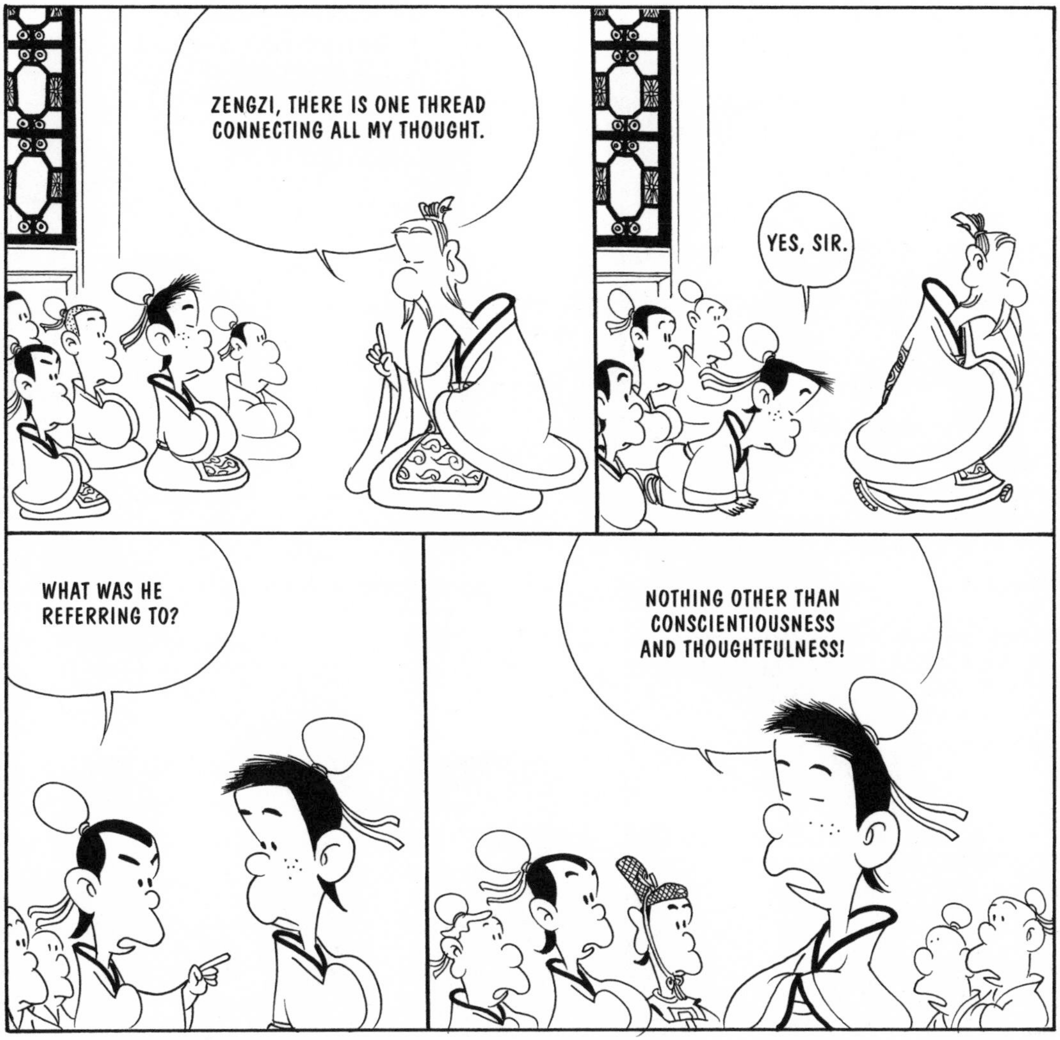
ZENGZI, THERE IS ONE THREAD CONNECTING ALL MY THOUGHT.
YES, SIR.
WHAT WAS HE REFERRING TO?
NOTHING OTHER THAN CONSCIENTIOUSNESS AND THOUGHTFULNESS!

曾參，南武城人，字子輿。少孔子四十六歲。孔子以為能通孝道，故授之業。作《孝經》。死於魯。

子曰：「參乎！吾道一以貫之。」曾子曰：「唯。」子出，門人問曰：「何謂也？」曾子曰：「夫子之道，忠恕而已矣。」

有若少孔子四十三歲。有若曰：「禮之用，和為貴，先王之道斯為美。小大由之，有所不行；知和而和，不以禮節之，亦不可行也。」「信近於義，言可復也；恭近於禮，遠恥辱也；因不失其親，亦可宗也。」孔子既沒，弟子思慕，有若狀似孔子，弟子相與共立為師，師之如夫子時也。

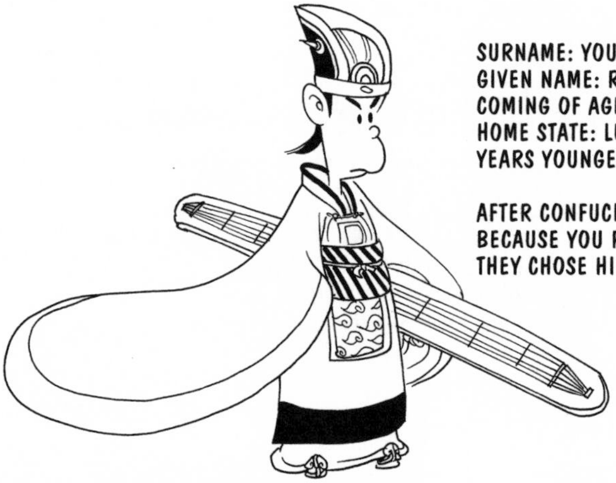

SURNAME: YOU
GIVEN NAME: RUO
COMING OF AGE NAME: ZIYOU
HOME STATE: LU
YEARS YOUNGER THAN CONFUCIUS: FORTY-THREE

AFTER CONFUCIUS DIED, HIS STUDENTS MISSED HIS PRESENCE. BECAUSE YOU RUO RESEMBLED CONFUCIUS IN APPEARANCE, THEY CHOSE HIM AS A REPLACEMENT.

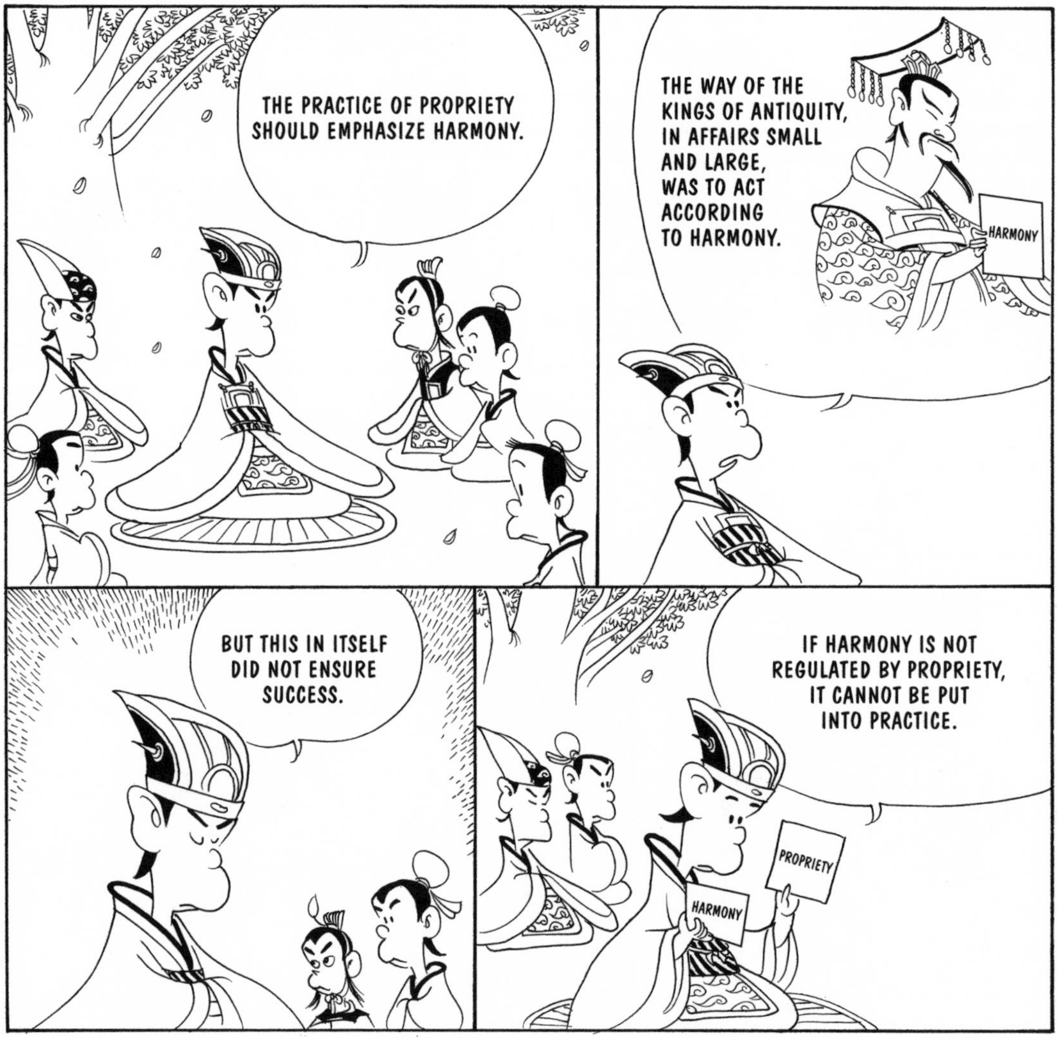
THE PRACTICE OF PROPRIETY SHOULD EMPHASIZE HARMONY.
THE WAY OF THE KINGS OF ANTIQUITY, IN AFFAIRS SMALL AND LARGE, WAS TO ACT ACCORDING TO HARMONY.
HARMONY
BUT THIS IN ITSELF DID NOT ENSURE SUCCESS.
IF HARMONY IS NOT REGULATED BY PROPRIETY, IT CANNOT BE PUT INTO PRACTICE.
PROPRIETY
HARMONY

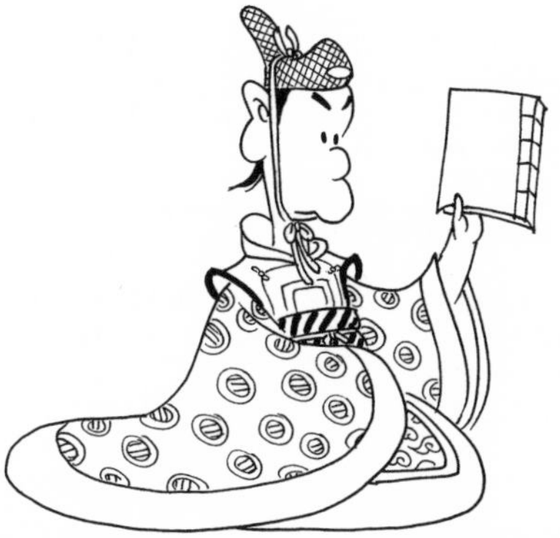

SURNAME: NANGONG
GIVEN NAME: KUO
COMING OF AGE NAME: ZIRONG
HOME STATE: LU
AGE DIFFERENCE WITH CONFUCIUS: UNKNOWN

CONFUCIUS SAID IN REGARD TO ZIRONG, "WHEN THE GOVERNMENT IS JUST, HE WILL CERTAINLY HOLD A POST. WHEN THE GOVERNMENT IS CORRUPT, HE WILL MAINTAIN HIS INTEGRITY AND PROTECT HIMSELF FROM HARM." CONFUCIUS GAVE HIS OWN NIECE TO ZIRONG IN MARRIAGE.

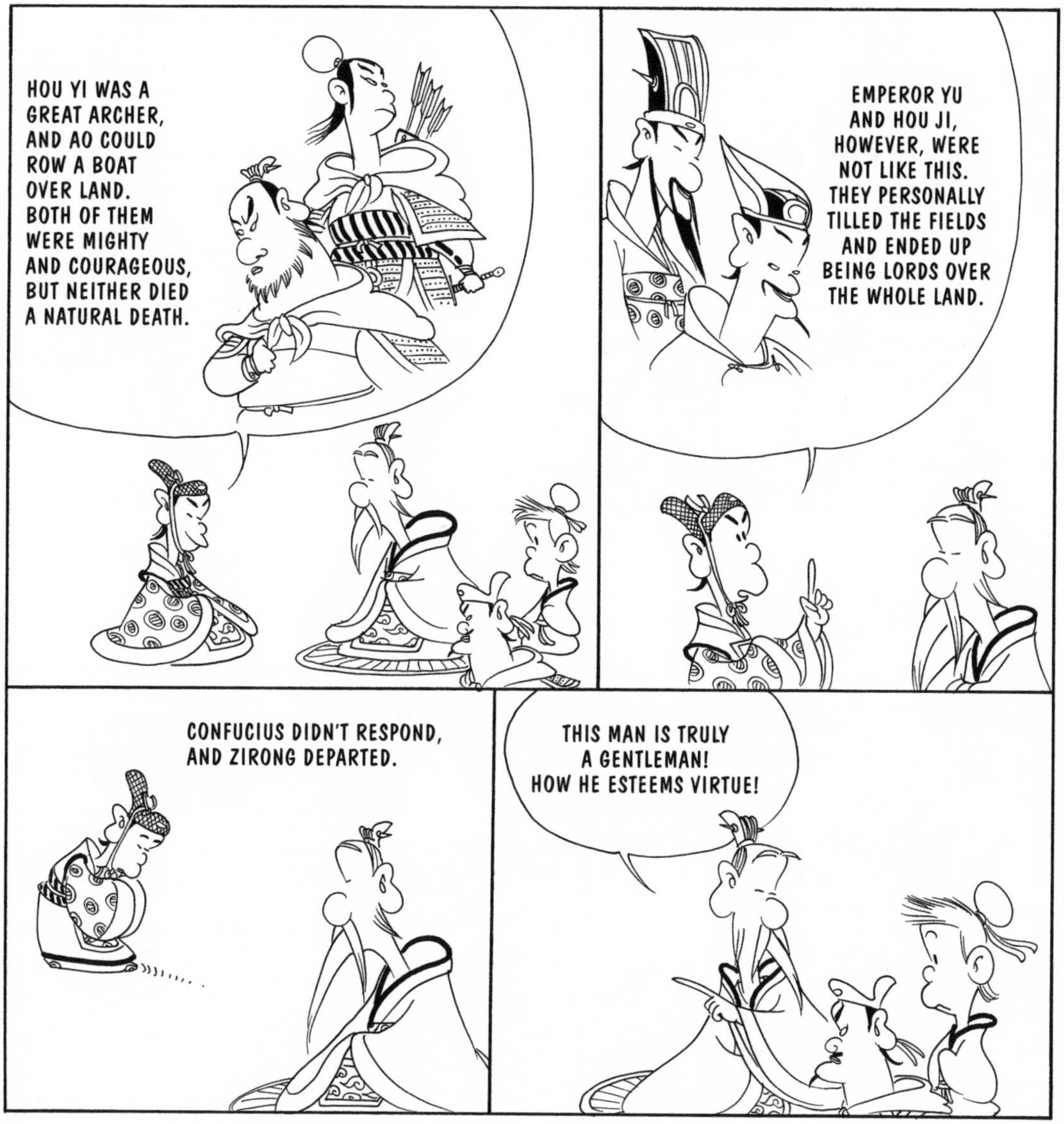
HOU YI WAS A GREAT ARCHER, AND AO COULD ROW A BOAT OVER LAND. BOTH OF THEM WERE MIGHTY AND COURAGEOUS, BUT NEITHER DIED A NATURAL DEATH.
EMPEROR YU AND HOU JI, HOWEVER, WERE NOT LIKE THIS. THEY PERSONALLY TILLED THE FIELDS AND ENDED UP BEING LORDS OVER THE WHOLE LAND.
CONFUCIUS DIDN'T RESPOND, AND ZIRONG DEPARTED.
THIS MAN IS TRULY A GENTLEMAN! HOW HE ESTEEMS VIRTUE!

南宮括字子容。

問孔子曰：「羿善射，奡盪舟，俱不得其死然；禹稷躬稼而有天下？」孔子弗答。容出，孔子曰：「君子哉若人！上德哉若人！」「國有道，不廢；國無道，免於刑戮。」三復「白珪之玷」，以其兄之子妻之。

公西赤字子華。少孔子四十二歲。
子華使於齊，冉有為其母請粟。孔子曰：「與之釜。」請益，曰：「與之庾。」冉子與之粟五秉。孔子曰：「赤之適齊也，乘肥馬，衣輕裘。吾聞君子周急不繼富。」

【史記・仲尼弟子列傳】

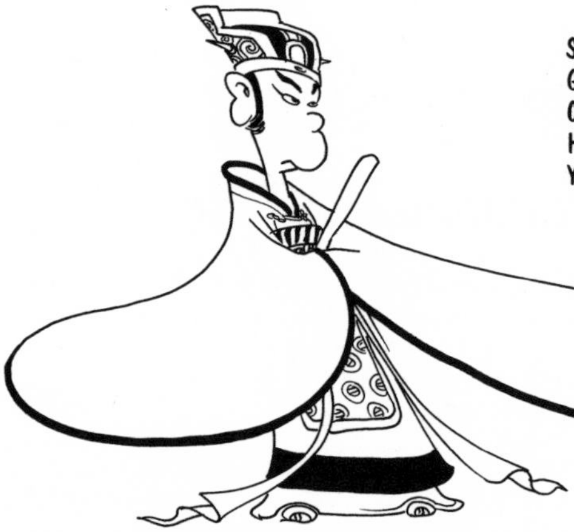

SURNAME: GONGXI
GIVEN NAME: CHI
COMING OF AGE NAME: ZIHUA
HOME STATE: LU
YEARS YOUNGER THAN CONFUCIUS: FORTY-TWO

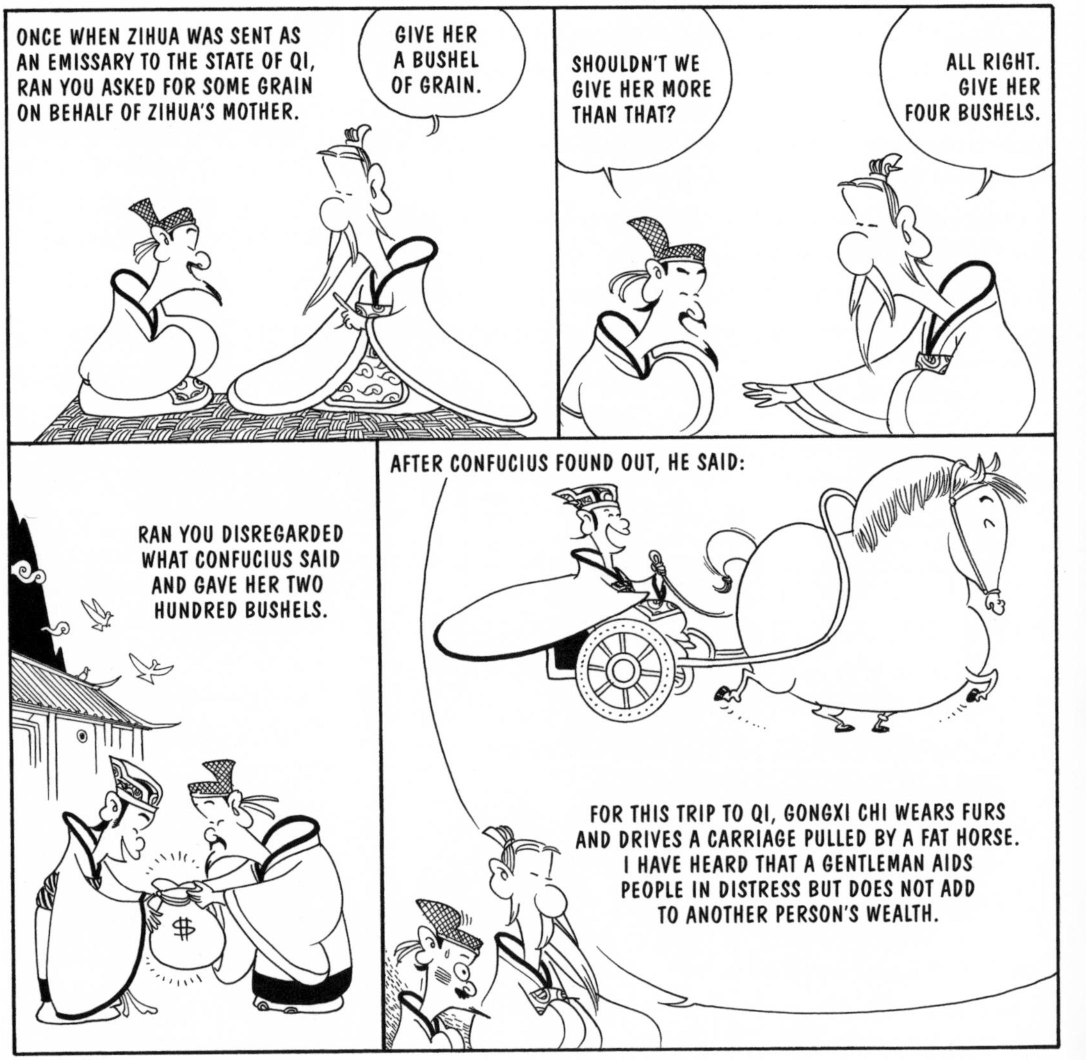
ONCE WHEN ZIHUA WAS SENT AS AN EMISSARY TO THE STATE OF QI, RAN YOU ASKED FOR SOME GRAIN ON BEHALF OF ZIHUA'S MOTHER.
GIVE HER A BUSHEL OF GRAIN.
SHOULDN'T WE GIVE HER MORE THAN THAT?
ALL RIGHT. GIVE HER FOUR BUSHELS.
RAN YOU DISREGARDED WHAT CONFUCIUS SAID AND GAVE HER TWO HUNDRED BUSHELS.
$
AFTER CONFUCIUS FOUND OUT, HE SAID:
FOR THIS TRIP TO QI, GONGXI CHI WEARS FURS AND DRIVES A CARRIAGE PULLED BY A FAT HORSE. I HAVE HEARD THAT A GENTLEMAN AIDS PEOPLE IN DISTRESS BUT DOES NOT ADD TO ANOTHER PERSON'S WEALTH.

Pronunciation Index

There are different systems of Romanization of Chinese words, but in all of these systems the sounds of the letters used do not necessarily correspond to those sounds which we are accustomed to using in English (for instance, would you have guessed that zh is pronounced like "jelly"—not as in "je ne sais quoi"?). Of course, these systems can be learned, but to save some time and effort for the reader who is not a student of Chinese, we have provided the following pronunciation guide. The Chinese words appear on the left as they do in the text and are followed by their pronunciations. Just sound them out and you will be quite close to the proper Mandarin Chinese pronunciation.

In addition, Chinese philosophical terms have been defined, and page numbers have been provided where every glossed term appears in the book.

NOTES

–dz is a combination of d and z in one sound, without the ee sound at the end; so it sounds kind of like a bee in flight with a slight d sound at the beginning.

–zh is pronounced like the j in "jelly" and not like the j in "je ne sais quoi."